Frequently Used Symbols in Financial Management

b (1) beta coefficient, a measure of an asset's riskiness;
     (2) the fraction of a firm's earnings retained rather than paid out

$CAPM$ capital asset pricing model

D dividend per share of stock *(DPS)*. D_t is the dividend in period t.

EPS earnings per share

$EBIT$ earnings before interest and taxes = net operating income *(NOI)*

$FVIF$ future value interest factor for a lump sum

$FVIFA$ future value interest factor for an annuity

g growth rate, especially growth rate in earnings, dividends, and stock prices

I interest (in dollars) on a bond

IRR internal rate of return

k a percentage discount rate, or cost of capital:

   k_d interest rate on debt (R_F = interest rate on risk-free debt)

   k_s cost of capital of common equity obtained by retaining earnings

   k_e cost of capital from sale of new common stock

   k_p cost of capital of preferred stock

   k_a weighted average cost of capital

   k_M cost of capital for "the market," or an "average" stock

   $\hat{k}$ "k hat" is an expected rate of return

MCC marginal cost of capital

NPV net present value

P price of a share of stock; P_0 = price of the stock today

P/E price/earnings ratio

PV present value

$PVIF$ present value interest factor for a lump sum

$PVIFA$ present value interest factor for an annuity

r (1) rate of return on investment; (2) the *IRR* on a new project

R_F rate of return on a risk-free security

R receipt, or cash flow

ROA return on assets

ROE return on equity

ROI return on investment

S sales

Σ summation sign (capital sigma)

σ standard deviation (lower case sigma)

t (1) tax rate, or (2) time, when used as a subscript.
     For example D_t = the dividend in year t

V value

FUNDAMENTALS OF FINANCIAL MANAGEMENT

FUNDAMENTALS OF FINANCIAL MANAGEMENT

Second Edition

EUGENE F. BRIGHAM
University of Florida

The Dryden Press
Hinsdale, Illinois

Library of Congress Catalog Card Number: 79-51055
ISBN: 0-03-054771-7
Printed in the United States of America
  2 039 98765

Acquiring Editor   Glenn Turner
Developmental Editor   Anne Boynton-Trigg
Project Editor   Jane Perkins
Art Director   Stephen Rapley
Production Manager   Peter Coveney

Copy editing by Judith Lynn Bleicher
Text and cover design by James A. Buddenbaum

PREFACE

Financial management has changed greatly in recent years. Strong inflationary pressures have pushed interest rates to unprecedented heights, and the resulting high cost of capital has led to profound changes in corporate financial policies and practices. Academic researchers have made significant advances, especially in the areas of capital budgeting and the cost of capital. At the same time, business practitioners are making increasing use of financial theory, and feedback from "the real world" has led to revisions in financial theory. To a large extent, these trends have dictated the revisions made in the second edition of *Fundamentals of Financial Management.*

The book begins with basic valuation concepts, focusing on stocks and bonds, and then goes on to show how the principles of financial management can be used to help maximize the value of a firm. Judging from students' reactions to the first edition, this organization produces three important benefits:

1. Developing valuation models at the beginning of the book gives students an early familiarity with the time value of money and with risk analysis, permitting the use of these concepts throughout the book. This usage, in turn, not only makes the institutional aspects of finance more interesting and meaningful but also reinforces through use students' understanding of risk and time value concepts.
2. Structuring the book around valuation concepts provides a continuity that is missing in many other texts. Most finance texts develop a series of topics in modular form, then attempt to integrate them in the later chapters. The present organization gives students a better and more continuous understanding of how the topics interact; it also minimizes the danger of running out of class time before all the pieces have been fitted into place.
3. Students—even those who do not plan to major in finance—generally enjoy studying investments. They like working with stock and bond values,

rates of return, and the like. Since people's ability to learn a subject is a function of their interest and motivation, and since *Fundamentals* begins by showing the direct relationship between security values and corporate finance, the new organization is better from a pedagogic standpoint.

The book is designed for use as an introductory text. In a one-quarter or one-semester course, the first seventeen chapters will typically be covered. To the extent that time permits, students can obtain breadth by going through the last six chapters on a self-study basis. Where the curriculum permits it, the text may be covered in a two-term sequence, with cases and readings being used to provide more depth and a better understanding of how financial theory and methodology are applied in practice. The book has been used in both ways, and its structure provides the flexibility necessary for each of them.

CHANGES IN THE SECOND EDITION

As a general rule, the most significant changes in textbooks occur between the first and second editions, and this book is no exception. Rough spots have been smoothed out; materials have been shifted around to provide better continuity; gaps have been filled; and end-of-chapter problems have been added and strengthened to better reinforce the text. The most significant changes are listed below:

1. Data have been updated to reflect current economic conditions and financial trends.
2. Chapter 2 has a greatly improved discussion of capital markets; it also incorporates recent tax law changes.
3. Chapter 3 (Time Value) now includes loan amortization schedules.
4. Chapter 4 (Stock and Bond Values) has a streamlined discussion of stock valuation models, which has permitted me to cover nonconstant growth models in the chapter rather than in an appendix.
5. Chapter 5 (Risk and Rates of Return) has been clarified, and the method of calculating betas has been clarified and moved from an appendix to the chapter proper.
6. Chapter 6 (Analysis of Financial Statements) has been greatly strengthened. Internal cash flows—including lags between purchases, production, sales, and collections—are now discussed, and a clear explanation of the sources and uses of funds statement is given. This change carries over into Chapter 7 (Financial Forecasting).
7. The section on credit policy in Chapter 9 (Accounts Receivable and Inventory) has been totally rewritten to show the incremental effects of changes in each credit policy variable on profits.
8. Major revisions have been made to the capital budgeting chapters. First,

Chapter 11 (The Basics of Capital Budgeting) has been streamlined. Second, and more important, Chapter 12, which deals largely with capital budgeting under uncertainty, has been greatly modified. Here the concept of beta risk in capital budgeting is developed and discussed, while the concepts of sensitivity analysis and computer simulation (which are what is really being done in industry today) are developed and explained in terms that introductory students can understand. Other additions to the capital budgeting section include explicit treatment of inflation, capital budgeting for projects that have different lives, and a discussion of how project financing and debt capacity affect capital budgeting decisions.

9. Chapters 15 and 16 (Capital Structure and Cost of Capital) have been improved in several respects: The trade-off between tax savings and "bankruptcy costs" as a determinant of the optimal capital structure has been made explicit; a brief section on preferred stock has been added; and the derivation of the MCC Schedule has been clarified greatly.

10. Because of the growing importance of multinational finance, an internationally recognized expert, Professor Hai Hong of Northwestern University, has revised the chapter on multinational financial management. The new chapter is truly one of the strong points of the text.

11. The Bankruptcy Act of 1978 has been incorporated into Chapter 20.

12. Chapter 22 (Warrants and Convertibles) has been greatly strengthened by the inclusion of a simplified, lucid version of the convertible bond model.

13. The end-of-chapter problems have been revised extensively. The number of problems has been increased, and their range of difficulty has been expanded. In chapters where a discussion approach is especially useful (for example, Chapter 14, Common Stock), longer, case-like problems have been added. Incidentally, arrangements have been made through Dryden Press to allow instructors who want to use a few cases, but not enough to warrant having students purchase a casebook, to reproduce selected cases. Also, a set of supplemental problems similar to the end-of-chapter problems is available to instructors from Dryden Press.

ANCILLARY MATERIALS

Several additional items are available as aids to students and instructors:

1. *Study Guide.* This supplement, coauthored with Robert T. LeClair, outlines the key sections of *Fundamentals,* offers students self-testing questions for each chapter, and provides a set of solved problems similar to those in the text.

2. *Casebooks.* Two casebooks, *Cases in Managerial Finance* and *Decisions in Financial Management: Cases,* can be used with the book.

3. *Readings books.* A number of readings books, including one designed

specifically for use with this book (*Issues in Managerial Finance,* edited by E. F. Brigham and R. E. Johnson), can be used as supplements.

4. *Instructor's Manual.* A very complete 400-page *Instructor's Manual* is available.

5. *Test bank.* A test bank of about 250 pages, with over 1,000 class-tested true/false and multiple choice exam questions and problems, is available to instructors.

6. *Lecture notes and transparencies.* A carefully constructed set of lecture notes, together with 100 acetate transparencies, is available to instructors who adopt the text. These notes were prepared on the basis of detailed student suggestions as to which parts of each chapter require the most explanation. Each instructor will want to modify the notes to suit his or her own situation, but the notes and transparencies can be used as the basis for lectures to both large and small classes.

7. *Supplemental problems.* Supplemental problems, which are similar to but generally somewhat more difficult than the end-of-chapter problems, are available to instructors.

ACKNOWLEDGMENTS

A great many people participated, directly or indirectly, in the preparation of this book, and I would like to acknowledge the help of the following:
M. Adler, E. Altman, A. Andrews, R. Angell, V. Apilado, Y. Atai, R. Aubey, G. Babcock, P. Bacon, T. Bankston, C. Barngrover, W. Beedles, M. Ben-Horim, W. Beranek, R. Bey, J. Bildersee, K. Boudreaux, D. Boyd, P. Boyer, K. Brigham, L. Brigham, S. Brigham, M. Broske, W. Brueggeman, R. Carleson, S. Celec, S. Choudhury, L. Chugh, P. Cooley, D. Crary, R. Crum, B. Dalrymple, D. Durst, E. Dyl, A. Edwards, M. Ertell, J. Ezzell, M. Ferri, J. Finnerty, J. Garvin, A. Gehr, F. Gile, J. Griggs, E. Grossnickle, J. Groth, M. Gupta, D. Hakala, C. Haley, R. Haugen, S. Hawk, R. Hehre, G. Hettenhouse, H. Heymann, L. Hill, R. Himes, H. Hong, C. Johnson, K. Johnson, R. Johnson, R. Jones, G. Kalogeras, S. Karp, J. Keenan, D. Knight, J. Komarynsky, H. Krogh, L. Lang, P. Lange, H. Lanser, R. LeClair, M. Ledford, W. Lee, J. Lewis, C. Linke, J. Longstreet, H. Magee, P. Malone, T. Martell, A. McCollough, K. McShane, L. Merville, J. Millar, J. Mills, C. Moerdyk, R. Moore, F. Morrissey, S. Myers, O. Nabe, T. Nantell, R. Nelson, W. Nelson, T. O'Brien, D. O'Conner, J. Pappas, G. Perritt, R. Pettit, R. Pettway, J. Pinkerton, G. Pogue, R. Potter, R. Powell, K. Price, H. Puckett, G. Racette, R. Radcliffe, R. Rainish, W. Regan, W. Reichenstein, R. Rentz, T. Rhoads, C. Rini, J. Ritchie, E. Rose, J. Rosenblum, D. Rowell, M. Sachlis, M. Scheuer, C. Schweser, S. Shalit, R. Shrieves, J. Sinkey, D. Shome, P. Smith, D. Sorenson, K. Stanley, D. Stevens, G. Strasburg, A. Sweetser, P. Swensen,

E. Swift, G. Tallman, G. Trivoli, M. Tysseland, H. Van Auken, P. Vandenburg, P. Van den Dool, P. Vanderheiden, J. Verbrugge, L. Wiltbank, D. Woods, C. Yang, J. Yeakel, and D. Ziegenbein. In addition, all or major parts of the manuscript were reviewed by the following executives: James Dunn, Financial Vice President, GT&E; Larry Hastie, Treasurer, Bendix Corporation; Victor Leavengood, Treasurer, General Telephone of Florida; Archie Long, Comptroller, General Motors; and James Taggart, Financial Vice President, Tampa Electric Company.

Special thanks are due Hai Hong, who wrote the chapter on multinational finance, and Art Herrmann, who wrote the bankruptcy chapter.

My colleagues at the University of Florida gave me many useful suggestions, and the Dryden Press staff—especially Glenn Turner, Anne Boynton-Trigg, Jo-Anne Naples, Stephen Rapley, and Jane Perkins—helped greatly in transforming the book from an idea to a bound book. I also wish to express my appreciation for the copy editing and proofreading done by Judith Lynn Bleicher and Beverly Peavler.

Last, but certainly not least, I owe a special debt to Fred Weston, both for teaching me much of what I know about finance and for permitting me to draw from our coauthored texts.

ERRORS IN THE TEXT

At this point in the preface, authors generally say something like this: "I appreciate all the help I received from the people listed above but any remaining errors are, of course, my own responsibility." And in many books there are plenty of remaining errors. Having experienced difficulties with errors myself, both as a student and as an instructor, I resolved to avoid this problem in *Fundamentals.* As a result of the error detection procedures used, I am convinced that it is freer of mistakes than any other book with which I have been associated.

Some of my colleagues suggested that if I am so confident about the book's accuracy, I should offer a reward to people who find errors. With this in mind, and also because I want to detect any remaining errors and correct them in subsequent printings, I hereby offer a reward of $5 per error (misspelled word, arithmetic mistake, and the like) to the first person who reports it to me. (Any error that has follow-through effects is counted as two errors only.) Two accounting students have set up a foolproof audit system to make sure I pay off. Accounting students tend to be skeptics!

CONCLUSION

Finance is, in a real sense, the cornerstone of the enterprise system, so good financial management is vitally important to the economic health of business firms and hence to the nation and the world. Because of its importance, finance should be widely and thoroughly understood; but this is easier said than done. The field is relatively complex, and it is undergoing constant change in response to shifts in economic conditions. All of this makes finance stimulating and exciting but also challenging and sometimes perplexing. I sincerely hope that *Fundamentals of Financial Management* will meet its own challenge by contributing to a better understanding of the financial system.

Eugene F. Brigham
College of Business
University of Florida
Gainesville, Florida 32611
November 1979

CONTENTS

I INTRODUCTION

Financial management can best be
understood if we begin with a brief
survey of the history of the field, a
summary of our goals, and a review of
the legal and economic framework
within which financial management is
practiced. These topics are covered
in Part I.

1 AN OVERVIEW OF FINANCIAL MANAGEMENT

The study of *financial management* has undergone significant changes over the years. When finance first emerged as a separate field of study in the early 1900s, the emphasis was on legalistic matters such as mergers, consolidations, the formation of new firms, and the various types of securities issued by corporations. Industrialization was sweeping the country, and the critical problem firms faced was obtaining capital for expansion. The capital markets were relatively primitive, making transfers of funds from individual savers to businesses quite difficult. Reports of earnings and asset values in accounting statements were unreliable, while stock trading by insiders and manipulators caused prices to fluctuate wildly. Consequently, investors were reluctant to purchase stocks and bonds. In this environment, it is easy to see why finance in the early 1900s concentrated so heavily on legal issues relating to the issuance of securities.

The emphasis remained on securities through the 1920s. However, radical changes occurred during the depression of the 1930s, when an unprecedented number of business failures caused finance to focus on bankruptcy and reorganization, on corporate liquidity, and on governmental regulation of securities markets. Finance was still a descriptive, legalistic subject, but the emphasis shifted from expansion to survival.

During the 1940s and early 1950s, finance continued to be taught as a descriptive, institutional subject, viewed from the outside rather than from the standpoint of management. However, methods of financial analysis designed to help firms maximize their profits and stock prices were beginning to receive attention.

The evolutionary pace quickened during the late 1950s. Whereas the right-hand side of the balance sheet (liabilities and capital) had received more attention in the earlier era, the major emphasis began to shift to asset analysis. Mathematical models were developed and applied to inventories, cash, accounts receivable, and fixed assets. Increasingly, the focus of finance shifted from the outsider's to the insider's point of view, as financial decisions within the firm were recognized to be the critical issue in corporate finance. Descriptive, institutional materials on capital markets and financing instruments were still studied, but these topics were considered within the context of corporate financial decisions.

The 1960s witnessed a renewed interest in the liabilities-capital side of the balance sheet, with a focus on (1) the optimal mix of securities and (2) the cost of capital. At the same time, the theory of asset selection by individual investors, or "portfolio management," and its implications for corporate finance were being developed. These trends have continued during the 1970s, and the result has been a merging of investments with corporate finance.

INCREASING IMPORTANCE OF FINANCIAL MANAGEMENT

These evolutionary changes have greatly increased the importance of financial management. In earlier times, the marketing manager would project sales, the engineering and production staffs would determine the assets necessary to meet these demands, and the financial manager would simply raise the money needed to purchase the plant, equipment, and inventories. This mode of operation is no longer prevalent. Today, decisions are made in a much more coordinated manner, with the financial manager having direct responsibility for the control process.

Northeast Utilities can be used to illustrate this change. A few years ago, Northeast's economic forecasters would project power demand on the basis of historic trends and then give these forecasts to the engineers, who would then proceed to build the new plants necessary to meet the forecasted demand. The finance group simply had the task of raising the capital the engineers told them was needed. However, inflation, environmental regulations, and other factors combined to double or even triple plant construction costs, and this caused a corresponding increase in the need for new capital. At the same time, rising fuel costs caused dramatic increases in electricity prices, which lowered demand and made some of the new construction unnecessary. Thus, Northeast found itself building plants that it did not need and unable to raise the capital necessary to pay for them. The price of the company's stock declined from $20 to $5. As a result of this experience, Northeast Utilities (and other utilities and industrial companies) now places a great deal more stress on the planning and control process, and this has greatly increased the importance of the finance staff.

The direction in which business is moving, as well as the increasing importance of finance, was described recently in *Fortune.* After pointing out that well over half of today's top executives majored in business administration, versus about 25 percent a few years earlier, *Fortune* continued:

Career patterns have followed the educational trends. Like scientific and technical schooling, nuts-and-bolts business experience seems to have become less important. The proportion of executives with their primary experience in production, operations, engineering, design, and R. and D. has fallen from a third of the total to just over a quarter. And the number of top officers with legal and financial backgrounds has increased more than enough to make up the difference. Lawyers and financial men now head two out of five corporations.

It is fair to assume the changes in training, and in the paths that led these men to the top, reflect the shifting priorities and needs of their corporations. In fact, the expanding size and complexity of corporate organizations, coupled with their continued expansion overseas, have increased the importance of financial planning and controls. And the growth of government regulation and of obligations companies face under law has heightened the need for legal advice. The engineer and the production man have become, in consequence, less important in management than the finance man and the lawyer.

Today's chief executive officers have obviously perceived the shift in emphasis, and many of them wish they had personally been better prepared for it. Interestingly enough, a majority of them say they would have benefited from additional formal training, mainly in business administration, accounting, finance, and law.[1]

These same trends are evident at lower levels within firms of all sizes, as well as in nonprofit and governmental organizations. Thus, it is becoming increasingly important for people in marketing, accounting, production, personnel, and other areas to understand finance in order to do a good job in their own fields. Marketing people, for instance, must understand how marketing decisions affect and are affected by funds availability, by inventory levels, by excess plant capacity, and so on. Accountants, to cite another example, must understand how accounting data are used in corporate planning and viewed by investors. The function of accounting is to provide quantitative financial information for use in making economic decisions, while the main functions of financial management are to plan for, acquire, and utilize funds in order to maximize the efficiency and value of the enterprise.[2]

Thus, there are financial implications in virtually all business decisions, and nonfinancial executives simply must know enough finance to work these implications into their own specialized analyses.[3] This point is amplified in the following section.

1 C. G. Burck, "A Group Profile of the Fortune 500 Chief Executive," *Fortune* (May 1976), p. 173.

2 American Institute of Certified Public Accountants, *Statement of the Accounting Principles Board No. 4* (New York, October 1970), p. 17.

3 It is an interesting fact that the course "Financial Analysis for Nonfinancial Executives" has the highest enrollment in most executive development programs.

Figure 1–1
Place of Finance in a Typical Business
Organization

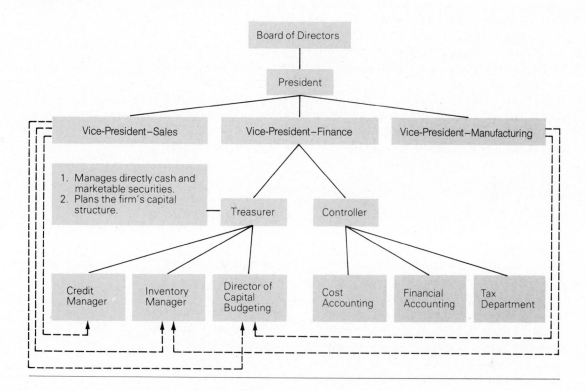

THE PLACE OF FINANCE IN A BUSINESS ORGANIZATION

Organization structures vary from firm to firm, but Figure 1–1 gives a fairly typical picture of the role of finance within a business. The chief financial officer, who has the title of vice-president: finance, reports to the president. Key subordinates are the treasurer and the controller. The treasurer has direct responsibility for managing the firm's cash and marketable securities, for planning the financial structure, and for selling stocks and bonds to raise capital. Under the treasurer (but in some firms under the controller) are the credit manager, the inventory manager, and the director of capital budgeting (who analyzes decisions relating to investments in fixed assets). The controller is responsible for the activities of the accounting and tax departments.

THE GOALS OF THE FIRM

Decisions are not made in a vacuum—they are made with some objective in mind. *Throughout this book, we operate on the assumption that management's primary goal is to maximize the wealth of its stockholders.* As we shall see, this translates into *maximizing the price of the common stock.* Firms do, of course, have other objectives—managers, who make the actual decisions, are interested in their own personal satisfaction, in employees' welfare, and in the good of the community and society at large. Still, for the reasons set forth below, *stock price maximization is probably the most important goal of most firms (except public utilities),* and it is a reasonable operating objective upon which to build decision rules in a book such as this one.

Why Managers Try to Maximize Stockholders' Wealth

Stockholders own the firm and elect the management team. Management, in turn, is supposed to operate in the best interests of the stockholders. We know, however, that because the stock of most large firms is widely held, the managers of such firms have a great deal of autonomy. This being the case, might not managements pursue goals other than maximization of stockholder wealth? For example, some argue that the management of a large. well-entrenched corporation could work to keep stockholder returns at a fair or "reasonable" level and then devote part of its efforts and resources to public service activities, to employee benefits, to higher management salaries, or to golf.

Similarly, an entrenched management might avoid risky ventures, even when the possible gains to stockholders were high enough to warrant taking the gamble. The theory behind this argument is that stockholders are generally well diversified, holding portfolios of many different stocks, so if one company takes a chance and loses, the stockholders lose only a small part of their wealth. Managers, on the other hand, are not diversified, so setbacks affect them more seriously. Accordingly, some maintain that corporate managers tend to "play it safe" rather than aggressively seek to maximize the prices of their firms' stocks.

It is extremely difficult to determine whether a particular management team is trying to maximize shareholder wealth or is merely attempting to keep stockholders satisfied while pursuing other goals. For example, how can we tell whether or not voluntary employee or community benefit programs are in the long-run best interests of the stockholders? Are relatively high management salaries really necessary to attract and retain excellent managers who, in turn, will keep the firm ahead of its competition? When a risky venture is turned down, does this reflect management conservatism, or is it a correct judgment regarding the risks of the venture versus its potential rewards?

It is impossible to give definitive answers to these questions. Several studies have suggested that managers are not completely stockholder-oriented, but the evidence is cloudy. It is true that more and more firms are tying management's compensation to the company's performance, and research suggests that this motivates managers to operate in a manner consistent with stock price maximization.[4] Additionally, in recent years tender offers and proxy fights have removed a number of supposedly entrenched managements; the recognition that such actions can take place has probably stimulated many other firms to attempt to maximize share prices.[5] Finally, a firm operating in a competitive market, or almost any firm during an economic downturn, will be forced to undertake actions that are reasonably consistent with shareholder wealth maximization. Thus, while managers may have other goals in addition to stock price maximization, there are reasons to view this as the dominant goal for most firms.

Social Responsibility

Another point that deserves consideration is social responsibility: should businesses operate strictly in the stockholders' best interest, or are firms also partly responsible for the welfare of society at large? In tackling this question, consider first those firms whose rates of return on investment are close to "normal," that is, close to the average for all firms. If such companies attempt to be social do-gooders, thereby increasing their costs over what they otherwise would have been, and if the other businesses in the industry do not follow suit, then the socially oriented firms will probably be forced to abandon their efforts. Thus, any socially responsible acts that raise costs will be difficult, if not impossible, in industries subject to keen competition.

What about firms with profits above normal levels—can they not devote resources to social projects? Undoubtedly they can; many large, successful firms do engage in community projects, employee benefit programs, and the like to a greater degree than would appear to be called for by pure profit or wealth maximization goals.[6] Still, publicly owned firms are constrained in such actions by capital market factors. Suppose a saver who has funds to invest is considering two alternative firms. One firm devotes a substantial part of its resources to social actions, while the other concentrates on profits and stock prices. Most investors are likely to shun the socially oriented firm, thus putting it at a disadvantage in the capital market. After

---

4 Wilbur G. Lewellen, "Management and Ownership in the Large Firm," *Journal of Finance* 24 (May 1969): 299–322. Lewellen concludes that managers seem to make decisions that are largely oriented toward stock price maximization.

5 A *tender offer* is a bid by one company to buy the stock of another, while a *proxy fight* involves an attempt to gain control by getting stockholders to vote a new management group into office. Both actions are facilitated by low stock prices, so self-preservation can lead management to try to keep the stock value as high as possible.

6 Even firms such as these often find it necessary to justify such programs at stockholder meetings by stating that they contribute to long-run profit maximization.

all, why should the stockholders of one corporation subsidize society to a greater extent than stockholders of other businesses? For all these reasons, even highly profitable firms (unless they are closely held rather than publicly owned) are generally constrained against taking unilateral cost-increasing social actions.

Does all this mean that firms should not exercise social responsibility? Not at all—it simply means that most cost-increasing actions may have to be put on a *mandatory* rather than a voluntary basis, at least initially, to insure that the burden of such action falls uniformly across all businesses. Thus, fair hiring practices, minority training programs, product safety, pollution abatement, antitrust actions, and the like are more likely to be effective if realistic rules are established initially and then enforced by government agencies. It is critical that industry and government cooperate in establishing the rules of corporate behavior and that firms follow the spirit as well as the letter of the law in their actions. Thus, the rules of the game become constraints, and firms should strive to maximize stock prices subject to these constraints. Throughout the book, we shall assume that managements operate in this manner.

If firms attempt to maximize stock prices, is this good or bad for society? In general, it is good. Aside from such illegal actions as attempting to form monopolies, violating safety codes, and failing to meet pollution control requirements—all of which are constrained by the government—*the same actions that maximize stock prices also benefit society.* First, stock price maximization requires efficient, low-cost operations that get the most value out of a given set of resources. Second, price maximization also requires the development of products that consumers want and need, so the profit motive leads to new technology, new products, and new jobs. Finally, price maximization requires efficient and courteous service, adequate stocks of merchandise, and well-located business establishments, because these things are all necessary to make sales, and sales are certainly necessary for profits. Therefore, the types of actions that help a firm increase the price of its stock are also directly beneficial to society at large. This is why profit-motivated enterprise economies have been so much more successful than other types of economic systems. Since financial management plays a crucial role in the operation of successful firms, and since successful firms are absolutely necessary for a healthy, productive economy, it is easy to see why finance is important from a social standpoint.[7]

---

7 People sometimes argue that firms, in their efforts to raise profits and stock prices, increase product prices and gouge the public. In a reasonably competitive economy, which we have, prices are constrained by competition and consumer resistance. If a firm raises its prices beyond reasonable levels, it will simply lose its market share. Even giant firms like General Motors lose business to the Japanese and Germans, as well as to Ford and Chrysler, if they do not set prices that merely cover production costs plus a "normal" profit. Of course, firms *want* to earn more, and they constantly try to cut costs, develop new products, and so on, and thereby earn excess profits. Yet these very excess profits attract competition, so the main beneficiary is the consumer.

What Can Managers Do to Maximize Stock Prices?

Assuming that a firm's management team does indeed seek to maximize its stock price, what types of actions should it take? First, consider the question of stock prices versus profits: will profit maximization result in stock price maximization? In answering this question, we must analyze the matter of total corporate profits versus earnings per share.

Suppose Company X had one million shares outstanding and earned $2 million, or $2 per share, and you owned 100 shares of the stock. Now suppose the company sold another one million shares and invested the funds received in assets which produced $1 million of income. Total income would have risen to $3 million, but earnings per share would have declined from $2 to $3,000,000/2,000,000 shares = $1.50. Now your own earnings would be only $150, down from $200. You (and the other original stockholders) would have suffered an earnings dilution, even though total corporate profits had risen. Therefore, other things held constant, *if management is interested in the well-being of its stockholders, it should concentrate on earnings per share rather than on total corporate profits.*

Will maximization of expected earnings per share always maximize stockholder welfare, or should other factors be considered? Think about the *timing of the earnings.* Suppose one project will cause earnings per share to rise by $0.20 per year for five years, or $1.00 in total, while another project has no effect on earnings for four years but increases earnings by $1.25 in the fifth year. Which project is better? The answer depends on which project adds the most to the value of the stock. This, in turn, depends on the time value of money to investors. In any event, timing is an important reason to concentrate on wealth as measured by the price of the stock rather than on earnings alone.

Still another issue relates to *risk.* Suppose one project is expected to increase earnings per share by $1.00, while another is expected to raise earnings by $1.20 per share. The first project is not very risky; if it is undertaken, earnings will almost certainly rise by about $1.00 per share. The other project is quite risky, so while our best guess is that earnings will rise by $1.20 per share, we must recognize the possibility that there may be no increase whatsoever. Depending on how averse stockholders are to risk, the first project may be preferable to the second.

The riskiness inherent in projected earnings per share (EPS) also depends on *how the firm is financed.* As we shall see, a large number of firms goes bankrupt every year, and the greater the use of debt, the greater the threat of bankruptcy. Consequently, *while the use of debt financing may increase projected EPS, debt also increases the riskiness of these projected earnings.*

Still another issue is the matter of paying dividends to stockholders versus retaining earnings and plowing them back into the business, thereby causing the earnings stream to grow over time. Stockholders like cash dividends, but they also like the growth in EPS that results from plowing earnings back into the business. The financial manager must decide exactly how much of current earnings should be paid out as dividends rather than retained and reinvested—this is called the *dividend policy decision.* The optimal dividend policy is the one that maximizes the firm's stock price.

We see, then, that the firm's stock price is dependent on the following factors:

1. projected earnings per share,
2. riskiness of projected earnings,
3. timing of the earnings stream,
4. the manner of financing the firm, and
5. dividend policy.

Every significant corporate decision should be analyzed in terms of its effect on these factors, hence on the price of the firm's stock. For example, a coal company may be considering opening a new mine. If the mine is opened, can it be expected to increase EPS? Is there a chance that costs will exceed estimates, that prices and output will fall below projections, and that EPS will be reduced because the new mine was opened? How long will it take for the new mine to start showing a profit? How should the capital required to open the mine be raised? If debt is used, how much will this increase the firm's riskiness? Should the firm reduce its current dividends and use the cash thus saved to finance the project, or should it finance the mine with external capital? Financial management is designed to help answer such questions as these, plus many more.

ORGANIZATION OF THE BOOK

Finance cannot be studied in a vacuum—financial decisions are made within an economic and social environment which has a profound influence on these decisions. An introduction to the economic side of the environment is provided in Part I.

Part II develops some models which can be used to help evaluate financial decisions. The specific tasks of financial managers include (1) coordinating the planning process, (2) administering the control process, and (3) handling the specialized finance functions such as raising capital and paying bills. To perform these tasks properly, it is necessary to estimate stockholders' reactions to alternative actions or events. Accordingly, our first task is to develop a stock valuation model which can be used to gain insights into how different actions are likely to affect the price of the firm's stock. The concepts and models developed in Part II are used extensively throughout the remainder of the book.

Next, since both long- and short-run plans are analyzed in terms of future financial statements, Part III considers how these statements are developed and used by both managers and investors. Here we concentrate first on analyzing reports of past operations, then on projecting financial statements into the future under different strategic plans and operating conditions.

In Part IV we move into the execution phase of the financial management process. Here we examine current, ongoing operations, looking first at the role of finance in insuring that cash, inventories, and current assets are used most effectively, and then considering the question of how current operations should be financed.

Part V takes up the vital subject of fixed asset acquisitions, or capital budgeting. Since major capital expenditures take years to plan and execute, and since decisions in this area are generally not reversible and affect operations for many years, their impact on the value of the firm is obvious.

Part VI focuses on raising long-term capital. What are the principal sources and forms of long-term capital, how much does each type cost, and how does the method of financing affect the value of the firm? This section utilizes most of the valuation concepts developed throughout the book, so it not only addresses such key issues as the optimal debt/equity mix and dividend policy, but it also serves to integrate the book and to show how the parts fit together.

Finally, in Part VII we consider some subjects that, while important, are best studied within the basic framework of financial management as developed in Parts I through VI. Included here are multinational operations, mergers, bankruptcy, small business finance, leasing, convertible securities, and warrants.

SUMMARY

This chapter has provided an overview of financial management. We began with a brief review of the evolution of finance as an academic discipline, tracing developments from 1900 to the present. We next examined the place of finance in the firm and saw that the financial manager has been playing an increasingly important role in the organization. We also considered the goals of financial management and concluded that *the key goal in most publicly owned firms is stock price maximization.* Managers do have other goals, both personal and social, but in a competitive economy, where managers serve at the pleasure of stockholders, stock price maximization must be the dominant goal (except for public utilities).

The book's organization reflects this primary goal. First, we shall develop valuation models that can be used to show how corporate actions affect stock prices. Then, in the remainder of the book, we shall examine actions that management can take to help maximize the price of the firm's stock.

Questions

1-1 Would the management of a firm in an oligopolistic or in a competitive industry be more likely to engage in what might be called "socially conscious" practices? Explain your reasoning.

1-2 What is the difference between stock price maximization and profit maximization? Would profit maximization not lead to stock price maximization?

1-3 If you were running a large, publicly owned corporation, would you make decisions to maximize stockholders' welfare or your own? What are some actions stockholders could take to insure that your interests and theirs coincided?

2 BACKGROUND INFORMATION: FORMS OF ORGANIZATION, CAPITAL MARKETS, AND TAXES

Financial management cannot be studied in a vacuum—if the value of a firm is to be maximized, the financial manager must understand the legal and economic environment in which financial decisions are made. Accordingly, this chapter presents some background information on forms of business organizations, interest rate patterns in the economy, and the federal income tax system.

ALTERNATIVE FORMS OF BUSINESS ORGANIZATION

There are three major forms of business organization: the sole proprietorship, the partnership, and the corporation. In terms of numbers, about 80 percent of business firms are operated as sole proprietorships, while the remainder are equally divided between partnerships and corporations. By dollar value of sales, however, about 80 percent of business is conducted by corporations, about 13 percent by sole proprietorships, and about 7 percent by partnerships.

Sole Proprietorship

A proprietorship is a business owned by one individual. To go into business as a single proprietor is very simple—one merely begins business operations. However, most cities require even the smallest establishments to be licensed, and occasionally state licenses are required as well.

The proprietorship has key advantages for small operations. It is easily and inexpensively formed; no formal charter for operations is required; and a proprietorship is subject to few government regulations. Further, the business pays no corporate income taxes, although all earnings of the firm are subject to personal income taxes, whether they are reinvested in the business or withdrawn.

The proprietorship also has important limitations. Most significant is its inability to obtain large sums of capital. Further, the proprietor has unlimited personal liability for the business's debts. Finally, the life of the proprietorship business is limited to the life of the individual who created it. For all of these reasons, the individual proprietorship is restricted primarily to small business operations. However, businesses are frequently started as proprietorships and then converted to corporations whenever their growth causes the disadvantages of the proprietorship form to outweigh its advantages.

Partnership

When two or more persons associate to conduct business, a partnership is said to exist. A partnership may operate under different degrees of formality, ranging from an informal oral understanding to a formal agreement filed with the secretary of the state. Like the proprietorship, the partnership has the advantages of ease and economy of formation, as well as freedom from special governmental regulations. Partnership profits are taxed as personal income in proportion to the partners' claims, whether they are distributed or retained in the business.

If a new partner comes into the business, the old partnership ceases to exist and a new one is created. The withdrawal or death of any one of the partners also dissolves the partnership. To prevent disputes under such circumstances, the articles of the partnership agreement should include terms and conditions under which assets are to be distributed upon dissolution. Of course, dissolution of the partnership does not necessarily mean the end of the business—the remaining partners may simply buy out the one who leaves the firm. To avoid financial pressures caused by the death of one of the partners, it is a common practice for each partner to carry life insurance naming the remaining partners as beneficiaries. The proceeds of such a policy may then be used to buy out the investment of the deceased partner.

Partnerships do have some drawbacks, including impermanence, difficulties of transferring ownership, and unlimited liability. Partners must risk their personal assets as well as their investments in the business, for under partnership law, the partners are liable for business debts. This means that if any partners are unable to meet their pro rata claims resulting from the bankruptcy of the partnership, the remaining partners must take over the unsatisfied claims, drawing on their personal assets if necessary.[1]

---

1 However, it is possible to limit the liabilities of certain partners by establishing a *limited partnership*, wherein certain partners are designated *general partners* and others *limited partners*. Limited partnerships are quite common in the area of real estate investment, but they do not work well with most types of businesses.

Corporation

A corporation is a legal entity created by a state. It is separate and distinct from its owners and managers. This separateness gives the corporation three major advantages: (1) It has an *unlimited life*—it can continue after its original owners and managers are dead. (2) It permits *easy transferability of ownership interest* in the firm, as ownership interests can be divided into shares of stock, which can be transferred far more easily than can partnership interests. (3) It permits *limited liability.* To illustrate, if you invested $10,000 in a partnership and the partnership went bankrupt owing a considerable sum of money, you could be assessed for a share of these debts. Thus, an investor in a partnership is exposed to unlimited liability. On the other hand, if you invested $10,000 in the stock of a corporation, your potential loss on the investment would be $10,000—your liability would be limited to the amount of your investment in the business.[2]

While a proprietorship or a partnership can commence operations without much paperwork, setting up a corporation is a bit more involved. The incorporators must prepare a *charter* and a set of *bylaws.* The charter includes the following information: (1) name of proposed corporation, (2) type of activities it will pursue, (3) amount of capital stock, (4) number of directors, (5) names and addresses of directors, and (6) duration (if limited). The charter is filed with the secretary of the state in which the firm will be headquartered, and when it is approved, the corporation is officially in existence.

The bylaws are a set of rules drawn up by the founders of the corporation to aid in governing the internal management of the company. Included are such points as (1) how directors are to be elected (all elected each year or, say, one-third each year); (2) whether the existing stockholders shall have the first right to buy any new stock the firm issues; and (3) what provisions there are for management committees, such as an executive committee or a finance committee, and their duties. Also included is the procedure for changing the bylaws themselves, should conditions require it.

The value of any business other than a very small one will probably be maximized if it is organized as a corporation. The reasons are outlined below:

1. Limited liability reduces risk to investors, and the lower the risk, other things held constant, the higher the value of the firm.
2. Value is dependent on growth opportunities, which in turn are dependent on a firm's ability to attract capital. Since corporations can attract capital more easily than unincorporated businesses, they have superior growth opportunities.

---

2 In the case of small corporations, the limited liability feature is often a fiction, as bankers and credit managers frequently require personal guarantees from the stockholders of small, weak businesses.

3. The value of an asset also depends on its *liquidity,* which means the ease of selling the asset and converting it to cash. Since an investment in the stock of a corporation is much more liquid than a similar investment in a proprietorship or partnership, this too means that the corporate organization can enhance the value of a business.

Since most firms are indeed managed with value maximization in mind, it is easy to see why most business is conducted by corporations.

THE CAPITAL MARKETS

Business firms, as well as individuals and government units, often need to raise capital. For example, suppose Tampa Electric Company forecasts an increase in the demand for power in its service area and decides to build a new power plant. It almost certainly will not have the $500 million necessary to pay for the plant, so it will have to raise this capital in the market. Or suppose that Mr. Jones, the proprietor of a local hardware store, decides to expand into appliances. Where will he get the money to buy the initial inventory of TV sets, washers, and freezers? Similarly, if a family wants to buy a home that costs $60,000 but has only $10,000 in savings, how can it raise the additional $50,000?

In all these cases, the firms or individuals must find some other firms, individuals, or government units with surplus funds. Tampa Electric is a corporation, and corporations obtain capital by borrowing or by selling additional shares of stock. If Tampa borrows, it can do so on either a short-term or a long-term basis. Since a short-term loan must be paid back fairly rapidly (often within ninety days), this will probably not be an appropriate way to finance a plant with a thirty year life. Therefore, long-term bonds will probably be sold. However, lenders generally insist that the owners of a business (its stockholders in the case of a corporation) put up some of the capital for a new venture, so Tampa Electric will probably have to raise part of the $500 million by selling additional shares of common stock. (If profits were high enough, the company might finance the equity portion of the plant by retaining earnings rather than by selling new shares of common stock.)

The primary source of capital for the hardware store will be the local bank, but the bank will probably insist that the proprietor raise part of the expansion capital as equity if the expansion is a large one. If the proprietor has savings, he can put some more of his own money into the business. If not, he can try to find a partner to bring into the firm. Often, expansion plans are restricted by a shortage of capital. This is especially true of small businesses.

The family will probably borrow money to purchase the house from a savings and loan association on a *mortgage loan.* The house itself can be used as collateral to secure the loan, but the family's income will have to be high enough to cover interest and principal payments on the loan.

The capital supplied in each of these instances will belong, directly or indirectly, to some individual or group of individuals. Tampa Electric will probably sell its bonds to individuals or to pension trusts which invest funds that are deducted from workers' salaries, while its new common stock will probably be sold to other individuals. The bank from which the hardware store proprietor borrows can actually create the money it lends, subject to controls imposed by the Federal Reserve System; but today most new bank capital is obtained in the form of interest-bearing deposits that people place with banks. Similarly, the money used to buy the house will have been placed in the savings and loan by people whose current income exceeds their current expenditures—that is, by savers.

Specialized Financial Institutions

A healthy economy is vitally dependent on efficient transfers of funds from savers to firms and individuals who need capital. Without such transfers, the city of Tampa would not have enough electricity, the local community would not have an appliance store, and the family would not have adequate housing. Also, unemployment would be higher, and savers would receive lower returns on their savings. Thus, an efficient financial system is absolutely necessary for an efficient economy.

The U.S. economy, as well as economies of other advanced nations, has a highly developed system of financial institutions. The commercial banks are like department stores; they supply many types of financial services, including long- and short-term loans, lease financing, consumer loans, checking accounts, credit cards, management of pension assets, and so on. Savings and loans, on the other hand, specialize in real estate financing, and credit unions specialize in consumer loans. Firms called *investment banks* handle the sale of common stocks and long-term bonds, and they also maintain *secondary markets* in which these securities are traded among investors after they have been issued by corporations. The New York Stock Exchange (NYSE) is a major secondary market; Merrill Lynch and other brokerage firms handle trades on the NYSE. Secondary markets are extremely important, for without them securities would be much less liquid, and this would make it harder to induce savers to make funds available to businesses and individuals who need capital.[3]

Our financial markets are regulated by government agencies. The banking system is regulated by several agencies, including the Federal Reserve

---

3 One of the biggest problems in developing nations is the establishment of efficient capital markets. There is a strong desire on the part of many savers in such countries to hold gold rather than financial assets. Yet without financial assets no mechanism exists for getting savings into the hands of the businesses which could develop the nation. Therefore, economic development requires the establishment of efficient capital markets.

System, which controls the volume of bank deposits (the money supply) in an effort to hold down inflation while still maintaining a growing economy. In addition, several other state and federal agencies try to insure the soundness of the banks and the safety of depositors' funds. The stock and bond markets are regulated by the Securities and Exchange Commission (SEC), which tries to insure (1) that investors are not given deceptive and misleading information and (2) that brokerage firms are financially sound. Savings and loans, life insurance companies, credit unions, and other institutions are all subject to similar regulation. The primary purpose of all this regulation is to maintain investor confidence, which is vital to an efficient financial system.

Interest Rates and the Cost of Capital

Capital in a free economy is allocated through the price system. The interest rate is the price paid for borrowed capital, while in the case of equity capital, investors expect compensation in the form of dividends and capital gains. Firms with the most profitable investment projects can pay the most for capital, so they tend to attract it away from inefficient firms or from those whose products are not in demand. Of course, our economy is not completely free in the sense of being influenced only by market forces. Thus, the federal government has agencies which help individuals or groups as stipulated by Congress to obtain credit on favorable terms. Among those eligible for this kind of assistance are small businesses, certain minorities, firms willing to build plants in areas with high unemployment, and so on. Still, most capital in the U.S. economy is allocated through the price system.

Figure 2–1 shows how supply and demand interact to determine interest rates in two capital markets. Markets A and B represent two of the many capital markets in existence. The going interest rate (k) is 10 percent for the low-risk securities in Market A—borrowers whose credit is strong enough to qualify for this market can obtain funds at a cost of 10 percent, and investors who want to put their money to work at low risk can obtain a 10 percent return. Riskier borrowers must obtain higher-cost funds in Market B, where investors who are more willing to take risks invest with the expectation of receiving a 12 percent return but also with the realization that they might receive much less.

If the demand for funds in a market declines, as it typically does during a business recession, the demand curve will shift to the left (or down) as shown by Curve D_2 in Market A. The market clearing, or equilibrium, interest rate (k) in this example will decline to 8 percent. You can also visualize what will happen if the Federal Reserve tightens credit: The supply curve (S_1) will shift to the left, and this will raise interest rates and lower the demand for funds.

Capital markets are interdependent. For example, assuming that Markets A and B were in equilibrium before the demand shift to D_2 in Market A, then investors were willing to accept the higher risk in Market B in exchange for

Figure 2–1
Interest Rates as a Function of Supply and
Demand for Funds

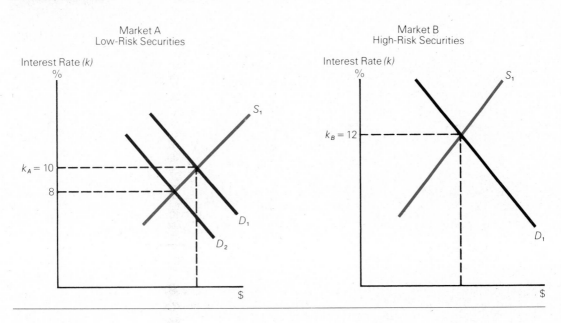

a *risk premium* of 12% − 10% = 2%. After the shift to D_2, the risk premium will immediately rise to 12% − 8% = 4%. In all likelihood, this much larger premium will induce some of the lenders in Market A to shift to Market B. This, in turn, will cause the supply curve in Market A to shift to the left (or up) and that in Market B to shift to the right. This transfer of capital between markets will raise interest rates in Market A and lower them in Market B.

There are many, many capital markets in the United States. U.S. firms also raise capital throughout the world, while foreign borrowers obtain capital in the U.S. There are markets in the U.S. for real estate loans; farm loans; business loans; federal, state, and local government loans; and consumer loans. Within each category, there are also regional markets, as well as submarkets. For example, in real estate there are separate markets for first and second mortgages and for owner-occupied homes, apartments, office buildings, shopping centers, vacant land, and so on. Within the business sector, there are dozens of types of debt (see Chapters 10 and 13) and a sharply differentiated market for common stocks as opposed to debt.

There are as many prices as there are types of capital, and these prices change over time with changes in supply and demand conditions. Figure 2–2 shows how long- and short-term interest rates to business borrowers have varied over the last twenty-five years. Notice that short-term interest rates are especially prone to rise during booms, then fall during recessions.

Figure 2–2
Long- and Short-Term Interest Rates, 1953–1979

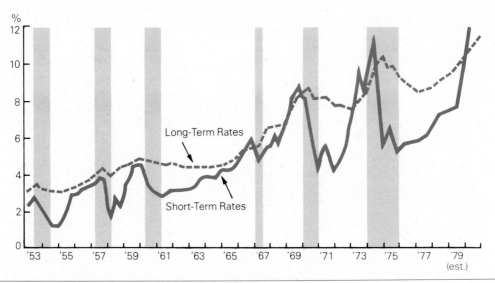

Note: The shaded areas designate business recessions. Short-term rates are measured by four- to six-month A-rated commercial paper and long-term rates by A-rated corporate bonds.
Source: Federal Reserve Bulletin, U.S. Department of Commerce, Moody's Investors Service.

(The shaded areas of the chart indicate recessions.) When the economy is expanding, firms need capital, and this pressure to borrow pushes rates up. Also, inflationary pressures are strongest during business booms, so at such times the Federal Reserve tends to tighten the money supply, which also exerts an upward pressure on rates. Just the reverse holds true during recessions—the Fed increases the money supply, slack business reduces the demand for credit, and the result is a drop in interest rates.

These tendencies do not hold exactly—the early part of the 1974–1975 recession is a case in point. The price of oil increased dramatically in 1974, exerting inflationary pressures on other prices and raising fears of serious, long-term inflation. These fears pushed rates to high levels; investors "looked over the valley" of the 1974–1975 recession, forecast a continued problem with inflation, and demanded an inflation premium that kept long-term rates high by historic standards.[4]

4 Short-term rates are responsive to current economic conditions, while long-term rates primarily reflect long-run expectations for inflation. As a result, short-term rates are sometimes above and sometimes below long-term rates. The relationship between long-term and short-term rates is called the *term structure of interest rates*. To understand the term structure relationships, one must understand how securities are valued in the marketplace. Therefore, a discussion of the term structure is deferred to Chapter 8.

Figure 2-3
**Relationship between Annual Inflation Rates
and Long-Term Interest Rates, 1960-1979**

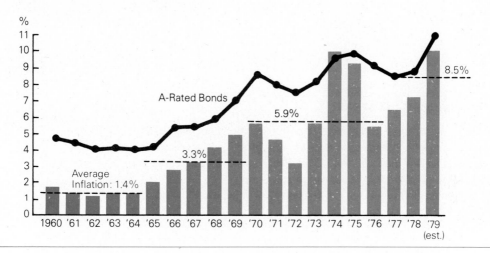

The relationship between inflation and long-term interest rates is highlighted in Figure 2-3, which plots rates of inflation along with long-term interest rates. From 1960 through 1964, when the average rate of inflation was 1.4 percent, interest rates on A-rated bonds ranged from 4 to 5 percent. As the war in Vietnam accelerated in the mid-1960s, the rate of inflation increased, and interest rates began to rise. The rate of inflation dropped after 1970, and so did long-term interest rates. However, the lifting of wage and price controls, in conjunction with the Arab oil embargo and a quadrupling of oil prices in 1974, caused a spurt in the price level, which drove interest rates to new record highs in 1974 and 1975. Inflationary pressures eased in late 1975 and 1976 but then rose again in 1977 and 1978. In 1979, as this is written, inflation rates are at the highest levels on record, with fears of continued double digit inflation having pushed interest rates up to historic highs.

Interest rates also vary depending on the riskiness of the borrower—the greater the risk, the higher the interest rate that lenders charge. Thus, had AAA bonds (which are less risky than A bonds) been used in Figures 2-2 and 2-3, the interest rate lines would have been somewhat lower. Also, as we shall see in Chapters 4 and 5, common stock represents an investment security much like a bond. Whereas the interest rate represents the "price" paid for debt capital, there is a similar "price" associated with capital supplied in the form of common stock. This "price," which is called the *cost of common equity,* moves up when interest rates go up and down when rates fall. Further, since a firm's common stock is riskier than its bonds, the cost of equity capital exceeds the cost of bonds. Therefore, if the cost of equity were plotted in Figure 2–3, it would lie somewhat above the line for A-rated bonds and move up and down with bond rates. These points are analyzed in depth in later chapters.

THE FEDERAL INCOME TAX SYSTEM

The value of any financial asset, including stocks, bonds, or even whole firms, depends on the stream of *usable* income produced by the asset. Usable income means income *after taxes.* Proprietorship and partnership income must be reported and taxed as personal income to the owners. Most corporations must first pay taxes on their own income, and stockholders must then pay taxes on corporate after-tax income distributed to them as dividends. Therefore, consideration must be given to both *personal* and *corporate* income taxes.

Federal income tax rates for individuals may be as high as 70 percent, and when state income taxes are included, the marginal tax rate on an individual's income can approach 90 percent. Business income is also taxed heavily. The income from partnerships and proprietorships is reported by the individual owners and taxed at their own rates, while corporate profits are subject to federal income tax rates of up to 46 percent, in addition to state income taxes. Because of the magnitude of the tax bite, taxes play an important role in many financial decisions.

Taxes are so complicated that university law schools offer master's degrees in taxation to practicing lawyers, many of whom also have CPAs. In a field complicated enough to warrant such detailed study, we can only cover the highlights. This is all that is really necessary, because business people and investors should and do rely on tax specialists rather than trust their own limited knowledge. Still, it is important to know the basic elements of the tax system as a starting point for discussions with tax experts.[5]

Individual Income Taxes

Individuals pay taxes on wages and salaries, on investment income (dividends, interest, and profits from the sale of securities), and on the profits of proprietorships and partnerships. Our tax rates are *progressive;* that is, the higher the income, the larger the percentage paid in taxes. Rates

5 It should be noted that Congress changes the tax laws fairly often. The provisions given here are those for 1979 as they existed in December 1979.

in 1979 ranged from 14 percent on the first $500 of taxable income to 70 percent on each dollar of income over $100,000, with a 50 percent limit on such earned income as salaries.[6]

The tax rate on the last unit of income is defined as the *marginal tax rate.* Thus, for a person with taxable income in excess of $100,000, the marginal tax rate is 70 percent. (The *average tax rate* on the $100,000 would be much lower than 70 percent.)

Taxes on Dividend and Interest Income Dividend and interest income is fully taxed at rates going up to 70 percent.[7] Since corporations pay dividends out of earnings that have already been taxed, there is *double taxation* of corporate income. To partially offset double taxation, the first $100 of dividend income ($200 for married couples with jointly owned stock) is *excluded* from personal income taxes.

Capital Gain versus Ordinary Income Assets such as stocks, bonds, and real estate are defined as *capital assets.* If you buy a capital asset and later sell it for more than your purchase price, the profit is defined as a *capital gain.* If you suffer a loss, it is called a *capital loss.*

An asset sold within one year of the time it was purchased produces a *short-term gain or loss,* while an asset held for more than one year produces a *long-term gain or loss.* Thus, if you buy 100 shares of GM stock for $70 per share and sell it for $80, you make a capital gain of 100 × $10, or $1,000. If you sell the stock for $60, you have a $1,000 capital loss. If you hold the stock for more than one year, the gain or loss is long-term; otherwise, it is short-term.

Long-term capital gains are generally taxed at much lower rates than short-term gains (or other ordinary income). As a rule, 60 percent of any long-term gain is deducted, so taxes are paid on only 40 percent of long-term gains income. Thus, if one individual has $1,000 of short-term capital gains (or dividends) and is in the 30 percent marginal tax bracket, the gains tax would be $300, while if another individual in the same bracket had $1,000 of long-term gains, the tax would be only 0.3 ($1,000 − $600) =

---

6 It is interesting to note what happens to taxes under inflation. Suppose you had a taxable income of $10,000. Your tax bill would be $2,090. Now suppose inflation causes prices to double, and your income, being tied to a cost of living index, rises to $20,000. Because our tax rates are progressive, your taxes would jump to $5,230. Your after-tax income has thus increased from $7,910 to $14,770, but, since prices have doubled, your real income has *declined* from $7,910 to $7,385 (calculated as 1/2 of $14,770). You are in a higher tax bracket, so you are paying a higher percentage of your real income in taxes. If this happens to everyone, and if Congress fails to change tax rates sufficiently, then the federal government gets a larger share of the national product. This is exactly what has been happening during the 1970s.

7 However, interest on state and local government bonds is not subject to federal income taxes. Thus, for a taxpayer in the 70 percent bracket, a 3.6 percent state bond would provide as much after-tax income as a 12 percent corporate bond:

Tax exempt yield = Taxable yield (1 − Tax rate) = 12% (0.3) = 3.6%.

$120. As a percentage, the long-term gains tax rate is 40 percent of the ordinary tax rate.[8]

The fact that capital gains income is taxed at a lower rate than dividend or interest income has an important bearing on financial management. As we shall see, most businesses have at least some flexibility in providing returns to investors in the form of dividends or of capital gains. Since the tax treatment of income from an asset has a significant effect on the value of the asset, personal income taxes must be taken into account by a firm seeking to maximize the value of its stock.

Corporate Income Taxes

The corporate tax structure is relatively simple. In 1979, corporations were required to pay 17 percent on the first $25,000 of taxable income, and the rates progressed up to 46 percent on all income over $100,000:

1st $25,000: 17%
2nd $25,000: 20%
3rd $25,000: 30%
4th $25,000: 40%
Over $100,000: 46%

Therefore, if a firm had $200,000 of taxable income, its tax bill would be

$$\begin{aligned} \text{Taxes} &= 0.17\,(\$25{,}000) + 0.20\,(\$25{,}000) + 0.30\,(\$25{,}000) \\ &\quad + 0.40\,(\$25{,}000) + 0.46\,(\$100{,}000) \\ &= \$4{,}250 + \$5{,}000 + \$7{,}500 + \$10{,}000 + \$46{,}000 \\ &= \$72{,}750. \end{aligned}$$

Thus, the corporate tax is very progressive up to $100,000 of income, but it is constant thereafter.[9] Also, note that the marginal corporate tax rate is 46 percent if a firm earns over $100,000.

Interest and Dividend Income Received by a Corporation Interest income received by a corporation is taxed as ordinary income at regular corporate tax rates. However, 85 percent of the dividends received by one corporation from another is excluded from taxable income. The remaining 15 percent of dividends received is taxed at the ordinary tax rate. Thus, a corporation earning over $100,000 and paying a 46 percent tax rate would pay $(0.15)\,(0.46) = 0.069 = 6.9$ percent of its dividend income as taxes. If this

---

8 Some complexities in long-term capital gains taxes are not discussed here: (1) Gains realized before October 31, 1978, are treated differently from those realized after that date. (2) Long-term gains are regarded as tax preference items; if tax preferences exceed $10,000, special tax rates apply. (3) Corporate capital gains are treated differently from the gains realized by individuals. (4) For individuals in very high tax brackets, the long-term capital gains tax is generally limited to 28 percent.
9 Corporate capital gains and losses are also subject to special (more favorable) tax treatment, but the rules are too complicated to be described in this book. The interested reader is referred to *Federal Tax Course* (Englewood Cliffs, N.J.: Prentice-Hall, 1979).

corporation passes its own after-tax income on to its stockholders as dividends, the income is ultimately subjected to *triple taxation*—the original corporation is first taxed, then the second corporation is taxed, and finally the individual who receives the dividend is taxed. This is the reason for the 85 percent exclusion on intercorporate dividends.

Notice that if a corporation has surplus funds which can be invested in marketable securities, the tax factor favors investment in stocks, which pay dividends, rather than bonds, which pay interest. For example, suppose a firm had $100,000 to invest and it could buy bonds which pay interest of $10,000 per year or stock which pays dividends of $10,000. If the firm is in the 46 percent tax bracket, its tax on the interest would be 0.46 ($10,000) = $4,600, and its after-tax income would be $5,400. If it bought stock, its tax would be (0.15) ($10,000) (0.46) = $690, and its after-tax income would be $9,310. Other factors might lead the firm to invest in bonds, but the tax factor favors stock investments when the investor is a corporation.

Interest and Dividends Paid by a Corporation A firm's operations can be financed with either debt or equity capital. If it uses debt, it must pay interest on this debt, while firms generally pay dividends to equity investors (stockholders). The interest paid by a corporation is deducted from operating income to obtain taxable income, but dividends paid are not deductible. Thus, interest is paid with before-tax dollars, while dividends are paid with after-tax dollars.

To illustrate, suppose a firm's assets produce $25,000 of income before taxes. If the firm were financed entirely by debt and had interest payments of $25,000, then, as we see in Table 2-1, taxable income to the firm would be zero, taxes would be zero, and investors would receive the entire $25,000. If the firm had no debt and was therefore financed only by stock, the $25,000 would be taxable income to the corporation, the tax would be $25,000 (0.17) = $4,250, and investors would receive only $20,750 versus $25,000 under debt financing. Of course, it is generally not possible to finance exclusively with debt capital, and the risk of doing so would offset the benefits of the

Table 2-1
Cash Flows to Investors under Bond and Stock Financing

	Use Bonds	Use Stock
Before-tax income	$25,000	$25,000
Interest	25,000	0
Taxable income	$ 0	$25,000
Taxes (17%)	0	4,250
After-tax income	$ 0	$20,750
Income to investors	$25,000	$20,750

higher expected income. *Still, the fact that interest is a deductible expense has a profound effect on the way businesses are financed—our tax system favors debt financing over equity financing.* This point is discussed in more detail in Chapters 15 and 16.

Corporate Loss Carry-Back and Carry-Forward Ordinary corporate operating losses can be carried back to each of the three preceding years and forward for the following seven years and used to offset taxable income in those years. For example, an operating loss in 1979 can be used to reduce taxable income in 1976, 1977, or 1978, and then any remaining losses can be carried forward and used in 1980, 1981, 1982, 1983, 1984, 1985, and 1986. The loss is first applied to the earliest year, then to the next earliest year, and so on.

To illustrate, suppose that the Detroit Dolphins, Inc., made $1 million every year except for 1979, when they had a bad season and lost $6 million. The Dolphins would use the carry-back feature to recompute taxes for 1976, using $1 million of the operating losses to reduce the 1976 profit to zero. This would permit them to recover the amount of taxes paid in 1976, so in 1980 the Dolphins would receive a refund of 1976 taxes because of the loss experienced in 1979. Since $5 million of unrecovered losses would still be available, the Dolphins would repeat this procedure for 1977 and 1978. Then in 1980, 1981, and 1982 they would apply the loss carry-forward to reduce profits to zero in each of these years. The purpose of permitting this loss averaging is, of course, to avoid penalizing corporations whose incomes fluctuate widely.

Improper Accumulation to Avoid Payment of Dividends Corporations could refrain from paying dividends to permit their stockholders to avoid personal income taxes on dividends. To prevent this, the tax code states that earnings accumulated by a corporation are subject to penalty rates *if the purpose of the accumulation is to enable stockholders to avoid the personal income tax.* Of income not paid out in dividends, a cumulative total of $150,000 (the balance sheet item "retained earnings") is by law exempted from the improper accumulation tax. This is a benefit primarily to small corporations.

Although there is a penalty rate on all amounts over $150,000 *shown to be unnecessary to meet the reasonable needs of the business,* many companies do indeed have legitimate reasons for retaining earnings over $150,000 and are thus not subject to the penalty rate. Earnings during a given year may be retained and used to pay off debt, to finance growth, and to provide the corporation with a cushion against possible cash drains caused by losses. How much a firm should properly accumulate for uncertain contingencies is a matter of judgment. We shall consider this matter again in Chapter 17, which deals with corporate dividend policy.

Consolidated Corporate Tax Returns If a corporation owns 80 percent or more of another corporation's stock, it can aggregate income and file one consolidated tax return. Thus, losses in one company can be used to offset profits in another company. (Similarly, one division's losses can offset another division's profits.) No business ever wants to incur losses (you can go broke losing $1 to save 46 cents in taxes), but tax offsets do make it more feasible for large, multidivisional corporations to undertake risky new ventures or ventures that will suffer losses during a developmental period.

Investment Tax Credit The investment tax credit (ITC) is designed to stimulate business investment. The ITC is figured as a percentage of the cost of certain new assets used in any corporation, partnership, or proprietorship. Congress varies the ITC depending on economic conditions. In 1979 it was 10 percent for an asset with a life of seven years or more, $6^2/_3$ percent for an asset with a life of five or six years, $3^1/_3$ percent for an asset with a life of three or four years, and zero for an asset with a life of less than three years.

   The ITC is a direct reduction of taxes. Suppose a firm estimates that its taxable income next year will be $100,000 and that its tax bill will be $26,750. Now it decides to buy equipment that costs $50,000 and has a ten year life. The company's tax bill will be reduced by (0.10) ($50,000) = $5,000. *Thus, the ITC reduces the effective cost of fixed assets, and this stimulates investment.*[10]

Taxation of Small Businesses: Subchapter S Corporations

Subchapter S of the Internal Revenue Code provides that small businesses which meet certain restrictions as spelled out in the code may be set up as corporations and thus receive the benefits of the corporate form of organization—especially limited liability—yet still be taxed as proprietorships or as partnerships rather than as corporations. There are several reasons for a small firm's electing to be taxed under the Subchapter S procedures, including the following:

1. If the firm is profitable, its income is reported on a pro rata basis by its owners. This avoids the double taxation that occurs when a corporation reports income, pays taxes, and then pays dividends that are taxable income to the stockholders.
2. If the firm has operating losses, these losses can be claimed on a pro rata

---

10 If a firm does not have sufficiently large income taxes, it cannot fully utilize the ITC immediately. The ITC can be carried forward and used in future years, but there are also financing arrangements that effectively transfer the ITC from low-profit to high-profit firms. The details are covered in the chapter on leasing. Note also that Congress can and does change the ITC rate from time to time to stimulate or slow down the economy.

basis by the stockholders as deductions against their ordinary income. This is an especially attractive feature for a new business that incurs heavy start-up costs and whose stockholders are in high marginal tax brackets because of income from other sources.

3. If the firm has investment tax credits, these credits can be passed along to the stockholders. Again, this is especially important for small, new firms that are making heavy capital investments yet whose income is insufficient to fully utilize the tax credits generated by these investments, but whose owners have outside income that can be offset by the firm's tax credits.

Many factors other than taxes bear on the question of whether or not a firm should be organized as a corporation. However, the existence of Subchapter S makes it possible for most small businesses to have the benefits of a corporation yet be taxed at the owners' personal tax rates.

SUMMARY

This chapter presented some background information on forms of business organizations, interest rates, and income taxes. First, we saw that firms may be organized as *proprietorships,* as *partnerships,* or as *corporations.* The first two types are easy and inexpensive to form. However, corporations have a major advantage in terms of risk reduction, growth possibilities, and investment liquidity. These features make it possible to maximize the value of any business except very small ones by using the corporate form of organization. Accordingly, corporations are the dominant form of business.

Interest rates represent the price of borrowed money. Rates have been rising for the past twenty-five years, pushed up by rising inflation rates. Short-term rates are generally lower than long-term rates, and short-term rates are also subject to wider swings. As a general rule, short-term rates fall during recessions, then rise when the economy is strong. An astute financial manager will recognize these tendencies and try to take advantage of them to finance growth with the lowest-cost capital. Such action, if successful, will help to maximize the value of the firm.

The value of any asset is dependent on the effective income it produces for its owner. *Effective income* means *after-tax income.* Since corporate income is taxed at rates going up to 46 percent, and since personal income is subjected to additional taxes of up to 70 percent, the tax consequences of various decisions have a most important impact on a firm's value. It is not necessary to memorize everything about taxes—indeed, this would be impossible. However, you should know the basic differences between corporate and personal taxes, that interest is a tax deduction to the payer of the interest, that capital gains and operating income are taxed differently, what the investment tax credit is, and so on. These matters will come up throughout the book as we examine various types of financial decisions.

Questions

2-1 What are the three principal forms of business organizations? What are the advantages and disadvantages of each?

2-2 Which fluctuate more, long-term or short-term interest rates?

2-3 You feel that the economy is just entering a recession. Your firm must raise capital immediately, and debt will be used. Would it be better to borrow on a long-term or a short-term basis? Explain.

2-4 What effect does inflation have on long-term interest rates?

2-5 Suppose you owned 100 shares of General Motors stock and the company just earned $6 per share. Suppose further that GM could either pay all its earnings out as dividends (in which case you would receive $600) or retain the earnings in the business, buy more assets, and cause the price of the stock to go up by $6 per share (in which case the value of your stock would rise by $600).

 a. How would the tax laws influence what you, as a typical stockholder, would want the company to do?

 b. Would your choice be influenced by how much other income you had?

 c. How might the corporation's decision with regard to dividend policy influence the price of its stock?

2-6 What does *double taxation of corporate income* mean?

2-7 If you were starting a business, what tax considerations might cause you to prefer to set it up as a proprietorship or a partnership rather than as a corporation?

2-8 Explain how the federal income tax structure affects the choice of financing (debt versus equity) used by U.S. business firms.

2-9 How can the federal government influence the level of business investment by adjusting the ITC?

Problems

2-1 The Oscar Minor Weenie Company had an income of $120,000 from operations after all operating costs but before (a) interest charges of $10,000, (b) dividends paid of $20,000, and (c) income taxes. What is Oscar Minor's income tax liability?

2-2 a. The Thomas Corporation had $100,000 of taxable income from operations. What is the company's federal income tax bill for the year?

 b. Assume Thomas receives an additional $10,000 interest income from some bonds it owns. What is the tax on this interest income?

 c. Now assume that Thomas does not receive the interest income but that it does receive an additional $10,000 as dividends on some stock it owns. What is the tax on this dividend income?

2-3 The Columbus Construction Company has made $100,000 before taxes for each of the last fifteen years, and it expects to make $100,000 a year before taxes in the future. However, this year (1980) Columbus incurred a loss of

$600,000. Columbus will claim a tax credit at the time it files its 1980 income tax returns and will receive a check from the U.S. Treasury. Show how it calculates this credit, and then indicate Columbus's tax liability for each of the next five years. Assume a 50 percent tax rate on *all* income to ease the calculations.

APPENDIX 2A   DEPRECIATION[1]

Depreciation is a deductible expense. Several different depreciation methods are permitted for tax purposes, and the choice of the tax depreciation method used can have a profound effect on a firm's tax liabilities. The four principal methods of depreciation—straight line, sum-of-years' digits, double declining balance, and units of production—and their effects on a firm's taxes are illustrated in this appendix. We will begin by assuming that a machine is purchased for $2,500 and has an estimated useful life of six years or 6,000 hours. It will have a scrap value of $400 after six years of use or after 6,000 hours, whichever comes first. Figure 2A–1 graphs the depreciation charges under straight line and double declining balance. Table 2A–1 illustrates each of the four depreciation methods and compares the depreciation charges under each method over the six year period.

Straight Line

With the straight line method, a uniform annual depreciation charge of $350 a year is allowed. This figure is arrived at by simply dividing the economic life into the total cost of the machine minus the estimated salvage value:

Figure 2A–1
Double Declining Balance versus Straight Line Depreciation

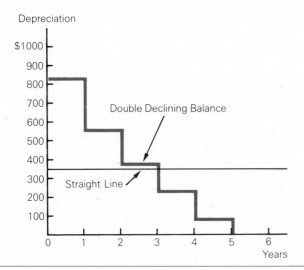

1 This appendix is included here because accelerated depreciation methods are used primarily for purposes of calculating taxable income. However, the appendix could just as logically be covered in connection with Chapter 6, which deals with financial statements, or with Chapter 11, which deals with capital budgeting.

Table 2A–1
Comparison of Depreciation
Methods for a Six Year,
$2,500 Asset with a $400
Salvage Value

Year	Straight Line	Double Declining Balance (DDB)	Sum-of-Years'-Digits (SYD)	Units of Production[a]
1	$ 350	$ 833	$ 600	$ 700
2	350	556	500	630
3	350	370	400	350
4	350	247	300	210
5	350	94[b]	200	140
6	350	—	100	70
Total	$2,100	$2,100	$2,100	$2,100

[a]The assumption is made that the machine is used the following number of hours: first year, 2,000; second year, 1,800; third year, 1,000; fourth year, 600; fifth year, 400; sixth year, 200.

[b]The maximum depreciation that can be taken is the value of cost minus salvage, or $2,100 in this example. Thus, $94 of depreciation in Year 5 exhausts the depreciation allowed under DDB.

$$\frac{\$2,500 \text{ cost} - \$400 \text{ salvage value}}{6 \text{ years}} = \$350 \text{ a year depreciation charge.}$$

If the estimated salvage value had been less than 10 percent of the original cost, it could have been ignored.

Double Declining Balance

The double declining balance (DDB) method of depreciation requires the application of a constant rate of depreciation each year to the undepreciated value of the asset at the close of the previous year. To calculate DDB depreciation, we first find the fraction $1/N$, where N is the life of the asset. In our example, $1/N = 1/6 = 0.1667$. This fraction is then doubled, giving 0.3333 in this case, and it is called the "depreciation rate." This rate is applied to the full purchase price of the machine, not to the cost less salvage value. Therefore, depreciation under the DDB method during the first year is calculated as follows:

$$0.3333 \ (\$2,500) = \$833.$$

Depreciation during the second year is calculated by applying the 33.33 percent rate (or 0.3333) to the undepreciated balance as follows:

$$0.3333(\$2,500 - \$833) = 0.3333(\$1,667) = \$556.$$

The process is continued for other years, until the total depreciation taken equals the cost of the asset less the estimated salvage value. Thus, in the illustrative case, the asset is fully depreciated during the fifth year.

The total amount of depreciation taken under the DDB method is equal to that under straight line, but under DDB the depreciation is taken faster, as it is under sum-of-years'-digits. Thus, DDB and sum-of-years'-digits are called *accelerated depreciation methods*.[2]

Sum-of-Years'-Digits

Under the sum-of-years'-digits (SYD) method, the yearly depreciation allowance is determined as follows:

1. Calculate the SYDs. In our example there is a total of 21 digits: $1 + 2 + 3 + 4 + 5 + 6 = 21$. This figure can also be arrived at by means of the sum of an algebraic progression equation, where N is the life of the asset:

$$\text{Sum} = N\left(\frac{N + 1}{2}\right)$$

$$= 6\left(\frac{6 + 1}{2}\right) = 21.$$

2. Divide the number of remaining years by the SYDs and multiply this fraction by the depreciable cost (total cost minus salvage value) of the asset:

$$\text{Year 1:} \quad \left(\frac{6}{21}\right)(\$2,100) = \$600 \text{ depreciation}$$

$$\text{Year 2:} \quad \left(\frac{5}{21}\right)(\$2,100) = \$500 \text{ depreciation}$$

$$\text{Year 6:} \quad \left(\frac{1}{21}\right)(\$2,100) = \$100 \text{ depreciation.}$$

Units of Production

Under the units of production method, the expected useful life of 6,000 hours is divided into the depreciable cost (purchase price minus salvage value) to arrive at an hourly depreciation rate of 35 cents. Since, in our example, the machine is run for 2,000 hours in the first year, the depreciation in that year is $700; in the second year it is $630; and so on. With this method, depreciation charges cannot be estimated precisely ahead of time; the firm must wait until the end of the year to determine what usage has been made of the machine and, hence, its depreciation.

---

2 It should also be noted that a firm may switch from DDB (or SYD) to straight line whenever it becomes advantageous to do so. The undepreciated balance, less the estimated salvage value, is divided by the remaining life to get the annual depreciation. If this value is larger than the DDB depreciation, then the switch should be made. In our example, it is not advantageous to switch. Had the salvage value been lower, then a switch would have been advantageous.

Effect of Depreciation on Taxes Paid

The effect of the accelerated methods on a firm's income tax payment is easily demonstrated. In the first year, if the firm chooses to use the straight line method, only $350 may be deducted from its earnings to arrive at earnings before taxes (the amount of earnings to which the tax rate applies). However, using any one of the other three methods, the firm would have a much greater deduction and, therefore, a lower tax liability.

This point is illustrated in Table 2A–2, which shows the cash flows a hypothetical firm will generate if it uses straight line versus double declining balance depreciation. In Year 1, taxes are lower under DDB depreciation, hence cash flows are higher. However, the situation changes over time—in later years, the depreciation tax shelter declines in the DDB case, causing taxes to rise and cash flows to decline.

Over the entire six year period, total cash flows are the same for the two cases. However, since cash received sooner is more valuable than cash received later, a firm that uses accelerated depreciation and thus speeds up the cash flows from

Table 2A–2
Cash Flow Effects: Straight Line versus DDB Depreciation

	Straight Line	DDB
Year 1		
Sales (all cash)	$2,000	$2,000
Costs other than depreciation (all cash)	1,000	1,000
Depreciation (not a cash charge)	350	833
Total deductible costs	$1,350	$1,833
Taxable income	650	167
Taxes (assume a 40% rate)	$ 260	$ 67
Cash flow = sales − other costs − taxes	$ 740	$ 933
Year 6		
Sales (all cash)	$2,000	$2,000
Costs other than depreciation (all cash)	1,000	1,000
Depreciation (not a cash charge)	350	—
Total deductible costs	$1,350	$1,000
Taxable income	650	1,000
Taxes (assume a 40% rate)	$ 260	$ 400
Cash flow = sales − other costs − taxes	$ 740	$ 600

operations will have a higher value than a similar firm that uses straight line depreciation. Similarly, an asset that can be depreciated by an accelerated method will have a higher value than one that must be depreciated by straight line.[3]

Changing the Depreciable Life of an Asset

Assets are depreciated over their estimated useful lives, which may be based on the firm's actual operating experience with similar assets or on guideline lives specified by the Internal Revenue Service for specific classes of assets (class life asset depreciation range [ADR] figures). If the ADR life is used, depreciation may be calculated by any one of the first three methods described, and the salvage value need not be included when calculating depreciation. However, assets may not be depreciated below a reasonable estimate of the salvage value; see Table 2A−1, DDB, for an illustration of this point.

Problem

2A-1 a. The Ajax Company acquires a machine tool that costs $50,000, has a five year life, and will have a zero salvage value. Calculate the depreciation schedule on the asset under the straight line, double declining balance, and sum-of-years'-digits methods.

b. Assume that Ajax earns $20,000 per year before depreciation and income taxes on the machine tool (sales − operating expenses = $20,000). What are Ajax's tax bill, profit after tax, and cash flow[4] in Year 1 and Year 5 under (1) straight line and (2) sum-of-years'-digits depreciation? For convenience, assume the company pays a 20 percent tax rate on *all* taxable income.

c. Suppose the investment tax credit is currently 9 percent on assets with lives of eight years or longer, 6 percent on assets with lives of six or seven years, and 3 percent on assets with lives of four or five years. How would the ITC affect Ajax's tax situation? (Assume that Ajax will be able to use the calculated credit in full.)

d. Consider the question of Ajax's changing depreciation, for example, from DDB to SYD, or from either DDB or SYD to straight line. (The IRS permits such switches under certain conditions.) Would a switch be appropriate for Ajax?

---

3 Firms may report profit to stockholders using straight line depreciation even though they use an accelerated depreciation method for tax purposes. The difference between taxes actually paid during the year (the actual tax bill) and the taxes that would have been paid had the firm used straight line for tax purposes is reported on the income statement as "deferred taxes," and the accumulated deferred taxes over the years is reported on the balance sheet as a liability item. This treatment, which is called "normalization" for timing differences in the reporting of depreciation for tax and book purposes, would keep our illustrative firm from having to report lower income just because it elected to use accelerated depreciation for tax purposes.

4 Cash flows, which are discussed in detail in Chapter 6, are equal to net income after taxes plus depreciation.

II FUNDAMENTAL CONCEPTS IN FINANCE: RISK, RETURN, AND VALUE

Each financial decision must be analyzed in terms of its effect on the value of the firm's stock. This requires a knowledge of how alternative decisions will impact on stock prices. A stock price model is essential to such knowledge. Accordingly, we develop in Part II a basic stock valuation model for use throughout the remainder of the book.

Part II begins with Chapter 3, which takes up the concept of the time value of money. Next, in Chapter 4, we use this concept to see how bond and stock values are determined. Finally, Chapter 5 discusses the concept of risk, including ways of measuring a security's risk and the impact risk has on stock prices and rates of return.

3   TIME VALUE OF MONEY

In Chapter 1 we saw that the primary goal of management is to maximize the value of a firm's stock. We also saw that stock values depend, in part, on the timing of the cash flows investors expect to receive—income expected soon is valued more highly than income expected far in the future. These concepts are extended and made more precise in this chapter, which shows how the timing of cash flows affects asset values and rates of return.

The principles of the time value of money as developed here also have many other applications, ranging from setting up schedules for paying off loans to making decisions about whether to acquire new equipment. *In fact, of all the techniques used in finance, none is more important than the time value of money.* This concept is used throughout the remainder of the book, so it is vital to understand the material in this chapter thoroughly before going on to other topics.

FUTURE VALUE (OR COMPOUND VALUE)

A dollar in hand today is worth more than a future dollar because, if you had it now, you could invest it and earn interest. To illustrate, suppose you had $100 and deposited it in a bank savings account that paid 5 percent interest compounded annually. How much would you have at the end of one year? Let us define terms as follows:

PV = present value of your account, or the beginning amount, $100.

k = interest rate the bank pays you = 5 percent per year, or, expressed as a decimal, 0.05.

I = dollars of interest you earn during the year.

FV_n = future value, or ending amount, of your account at the end of n years. Whereas PV is the value now, at the *present* time, FV_n is the value n years into the future, after compound interest has been earned. Note also that FV_0 is the future value *zero* years into the future, which is the *present,* so $FV_0 = PV$.

In our example, $n = 1$, so $FV_n = FV_1$, and it is calculated as follows:

$$FV_1 = PV + I$$
$$= PV + PV(k)$$
$$= PV(1 + k). \tag{3-1}$$

We can now use Equation 3–1 to find how much your account is worth at the end of one year:

$$FV_1 = \$100(1 + 0.05) = \$100(1.05) = \$105.$$

Your account earned $5 of interest ($I = \$5$), so you have $105 at the end of the year.

Now suppose you leave your funds on deposit for five years; how much will you have at the end of the fifth year? The answer is $127.63; this value is worked out in Table 3–1.

Table 3–1
Compound Interest Calculations

Year	Beginning Amount, PV	×	(1 + k)	=	Ending Amount, FV_n
1	$100.00		1.05		$105.00
2	105.00		1.05		110.25
3	110.25		1.05		115.76
4	115.76		1.05		121.55
5	121.55		1.05		127.63

Notice that the Table 3–1 value for FV_2, the value of the account at the end of Year 2, is equal to

$$FV_2 = FV_1(1 + k) = PV(1 + k)(1 + k) = PV(1 + k)^2.$$

Continuing, we see that FV_3, the balance after three years, is

$$FV_3 = FV_2(1 + k) = PV(1 + k)^3.$$

In general, FV_n, the future value at the end of n years, is found as follows:

$$FV_n = PV(1 + k)^n. \tag{3-2}$$

Applying Equation 3–2 to our five year, 5 percent case, we obtain

$$FV_5 = \$100(1.05)^5$$
$$= \$100(1.2763)$$
$$= \$127.63,$$

which is the same as the value worked out in Table 3–1.

If an electronic calculator is handy, it is easy enough to calculate $(1 + k)^n$ directly.[1] However, tables have been constructed for values of $(1 + k)^n$ for wide ranges of k and n. Table 3–2 is illustrative. Notice that we have used the term *period* rather than *year* in Table 3–2. As we shall see later in the chapter, compounding can occur over periods of time different from one year. Thus, while compounding is often on an annual basis, it can be quarterly, semiannually, monthly, or for any other period.

Table 3–2
Future Value of $1 at the End of n Periods:
$$\text{FVIF}_{k,n} = (1 + k)^n$$

Period (n)	1%	2%	3%	4%	5%	6%	7%	8%	9%	10%
0	1.0000	1.0000	1.0000	1.0000	1.0000	1.0000	1.0000	1.0000	1.0000	1.0000
1	1.0100	1.0200	1.0300	1.0400	1.0500	1.0600	1.0700	1.0800	1.0900	1.1000
2	1.0201	1.0404	1.0609	1.0816	1.1025	1.1236	1.1449	1.1664	1.1881	1.2100
3	1.0303	1.0612	1.0927	1.1249	1.1576	1.1910	1.2250	1.2597	1.2950	1.3310
4	1.0406	1.0824	1.1255	1.1699	1.2155	1.2625	1.3108	1.3605	1.4116	1.4641
5	1.0510	1.1041	1.1593	1.2167	1.2763	1.3382	1.4026	1.4693	1.5386	1.6105
6	1.0615	1.1262	1.1941	1.2653	1.3401	1.4185	1.5007	1.5869	1.6771	1.7716
7	1.0721	1.1487	1.2299	1.3159	1.4071	1.5036	1.6058	1.7138	1.8280	1.9487
8	1.0829	1.1717	1.2668	1.3686	1.4775	1.5938	1.7182	1.8509	1.9926	2.1436
9	1.0937	1.1951	1.3048	1.4233	1.5513	1.6895	1.8385	1.9990	2.1719	2.3579
10	1.1046	1.2190	1.3439	1.4802	1.6289	1.7908	1.9672	2.1589	2.3674	2.5937
11	1.1157	1.2434	1.3842	1.5395	1.7103	1.8983	2.1049	2.3316	2.5804	2.8531
12	1.1268	1.2682	1.4258	1.6010	1.7959	2.0122	2.2522	2.5182	2.8127	3.1384
13	1.1381	1.2936	1.4685	1.6651	1.8856	2.1329	2.4098	2.7196	3.0658	3.4523
14	1.1495	1.3195	1.5126	1.7317	1.9799	2.2609	2.5785	2.9372	3.3417	3.7975
15	1.1610	1.3459	1.5580	1.8009	2.0789	2.3966	2.7590	3.1722	3.6425	4.1772

We define the term *future value interest factor* ($\text{FVIF}_{k,n}$) to equal $(1 + k)^n$. Therefore, Equation 3–2 may be written as $\text{FV}_n = \text{PV}(\text{FVIF}_{k,n})$. It is necessary only to go to an appropriate interest table to find the proper interest factor. For example, the correct interest factor for our five year, 5 percent illustration can be found in Table 3–2. We look down the period column to 5, then across this row to the 5 percent column to find the interest factor, 1.2763. Then, using this interest factor, we find the value of $100 after five years as $\text{FV}_n = \text{PV}(\text{FVIF}_{k,n}) = \$100(1.2763) = \$127.63$, which is identical to the value obtained by the long method in Table 3–1.

---

1 For example, to calculate $(1 + k)^n$ for $k = 5\% = 0.05$ and $n = 5$ years, we multiply $(1 + k) = (1.05)$ times (1.05); multiply this product by (1.05); and so on:

$$(1 + k)^n = (1.05)(1.05)(1.05)(1.05)(1.05) = (1.05)^5 = 1.2763.$$

Graphic View of the Compounding Process: Growth

Figure 3–1 shows how $1 (or any other sum) grows over time at various rates of interest. The points plotted on the 5 percent and 10 percent curves are taken from the appropriate columns of Table 3–2. The higher the rate of interest, the faster the rate of growth. The interest rate is, in fact, the growth rate; if a sum is deposited and earns 5 percent, then the funds on deposit grow at the rate of 5 percent per period.

Figure 3–1
Relationship between Future Value Interest Factors, Interest Rates, and Time

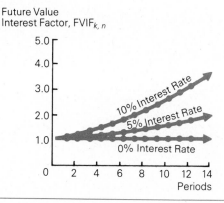

PRESENT VALUE

Suppose you are offered the alternative of receiving either $127.63 at the end of five years or X dollars today. There is no question that the $127.63 will be paid in full (perhaps the payer is the United States government). Having no current need for the money, you would deposit it in a bank account that pays 5 percent interest. (Five percent is defined to be your "opportunity cost," or the rate of interest you could earn on alternative investments of equal risk.) What value of X would make you indifferent between X dollars today and the promise of $127.63 five years hence?

Table 3–1 shows that the initial amount of $100 growing at 5 percent a year yields $127.63 at the end of five years. Thus, you should be indifferent in your choice between $100 today and $127.63 at the end of five years. The $100 is defined as the present value, or PV, of $127.63 due in five years when the applicable interest rate is 5 percent. Therefore, if X is anything less than $100, you would prefer the promise of $127.63 in five years to X dollars today.

In general, the present value of a sum due n years in the future is the amount which, if it were on hand today, would grow to equal the future sum. Since $100 would grow to $127.63 in five years at a 5 percent interest rate, $100 is defined to be the present value of $127.63 due five years in the future when the appropriate interest rate is 5 percent.

Finding present value (or *discounting,* as it is commonly called) is simply the reverse of compounding, and Equation 3–2 can readily be transformed into a present value formula:

$$FV_n = PV(1 + k)^n, \qquad (3\text{–}2)$$

which, when solved for PV, gives

$$PV = \frac{FV_n}{(1 + k)^n} = FV_n\left[\frac{1}{(1 + k)}\right]^n. \qquad (3\text{–}3)$$

Tables have been constructed for the term in brackets for various values of k and n; Table 3–3 is an example. For a more complete table, see Table A–1 at the end of the book. For the illustrative case being considered, look down the 5 percent column in Table 3–3 to the fifth row. The figure shown there, 0.7835, is the *present value interest factor* ($PVIF_{k,n}$) used to determine the present value of $127.63 payable in five years, discounted at 5 percent:

$$PV = FV_5(PVIF_{k,n})$$
$$= \$127.63(0.7835)$$
$$= \$100.$$

Table 3–3
Present Values of $1 Due at the End of n Periods:

$$PVIF_{k,n} = \frac{1}{(1 + k)^n} = \left[\frac{1}{(1 + k)}\right]^n$$

Period (n)	1%	2%	3%	4%	5%	6%	7%	8%	9%	10%	12%	14%	15%
1	.9901	.9804	.9709	.9615	.9524	.9434	.9346	.9259	.9174	.9091	.8929	.8772	.8696
2	.9803	.9612	.9426	.9246	.9070	.8900	.8734	.8573	.8417	.8264	.7972	.7695	.7561
3	.9706	.9423	.9151	.8890	.8638	.8396	.8163	.7938	.7722	.7513	.7118	.6750	.6575
4	.9610	.9238	.8885	.8548	.8227	.7921	.7629	.7350	.7084	.6830	.6355	.5921	.5718
5	.9515	.9057	.8626	.8219	.7835	.7473	.7130	.6806	.6499	.6209	.5674	.5194	.4972
6	.9420	.8880	.8375	.7903	.7462	.7050	.6663	.6302	.5963	.5645	.5066	.4556	.4323
7	.9327	.8706	.8131	.7599	.7107	.6651	.6227	.5835	.5470	.5132	.4523	.3996	.3759
8	.9235	.8535	.7894	.7307	.6768	.6274	.5820	.5403	.5019	.4665	.4039	.3506	.3269
9	.9143	.8368	.7664	.7026	.6446	.5919	.5439	.5002	.4604	.4241	.3606	.3075	.2843
10	.9053	.8203	.7441	.6756	.6139	.5584	.5083	.4632	.4224	.3855	.3220	.2697	.2472

Graphic View of the Discounting Process

Figure 3–2 shows how the interest factors for discounting decrease as the discounting period increases. The curves in the figure were plotted with data taken from Table 3–3; they show that the present value of a sum to be received at some future date decreases (1) as the payment date is extended further into the future and (2) as the discount rate increases. If relatively high discount rates apply, funds due in the future are worth very little today. Even at relatively low discount rates, the present values of funds due in the distant future are quite small. For example, $1 due in ten years is worth about 61 cents today if the discount rate is 5 percent, but it is worth only 25 cents today at a 15 percent discount rate. Similarly, $1 due in five years at 10 percent is worth 62 cents today, but at the same discount rate $1 due in ten years is worth only 39 cents today.

Figure 3–2
Relationship between Present Value Interest Factors, Interest Rates, and Time

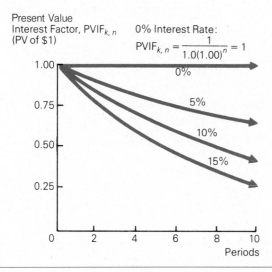

Present Value
Interest Factor, $PVIF_{k,n}$
(PV of $1)

0% Interest Rate:

$$PVIF_{k,n} = \frac{1}{1.0(1.00)^n} = 1$$

FUTURE VALUE VERSUS PRESENT VALUE

Notice that Equation 3–2, the basic equation for compounding, was developed from the logical sequence set forth in Table 3–1; the equation merely presents in mathematical form the steps outlined in the table. The present value interest factor ($PVIF_{k,n}$) in Equation 3–3, the basic equation for discounting or finding present values, was found as the *reciprocal* of the future value interest factor ($FVIF_{k,n}$) for the same *k,n* combination. In other words,

$$PVIF_{k,n} = \frac{1}{FVIF_{k,n}}.$$

For example, the *future value* interest factor for 5 percent over five years is seen in Table 3–2 to be 1.2763. The *present value* interest factor for 5 percent over five years must be the reciprocal of 1.2763:

$$PVIF_{5\%,\ 5\ years} = \frac{1}{1.2763} = 0.7835.$$

The $PVIF_{k,n}$ found in this manner does, of course, correspond with the $PVIF_{k,n}$ shown in Table 3–3.

The reciprocal nature of the relationship between present value and future value permits us to find present values in two ways—by multiplying or by dividing. Thus, the present value of $1,000 due in five years and discounted at 5 percent may be found as

$$PV = FV_n(PVIF_{k,n}) = FV_n\left[\frac{1}{1+k}\right]^n = \$1,000(0.7835) = \$783.50,$$

or as

$$PV = \frac{FV_n}{FVIF_{k,n}} = \frac{FV_5}{(1+k)^5} = \frac{\$1,000}{1.2763} = \$783.50.$$

To conclude this comparison of present and future values, compare Figures 3–1 and 3–2. Notice that the vertical intercept is at 1.0 in each case, but future value interest factors rise, while present value interest factors decline.[2]

FUTURE VALUE OF AN ANNUITY

An annuity is defined as a series of payments of a fixed amount for a specified number of periods. If payments occur at the end of each period, as they typically do, then we have a *regular annuity,* or a *deferred payment annuity* as it is sometimes called. If payments are made at the beginning of each period, then we have an *annuity due.* Since regular (or deferred) annuities are far more common in finance, when the word *annuity* is used in this book, you may assume that payments are received at the end of each period unless otherwise indicated.

A promise to pay $1,000 a year for three years is a three year annuity. If

---

2 Notice that Figure 3–2 is not a mirror image of Figure 3–1. The curves in Figure 3–1 approach ∞ as *n* increases; in Figure 3–2 the curves approach zero, not $-\infty$.

you were to receive such an annuity and were to deposit each annual payment in a savings account paying 4 percent interest, how much would you have at the end of three years? The answer is shown graphically as a *time line* in Figure 3–3. The first payment is made at the end of Year 1, the second at the end of Year 2, and the third at the end of Year 3. The last payment is not compounded at all; the second payment is compounded for one year; and the first is compounded for two years. When the future values of each of the payments are added, their total is the sum of the annuity. In the example, this total is $3,121.60.[3]

Figure 3–3
Time Line for an Annuity: Future Value
with $k = 4\%$

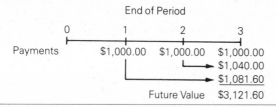

End of Period

	0	1	2	3
Payments		$1,000.00	$1,000.00	$1,000.00
				$1,040.00
				$1,081.60
			Future Value	$3,121.60

Expressed algebraically, with S_n defined as the future value of the annuity, R as the periodic receipt, n as the length of the annuity, and $\text{FVIFA}_{k,n}$ as the future value interest factor for an annuity, the formula for S_n is

$$S_n = R(1 + k)^{n-1} + R(1 + k)^{n-2} + \cdots + R(1 + k)^1 + R(1 + k)^0$$

$$= R[(1 + k)^{n-1} + (1 + k)^{n-2} + \cdots + (1 + k)^1 + (1 + k)^0]$$

$$= R \sum_{t=1}^{n} (1 + k)^{n-t}$$

$$= R[\text{FVIFA}_{k,n}].$$

The expression in brackets, $\text{FVIFA}_{k,n}$, has been calculated for various combinations of k and n.[4] An illustrative set of these annuity interest factors

---

3 Had the annuity been an annuity due, the first $1,000 payment would have occurred at time $t = 0$, the second at $t = 1$, and the third at $t = 2$. Thus, each payment would have been compounded for an extra year, so the future value would have been larger. (It would have been $3,246.46.)

4 The third equation is simply a shorthand expression in which sigma (Σ) signifies "sum up" or add the values of n factors. If $t = 1$, then $(1 + k)^{n-t} = (1 + k)^{n-1}$; if $t = 2$, then $(1 + k)^{n-t} = (1 + k)^{n-2}$; and so on until $t = n$, the last year the annuity provides any returns.

The symbol $\sum_{t=1}^{n}$ simply says, "Go through the following process: Let $t = 1$ and find the first factor.

Then let $t = 2$ and find the second factor. Continue until each individual factor has been found, and then add these individual factors to find the value of the annuity."

is given in Table 3–4.[5] To find the answer to the three year, $1,000 annuity problem, simply refer to Table 3–4, look down the 4 percent column to the row of the third period, and multiply the factor 3.1216 by $1,000. The answer is the same as the one derived by the long method illustrated in Figure 3–3:

$$S_n = R(\text{FVIFA}_{k,n}) \tag{3–4}$$

$$S_3 = \$1,000(3.1216) = \$3,121.60.$$

Notice that for all positive interest rates, the $\text{FVIFA}_{k,n}$ for the sum of an annuity is always equal to or greater than the number of periods the annuity runs.[6]

Table 3–4
Sum of an Annuity of $1 per Period for n Periods:

$$\text{FVIFA}_{k,n} = \sum_{t=1}^{n} (1 + k)^{n-t}$$

$$= \frac{(1 + k)^n - 1}{k}$$

Number of Periods	1%	2%	3%	4%	5%	6%	7%	8%
1	1.0000	1.0000	1.0000	1.0000	1.0000	1.0000	1.0000	1.0000
2	2.0100	2.0200	2.0300	2.0400	2.0500	2.0600	2.0700	2.0800
3	3.0301	3.0604	3.0909	3.1216	3.1525	3.1836	3.2149	3.2464
4	4.0604	4.1216	4.1836	4.2465	4.3101	4.3746	4.4399	4.5061
5	5.1010	5.2040	5.3091	5.4163	5.5256	5.6371	5.7507	5.8666
6	6.1520	6.3081	6.4684	6.6330	6.8019	6.9753	7.1533	7.3359
7	7.2135	7.4343	7.6625	7.8983	8.1420	8.3938	8.6540	8.9228
8	8.2857	8.5830	8.8923	9.2142	9.5491	9.8975	10.2598	10.6366
9	9.3685	9.7546	10.1591	10.5828	11.0266	11.4913	11.9780	12.4876
10	10.4622	10.9497	11.4639	12.0061	12.5779	13.1808	13.8164	14.4866

5 The equation given with Table 3–4 recognizes that an FVIFA factor is the sum of a geometric progression. The proof of this equation is given in all college algebra texts. Notice that it is easy to use the equation to develop annuity factors. This is especially useful if you need the FVIFA for some interest rate not given in the tables, for example, 6.5 percent. The equation is also useful for finding factors for fractional periods—for example, $2\frac{1}{2}$ years—but one really needs a calculator with an exponential function for this. See Problem 3-22 for an example.

6 It is worth noting that the entry for each period t in Table 3–4 is equal to the sum of the entries in Table 3–2 up to Period $n - 1$. For example, the entry for Period 3 under the 4 percent column in Table 3–4 is equal to $1.000 + 1.0400 + 1.0816 = 3.1216$.

    Also, had the annuity been an *annuity due*, then the three payments would have occurred at $t = 0$, $t = 1$, and $t = 2$. To find the future value of an annuity due, (1) look up the $\text{FVIFA}_{k,n}$ for $n + 1$ years, then subtract 1.0 from the amount to get the $\text{FVIFA}_{k,n}$ for the annuity due. In the example, the annuity due $\text{FVIFA}_{k,n}$ is $4.2465 - 1.0 = 3.2465$ versus 3.1216 for a regular annuity. Because payments on an annuity due come earlier, it is a little more valuable than a regular (deferred) annuity.

PRESENT VALUE OF AN ANNUITY

Suppose you were offered the following alternatives: a three year annuity of $1,000 a year or a lump sum payment today. You have no need for the money during the next three years, so if you accept the annuity you would simply deposit the receipts in a savings account paying 4 percent interest. How large must the lump sum payment be to make it equivalent to the annuity? The time line shown in Figure 3–4 will help explain the problem.

Figure 3–4
Time Line for an Annuity: Present Value with
$k = 4\%$

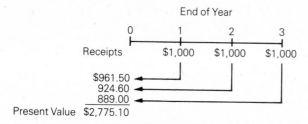

The present value of the first receipt is $R[1/(1 + k)]$, the second is $R[1/(1 + k)]^2$, and so on. Defining the present value of an annuity of n years as A_n, and with $PVIFA_{k,n}$ defined as the present value interest factor for an annuity, we may write the following equation:

$$A_n = R\left(\frac{1}{1 + k}\right)^1 + R\left(\frac{1}{1 + k}\right)^2 + \cdots + R\left(\frac{1}{1 + k}\right)^n$$

$$= R\left(\frac{1}{(1 + k)} + \frac{1}{(1 + k)^2} + \cdots + \frac{1}{(1 + k)^n}\right)$$

$$= R\sum_{t=1}^{n}\left(\frac{1}{1 + k}\right)^t$$

$$= R(PVIFA_{k,n}). \qquad (3-5)$$

Again, tables have been worked out for $PVIFA_{k,n}$, the term in parentheses. Table 3–5 is illustrative; a more complete listing is found in Table A–2 in Appendix A. From Table 3–5, the $PVIFA_{k,n}$ for a three year, 4 percent annuity is found to be 2.7751. Multiplying this factor by the $1,000 annual receipt gives $2,775.10, the present value of the annuity. This figure is identical to the long-method answer shown in Figure 3–4:

Table 3–5
Present Value of an Annuity of $1 per Period
for _n_ Periods:

$$\text{PVIFA}_{k,n} = \sum_{t=1}^{n} \frac{1}{(1+k)^t} = \frac{1 - \frac{1}{(1+k)^n}}{k}$$

Number of Payments (n)	1%	2%	3%	4%	5%	6%	7%	8%	9%	10%
1	0.9901	0.9804	0.9709	0.9615	0.9524	0.9434	0.9346	0.9259	0.9174	0.9091
2	1.9704	1.9416	1.9135	1.8861	1.8594	1.8334	1.8080	1.7833	1.7591	1.7355
3	2.9410	2.8839	2.8286	2.7751	2.7232	2.6730	2.6243	2.5771	2.5313	2.4869
4	3.9020	3.8077	3.7171	3.6299	3.5460	3.4651	3.3872	3.3121	3.2397	3.1699
5	4.8534	4.7135	4.5797	4.4518	4.3295	4.2124	4.1002	3.9927	3.8897	3.7908
6	5.7955	5.6014	5.4172	5.2421	5.0757	4.9173	4.7665	4.6229	4.4859	4.3553
7	6.7282	6.4720	6.2303	6.0021	5.7864	5.5824	5.3893	5.2064	5.0330	4.8684
8	7.6517	7.3255	7.0197	6.7327	6.4632	6.2098	5.9713	5.7466	5.5348	5.3349
9	8.5660	8.1622	7.7861	7.4353	7.1078	6.8017	6.5152	6.2469	5.9952	5.7590
10	9.4713	8.9826	8.5302	8.1109	7.7217	7.3601	7.0236	6.7101	6.4177	6.1446

$$A_n = R(\text{PVIFA}_{k,n}) \qquad\qquad (3\text{–}6)$$

$$A_3 = \$1,000(2.7751)$$

$$= \$2,775.10.$$

Notice that the entry for each period _n_ in Table 3–5 is equal to the sum of the entries in Table 3–3 up to and including period _n_. For example, the PVIFA for 4 percent, three periods as shown in Table 3–5 could have been calculated by summing values from Table 3–3:

$$0.9615 + 0.9246 + 0.8890 = 2.7751.$$

Notice also that for all positive interest rates, PVIFA$_{k,n}$ for the _present value_ of an annuity is always less than the number of periods the annuity runs, whereas FVIFA$_{k,n}$ for the _sum_ of an annuity is equal to or greater than the number of periods.[7]

---

7 Had the annuity been an _annuity due,_ then in Figure 3–4 each $1,000 payment would have occurred one year earlier. Therefore, the PV of each individual payment would have been larger, and the PV of the annuity due, using the method in Figure 3–4, would have been $2,886.10 versus $2,775.10 for the regular annuity. Also, to find the PVIFA$_{k,n}$ for an _annuity due,_ go through these steps: (1) look up the PVIFA$_{k,n}$ for $n-1$ periods, then (2) add 1.0 to this amount to obtain the PVIFA$_{k,n}$ for the annuity due. In the example, the PVIFA$_{k,n}$ for a 4 percent, three year annuity due is 1.8861 + 1.0 = 2.8861.

PRESENT VALUE OF AN UNEVEN SERIES OF RECEIPTS

The definition of an annuity includes the words *fixed amount*—in other words, annuities involve situations where cash flows are *identical* in every year. Although many financial decisions do involve constant cash flows, some important decisions are concerned with uneven flows of cash. In particular, common stock investments ordinarily involve uneven, hopefully increasing, dividend payments over time. Consequently, it is necessary to expand our analysis to deal with varying payment streams.

The PV of an uneven stream of future income is found as the sum of the PVs of the individual components of the stream. For example, suppose we are trying to find the PV of the stream of receipts shown in Table 3–6, discounted at 6 percent. As shown in the table, we multiply each receipt by the appropriate $PVIF_{k,n}$, then sum these products to obtain the PV of the stream, $1,413.24. Figure 3–5 gives a graphic view of the cash flow stream.[8]

Table 3–6
Present Value of an Uneven Stream of Receipts

	Stream of Receipts	×	$PVIF_{k,n}$ (6%)	=	PV of Individual Receipts
Year 1	$ 100		0.9434		$ 94.34
Year 2	200		0.8900		178.00
Year 3	200		0.8396		167.92
Year 4	200		0.7921		158.42
Year 5	200		0.7473		149.46
Year 6	0		0.7050		0
Year 7	1,000		0.6651		665.10
			PV = sum =		$1,413.24

The PV of the receipts shown in Table 3–6 and Figure 3–5 can also be found by using the annuity equation; the steps in this alternative solution process are outlined below:

Step 1. Find PV of $100 due in Year 1:

$$\$100(0.9434) = \$94.34.$$

[8] This general equation may be used to find the PV of an uneven series of payments:

$$PV = \sum_{t=1}^{n} R_t \left(\frac{1}{1+k} \right)^t = \sum_{t=1}^{n} R_t (PVIF_{k,t}),$$

where R_t is the payment in any year t.

Figure 3–5
Time Line for an Uneven Cash Flow Stream with
k = 6%

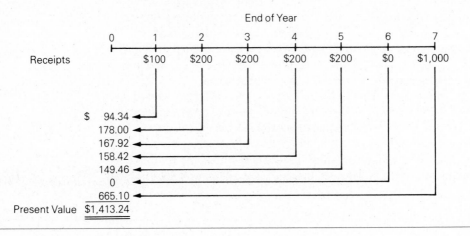

Step 2. Recognize that a $200 annuity will be received during Years 2 through 5. Thus, we could determine the value of a five year annuity, subtract from it the value of a one year annuity, and have remaining the value of a four year annuity whose first payment is due in two years. This result is achieved by subtracting the PVIFA for a one year, 6 percent annuity from the PVIFA for a five year annuity and then multiplying the difference by $200:

$$
\begin{aligned}
\text{PV of the annuity} &= \$200 \,(\text{PVIFA}_{6\%,\ 5\ \text{yrs.}}) - \$200\,(\text{PVIFA}_{6\%,\ 1\ \text{yr.}}) \\
&= \$200\,(\text{PVIFA}_{6\%,\ 5\ \text{yrs.}} - \text{PVIFA}_{6\%,\ 1\ \text{yr.}}) \\
&= \$200\,(4.2124 - 0.9434) \\
&= \$653.80.
\end{aligned}
$$

Thus, the present value of the annuity component of the uneven stream is $653.80.

Step 3. Find the PV of the $1,000 due in Year 7:

$$\$1,000(0.6651) = \$665.10.$$

Step 4. Sum the components:

$$\$94.34 + \$653.80 + \$665.10 = \$1,413.24.$$

Either of the two methods can be used to solve problems of this type. However, the alternative (annuity) solution is easier if the annuity component runs for many years. For example, the alternative solution would be clearly superior for finding the PV of a stream consisting of $100 in Year 1, $200 in Years 2 through 29, and $1,000 in Year 30.[9]

DETERMINING INTEREST RATES

We can use the basic equations developed above to determine the interest rates implicit in financial contracts.

Example 1. A bank offers to lend you $1,000 if you sign a note to repay $1,610.50 at the end of five years. What rate of interest are you paying?

1. Recognize that $1,000 is the PV of $1,610.50 due in five years:

$$PV = \$1,000 = \$1,610.50(PVIF_{k,5}).$$

2. Solve for $PVIF_{k,5}$:

$$PVIF_{k,5} = \$1,000/\$1,610.50 = 0.6209.$$

3. Now turn to Table 3–3 (or Table A–1). Look across the row for Period 5 until you find the value 0.6209. It is in the 10 percent column, so you would be paying a 10 percent rate of interest if you were to take out the loan.

Example 2. A bank offers to lend you $25,000 to buy a home. You must sign a mortgage calling for payments of $2,545.16 at the end of each of the next twenty-five years. What interest rate is the bank charging you?

1. Recognize that $25,000 is the PV of a twenty-five year, $2,545.16 annuity:

$$PV = \$25,000 = \sum_{t=1}^{25} \$2,545.16\left[\frac{1}{(1 + k)^t}\right] = \$2,545.16(PVIFA_{k,n}).$$

2. Solve for $PVIFA_{k,n}$:

$$PVIFA_{k,n} = \$25,000/\$2,545.16 = 9.8226.$$

3. Turn to Table A–2. Looking across the row for twenty-five periods, you find

---

9 The future value of a series of uneven payments, often called the *terminal value,* is found by compounding each payment, then summing the individual future values:

$$FV = \sum_{t=1}^{n} R_t(1 + k)^{n-t}.$$

9.8226 under the column for 9 percent. Therefore, the rate of interest on this mortgage loan is 9 percent.[10]

While the tables can be used to find the interest rate implicit in single payments and annuities, it is more difficult to find the interest rate implicit in an uneven series of payments. One can use a trial-and-error procedure, use more efficient but more complicated analytic procedures, or use a computer. We shall defer further discussion of this problem for now, but we will take it up later in our discussion of bond values and again in the capital budgeting chapters.

SEMIANNUAL AND OTHER COMPOUNDING PERIODS

In all the examples used thus far, it has been assumed that returns were received once a year, or annually. Suppose, however, that you put your $1,000 in a bank that advertises that it pays 6 percent interest *semiannually.* How much will you have at the end of one year? Semiannual compounding means that interest is actually paid each six months; the procedures are illustrated in the tabular calculations in Table 3–7. Here the annual interest rate is divided by 2, but twice as many compounding periods are used, because interest is paid twice a year. Comparing the amount on hand at the end of the second six month period, $1,060.90, with what would have been on hand under annual compounding, $1,060, shows that semiannual compounding is better from the standpoint of the saver. This result occurs because you earn *interest on interest* more frequently.

Throughout the economy, different types of investments use different compounding periods. For example, bank and savings and loan accounts generally pay interest quarterly; most bonds pay interest semiannually; and a few bonds pay annual interest. Thus, if we are to compare securities with different compounding periods, we need to put them on a common basis. This need has led to the development of the terms *nominal, or stated, interest rate* and *effective annual, or annual percentage, rate* (APR). The

---

10 Suppose the mortgage called for annual payments of $2,400. Then $PVIFA_{k,n}$ = $25,000/$2,400 = 10.4167. This value lies between the $PVIFA_{k,n}$ for 8 percent and 9 percent, but closer to 8 percent. The approximate rate for the mortgage could be found by using more extensive tables, by using one of the better hand-held calculators, or by "linear interpolation." To interpolate, we go through the following steps:
  Step 1. Find the difference between 10.6748, the $PVIFA_{k,n}$ for 8 percent, and 9.8226, the $PVIFA_{k,n}$ for 9 percent. This difference is 0.8522.
  Step 2. Find the difference between the calculated value, 10.4167, and 9.8226, the $PVIFA_{k,n}$ for 9 percent. This difference is 0.5941.
  Step 3. Divide 0.5941 by 0.8522 to obtain 0.6971, the ratio expressing the distance of the calculated $PVIFA_{k,n}$ from the upper end of the range.
  Step 4. The calculated $PVIFA_{k,n}$, 10.4167, represents 69.71 percent of the difference between 8 percent and 9 percent. Thus the interest rate represented by the $PVIFA_{k,n}$ of 10.4167 is 9% − 0.6971% = 8.3029%. (The exact rate, determined with a calculator, is 8.2887 percent.)

stated, or nominal, rate is the quoted rate; thus, in our example the nominal rate is 6 percent. *The annual percentage rate is the rate that would have produced the final compound value, $1,060.90, under annual rather than semiannual compounding.* In this case, the effective annual rate is 6.09 percent:

$$\$1,000(1 + k) = \$1,060.90$$

$$k = \frac{\$1,060.90}{\$1,000} - 1 = 0.0609 = 6.09\%.$$

Thus, if one bank offered 6 percent with semiannual compounding, while another offered 6.09 percent with annual compounding, they would both be paying the same effective rate of interest.

Table 3–7
Future Value Calculations with Semiannual Compounding

Period	Beginning Amount, PV	× (1 + k/2)	= Ending Amount, FV_n
1	$1,000.00	(1.03)	$1,030.00
2	1,030.00	(1.03)	1,060.90

In general, we can determine the effective annual percentage rate, or APR, given the nominal rate, by solving Equation 3–7:

$$\text{Annual percentage rate (APR)} = \left(1 + \frac{k_{nom}}{m}\right)^m - 1.0. \qquad (3\text{–}7)$$

Here k_{nom} is the nominal rate, and m is the number of compounding periods per year. For example, to find the effective annual rate if the nominal rate is 6 percent, compounded semiannually, we make the calculations below:

$$\begin{aligned}
\text{Effective annual rate (APR)} &= \left(1 + \frac{0.06}{2}\right)^2 - 1.0 \\
&= (1.03)^2 - 1.0 \\
&= 1.0609 - 1.0 \\
&= 0.0609 \\
&= 6.09\%.
\end{aligned}$$

The points made about semiannual compounding can be generalized as follows. When compounding periods are more frequent than once a year, we use a modified version of Equation 3–2:

$$\text{Annual compounding:} \qquad FV_n = PV(1 + k)^n. \qquad (3\text{–}2)$$

$$\text{More frequent compounding:} \quad FV_n = PV\left(1 + \frac{k_{nom}}{m}\right)^{mn}. \qquad (3\text{–}2a)$$

Here *m* is the number of times per year compounding occurs. When banks compute daily interest, the value of *m* is set at 365, and Equation 3–2a is applied.

The interest tables can be used when compounding occurs more than once a year. Simply divide the nominal, or stated, interest rate by the number of times compounding occurs, and multiply the years by the number of compounding periods per year. For example, to find the amount to which $1,000 will grow after five years if semiannual compounding is applied to a stated 4 percent interest rate, divide 4 percent by 2 and multiply the five years by 2. Then look in Table 3–2 under the 2 percent column and in the row for Period 10. You find an interest factor of 1.2190. Multiplying this by the initial $1,000 gives a value of $1,219, the amount to which $1,000 will grow in five years at 4 percent compounded semiannually. This compares with $1,216.70 for annual compounding.[11]

The same procedure is applied in all the cases covered—compounding, discounting, single payments, and annuities. To illustrate semiannual discounting in finding the present value of an annuity, consider the case described in the section "Present Value of an Annuity": $1,000 a year for three years, discounted at 4 percent. With annual discounting, the interest factor is 2.7751 and the present value of the annuity is $2,775.10. For semiannual discounting, look under the 2 percent column and in the Period 6 row of Table 3–5 to find an interest factor of 5.6014. This is now multiplied by half of $1,000, or the $500 received each six months, to get the present value of the annuity, $2,800.70. The payments come a little more rapidly—the first $500 is paid after only six months (similarly with other payments), so the annuity is a little more valuable if payments are received semiannually rather than annually.

By letting *m* approach infinity, Equation 3–2a can be modified to the special case of *continuous compounding.* Continuous compounding is extremely useful in theoretical finance, and it also has practical applications. For example, banks and savings associations in New York and many other states pay interest on a continuous basis.[12]

AMORTIZED LOANS

One of the most important applications of compound interest concepts involves loans that are to be paid off in installments over time. Examples include automobile loans, home mortgage loans, and most business debt

---

11 Another approach: APR $= (1 + 0.04/2)^2 - 1.0 = 0.0404$ or 4.04%. FV $= PV(1 + APR)^n =$
   $1,000(1.0404)^5 = 1,000(1.218894) = 1,219$.
12 Continuous compounding is discussed in Appendix 3A.

other than very short-term debt. If a loan is to be repaid in equal periodic amounts (monthly, quarterly, or annually), then it is said to be an *amortized loan.*[13]

To illustrate, suppose a firm borrows $1,000 to be repaid in three equal payments at the end of each of the next three years. The lender is to receive 6 percent interest on funds outstanding. The first task is to determine the amount the firm must repay each year, or the annual payment. To find this amount, recognize that the $1,000 represents the present value of an annuity of R dollars per year for 3 years, discounted at 6 percent:

$$\$1,000 = \text{PV of annuity} = R(\text{PVIFA}_{6\%,\ 3\ \text{yrs.}}). \qquad (3-5)$$

The PVIFA is 2.6730, so

$$\$1,000 = R(2.6730).$$

Solving for R, we obtain

$$R = \$1,000/2.6730 = \$374.11.$$

If the firm pays the lender $374.11 at the end of each of the next three years, the percentage cost to the borrower, and the return to the lender, will be 6 percent.

Each payment consists partly of interest and partly of a repayment of principal. This breakdown is given in the *amortization schedule* shown in Table 3–8. The interest component is largest in the first year, and it declines as the outstanding balance of the loan goes down. For tax purposes, the borrower reports as a deductible cost each year the interest payments in Column 2, while the lender reports these same amounts as taxable income.

Table 3–8
Loan Amortization Schedule

Year	Payment (1)	Interest[a] (2)	Repayment of Principal[b] (3)	Remaining Balance (4)
1	$ 374.11	$ 60.00	$ 314.11	$685.89
2	374.11	41.15	332.96	352.93
3	374.11	21.18	352.93	0
	$1,122.33	$122.33	$1,000.00	

[a]Interest is calculated by multiplying the loan balance at the beginning of the year by the interest rate. Therefore, interest in Year 1 is $1,000(0.06) = $60; in Year 2 interest is $685.89(0.06) = $41.15; and in Year 3 interest is $352.93(0.06) = $21.18.

[b]Repayment of principal is equal to the payment of $374.11 minus the interest charge.

13 The word *amortized* comes from the Latin "mort," meaning dead, so an amortized loan is one that is "killed off" over time.

SUMMARY

Financial decisions often involve determining the present value of a stream of future cash flows—this is true in stock, bond, and real estate valuation. Also, we often need to know the amount to which funds now on hand will grow during a specified time period. At other times we must calculate the interest rate built into a bond or loan contract. The basic concepts involved in these processes are called the "math of finance," which is the subject of this chapter.

The key procedures covered in the chapter are summarized below:

Future Value $FV_n = PV(1 + k)^n$, where FV_n is the future value of an initial amount, PV, compounded at the rate k percent for n periods. The term $(1 + k)^n$ is defined as $FVIF_{k,n}$, the "future value interest factor." Values for FVIF are contained in tables.

Present Value $PV = FV_n \left[\dfrac{1}{(1 + k)} \right]^n$. This equation is simply a transformation of the future value equation. The term $\left[\dfrac{1}{(1 + k)} \right]^n$ is defined as $PVIF_{k,n}$, the "present value interest factor." The term k, when used to find present values, is often called the *discount rate*.

Future Value of an Annuity An annuity is defined as a series of constant or equal payments of R dollars per period. The sum, or future value of an annuity, is given the symbol S_n, and it is found as follows:

$$S_n = R \left[\sum_{t=1}^{n} (1 + k)^{n-t} \right].$$ The term $\left[\sum_{t=1}^{n} (1 + k)^{n-t} \right]$ is defined as $FVIFA_{k,n}$, the

"future value interest factor for an annuity."

Present Value of an Annuity The present value of an annuity is given the symbol A_n, and it is found as follows:

$$A_n = R \left[\sum_{t=1}^{n} \left(\frac{1}{1 + k} \right)^t \right].$$ The term $\left[\sum_{t=1}^{n} \left(\frac{1}{1 + k} \right)^t \right] = PVIFA_{k,n}$ is defined as the

"present value interest factor for an annuity."

These four basic equations can be used to find the present or the future value of any lump sum or series of cash flows and also the interest rate built into any financial contract. These concepts will be used throughout the remainder of the book. In Chapter 4 we apply present value concepts to the process of valuing stocks and bonds. This discussion is extended in Chapter 5, where we examine the determinants of k, the interest rate, and in Chapter

6, where we analyze ways of estimating future cash flows. Then, in later chapters, the same basic concepts are applied to corporate decisions involving expenditures on capital assets as well as to decisions involving the types of capital that should be used to pay for assets.

Questions

3-1 Is it true that for all positive interest rates, the following conditions hold: $FVIF_{k,n} \geq 1.0$; $PVIF_{k,n} < 1.0$; $FVIFA_{k,n} \geq$ number of periods the annuity lasts; $PVIFA_{k,n} <$ number of periods the annuity lasts?

3-2 An annuity is defined as a series of payments of a fixed amount for a specific number of periods. Thus $100 a year for 10 years is an annuity, but $100 in Year 1, $200 in Year 2, and $400 a year in Years 3 through 10 is *not* an annuity. However, the second series *contains* an annuity. Is this statement true or false?

3-3 If a firm's earnings per share grew from $1 to $2 over a ten year period, the *total growth* was 100 percent, but the *annual growth rate* was *less than* 10 percent. Why is this so?

3-4 Would you rather have a deposit in a bank that uses annual, semiannual, or quarterly compounding? Explain.

3-5 To find the present value of an uneven series of payments, you must use the $PVIF_{k,n}$ tables; the $PVIFA_{k,n}$ tables can never be of use, even if some of the payments constitute an annuity (for example, $100 each for Years 3, 4, 5, and 6), because the entire series is not an annuity. Is this statement true or false?

Problems

3-1 Find the following values *without using tables,* then work the problems *with tables* to check your answers. Disregard rounding errors.
   a. An initial $100 compounded for one year at 5 percent.
   b. An initial $100 compounded for two years at 5 percent.
   c. The present value of $100 due in one year at a discount rate of 5 percent.
   d. The present value of $100 due in two years at a discount rate of 5 percent.

3-2 Use the tables to find the following values:
   a. An initial $100 compounded for ten years at 5 percent.
   b. An initial $100 compounded for ten years at 10 percent.
   c. The present value of $100 due in ten years at a 5 percent discount rate.
   d. The present value of $259.40 due in ten years at a 10 percent discount rate.

3-3 To the closest year, how long will it take $100 to double if it is deposited and earns the following rates?
   a. 10 percent.

   b. 15 percent.
   c. 100 percent.
3-4 Find the *future value* of the following annuities. The first payment in these
   annuities is made at the *end* of Year 1:
   a. $100 per year for ten years at 10 percent.
   b. $200 per year for five years at 5 percent.
   c. $100 per year for five years at 0 percent.
3-5 Find the *present value* of the following annuities:
   a. $100 per year for ten years at 10 percent.
   b. $200 per year for five years at 5 percent.
   c. $100 per year for five years at 0 percent.
3-6 a. Find the present values of the following cash flow streams; the
   appropriate discount rate is 8 percent:

Year	Cash Stream A	Cash Stream B
1	$100	$300
2	$200	$200
3	$200	$200
4	$200	$200
5	$300	$100

   b. What is the value of each cash flow stream at a zero percent discount
   rate?
3-7 Find the present value of the following cash flow stream, discounted at 5
   percent: Year 1, $200; Years 2 to 20, $100.
3-8 Last year Union Chemical's sales were $2 million. Sales were $1 million
   five years earlier. To the nearest percentage point, at what rate have sales
   been growing?
3-9 Suppose someone calculated the sales growth rate for Union Chemical in
   Problem 3-8 as follows: "Sales doubled in five years. This represents a
   growth of 100 percent in five years; so dividing 100 percent by 5, we find
   the growth rate to be 20 percent per year." Explain what is wrong with this
   calculation.
3-10 Find the interest rates, or rates of return, on each of the following:
   a. You borrow $100 and promise to pay back $105 at the end of one year.
   b. You lend $100, and you receive a promise of $105 at the end of one
   year.
   c. You borrow $10,000 and promise to pay back $16,289 at the end of ten
   years.
   d. You borrow $1,000 and promise to make payments of $257.09 per year
   for five years.
3-11 The Compound Company buys a machine for $10,000 and expects a return
   of $2,385.21 per year for the next ten years. What is the expected rate of
   return on the machine?

3-12 Apex Orchards invests $100,000 to clear a tract of land and set out some young apple trees. The trees will mature in ten years, at which time Apex plans to sell the orchard at an expected price of $300,000. What is Apex's expected rate of return?

3-13 Your broker offers to sell you a note for $2,395.62 that will pay $600 per year for five years. If you buy the note, what rate of interest will you be earning?

3-14 A mortgage company offers to lend you $25,000; the loan calls for payments of $2,738.68 per year for twenty years. What interest rate is the mortgage company charging you?

3-15 To enable you to complete your last year in the business school and then go through law school, you will need $5,000 per year for four years, starting next year (that is, you need the first payment of $5,000 one year from today). Your rich uncle offers to deposit a sum of money sufficient to put you through school in a bank time deposit that pays 5 percent interest; the deposit will be made today.
   a. How large must the deposit be?
   b. How much will be in the account immediately after you make the first withdrawal? After the last withdrawal?

3-16 Find the amount to which $100 will grow under each of the following conditions:
   a. 8 percent compounded annually for four years.
   b. 8 percent compounded semiannually for four years.
   c. 8 percent compounded quarterly for four years.
   d. 12 percent compounded monthly for one year.

3-17 Find the present values of $100 due in the future under each of the following conditions:
   a. 8 percent nominal rate, semiannual compounding, discounted back four years.
   b. 8 percent nominal rate, quarterly compounding, discounted back four years.
   c. 12 percent nominal rate, monthly compounding, discounted back one year.

3-18 Find the indicated value of the following annuities:
   a. FV of $100 each six months for four years at a nominal rate of 8 percent.
   b. PV of $100 each three months for four years at a nominal rate of 8 percent.

3-19 The First National Bank pays 9 percent interest compounded annually on time deposits. The Second National Bank pays 8 percent interest compounded quarterly.
   a. In which bank would you prefer to deposit your money?
   b. Could your choice of banks be influenced by the fact that you might want to withdraw your funds during the year as opposed to the end of a year? In answering this question, assume that funds must be left on deposit during the entire compounding period in order to receive any interest.

3-20 Set up an amortization schedule for a $10,000 loan to be repaid in equal installments at the end of each of the next three years. The interest rate is 10 percent.

(These next three problems are quite difficult. Most introductory students cannot work them without guidance, so do not be surprised if you have trouble!)

3-21 As a financial consultant, you are helping a client who just won a fortune at Las Vegas plan his retirement. He will make a deposit today (January 1, 1980) in a time deposit that pays 5 percent interest, compounded annually. He will retire in twenty-five years (on January 1, 2005), and he expects to live for another thirty years beyond his retirement (until December 31, 2034). His wife is expected to live an additional five years (until December 31, 2039). He wants a retirement income of $20,000 per year during his retirement years, the first payment to be received on January 1, 2005, and the last on January 1, 2034. Further, he wants his wife to have an income of $10,000 after he is dead, or $10,000 on each January 1 from 2035 through 2039. Finally, he plans to take a trip to the moon in 2010 and be gone for two years, so he wants to receive $40,000 on January 1, 2010, and nothing on January 1, 2011.

    a. How much must he deposit on January 1, 1980, in order to attain his retirement goal? (*Hint:* Use a time line.)

    b. In terms of current dollars, how much will his $20,000 of income in 2005 be worth in 1980 if we experience a constant 8 percent rate of inflation?

    c. What are the major weaknesses of this financial plan? Assume this is the only source of retirement income, and question the assumptions used in the problem.

3-22 Assume that you deposited $100 in a bank time deposit account on January 1, 1970, and an additional $100 each six months thereafter until July 1, 1979. Thus, you made a total of twenty deposits of $100 each. The bank paid interest at the rate of 4 percent, compounded quarterly, from January 1, 1970, through December 31, 1972. The rate of interest went to 6 percent, compounded semiannually, on January 1, 1973, and remained at that level until December 31, 1977. The interest rate then became 8 percent, compounded annually, on January 1, 1978, and stayed at that level until December 31, 1979. How much will you have in your account on January 1, 1980?

(*Hints:* [1] This problem requires the use of a calculator with an exponential function. [2] Work the problem assuming that the deposits are $1 rather than $100, and then multiply by 100 to get the final answer. [3] Although it is possible to use annuity formulas to help solve this problem, it is probably easier for most people not to use them. However, the deferred annuity equation might be used for the period January 1, 1973, through December 31, 1977.)

3-23 Assume that your father is now fifty and plans an early retirement in eight years at age fifty-eight. He will be able to save $6,000 per year for the next four years, while he puts you through law school, and $20,000 per year for the following four years. In addition, he has $300,000 currently invested in undeveloped real estate.

a. If his annual savings over the next eight years are deposited in a bank account that pays 6 percent compounded annually, while the value of his real estate appreciates at the rate of 10 percent per year, how much will your father have upon retirement at age fifty-eight? (Disregard taxes.)

b. If your father expects to live to be eighty-eight, that is, he expects to live for thirty years after retirement, and at age fifty-eight he deposits all his wealth in a savings and loan account that pays 7 percent annual interest, how much can he withdraw each year to end up with a zero balance?

c. Assume all the conditions in Part b except that your father wants to leave an estate of $200,000 when he dies. How much can he draw out of the account each year after he reaches age fifty-eight?

d. How much will be in the account after one year of retirement but just before your father makes his first withdrawal?

e. Continuing Part d, how much will be in the account immediately after your father's first withdrawal? Assume he wishes to provide the estate as described in Part c.

f. Of your father's annual withdrawal at the end of Year 1, which was calculated in Part c and used in Part e, how much constituted withdrawal of principal, and how much was interest? Will this breakdown between principal and interest remain constant over the thirty years of your father's retirement?

APPENDIX 3A   CONTINUOUS COMPOUNDING AND DISCOUNTING

Continuous Compounding

In Chapter 3, we implicitly assumed that growth occurs at discrete intervals—annually, semiannually, and so forth. For some purposes it is better to assume instantaneous, or *continuous,* growth. The relationship between discrete and continuous compounding is illustrated in Figure 3A–1. Figure 3A–1a shows the annual compounding case, where interest is added once a year; in Figure 3A–1b compounding occurs twice a year; in Figure 3A–1c interest is earned continuously. As the graph shows, the more frequent the compounding period, the larger the final compound amount, because interest is earned on interest more often.

Figure 3A–1
Annual, Semiannual, and Continuous
Compounding (25 Percent Rate)

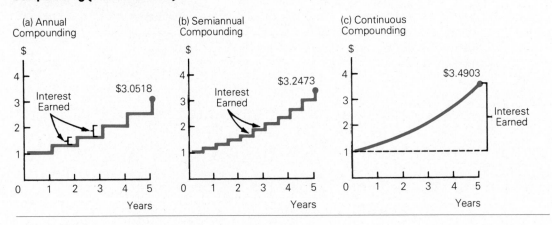

In Chapter 3, Equation 3–2a was developed to allow for any number of compounding periods per year:

$$FV_n = PV\left(1 + \frac{k}{m}\right)^{m \cdot n}$$ (3–2a)

where k = the stated interest rate, m = the number of corresponding periods per year, and n = the number of years. To illustrate, let PV = $100, k = 10%, and n = 5. At various compounding periods per year, we obtain the following future values:

Annual: $\quad FV_5 = \$100\left(1.0 + \dfrac{0.10}{1}\right)^{1\cdot5} = \$100(1.10)^5 = \$161.05.$

Semiannual: $FV_5 = \$100\left(1.0 + \dfrac{0.10}{2}\right)^{2\cdot5} = \$100(1.05)^{10} = \$162.89.$

Monthly: $\quad FV_5 = \$100\left(1.0 + \dfrac{0.10}{12}\right)^{12\cdot5} = \$100(1.0083)^{60} = \$164.53.$

Daily: $\quad FV_5 = \$100\left(1.0 + \dfrac{0.10}{365}\right)^{365\cdot5} = \$164.86$

Hourly: $\quad FV_5 = \$100\left(1.0 + \dfrac{0.10}{8,760}\right)^{365\cdot24\cdot5} = \$164.87.$

We could keep going, compounding every minute, every second, every 1/1000th of a second, and so on. At the limit, we could compound every instant, or *continuously*. The equation for continuous compounding is

$$FV_n = PV(e^{k\cdot n}), \tag{3A-1}$$

where e is the value $2.7183\cdots$.[1] In our example, FV_5 is computed as follows:[2]

$$\text{\textit{Continuous:} } FV_5 = \$100(e^{0.10\cdot5}) = \$100(2.7183\cdots)^{0.5}$$

$$= \$164.872.$$

---

1 To derive Equation 3A-1, we proceed as follows:
  1. We begin with Equation 3-2a:

$$FV_n = PV\left(1 + \frac{k}{m}\right)^{m\cdot n}. \tag{3-2a}$$

  2. Multiply mn by k/k, obtaining $mn = mn(k/k) = (m/k)(kn)$.
  3. Substitute $(m/k)(kn)$ for mn in Equation 3-2a:

$$FV_n = PV\left[\left(1 + \frac{k}{m}\right)^{m/k}\right]^{kn}. \tag{3A-2}$$

  4. Define $x = m/k$ and note that $k/m = 1/(m/k) = 1/x$. Now rewrite Equation 3A-2 as follows:

$$FV_n = PV\left[\left(1 + \frac{1}{x}\right)^{x}\right]^{kn}. \tag{3A-3}$$

  5. As the number of compounding periods, m, increases, x also increases; this causes the term in brackets in Equation 3A-3 to increase. At the limit, when m and x approach infinity (and compounding is instantaneous, or continuous), the term in brackets approaches the value $2.7183\cdots$. The value e is defined as this limiting case:

$$e = \lim_{x\to\infty}\left(1 + \frac{1}{x}\right)^{x} = 2.7183\cdots. \tag{3A-4}$$

  6. We can substitute e for the bracketed term in Equation 3A-3 to obtain the following expression:

$$FV_t = (PV)e^{kn}. \tag{3A-1}$$

2 Scientific or financial calculators with exponential functions can be used to evaluate Equation 3A-1.

Continuous Discounting

Equation 3A–1 can be transformed into Equation 3A–2 and used to determine
present values under continuous compounding:

$$PV = \frac{FV_t}{e^{kn}} = FV_t e^{-kn}. \qquad (3A-2)$$

Thus, if $1,649 is due in ten years and if the appropriate *continuous* discount rate,
k, is 5 percent, the present value of this future payment is

$$PV = \$1,649 \left[\frac{1}{(2.7183\cdots)^{0.5}} \right] = \frac{\$1,649}{1.649} \approx \$1,000.$$

4 STOCK AND BOND VALUES

In the last chapter we examined the time value of money. The concepts developed there can be used to analyze the value of any financial asset (that is, any asset which provides cash flows in some future period), including real estate, factories, machinery, oil wells, coal mines, farmland, stocks, or bonds. In this chapter we use the time value concept to show how investors establish the values of stocks and bonds. The materials covered in the chapter are obviously important to investors and potential investors, and they are also important to corporate decision makers. *All important corporate decisions should be analyzed in terms of how a particular decision will affect the price of the firm's stock, so it is clearly important to know what determines stock prices.*

BOND VALUES

Corporations raise capital in two primary forms—debt and common equity. Our first task in this chapter is to examine the valuation process for the primary type of long-term debt, bonds.

A *bond* is a promissory note issued by a business or governmental unit. For example, on October 1, 1979, the Carter Chemical Company borrowed $150 million by selling 150,000 individual bonds for $1,000 each. As a first step in explaining how bond values are determined, we need to define some of the terms associated with these securities.

1. *Par value*   This is the stated face value of the bond, and it is usually set at $1,000. The par value generally represents the amount of money that the firm borrows and promises to repay at some future date.
2. *Coupon interest rate*   The bond states that the issuer will pay a specified number of dollars of interest each year (or perhaps each six months). When this *coupon payment,* as it is called, is divided by the par value, the

result is the *coupon interest rate.* For example, Carter Chemical's bonds have a $1,000 par value and pay $90 each year. The bond's coupon interest is $90, so its coupon interest rate is 9 percent. The $90 is the yearly "rent" on the $1,000 loan. This payment, which is fixed at the time the bond is issued, remains in force, by contract, during the life of the bond.

3. *Maturity date*   Bonds generally mature at a specified date; at maturity, the par value is repaid to each bondholder. Carter's bonds, which were issued in 1979, will mature in 1994. Thus, they had a fifteen year maturity at time of issue. Most bonds have maturities of from fifteen to forty years, but this is not a hard and fast rule.[1]

4. *New issues* versus *outstanding bonds*   As we shall see below, a bond's market price is determined in large part by its coupon interest payment—the higher the coupon, other things held constant, the higher the market price of the bond. At the time a bond is issued, the coupon is generally set at a level that will force the market price of the bond to equal its par value. If a lower coupon were set, investors simply would not be willing to pay $1,000 for the bond, while if a higher coupon were set, investors would clamor for the bond and bid its price up over $1,000. Issuers can judge quite precisely the coupon rate which will cause the bond to sell at its $1,000 par value.

A bond that has just been issued is defined as a *new issue.* (The *Wall Street Journal* classifies a new bond as a new issue for about two weeks after it has first been issued.) Once the bond has been on the market for a while, it is classified as an *outstanding* bond, also called a *seasoned issue.* As we shall see below, although newly issued bonds do generally sell at par, outstanding bonds do not always sell at par. Their coupon interest payments are constant, but economic conditions change, so although a bond with a $90 coupon may sell at par when it is issued, it can sell for more or less than $1,000 thereafter.

The Basic Bond Valuation Model[2]

As noted above, bonds call for the payment of a specified amount of interest for a stated number of years, and for the repayment of the par value on the bond's maturity date.[3] Thus, a bond represents an annuity plus a lump sum, and its value is found as the present value of this payment stream.

---

1 Some bonds have a provision whereby the issuer may pay them off prior to maturity. This feature is termed a *call provision,* and it is discussed in detail in Chapter 13. If a bond is callable, and if interest rates on new bonds fall substantially below the coupon rate on the old bond, then the company will sell a new issue of low interest rate bonds and use the proceeds to retire the old high interest rate issue. See Appendix 13B.

2 In finance the term *model* refers to an equation or set of equations designed to show how one or more variables affect some other variable. Thus, a bond valuation model shows the mathematical relationship between a bond's price and the set of variables that determines this price.

3 Actually, most bonds pay interest semiannually, not annually, which makes it necessary to modify our valuation equation slightly. We abstract from semiannual compounding at this point to avoid unnecessary detail. However, the subject is discussed later in the chapter.

The following equation is used to find a bond's value:

$$\text{Value} = V = \sum_{t=1}^{n} I \left(\frac{1}{1 + k_d}\right)^t + M \left(\frac{1}{1 + k_d}\right)^n$$

$$= I(\text{PVIFA}_{k_d,n}) + M(\text{PVIF}_{k_d,n}). \quad\quad (4-1)$$

Here:

I = dollars of interest paid each year = coupon interest rate $\times$ par value.
M = the par value, or maturity value, which is typically $1,000.
k_d = the appropriate rate of interest on the bond.[4]
n = the number of years until the bond matures; n declines each year after the bond is issued.

We can use the equation to find the value of Carter Chemical's bonds. Simply substitute in $90 for I, $1,000 for M, and the values for PVIFA and PVIF at 9 percent, 15 periods, as found in Tables A–1 and A–2 at the end of the book:

$$V = \$90(8.0607) + \$1,000(0.2745)$$

$$= \$725.46 + \$274.50$$

$$= \$999.96 \approx \$1,000 \text{ when } k_d = 9\%.$$

Figure 4–1 gives a graphic view of the bond valuation process.

If k_d remained constant at 9 percent, what would the value of the bond be one year after it was issued? We can find this value using the same valuation formula, but now the term to maturity is only fourteen years; that is, $n = 14$:

$$V = \$90(7.7862) + \$1,000(0.2992)$$

$$= \$999.96 \approx \$1,000.$$

This same result will hold for every year so long as the appropriate interest rate for the bond remains constant at 9 percent.[5]

Now suppose interest rates in the economy rose after the Carter Chemical bonds were issued, and as a result k_d increased from 9 percent to 10 percent. Both the coupon interest payment and the maturity value would

---

4 The matter of how the *appropriate interest rate* is determined will be taken up in the next chapter. The bond's riskiness and years to maturity, as well as supply and demand conditions in the capital markets, all have an influence. We shall go into detail on these points later, but for now just accept the statement that k_d is the appropriate interest rate for the bonds. k_d is also called the *required rate of return*, and on any risky investment it is equal to the rate of return on riskless investments (such as U.S. Treasury Securities), given the symbol R_F, *plus a risk premium*, ρ, pronounced "rho." All this is discussed in depth in Chapter 5.

5 The bond prices quoted by brokers are calculated as described. However, if you bought a bond, you would have to pay this basic price plus accrued interest. Thus, if you purchased a Carter Chemical bond six months after it was issued, your broker would send you an invoice stating that you must pay $1,000 as the basic price of the bond plus $45 interest, representing one-half the annual interest of $90. The seller of the bond would receive $1,045. If you bought the bond the day before its interest payment date, you would pay $1,000 + 364/365 ($90) = $1,089.75. Of course, you would receive an interest payment of $90 at the end of the next day.

Figure 4–1
Time Line for Carter Chemical Bonds

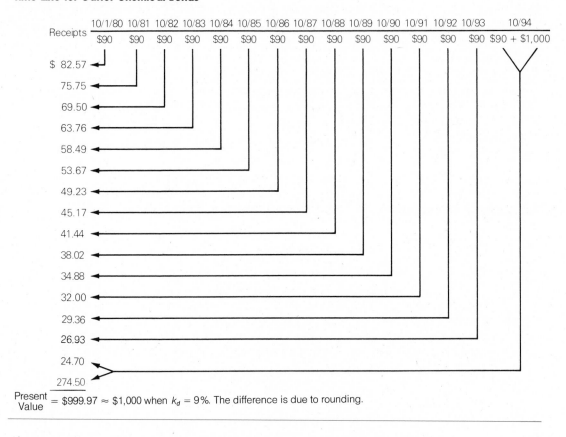

Present Value $= \$999.97 \approx \$1,000$ when $k_d = 9\%$. The difference is due to rounding.

remain constant, but now 10 percent values for PVIF and PVIFA would have to be used in Equation 4–1. The value of the bonds at the end of the first year would be

$$
\begin{aligned}
V &= \$90(\text{PVIFA}_{10\%,\ 14\ years}) + \$1,000(\text{PVIF}_{10\%,\ 14\ years}) \\
&= \$90(7.3667) + \$1,000(0.2633) \\
&= \$663.00 + \$263.30 \\
&= \$926.30 \text{ when } k_d = 10\%.
\end{aligned}
$$

Thus, the bond sells at a *discount* below its par value.

The arithmetic of the bond price decline should be clear, but what is the logic behind the decline? The reason for it is simple. The fact that k_d has risen to 10 percent means that, if you had $1,000 to invest, you could buy bonds like Carter's except that they would pay $100 of interest each year rather than $90. Naturally, you would prefer $100 to $90, so you would not be willing to pay $1,000 for Carter bonds when the $1,000 could buy you a higher-yielding bond. All investors would recognize these facts, and as a result the Carter bonds would be bid down in price to $926.30, at which price the Carter bonds would provide the same rate of return as the new bonds, 10 percent.

Assuming that interest rates remain constant at 10 percent for the next fourteen years, what will happen to the value of these bonds? It will rise gradually from $926.30 at present to $1,000 at maturity, when Carter Chemical must redeem each bond for $1,000. This point is illustrated by calculating the value of the bond one year later, when it has thirteen years remaining to maturity:

$$V = \$90(PVIFA_{10\%, \; 13 \; years}) + \$1,000(PVIF_{10\%, \; 13 \; years})$$

$$= \$90(7.1034) + \$1,000(0.2897) = \$929.01.$$

Thus, the value of the bond has risen from $926.30 to $929.01, or by $2.71. If you were to calculate the value of the bond at other dates, the price would continue to rise as the maturity date approached.

Notice also that, if you purchased the bond at a price of $926.30 and then sold it one year later, you would receive $90 of interest income plus a capital gain of $2.71, or a total return of $92.71. Your percentage rate of return would consist of an *interest yield* (also called *current yield*) plus a *capital gains yield* calculated as follows:

$$
\begin{aligned}
\text{Interest or current yield} &= \quad \$90/\$926.30 = 0.0971 = \quad 9.71\% \\
\text{Capital gains yield} &= \quad \$2.71/\$926.30 = 0.0029 = \quad \underline{0.29\%} \\
\text{Total rate of return or yield} &= \$92.71/\$926.30 = 0.1000 = \underline{10.00\%}
\end{aligned}
$$

Had interest rates fallen during the first year to 8 percent rather than risen, the value of Carter's bonds would have increased to $1,082.48:

$$V = \$90(8.2442) + \$1,000(0.3405)$$

$$= \$741.98 + \$340.50$$

$$= \$1,082.48 \text{ when } k_d = 8\%.$$

In this case, the bond would sell at a *premium* above its par value. Its total yield would again consist of a current interest yield and a capital gains yield, but the capital gains yield would be *negative* as the premium was amortized over time. The total yield would, of course, be 8 percent.

Figure 4–2 graphs the value of the bond over time, assuming that interest rates remain constant at 9 percent, rise to 10 percent, or fall to 8 percent. Of course, if interest rates do *not* remain constant, then the price of the bond will fluctuate. However, regardless of what interest rates do, the bond's price will approach $1,000 as the maturity date comes nearer (barring bankruptcy, in which case the bond's value might drop to zero).

Figure 4–2
Time Path of the Value of a 9% Coupon,
$1,000 Par Value Bond When Interest Rates
Are 8%, 9%, and 10%

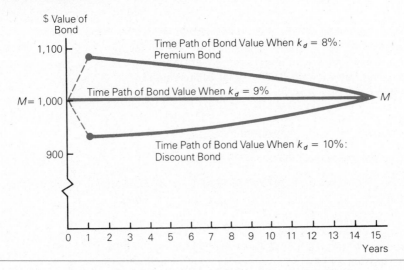

Note: The curves for 8% and 10% appear to be straight, but they actually have a slight bow.

Figure 4–2 illustrates the following key points:

1. Whenever the going rate of interest (k_d) is equal to the coupon rate, a bond will sell at its par value.
2. Whenever the going rate of interest is above the coupon rate, a bond will sell below its par value. Such a bond is called a *discount bond.*
3. Whenever the going rate of interest is below the coupon rate, a bond will sell above its par value. Such a bond is said to sell at a *premium.*
4. An increase in interest rates will cause the prices of outstanding bonds to fall, while a decrease in rates will cause bond prices to rise.
5. The market value of a bond will approach its par value as its maturity date approaches.

These points are very important to investors, for they show that bondholders may suffer capital losses or make capital gains depending on whether interest rates rise or fall. And, as we saw in Chapter 2, interest rates do indeed change over time.

Finding the Interest Rate on a Bond: Yield to Maturity

Suppose you were offered a fourteen year, 9 percent coupon, $1,000 par value bond at a price of $1,082.48. What rate of interest would you earn if you bought the bond and held it to maturity? This rate is defined as the bond's *yield to maturity,* and it is the interest rate discussed by bond traders when they talk about rates of return. To find the yield to maturity, often called the YTM, you could solve the following equation for k_d:

$$V = \$1,082.48$$

$$= \frac{\$90}{(1 + k_d)^1} + \frac{\$90}{(1 + k_d)^2} + \cdots + \frac{\$90}{(1 + k_d)^{14}} + \frac{\$1,000}{(1 + k_d)^{14}}$$

$$= \$90(\text{PVIFA}_{k,n}) + \$1,000(\text{PVIF}_{k,n}).$$

We can substitute in values for PVIFA and PVIF until we find a pair that "works" and makes

$$\$1,082.48 = \$90(\text{PVIFA}_{k,n}) + \$1,000(\text{PVIF}_{k,n}).$$

What would be a good interest rate to use as a starting point? First, referring to Point 3 in the preceding subsection, we know that since the bond is selling at a premium over its par value ($1,082.48 vs. $1,000), the bond's yield is *below* the 9 percent coupon rate. Therefore, we might try a rate of 7 percent. Substituting in factors for 7 percent, we obtain

$$\$90(8.7455) + \$1,000(0.3878) = \$1,174.90 \neq \$1,082.48.$$

Our calculated bond value, $1,174.90, is *above* the actual market price, so the yield to maturity is *not* 7 percent. To lower the calculated value, we must *raise* the interest rate used in the process. Inserting factors for 8 percent, we obtain

$$\begin{aligned} V &= \$90(8.2442) + \$1,000(0.3405) \\ &= \$741.98 + \$340.50 \\ &= \$1,082.48. \end{aligned}$$

This calculated value is exactly equal to the market price of the bond; thus, 8 percent is the bond's yield to maturity.[6]

The yield to maturity is identical to the total rate of return we calculated in the preceding section. The YTM for a bond that sells at par consists entirely

---

6 We found the yield to maturity on this bond by trial and error. In Chapter 11 we will examine more efficient procedures for zeroing in on interest rates. It should also be noted that specialized hand-held calculators can be used to find the yield to maturity on a bond with very little effort. A few years ago traders all had specialized tables called *bond tables* that gave yields on bonds of different maturities selling at different premiums and discounts. Because the calculators are so much more efficient (and accurate), bond tables are rarely used any more.

There is also a formula that can be used to find the approximate yield to maturity on a bond:

$$k_d = \text{YTM} = \frac{I + (M - V)/n}{(M + V)/2}.$$

In the situation where $I = \$90$, $M = \$1,000$, $V = \$1,082.48$, and $n = 14$,

$$k_d = \frac{\$90 + (\$1,000 - \$1,082.48)/14}{(\$1,000 + \$1,082.48)/2} = 0.0808 = 8.08\%.$$

This is close to the exact value, 8 percent. This formula can also be used to obtain a starting point for the trial-and-error method.

of an interest yield, but if the bond sells at a price other than its par value, YTM consists of a positive or negative capital gains yield plus the interest yield. Note also that a bond's YTM changes whenever interest rates in the economy change, and this is almost daily. One who purchases a bond and holds it until it matures will receive the YTM that existed on the purchase date, but the bond's YTM will change frequently.

Interest Rate Risk on a Bond

As we saw in Chapter 2, Figure 2–2, interest rates go up and down over time, and as interest rates change, the values of outstanding bonds also fluctuate. Suppose that you bought some 9 percent Carter bonds at a price of $1,000 and interest rates subsequently rose to 10 percent. The price of the bonds would fall to $926.30, so the value of the bonds would decline by $73.70 per bond. Interest rates can and do rise, and rising rates will cause a loss of value for bondholders. Thus, people or firms who invest in bonds are exposed to risk from changing interest rates, or *interest rate risk.*

One's exposure to interest rate risk is higher on bonds with long maturities than on those maturing in the near future. This point can be demonstrated by showing how the value of a one year, 9 percent coupon bond changes with changes in k_d, and then comparing these changes with those on a fourteen year bond as calculated above. The one year bond values at different interest rates are shown below.

Value at k_d = 8%:
$$V = \$90(PVIFA_{8\%, \, 1 \text{ year}}) + \$1,000(PVIF_{8\%, \, 1 \text{ year}})$$
$$= \$90(0.9259) + \$1,000(0.9259)$$
$$= \$83.33 + \$925.90 = \$1,009.23.$$

Value at k_d = 9%:
$$V = \$90(0.9174) + \$1,000(0.9174)$$
$$= \$82.57 + \$917.40 = \$999.97 \approx \$1,000.$$

Value at k_d = 10%:
$$V = \$90(0.9091) + \$1,000(0.9091)$$
$$= \$81.82 + \$909.10 = \$990.92.$$

The values of the one year and fourteen year bonds, at different current market interest rates, are summarized in Table 4–1, and they are plotted in Figure 4–3. Notice how much more sensitive the price of the long-term bond is to changes in interest rates. At a 9 percent interest rate, both the long- and short-term bonds are valued at $1,000. When rates rise to 10 percent, the long-term bond falls to $926.30, while the short-term bond falls only to $990.92. A similar situation occurs when rates fall below 9 percent.

This *differential responsiveness to changes in interest rates always holds true — the longer the maturity of a security, the greater its price change in response to a given change in interest rates.* Thus, even if the risk of default on two bonds is exactly the same, the one with the longer maturity is exposed to more risk from a rise in interest rates.[7]

Table 4–1
Values of Long-Term and Short-Term, 9%
Coupon Rate Bonds at Different Market
Interest Rates

Current Market Interest Rate (k_d)	Current Market Value	
	One Year Bond	Fourteen Year Bond
8%	$1,009.23	$1,082.48
9%	1,000.00	1,000.00
10%	990.92	926.30

The logical explanation for this difference in interest rate risk is simple. Suppose you bought a fifteen year bond that yielded 9 percent, or $90 a year. Now suppose interest rates on bonds of comparable risk rose to 10 percent. You would be stuck with only $90 interest for the next fifteen years. On the other hand, had you bought a one year bond, you would only have a low return for one year. At the end of the year, you would get your $1,000 back, and you could then reinvest it and receive 10 percent, or $100 per year, for the next fourteen years. Thus, interest rate risk reflects the length of time one is committed to a given investment.[8]

---

7 The discount or premium on a bond may also be calculated as follows:

$$\begin{matrix} \text{Discount or} \\ \text{premium} \end{matrix} = \begin{pmatrix} \text{Interest payment} \\ \text{on old bond} \end{pmatrix} - \begin{pmatrix} \text{Interest payment} \\ \text{on new bond} \end{pmatrix} \left(PVIFA_{k_d, n} \right),$$

where n = years to maturity on the old bond and k_d = current rate of interest, or yield to maturity, on the new bond. For example, when interest rates rose to 10 percent one year after they were issued, the discount on the Carter bonds could be calculated as follows:

Discount = ($90 − $100) (7.3667) = −$73.67. (The minus sign indicates discount.)

This value agrees (except for a rounding error) with the value calculated above:

Discount = Par value − Price = $1,000 − $926.30 = $73.70.

In this form, we see that the discount is equal to the present value of the interest payment one sacrifices to buy a low-coupon old bond rather than a high-coupon new bond. The longer the bond has to run, the greater the sacrifice, hence the greater the discount.

8 If a ten year bond were plotted in Figure 4–3, its curve would lie between those of the fourteen year bond and the one year bond. The curve of a one month bond would be almost horizontal, indicating that its price changes very little in response to interest rate changes.

Figure 4–3
Values of Long-Term and Short-Term, 9%
Coupon Rate Bonds at Different Market
Interest Rates

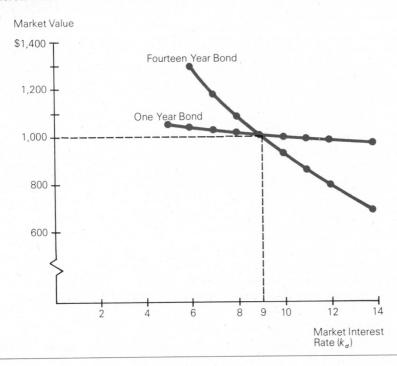

BOND VALUES WITH SEMIANNUAL COMPOUNDING

Although many bonds do pay interest annually, most actually pay interest
semiannually. To evaluate these bonds, we must modify the valuation
formula as follows:

1. Divide the annual coupon interest payment by 2 to determine the interest
   paid each six months.
2. Determine the number of periods by multiplying the years to maturity,
   n, by 2.
3. Determine the semiannual interest rate by dividing the annual rate, k_d, by 2.

With these changes made, we can apply Equation 4–1 to find the value of a
bond that pays interest semiannually.

   To illustrate, assume that Carter Chemical's bonds pay $45 interest each
six months rather than $90 at the end of each year. Thus, each interest

payment is only half as large, but there are twice as many of them. When the going rate of interest is 8 percent, the value of this fifteen year bond is found as follows:

$$V = \sum_{t=1}^{2n} \frac{I}{2} \left(\frac{1}{1 + \dfrac{k_d}{2}} \right)^t + M \left(\frac{1}{1 + \dfrac{k_d}{2}} \right)^{2n}$$

$$= \$45(\text{PVIFA}_{4\%,\ 30}) + \$1{,}000(\text{PVIF}_{4\%,\ 30})$$
$$= \$45(17.2920) + \$1{,}000(0.3083)$$
$$= \$778.14 + \$308.30$$
$$= \$1{,}086.44.$$

The \$1,086.44 value with semiannual interest payments is slightly larger than \$1,085.56, the value when interest is paid annually. This higher value occurs because interest payments are received somewhat faster under semiannual compounding.

Students sometimes discount the maturity value at 8 percent over fifteen years, rather than at 4 percent over thirty six-month periods. This is incorrect—logically, all cash flows in a given contract must be discounted on the same basis, semiannually in this instance. Notice that the \$45 of interest due at the end of the fifteenth year is, as part of the annuity, discounted back thirty periods at 4 percent; that is, the PV of this \$45 is based on $(1/1.04)^{30}$, not on $(1/1.08)^{15}$. For consistency, bond traders *must* apply semiannual compounding to the maturity value, and they do.

COMMON STOCK VALUATION

Common stock represents ownership of a corporation, but to the typical investor, a share of common stock is simply a piece of paper distinguished by two important features:

1. It entitles its owner to dividends.
2. It can be sold at some future date, hopefully for more than its purchase price.

If the stock is sold at a price above its purchase price, the investor will receive a *capital gain.* Generally, at the time people buy common stocks, they do expect to receive capital gains; otherwise, they would not buy the stocks.

In Chapter 14 we shall discuss the rights and privileges of the common stockholder, the process by which new shares are issued, and the markets in which outstanding shares are traded. Our purpose in this chapter, however, is simply to analyze models that help explain how stock prices are determined.

Definitions of Terms Used
in the Stock Valuation Models

Common stocks provide an expected future cash flow stream, and stock values are found like the values of other financial assets, namely, as the present value of a future stream of income. The expected cash flows consist of two elements: (1) the dividend expected in each year and (2) the price investors expect to receive when they sell the stock. The final stock price includes the return of the original investment plus a capital gain (or minus a capital loss).

We shall develop some models to help determine the value of a share of stock under several different sets of conditions, but let us first define the following terms:

D_t = the dividend the stockholder expects to receive at the end of year t.[9] D_0 is the most recent dividend, which has already been paid; D_1 is the next dividend, which will be paid at the end of this year; D_2 is the dividend expected at the end of two years, and so forth. D_1 represents the first cash flow a new purchaser of the stock will receive.

P_t = the price of the stock at the end of each year t. P_0 is the price of the stock today; P_1 is the price expected at the end of one year; and so on.

g = the expected rate of growth in the stock price. (In most of our models, g is also the expected rate of growth in earnings and dividends. In addition, we generally assume that g is expected to be constant over time.)

k_s = the minimum acceptable or *required rate of return* on the stock, considering both its riskiness and the returns available on other investments. The determinants of k_s will be discussed in detail in Chapter 5.

$\hat{k}_s$ = (pronounced "k hat") the *expected rate of return* which the individual who buys the stock actually expects to receive. The caret, or "hat," is used to indicate that $\hat{k}_s$ is a predicted value. $\hat{k}_s$ could be above or below k_s, but one would buy the stock only if $\hat{k}_s$ were equal to or greater than k_s.

D_1/P_0 = the expected *dividend yield* on the stock during the coming year. If the stock is expected to pay a dividend of $1 during the next twelve months, and if its current price is $10, then the dividend yield is $1/$10 = 0.10 = 10%.

---

9 We could speak here of periods rather than years, but in stock valuation it is typical to work on an annual rather than on a quarterly, semiannual, or other basis. The data used in stock valuation are simply not precise enough to warrant such refinements.

$\dfrac{P_1 - P_0}{P_0}$ = the expected *capital gains yield* on the stock during the coming year. If the stock sells for $10 today, and if it is expected to rise to $10.50 at the end of one year, then the expected capital gain is $P_1 - P_0 = \$10.50 - \$10.00 = \$0.50$, and the expected capital gains yield is $0.50/\$10 = 0.05 = 5\%$. If the stock price grows at a constant rate, then the growth rate, g, is equal to the capital gains yield.

$\dfrac{\text{Total}}{\text{return}}$ = The dividend yield plus the capital gains yield = $\hat{k}_s$ as defined above.

Expected Dividends as the Basis for Stock Values

In our discussion of bonds, we found the value of a bond as the present value of interest payments over the life of the bond plus the present value of the bond's maturity value, or par value:

$$V = \frac{I}{(1 + k_d)} + \frac{I}{(1 + k_d)^2} + \cdots + \frac{I}{(1 + k_d)^n} + \frac{M}{(1 + k_d)^n}.$$

Stock prices are determined as the present value of a stream of cash flows, and the basic stock valuation model turns out to be very similar to the bond value equation. What are the cash flows that corporations provide to their stockholders? First, think of yourself as an investor who buys a stock with the intention of holding it (in your family) forever. In this case, all you will receive is a stream of dividends, and the value of the stock is calculated as the present value of an infinite stream of dividends:

$$\text{Value of stock} = P_0 = \text{PV of expected future dividends}$$

$$= \frac{D_1}{(1 + k_s)^1} + \frac{D_2}{(1 + k_s)^2} + \cdots + \frac{D_\infty}{(1 + k_s)^\infty}. \qquad (4\text{-}2)$$

What about the more general case, where you expect to hold the stock for a finite period, then to sell it? What will be the value of P_0 in this case? *The value of the stock is again determined by Equation 4–2.* To see this, recognize that for any individual investor, cash flows consist of dividends plus the sale price of the stock, but for all present and future investors in total, expected cash flows consist only of future dividends—unless a firm is liquidated or is sold to another concern, the cash flows it provides to its stockholders consist only of a stream of dividends. Thus, the value of a share of common stock may be established as the present value of its stream of dividends.

The generalized nature of Equation 4–2 can also be seen by asking this question: Suppose I buy a stock expecting to hold it for one year. I will receive dividends during the year, and the value P_1 when I sell the stock at the end of the year. But what will determine the value of P_1? It will be determined as the present value of the dividends during Year 2 plus the stock price at the end of Year 2, which, in turn, will be determined as the present value of another set of future dividends and an even more distant stock price. This process can be continued ad infinitum, and the ultimate result is Equation 4–2.[10]

Equation 4–2 is a generalized stock valuation model in the sense that the time pattern of D_t can be anything: D_t can be rising, falling, constant, or it can even fluctuate randomly, and Equation 4–2 will still hold. For many purposes, however, it is useful to estimate a particular time pattern for D_t and then develop a simplified (that is, easier to evaluate) version of the stock valuation model expressed in Equation 4–2. In the following sections we consider the cases of zero growth, constant growth, and nonconstant (or "supernormal") growth.

Stock Values with Zero Growth

Suppose dividends are not expected to grow—they are expected to remain constant, so we have a *zero growth stock.* In this case, the dividends expected in each future year are equal to some constant amount, $D_1 = D_2 = D_3$ and so on. Therefore, we can drop the subscript and rewrite Equation 4–2 as follows:

$$P_0 = \frac{D}{(1 + k_s)^1} + \frac{D}{(1 + k_s)^2} + \cdots + \frac{D}{(1 + k_s)^n} + \cdots + \frac{D}{(1 + k_s)^\infty}. \quad (4\text{–}2a)$$

A security that is expected to pay a constant amount each period forever is defined as a *perpetuity,* so a zero growth stock may be thought of as a perpetuity.

The stock is expected to provide an infinite stream of future dividends, but each one has a smaller present value than the preceding one, and as n gets very large, the present value of the individual future dividends approaches zero. To illustrate, suppose $D = \$1.92$ and $k_s = 9\% = 0.09$. We can rewrite Equation 4–2a as follows:

$$P_0 = \frac{\$1.92}{(1.09)^1} + \frac{\$1.92}{(1.09)^2} + \frac{\$1.92}{(1.09)^3} + \cdots + \frac{\$1.92}{(1.09)^{50}} + \cdots + \frac{\$1.92}{(1.09)^{100}} + \cdots$$

$$= \$1.76 + \$1.62 + \$1.48 + \cdots + \$0.03 + \cdots + \$0.0003 + \cdots.$$

We can also show the perpetuity in graph form, as in Figure 4–4. The horizontal line shows the constant dividend stream, $D_t = \$1.92$. The step function curve shows the present value of each future dividend. If we

---

10 Investors periodically lose sight of the long-run nature of stocks as investments and forget that in order to sell a stock at a profit, one must find a buyer who will pay the higher price. If you analyze a stock's value in accordance with Equation 4–2, conclude that the stock's market price exceeds a reasonable value, and then buy the stock anyway, then you are following the "bigger fool theory of investment." You think that you may be a fool to buy the stock at its excessive price, but you also think that when you get ready to sell it, you can find someone who is an even bigger fool. The bigger fool theory was widely followed in 1929.

Figure 4–4
Present Values of Dividends of a Perpetuity
(Zero Growth Stock)

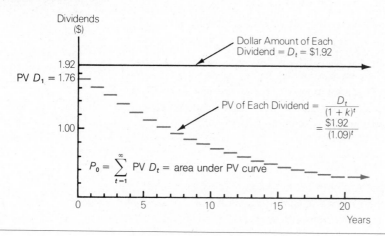

extended the analysis on out to infinity and then summed the PVs of all future dividends, the sum would be equal to the value of the stock.

It can be shown that Equation 4–2a, hence the value of a zero growth stock, reduces to this formula:[11]

$$P_0 = \frac{D_1}{k_s}. \qquad (4–3)$$

Therefore, in our example, the value of the stock is $21.33:

$$P_0 = \frac{\$1.92}{0.09} = \$21.33.$$

Thus, if you were to extend Figure 4–4 on out forever, then add up the present values of each individual dividend, you would end up with the value of the stock, $21.33.[12]

We could transpose the P_0 and the k_s in Equation 4–3 to solve for k_s. We could then look up the value of the stock and the latest dividend, P_0 and D, in the newspaper, and the value $k = D/P_0$ would be the rate of return we would expect to earn if we bought the stock. Since we are dealing with an *expected rate of return,* we put a "hat" on the k value to produce Equation 4–4:

11 The derivation of the formula in Equation 4–3 is shown in Appendix 4A.
12 If you think that having a stock pay dividends forever is unrealistic, then think of it as lasting only for 50 or 100 years. Here we would have an annuity of $1.92 per year for 50 or 100 years. The PV of a 50 year annuity would be $1.92 (10.9617) = $21.01, while the PV of a 100 year annuity would be $21.329, versus $21.33 for the infinite annuity. Thus, the years from 50 to infinity do not contribute much to the value of the stock!

$$\hat{k}_s = \frac{D_1}{P_0}. \tag{4-4}$$

Thus, if we bought the stock at a price of $21.33 and expected to receive a constant dividend of $1.92, our expected rate of return would be

$$\hat{k}_s = \frac{\$1.92}{\$21.33} = 0.09 = 9\%.$$

Before leaving this section, we should note that Equations 4-3 and 4-4 are applicable to *preferred stock,* a type of stock that pays a constant dividend. Preferred stock is discussed in detail in Chapter 13.

"Normal," or Constant, Growth

Although the zero growth model is applicable to some companies, the earnings and dividends of most companies increase each year. In general, this growth is expected to continue in the foreseeable future at about the same rate as that of the gross national product. On this basis, it is expected that an average, or "normal," company will grow at a rate of about 6 percent a year, and this rate will rise if the inflation rate increases. Thus, if such a company's last dividend, which has already been paid, was D_0, its dividend in any future year t may be forecast as $D_t = D_0 (1 + g)^t$, where g is the expected rate of growth. For example, if Carter Chemical just paid a dividend of $1.92 (that is, $D_0 = \$1.92$) and investors expect a 4 percent growth rate, the estimated dividend one year hence will be $D_1 =$ ($1.92)(1.04) = $2; D_2 will be $2.08; and the estimated dividend five years hence will be

$$D_t = D_0(1 + g)^t$$
$$= \$1.92(1.04)^5$$
$$= \$2.34.$$

Using this method of estimating future dividends, the current price, P_0, is determined by Equation 4-2, as described earlier. In other words, we find the expected future cash flow stream (the dividends), get the present value of each dividend payment, and sum them. The summation is the value of the stock. Thus, the stock price is equal to the present value of the expected future dividends.

If g is constant, Equation 4-2 may be simplified as follows:[13]

$$P_0 = \frac{D_1}{k_s - g}. \tag{4-5}$$

Inserting values into the equation, we find the price of this stock to be $40:

---

13 The proof of Equation 4-5 is given in Appendix 4A.

$$P_0 = \frac{\$1.92(1.04)}{0.09 - 0.04} = \frac{\$2}{0.05} = \$40.$$

The constant growth model expressed in Equation 4–5 is often called the Gordon Model, after Myron J. Gordon, who did much to develop and popularize it.

Note that Equation 4–5 is sufficiently general to encompass the no-growth case described above: if growth is zero, this is simply a special case, and Equation 4–5 is equal to Equation 4–3. Note also that a necessary condition for the derivation of Equation 4–5 is that k_s be greater than g. If the equation is used where k_s is not greater than g, the results are meaningless.

The concept underlying the stock valuation process is graphed in Figure 4–5 for the case of a 4 percent growth rate. Dividends grow, but since $k_s > g$, the present value of each future dividend (the lower step-function curve) is declining. For example, the dividend in Year 1 is $D_1 = D_0(1 + g)^1 = \$1.92(1.04) = \$2.00$. The present value of this dividend, discounted at 9 percent, is PV $D_1 = \$2.00/(1.09)^1 = \$2.00/1.09 = \$1.83$. The dividend expected in Year 2 is $D_2 = \$2.08$, and the PV of this dividend is $1.75.

Figure 4–5
Growing Dividend Stream and Present Value
of the Stream: $D_0 = \$1.92$, $g = 4\%$, $k_s = 9\%$

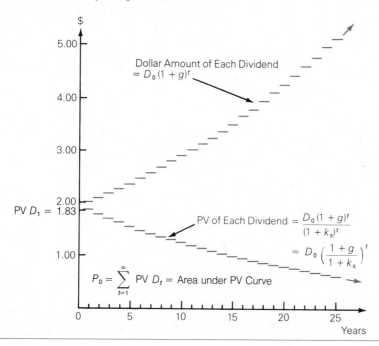

Continuing, $D_3 = \$2.16$ and PV $D_3 = \$1.67$. Thus, the expected dividends are growing, but the PV of the successive dividends is declining because $k_s > g$.

If we added up the PVs of each future dividend, this summation would be the value of the stock, P_0. And, as we saw above, when g is a constant, this summation is equal to $D_1/(k_s - g)$, so

$$P_0 = \frac{D_1}{k_s - g}. \qquad (4\text{--}5)$$

If we extended the lower step-function curve in Figure 4–5 on out to infinity and added up the present values of each future dividend, the summation would be identical to the value given by the formula.

The Expected Rate of Return on a Constant Growth Stock

We could solve Equation 4–5 for k_s, again using the hat to denote that we are dealing with an expected rate of return:[14]

$$\hat{k}_s = \frac{D_1}{P_0} + g. \qquad (4\text{--}6)$$

Thus, if you buy a stock for a price $P_0 = \$40$, and if the stock is expected to pay a dividend $D_1 = \$2$ next year and to grow at a constant rate $g = 4\%$ in the future, then your expected rate of return is 9 percent on your $40 investment:

$$\hat{k}_s = \frac{\$2}{\$40} + 4\% = 5\% + 4\% = 9\%.$$

In this form we see that $\hat{k}_s$ is the *expected total return* and that it consists of $D_1/P_0 = 5\%$, the *expected dividend yield*, and $g = 4\%$, the *expected growth rate or capital gains yield*.

Suppose the analysis above had been conducted on January 1, 1980, so $P_0 = \$40$ was the January 1, 1980, stock price and $D_1 = \$2$ was the dividend expected during 1980. What would the stock price be at the end of 1980 (or the beginning of 1981)? We would again apply Equation 4–5, but this time with the 1981 dividend, $D_2 = D_1 (1 + g) = \$2(1.04) = \$2.08$:

$$P_{1/1/81} = \frac{D_{1981}}{k_s - g} = \frac{\$2.08}{0.09 - 0.04} = \$41.60.$$

14
$$P_0 = \frac{D_1}{k_s - g} \qquad (4\text{--}5)$$

$$k_s P_0 - g P_0 = D_1$$

$$k_s P_0 = D_1 + g P_0$$

$$k_s = \frac{D_1}{P_0} + g. \qquad (4\text{--}6)$$

Now notice that $41.60 is exactly 4 percent greater than P_0, the $40 price on 1/1/80:

$$\$41.60 = \$40(1.04).$$

Thus, we expect to make a capital gain of $41.60 − $40 = $1.60 during the year, for a capital gains yield of 4 percent:

$$\text{Capital gains yield} = \frac{\$1.60}{\$40} = 0.04 = 4\%.$$

We could extend the analysis on out, and in each future year the expected capital gains yield would always equal g, the expected dividend growth rate.

The dividend yield in 1981 can be estimated as follows:

$$\text{Dividend yield}_{1981} = \frac{D_{1981}}{P_{1/1/81}} = \frac{\$2.08}{\$41.60} = 0.05 = 5\%.$$

The capital gains yield could again be calculated, and it would again be 4 percent. Thus, for a constant growth stock, (1) the dividend grows at a constant rate; (2) the stock price grows at this same rate; (3) the dividend yield is a constant; (4) the capital gains yield is also a constant, and it is equal to g, the expected dividend growth rate; and (5) the expected total rate of return, $\hat{k}_s$, is equal to the expected dividend yield plus the expected capital gains yield.

Nonconstant, or "Supernormal," Growth[15]

Firms typically go through "life cycles" during part of which their growth is much faster than that of the economy as a whole. Automobile manufacturers in the 1920s and computer and office equipment manufacturers in the 1970s are examples. Figure 4–6 illustrates such nonconstant, or "supernormal," growth and compares it with normal growth, zero growth, and negative growth.[16]

The dividends of the supernormal growth firm are expected to grow at a 20 percent rate for three years, after which the growth rate is expected to fall to 4 percent, the assumed norm for the economy. The value of this firm, like any other, is the present value of its expected future dividends as determined by Equation 4–2. In the case where D_t is growing at a constant rate, Equation 4–2 may be simplified to $P_0 = D_1/(k_s - g)$. In the supernormal case, however, the expected growth rate is not a constant—it declines at the end of the period of supernormal growth. To find the value of such a stock, we proceed in three steps:

1. Find the PV of the dividends during the period of supernormal growth.

---

15 This section is relatively technical and may be omitted at the option of the instructor without loss of continuity.

16 A negative growth rate indicates a declining company. A mining company whose profits are falling because of a declining ore body is an example.

2. Find the price of the stock at the end of the supernormal growth period, and then discount this price back to the present.
3. Add these two components to find the present value of the stock, P_0.

Figure 4–6
Illustrative Dividend Growth Rates

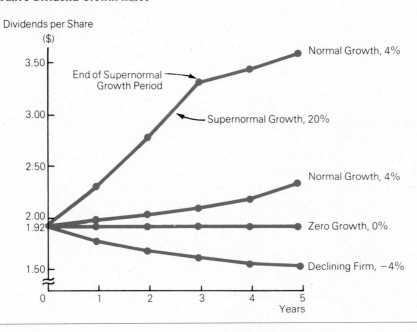

To illustrate the process of growth stock valuation, suppose the following facts exist:

k_s = stockholders' required rate of return = 9 percent.
N = years of supernormal growth = 3.
g_s = rate of earnings and dividend growth during supernormal growth period = 20 percent.
g_n = rate of growth after supernormal period = 4 percent.
D_0 = last dividend that the company paid = $1.92.

Step 1. Find the PV of dividends paid (PV D) at the end of Years 1 to 3 using this formula:

$$PV\ D_t = D_0(1 + g_s)^t\left(\frac{1}{1 + k_s}\right)^t = D_0(FVIF_{g_s,t})(PVIF_{k_s,t}).$$

D_0	$\times$	$FVIF_{20\%,t}$	=	D_t ;	D_t	$\times$	$PVIF_{9\%,t}$	=	PV D_t
D_1: $1.92	$\times$	(1.200)	=	$2.304;	$2.304	$\times$	0.9174	=	$2.1137
D_2: 1.92	$\times$	(1.440)	=	2.765;	2.765	$\times$	0.8417	=	2.3273
D_3: 1.92	$\times$	(1.728)	=	3.318;	3.318	$\times$	0.7722	=	2.5622
				Sum of PVs of supernormal period dividends				=	$7.0032

Step 2. Find the PV of the stock's price (PV P) at the end of Year 3:

a.
$$P_3 = \frac{D_4}{k_s - g_n} = \frac{D_3(1 + g_n)}{0.09 - 0.04} = \frac{\$3.318(1.04)}{0.05}$$

$$= \frac{\$3.45}{0.05} = \$69.$$

b.   PV P_3 = $69 (PVIF$_{9\%,\ 3\ yr.}$) = $69(0.7722) = $53.28.

Step 3. Sum to find P_0, the value of the stock today:

$$P_0 = \$7 + \$53.28 = \$60.28.$$

A graphic view of this process, using a time line diagram, is given in Figure 4–7.

**Figure 4–7
Time Line for Finding the Value of a
Supernormal Growth Stock**

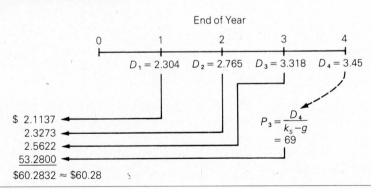

We have now calculated the illustrative firm's stock price today ($P_0 =$ $60.28) and three years from now ($P_3 = $69). We could estimate the price for other years. For example, P_1, the price at the end of Year 1 (just after D_1 has been paid), is \$63.43, calculated as follows:[17]

$$P_1 = PV\ D_2 + PV\ D_3 + PV\ P_3$$
$$= D_0(1 + g_s)^2(PVIF_{9\%,\ 1\ year}) + D_0(1 + g_s)^3(PVIF_{9\%,\ 2\ years}) + P_3(PVIF_{9\%,\ 2\ years})$$
$$= 1.92(1.44)(0.917) + \$1.92(1.728)(0.842) + \$69(0.842)$$
$$= \$2.535 + \$2.794 + \$58.10$$
$$= \$63.43.$$

Note that D_2 is discounted back one year, while D_3 and P_3 are discounted back two years, in order to find the stock price at $t = 1$.

The value of the stock at the end of Year 2, P_2, is found as follows:

$$P_2 = PV\ D_3 + PV\ P_3$$
$$= D_0\ (1 + g_s)^3(PVIF_{9\%,\ 1\ year}) + P_3(PVIF_{9\%,\ 1\ year})$$
$$= \$1.92(1.728)\ (0.917) + 69\ (0.917)$$
$$= \$66.32.$$

The price of the stock at the end of Year 4, when the stock is a "normal growth stock" is

$$P_4 = \frac{D_5}{k_s - g_n} = \frac{D_3(1 + g_n)^2}{0.09 - 0.04}$$

$$= \frac{\$3.318(1.082)}{0.05} = \frac{\$3.59}{0.05} = \$71.80.$$

Through this process, we can estimate the stock price in any future year; the values at the end of Years 1, 2, 3, and 4 are summarized below:

End of Year	Estimated Stock Price
0	\$60.28
1	63.43
2	66.32
3	69.00
4	71.80

---

17 An equation that summarizes the supernormal growth stock calculations is

$$P_0 = \sum_{t=1}^{N} \frac{D_0(1 + g_s)^t}{(1 + k_s)^t} + \frac{D_{N+1}}{k_s - g_n} \left(\frac{1}{1 + k_s}\right)^N.$$

A general equation for supernormal stock valuation, where the growth rate is allowed to decline gradually rather than suddenly, is given in E. F. Brigham and J. L. Pappas, "Duration of Growth, Changes in Growth Rates, and Corporate Share Prices," *Financial Analysts' Journal,* vol. 24 (May–June 1966), 157–162.

Dividends and Capital Gains on Supernormal Growth Stocks As we have seen, the expected rate of return on a constant growth stock consists of a dividend yield plus a growth or capital gains yield: $\hat{k}_s = D_1/P_0 + g$. Supernormal growth stocks are also expected to provide dividend yields plus capital gains yields, but, whereas the D/P and g components are both constant for a constant growth stock, these components change under conditions of supernormal growth. This point can be illustrated with the data we have developed. First, note that the capital gains yield in any year consists of the capital gain during the year, $P_t - P_{t-1}$, divided by the beginning price, P_{t-1}. Thus, for our illustrative stock, the capital gains yield expected during the first year is 5.2 percent:

$$\text{Capital gains yield} = \frac{P_1 - P_0}{P_0} = \frac{\$63.43 - \$60.28}{\$60.28} = \frac{\$3.15}{\$60.28}$$

$$= 0.052 = 5.2\%.$$

The dividend yield expected during Year 1 is 3.8 percent:

$$\text{Dividend yield} = \frac{D_1}{P_0} = \frac{\$2.304}{\$60.28} = 3.8\%.$$

The dividend yield plus the capital gains yield equals the total expected return on the stock:

$$\text{Total expected return} = \hat{k}_s = 3.8\% + 5.2\% = 9.0\%.$$

Similarly, the capital gains yield expected during Year 2 is 4.6 percent:

$$\text{Capital gains yield} = \frac{P_2 - P_1}{P_1} = \frac{\$66.32 - \$63.43}{\$63.43}$$

$$= 0.046 = 4.6\%,$$

while the dividend yield expected during Year 2 is 4.4 percent:

$$\text{Dividend yield} = \frac{D_2}{P_1} = \frac{\$2.765}{\$63.43} = 0.044 = 4.4\%.$$

Dividend yields, capital gains yields, and total returns for the illustrative supernormal growth stock are given below for Years 1 through 5:

Year	Dividend Yield	Capital Gains Yield	Total Return
1	3.8%	5.2%	9%
2	4.4	4.6	9
3	5.0	4.0	9
4	5.0	4.0	9
5	5.0	4.0	9

Notice that the dividend yield is relatively low during the early years of the stock's period of supernormal growth, while the capital gains yield is relatively high. As the end of the supernormal growth period approaches, the capital gains yield declines, while the dividend yield increases. The total expected return remains constant at $\hat{k}_s = 9\%$.

Comparing Companies with Different Expected Growth Rates

It is useful to summarize our discussion of stock valuation models by comparing companies with the four growth situations graphed in Figure 4–6. Here we had a zero growth company, one with a constant 4 percent expected growth rate, one whose earnings are expected to decline at the rate of 4 percent a year, and one whose growth rate is not a constant.

We can use the valuation equations developed above to determine the stock prices, dividend yields, capital gains yields, total expected returns, and price/earnings ratios (P/E ratios)[18] for the four companies. These data are shown in Table 4–2. We assume that each firm had earnings per share (EPS) of $3.60 during the preceding reporting period (that is, $EPS_0 = \$3.60$) and paid out 53.3 percent of its reported earnings as dividends. Therefore, dividends per share last year, D_0, were $1.92 for each company, but the values of D_1 differ among the companies.

The expected and required return is 9 percent on each of the stocks; thus, $\hat{k}_s = k_s = 9\%$. For a declining firm this return consists of a relatively high current dividend yield combined with a capital loss amounting to 4 percent a year. For the no growth firm there is neither a capital gain nor a capital loss expectation, so the 9 percent return must be obtained entirely from the dividend yield. The normal growth firm provides a relatively low current dividend yield, but a 4 percent per year capital gains expectation. Finally, the supernormal growth firm has the lowest current dividend yield but the highest capital gains expectation.

What is expected to happen to the prices of the four illustrative firms' stocks over time? Three of the four cases are straightforward: The zero growth firm's price is expected to be constant (that is, $P_t = P_{t+1}$); the declining firm is expected to have a falling stock price; and the constant growth firm's stock is expected to grow at a constant rate, 4 percent. As we

---

18 Price/earnings ratios relate a stock's price to its earnings per share (EPS). The higher the P/E ratio, the more investors are willing to pay for a dollar of the firm's current earnings. Other things held constant, investors will pay more for a dollar of current earnings of a rapidly growing firm than for one of a slow growth company; hence, rapid growth companies generally have high P/E ratios. These ratios are discussed in more detail in Chapters 6 and 15. The relationships among the P/E ratios, shown in the last column of Table 4–2, are similar to what one would intuitively expect—the higher the expected growth (all other things the same), the higher the P/E ratio.

   We should note, too, that differences in P/E ratios among firms can also arise from differences in the required rates of return, k_s, which investors use in capitalizing the future dividend streams. If one company has a higher P/E than another, this could be caused by a higher g, a lower k_s, or a combination of these two factors.

saw in the preceding section, the supernormal firm's stock price growth rate is identical to its capital gains yield, which starts at 5.2 percent per year but declines to 4 percent as the supernormal growth period ends. So, the supernormal firm's stock price grows at a declining rate that levels off at 4 percent at the end of the supernormal growth period, when it becomes a "normal growth stock."

Table 4–2
Prices, Dividend Yields, and Price/Earnings
Ratios for 9 Percent Returns under Different
Growth Assumptions

				Current Dividend	Capital Gains Yield in Year 1	Total Expected	P/E
			Price	Yield (D_1/P_0)	[($P_1 - P_0$)/P_0]	Return	Ratio[a]
Declining firm (−4%)	$P_0 = \dfrac{D_1}{k_s - g} = \dfrac{\$1.84}{0.09 - (-0.04)}$		= $14.15	13%	−4.0%	9%	3.9
No growth firm (0%)	$P_0 = \dfrac{D_1}{k_s} = \dfrac{\$1.92}{0.09}$		= 21.33	9	0.0	9	5.9
Normal growth firm (4%)	$P_0 = \dfrac{D_1}{k_s - g} = \dfrac{\$2.00}{0.09 - 0.04}$		= 40.00	5	4.0	9	11.1
Supernormal growth firm	$P_0 = $ (see earlier section)		= 60.28	3.8	5.2	9	16.7

[a]It was assumed at the beginning of this example that each company is earning $3.60 initially. This $3.60, divided into the various prices, gives the indicated P/E ratios.

We might also note that as the supernormal growth rate declines toward the normal rate (or as the time when this decline will occur becomes more imminent), the high P/E ratio must approach the normal P/E ratio; that is, the P/E of 16.7 will decline year by year and equal 11.1, that of the normal growth company, in the third year.

Note also that D_1 differs for each firm, being calculated as follows:

$$D_1 = EPS_0(1 + g)(\text{Percentage of earnings paid out}) = \$3.60(1 + g)(0.533).$$

For the declining firm, $D_1 = \$3.60\,(0.96)\,(0.533) = \$1.84.$

SUMMARY

Corporate decisions should be analyzed in terms of how alternative courses of action will affect the value of the firm's stock. Clearly, it is necessary to know how stock prices in general are established before attempting to measure how a given decision will affect a specific firm's stock price. Accordingly, this chapter shows how bond and stock values are established, as well as how investors go about estimating the rates of return they will receive on these securities if they purchase them at the existing market prices. In all cases, security values were found to be *the present value of the future cash flows expected from the security.* The cash flows from a bond consist of interest payments and the bond's maturity value, while stocks provide a stream of dividends plus a sale price which can include capital gains or losses.

The following equation is used to find the value of a bond:

$$V = I\,(\text{PVIFA}_{k_d,n}) + M\,(\text{PVIF}_{k_d,n}).$$

Here V is the value of the bond; I is the annual interest payment, or coupon; n is years to maturity; k_d is the appropriate interest rate; and M is the bond's maturity value, generally \$1,000. This equation can also be solved for k_d, which is called the *yield to maturity.*

Several different stock valuation formulas were developed; the ones for zero and for constant growth are given below:

Zero growth stock
$$P_0 = \frac{D_1}{k_s}.$$

Constant, or normal, growth stock
$$P_0 = \frac{D_1}{k_s - g}.$$

Here P_0 is the current price of the stock; D_1 is the dividend expected during the next year; k_s is the required rate of return on the stock; and g is the expected growth rate. In this equation, g is a constant; if g is not a constant, then the supernormal growth formula must be used to find the stock's value.

We can express the equation for the expected rate of return as follows:

$$\hat{k}_s = \frac{D_1}{P_0} + g.$$

In this form, we see that $\hat{k}_s$ is a total expected return, consisting of an *expected dividend yield* plus an *expected capital gains yield.* For a constant growth stock, the dividend and capital gains components of total yield are constant over time. For supernormal growth stocks, the dividend yield rises over time, while the capital gains component declines, with the total yield remaining constant.

Throughout the chapter we simply take as given both the "appropriate discount rate," k_s, and the expected growth rate of dividends and stock prices. In Chapter 5 we shall examine the factors that determine the discount rates, and in Chapter 6 we take up methods of estimating future growth. Then, in the remainder of the book, we consider the types of actions that a firm's financial manager can take to lower the discount rate and to increase the expected growth rate, thus increasing the value of the firm's stock.

Questions

4-1 If a corporation sells a certificate under which it promises to pay $60 per year for twenty years, plus $1,000 at the end of twenty years, what is the certificate called?

4-2 A bond that pays interest forever and has no maturity date is a perpetual bond. In what respect is a perpetual bond similar to a no growth stock and to a share of preferred stock?

4-3 Is it true that the following equation can be used to find the value of an n-year bond that pays interest once a year?

$$\text{Value} = \sum_{t=1}^{n} \frac{\text{Annual interest}}{(1 + k_d)^t} + \frac{\text{Par value}}{(1 + k_d)^n}.$$

4-4 "The values of outstanding bonds change whenever the going rate of interest changes. In general, short-term bond prices are more sensitive to interest rate changes than are long-term bond prices." Is this statement true or false? Explain.

4-5 The rate of return you would get if you bought a bond and held it to its maturity date is defined as the bond's yield to maturity (YTM). If interest rates in the economy rise after a bond has been issued, what will happen to the YTM? Does it matter how long the bond has before maturity?

4-6 If you buy a share of common stock, you will typically expect to receive dividends plus capital gains. Would you expect the distribution between dividends and capital gains to be influenced by a firm's decision to pay more dividends rather than retain and reinvest more earnings?

4-7 The next expected dividend, D_1, divided by the current price of a share of stock, P_0, is defined as the stock's expected dividend yield. What is the relationship between the dividend yield, the total yield, and the remaining years of supernormal growth for a supernormal growth firm?

4-8 Is it true that the following expression can be used to find the value of a constant growth stock?

$$P_0 = \frac{D_0}{k_s - g}.$$

4-9 Is it true that the following expression can be used to find the expected rate of return on a share of stock that is expected to grow at a constant rate?

$$\hat{k}_s = \frac{D_1}{P_0} + g.$$

Problems

4-1 a. The Signal Company's bonds pay $100 annual interest, mature in ten years, and pay $1,000 on maturity. What will be the value of these bonds when the going rate of interest is (1) 6 percent, (2) 9 percent, and (3) 12 percent?

b. Now suppose Signal has some other bonds that pay $100 interest per year, $1,000 at maturity, and mature in one year. What will be the value of these bonds at a going rate of interest of (1) 6 percent, (2) 9 percent, and (3) 12 percent? Assume there is only one more interest payment to be made.

c. Why do the longer-term bonds fluctuate more when interest rates change than do the shorter-term bonds (the one year bonds)?

4-2 a. The Williams Company's bonds have three years remaining to maturity. Interest is paid annually, the bonds have a $1,000 par value, and the coupon interest rate is 7 percent. What is the yield to maturity at a current market price (1) of $974 or (2) of $1,027?

b. Would you pay $974 for the bond described in Part a if you felt that the appropriate rate of interest for these bonds is $7^1/2$ percent; that is, $k_d = 7^1/2\%$? Explain your answer.

4-3 Suppose General Motors sold an issue of bonds with a ten year maturity, a $1,000 par value, a 10 percent coupon rate, and semiannual interest payments.

a. Two years after the bonds were issued, the going rate of interest on bonds such as these fell to 8 percent. At what price would the bonds sell?

b. Suppose that, two years after issue, the going interest rate had risen to 12 percent. At what price would the bonds sell?

c. Suppose the conditions in Part a existed; that is, interest rates fell to 8 percent two years after the issue date. Suppose, further, that the interest rate remained at 8 percent for the next eight years. What would happen to the price of the GM bond over time?

4-4 Your broker offers to sell you a share of common stock that paid a dividend of $2 *last year.* You expect the dividend to grow at the rate of 5 percent per year for the next three years, and you plan to hold the stock for three years, then to sell it, if you do indeed buy the stock.

a. What is the expected dividend for each of the next three years; that is, calculate D_1, D_2, and D_3. Note that $D_0 = \$2$.

b. If the appropriate discount rate is 10 percent, and the first of these dividend payments will occur one year from now, what is the present value of the dividend stream; that is, calculate the PV of D_1, D_2, and D_3, and sum these PVs.

c. You expect the price of the stock to be $48.62 three years from now; that is, you expect P_3 to equal $48.62. Discounted at a 10 percent rate, what is the present value of this expected future stock price; that is, calculate the PV of $48.62.

d. If you plan to buy the stock, hold it for three years, and then sell it for $48.62, what is the most you should pay for it?

e. Use Equation 4–5 to calculate the present value of this stock. Assume that $g = 5\%$ and is a constant.

f. Is the value of this stock to you dependent upon how long you plan to hold it? In other words, if your planned holding period were two years or five years rather than three years, would this affect the value of the stock today, P_0?

4-5 You buy a share of stock for $42. You expect the stock to pay dividends of $2.10, $2.205, and $2.315 in Years 1, 2, and 3, respectively, and you expect to sell the stock at a price of $48.62 at the end of three years.

a. Calculate the growth rate in dividends.

b. Calculate the current dividend yield.

c. Assuming the calculated growth rate is expected to continue, you can add the dividend yield to the expected growth rate to get the expected total rate of return. What is this expected total rate of return?

4-6 a. Investors require a 15 percent rate of return on Company X's stock ($k_s = 15\%$). At what price will the stock sell if the previous dividend was $D_0 = \$1$ and investors expect dividends to grow at a constant compound annual rate of (1) minus 5 percent, (2) 0 percent, (3) 5 percent, and (4) 14 percent? (*Hint:* Use $D_1 = D_0(1 + g)$, not D_0, in the formula.)

b. In Part a, what is the "formula price" for Company X's stock if the required rate of return is 15 percent and the expected growth rate is (1) 15 percent or (2) 20 percent? Are these reasonable results? Explain.

4-7 In February 1956 the Los Angeles Airport authority issued a series of 3.4 percent, thirty year bonds. Interest rates rose substantially in the years following the issue, and as rates rose, the price of the bonds declined. In February 1969, thirteen years later, the price of the bonds had dropped from $1,000 to $650. Assume annual interest payments.

a. Each bond originally sold at its $1,000 par value. What was the bond's yield to maturity at time of issue?

b. Calculate the yield to maturity in February 1969. (*Hint:* Use the formula in Footnote 6 to get started. Also, note that the bond has seventeen years remaining to maturity.)

c. Assume that interest rates stabilize at the 1969 level and remain at this level for the remainder of the bond's life. What will be the bond's price in February 1979, when it has seven years remaining to maturity?

d. What will the bond's price be the day before it matures in 1986?

e. In 1969 the Los Angeles Airport bonds were called "discount bonds." What will happen to the price of discount bonds as they approach maturity? Is there a "built-in capital gain" on discount bonds?

f. The coupon interest divided by the market price of a bond is defined as the bond's *current yield*. What is the Los Angeles Airport bond's current yield (1) in February 1969 and (2) in February 1979? What are the bond's capital gains yields and total yields (total yield equals yield to maturity) on those same two dates?

4-8 Pittsburgh Mining Company's ore reserves are being depleted, and its costs of recovering a declining quantity of ore are rising each year. As a result, the company's earnings and dividends are declining at the rate of 10 percent per year. If $D_0 = \$5$ and $k_s = 11\%$, what is the value of Pittsburgh Mining's stock?

4-9 It is now January 1, 1980. Apex Oil's 1979 dividend, which was paid yesterday, was $1, that is, $D_0 = \$1$. Earnings and dividends are expected to grow at a rate of 15 percent per year for the next three years (that is, during 1980, 1981, and 1982) and thereafter to grow indefinitely at the same rate as the national economy, 6 percent. Thus $g_s = 15\%$ and $g_n = 6\%$, and the period of supernormal growth is three years. The required rate of return on the stock, k_s, is 12 percent.

a. Calculate the expected dividends for 1980, 1981, and 1982.

b. Calculate the price of the stock today. This is P_0. Proceed by finding the present value of the dividends expected during 1980, 1981, and 1982, plus the present value of the stock price at the end of 1982. The year-end 1982 stock price can be found by use of the constant growth equation. Notice that, to find the 12/31/1982 price, you use the dividend expected in 1983, which is 6 percent greater than the 1982 dividend.

c. You have now calculated the present price of the stock and its expected price three years from now. Calculate its price two years from now; that is, the 12/31/1981 price. The price one year from now, on 12/31/1980, should be $23.81.

d. Calculate the current dividend yield, D_1/P_0, the capital gains yield expected in 1980, $(P_1 - P_0)/P_0$, and the expected total return (dividend yield plus capital gains yield) for 1980. Also, calculate these same three yields for 1983. The yields for 1981 and 1982 are as follows:

Year	Dividend Yield	Capital Gains Yield	Total Expected Yield
1981	5.56%	6.47%	≈12%
1982	6.00	6.00	≈12

e. How might an investor's tax situation affect the decision to purchase stocks of companies in the early stages of their lives, when they are growing rapidly, versus stocks of older, more mature firms? When does Apex Oil's stock become "mature" in this example?

4-10 a. Electronic Memories, Inc. (EMI), has been growing at a rate of 20 percent per year in recent years. This same growth rate is expected to last for another two years. If $D_0 = \$1$, $k_s = 14\%$, and $g_n = 6\%$, what is EMI's stock worth today?

b. Now assume that EMI's period of supernormal growth is five years rather than two years.

(1) Calculate EMI's expected dividend in each of the next six years.

(2) Calculate EMI's stock price today, P_0, and the stock price in five years, P_5. Stock prices in other years are as follows: $P_1 = \$24.99$; $P_2 = \$27.04$; $P_3 = \$29.10$; $P_4 = \$31.10$.

(3) Now calculate EMI's dividend yield, capital gains yield, and total yield for Years 1 and 4. These yields for other years are as follows (disregard rounding errors):

Year	D_t/P_{t-1}	+	$(P_t - P_{t-1})/P_{t-1}$	=	Total Yield
1					
2	5.76%		8.20%		13.96%
3	6.39		7.62		14.01
4					
5	8.00		6.01		14.01

c. Of what interest to investors is the changing relationship between dividend yield and capital gains yield over time?

APPENDIX 4A
DERIVATION OF VALUATION EQUATIONS

The derivation of the formula for the value of a zero growth stock, $P_0 = D/k_s$ (Equation 4–3), is as follows:

$$P_0 = \frac{D}{(1 + k_s)^1} + \frac{D}{(1 + k_s)^2} + \cdots + \frac{D}{(1 + k_s)^\infty}. \qquad (4A–1)$$

Equation 4A–1 may be rewritten as follows:

$$P_0 = D\left[\frac{1}{(1 + k_s)^1} + \frac{1}{(1 + k_s)^2} + \cdots + \frac{1}{(1 + k_s)^N}\right]. \qquad (4A–2)$$

Multiply both sides of Equation 4A–2 by $(1 + k_s)$:

$$P_0 (1 + k_s) = D\left[1 + \frac{1}{(1 + k_s)^1} + \frac{1}{(1 + k_s)^2} + \cdots + \frac{1}{(1 + k_s)^{N-1}}\right]. \qquad (4A–3)$$

Subtract Equation 4A–2 from Equation 4A–3, obtaining

$$P_0 (1 + k_s - 1) = D\left[1 - \frac{1}{(1 + k_s)^N}\right]. \qquad (4A–4)$$

As $N \to \infty$, $\dfrac{1}{(1 + k_s)^N} \to 0$, so Equation 4A–4 approaches

$$P_0 (k_s) = D,$$

and

$$P_0 = \frac{D}{k_s}. \qquad (4–3)$$

The proof for Equation 4–5, the formula for the value of a constant growth stock, $P_0 = D_1/(k_s - g)$, is developed as follows. Rewrite Equation 4–2 as

$$\text{Value} = P_0 = \frac{D_0(1 + g)^1}{(1 + k_s)^1} + \frac{D_0(1 + g)^2}{(1 + k_s)^2} + \frac{D_0(1 + g)^3}{(1 + k_s)^3} + \cdots$$

$$= D_0\left[\frac{(1 + g)}{(1 + k_s)} + \frac{(1 + g)^2}{(1 + k_s)^2} + \frac{(1 + g)^3}{(1 + k_s)^3} + \cdots + \frac{(1 + g)^N}{(1 + k_s)^N}\right]. \qquad (4A–5)$$

Multiply both sides of Equation 4A–5 by $(1 + k_s)/(1 + g)$:

$$\left[\frac{(1 + k_s)}{(1 + g)}\right]P_0 = D_0\left[1 + \frac{(1 + g)}{(1 + k_s)} + \frac{(1 + g)^2}{(1 + k_s)^2} + \cdots + \frac{(1 + g)^{N-1}}{(1 + k_s)^{N-1}}\right]. \qquad (4A–6)$$

Subtract Equation 4A–5 from Equation 4A–6 to obtain

$$\left[\frac{(1 + k_s)}{(1 + g)} - 1\right]P_0 = D_0\left[1 - \frac{(1 + g)^N}{(1 + k_s)^N}\right].$$

$$\left[\frac{(1 + k_s) - (1 + g)}{(1 + g)}\right]P_0 = D_0\left[1 - \frac{(1 + g)^N}{(1 + k_s)^N}\right].$$

Assuming $k_s > g$, as $N \rightarrow \infty$ the term in brackets on the right-hand side of the equation $\rightarrow 1.0$, leaving

$$\left[\frac{(1 + k_s) - (1 + g)}{(1 + g)} \right] P_0 = D_0,$$

which simplifies to

$$(k_s - g) P_0 = D_0 (1 + g) = D_1$$

$$P_0 = \frac{D_1}{k_s - g}. \qquad\qquad (4\text{--}5)$$

5 RISK AND RATES OF RETURN

In Chapter 4, we referred frequently to the terms *appropriate interest rate on debt, k_d,* and *appropriate (or required) rate of return on a share of common stock, k_s.* These rates, which we used to help determine the values of bonds and stocks, depend primarily on the riskless rate of interest, R_F, and on the riskiness of the security in question. In this chapter, we define the term *risk* as it relates to securities, discuss procedures for measuring it, and then discuss the relationships between risk, returns, and security prices.

DEFINING AND MEASURING RISK

Risk is defined in *Webster's* as "a hazard; a peril; exposure to loss or injury." Thus, risk refers to the chance that some unfavorable event will occur. If you engage in skydiving, you take a chance with your life—skydiving is risky. If you bet on the horses, you risk losing your money. If you invest in speculative stocks (or, really, *any* stock), you are taking a risk in the hope of making an appreciable capital gain.

To illustrate the riskiness of financial assets, suppose an investor buys $100,000 of short-term government bonds with an interest rate of 5 percent. In this case, the yield to maturity on the investment, 5 percent, can be estimated quite precisely, and the investment is defined as being risk-free. However, if the $100,000 is invested in the stock of a company just being organized to prospect for oil in the mid-Atlantic, then the investment's return cannot be estimated precisely. The rate of return could range from some extremely large positive figure to minus 100 percent, and because there is a significant danger of loss, the stock is described as being relatively risky.

Investment risk, then, is associated with the probability of losses—the greater the chance of loss, the riskier the investment. However, we can define risk more precisely, and it is useful to do so.

Probability Distributions

An event's *probability* is defined as the chance that the event will occur. For example, a weather forecaster may state, "There is a 40 percent chance of rain today and a 60 percent chance that it will not rain." If all possible events, or outcomes, are listed, and if a probability is assigned to each event, then the listing is defined as a *probability distribution.* For our weather forecast, we could set up the following probability distribution:

Outcome (1)	Probability (2)
Rain	0.4 = 40%
No rain	0.6 = 60%
	1.0 = 100%

The possible outcomes are listed in Column 1, while the probabilities of these outcomes, expressed both as decimals and as percentages, are given in Column 2. Notice that the probabilities must sum to 1.0, or 100 percent.

In Chapter 4 we defined the expected rate of return on a stock, $\hat{k}_s$, as the sum of the expected dividend yield plus the expected capital gain: $\hat{k}_s = D_1/P_0 + g$. We now examine the probability distribution concept as related to rates of return. To begin, consider the possible rates of return (dividend yield plus capital gain or loss) that you might earn next year on a $10,000 stock investment in Kelly Services, Inc., or on a $10,000 investment in U.S. Telephone stock:

1. Kelly Services

State of the Economy	Probability of This State Occurring	Rate of Return on Kelly Services' Stock under This State
Boom	0.3	100%
Normal	0.4	15
Recession	0.3	−70
	1.0	

2. U.S. Telephone

State of the Economy	Probability of This State Occurring	Rate of Return on U.S. Telephone's Stock under This State
Boom	0.3	20%
Normal	0.4	15
Recession	0.3	10
	1.0	

Here we see that there is a 30 percent chance of a boom, in which case both companies will have high earnings, pay high dividends, and enjoy capital gains; a 40 percent probability of a "normal" economy and moderate returns; and a 30 percent probability of a recession, which will mean low earnings and dividends, and also capital losses. Notice, however, that Kelly Services' rate of return could vary far more widely than that of U.S. Telephone. There is a fairly high probability that the value of the Kelly stock will drop by 70 percent, or from $10,000 to $3,000, while there is no chance of a loss on U.S. Telephone.[1]

Expected Rate of Return

If we multiply each possible outcome by its probability of occurrence and then sum these products, we have a *weighted average* of outcomes. The weights are the probabilities, and the weighted average is defined as the *expected rate of return.* The expected rate of return for Kelly Services is shown in Table 5–1 to be 15 percent; this table is known as a "payoff matrix."

**Table 5–1
Calculation of Expected Rate of Return for
Kelly Services**

State of the Economy (1)	Probability of This State Occurring (2)	Rate of Return If This State Occurs (3)	(2) × (3) (4)
Boom	0.3	100%	30%
Normal	0.4	15	6
Recession	0.3	−70	−21
	1.0		Expected Rate of Return = 15%

The expected rate of return calculation can also be expressed in equation format:

$$\text{Expected rate of return} = \hat{k} = \sum_{i=1}^{n} P_i k_i. \qquad (5\text{--}1)$$

Here k_i is the ith possible outcome, P_i is the probability of the ith outcome, and n is the number of possible outcomes. Thus, $\hat{k}$ is a weighted average of

1 It is, of course, completely unrealistic to think that any stock has no chance of a loss! Only in hypothetical instances could this occur. To illustrate, the price of AT&T's stock dropped from $75 in 1964 to $39 in 1974, a decline of 48 percent. Don't tell people who bought AT&T in 1964 that the stock has no chance of a loss.

the possible outcomes (the k_i values), with each outcome's weight being equal to its probability of occurrence.[2]

Using the data for Kelly Services, we obtain its expected rate of return as follows:

$$\hat{k} = P_1(k_1) + P_2(k_2) + P_3(k_3)$$
$$= 0.3(100\%) + 0.4(15\%) + 0.3(-70\%)$$
$$= 15\%.$$

Equation 5–1 expresses the same operations as does the table, so we can use the equation to determine U.S. Telephone's expected rate of return:

$$\hat{k} = 0.3(20\%) + 0.4(15\%) + 0.3(10\%) = 15\%.$$

We can graph the rates of return to obtain a picture of the variability of possible outcomes; this is shown in the bar charts in Figure 5–1. The height

Figure 5–1
Probability Distributions of Kelly Services' and U.S. Telephone's Rates of Return

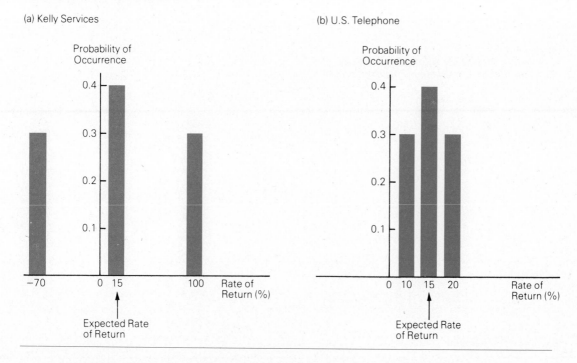

(a) Kelly Services

(b) U.S. Telephone

2 In this section we discuss only returns on stock. Thus, the subscript s is unnecessary, and we use the term k rather than k_s. Also, keep in mind that $\hat{k} = D_1/P_0 + g$:

$$\hat{k} = D_1/P_0 + g = \sum_{i=1}^{n} P_i k_i .$$

of each bar signifies the probability that a given outcome will occur. The range of probable returns for Kelly Services is from 100 to −70 percent, with an average or expected return of 15 percent. The expected return for U.S. Telephone is also 15 percent, but its range is much narrower.

Continuous Probability Distributions

Thus far we have assumed that only three states of the economy can exist: recession, normal, and boom. Actually, of course, the state of the economy could range from a deep depression to a fantastic boom, and there are an unlimited number of possibilities in between. Suppose we had the time and patience to assign a probability to each possible state of the economy (with the sum of the probabilities still equaling 1.0), and to assign a rate of return to each stock for each state of the economy. We would have a table similar to Table 5–1 except that it would have many more entries in each column. This table could be used to calculate expected rates of return as shown above, and the probabilities and outcomes could be approximated by the continuous curves presented in Figure 5–2. Here we have changed the assumptions so that there is essentially a zero probability that Kelly Services'

Figure 5–2
Continuous Probability Distributions of Kelly Services' and U.S. Telephone's Rates of Return

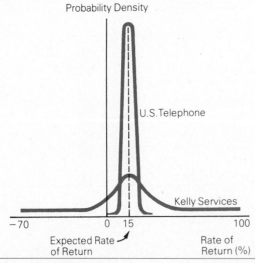

Note: The assumptions regarding the probabilities of various outcomes have been changed from those in Figure 5–1. The probability of obtaining exactly 15 percent was 40 percent in Figure 5–1; in Figure 5–2 it is *much smaller,* because here there are many possible outcomes instead of just three. With continuous distributions such as in Figure 5–2, it is more appropriate to ask what the probability is of obtaining *at least* some specified rate of return than to ask what the probability is of obtaining exactly that rate of return. This cumulative probability is equal to the area under the probability distribution curve to the right of the point of interest or 1 minus the area under the curve up to the point of interest. This topic is covered in more detail later in the chapter.

return will be less than -70 percent or more than 100 percent, or that U.S. Telephone will return less than 10 percent or more than 20 percent.

The tighter the probability distribution, the more likely it is that the actual outcome will be close to the expected value, and the less likely it is that the actual return will be far below the expected return. Thus, the tighter the probability distribution, the lower the risk assigned to a stock. Since U.S. Telephone has a relatively tight probability distribution, its *actual return* is likely to be closer to the 15 percent *expected return* than is that of Kelly Services.[3]

Measuring Risk: The Standard Deviation

Risk is a difficult concept to grasp, and a great deal of controversy has surrounded attempts to define and measure it. However, a common definition, and one that is satisfactory for many purposes, is stated in terms of probability distributions such as those presented in Figure 5–2: *The tighter the probability distribution of expected future returns, the smaller the risk of a given investment.* According to this definition, U.S. Telephone is less risky than Kelly Services *because the chances of a large loss on U.S. Telephone are smaller than the chances of a similar loss on Kelly Services.*

To be most useful, any measure of risk should have a definite value—we need a measure of the tightness of the probability distribution. One such measure is the *standard deviation,* the symbol for which is σ, pronounced "sigma." The smaller the standard deviation, the tighter the probability distribution and, accordingly, the lower the riskiness of the stock. To calculate the standard deviation, we proceed as follows:

1. Calculate the expected rate of return:

$$\text{Expected rate of return} = \hat{k} = \sum_{i=1}^{n} P_i k_i. \qquad (5\text{--}1)$$

2. Subtract the expected rate of return from each possible outcome to obtain a set of deviations about the expected rate of return:

$$\text{Deviation}_i = k_i - \hat{k}.$$

3. Square each deviation, multiply the squared deviation by the probability of occurrence for its related outcome, and sum these products to obtain the *variance* of the probability distribution:

$$\text{Variance} = \sigma^2 = \sum_{i=1}^{n} (k_i - \hat{k})^2 P_i. \qquad (5\text{--}2)$$

3 Since we define risk in terms of the chance of a loss, it would seem logical to measure risk in terms of the probability of losses, or at least of returns below the expected return, rather than by the entire distribution. Measures of below-expected returns, which are known as *semivariance measures,* have been developed, but they are difficult to analyze. In addition, such measures are unnecessary if the distribution of future returns is reasonably symmetric about the expected return, as empirical studies show that it is (at least for diversified portfolios).

4. The standard deviation is found by obtaining the square root of the variance:

$$\text{Standard deviation} = \sigma = \sqrt{\sum_{i=1}^{n}(k_i - \hat{k})^2 P_i}. \qquad (5-3)$$

5. We can illustrate these procedures by calculating the standard deviation for Kelly Services:
   a. The expected rate of return, or the mean, was found in Table 5–1 to be 15 percent.
   b. Set up a table to work out the value for Equation 5–3:

$k_i - \hat{k}$	=	$(k_i - \hat{k})$	$(k_i - \hat{k})^2$	$(k_i - \hat{k})^2 P_i$	
100–15		85	7,225	(7,225)(0.3) =	2,167.5
15–15		0	0	(0)(0.4) =	0
–70–15		–85	7,225	(7,225)(0.3) =	2,167.5
				Variance = σ_k^2 =	4,335.0

$$\text{Standard deviation} = \sigma_k = \sqrt{\sigma_k^2} = \sqrt{4,335} = 65.84\%.$$

Using these same procedures, we find U.S. Telephone's standard deviation to be 3.87 percent. Since Kelly's standard deviation is larger, it is the riskier stock according to this criterion.

If a probability distribution is normal, the *actual* return will lie within ±1 standard deviation of the *expected* return 68 percent of the time. Figure 5–3 illustrates this point and also shows the situation for ±2σ and ±3σ. For Kelly Services, $\hat{k}$ = 15 percent and σ = 65.84 percent. Thus, there is a 68.26 percent probability that the actual return will be in the range of 15 percent ±65.84 percent, or from −50.84 to 80.84 percent. For U.S. Telephone, the 68 percent range is 15 percent ±3.87 percent, or from 11.13 to 18.87 percent. With such a small σ, there is a small probability that U.S. Telephone's return will be very low; hence the stock is not very risky. For the average firm listed on the New York Stock Exchange, σ has been close to 30 percent in recent years.

Risk Aversion

Suppose you have worked hard and saved $1 million, which you now plan to invest. You can buy a 6 percent Treasury note, and at the end of one year you will have a sure $1,060,000, which is your original investment plus $60,000 in interest. Alternatively, you can buy stock in R&D Enterprises. If R&D's research programs are successful, your stock will increase in value to $2.12 million; however, if the research is a failure, the value of your stock will go to zero. You regard the chances of success or failure as being 50–50, so the expected value of the stock investment is 0.5($0) + 0.5($2.12 million) = $1,060,000. Subtracting out the $1 million cost of the stock, you will have an expected profit of $60,000, or an expected (but risky) 6 percent rate of return.

Figure 5-3
Probability Ranges for a Normal Distribution

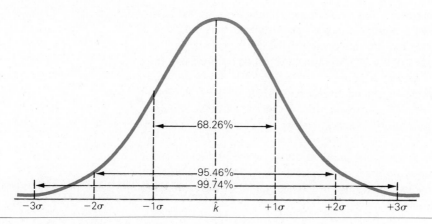

Notes:
a. The area under the normal curve equals 1.0, or 100 percent. *Thus, the areas under any pair of normal curves drawn on the same scale, whether they are peaked or flat, must be equal.*
b. Half of the area under a normal curve is to the left of the mean, indicating that there is a 50 percent probability that the actual outcome will be less than the mean and a 50 percent probability that it will be greater than the mean, or to the right of $\hat{k}$.
c. Of the area under the curve, 68.26 percent is within $\pm 1\sigma$ of the mean, indicating that the probability is 68.26 percent that the actual outcome will be within the range $\hat{k} - 1\sigma$ to $\hat{k} + 1\sigma$.
d. Procedures are available for finding the probability of other earnings ranges. These procedures are covered in statistics courses.
e. For a normal distribution, the larger the value of σ, the greater the probability that the actual outcome will vary widely from, hence perhaps be far below, the expected, or most likely, outcome. *Since the probability of having the actual results turn out to be bad is our definition of risk, and since σ measures this probability, we can use σ as a measure of risk.* This definition may not be a good one, however, if we are dealing with an asset held in a diversified portfolio. This point is covered later in the chapter.

Thus, you have a choice between a *sure* $60,000 profit (a 6 percent rate of return) on the Treasury note, or a *risky* expected $60,000 profit (also a 6 percent expected rate of return) on the stock. Which one would you choose? *If you choose the less risky investment, you are risk averse. Most investors are indeed risk averse, and certainly the average investor is risk averse. Since this is a well-documented fact, we shall assume risk aversion throughout the remainder of the book.*

What are the implications of risk aversion for security prices and rates of return? The answer is that, other things held constant, the higher a security's risk, (1) the lower its price and (2) the higher its expected return. To see how this works, we can analyze the situation with U.S. Telephone and Kelly Services stocks. Suppose each stock sold for $100 per share and each had an expected dividend of $15 per share. No growth is anticipated, so the expected rate of return on each stock is $15/$100 = 0.15 = 15 percent. Investors are averse to risk, so there would be a general preference for U.S. Telephone. People with money to invest would bid for Telephone rather than Kelly stock, and Kelly stockholders would start selling it and buying Telephone stock. The buying pressure would tend to drive up the price of Telephone stock, and the selling pressure would cause Kelly's price to decline.

These price changes, in turn, would cause changes in the expected rates of return on the two securities. Suppose, for example, that the price of Telephone stock was bid up from $100 to $150, while the price of Kelly stock declined from $100 to $75. With the $15 expected dividend, this would cause Telephone's expected return to fall to $15/$150 = 0.10 = 10 percent, while Kelly's expected return would rise to $15/$75 = 0.20 = 20 percent. The difference in returns, 20% − 10% = 10%, is defined as a *risk premium,* which is the compensation investors require for assuming the additional risk on Kelly stock.

This example demonstrates a very important principle: *Riskier securities have higher expected returns than less risky ones.* We will consider the question of *how much* higher later in the chapter, after we examine in more depth how risk should be measured.

PORTFOLIO RISK AND
THE CAPITAL ASSET PRICING MODEL

In the preceding section, we considered the riskiness of a stock held in isolation. Now we analyze the riskiness of stocks held in portfolios.[4] As we shall see, a stock held as part of a portfolio is less risky than the same stock held in isolation. This fact has been incorporated into a generalized framework for analyzing the relationship between risk and rates of return; this framework is called the *Capital Asset Pricing Model,* or CAPM. The CAPM framework is, as we shall see, an extremely important analytical tool in both financial management and investment analysis.

Portfolio Risk

Most financial assets are not held in isolation; rather, they are held as parts of portfolios. Banks, pension funds, insurance companies, mutual funds, and other financial institutions are required by law to hold diversified portfolios. Even individual investors—at least those individuals whose security holdings constitute a significant part of their total wealth—generally hold stock portfolios, not just the stock of one firm. This being the case, from an investor's standpoint the fact that a particular stock goes up or down is not

---

4 A *portfolio* is a collection of investment securities. If you owned some General Motors stock, some Exxon stock, and some IBM stock, you would be holding a three-stock portfolio. For reasons set forth in this section, the vast majority of all stocks are held as parts of portfolios.

very important; *what is important is the value of the portfolio and the portfolio's return.*

To illustrate this point, suppose you have $100,000 to invest. You are considering two stocks, Atlas Industries and Walker Products, whose total returns (dividend yield plus capital gains or minus capital losses) over the last four years are shown in Columns 2 and 3 below:

Year (1)	Rates of Return Atlas (2)	Walker (3)	Portfolio (4)
1976	40%	−20%	10%
1977	−10	50	20
1978	35	−9	13
1979	−5	39	17
Average return	15%	15%	15%
Standard deviation	26%	35%	4%

If you invested your entire $100,000 in either Atlas or Walker, and if returns in the future varied as they have in the past, then your *expected return* on this one-stock portfolio would be $15,000, or 15 percent. However, your *actual return* could easily be negative. On the other hand, if you put half of your money into each stock, your expected return would still be $15,000, or 15 percent, but this return would be much less risky. These results are graphed in Figure 5–4, where we see that the ups and downs in the portfolio's returns are not nearly so pronounced as are those on the individual stocks.

What conditions are necessary for diversification to cause the riskiness of a portfolio to be less than the riskiness of the individual assets contained in the portfolio? The only condition necessary is that the returns on the stocks in the portfolio do not move exactly together. If Atlas's and Walker's returns always moved in the same direction and by the same amount, then diversification into these two stocks would do no good. *In technical terms, this means that for diversification to be effective, returns must not be perfectly positively correlated.* Since most stocks are not perfectly correlated, diversification generally reduces, but does not eliminate, portfolio risk.[5]

To see better how diversification affects portfolio risk, consider Figure 5–5, which shows that the riskiness of a portfolio declines as more and

---

5 *Correlation* is defined as the tendency of two variables to move together. The *correlation coefficient, r,* measures this tendency and can range from +1.0, denoting that the two variables move up and down in perfect synchronization, to −1.0, denoting that the variables always move in exactly opposite directions. A correlation coefficient of zero suggests that the two variables are not related to one another, that is, changes in one variable are independent of changes in the other. If stocks were negatively correlated, or if there were zero correlation, then a properly constructed portfolio would have very little risk. However, stocks tend to be positively (but less than perfectly) correlated with one another, so all stock portfolios tend to be somewhat risky.

Figure 5–4
Rates of Return on Atlas Industries, Walker Products, and Portfolio Consisting of 50% in Each Stock

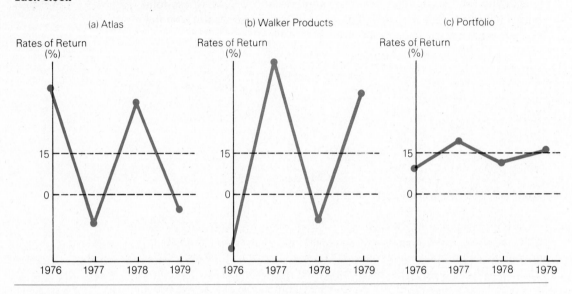

(a) Atlas

(b) Walker Products

(c) Portfolio

Figure 5–5
Reduction of Portfolio Risk through Diversification

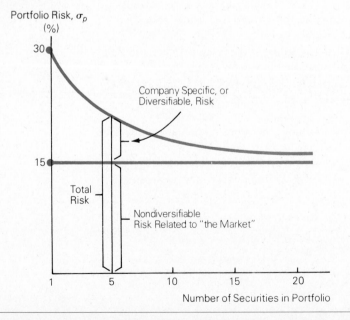

more stocks are added.[6] Here risk is measured by the standard deviation of annual returns on the portfolio, σ_p. With just one stock such as Stock S in the portfolio, σ_p equals the standard deviation of returns on Stock S, or 30 percent. Notice, however, that as more stocks are added, the portfolio's risk declines and approaches a limit, 15 percent in this example. (It is a coincidence that σ_p and k are both 15 percent.) Adding more and more stocks (diversification) can eliminate some of the riskiness of a portfolio, but not all of it. Thus, risk consists of two parts: (1) *company specific, or diversifiable, risk,* which can be eliminated by adding enough securities to the portfolio, and (2) *market,* or nondiversifiable, risk, which is related to broad swings in the stock market and which cannot be eliminated by diversification.[7]

Company risk is caused by such things as lawsuits, strikes, successful and unsuccessful marketing programs, winning and losing major contracts, and other events that are unique to a particular firm. Since these events are essentially random, their effects on a portfolio can be eliminated by diversification—bad events in one firm will be offset by good events in another. *Market risk,* on the other hand, stems from such things as inflation, recessions, and high interest rates, factors which affect all firms simultaneously. Since all firms are affected simultaneously by these factors, this type of risk cannot be eliminated by diversification.

We know that investors demand a premium for bearing risk; that is, the higher the riskiness of a security, the higher its expected return must be in order to induce investors to buy (or to hold) it. But if investors are primarily concerned with *portfolio risk* rather than the risk of the individual securities in the portfolio, how should the riskiness of the individual stocks be measured? The answer is this: The *relevant riskiness of an individual stock is its contribution to the riskiness of a well-diversified portfolio.* In other words, the riskiness of Stock X to a doctor who has a portfolio of 30 stocks, or to a trust officer managing a 150-stock portfolio, is the contribution that Stock X makes to the portfolio's riskiness. The stock might be quite risky if held by itself, but if most of its risk can be eliminated by diversification, the stock's *relevant risk,* which is its contribution to the *portfolio's risk,* may be small.

A simple example will help make this point clear. Suppose you can flip a coin once. If a head comes up, you win $10,000, but you lose $9,500 if it comes up tails. Although this may be considered to be a good bet—the expected return is $250—it is a highly risky proposition. Alternatively, suppose you can flip 100 coins and win $100 for each head but lose $95 for each tail. It is possible that you would hit all heads and win $10,000, and it is also possible that you would flip all tails and lose $9,500, but the chances

6 The data used in this example are adapted from W. H. Wagner and S. C. Lau, "The Effect of Diversification on Risk," *Financial Analysts' Journal,* November–December 1971, pp. 48–53. Wagner and Lau divided a sample of 200 New York Stock Exchange stocks into six subgroups based on quality ratings. Then they constructed portfolios from each of the subgroups, using from one to twenty randomly selected securities, and applied equal weights to each security.

7 Market risk is sometimes called "systematic risk," while company risk is called "unsystematic risk."

are very high that you would actually flip about 50 heads and about 50 tails, winning a net $250. Although each individual flip is a risky bet, collectively you have a very low-risk proposition because you have diversified away most of the risk. This is the idea behind holding portfolios of stocks rather than just one stock, except that with stocks all of the risk cannot be eliminated by diversification—those risks related to broad changes in the stock market as reflected in the Dow Jones Index and other stock market averages will remain.

Are all stocks equally risky in the sense that adding them to a well-diversified portfolio would have the same effect on the portfolio's riskiness? The answer is no—different stocks will affect the portfolio differently; hence, different securities have different degrees of relevant risk.

How can the relevant risk of a stock be measured? As we saw above, all risk except that related to broad market movements can, and presumably will, be diversified away. After all, why accept risk that can easily be eliminated? *The risk that remains after diversifying is market risk, or risk that is inherent in the market, and this risk can be measured by the degree to which a given stock tends to move up and down with the market.*

The Concept of Beta

The tendency of a stock to move with the market is reflected in its *beta coefficient,* which is a measure of the stock's *volatility* relative to an average stock. Betas are discussed at an intuitive level in this section, then in more detail later in the chapter.

An *average risk stock* is defined as one which tends to move up and down in step with the general market as measured by some index such as

Table 5–2
Illustrative List of Beta Coefficients

Stock	Beta
Campbell Soup Company	0.69
Caterpillar Tractor	1.13
Data 100 Corporation	2.02
Dean Foods Company	0.88
Eastman Kodak	1.24
General Electric	1.40
General Motors	0.76
Olympia Brewing Company	0.67
Oceanic Drilling & Exploration	1.96
Polaroid	2.17
Safeway Stores	0.70
St. Regis Paper	1.21

Source: Merrill Lynch, Pierce, Fenner & Smith, November 1979.

the Dow Jones or the New York Stock Exchange Index. Such a stock will have a beta (b) of 1.0, which indicates that, in general, if the market moves up 10 percent, the stock will also move up by 10 percent, and that if the market falls by 10 percent, the stock will likewise fall by 10 percent. A portfolio of such $b = 1.0$ stocks will move up and down with the broad market averages and will be just as risky as the averages. If $b = 0.5$, the stock is only half as volatile as the market—it will rise and fall only half as much—and a portfolio of such stocks is half as risky as a portfolio of $b = 1.0$ stocks. On the other hand, if $b = 2.0$, the stock is twice as volatile as an average stock, so a portfolio of such stocks will be twice as risky as an average portfolio.

Betas are calculated and published by Merrill Lynch, Value Line, and numerous other organizations. The beta coefficients of some well-known companies, as calculated by Merrill Lynch, are shown in Table 5–2. Most stocks have betas in the range of 0.75 to 1.50. The average for all stocks is 1.0 by definition.[8]

If a high beta stock (one whose beta is greater than 1.0) is added to an average risk ($b = 1.0$) portfolio, both the beta and the riskiness of the portfolio will increase. Conversely, if a low beta stock (one whose beta is less than 1.0) is added to an average risk portfolio, the portfolio's beta and risk will decline. *Thus, since a stock's beta measures its contribution to the riskiness of any portfolio, beta is the appropriate measure of the stock's riskiness.*

Figure 5–6 shows graphically the relationship between a portfolio's risk and the betas of the stocks contained in the portfolio. High beta stocks tend to be risky individually, and even a large portfolio of such stocks will have a high degree of risk. Conversely, low beta stocks tend not to be very risky when held individually, and portfolios of low beta stocks are even less risky.

We can summarize our analysis to this point as follows:

1. A stock's risk consists of two components, market and company risk.
2. The company risk can be eliminated by diversification, and most investors do indeed diversify. We are left, then, with market risk, which is caused by general movements in the stock market. This market risk is the only relevant risk to a rational, diversified investor.
3. The market risk of a stock is measured by its beta coefficient, which is an index of the stock's relative volatility. Some benchmark betas are given below:

$b = 0.5$: Stock is only half as volatile, or risky, as the average stock.
$b = 1.0$: Stock is of average risk.
$b = 2.0$: Stock is twice as risky as the average stock.

---

8 These betas are called "historic" or "ex post" betas because they are based strictly on historic, or past, data. Another type of beta, the "fundamental beta," which is based partly on past actions and partly on expected future conditions not yet reflected in historic data, is also in wide use today. For a discussion, see Barr Rosenberg and James Guy, "Beta and Investment Fundamentals," *Financial Analysts' Journal,* May–June 1976, pp. 60–72.

Figure 5–6
**Market and Company Risk for Portfolios of
High Beta, Average Beta, and Low Beta Stocks**

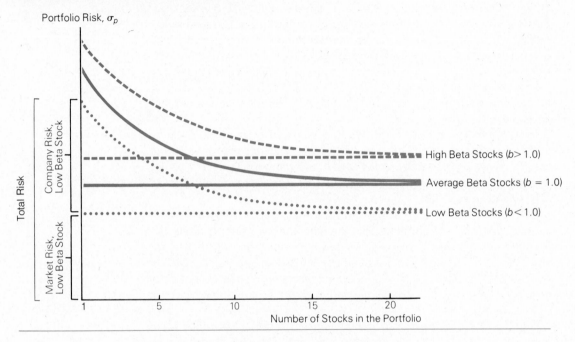

4. *Since a stock's beta coefficient determines how it affects the riskiness of a
   diversified portfolio, beta is the most relevant measure of a stock's risk.
   Henceforth, we shall rely heavily on beta coefficients to measure security
   risk.*[9]

In the following section, we discuss the process of calculating beta
coefficients for individual stocks.

Calculating Beta Coefficients[10]

Professor William F. Sharpe developed the concept of beta coefficients and
pioneered their use in separating the standard deviation of returns on
individual stocks into market and company risk components.[11] Sharpe noted

---

9 It should be noted that beta analysis in practice is not nearly as simple as this discussion makes it
   sound. Actually, a great deal of controversy has surrounded attempts to apply the theory.
10 This section is relatively technical, and it can be omitted at the option of the instructor. If it is omitted,
   the next section taken up should be "The Relationship between Risk and Rates of Return."
11 William F. Sharpe, "Capital Asset Prices: A Theory of Market Equilibrium under Conditions of Risk,"
   Journal of Finance 19 (September 1964): 425–442. It should also be noted that Sharpe, in his early
   work, defined market risk as "systematic risk" and company specific risk as "unsystematic risk." These
   terms are still found in much of the finance literature, but Sharpe and others are now using the
   terminology employed here.

that the market risk of a given stock can be measured by its tendency to move with the general market. Using the data given in Table 5–3, his procedure for determining market risk is illustrated in Figure 5–7. The table and figure are explained in the following paragraphs.

Table 5–3
Returns on Stock J and on the Market,
1975–1979

| Year | Historic Rate of Return[a] | |
	Stock J ($\bar{k}_J$)	The Market ($\bar{k}_M$)
1975	(13.20%)	(18.41%)
1976	14.97	13.94
1977	2.72	1.44
1978	6.12	20.25
1979	11.55	7.11
Mean	4.43%	4.87%
Standard deviation	10.94%	14.81%

[a]Rate of return is equal to dividend yield plus any capital gain or minus any capital loss. Here the market is measured by an index such as the New York Stock Exchange Index.

Figure 5–7
Relationship of Stock J to the Market

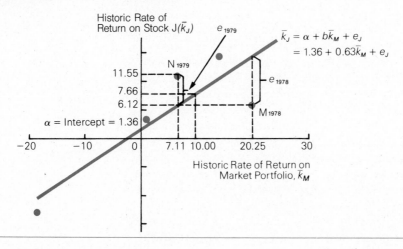

First, familiarize yourself with the definitions of the terms used in Figure 5–7:

$\bar{k}_J$ = Historic realized rate of return on Stock J.

$\bar{k}_M$ = Historic realized rate of return on the market.

α = Vertical axis intercept term, pronounced "alpha."

b = Slope coefficient, called the "beta coefficient."

e_J = Random error, reflecting the difference between the actual return on
Stock J in a given year and the return predicted by the regression
equation or line.

Each of these definitions is expanded in the explanation below.

To begin, if you have ever invested in stocks, you are well aware that
there is often a big difference between expected returns ($\hat{k}$) and the actual
returns that are realized on an investment. Accordingly, it is useful to define
the term *historic rate of return, $\bar{k}_J$*, called "k bar," as the dividend yield plus
capital gain or minus capital loss that actually occurred for Stock J in a
given year. For example, people who bought General Public Utilities (GPU)
stock at $18 per share in 1979, just prior to the accident at its Three Mile
Island nuclear plant, expected to receive a dividend yield of about
$1.87/$18 = 10.4% plus a capital gains yield of about 4%, for a total return
$\hat{k}_{GPU}$ = 14.4%. However, after the accident, the company was forced to
reduce the dividend to $1, and the stock price fell from $18 to $7, so the
yield actually realized in 1979 on the $18 investment was

$$\bar{k}_{GPU} = D_1/P_0 + g$$

$$= \frac{\$1}{\$18} + \frac{\$7 - \$18}{\$18}$$

$$= 0.056 - 0.611 = -0.555 = -55.5\%.$$

This demonstrates that realized or historic returns are not necessarily equal
to expected returns for risky assets like stocks.

The historic returns on Stock J were given in Table 5–3, along with
historic returns on "the market," $\bar{k}_M$, which may be thought of as a mutual
fund that holds a portfolio with some of each company's stock.

We now plot the data contained in Table 5–3 as the scatter diagram
shown in Figure 5–7 to highlight the relationship between Stock J and the
market. For example, the data for 1979 are plotted as Point N, while those
for 1978 are plotted as Point M. Notice that when returns on the market are
high, returns on Stock J likewise tend to be high, and when the market is
down, Stock J's returns are low. This general relationship is expressed more
precisely in the regression line shown in Figure 5–7.

Recall what the term *regression line* or *regression equation* means: the
equation $Y = a + bX$ is the standard form of a simple linear regression. It
states that the dependent variable, Y, is equal to a constant, a, plus b times
X, where X is the "independent" variable. Thus, the rate of return on the
stock during a given time period depends on what happens to the general
stock market, which is measured by $\bar{k}_M$.

The regression equation is obtained by plotting the data points on *graph paper* and then drawing a line through the scatter of points "by eye."[12] There is a mathematical line of best fit, the *least squares regression line,* but unless the data points all line up neatly, the "by eye" regression line may differ from the least squares line, and different students will draw in somewhat different lines. The procedure for obtaining least squares estimates is explained in statistics courses.

Once the line has been drawn on the graph paper, we can estimate its intercept and slope, the a and b values in $Y = a + bX$. The intercept, a, is simply the point where the line cuts the vertical axis. The slope coefficient, b, can be estimated by the "rise over run" method. This involves calculating the amount by which $\bar{k}_J$ increases for a given increase in $\bar{k}_M$. For example, we observe (in Figure 5–7) that $\bar{k}_J$ increases from 1.36 percent to 7.66 percent (the "rise") when $\bar{k}_M$ increases from 0 to 10.00 (the "run"). Thus, the b, or beta coefficient, can be measured as follows:

$$b = \text{Beta} = \frac{\text{Rise}}{\text{Run}} = \frac{\Delta Y}{\Delta X} = \frac{7.66 - 1.36}{10.00 - 0.00} = \frac{6.30}{10.00} = 0.63.$$

Note that the "rise over run" is a ratio, and it would be the same if measured using any two arbitrarily selected points on the line.

The regression line or equation enables us to predict a rate of return for Stock J, given a value of $\bar{k}_M$. For example, if $\bar{k}_M = 15\%$, we would predict $\bar{k}_J = 1.36\% + 0.63(15\%) = 10.81\%$. The actual return will probably differ from the predicted return. This deviation is the error term, e, for the year, and it varies randomly from year to year. The least squares method of fitting the line is designed to produce the smallest errors.

Some Observations about Betas

Now that we have plotted the scatter diagram and estimated the regression equation and the beta coefficient, we can note the following points: First, expected future returns of any stock (J) are presumed to bear a linear relationship of the following form to those of the market:

$$\hat{k}_J = \alpha_J + b_J \hat{k}_M + e_J$$

$$= 1.36 + 0.63 \hat{k}_M + e_J.$$

In words, the expected return on the stock, $\hat{k}_J$, is equal to an intercept term, α (pronounced alpha), plus a regression coefficient, b_J, times the expected future market portfolio return, $\hat{k}_M$, plus a random error term, e_J. The term b_J, called the *beta coefficient,* is generally positive, indicating that if the market return is expected to be high, the return on Stock J is also expected to be high, and conversely.

Second, in addition to general market movements, each firm also faces events that are peculiar to it and independent of the general economic

---

12 In real-world applications, the regression equation would always be fitted by the method of least squares, using one of the sophisticated hand-held calculators or a computer.

climate. Such events tend to cause the returns on any Firm J's stock to move at least somewhat independently of those for the market as a whole. For example, GPU suffered a sharp price decline in 1979 despite a generally rising stock market. Such an event is accounted for by the random error term e_J. (If the random error is especially large, as was that of GPU in 1979, e_J is called a *shock term.*)

Third, the regression coefficient, *b,* or the beta coefficient as it is generally called, is a *market sensitivity index; it measures the relative volatility of a given stock* (J) *versus the average stock, or the "market."* If a firm's beta is 1.0, then on average we would expect its rate of return to rise or fall in direct proportion to changes in market returns. Thus, if the market return falls one year by one percentage point, say from a 10 percent return to a 9 percent return, we would expect the firm's rate of return to experience a similar decline. This tendency of an individual stock to move with the market constitutes a risk, because the market does fluctuate, and these fluctuations cannot be diversified away. *This component of total risk is the stock's market, or nondiversifiable, risk.*

As noted earlier, a beta of 1.0 indicates a stock with "average" market risk —on the average, such a stock rises and falls by the same percentage as the market. What does $b = 0.5$ indicate? This means that if the market return rises or falls by *X* percentage points, the firm's rate of return rises or falls by only 0.5 *X,* so this stock has less market risk than the average stock. Conversely, if beta $= 2.0$, then the stock's rate of return fluctuates twice as much as the market rate of return, so it has more than the average market risk. *From this it follows that the size of beta is an indicator of market risk: The larger the value of beta, the greater a stock's market, or nondiversifiable, risk.*

Finally, the relationship between a stock's total risk, market risk, and company risk can be expressed as follows:

Total risk = Market risk + Company specific risk.

The company specific risk should be eliminated by diversification, so we are left with the following:

Relevant risk = Market risk.

Several points about total and relevant risk are significant:

1. If, in a graph such as Figure 5–7, all the points plotted exactly on the regression line, then the error term would be zero and all of the stock's risk would be market related. On the other hand, if the points were widely scattered about the regression line, much of the stock's risk would be company specific. The shares of a large, well-diversified mutual fund would plot very close to the regression line, as would those of a highly diversified "conglomerate" corporation.
2. If the stock market never fluctuated, then stock would have no market risk. Of course, the market does fluctuate, so market risk is present. In recent

years the standard deviation of market returns, σ_M, has generally run about 15 to 20 percent annually, meaning that actual returns could easily be 20 percent below the expected return. Back in the "wild" days of the 1920s, before the SEC and other forces helped stabilize the market, fluctuations were even greater.

3. Although it is not demonstrated here, the market risk of any individual stock can be measured as follows:

$$\text{Market risk for Stock J} = b_J\sigma_M.$$

Therefore, for any given level of market volatility as measured by the standard deviation, σ_M, the higher a stock's beta, the higher its market risk. If beta were zero, the stock would have no market risk, while if beta were negative (the regression line in Figure 5-7 had a negative slope), the market risk would also be negative. As we shall see in Problems 5-5 and 5-6, a negative beta has interesting implications.

4. If a given stock has $b = 0.5$, and if $\sigma_M = 20$ percent, then the stock's relevant risk equals $b_J\sigma_M = 0.5(20\%) = 10\%$. A portfolio of such low beta stocks would have a standard deviation of expected returns of $\sigma_P = 10\%$, or one-half the standard deviation of expected returns on a portfolio of average ($b = 1.0$) stocks. Had Stock J been a high beta stock ($b = 2.0$), then its relevant risk would have been $b_J\sigma_M = 2.0(20\%) = 40\%$. A portfolio of $b = 2.0$ stocks would have $\sigma_P = 40\%$, so such a portfolio would be twice as risky as a portfolio of average stocks.

Portfolio Beta Coefficients

A portfolio consisting of low beta securities will itself have a low beta, as the beta of any set of securities is a weighted average of the individual securities' betas:

$$b_p = \sum_{J=1}^{n} x_J b_J.$$

Here b_p is the beta of the portfolio, which reflects how volatile the portfolio is in relation to the market index; x_J is the percentage of the portfolio invested in the Jth stock; and b_J is the beta coefficient of the Jth stock.

If an investor holds a $100,000 portfolio consisting of $10,000 invested in each of ten stocks, and if each stock has a beta of 0.8, then the portfolio will have $b_p = 0.8$. Thus, the portfolio is less risky than the market, and it should experience relatively narrow price swings and have small rate of return fluctuations.

Now suppose one of the existing stocks is sold and replaced by a stock with $b = 2.0$. This action will increase the riskiness of the portfolio from $b_{p1} = 0.8$ to $b_{p2} = 0.92$:

$$b_{p2} = \sum_{J=1}^{n} x_J b_J = 0.9(0.8) + 0.1(2.0) = 0.92.$$

Had a stock with $b = 0.6$ been added, the portfolio beta would have declined from 0.8 to 0.78.

A Word of Caution

A word of caution about betas and the capital asset pricing model is in order. Although these concepts are very logical, the entire theory is based on *ex ante,* or expected, conditions, yet we have available only *ex post,* or past, data. Thus, the betas we calculate show how volatile a stock has been in the *past,* but conditions may change and alter its *future* volatility, which is the item of real concern to investors. This problem and others involved in actually using the CAPM are covered in depth in advanced finance courses.

THE RELATIONSHIP BETWEEN RISK AND RATES OF RETURN

Now that we have established beta as an appropriate measure of most stocks' risks, the next step in the capital asset pricing model (CAPM) framework is to specify the relationship between risk and return. This relationship is known as the *Security Market Line (SML),* and it is given by this equation:

$$k = R_F + b(k_M - R_F). \tag{5-4}$$

Here:

$k =$ the required rate of return on the stock in question. If the expected future return, $\hat{k}$, is less than k, then you would not purchase this stock, or you would sell it if you owned it.

$R_F =$ the riskless rate of return, generally measured by the rate of return on U.S. Treasury securities.

$b =$ the beta coefficient of the stock in question.

$k_M =$ the required rate of return on an average ($b = 1.0$) stock. k_M is also the required rate of return on a portfolio consisting of all stocks.

$(k_M - R_F) =$ the market risk premium, or the price of risk for an average stock. It is the additional return over the riskless rate required to compensate investors for assuming an "average" amount of risk.

$b(k_M - R_F) =$ the risk premium on the stock in question. The stock's risk premium is less than, equal to, or greater than the premium on an average stock depending on whether its beta is less than, equal to, or greater than 1.0.

In words, the SML equation shows that the required rate of return on a given stock, k, is equal to the return required in the marketplace for securities that have no risk, R_F, plus a risk premium equal to the risk premium demanded on an average stock, $k_M - R_F$, scaled up or down by the relative riskiness of the firm as measured by its beta coefficient. Thus, if $R_F = 8\%$, $b = 0.5$, and $k_M = 12\%$, then

$$k = 8\% + 0.5(12\% - 8\%)$$
$$= 8\% + 0.5(4\%)$$
$$= 10\%.$$

An average firm, with $b = 1.0$, would have

$$k = 8\% + 1.0(4\%) = 12\%,$$

while a riskier firm, with $b = 2.0$, would have

$$k = 8\% + 2.0(4\%) = 16\%.$$

Figure 5–8 gives a graph of the SML and the required returns on the three illustrative stocks. Figure 5–8 is related to Figure 5–5, which showed that the relevant risk of a portfolio of average stocks (i.e., stocks with $b = 1.0$) is

Figure 5–8
The Security Market Line (SML)

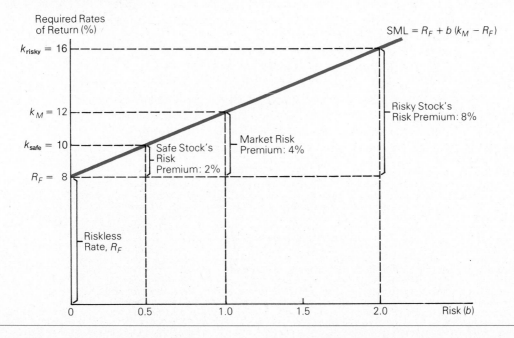

the portfolio's standard deviation, σ_p = 15%. Since each of these average stocks has b = 1.0, each contributes equally to the portfolio's risk. In Figure 5–8 we see that the required return on an average stock is 12 percent, reflecting the 8 percent required return for riskless assets plus a 4 percent risk premium needed to induce investors to accept the level of risk in a portfolio of these average, or b = 1.0, stocks, with σ_p = 15%.[13]

The Impact of Inflation

Interest amounts to "rent" on borrowed money, or the "price" of money. Thus, R_F is the price of money to a riskless borrower. The existing market risk-free rate is called the *nominal rate,* and it consists of two elements: (1) *a real or inflation-free rate of return, RR_F,* and (2) an *inflation premium, IP,* equal to the anticipated rate of inflation.[14] Thus, $R_F = RR_F + IP$. The real rate on risk-free government bonds has, historically, ranged from 2 to 4 percent, with a mean of about 3 percent. Thus, if no inflation were expected, government bonds would tend to yield about 3 percent.[15] However, as the expected rate of inflation increases, a premium must be added to the real rate of return to compensate investors for the loss of purchasing power that results from inflation.

To illustrate the effects of inflation, if you loaned the government $1,000 at 4 percent, you would have $1,040 at the end of the year. If inflation occurred at the rate of 5 percent during the year, you would end up with a purchasing power *loss* of 1 percent—your real rate of return would be *minus* 1 percent. If you (and other investors) anticipated a 5 percent inflation rate, you would add a 5 percent inflation premium to the 3 percent real required rate of return to produce a nominal R_F of about 8 percent. Thus, the 8 percent R_F shown in Figure 5–8 may be thought of as consisting of a 3 percent real rate of return plus a 5 percent inflation premium: $R_F = RR_F + IP = 3\% + 5\% = 8\%$.

If the expected rate of inflation rose to 7 percent, this would cause R_F to rise to 10 percent. Such a change is shown in Figure 5–9. Notice that the increase in R_F also causes an increase in the rate of return on all risky assets. For example, the rate of return on an average stock, k_M, increases

---

13 The risk premium of an average stock, $k_M - R_F$, cannot be measured with great precision because it is impossible to observe expected returns. However, empirical studies suggest that, where long-term U.S. Treasury bonds are used to measure R_F and where k_M is the return on the S&P 400 Industrial Stocks, the market risk premium varies somewhat from year to year, but it has averaged $5\frac{1}{2}$ percent during the last twenty years. (E. F. Brigham and D. K. Shome, *Risk Premiums on Common Stocks* [Gainesville, Fla.: University of Florida, Public Utility Research Center, 1979].)

14 The terminology employed here is standard economics notation. We should note, however, that in accounting terminology *nominal rate of return* means what we call the *coupon interest rate.* As economists use the term, nominal rate of return is identical to yield to maturity.

15 The real rate of return depends upon the supply of and demand for money, which in turn depend upon people's willingness to defer consumption (save), rates of return on investments in manufacturing plants, Federal Reserve policy, and so on. For example, during the depression of the 1930s, when investment opportunities were poor, the real rate of return was quite low. In a more booming period the expected real rate tends to be high. RR_F cannot be measured with precision.

Figure 5-9
Shift in the SML Caused by an Increase in Inflation

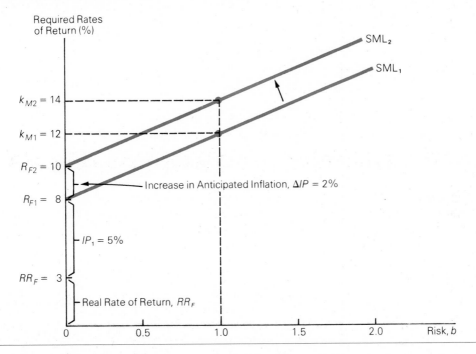

from 12 to 14 percent. Other risky securities' returns also rise by two percentage points.

Changes in Risk Aversion

The slope of the Security Market Line (SML) reflects the extent to which investors are averse to risk—the steeper the slope of the line, the greater the average investor's risk aversion. If investors were not at all averse to risk, and if R_F were 8 percent, then risky assets would also sell to provide an expected return of 8 percent—with no risk aversion, there would be no risk premium, and the SML would be horizontal. As risk aversion increases, so does the risk premium and, thus, the slope of the SML.

Figure 5-10 illustrates an increase in risk aversion. The market risk premium rises from 4 percent to 6 percent, and k_M rises from 12 percent to 14 percent. The returns on other risky assets also rise, with the impact of this shift in risk aversion being more pronounced on riskier securities. For example, the required return on a stock with $b = 0.5$ increases by only one percentage point, from 10 to 11 percent, while the required return on a stock with $b = 1.5$ increases by three percentage points, from 14 to 17 percent.

Figure 5–10
**Shift in the SML Caused by Increased Risk
Aversion**

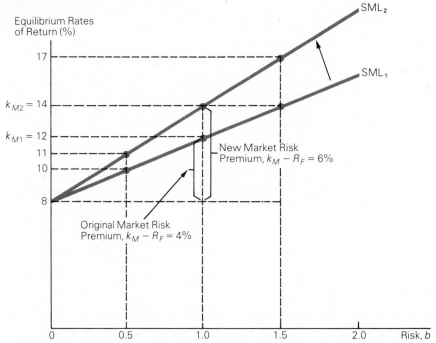

Changes in a Stock's Beta Coefficient

As we shall see later in the book, a firm can affect its market, or beta, risk
through changes in the nature and composition of its assets, and also
through its use of debt financing. A company's beta can also change as a
result of increased competition in its industry, the expiration of basic
patents, a change in management, and the like. When such changes occur,
the demanded or required rate of return also changes, and this will affect
the price of the firm's stock. For example, suppose some action occurred
that caused Carter Chemical's beta to increase from 1.0 to 1.5. If the
conditions depicted in Figure 5–8 held, Carter's required rate of return
would increase from

$$k_1 = R_F + b(k_M - R_F) = 8\% + 1.0(12\% - 8\%) = 12\%$$

to

$$k_2 = 8\% + 1.5(12\% - 8\%) = 14\%.$$

This change in k would cause a change in Carter's stock price, other things held constant:[16]

$$\text{Old price} = P = \frac{D_1}{k - g} = \frac{\$2.00}{0.12 - 0.05} = \$28.57.$$

$$\text{New price} = P = \frac{\$2.00}{0.14 - 0.05} = \$22.22.$$

Notice that at its new equilibrium price of $22.22, Carter's new expected rate of return is exactly equal to its new 14 percent required rate of return:

$$\hat{k} = \frac{D_1}{P_0} + g = \frac{\$2.00}{\$22.22} + 5\% = 14\% = R_F + 1.5(12\% - 8\%).$$

Since the expected rate of return is equal to the required return, we know that $22.22 is Carter's new equilibrium stock price.

SECURITY MARKET EQUILIBRIUM

Suppose a "typical" investor's required rate of return on some high risk Stock X is 16 percent, determined as follows:

$$k_X = R_F + b_X(k_M - R_F)$$
$$= 8\% + 2.0(12\% - 8\%)$$
$$= 16\%.$$

This 16 percent required return is indicated in Figure 5–11.

Our typical investor will want to buy X if the expected rate of return is more than 16 percent, will want to sell it if the expected rate of return is less than 16 percent, and will be indifferent if the expected return is exactly 16 percent. Now suppose the investor, whose portfolio contains X, analyzes the stock's prospects and concludes that its earnings, dividends, and price can be expected to grow at the rate of 5 percent per year. The last dividend was $D_0 = \$2.8571$, so the next expected dividend is

$$D_1 = \$2.8571(1.05) = \$3.$$

The investor observes that the present price of the stock, P_0, is $30. Should more of Stock X be purchased, should the present holdings be sold, or

---

16 Companies do sometimes deliberately increase their risk, but only if the action that raises risk also raises the expected earnings and the expected growth rate. Trying to determine the effects of a given action on risk and profitability, which affects growth, is one of the financial manager's central tasks.

should the present position be maintained? This investor can calculate Stock X's expected rate of return as follows:

$$\hat{k}_x = \frac{D_1}{P_0} + g = \frac{\$3}{\$30} + 5\% = 15\%.$$

The point is plotted on Figure 5–11 as Point X, which is below the SML.

Since the expected rate of return is less than the required return, this typical investor will want to sell the stock, as will other holders. However, few people will want to buy at the $30 price, so present owners will only be able to find buyers if they cut the price of the stock. Thus, the price will decline until it reaches $27.27, at which point the expected rate of return, 16 percent, is equal to the required rate of return:

$$\hat{k}_x = \frac{\$3}{\$27.27} + 5\% = 16\% = k_x.$$

Had the stock initially sold for less than $27.27, then events would have been reversed. Investors would have wanted to buy the stock, because its expected return would have exceeded its required rate of return. These buy orders would have driven the stock's price up to $27.27.

Figure 5–11
Expected and Required Returns on Stock X

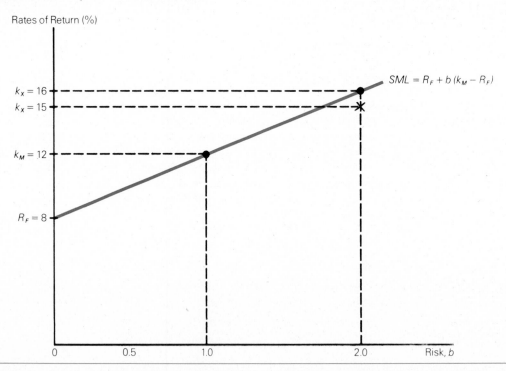

The price of $27.27 is defined as Stock X's *equilibrium price* because, given investors' feelings about the stock, this is the only stable price. If the price had exceeded $27.27, market forces would have driven it down, while if the current price had been less than $27.27, market forces would have driven it up.

Changes in Equilibrium Stock Prices

Stock market prices are *not* constant—they undergo violent changes at times. Let us assume that Stock X is in equilibrium, selling at a price of $27.27 per share. If all expectations were exactly met, over the next year the price would gradually rise to $28.63, or by 5 percent. However, many different events could occur to cause a change in the equilibrium price of the stock. To illustrate the forces at work, consider again the set of inputs used to develop Stock X's price of $27.27, and a new set of assumed input variables:

	Variable Value	
	Original	New
Riskless rate, R_F.	8%	7%
Market risk premium, $k_M - R_F$	4%	3%
Stock X's beta coefficient, b_X	2.0	1.0
Stock X's expected growth rate, g_X	5%	6%

The first three variables influence k_X, which declines as a result of the new set of variables from 16 to 10 percent:

$$\text{Original:} \quad k_X = 8\% + 2(4\%) = 16\%.$$
$$\text{New:} \quad k_X = 7\% + 1(3\%) = 10\%.$$

Using these values, together with the new D and g values, we find that P_0 rises from $27.27 to $75.71.[17]

$$\text{Original:} \quad P_0 = \frac{\$2.8571(1.05)}{0.16 - 0.05} = \frac{\$3}{0.11} = \$27.27.$$

$$\text{New:} \quad P_0 = \frac{\$2.8571(1.06)}{0.10 - 0.06} = \frac{\$3.0285}{0.04} = \$75.71.$$

At the new price, the expected and required rates of return will be equal:

$$\hat{k}_X = \frac{\$3.0285}{\$75.71} + 6\% = 10\% = k_X.$$

Evidence suggests that securities adjust quite rapidly to disequilibrium situations. Consequently, equilibrium ordinarily exists for any given stock,

---

17 A price change of this magnitude is by no means rare. The prices of *many* New York Stock Exchange stocks double or halve during a year, and almost every day some stock goes up or down by 15 percent or more.

and in general the required and expected returns are equal. Stock prices certainly change, sometimes violently and rapidly, but this simply reflects changing conditions and expectations. There are, of course, times when a stock continues to react for several months to a favorable or unfavorable development, but this does not signify a long adjustment period; rather, it simply illustrates that as more new bits of information about the situation become available, the market adjusts to them.[18]

SUMMARY

The primary goals of this chapter were (1) to show how risk is measured in financial analysis and (2) to explain how risk affects security prices and rates of return. We began by showing that risk is related to variability of expected future returns. However, we soon saw that most rational investors hold *portfolios of stocks,* and that such investors are more concerned with the risks of their portfolios than with the risks of individual stocks.

Next, we saw that the riskiness of a given stock can be split into two components—*market risk,* which is caused by changes in the broad stock market and which cannot be eliminated by diversification, and *company specific risk,* which can be eliminated by holding a diversified portfolio. Since investors do diversify and eliminate company risk, the most *relevant risk* inherent in stocks is their market risk, which is measured by the *beta coefficient.*

Betas measure the tendency of stocks to move up and down with the market— a high beta stock is more volatile than the market, while a low beta stock is less volatile than average. An average stock has $b = 1.0$ by definition.

The required rate of return on a stock consists of the rate of return on riskless bonds, R_F, plus a risk premium that depends on the stock's beta coefficient:

$$k = R_F + b(k_M - R_F).$$

This formula is called the *Security Market Line (SML) equation,* or sometimes the *Capital Asset Pricing Model (CAPM) equation,* and it is of fundamental importance in finance.

We also saw that stocks are typically in equilibrium, with their expected and required rates of return equal to one another:

$$\hat{k} = \frac{D_1}{P_0} + g = R_F + b(k_M - R_F) = k.$$

18 A theory called the *efficient markets hypothesis* (EMH) holds that stocks are always in equilibrium and that they are always "fairly priced," so it is impossible for an investor to "beat the market" except by luck. Though the EMH has not been proven without a doubt, there is a good bit of evidence that suggests that it is largely true except for people with "inside information."

Although stocks are generally in equilibrium, a number of things can happen to cause prices to change. The riskless rate can change because of changes in anticipated inflation; a stock's beta can change; or its rate of expected growth can increase or decrease. In the remainder of this book we will examine ways a firm's management can influence its stock's riskiness and expected growth rate, hence its price.

Questions

5-1 Define the following terms, using graphs or equations to illustrate your answers wherever feasible:
   a. Uncertainty
   b. Probability distribution
   c. *Expected* versus *required* versus *historic* rate of return
   d. Standard deviation
   e. SML
   f. Market risk
   g. Company specific risk
   h. Beta coefficient
   i. "Relevant risk"
   j. CAPM
   k. Risk premium
   l. Inflation premium
   m. Risk aversion
   n. Market equilibrium

5-2 The probability distribution of a less risky expected return is more peaked than that of a risky return. What shape would the probability distribution have (1) for completely certain returns and (2) for completely uncertain returns?

5-3 Security A has an expected return of 6 percent, a standard deviation of expected returns of 30 percent, a correlation coefficient with the market of minus 0.25, and a beta coefficient of minus 0.5. Security B has an expected return of 11 percent, a standard deviation of returns of 10 percent, a correlation with the market of 0.75, and a beta coefficient of 0.10. Which security is more risky? Why?

5-4 a. If you owned a portfolio consisting of $500,000 worth of long-term U.S. government bonds, would your portfolio be riskless?
   b. Suppose you held a portfolio consisting of $500,000 worth of thirty-day Treasury bills. Every thirty days, your bills mature and you reinvest the proceeds ($500,000) in a new batch of bills. Would your portfolio be truly riskless? (*Hint:* Assume that you live on the investment income from your portfolio, and that you want to maintain a constant standard of living.)
   c. You should have concluded that both long-term and short-term portfolios of government securities have some element of risk. Can you think of any asset that would be completely riskless?

5-5 An insurance policy is a financial asset. The investment cost is the premium paid.
    a. How do you calculate the expected return on a life insurance policy?
    b. Suppose the owner of the life insurance policy has no other financial assets—the person's only other asset is "human capital" or lifetime earnings capacity. What is the correlation coefficient between returns on the insurance policy and returns on the policyholder's human capital?
    c. Life insurance companies have administrative costs and sales representatives' commissions; hence, the expected rate of return on insurance premiums is low or even negative. Use the portfolio concept to explain why people buy life insurance in spite of negative expected returns.

5-6 If investors' aversion to risk increases, would the risk premium on a high beta stock increase more or less than that on a low beta stock? Explain.

Problems

5-1 Stocks A and B have the following probability distributions of expected future returns:

Probability	A	B
0.1	−10	−30
0.2	5	0
0.4	10	12
0.2	15	24
0.1	30	54

    a. Calculate the expected rate of return, $\hat{k}$, for Stock B. $\hat{k}_A = 10\%$.
    b. Calculate the standard deviation of expected returns for Stock A. That for Stock B is 20.3 percent. Is it possible that most investors might regard Stock B as being *less* risky than Stock A? Explain.

5-2 a. Suppose $R_F = 8\%$, $k_M = 12\%$, and $b_A = 1.4$. What is k_A, the required rate of return on Stock A?
    b. Now suppose R_F (1) increases to 9 percent, or (2) decreases to 7 percent. The slope of the SML remains constant. How will this affect k_M and k_A?
    c. Now assume R_F remains at 8 percent, but k_M (1) increases to 13 percent, or (2) falls to 11 percent. The slope of the SML does *not* remain constant. How will this affect k_A?
    d. Now assume that R_F remains at 8 percent and k_M at 12 percent, but beta (1) rises to 1.6, or (2) falls to 0.75. How will this affect k_A?

5-3 Suppose you are offered (a) $1 million or (b) a gamble where you get $2 million if a head is flipped but zero if a tail comes up.
    a. What is the expected value of this gamble?
    b. Would you take the sure $1 million or the gamble?

c. If you take the sure $1 million, are you a risk averter or a risk seeker?

d. Suppose you actually take the $1 million. You can invest it in either a U.S. Treasury bond that will return $1,075,000 at the end of a year or common stock that has a 50-50 chance of being either worthless or worth $2,300,000 at the end of the year.

  (1) What is the expected profit on the stock investment? The expected profit on the bond investment is $75,000.

  (2) What is the expected rate of return on the stock investment? The expected rate of return on the bond investment is 7.5 percent.

  (3) Would you invest in the bond or the stock?

  (4) Just how large would the expected profit and the expected rate of return have to be on the stock investment to make you invest in the stock?

  (5) How might your decision be affected if, rather than buying one stock for $1 million, you could construct a portfolio consisting of 100 stocks with $10,000 in each? Each of these stocks has the same return characteristics as the one stock, that is, a 50-50 chance of being worth either zero or $23,000 at year end. Would the correlation of returns on these stocks matter?

5-4 a. The risk-free rate of return is 8 percent, the required rate of return on the market, k_M, is 12 percent, and Stock X has a beta coefficient of 1.4. If the dividend expected during the coming year, D_1, is $2.50 and $g = 5\%$, at what price should Stock X sell?

b. Now suppose the Federal Reserve Board increases the money supply, causing the riskless rate to drop to 7 percent. What will this do to the price of the stock?

c. In addition to the change in Part b, suppose investors' risk aversion declines; this fact, combined with the decline in R_F, causes k_M to fall to 10 percent. At what price will Stock X sell?

d. Now suppose Firm X has a change in management. The new group institutes policies that increase the growth rate to 6 percent. Also, the new management stabilizes sales and profits, and thus causes the beta coefficient to decline from 1.4 to 1.1. After all these changes, what is Stock X's new equilibrium price? (Note: D_1 goes to $2.52.)

5-5 a. Suppose Carter Chemical Company's management conducts a study and concludes that, if Carter expands its consumer products division (which is less risky than its primary business, industrial chemicals), the firm's beta will decline from 1.1 to 0.9. However, consumer products have a somewhat lower profit margin, and this will cause Carter's growth rate in earnings and dividends to fall from 7 percent to 6 percent. Should management make the change? Assume the following: $k_M = 11\%$; $R_F = 7.5\%$; $D_0 = $2.$

b. Assume all the facts as given in Part a except the one about the changing beta coefficient. By how much would the beta have to decline to cause the expansion to be a good one? (Hint: Set P_0 under the new policy equal to P_0 under the old one, and find the new beta that produces this equality.)

5-6 The beta coefficient for Stock C is $b_C = 0.4$, while that for Stock D is $b_D = -0.5$. (Stock D's beta is negative, indicating that its rate of return rises whenever returns on most other stocks fall. There are very few negative beta stocks, although gold mining stocks are often cited as an example.)

a. If the risk-free rate is 7 percent, and the expected rate of return on an average stock is 11 percent, what are the required rates of return on Stocks C and D?

b. For Stock C, suppose the current price, P_0, is $25, the next expected dividend, D_1, is $1.50, and the stock's expected growth rate is 4 percent. Is the stock in equilibrium? Explain, and describe what will happen if the stock is not in equilibrium.

5-7 The Myers Investment Fund has a total investment of $200 million in five stocks:

Stock	Investment	Stock's Beta Coefficient
A	$60 million	0.5
B	50 million	2.0
C	30 million	4.0
D	40 million	1.0
E	20 million	3.0

The beta coefficient for a fund such as this can be found as a weighted average of the fund's investments. The current risk-free rate is 5 percent, while expected market returns, k_M, have the following probability distribution for the next period:

Probability	Market Return
0.1	6%
0.2	8
0.4	10
0.2	12
0.1	14

a. What is the estimated equation for the security market line (SML)?

b. Compute the required rate of return on the Myers Fund for the next period.

c. Suppose management receives a proposal for a new stock. The investment needed to take a position in the stock is $50 million; it will have an expected return of 15 percent, and its estimated beta coefficient is 2.5. Should the new stock be purchased? At what expected rate of return would management be indifferent to purchasing the stock?

5-8 You are given the following set of data:

Year	Historic Rates of Return $(\bar{k})$	
	The Market	Stock X
1967	0	3
1968	25	15
1969	(8)	6
1970	22	13
1971	16	17
1972	12	14
1973	(10)	5
1974	23	18
1975	11	7
1976	(4)	2
1977	4	5
1978	14	13
1979	11	10
Mean	8.9%	9.8%

a. Construct a "standard" graph showing the relationship between returns on Stock X and the market, then draw a freehand approximation of the regression line. What is the approximate value of the beta coefficient?

b. Give a verbal interpretation of what the regression line and the beta coefficient show about Stock X's volatility and relative riskiness as compared to other stocks.

c. Suppose the scatter of points had been more spread out, but the regression line was exactly where your present graph shows it. How would this affect (1) the firm's risk if the stock is held in a one-asset portfolio and (2) the actual risk premium on the stock if the CAPM holds exactly?

d. Suppose the regression line had been downward-sloping, and the beta coefficient had been negative. What would this imply about (1) Stock X's relative riskiness, (2) its correlation with k_M, and (3) its probable risk premium?

e. Construct an illustrative probability distribution graph of returns on portfolios consisting of (1) only Stock X; (2) one percent each of 100 stocks with beta coefficients similar to that of Stock X; and (3) all stocks (that is, the distribution of returns on the market). Use as the expected rate of return the arithmetic mean as given above for both Stock X and the market, and assume that the distributions are normal. Are the expected returns "reasonable," that is, is it reasonable for $\hat{k}_X = 9.8\% > \hat{k}_M = 8.9\%$?

5-9 You are given the following data on market returns, k_M, and the returns on Stocks A and B:

Year	$\overline{k}_M$	$\overline{k}_A$	$\overline{k}_B$
1973	7.5%	7.5%	6.25%
1974	2.5	2.5	3.75
1975	−5.0	−5.0	0
1976	12.5	12.5	8.75
1977	15.0	15.0	10.00
1978	−2.5	−2.5	1.25

R_F, the riskless rate, is 6 percent. Your probability distribution for $\hat{k}_M$ for next year is as follows:

Probability	$\hat{k}_M$
0.1	6%
0.2	8
0.4	10
0.2	12
0.1	14

a. Determine graphically the beta coefficients for Stocks A and B.

b. Graph the market line, and give the equation for the SML.

c. Calculate the required rate of return on Stocks A and B.

d. Suppose Stock C has $b = 2$, $D_1/P_0 = 8\%$, and an expected growth rate of 8 percent. Is the stock in equilibrium? Explain, and if the stock is not in equilibrium, explain how equilibrium will be restored.

e. What percentage of Stock A's total risk is market risk? Explain.

III

FINANCIAL STATEMENTS AND FINANCIAL FORECASTING

In order to use the valuation models developed in Part II, investors need information on companies' expected earnings, dividends, and growth rates, and on the riskiness of these items. The sources of this information are described in Chapter 6. Then, in Chapter 7, we see how financial managers make projections of future financial statements and use these projections to help plan future operations.

6 ANALYSIS OF FINANCIAL STATEMENTS

In Part II, we examined compound interest and the time value of money, developed bond and stock valuation models, discussed the concept of risk, and saw that risk affects the value of financial assets. Investors use risk-adjusted valuation models when making decisions to buy or sell securities, and corporate managers use these models to analyze the potential effects of different actions on their firms' expected profits, riskiness, and stock prices. Up to this point, however, we have abstracted from the actual data used in financial analysis. In this chapter we examine the *basic financial data* available to managers and investors, as well as the *techniques of financial analysis* used by investors to appraise firms' relative riskiness, profit potential, and general management competence. Managers also use these same analytical techniques to measure and improve their own performance. As always, performance is judged in terms of the extent to which specific operations are contributing to the firm's overall goal of stock price maximization.

THE BASIC FINANCIAL STATEMENTS

Of the various reports corporations issue to their stockholders, the *annual report* is by far the most important. Two types of information are given in this report. First, there is a verbal statement that describes the firm's operating results during the past year and discusses new developments that will affect future operations. Second, the report presents four basic financial statements—the *income statement,* the *balance sheet,* the *statement of retained earnings,* and the *statement of changes in financial position.* Taken together, these statements give an accounting picture of the firm's operations and financial position. Detailed data are provided for the two most recent years, along with historical summaries of key operating statistics for the past ten years.[1]

The quantitative information and the verbal information are equally important. The financial statements report *what has actually happened* to earnings and dividends over the past few years, while the verbal statements represent an attempt to explain why things turned out the way they did. For example, suppose earnings dropped sharply last year. Management may report that the drop resulted from a strike at a key facility at the height of the busy season, but then go on to state that the strike has now been settled and that future profits are expected to bounce back. Of course, this return to profitability may not occur, and investors will want to compare management's past statements with subsequent results. *In any event, the information contained in the annual report is used by investors to form expectations about future earnings and dividends, and about the riskiness of these expected cash flows.* Therefore, the annual report is obviously of great interest to investors.

The Income Statement

Table 6–1 gives the 1978 and 1979 income statements for Carter Chemical Company, a major producer of industrial and consumer chemical products. Given at the top of the statements are net sales, from which various costs, including income taxes, are subtracted to obtain the net income available to common stockholders.[2] A report on earnings and dividends per share is given at the bottom of the statement. In financial management, earnings per share (EPS) is called "the bottom line," denoting that of all the items on the income statement, EPS is the most important.[3] Carter earned $2.40 per share in 1979, down from $2.60 in 1978, but it raised the dividend from $1.80 to $2.00.

The Balance Sheet

The left-hand side of Carter's balance sheet, which is given in Table 6–2, shows the firm's assets, while the right-hand side of the statement shows claims against these assets. The assets are listed in order of their "liquidity," or the length of time it typically takes to convert them to cash.

1 Larger firms file even more detailed statements, giving the particulars of each major division or subsidiary, with the U.S. Securities and Exchange Commission (SEC). These reports, called *10-K reports,* are made available to stockholders upon request to a company's secretary.
2 We shall not devote much time to the question of the accounting methods used to calculate net income. It should, however, be noted that the methods for calculating depreciation, valuing inventory, determining pension fund liabilities, and so on have significant impacts on reported profits. Accounting methods are reported in detail in notes to the financial statements, especially in the 10-K report to the SEC, and security analysts are well aware of the degree of conservatism used to produce reported profits. In other words, analysts recognize differences in the "quality" of reported earnings, and these quality differences are reflected in k_s and consequently in stock prices.
3 Dividends are important too, but the firm's ability to pay dividends is dependent on its earnings.

Table 6-1
Carter Chemical Company: Income Statement for Year Ending December 31 (Millions of Dollars, except per Share Data)

	1979	1978
Net sales	$3,000	$2,850
Costs and expenses		
Labor and materials	$2,544	$2,413
Depreciation	100	90
Selling	22	20
General and administrative	40	35
Lease payments on buildings	28	28
Total costs	$2,734	$2,586
Net operating income, or earnings before interest and taxes (EBIT)	$ 266	$ 264
Less interest expense		
Interest on notes payable	$ 8	$ 2
Interest on first mortgage bonds	40	42
Interest on debentures	18	3
Total interest	$ 66	$ 47
Earnings before tax	$ 200	$ 217
Federal income tax (at 40%)	80	87
Net income after taxes available to common stockholders	$ 120	$ 130
Disposition of net income		
Dividends to common stockholders	$ 100	$ 90
Addition to retained earnings	$ 20	$ 40
Per share of common stock		
Earnings per share (EPS)[a]	$ 2.40	$ 2.60
Dividends per share (DPS)[a]	$ 2.00	$ 1.80

[a]50 million shares are outstanding: see Table 6-2. Calculations of EPS and DPS for 1979 are as follows:

$$EPS = \frac{Net\ income\ after\ tax}{Shares\ outstanding} = \frac{\$120,000,000}{50,000,000} = \$2.40.$$

$$DPS = \frac{Dividends\ paid\ to\ common\ stockholders}{Shares\ outstanding} = \frac{\$100,000,000}{50,000,000} = \$2.00.$$

Table 6–2
Carter Chemical Company: Balance Sheet as
of December 31 (Millions of Dollars)

Assets	1979	1978	Claims on Assets	1979	1978
Cash	$ 50	$ 55	Accounts payable	$ 60	$ 30
Marketable securities	0	25	Notes payable	100	60
Accounts receivable	350	315	Accrued wages	10	10
Inventories	300	215	Accrued federal income taxes	130	120
Total current assets	$ 700	$ 610	Total current liabilities	$ 300	$ 220
Gross plant and equipment	$1,800	$1,470	First mortgage bonds[a]	$ 500	$ 520
Less depreciation	500	400	Debentures	300	60
			Total long-term debt	$ 800	$ 580
Net plant and equipment	$1,300	$1,070	Stockholders' equity:		
			Common stock		
			(50,000,000 shares, $1 par)	$ 50	$ 50
			Additional paid-in capital	100	100
			Retained earnings	750	730
			Total stockholders' equity (common net worth)	$ 900	$ 880
Total assets	$2,000	$1,680	Total claims on assets	$2,000	$1,680

[a]The sinking fund requirement for the first mortgage bonds is $20 million a year. Sinking funds are discussed in Chapter 13, but, in brief, a sinking fund simply involves the repayment of long-term debt. Thus Carter Chemical is required to pay off $20 million each year. Accordingly, mortgage bonds outstanding declined by $20 million from 12/31/78 to 12/31/79. The current portion of the long-term debt is included in notes payable here, although in a more detailed balance sheet it would be shown as a separate item.

The claims are listed in the order in which they must be paid: Trade accounts must generally be paid within thirty days; notes are payable within ninety days; and so on down to the stockholders' equity accounts, which represent ownership and need never be "paid off."

Some additional points about the balance sheet are significant:

1. *Cash versus Other Assets.* Although the assets are all stated in terms of dollars, *only cash* represents actual money. Receivables are bills others owe Carter; inventories consist of raw materials, work in process, and finished goods available for sale; and fixed assets consist of Carter's plants and equipment. Carter can write checks at present for a total of $50 million (versus current liabilities of $300 million due within a year). The noncash assets will presumably be converted to cash eventually, but they do not represent cash-in-hand.

2. *Liabilities versus Stockholders' Equity.* The claims against assets are of

two types—liabilities, or money the company owes, and the stockholders' ownership position.[4] The equity, or net worth, is a residual; that is,

$$\text{Assets} - \text{Liabilities} = \text{Stockholders' equity.}$$

$$\$2{,}000{,}000{,}000 - \$1{,}100{,}000{,}000 = \$900{,}000{,}000.$$

Suppose assets decline in value—for example, suppose some of the accounts receivable are written off as bad debts. Liabilities remain constant, so the value of the net worth declines. Therefore, the risk of asset value fluctuations is borne entirely by the stockholders. Note, however, that if asset values rise, these benefits accrue exclusively to the stockholders.

3. *Breakdown of the Stockholders' Equity Account.* A detailed discussion of the equity accounts is given in Chapter 14, "Common Stock," but a brief preview of that discussion is useful here. First, note that the equity section is divided into three accounts—*common stock, paid-in capital,* and *retained earnings.* As explained below, the retained earnings account is built up over time by the firm's "saving" a part of its earnings rather than paying all earnings out as dividends. The other two accounts arise from the sale of stock by the firm to raise capital. Accountants generally assign a *par value* to common stock—Carter Chemical's stock has a par value of $1.[5] Now suppose Carter were to sell 1 million additional shares at a price of $30 per share. The company would raise $30 million, and the cash accounts would go up by this amount. Of the total, $1 million would be added to common stock, and $29 million would be added to paid-in capital. Thus, after the sale, common stock would show $51 million, paid-in capital would show $129 million, and there would be 51 million shares outstanding.

   The breakdown of the equity accounts is important for some purposes but not for others. For example, a potential stockholder would want to know if the company had earned the funds in its equity accounts, or if they had come mainly from selling stock. A potential creditor, on the other hand, would be more interested in the amount of money the owners had put up than in the form in which they put it up. In the remainder of this chapter, we generally aggregate the three equity accounts and call this sum *equity* or *net worth.*[6]

4. *The Time Dimension.* The balance sheet may be thought of as a snapshot of the firm's financial position *at a point in time*—for example, on December 31, 1979. The income statement, on the other hand, reports on operations *over a period of time*—for example, during the calendar year 1979.

---

4 One could divide liabilities into (1) debts owed to someone and (2) other items such as deferred taxes, reserves, etc. We do not make this distinction, so the terms *debt* and *liabilities* are used synonymously.
5 See Chapter 14 for a discussion of par value.
6 In Chapter 14 we will differentiate between *total equity,* which includes preferred stocks, and *common equity,* which does not.

The Cash Flow Cycle

Figure 6–1 shows the cash flow cycle within a firm. Rectangles represent balance sheet accounts—assets and claims against assets—while circles represent actions taken by the firm. The diagram is by no means a complete representation of the cash flow cycle: To avoid undue complexity, it shows only the major flows.

The cash account is the focal point of the graph. Certain events, such as collecting accounts receivable or borrowing money from the bank,

Figure 6–1
Cash and Materials Flows within the Firm

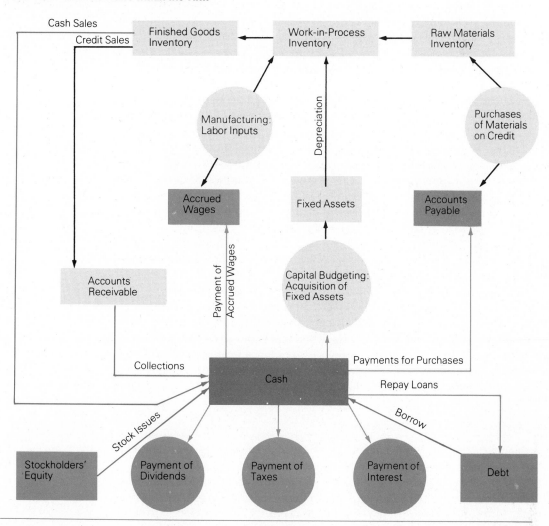

will cause the cash account to increase, while the payment of taxes, interest, and so on will cause the cash account to decline. Similar comments could be made about all the balance sheet accounts—their balances rise, fall, or remain constant depending on events that occur during the period under study, which for Carter Chemical is December 31, 1978, through December 31, 1979.

Projected sales increases may require the firm to raise cash by borrowing from its bank or selling new stock. For example, if the firm anticipates an increase in sales, it will (1) expend cash to buy or build fixed assets, (2) step up purchases, thereby increasing raw materials inventories and accounts payable, (3) increase production, which causes an increase in accrued wages and work-in-process, and (4) eventually build up its finished goods inventory. Some cash will have been expended, and the firm will have obligated itself to expend still more cash to pay off its accounts payable and accrued wages. These events will have occurred *before* any cash has been generated. Even when the expected sales do occur, there will still be a lag in the generation of cash until receivables are collected. Depending on how much cash the firm had at the beginning of the build-up, on the length of its production-sales-collection cycle, and on how long it can delay payment of its own payables and accrued wages, the firm may have to obtain significant amounts of additional cash by selling stock or bonds.

If the firm is profitable, its sales revenues will exceed its costs, and its cash inflows will eventually exceed its cash outlays. However, even a profitable firm can experience a cash shortage if it is growing rapidly. It may have to pay for plant, materials, and labor before cash from the expanded sales starts flowing in. For this reason, rapidly growing firms often require large bank loans or capital from other sources.

An unprofitable firm will have larger cash outlays than inflows. This, in turn, will typically cause a slowdown in the payment of accrued wages and accounts payable, and it may also lead to heavy borrowings. Thus, liabilities build up to excessive levels in unprofitable firms. Similarly, an overly ambitious expansion plan will be reflected in an excessive buildup of inventories and fixed assets, while a poor credit/collection policy will produce bad debts and reduced profits that first show up as high accounts receivable. Financial analysts are well aware of these relationships, and they use the analytical techniques discussed in the remainder of this chapter to help discover problems before they become too serious.

Statement of Retained Earnings

Changes in the equity accounts between balance sheet dates are reported in the statement of retained earnings; Carter's statement is shown in Table 6–3. The company earned $120 million during 1979, paid out $100 million in dividends, and plowed $20 million back into the business. Thus, the balance sheet item "retained earnings" increased from $730 million at the end of 1978 to $750 million at the end of 1979.

Table 6–3
Carter Chemical Company: Statement of
Retained Earnings for Year Ending
December 31, 1979 (Millions of Dollars)

Balance of retained earnings, December 31, 1978	$730
Add: Net income, 1979	120
Less: Dividends to stockholders	(100)
Balance of retained earnings, December 31, 1979	$750

Note that the balance sheet account "retained earnings" represents a *claim against assets,* not assets per se. Further, firms retain earnings primarily to expand the business. This means investing in plant and equipment, inventories, and so on, *not* in a bank account. *Thus, retained earnings as reported on the balance sheet do not represent cash and are not "available" for the payment of dividends or anything else.*[7]

Statement of Changes in Financial Position

The graphic analysis given in Figure 6–1 is converted into numerical form and reported in annual reports as the *statement of changes in financial position,* often called the *sources and uses of funds statement.* This statement is designed to show how funds were obtained and how they were used. It helps answer questions such as these: Was the expansion program financed by sale of debt or equity? How much of its required capital has the firm been able to generate internally? Has the firm been building up its liquid assets, or is it becoming less liquid? Information such as this is useful both for investment analysis and for corporate planning, so the statement of changes in financial position is an important part of the annual report.

The Role of Depreciation Before we discuss the statement of changes in financial position in detail, we should pause to consider one of its most important elements—depreciation. First, what is depreciation? In effect, it is

---

7 Recall that the amount recorded in the retained earnings account is *not* an indication of the amount of cash the firm has. That amount (as of the balance sheet date) is found in the cash account—an asset account. A positive number in the retained earnings account indicates only that, in the past, according to generally accepted accounting principles, the firm has earned an income and its dividends have been less than that reported income. Also, recall the difference between accrual and cash accounting. Even though a company reports record earnings and shows an increase in the retained earnings account, it may still be short of cash.

an annual charge against income which reflects a rough estimate of the dollar cost of the capital equipment used in the production process. For example, suppose a machine with an expected useful life of ten years and a zero expected salvage value was purchased in 1978 for $100,000. This $100,000 cost must be charged against production over the machine's ten year life; otherwise, profits will be overstated. If the machine is depreciated by the straight-line method, the annual charge is $10,000. This amount is deducted from sales revenues, along with such other costs as labor and raw materials, to determine income. However, depreciation is not a cash outlay; funds were expended back in 1978, so the depreciation charged against the income in years 1979 through 1988 is not a cash outlay, as are labor or raw materials charges. *Depreciation is a noncash charge.*

This point is illustrated with data for Carter Chemical Company in Table 6–4. Here Column 1 shows an abbreviated version of Carter's income statement, while Column 2 shows the statement on a cash flow basis. Assume for the moment that (1) all sales are for cash, (2) all costs except depreciation were paid during 1979, and (3) no build-ups occurred in inventories or other assets. How much cash would have been generated from operations? From Column 2 we see that the answer is $220 million. The sales are all for cash, so the firm took in $3,000,000,000 in cash money. Its costs other than depreciation were $2,634,000,000, and these were paid in cash, leaving $366 million. Depreciation is *not* a cash charge—the firm does not pay out the $100 million of depreciation expenses—so $366 million of cash money is still left after depreciation. Taxes and interest, however, are paid in cash, so $66 million for interest and $80 million for taxes must be deducted from the $366 million EBIT cash flow, leaving a net cash flow from operations of $220 million. As shown in Column 1, this $220 million is, of

---

Table 6–4
Carter Chemical Company: Cash Flows for 1979 (Millions of Dollars)

	Income Statement (1)	Cash Flows (2)
Sales	$3,000	$3,000
Costs and expenses:		
All costs except depreciation	2,634	2,634
Depreciation (D)	100	—
Earnings before interest and taxes (EBIT)	$ 266	$ 366
Interest expense	66	66
Earnings before taxes	$ 200	$ 300
Taxes	80	80
Net income (NI)	$ 120	
Cash flow: $CF = NI + D = \$120 + \$100 =$	$ 220	$ 220

course, exactly equal to profit after tax plus depreciation: $120 million plus $100 million equals $220 million. Thus, since depreciation is a noncash charge and is added back to net income to approximate cash flows from operations, it is included as a source of funds in the statement of changes in financial position.

Before leaving the subject of depreciation, we should sound a word of caution. Depreciation does not *really* provide funds; it is simply a noncash charge. Hence, it is added back to net income to obtain an estimate of the cash flow from operations. However, if the firm made no sales, then depreciation would certainly not provide cash flows. To see this point more clearly, consider the situation of Communications Satellite Corporation (Comsat), which derives its income principally from two satellites, one positioned over the Atlantic and one over the Pacific. Comsat's cash flows are approximately equal to its net income plus its depreciation charges. Yet, if its satellites stopped working, sales would vanish, and while accountants might still calculate depreciation, this depreciation would provide no cash flows (except possibly some tax loss carrybacks).

Preparing the Statement of Changes in Financial Position The statement of changes in financial position is designed to answer at a glance these three questions: (1) Where did the firm get its funds during the year? (2) What did it do with its available funds? (3) Did operations during the year tend to increase or decrease the firm's liquidity as measured by the change in net working capital? (*Net working capital* is defined as current assets minus current liabilities. In general, the firm's financial position is stronger if net working capital increases, weaker if it decreases.)

The starting point in preparing a statement of changes in financial position is to determine the change in each balance sheet item, and then to record it as either a source or a use of funds in accordance with the following rules:

Sources: (1) *Increase* in a claim, that is, in a liability or capital account.
(2) *Decrease* in an asset account.

Uses: (1) *Decrease* in a claim against assets.
(2) *Increase* in an asset account.

Thus, sources of funds include bank loans and retained earnings, as well as money generated by selling assets, collecting receivables, and even drawing down the cash account. Uses include acquiring fixed assets, building up inventories, and paying off debts.

Table 6–5 shows the changes in Carter Chemical Company's balance sheet accounts during the calendar year 1979, with each change designated as a source or a use. Sources and uses each total $470 million.[8]

---

8 Adjustments must be made if fixed assets were sold or retired during the year. Carter had no sales of assets or major retirements during 1979.

The data contained in Table 6–5 are next used to prepare the formal statement of changes in financial position, or sources and uses of funds statement; the one contained in Carter Chemical's annual report is shown in Table 6–6. Notice that the statement provides answers to the three questions asked above: (1) the top section reports Carter's major sources of funds; (2) the middle section shows how Carter used funds; and (3) the lower section, which deals with current assets and liabilities, shows how the company's liquidity position changed during the year. We see that Carter's major sources of funds were net income, depreciation, and the sale of debentures (a type of long-term debt which is described in Chapter 13). These funds were used to reduce the mortgage debt, to increase fixed assets, and to pay dividends on common stock. Also, $10 million was used to increase net working capital.

Table 6–5
Carter Chemical Company: Changes in
Balance Sheet Accounts during 1979 (Millions
of Dollars)

	12/31/79	12/31/78	Change Source	Use
Cash	$ 50	$ 55	$ 5	$
Marketable securities	0	25	25	
Accounts receivable	350	315		35
Inventories	300	215		85
Gross plant and equipment	1,800	1,470		330
Accumulated depreciation[a]	500	400	100	
Accounts payable	60	30	30	
Notes payable	100	60	40	
Accrued wages	10	10		
Accrued taxes	130	120	10	
Mortgage bonds	500	520		20
Debentures	300	60	240	
Common stock	50	50		
Paid-in capital	100	100		
Retained earnings	750	730	20	
Totals			$470	$470

[a]Depreciation is a "contra-asset," not an asset. Hence, an increase in depreciation is a source of funds.

As shown in the bottom section, Carter decreased its cash and marketable securities but increased accounts receivable and inventories, for a net increase in current assets of $90 million. Current liabilities increased by $80

Table 6–6
Carter Chemical Company:
Statement of Changes in Financial Position
(Millions of Dollars)

Sources of funds:

Net income after taxes	$120
Depreciation	100
Funds from operations	$220
Proceeds from sale of debentures	240
Total sources	$460

Uses of funds:

Repayment of mortgage bonds	$ 20
Increase in gross fixed assets	330
Dividend payments to common stockholders	100
Net increase in working capital (see detail below)	10
Total uses	$460

- -

Analysis of changes in working capital[a]

Increase (decrease) in current assets:

Cash	($ 5)[b]
Marketable securities	(25)
Accounts receivable	35
Inventories	85
Net increase in current assets	$90

Increase (decrease) in current liabilities:

Accounts payable	$30
Notes payable	40
Accrued taxes	10
Net increase in current liabilities	$80
Net increase (decrease) in working capital	$10

[a]*Net working capital* is defined as current assets minus current liabilities.
[b]Parentheses denote negative numbers here and throughout the book.

million, so there was an increase of $10 million in net working capital (current assets minus current liabilities). This net increase in working capital is reported as a use in the middle section.

Notice also that every item in the "change" columns of Table 6–5 is carried over to Table 6–6 *except retained earnings.* The statement of changes in financial position reports net income as a source and dividends as a use, rather than netting these items out and just reporting the increase in retained earnings.

Carter Chemical is a strong, well-managed company, and its sources and uses statement shows nothing unusual or alarming. One does, however, occasionally see situations where huge increases in fixed assets are financed primarily by short-term debt, which must be repaid within a few months if the lender demands repayment. This would show up in the lower

third of the table as a decrease in net working capital, and it is, as we shall
see in detail later in the book, a dangerous situation.[9]

Eleven Year Earnings, Dividend, and Stock Price Record

In addition to the four statements described, most annual reports today also
give a summary of earnings, dividends, and stock prices over the last few
years. For Carter Chemical, these data are given in Table 6–7 and plotted in
Figure 6–2. Earnings were variable, but there was a definite upward trend
over the period. In 1979 a strike caused earnings to drop somewhat, but
management expects the growth trend to resume in 1980.

Table 6–7
Carter Chemical Company: Eleven Year
Earnings, Dividend, and Stock Price Record,
1969–1979

Year	Average Stock Price	Earnings per Share	Dividends per Share
1969	$20	$1.53	$1.25
1970	22	1.55	1.30
1971	22	1.80	1.35
1972	23	1.65	1.40
1973	24	2.00	1.50
1974	21	1.80	1.55
1975	30	1.25	1.65
1976	31	2.40	1.70
1977	30	2.43	1.75
1978	37	2.60	1.80
1979	33	2.40	2.00

Ten year growth rate[a]: EPS 5%
                          DPS 5%

[a]Growth rates were obtained by linear regression. The logs of EPS and DPS were regressed against
years, and the slope coefficient represents the growth rate. The graphs in Figure 6–2 give plots of EPS
and DPS over time and a trend line for EPS fitted by least squares regression. (The DPS growth is so
smooth that a trend line is unnecessary.) By dividing the trend line figure for EPS in 1979 ($2.43) into
the trend line figure for 1969 ($1.49), we obtain a PVIF for ten years (not eleven years; eleven years
of data are needed to estimate ten years of *growth*). We can look up PVIF = $1.49/$2.43 = 0.6132
in Table A–1, across the row for 10 periods. The calculated interest factor is approximately
equal to 0.6139, the factor for 5 percent. Thus, the growth rate in EPS is approximately 5 percent.
   Calculated growth rates can be highly sensitive to the beginning and ending points. For example,
Carter's growth rate in EPS was negative from 1969 to 1975, but positive from 1969 to 1979. A
great deal of judgment, plus qualitative information about the company, is needed when interpreting past
trends and forecasting future EPS growth rates.

9 It should be noted that statements of changes in financial position are especially useful for planning
   purposes. More will be said about this in Chapter 7, which deals with the analysis of projected
   financial statements.

Although dividends and dividend policy are discussed in detail in Chapter 17, we can make several comments about dividends at this point:

1. Dividends per share (DPS) represent the basic cash flows passed from the firm to its stockholders. As such, dividends are a key element in the stock valuation models developed in earlier chapters.
2. DPS in any given year can exceed EPS, but in the long run dividends are paid from earnings, so normally DPS is smaller than EPS. The percentage of earnings paid out in dividends, or the ratio of DPS to EPS, is defined as the *dividend payout ratio.* Carter Chemical's payout ratio has varied somewhat from year to year, but it has averaged about 80 percent.
3. In a graph such as Figure 6–2, the DPS line is typically below the EPS line, while the two lines generally have about the same slope, indicating that EPS and DPS are growing at about the same rate. As the data in Table 6–7 indicate, Carter's earnings and dividends have both been growing at an average rate of 5 percent per year. If the type of analysis

Figure 6–2
Carter Chemical Company: Eleven Year
Earnings and Dividend Record, 1969–1979

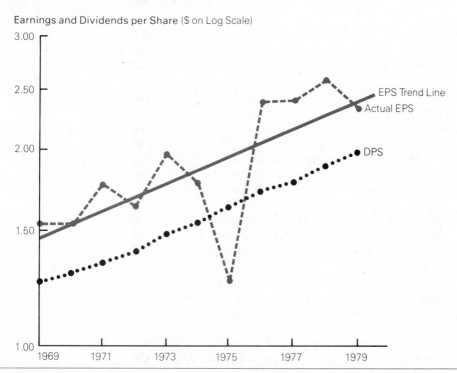

Note: See Table 6–7 for data and trend calculations.

undertaken in the next section suggests that this trend will continue, then 5 percent is the value of *g* that will be used in the valuation model to calculate Carter's stock price.

ANALYSIS OF THE FINANCIAL STATEMENTS

Financial statements report both on a firm's position at a point in time and on its operations over some past period. However, their real usefulness lies in the fact that they can be used to help predict the firm's future earnings and dividends, as well as the riskiness of these cash flows. From an investor's standpoint, *predicting the future is what financial statement analysis is all about.* From management's standpoint, *financial statement analysis is useful both as a way to anticipate future conditions and, more importantly, as a starting point for planning actions that will influence the future course of events.* In the remainder of this chapter we discuss procedures used by both investors and managers to analyze and interpret financial statements.

RATIO ANALYSIS[10]

Financial ratios are designed to show relationships among financial statement accounts. Ratios put numbers into perspective. For example, Firm A might have $5,248,760 of debt and annual interest charges of $419,900, while Firm B's debt totals $52,647,980 and its interest charges are $3,948,600. The true burden of these debts, and the companies' ability to repay them, can only be ascertained by comparing each firm's debt to its assets, and its interest charges to the income available for payment of interest. Such comparisons are made by *ratio analysis.*

Ratios may be categorized into five groups: (1) liquidity ratios, (2) asset management ratios, (3) debt management ratios, (4) profitability ratios, and (5) market value ratios. Some of the most useful ones in each category are discussed next.

---

10 In addition to the ratios discussed in this section, financial analysts also employ a tool known as *common size* balance sheets and income statements. To form a common size balance sheet, one simply divides each asset and liability item by total assets and expresses the result as a percentage. The resultant percentage statement can be compared with those of larger or smaller firms, or for the same firm over time. To form a common size income statement, one simply divides each item by sales.

Liquidity Ratios

One of the first concerns of the financial analyst is liquidity: Will the firm be able to meet its maturing obligations? Carter Chemical has debts totaling $300 million that must be paid off within the coming year. Can those obligations be satisfied? A full liquidity analysis requires the use of cash budgets (described in Chapter 8); however, by relating the amount of cash and other current assets to the current obligations, ratio analysis provides a quick and easy-to-use measure of liquidity. Two commonly used liquidity ratios are presented below.

Current Ratio The current ratio is computed by dividing current assets by current liabilities. Current assets normally include cash, marketable securities, accounts receivable, and inventories; current liabilities consist of accounts payable, short-term notes payable, current maturities of long-term debt, accrued income taxes, and other accrued expenses (principally wages).

If a company is getting into financial difficulty, it begins paying its bills (accounts payable) slowly, building up bank loans, and so on. If these current liabilities are rising faster than current assets, the current ratio will fall, and this could spell trouble. Accordingly, the current ratio is the most commonly used measure of short-term solvency, since it provides the best single indicator of the extent to which the claims of short-term creditors are covered by assets that are expected to be converted to cash in a period roughly corresponding to the maturity of the claims.

The calculation of the current ratio for Carter Chemical at year-end 1979 is shown below. (All dollar amounts in this section are in millions.)

$$\text{Current ratio} = \frac{\text{Current assets}}{\text{Current liabilities}} = \frac{\$700}{\$300} = 2.3 \text{ times.}$$

$$\text{Industry average} = 2.5 \text{ times.}$$

Carter's current ratio is slightly below the average for the industry, 2.5, but not low enough to cause concern. It appears that Carter is about in line with most other chemical firms. Since current assets are scheduled to be converted to cash in the near future, it is highly probable that they could be liquidated at close to their stated value. With a current ratio of 2.3, Carter could liquidate current assets at only 43 percent of book value and still pay off current creditors in full.[11]

Although industry average figures are discussed later in some detail, it should be stated at this point that an industry average is not a magic number that all firms should strive to maintain. In fact, some very well-managed firms will be above it, and other good firms will be below it.

---

11 (1/2.3) = 0.43, or 43 percent. Note that (0.43) ($700) ≈ $300, the amount of current liabilities.

However, if a firm's ratios are very far removed from the average for its industry, the analyst must be concerned about why this variance occurs. Thus, a deviation from the industry average should signal the analyst to check further.

Note also that Carter's current ratio declined to 2.3 in 1979 from 2.8 in 1978. Thus, the *trend* is poor, and this could indicate potential future difficulties. More will be said about *trend analysis* later in the chapter.

Quick Ratio or Acid Test The quick ratio is calculated by deducting inventories from current assets and dividing the remainder by current liabilities. Inventories are typically the least liquid of a firm's current assets, hence the assets on which losses are most likely to occur in the event of liquidation. Therefore, this measure of the firm's ability to pay off short-term obligations without relying on the sale of inventories is important.

$$\text{Quick, or acid test, ratio} = \frac{\text{Current assets} - \text{Inventory}}{\text{Current liabilities}} = \frac{\$400}{\$300}$$

$$= 1.3 \text{ times.}$$

$$\text{Industry average} = 1.0 \text{ times.}$$

The industry average quick ratio is 1.0, so Carter's 1.3 ratio compares favorably with other firms in the industry. If the accounts receivable can be collected, the company can pay off current liabilities even without selling any inventory. Again, however, it should be noted that the trend is downward: 1.3 in 1979 versus 1.8 in 1978.

Asset Management Ratios

The second group of ratios is designed to measure how effectively the firm is managing its assets. In particular, the asset management ratios answer this question: Does the total amount of each type of asset as reported on the balance sheet seem "reasonable," too high, or too low in view of current and projected operating levels? Carter Chemical and other companies must borrow or obtain capital from other sources in order to acquire assets. If they have too many assets, then their interest expenses are too high, hence profits are too low. If assets are too low, then operations will not be as efficient as possible.

Inventory Utilization The inventory utilization ratio, sometimes called the *inventory turnover ratio,* is defined as sales divided by inventories.

$$\begin{array}{c}\text{Inventory utilization} \\ \text{(or turnover)}\end{array} = \frac{\text{Sales}}{\text{Inventory}} = \frac{\$3,000}{\$300} = 10 \text{ times.}$$

$$\text{Industry average} = 9 \text{ times.}$$

Carter's ratio of 10 compares favorably with an industry average of 9 times. This suggests that the company does not hold excessive stocks of inventory; excess stocks are, of course, unproductive and represent an investment with a low or zero rate of return. This high inventory utilization ratio also reinforces our faith in the current ratio. If the turnover were low—say 3 or 4 times—we might wonder whether the firm was holding damaged or obsolete materials not actually worth their stated value.

Two problems arise in calculating and analyzing the inventory utilization ratio. First, sales are at market prices; if inventories are carried at cost, as they generally are, it would be more appropriate to use cost of goods sold in place of sales in the numerator of the formula. Established compilers of financial ratio statistics such as Dun & Bradstreet, however, use the ratio of sales to inventories carried at cost. To develop a figure that can be compared with those developed by Dun & Bradstreet, it is therefore necessary to measure inventory utilization with sales in the numerator, as we do here.

The second problem lies in the fact that sales occur over the entire year, whereas the inventory figure is for one point in time. This makes it better to use an average inventory.[12] If it is determined that the firm's business is highly seasonal, or if there has been a strong upward or downward sales trend during the year, it becomes essential to make some such adjustment. To maintain comparability with industry averages, we did not use the average inventory figure.

Average Collection Period The average collection period, which is used to appraise the accounts receivable, is computed by dividing average daily sales into accounts receivable to find the number of days' sales tied up in receivables.[13] This is defined as the *average collection period* (ACP), because it represents the average length of time that the firm must wait after making a sale before receiving cash. The calculations for Carter show an average collection period of forty-two days, slightly above the thirty-six day industry average.

---

12 Preferably, the average inventory would be calculated by summing the monthly figures during the year and dividing by 12. If monthly data are not available, one can add the beginning and ending figures and divide by 2; this will adjust for secular trends but not for seasonal fluctuations.

13 Because information on credit sales is generally unavailable, total sales must be used. Since all firms do not have the same percentage of credit sales, there is a good chance that the average collection period will be somewhat in error. Also, note that for convenience, the financial community generally uses 360 rather than 365 as the number of days in the year for purposes such as these. Finally, it would be better to use *average* receivables = (Beginning + Ending)/2 = (315 + 350)/2 = $332.5 in the formula. Had this been done, the ACP would have been $332.5/$8.333 = 40 days. The 40-day figure is the more accurate one, but since the industry average was based on year-end receivables, we used 42 days for the comparison.

$$\text{Average collection period} = \frac{\text{Receivables}}{\text{Average sales per day}} = \frac{\text{Receivables}}{\text{Annual sales/360}}$$

$$= \frac{\$350}{\$3,000/360} = \frac{\$350}{\$8.333} = 42 \text{ days.}$$

Industry average = 36 days.

This ratio can also be evaluated by comparison with the terms on which the firm sells its goods. For example, Carter's sales terms call for payment within thirty days, so the forty-two day collection period indicates that customers, on the average, are not paying their bills on time. If the trend in the collection period over the past few years had been rising while the credit policy had not changed, this would be even stronger evidence that steps should be taken to expedite the collection of accounts receivable.

Fixed Asset Utilization The ratio of sales to fixed assets, often called the fixed asset turnover ratio, measures the utilization of plant and equipment:

$$\text{Fixed assets utilization} = \frac{\text{Sales}}{\text{Net fixed assets}} = \frac{\$3,000}{\$1,300} = 2.3 \text{ times.}$$

Industry average = 3.0 times.

Carter's ratio of 2.3 times compares poorly with the industry average of 3 times, indicating that the firm is not using its fixed assets to as high a percentage of capacity as are the other firms in the industry. The financial manager should bear this fact in mind when production people request funds for new capital investments.

Total Assets Utilization The final asset ratio measures the utilization or turnover of all the firm's assets—it is calculated by dividing sales by total assets.

$$\text{Total assets utilization} = \frac{\text{Sales}}{\text{Total assets}} = \frac{\$3,000}{\$2,000} = 1.5 \text{ times.}$$

Industry average = 1.8 times.

Carter's ratio is somewhat below the industry average. The company is not generating a sufficient volume of business for the size of its asset investment. Sales should be increased, or some assets should be disposed of, or both steps should be taken.

Debt Management Ratios

The extent to which a firm uses debt financing, or financial leverage, has a number of implications. First, creditors look to the equity, or owner-supplied funds, to provide a margin of safety. Second, if owners have provided only a small proportion of total financing, the risks of the enterprise are borne mainly by the creditors. Third, by raising funds through debt, the owners gain the benefits of maintaining control of the firm with a limited investment. And fourth, if the firm earns more on the borrowed funds than it pays in interest, then the return on the owners' capital is magnified.

To illustrate the last point, if the assets of a firm earned 10 percent while its debt cost only 8 percent, there would be a 2 percent differential accruing to the stockholders. If the firm had $200 in assets and was financed totally with common equity, then its operating income would be (0.10) ($200) = $20, and its return on equity would be $20/$200 = 10%. However, if the firm used $150 of debt and only $50 of equity, its return on equity (ROE) would be

$$ROE = \frac{Operating\ income - Interest}{Common\ equity}$$

$$= \frac{Income\ available\ to\ common\ stockholders}{Common\ equity}$$

$$= \frac{0.10\ (\$200) - 0.08\ (\$150)}{\$50}$$

$$= \frac{\$20 - \$12}{\$50} = \frac{\$8}{\$50} = 16\%.$$

Thus, financial leverage can greatly increase the rate of return on common stockholders' equity. However, financial leverage cuts both ways. In our example, if the return on assets fell to 5 percent, the differential between that return and the cost of debt would have to be made up from equity's share of total profits, resulting in

$$ROE = \frac{0.05\ (\$200) - 0.08\ (\$150)}{\$50} = \frac{\$10 - \$12}{\$50} = -4\%.$$

Thus, if operating income was low, financial leverage would reduce equity returns below the rate of return on assets. If the return on assets stayed at the 5 percent level, the firm would be unable to meet interest payments, which would eventually force it into bankruptcy and would result in total losses to the common stockholders.

We see, then, that firms with low amounts of debt have less risk of loss when the economy is in a recession, but they also have lower expected returns when the economy booms. Conversely, firms with high leverage ratios run the risk of large losses but also have a chance of gaining high profits. The prospects of high returns are desirable, but investors are averse to risk. Decisions about the use of leverage, then, must balance higher expected returns against increased risk.[14]

---

14 The problem of determining the optimum leverage for a firm is examined extensively in Chapters 15 and 16.

In practice, leverage is approached in two ways. One approach examines balance sheet ratios and determines the extent to which borrowed funds have been used to finance the firm. The other approach measures the risks of debt by income statement ratios designed to determine the number of times fixed charges are covered by operating profits. These sets of ratios are complementary, and most analysts examine both types of leverage ratios.

Total Debt to Total Assets The ratio of total debt to total assets, generally called the *debt ratio,* measures the percentage of total funds provided by creditors. Debt includes current liabilities and all bonds. Creditors prefer low debt ratios, since the lower the ratio, the greater the cushion against creditors' losses in the event of liquidation. The owners, on the other hand, may seek high leverage either (1) to magnify earnings or (2) because selling new stock means giving up some degree of control.

$$\text{Debt ratio} = \frac{\text{Total debt}}{\text{Total assets}} = \frac{\$1,100}{\$2,000} = 55\%.$$

$$\text{Industry average} = 40\%.$$

Carter's debt ratio is 55 percent; this means that creditors have supplied more than half the firm's total financing. Since the average debt ratio for this industry—and for manufacturing generally—is about 40 percent, Carter would find it difficult to borrow additional funds without first raising more equity capital. Creditors would be reluctant to lend the firm more money, and management would probably be subjecting the firm to the risk of bankruptcy if it sought to increase the debt ratio still more by borrowing.[15]

Times Interest Earned The times-interest-earned ratio (TIE) is determined by dividing earnings before interest and taxes (EBIT in Table 6–1) by the interest charges. The TIE ratio measures the extent to which earnings can decline without resultant financial embarrassment to the firm because of an inability to meet annual interest costs. Failure to meet this obligation can bring legal action by the creditors, possibly resulting in bankruptcy. Note that the before-tax profit figure is used in the numerator. Because income taxes are computed after interest expense is deducted, the ability to pay current interest is not affected by income taxes.

---

15 The ratio of debt to equity is also used in financial analysis. The debt to assets *(D/A)* and debt to equity *(D/E)* ratios are simply transformations of one another.

$$D/E = \frac{D/A}{1 - D/A} \text{ and } D/A = \frac{D/E}{1 + D/E}.$$

Both ratios increase as a firm of a given size (total assets) uses a greater proportion of debt, but *D/A* rises linearly and approaches a limit of 100 percent, while *D/E* rises exponentially and approaches infinity.

$$\text{TIE} = \frac{\text{EBIT}}{\text{Interest charges}} = \frac{\$266}{\$66} = 4 \text{ times.}$$

$$\text{Industry average} = 6 \text{ times.}$$

Carter's interest is covered 4 times. Since the industry average is 6 times, the company is covering its interest charges by a minimum margin of safety and deserves only a fair rating. This ratio reinforces the conclusion based on the debt ratio that the company might face some difficulties if it attempts to borrow additional funds.[16]

Profitability Ratios

Profitability is the net result of a large number of policies and decisions. The ratios examined thus far reveal some interesting things about the way the firm is operating, but the profitability ratios show the combined effects of liquidity, asset management, and debt management on operating results.

Profit Margin on Sales The profit margin on sales, computed by dividing net income after taxes by sales, gives the profit per dollar of sales.

$$\text{Profit margin} = \frac{\text{Net profit after taxes}}{\text{Sales}} = \frac{\$120}{\$3,000} = 4\%.$$

$$\text{Industry average} = 5\%.$$

Carter's profit margin is somewhat below the industry average of 5 percent, indicating that the firm's sales prices are relatively low or that its costs are relatively high, or both.

Return on Total Assets The ratio of net profit to total assets measures the return on total assets.

$$\text{Return on total assets} = \frac{\text{Net profit after taxes}}{\text{Total assets}} = \frac{\$120}{\$2,000} = 6\%.$$

$$\text{Industry average} = 9\%.$$

Carter's 6 percent return is well below the 9 percent average for the industry. This low rate results from three primary factors: (1) the low profit margin on sales, (2) the low utilization of total assets, and (3) Carter's above

---

16 More complete coverage ratios, which take account of mandatory lease payments, sinking fund payments, and other fixed financial charges, are also used in financial analysis. These refinements are covered in Chapter 13, which deals specifically with long-term debt.

average use of debt, which causes its interest payments to be high and its profits to be reduced.[17]

Return on Common Equity The ratio of net profit after taxes to common equity measures the rate of return on the stockholders' investment, ROE.

$$\text{Return on common equity (ROE)} = \frac{\text{Net profit after taxes}}{\text{Common equity}} = \frac{\$120}{\$900} = 13.3\%.$$

$$\text{Industry average} = 15.0\%.$$

Carter's 13.3 percent return is below the 15.0 percent industry average, but not as far below as the return on total assets. This results from Carter's greater use of debt, a point analyzed in detail later in the chapter.

Market Value Ratios

A final group of ratios relates the firm's stock price to its earnings and book value per share. These ratios give management an indication of what investors think of the company's past performance and future prospects. If the firm's liquidity, asset management, debt management, and profitability ratios are all good, then its market value ratios will be high, and the stock price will probably be as high as can be expected.

Price/Earnings Ratios The P/E ratio, which was discussed in Chapter 4, shows how much investors are willing to pay per dollar of reported profits. Carter's stock sells for $28.50, so with an EPS of $2.40, its P/E ratio is 11.9.

$$\text{Price/earnings ratio} = \frac{\text{Price per share}}{\text{Earnings per share}} = \frac{\$28.50}{\$2.40} = 11.9 \text{ times.}$$

$$\text{Industry average} = 12.5 \text{ times.}$$

As we saw in Chapter 4, P/E ratios are higher for firms with high growth prospects, but lower for riskier firms. Carter's P/E ratio is slightly below those of other large chemical producers, which suggests that the company is regarded as being somewhat riskier than most, as having poorer growth prospects, or both.

---

17 In calculating the return on total assets, it is sometimes desirable to add interest to net profits after taxes to form the numerator of the ratio. The theory here is that since assets are financed by both stockholders and creditors, the ratio should measure the productivity of assets in providing returns to both classes of investors. Alternatively, one can calculate a "basic earning power" ratio:

$$\text{Basic earning power} = \frac{\text{Earnings before interest and taxes}}{\text{Total assets}}.$$

Also, if assets grew rapidly during the year, it would improve the analysis if average assets (beginning assets plus ending assets divided by 2) were used in the denominator. We have not made these adjustments because the published averages we use for comparative purposes do not include them.

Price/Book Ratios The ratio of a stock's market price to its book value gives another indication of how investors regard the company. Companies with high rates of return on equity generally sell at higher multiples of book value than those with low returns. Carter's book value per share is $18.00:

$$\text{Book value per share} = \frac{\text{Stockholders' equity}}{\text{Shares outstanding}} = \frac{\$900}{50} = \$18.00.$$

Dividing this value into the price per share gives a price/book ratio of 1.6 times:

$$\text{Price/book ratio} = \frac{\$28.50}{\$18.00} = 1.6 \text{ times}.$$

$$\text{Industry average} = 1.8 \text{ times}.$$

Investors are willing to pay slightly less for Carter's book value than for that of an average chemical company.[18]

The typical railroad, which has a very low rate of return on assets, has a market value/book value ratio of less than 0.5. Very successful firms such as IBM achieve high rates of return on their assets and have market values that are four or five times their book values.

Trend Analysis

It is important to analyze trends in ratios as well as their absolute levels, for the trends give clues as to whether the financial situation is improving or

Figure 6–3
Rate of Return on Common Equity, 1975–1979

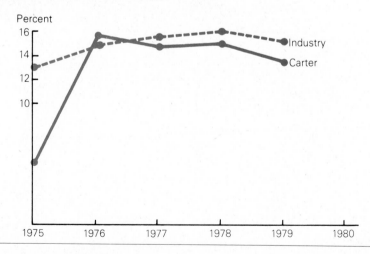

---

18 The degree of conservatism used by the company's accountants can also affect the price/book ratio. The more conservative the accountants, the higher the price/book ratio will be, other things held constant. The same holds true for the P/E ratio.

deteriorating. To do a trend analysis, one simply graphs a ratio against years, as shown in Figure 6–3. This graph shows that Carter's rate of return on common equity has been declining since 1976, even though the industry average has been relatively stable. Other ratios could be analyzed similarly.

Summary of Ratio Analysis: The du Pont System

Table 6–8 summarizes Carter Chemical's ratios, while Figure 6–4, which is called a *du Pont chart* because that company's managers developed the general approach, shows the relationships among debt, asset utilization, and profitability ratios. The left-hand side of the chart develops the *profit margin on sales.* The various expense items are listed, then summed to obtain Carter's total costs. Subtracting costs from sales yields the company's net income, which, when divided by sales, indicates that 4 percent of each sales dollar is left over for stockholders.

The right-hand side of the chart lists the various categories of assets,

Figure 6–4
Modified du Pont Chart Applied to Carter
Chemical Company (Millions of Dollars)

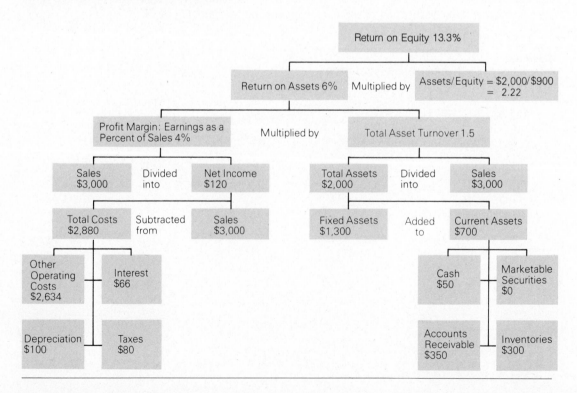

Table 6–8
Summary of Carter Chemical's Ratios

Ratio	Formula for Calculation	Calculation	Ratio	Industry Average	Evaluation
Liquidity					
Current	$\dfrac{\text{Current assets}}{\text{Current liabilities}}$	$\dfrac{\$\ 700}{\$\ 300}$ =	2.3 times	2.5 times	Good
Quick, or acid test	$\dfrac{\text{Current assets} - \text{Inventory}}{\text{Current liabilities}}$	$\dfrac{\$\ 400}{\$\ 300}$ =	1.3 times	1.0 times	Good
Asset management					
Inventory turnover	$\dfrac{\text{Sales}}{\text{Inventory}}$	$\dfrac{\$3,000}{\$\ 300}$ =	10 times	9 times	Good
Average collection period	$\dfrac{\text{Receivables}}{\text{Sales}/360}$	$\dfrac{\$\ 350}{\$8.333}$ =	42 days	36 days	Slightly high
Fixed assets utilization	$\dfrac{\text{Sales}}{\text{Fixed assets}}$	$\dfrac{\$3,000}{\$1,300}$ =	2.3 times	3.0 times	Low
Total assets utilization	$\dfrac{\text{Sales}}{\text{Total assets}}$	$\dfrac{\$3,000}{\$2,000}$ =	1.5 times	1.8 times	Low
Debt management					
Debt to total assets	$\dfrac{\text{Total debt}}{\text{Total assets}}$	$\dfrac{\$1,100}{\$2,000}$ =	55 percent	40 percent	High
Times interest earned	$\dfrac{\text{Earnings before interest and taxes}}{\text{Interest charges}}$	$\dfrac{\$\ 266}{\$\ 66}$ =	4.0 times	6 times	Low
Profitability					
Profit margin on sales	$\dfrac{\text{Net profit after taxes}}{\text{Sales}}$	$\dfrac{\$\ 120}{\$3,000}$ =	4 percent	5.0 percent	Low
Return on total assets	$\dfrac{\text{Net profit after taxes}}{\text{Total assets}}$	$\dfrac{\$\ 120}{\$2,000}$ =	6 percent	9.0 percent	Low
Return on common equity	$\dfrac{\text{Net profit after taxes}}{\text{Common equity}}$	$\dfrac{\$\ 120}{\$\ 900}$ =	13.3 percent	15.0 percent	Low
Market value					
Price/earnings	$\dfrac{\text{Price per share}}{\text{Earnings per share}}$	$\dfrac{\$28.50}{\$\ 2.40}$ =	11.9 times	12.5 times	Low
Price/book	$\dfrac{\text{Price per share}}{\text{Book value per share}}$	$\dfrac{\$28.50}{\$18.00}$ =	1.6 times	1.8 times	Low

which are summed and then divided into sales to find the number of times Carter "turns its assets over" each year. Carter's total asset utilization, or "turnover," ratio is 1.5 times.

The profit margin times the total asset turnover ratio is defined as the *du Pont equation,* which gives the rate of return on assets, ROA:

$$\text{ROA} = \frac{\text{Rate of return}}{\text{on assets}} = \text{Profit margin} \times \text{Total asset turnover}$$

$$= \frac{\text{Net profit after taxes}}{\text{Sales}} \times \frac{\text{Sales}}{\text{Total assets}}$$

$$= 4\% \times 1.5 = 6\%.$$

Carter makes 4 percent, or four cents, on each dollar of sales. Assets were "turned over" 1.5 times during the year, so Carter earned a return of 6 percent on its assets.[19]

If Carter used only equity, the 6 percent rate of return on assets would equal the rate of return on equity. However, 55 percent of the firm's capital is supplied by creditors. Since the 6 percent return on *total* assets all goes to stockholders, who put up only 45 percent of the capital, the return on equity is higher than 6 percent. Specifically, the rate of return on assets (ROA) must be multiplied by the *equity multiplier,* which is the ratio of assets to common equity, to obtain the rate of return on equity, ROE:

$$\text{ROE} = \text{ROA} \times \text{Equity multiplier}$$

$$= \frac{\text{Net income}}{\text{Assets}} \times \frac{\text{Assets}}{\text{Common equity}}$$

$$= 6\% \times (\$2{,}000/\$900)$$

$$= 6\% \times 2.22 = 13.3\%.$$

This 13.3 percent rate of return could, of course, be calculated directly: net income after taxes/common equity = \$120/\$900 = 13.3 percent. However, the du Pont equation shows how the rate of return on assets and the use of debt interact to determine the return on equity.[20]

---

19 The term *turnover* goes back to the days of the Yankee peddler. See Footnote 1, Chapter 8, for an explanation.

20 Another ratio that is frequently used is the following:

$$\text{Rate of return on invested capital} = \frac{\text{Net income after taxes} + \text{Interest}}{\text{Debt} + \text{Equity}}.$$

This ratio is especially important in the public utility industries, where regulators are concerned about the companies' using their monopoly positions to earn excessive returns on invested capital. In fact, regulators try to set utility prices (service rates) at levels that will force the return on invested capital to equal a company's cost of capital as defined in Chapter 16.

Management can use the du Pont system to analyze ways of improving the firm's performance. On the left, or "profit margin," side of the chart, marketing people can study the effects of raising sales prices (or lowering them to get greater volume), of moving into new products or markets with higher margins, and so on. Cost accountants can study the expense items and, working with engineers, purchasing agents, and other operating personnel, seek ways of holding costs down. On the "turnover" side, financial analysts, working with both production and marketing people, can investigate ways of reducing the investment in various types of assets. At the same time, the treasurer can analyze the effects of alternative financing strategies, seeking to hold down interest expenses and the risks of debt while still using debt to increase the rate of return on equity.

COMPARATIVE RATIOS

The preceding analysis of Carter Chemical Company pointed out the usefulness of comparing a company's ratios with those of other firms in its industry. Comparative ratios are available from a number of sources. One useful set of comparative data is compiled by Dun and Bradstreet, Inc. D & B provides fourteen ratios calculated for a large number of industries. Useful ratios can also be found in the *Annual Statement Studies* published by Robert Morris Associates, the national association of bank loan officers. The Federal Trade Commission's *Quarterly Financial Report,* which is found in most libraries, gives a set of ratios for manufacturing firms by industry group and size of firm. Trade associations and individual firms' credit departments also compile industry average financial ratios. Finally, financial statement data are available on magnetic tapes for thousands of corporations, and since most of the larger brokerage houses, banks, and other financial institutions have access to these data, security analysts can and do generate comparative ratios tailored to their own individual needs.

Each of these organizations uses a somewhat different set of ratios, designed for the organization's own purposes. For example, D & B deals mainly with small firms, many of which are proprietorships, and they are concerned largely with the creditors' viewpoint. Accordingly, their ratios emphasize current assets and liabilities, and D & B is completely unconcerned with market value ratios. Therefore, when you select your comparative data source, you should be sure that your emphasis is similar to that of the agency, or else recognize the limitations of their ratios for your purposes.

LIMITATIONS OF RATIO ANALYSIS

Although ratio analysis is useful in finance, it does have limitations, some of which are listed below.

1. Many large firms actually operate a number of different divisions in quite different industries, making it difficult to develop a meaningful set of industry averages for comparative purposes. This tends to make ratio analysis more useful for small than for large firms.
2. Most firms want to be better than average (although about half will be above and half below), so merely attaining average performance is not necessarily good. As a target for high-level performance, it is preferable to look at industry leaders' ratios.
3. The ratios can be distorted. For example, the inventory turnover ratio for a food processor will be radically different if the balance sheet figure used for inventory is the one just before versus just after the close of the canning season. This problem can be minimized by using average inventory figures.

    Also, firms can employ "window dressing" techniques to make their financial statements look better to credit analysts. Recently, a firm sold its corporate aircraft for cash just prior to issuing a quarterly statement. This substantially improved its cash balance in time for the quarterly report.
4. Different operating and accounting practices distort comparisons. For example, if one firm leases a substantial amount of its productive equipment (and some airlines lease about half of their planes whereas others own virtually all equipment), then its assets may be low relative to sales because leased assets may not appear on the balance sheet. This improves turnover ratios. The accounting profession has recently taken steps which reduce but do not eliminate this problem.
5. It is difficult to generalize about whether a particular ratio is "good" or "bad." For example, a high current ratio may show a strong liquidity position, which is good, or excessive cash, which is bad because excess cash in the bank is a nonearning asset. Similarly, high asset utilization ratios may denote either a firm that uses assets efficiently or an undercapitalized firm that simply cannot afford to buy enough assets.
6. A firm may have some ratios which look "good" and others which look "bad," making it difficult to tell whether the firm is, on balance, in a strong or a weak position. A procedure called *discriminant analysis* can be used to analyze the net effects of a set of ratios, but a discussion of this topic goes beyond the scope of this book.[21]

Ratio analysis is useful in spite of these problems, but analysts should be aware of them and make adjustments as necessary. Ratio analysis

---

21 See Appendix 6A to the Second Edition of *Financial Management* for a discussion of discriminant analysis as applied to financial ratios.

conducted in a mechanical, unthinking manner is dangerous, but, used intelligently, and with good judgment, ratios can provide useful insights into a firm's operations. Your judgment in interpreting a set of ratios is probably weak at this point, but it will be greatly enhanced as we go through the remainder of the book.

SUMMARY

The primary purposes of this chapter were (1) to describe the basic financial statements and (2) to discuss techniques used by investors and managers to analyze these statements. Four basic statements were covered: *the income statement, the balance sheet, the statement of retained earnings, and the statement of changes in financial position.*

Financial analysis is designed to determine the relative strengths and weaknesses of a company—whether the firm is financially sound and profitable relative to other firms in its industry, and whether its position is improving or deteriorating over time. Investors need such information in order to estimate both future cash flows from the firm and the riskiness of these flows. Managers need to be aware of their firms' financial positions in order to detect and strengthen weaknesses in a continuous quest for improvement.

Our study of financial analysis concentrated on a set of ratios designed to highlight the key aspects of a firm's operations. These ratios were broken down into five categories: (1) liquidity ratios, (2) asset management ratios, (3) debt management ratios, (4) profitability ratios, and (5) market value ratios. The ratios for a given firm are calculated, then compared with those of other firms in the same industry to judge the relative strength of the firm in question. Trends in the ratios are also analyzed, and the du Pont system is used to pinpoint the cause of any weakness that is uncovered. Ratio analysis has limitations, but used with care and judgment, it can be most helpful.

Questions

6-1 What four statements are contained in most annual reports?

6-2 Is it true that if a "typical" firm reports $20 million of retained earnings on its balance sheet, that firm's directors could declare a $20 million cash dividend without any qualms whatsoever?

6-3 a. What would Carter Chemical's balance sheet item "retained earnings" for 1979 have been if, during 1978, the company had paid dividends of $150 million? (See Tables 6–1 and 6–2.)

  b. What would Carter Chemical's 1979 EPS have been had net income for that year been $150 million rather than $120 million?

c. Suppose you knew that Carter's EPS was $2.40 and that net income was $120 million. Could you use this information to determine the number of shares outstanding?

d. If Carter sold inventories carried at $200 million for only $50 million, what effects would this have on the firm's balance sheet? (Disregard tax effects.)

e. Could the DPS line in Figure 6–2 rise more steeply (that is, have a steeper slope) than the EPS line (1) over a ten year period, (2) in the "long run" (that is, forever)?

f. (1) Examine Figure 6–4, and then explain how a reduction in other operating costs from $2,634 million to $2,534 million would affect the rate of return on equity.

  (2) Then, holding other operating costs at the original $2,634 million, show how a reduction of total assets from $2 billion to $1.8 billion, with an offsetting reduction in equity by payment of a $200 million extra dividend, would affect the rate of return on equity.

  (3) Finally, use the stock price model developed in Chapter 4 to explain how these actions could affect the growth rate of EPS and DPS, hence the value of the firm's stock.

g. Suppose Carter's profit margin had been 5 percent, its total assets turnover 2 times, and its assets/equity ratio 1.49 times. What would Carter's rate of return on equity have been?

h. Had Carter's accountants decided to *shorten* the average life used to calculate depreciation, this would have increased the company's depreciation expense. Would this action have affected the company's cash flows? If so, how?

6-4 What is the relationship between each rectangle in Figure 6–1 and each individual source and use in a sources and uses of funds statement? Think of each rectangle as being a "reservoir" of assets or liabilities, and then think of changes in the levels of these reservoirs.

6-5 How might (a) seasonal factors and (b) different growth rates over time or across companies distort a comparative ratio analysis? Give some examples.

Problems

6-1 Data for the Wiggins Wheel Company, and its industry averages, are given below.

a. Calculate the indicated ratios for Wiggins Wheel.

b. Outline Wiggins Wheel's strengths and weaknesses as revealed by your analysis.

c. Suppose Wiggins had doubled its sales and also its inventories, accounts receivable, and common equity during 1979. How would that information affect the validity of your ratio analysis?

**Wiggins Wheel Company: Balance Sheet,
December 31, 1979**

Cash	$110,000	Accounts payable	$ 82,500
Receivables	137,500	Notes payable	110,000
Inventory	412,500	Other current liabilities	55,000
Total current assets	$660,000	Total current liabilities	$247,500
Net fixed assets	302,500	Long-term debt	110,000
		Common equity	605,000
Total assets	$962,500	Total claims on assets	$962,500

**Wiggins Wheel Company: Income Statement
for Year Ended December 31, 1979**

Sales		$1,375,000
Cost of goods sold		
Materials	$522,500	
Labor	330,000	
Heat, light, and power	49,500	
Indirect labor	82,500	
Depreciation	30,250	1,014,750
Gross profit		360,250
Selling expenses		137,500
General and administrative expenses		158,400
Earnings before interest and taxes		$ 64,350
Less interest expense		6,600
Net profit before taxes		$ 57,750
Less federal income taxes (50%)		28,875
Net profit		$ 28,875

	Ratios	
Ratio	**Wiggins**	**Industry Averages**
Current assets/current liabilities	_____	2.4×
Average collection period	_____	43 days
Sales/inventories	_____	9.8×
Sales/total assets	_____	2×
Net profit/sales	_____	3.3%
Net profit/total assets	_____	6.6%
Net profit/net worth	_____	18.1%
Total debt/total assets	_____	63.5%

6-2 The Williamsburg Furniture Company, a manufacturer and wholesaler of high-quality home furnishings, has been experiencing low profitability in recent years. As a result, the Board of Directors has replaced the president of the firm with a new president, John Sharpe, who asks you to make an analysis of the firm's financial position using the du Pont system. The most recent financial statements are reproduced below.

a. Calculate some ratios which you feel would be useful in this case.
b. Do the balance sheet accounts or the income statement figures seem to be primarily responsible for the low profits?
c. Which specific accounts seem to be most out of line in relation to other firms in the industry?
d. If Williamsburg had a pronounced seasonal sales pattern, or if it grew rapidly during the year, how might this affect the validity of your ratio analysis? How might you correct for such potential problems?

Industry Average Ratios

Current ratio	2×	Sales/fixed assets	6×
Debt/total assets	30%	Sales/total assets	3×
Times interest earned	7×	Net profit on sales	3%
Sales/inventory	10×	Return on total assets	9%
Average collection period	24 days	Return on common equity	12.8%

Williamsburg Furniture Company: Balance Sheet, December 31, 1979 (Millions of Dollars)

Cash		$ 30	Accounts payable	$ 30
Marketable securities		22	Notes payable	30
Net receivables		44	Other current liabilities	14
Inventories		106	Total current liabilities	$ 74
Total current assets		$202	Long-term debt	16
			Total liabilities	$ 90
Gross fixed assets	$150			
Less depreciation	52		Common stock	$ 76
Net fixed assets		98	Retained earnings	134
			Total stockholder equity	210
Total assets		$300	Total claims on assets	$300

**Williamsburg Furniture Company: Income
Statement for Year Ended December 31, 1979
(Millions of Dollars)**

Net sales	$530	
Cost of goods sold	440	
Gross profit		$90
Operating expenses	49	
Depreciation expense	8	
Interest expense	3	
Total expenses		60
Net income before tax		$30
Taxes (50%)		15
Net income		$15

6-3 The consolidated balance sheets for the Apex Corporation at the beginning
and end of 1979 are shown below. The company bought $75 million worth of
fixed assets. The charge for depreciation in 1979 was $15 million. Earnings
after taxes were $38 million, and the company paid out $10 million in
dividends.

a. Fill in the amount of source or use in the appropriate column.

**Apex Corporation: Balance Sheet, Beginning
and End of 1979 (Millions of Dollars)**

			Change	
	Jan. 1	Dec. 31	Source	Use
Cash	$ 15	$ 7	_____	_____
Marketable securities	11	0	_____	_____
Net receivables	22	30	_____	_____
Inventories	53	75	_____	_____
Total current assets	$101	$112	_____	_____
Gross fixed assets	75	150	_____	_____
Less: Depreciation	(26)	(41)	_____	_____
Net fixed assets	49	109	_____	_____
Total assets	$150	$221	_____	_____

	Jan. 1	Dec. 31	Change Source	Use
Accounts payable	$ 15	$ 18	———	———
Notes payable	15	3	———	———
Other current liabilities	7	15	———	———
Long-term debt	8	26	———	———
Common stock	38	64	———	———
Retained earnings	67	95	———	———
Total claims on assets	$150	$221	———	———

b. Prepare a statement of changes in financial position.

c. Briefly summarize your findings.

6-4 Indicate the effects of the transactions listed below on each of the following: total current assets, net working capital, current ratio, and net profit. Use (+) to indicate an increase, (−) to indicate a decrease, and (0) to indicate no effect or indeterminate effect. State necessary assumptions and assume an initial current ratio of more than 1 to 1.

	Total Current Assets	Net Working Capital[a]	Current Ratio	Effect on Net Profit
1. Cash is acquired through issuance of additional common stock.	———	———	———	———
2. Merchandise is sold for cash.	———	———	———	———
3. Federal income tax due for the previous year is paid.	———	———	———	———
4. A fixed asset is sold for less than book value.	———	———	———	———
5. A fixed asset is sold for more than book value.	———	———	———	———
6. Merchandise is sold on credit.	———	———	———	———
7. Payment is made to trade creditors for previous purchases.	———	———	———	———
8. A cash dividend is declared and paid.	———	———	———	———
9. Cash is obtained through bank loans.	———	———	———	———
10. Short-term notes receivable are sold at a discount.	———	———	———	———
11. Previously issued stock rights are exercised by company stockholders.	———	———	———	———
12. A profitable firm increases its rate of depreciation on fixed assets.	———	———	———	———
13. Marketable securities are sold below cost.	———	———	———	———
14. Uncollectible accounts are written off against the bad debt reserve.	———	———	———	———
15. Advances are made to employees.	———	———	———	———

[a]Net working capital is defined as current assets minus current liabilities.

	Total Current Assets	Net Working Capital	Current Ratio	Effect on Net Profit
16. Current operating expenses are paid.	———	———	———	———
17. Short-term promissory notes are issued to trade creditors for prior purchases.	———	———	———	———
18. Ten-year notes are issued to pay off accounts payable.	———	———	———	———
19. A fully depreciated asset is retired.	———	———	———	———
20. A *cash* sinking fund for the retirement of bonds is created; a reserve for a bond sinking fund is also created.	———	———	———	———
21. Bonds are retired by use of the cash sinking fund.	———	———	———	———
22. Accounts receivable are collected.	———	———	———	———
23. A stock dividend is declared and paid.	———	———	———	———
24. Equipment is purchased with short-term notes.	———	———	———	———
25. The allowance for doubtful accounts is increased.	———	———	———	———
26. Merchandise is purchased on credit.	———	———	———	———
27. Controlling interest in another firm is acquired by the issuance of additional common stock.	———	———	———	———
28. Earnings are added to the reserve for a bond sinking fund.	———	———	———	———
29. An unconsolidated subsidiary pays the firm a cash dividend from current earnings.	———	———	———	———
30. The estimated taxes payable are increased.	———	———	———	———

6-5 The record of earnings and dividends per share for the American Container Company (ACC) is given below:

Year	EPS	DPS
1969	$2.00	$0.80
1970	2.15	0.80
1971	2.30	0.80
1972	2.45	1.30
1973	2.60	1.30
1974	2.75	1.30
1975	3.25	1.60
1976	2.95	1.60
1977	3.44	2.00
1978	4.00	2.00
1979	3.62	2.00

a. Calculate ACC's growth rates in EPS and DPS. (Round to nearest percent.)

b. Suppose you conclude that ACC's growth rate in EPS will probably be maintained into the indefinite future. Which growth rate, that of EPS or DPS, would you use in the stock valuation equation $P = D_1/(k_s - g)$?

c. Consider now how certain financial decisions would probably affect the following factors. Use (+) to indicate an increase, (−) to indicate a decrease, and (0) to indicate either no effect or an unpredictable effect. *Note:* This question is designed to encourage discussion, not to produce precise answers. While some of the answers are clear-cut, finance professors would argue among themselves about others!

	ACC's Expected EPS and Growth in EPS during the Coming Year	ACC's Required Rate of Return on Stock, k_s	ACC's Cost of Debt, k_d	Market Price of ACC's Stock
1. ACC increases its debt/ assets ratio.	_____	_____	_____	_____
2. ACC decides to increase its cash position by selling long-term bonds.	_____	_____	_____	_____
3. Inventories are reduced by the introduction of a new control system.	_____	_____	_____	_____
4. ACC acquires through merger a firm whose beta is twice that of ACC.	_____	_____	_____	_____
5. The Federal Reserve System takes actions to lower interest rates in the economy.	_____	_____	_____	_____
6. ACC decides to pay out all of its earnings, each year, as dividends.	_____	_____	_____	_____
7. Optional question for accountants: ACC's "conservative" accountants are replaced by a group of more "liberal" accountants.	_____	_____	_____	_____

7 FINANCIAL FORECASTING

As noted in Chapter 6, both managers and investors are vitally concerned with *future* financial statements. Also, managers regularly construct *pro forma,* or projected, statements and consider alternative courses of action in terms of the actions' effects on these projections. In this chapter we discuss briefly how pro forma statements are constructed and how they are used to help estimate the need for capital.

DEMAND FORECASTS

The most important element in financial planning is a demand (or sales) forecast. Because such forecasts are critical for production scheduling, for plant design, for financial planning, and so on, the entire management team participates in their preparation. In fact, most of the larger firms have a *planning group* or *planning committee,* with its own staff of economists, which coordinates the corporation's sales forecast. Since demand forecasting is a rather specialized subject, we will not consider the mechanics of the forecasting process in this chapter. Rather, we will simply take the sales forecast as given and then use it to illustrate various types of financial decisions.[1]

---

1 A sales forecast is actually the *expected value of a probability distribution* of possible levels of sales. Because any sales forecast is subject to a greater or lesser degree of uncertainty, for financial planning we are often just as interested in the degree of uncertainty inherent in the sales forecast (σ sales) as we are in the expected value of sales. See J. L. Pappas and E. F. Brigham, *Managerial Economics,* Chapter 5: "Demand Estimation" (Hinsdale, Ill.: Dryden Press, 1979), for a detailed discussion of procedures for making demand forecasts.

FORECASTING FINANCIAL REQUIREMENTS: THE PERCENTAGE OF SALES METHOD

To use this simple but often practical method of forecasting financial requirements, we first express the various balance sheet items as a percentage of sales, then use these percentages, together with expected future sales, to construct pro forma balance sheets. To illustrate, consider the Arinson Products Company, whose December 31, 1979, balance sheet is given in Table 7–1. Arinson is operating at full capacity. Its 1979 sales were $400,000; its profit margin on sales was 10 percent; and Arinson distributed 60 percent of its after-tax profits to stockholders as dividends. If Arinson Products expects sales to increase to $600,000 in 1980, what will be its pro forma December 31, 1980, balance sheet, and how much additional financing will the company require?

Table 7–1
Arinson Products Company: Balance Sheet,
December 31, 1979 (Thousands of Dollars)

Cash	$ 10	Accounts payable	$ 40
Receivables	90	Notes payable	10
Inventories	200	Accrued wages and taxes	50
Total current assets	$300	Total current liabilities	$100
Net fixed assets	300	Mortgage bonds	150
		Common stock	50
		Retained earnings	300
Total assets	$600	Total claims	$600

Current ratio = 300/100 = 3:1; Industry average = 2.6:1.
Total debt/total assets = 250/600 = 42%; Industry average = 45%.

Our first step is to isolate those balance sheet items that vary directly with sales. Since Arinson is operating at full capacity, each asset item must increase if the higher level of sales is to be attained. More cash will be needed for transactions; receivables will be higher; additional inventory must be stocked; and new plant must be added.[2]

If assets are to increase, liabilities and net worth must likewise rise—the balance sheet must balance, and increases in assets must be financed in some manner. Accounts payable and accruals will rise *spontaneously* with sales: as sales increase, so will purchases, and larger purchases will result in

_____
2 Assets such as marketable securities, which are not tied directly to operations, do not vary directly with sales.

higher levels of accounts payable. Thus, if sales double, accounts payable will also double. Similarly, a higher level of operations will require more labor, so accrued wages will increase, and assuming profit margins are maintained, an increase in profits will pull up accrued taxes. Retained earnings will also increase, but not in direct proportion to the increase in sales. Neither notes payable, mortgage bonds, nor common stock will rise spontaneously with sales—higher sales do not *automatically* trigger increases in these items.

We can use this information to construct a pro forma balance sheet for December 31, 1980, proceeding as outlined below.

Step 1. In Table 7–2, Column 1, we express those balance sheet items that vary directly with sales as a percentage of sales. An item such as

Table 7–2
Arinson Products Company: 12/31/1979
Balance Sheet Expressed as a Percentage of
Sales and 12/31/1980 Pro Forma Balance
Sheet (Dollars in Thousands)

	Balance Sheet Items on 12/31/1979 (as a % of the $400 1979 Sales) (1)	Pro Forma Balance Sheet on 12/31/1980 (= Projected Sales of $600 Times Column 1) (2)
Cash	2.5%	$ 15
Receivables	22.5	135
Inventories	50.0	300
Total current assets	75.0%	$450
Net fixed assets	75.0	450
Total assets	150.0%	$900
Accounts payable	10.0%	$ 60
Notes payable	n.a.[a]	10[b]
Accrued wages and taxes	12.5	75
Total current liabilities	22.5%	$145
Mortgage bonds	n.a.	150[b]
Common stock	n.a.	50[b]
Retained earnings	n.a.	324[c]
	22.5% Funds available	$669
	Additional funds needed[d]	231
		$900

[a]n.a. = not applicable.
[b]1980 projections picked up from 12/31/1979 balance sheet.
[c]12/31/1979 balance in retained earnings plus 1980 addition to retained earnings.
[d]"Additional funds needed" is a balancing figure: $900 − $669 = $231.

notes payable that does not vary directly with sales is designated n.a., or "not applicable."

Step 2. Next, we multiply these percentages by the $600,000 projected 1980 sales to obtain the projected amounts as of December 31, 1980; these are shown in Column 2 of the table.

Step 3. We simply insert figures for notes payable, mortgage bonds, and common stock from the 12/31/1979 balance sheet. At least one of these accounts may have to be changed later in the analysis.

Step 4. We next add the addition to retained earnings estimated for 1980 to the figure shown on the December 31, 1979, balance sheet to obtain the 12/31/1980 projected retained earnings. Recall that Arinson expects to earn 10 percent on sales of $600,000, or $60,000, and to pay 60 percent of this out in dividends to stockholders. (The *dividend payout ratio* is 60 percent.) Thus, retained earnings for the year are projected to be $60,000 − 0.6($60,000) = $24,000. Adding the $24,000 addition to retained earnings to the $300,000 beginning balance gives the $324,000 projected retained earnings shown in Column 2.

Step 5. Next, we sum the asset accounts, obtaining a total projected assets figure of $900,000, and also add the projected liabilities and net worth items to obtain $669,000, the estimate of available funds. Since liabilities and net worth must total $900,000, but only $669,000 is projected, we have a shortfall of $231,000 "additional funds needed," which will presumably be raised by selling securities. For simplicity, we disregard depreciation by assuming that cash flows from depreciation are reinvested in fixed assets.

Step 6. Arinson could use short-term notes, mortgage bonds, common stock, or a combination of these securities to make up the shortfall. Ordinarily, it would make this choice on the basis of the relative costs of these different types of securities. However, in this case the company has a contractual agreement with its bondholders to keep total debt at or below 50 percent of total assets, and also to keep the current ratio at a level of 3.0 or greater. These provisions restrict the financing choices as follows:[3]

1. *Restriction on Additional Debt*

$$\text{Maximum debt permitted} = 0.5 \times \text{Total assets}$$
$$= 0.5 \times \$900,000 = \$450,000$$

Less debt already projected for 12/31/80:

Current liabilities	$145,000	
Mortgage bonds	150,000	= 295,000
Maximum additional debt		$155,000

---

3 As we shall see in Chapter 13, restrictions such as these are contained in virtually all long-term debt agreements. They are designed to protect bondholders against imprudent managerial decisions that would increase the risk the bondholders face.

2. *Restriction on Additional Current Liabilities*

$$\text{Maximum current liabilities} = \frac{1}{3} \text{ of current assets}$$

$= \quad \$450,000 \div 3 = \$150,000$	
Current liabilities already projected	145,000
Maximum additional current liabilities	$ 5,000

3. *Common Equity Requirements*

Total external funds required (from Table 7–2)	$231,000
Maximum additional debt permitted	155,000
Common equity funds required	$ 76,000

We see, then, that Arinson needs a total of $231,000 from external sources. Its existing debt contract limits new debt to $155,000, and of that amount only $5,000 can be short-term debt. Thus, Arinson must plan to sell common stock in the amount of $76,000, in addition to some debt financing, to cover its financial requirements.

Projected Financial Statements and Ratios

Arinson's financial manager can now construct a set of projected, or pro forma, financial statements and then analyze the ratios that are implied by these statements. Table 7–3 gives abbreviated versions of the final projected

---

Table 7–3
Arinson Products Company:
Projected Financial
Statements for 1980
(Dollars in Thousands)

I. Projected Balance Sheet, 12/31/80

Cash	$ 15	Accounts payable	$ 60
Accounts receivable	135	Notes payable[a]	15
Inventories	300	Accruals	75
Total current assets	$450	Total current liabilities	$150
Net fixed assets	$450	Long-term debt[b]	$300
		Common stock[c]	126
		Retained earnings	324
		Total equity	$450
Total assets	$900	Total claims	$900

[a]Assumes $5,000 additional is borrowed from bank. This is the maximum permissible increase in short-term debt.

[b]Assumes $150,000 additional long-term debt is sold. This is the maximum permissible increase in long-term debt, given the $5,000 increase in notes payable.

[c]Assumes $76,000 additional common stock is sold.

Table 7–3 continued

II. Projected Income Statement, 1980

Sales	$600
Total costs	500
Taxable income	$100
Taxes (40%)	40
Net income after taxes	$ 60
Dividends	36
Addition to retained earnings	$ 24

III. Projected Statement of Changes in Financial Position, 1980

Sources of funds:

Net income	$ 60
Funds from operations[d]	60
Proceeds from sale of bonds	150
Proceeds from sale of common stock	76
Total sources	$286

Uses of funds:

Increase in net fixed assets	$150
Dividend payments	36
Increase in net working capital (See detail below.)	100
Total uses	$286

Analysis of Changes in Working Capital
Increase (decrease) in current assets:

Cash	$ 5
Accounts receivable	45
Inventories	100
Net increase (decrease) in current assets	$150

Increase (decrease) in current liabilities:

Accounts payable	$ 20
Notes payable	5
Accruals	25
Net increase (decrease) in current liabilities	$ 50
Increase (decrease) in net working capital	$100

IV. Key Ratios Projected for 12/31/80

1. Current ratio	3.0 times
2. Total debt/total assets	50%
3. Rate of return on equity	13.3%

(Other ratios could be calculated and analyzed by the du Pont system.)

[d]*Funds from operations* normally includes depreciation. Here we have assumed that depreciation is reinvested in fixed assets; i.e., depreciation is netted out against fixed asset additions.

balance sheet, income statement, statement of changes in financial position, and a few key ratios. These statements, in turn, can be used by the financial manager to show the other executives the implications of the planned sales increase. For example, the projected rate of return on equity is 13.3 percent. Is this a reasonable target, or can it be improved? Also, the preliminary forecast calls for the sale of some common stock—but does top management really want to sell any new stock? Suppose Arinson Products is owned entirely by John Arinson, who does not want to sell any stock and thereby lose his exclusive control of the company. How then can the needed funds be raised, or what adjustments should be made? In the remainder of the chapter, we look at approaches to answering questions such as these.

The Relationship between Growth in Sales and Capital Requirements

Although the forecast of capital requirements can be made by constructing pro forma balance sheets as described above, it is often easier to use a simple forecasting formula. In addition, the formula can be used to make clear the relationship between sales growth and financial requirements:

$$\begin{bmatrix} \text{External} \\ \text{funds} \\ \text{needed} \end{bmatrix} = \begin{bmatrix} \text{Required} \\ \text{increase} \\ \text{in assets} \end{bmatrix} - \begin{bmatrix} \text{Spontaneous} \\ \text{increase in} \\ \text{liabilities} \end{bmatrix} - \begin{bmatrix} \text{Increase in} \\ \text{retained} \\ \text{earnings} \end{bmatrix}.$$

$$EFN = \frac{A}{S}(\Delta S) - \frac{L}{S}(\Delta S) - MS_1(1 - d). \qquad (7\text{–}1)$$

Here,

EFN = external funds needed.

$\dfrac{A}{S}$ = assets that increase spontaneously with sales as a percent of sales, or required dollar increase in assets per $1 increase in sales. A/S = 150%, or 1.5, for Arinson.

$\dfrac{L}{S}$ = liabilities that increase spontaneously with sales as a percent of sales, or spontaneously generated financing per $1 increase in sales. L/S = 22.5%, or 0.225, for Arinson.

S_1 = total sales projected for next year. Note that S_0 = last year's sales. S_1 = $600,000 for Arinson.

ΔS = change in sales = $S_1 - S_0$ = $600,000 - $400,000 = $200,000 for Arinson.

M = profit margin, or rate of profits per $1 of sales. M = 10%, or 0.10, for Arinson.

d = percentage of earnings paid out in dividends, or the dividend payout ratio; d = 60%. Notice that $1 - d$ =

1.0 − 0.6 = 0.4, or 40 percent. This is the percentage of earnings that Arinson retains, often called the *retention rate* or *retention ratio*.

Inserting values for Arinson Products into Equation 7−1, we find the external funds needed as follows:

$$EFN = 1.5\,(\Delta S) - 0.225(\Delta S) - 0.1(S_1)\,(1 - 0.6)$$
$$= 1.5(\$200{,}000) - 0.225(\$200{,}000) - 0.1(\$600{,}000)\,(0.4)$$
$$= \$300{,}000 - \$45{,}000 - \$24{,}000$$
$$= \$231{,}000.$$

To increase sales by $200,000, Arinson must increase assets by $300,000. The $300,000 of new assets must be financed in some manner. Of the total, $45,000 will come from a spontaneous increase in liabilities, while another $24,000 will be raised from retained earnings. The remaining $231,000 must be obtained from external sources. This value must, of course, agree with the figure developed in Table 7−2.

Graph of the Relationship between Growth and Funds Requirements

The faster Arinson's growth rate in sales, the greater its need for external financing; we can use Equation 7−1 to indicate this relationship. Consider Table 7−4, which shows Arinson Products' external financial requirements at various growth rates. These data also are plotted in Figure 7−1. Several points are apparent from the exhibits; they are discussed below.

Financial Planning At low growth rates Arinson needs no external financing. However, if the company grows faster than 3.239 percent, it must raise capital from outside sources. If for any reason management foresees difficulties in raising this capital—perhaps because Arinson's owners do not want to sell additional stock—then the company might need to reconsider the feasibility of its expansion plans.

The Effect of Dividend Policy on Financing Needs Dividend policy also affects external capital requirements, so if Arinson foresees difficulties in raising capital, it might want to consider a reduction in the dividend payout ratio. This would lower, or shift to the right, the line in Figure 7−1, indicating lower external capital requirements at all growth rates. However, before making this decision, management should consider the effects of changes in dividends on stock prices. These effects are described in Chapter 17.

Notice that the line in Figure 7−1 does *not* pass through the origin; thus, at low growth rates surplus funds (negative external requirements) will be produced, because new retained earnings plus spontaneous funds will

Table 7–4
Relationship between Growth in Sales and
Financial Requirements, Assuming $S_0 =$
$400,000

Growth Rate in Sales (%) (1)	Dollar Increase (Decrease) in Sales (ΔS in Thousands) (2)	New Sales (S_1 in Thousands) (3)	External Fund Requirements (Surplus in Thousands) (4)
100%	$400	$800	$478.0
50	200	600	231.0
25	100	500	107.5
10	40	440	33.4
3.239	12.956	412.956	0.0
0	0	400	(16.0)
−10	(40)	360	(65.4)
−25	(100)	300	(139.5)

Note: *Explanation of Columns*

Col. 1 Growth rate in sales, g.
Col. 2 Increase (decrease) in sales, $\Delta S = g(S_0)$.
Col. 3 New sales, $S_1 = S_0 + g(S_0) = S_0(1 + g)$.
Col. 4 External funds required $= 1.5(\Delta S) - 0.225(\Delta S) - 0.04(S_1)$
$\qquad\qquad\qquad = 1.275(\Delta S) - 0.04(S_1)$
$\qquad\qquad\qquad = 1.275(g)(S_0) - 0.04(S_0)(1 + g)$
$\qquad\qquad\qquad = 510g - 16 - 16g$
$\qquad\qquad\qquad = -16 + 494g$
$\qquad\qquad\qquad =$ equation plotted in Figure 7–1.

Example: If $g = 10\%$, or 0.10, then
External funds required $= -16 + 494g$
$\qquad\qquad\qquad = -16 + 494(0.10)$
$\qquad\qquad\qquad = 33.4$ or $33,400.

The maximum growth rate that can be financed without external funds is found by setting the equation equal to zero:

External funds required $= 0 = -16 + 494g$
$\qquad\qquad 494g = 16$
$\qquad\quad g = 16/494 = 0.03239$ or 3.239%.

exceed the required asset increases. Only if the dividend payout ratio is 100 percent, meaning that the firm does not retain any of its earnings, will the "funds required" line pass through the origin.

Capital Intensity The amount of assets required per dollar of sales, A/S in Equation 7–1, is often called the *capital intensity ratio*. This factor has a major effect on capital requirements per unit of sales growth. If the capital intensity ratio is low, then sales can grow rapidly without much outside capital. However, if the firm is capital intensive, even a small growth in output will require a great deal of outside capital. This is precisely the problem facing the utility industry today. Utilities are very capital intensive, so they require large amounts of capital to expand output. Further, a

Figure 7–1
Relationship between Arinson's Growth in
Sales and Financial Requirements

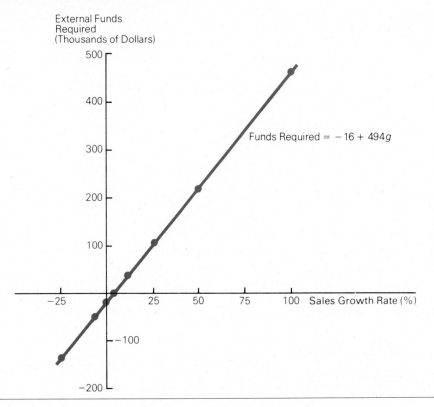

External Funds
Required
(Thousands of Dollars)

Funds Required $= -16 + 494g$

Sales Growth Rate (%)

conversion from an oil-based economy to one based more heavily on coal
and nuclear energy will mean a substantial growth in demand for electricity.
Since all this is coming at a time of tight money and high interest rates,
financial executives in the utility industry have their work cut out for them.

The Profit Margin and the Need for External Funds The profit margin, *M,*
is also an important determinant of the funds required equation—the higher
the margin, the lower the funds requirements, other things held constant.
Arinson's profit margin was 10 percent. Now suppose *M* increased to 15
percent. This new value could be inserted into the funds required formula,
and the following relationship between funds needs and growth would
result: $EFN = -24 + 486g$. Thus, we see that an increase in the profit
margin lowers both the intercept term and the slope coefficient, so for all
positive growth rates there is a reduction in external funds needed. Because
of the relationship between profit margins and external capital requirements,

some very rapidly growing firms do not need much external capital. Thus, for example, Xerox grew very rapidly with very little borrowing or stock sales. However, as the company lost patent protection, and as competition intensified in the copier industry, Xerox's profit margin declined, its needs for external capital rose, and it began to borrow heavily from banks and other sources.

Excess Capacity We assumed that Arinson was initially operating at full capacity. Therefore, any increase in sales required an increase in assets. However, had excess capacity existed initially, some level of sales expansion could have occurred with no increase in assets. Thus, Equation 7–1 cannot be used to forecast financial requirements if excess capacity exists. Forecasting procedures when excess capacity exists are discussed in a later section.

Changing Ratios If the ratios of either assets or liabilities to sales are changing over time, then Equation 7–1 cannot be used to forecast financial requirements. Procedures for dealing with this situation are also discussed in the next section.

FORECASTING FINANCIAL REQUIREMENTS WHEN THE BALANCE SHEET RATIOS ARE SUBJECT TO CHANGE

To this point we have been assuming that the balance sheet ratios (A/S and L/S) are constant at all levels of sales. For the ratios to remain constant, each asset and liability item must increase at the same rate as sales. In graph form, this assumption suggests the existence of the type of relationship indicated in Figure 7–2: a relationship that is linear and passes through the origin. The assumption of a constant ratio may or may not be appropriate, and certainly this is one of the things that should be discussed during the planning process.

Suppose, for example, that a ratio comparison showed that other firms in the industry had inventory-to-sales ratios of only 25 percent versus Arinson's 50 percent. If Arinson could reduce inventories to the industry average, its 12/31/80 inventory forecast would be $150,000 rather than $300,000. This would reduce financial requirements by $150,000. (See Table 7–2.) Further, if the assets side of the balance sheet were reduced by $150,000, so would be the claims side. This would mean less debt, hence lower interest charges, or less equity, hence a higher rate of return on equity.

In many firms it is completely unrealistic to think that fixed assets will ever be a stable percentage of sales. For example, if the production process is such that fixed assets are added in "lumpy" increments at infrequent

Figure 7–2
Relationship between Assets and Sales If the
Assets/Sales Ratio Is Constant for All Levels of
Sales

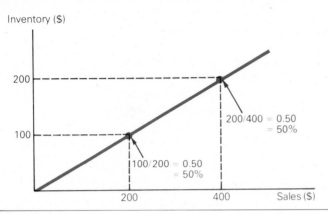

intervals, then the fixed assets/sales ratio will be low just *before* new capacity is added and high just *after* a new plant is put on line. Also, since sales tend to fluctuate over the business cycle, at the start of some years a firm will have excess manufacturing capacity and thus be able to expand sales greatly with little or no additions to fixed assets. On the other hand, if the firm is operating close to capacity, and if fixed assets are lumpy, then even a small increase in sales may require a large increase in fixed assets.[4]

All of the asset accounts, including fixed assets, should be carefully analyzed during the planning process, and the implications of changes should be examined through the use of projected financial statements. Smaller firms typically generate projected statements "by hand," but many larger firms have computerized the process. Computerized financial planning models have been developed to show the effects of different sales levels, different ratios of sales to operating assets, and even different assumptions about sales prices and input costs (labor, materials, and so forth). Plans are then made regarding how financial requirements are to be met—through bank loans, thus increasing short-term notes payable; by selling long-term bonds; or by selling new common stock. Pro forma balance sheets and income statements are generated under the different financing plans, and earnings per share are projected, along with such risk measures as the current ratio, the debt/assets ratio, and the times interest earned ratio.

Depending on how these projections look, management may modify its initial plans. For example, the firm may conclude that its sales forecast must

---

4 Current assets/sales ratios are much more stable than fixed assets/sales ratios because it is much easier to increase or decrease current assets as demand changes.

be cut because the requirements for external capital exceed the firm's ability to raise money. Or, management may decide to reduce dividends and thus generate more funds internally. Alternatively, the company may decide to investigate production processes that require fewer fixed assets, or to consider the possibility of buying rather than manufacturing certain components, thus eliminating raw materials and work-in-process inventories, as well as certain manufacturing facilities.

In subsequent chapters we will look in detail at ways of analyzing policy changes such as those mentioned above. In all such considerations, the basic issue is the effect that a specific action will have on future earnings, on the riskiness of these earnings, and, hence, on the price of the firm's stock. Since computerized models help management assess these effects, such planning models are playing an ever increasing role in corporate management.[5]

SUMMARY

This chapter described in broad outline how firms go about projecting their financial statements and determining their overall financial requirements. In brief, management establishes a target balance sheet based on the type of ratio analysis discussed in Chapter 6. Assuming that each balance sheet ratio is at the desired level and that the optimal levels for these ratios are stable, the *percentage of sales method* can be used to forecast the external financial requirements associated with any given increase in sales. If the balance sheet ratios are subject to change, as they will be if excess capacity exists, then each item in the projected balance sheet must be forecasted separately.

The type of forecasting described here is important for several reasons. First, if the projected operating results look poor, management can "go back to the drawing board" and reformulate its plans for the coming year. Second, it is possible that the funds required to meet the sales forecast simply cannot be obtained. If so, it is obviously better to know this in advance and to scale back the projected level of operations. And third, even if the required funds can be raised, it is desirable to plan for the acquisition of these funds well in advance. As we shall see in later chapters, raising capital takes time and is expensive, and both time and money can be saved by careful forward planning.

---

5 Corporations can develop their own computerized models, but excellent and easy-to-use planning models are also available from a number of specialized computer software companies. One such model—Interactive Financial Planning System (IFPS)—is installed on the computer system at the University of Florida. IFPS is also used by several hundred companies, including 3M Corporation, Shell Oil, and Florida Power & Light. Further discussion of computer models is deferred to Chapter 12, where their use in capital budgeting is considered.

Questions

7-1 Certain liability and net worth items generally increase spontaneously with increases in sales. Put a check ($\checkmark$) by those items that typically increase spontaneously:

Accounts payable ____
Notes payable to banks ____
Accrued wages ____
Accrued taxes ____
Mortgage bonds ____
Common stock ____
Retained earnings ____
Marketable securities ____

7-2 The following equation can, under certain assumptions, be used tó forecast financial requirements:

$$\text{External funds needed} = \frac{A}{S}(\Delta S) - \frac{L}{S}(\Delta S) - MS_1(1 - d).$$

Under what conditions does the equation give satisfactory predictions, and when should it not be used?

7-3 Assume that an average firm in the office supply business has a 6 percent after-tax profit margin, a 40 percent debt/assets ratio, a turnover of 2 times, and a dividend payout ratio of 40 percent. Is it true that if such a firm is to have *any* sales growth ($g > 0$), it will be forced to sell either bonds or common stock; that is, it will need some nonspontaneous external capital, and this will be true even if g is very small?

7-4 Is it true that computerized corporate planning models were a fad during the 1960s, but, because of a need for flexibility in corporate planning, they have been dropped by most firms?

7-5 Suppose a firm makes the following policy changes. If the change means that external, nonspontaneous financial requirements for any rate of growth will increase, indicate this by a ($+$); indicate decreases by a ($-$); and indicate indeterminant and/or no effect by a (0). Think in terms of the immediate, short-run effect on funds requirements.

a. The dividend payout ratio is increased. ____
b. The firm contracts to buy rather than make certain components used in its products. ____
c. The firm decides to pay all suppliers on delivery, rather than after a thirty day delay, in order to take advantage of discounts for rapid payment. ____
d. The firm begins to sell on credit; previously, all sales had been on a cash basis. ____
e. The firm's profit margin is eroded by increased competition. ____

f. Advertising expenditures are stepped up. ———
g. A decision is made to substitute long-term mortgage
    bonds for short-term bank loans. ———
h. The firm begins to pay employees on a weekly basis;
    previously, it paid at the end of each month. ———

Problems

7-1 Continental Foods, Inc., is planning to set up a subsidiary to package and
distribute frozen fish. To help plan the new operation's financial requirements,
Continental is constructing a pro forma balance sheet for 12/31/80, the end of
the first year of operations. Sales for 1980 are projected at $10 million, and
the following are industry average ratios for frozen fish companies.

Sales to common equity	5×
Current debt to equity	50%
Total debt to equity	80%
Current ratio	2.2×
Net sales to inventory	9×
Accounts receivable to sales	10%
Fixed assets to equity	70%
Profit margin	3%
Dividend payout ratio	30%

a. Complete the pro forma balance sheet below, assuming the fish
    subsidiary's 1980 sales are $10 million.
b. If Continental Foods supplies all the new firm's equity, how much capital
    will Continental be required to have put up by 12/31/80?

**Frozen Fish Subsidiary: Pro Forma Balance
Sheet, December 31, 1980 (Millions of Dollars)**

Cash	$————	Current debt	$————
Accounts receivable	————	Long-term debt	————
Inventories	————	Total debt	————
Total current assets	————	Equity	————
Fixed assets	————		
Total assets	$————	Total claims	$————

7-2 Allied Grocers is a wholesale concern. It makes bulk purchases of grocery
products, stocks them in conveniently located warehouses, and then ships to
retailers on demand. Allied's balance sheet as of 12/31/1979 is shown below
(in millions of dollars):

Cash	$ 1.0	Accounts payable	$ 2.5
Receivables	7.5	Notes payable	5.0
Inventories	16.5	Accruals	2.5
Total current assets	$25.0	Total current liabilities	$10.0
Net fixed assets	10.1	Mortgage loan	1.7
		Common stock	4.2
		Retained earnings	19.2
Total assets	$35.1	Total liabilities and net worth	$35.1

Sales for 1979 were $100 million, while net income after taxes for the year was $2,835,000. Allied paid dividends of $1,134,000 to common stockholders. The firm is operating at full capacity.

a. If sales are projected to increase by $25 million, or by 25 percent, during 1980, what are Allied Grocers' projected external capital requirements?

b. Construct Allied Grocers' pro forma balance sheet for 12/31/1980. Assume that all external capital requirements are met by bank loans and are reflected in notes payable.

c. Now calculate the following ratios, based on your projected 12/31/1980 balance sheet. Allied's 1979 ratios and industry average ratios are shown below for comparison.

	Allied Grocers 12/31/80	Allied Grocers 12/31/79	Industry Average 12/31/79
Current ratio	_____	2.5×	3×
Debt/total assets	_____	33.3%	30%
Rate of return on net worth	_____	12.1%	12%

d. Now assume that Allied Grocers grows by the same $25 million, but that the growth is spread over five years; that is, sales grow by $5 million each year.

   (1) Calculate total external financial requirements over the five year period.

   (2) Construct a pro forma balance sheet as of 12/31/1984, using notes payable as the balancing item.

   (3) Calculate the current ratio, debt/assets ratio, and rate of return on net worth as of 12/31/84.

   Hint: Be sure to use *total sales,* which amount to $575 million, to calculate retained earnings, but 1984 profits to calculate the rate of return on net worth; that is, (1984 profits)/(12/31/84 net worth).

e. Do the plans outlined in Parts c and d seem feasible to you; that is, do you think Allied could borrow the required capital, and would the company be raising the odds on its bankruptcy in the event of some temporary misfortune to an excessive level?

7-3 The Watkins-Jensen Company's 1979 sales were $24 million. The percentage of sales of each balance sheet item that varies directly with sales is given below:

Cash	3%
Receivables	20
Inventories	25
Net fixed assets	40
Accounts payable	15
Accruals	10
Profit rate (after taxes) on sales	5

The dividend payout ratio is 40 percent; the 12/31/1978 balance sheet account for retained earnings was $8.2 million; and both common stock and mortgage bonds are constant and equal to the amounts shown on the balance sheet below.

a. Complete the following balance sheet:

Watkins-Jensen Company: Balance Sheet, December 31, 1979 (Thousands of Dollars)

Cash	$	Accounts payable	$
Receivables		Notes payable	2,200
Inventories	————	Accruals	————
Total current		Total current	
assets		liabilities	
Net fixed assets	————	Mortgage bonds	2,000
		Common stock	2,000
		Retained earnings	————
		Total liabilities	
Total assets	$————	and net worth	$————

---

b. Now suppose that 1980 sales increase by 10 percent over 1979 sales. How much additional external capital will be required? The company was operating at full capacity in 1979. Use Equation 7–1 to answer this question.

c. Develop a pro forma balance sheet for 12/31/1980. Assume that any required financing is borrowed as notes payable.

d. What would happen to external fund requirements under each of the following conditions? Answer in words, without calculations.

  (1) The profit margin went (i) from 5 percent to 6 percent, (ii) from 5 percent to 3 percent.

  (2) The dividend payout rate (i) was raised from 40 to 90 percent, (ii) was lowered from 40 to 20 percent.

  (3) Credit terms on sales were relaxed substantially, giving customers longer to pay.

  (4) The company had excess manufacturing capacity at 12/31/79.

7-4 Western Carolina Mills' 1979 sales were $72 million. The percentage of sales of each balance sheet item except notes payable, mortgage bonds, and common stock is given below:

Cash	4%
Receivables	25
Inventories	30
Net fixed assets	50
Accounts payable	15
Accruals	5
Profit margin (after taxes) on sales	5

The dividend payout ratio is 60 percent; the 12/31/1978 balance sheet account for retained earnings was $41.8 million; and both common stock and mortgage bonds are constant and equal to the amounts shown on the following balance sheet.

a. Complete the following balance sheet:

**Western Carolina Mills: Balance Sheet,
December 31, 1979 (Thousands of Dollars)**

Cash	$	Accounts payable	$
Receivables		Notes payable	6,840
Inventories	————	Accruals	————
Total current		Total current	
assets		liabilities	
Net fixed assets	————	Mortgage bonds	10,000
		Common stock	4,000
		Retained earnings	————
		Total liabilities	
Total assets	$————	and net worth	$————

---

b. Assume that the company was operating at full capacity in 1979 with regard to all items *except* fixed assets; had the fixed assets been used to full capacity, the fixed assets/sales ratio would have been 40 percent in 1979. By what percentage could 1980 sales increase over 1979 sales without the need for an increase in fixed assets?

c. Now supppose that 1980 sales increase by 20 percent over 1979 sales. How much additional external capital will be required? Assume that WCM cannot sell any fixed assets. (*Hint:* Equation 7–1 can no longer be used. You must develop a pro forma balance sheet as in Table 7–2.) Assume that any required financing is borrowed as notes payable.

d. Suppose the industry averages for receivables and inventories are 20 percent and 25 percent, respectively, and that WCM matches these figures in 1980 and then uses the funds released to reduce equity. (It could pay a special dividend out of retained earnings.) What would this do to the rate of return on year-end 1980 equity?

IV WORKING CAPITAL MANAGEMENT

Up to now we have discussed financial management in a generalized sense. In the remainder of the book we look at specific financial decisions, beginning in Part IV with decisions related to working capital management. Chapter 8 analyzes the management of cash and marketable securities; Chapter 9 considers accounts receivable and inventories; and Chapter 10 discusses the various types of short-term credit that can be used to finance current assets.

8 CASH AND MARKETABLE SECURITIES

In Part III we saw (1) that a firm's assets are closely related to actual and projected sales, (2) that the various liability and equity accounts must be analyzed in terms of their relationships to assets, and (3) that risk, profitability, and consequently stock prices are all dependent upon decisions relating to acquiring and financing assets. However, this discussion was very general, and we looked more at industry averages than at specific economic determinants of the different types of assets. Now, in Part IV, we examine the optimal levels of current assets and current liabilities.

WORKING CAPITAL POLICY AND MANAGEMENT

Before taking up the topics of primary interest in this chapter, cash and marketable securities, it is useful to take an overview of the concepts of working capital and working capital management. We begin by defining the following key terms:

1. *Working capital,* sometimes called gross working capital, simply refers to current assets.[1]
2. *Net working capital* is defined as current assets minus current liabilities.
3. *Working capital policy* refers to basic policy decisions regarding target levels for each category of current assets, and to the financing of these assets.
4. *Working capital management* involves the administration, within policy guidelines, of current assets and current liabilities.

---

1 The term *working capital* originated with the old Yankee peddler, who would load up his wagon with goods, then go off on his route to peddle his wares. The merchandise was defined as his "working capital" because it was what he actually sold or "turned over" to produce his profits.

Whereas working capital policy relates to setting long-run targets, working capital management deals with the implementation of policy. Both are critically important, because working capital is used to make adjustments in operations to account for changing economic conditions. If demand begins to rise or fall, the immediate response is in the working capital accounts, and the appropriateness of the response can spell success or failure for the firm. For example, when its sales began to decline in 1974, Chrysler decided that the decline was only a temporary dip, so production levels were maintained. By the time it became clear that the "dip" was really a major recession, Chrysler had built up huge inventories of new cars. The company had borrowed heavily to finance this inventory buildup, and these loans had to be repaid. The only choice was to slash prices below costs in order to move the cars. This poor management of working capital resulted in hundreds of millions of dollars of losses, and to this time it is still unclear whether or not Chrysler will ever recover.

The types of credit available to finance current assets will be discussed in detail in Chapter 10. At this point, it is necessary only to know (1) that a major element of working capital policy and management relates to the financing of current assets and (2) that lining up sources of short-term credit, minimizing the cost of this credit, and making sure that it can be repaid on schedule is an important part of working capital operations.

With this background, we are now in a position to consider policy and management decisions relating to specific types of current assets and to the types of credit available to finance these assets. We begin with cash and marketable securities.

CASH MANAGEMENT

Approximately 1.5 percent of the average industrial firm's assets are held in the form of cash, which is defined as the total of bank demand deposits plus currency. However, cash balances vary widely not only among industries but also among the firms within a given industry, depending on the individual firms' specific conditions and on their owners' and managers' aversion to risk. In this section, we analyze the factors that determine firms' cash balances. These same factors, incidentally, apply to the cash holdings of individuals and nonprofit organizations, including government agencies.

Reasons for Holding Cash

Firms hold cash for four primary reasons:

1. *Transactions.* Cash balances are necessary to conduct business. Payments must be made, and receipts are deposited in the cash account. Cash

balances associated with payments and collections are known as *transactions balances.*

2. *Precaution.* Cash inflows and outflows are somewhat unpredictable, with the degree of predictability varying among firms and industries. Cash balances held in reserve for random, unforeseen fluctuations in inflows and outflows are defined as *precautionary balances.* The less predictable the firm's cash flows, the larger the necessary cash balances. However, if the firm has easy access to borrowed funds— that is, if the firm can borrow on short notice—then it need not hold much, if any, cash for precautionary purposes. Also, as shall be noted later in this chapter, firms that do need precautionary balances tend to hold them as highly liquid marketable securities; such holdings accomplish the same purposes as cash balances while providing income in the form of interest received.

3. *Speculation.* Some cash balances may be held to enable the firm to take advantage of any bargain purchases that might arise; these are defined as *speculative balances.* However, as with precautionary balances, firms today are more likely to rely on reserve borrowing power and on marketable securities portfolios than on actual cash holdings for speculative purposes.

4. *Compensation to banks for providing loans and services.* This type of balance, defined as a *compensating balance,* is discussed in detail later in this chapter.

Although the actual cash balance can be thought of as consisting of transactions balances, speculative balances, precautionary balances, and compensating balances, we cannot calculate the amount needed for each type, add them together, and produce a total desired cash balance, because the same money serves all four purposes. Firms do, however, consider these four factors when establishing their target cash positions.

While there are good reasons for holding *adequate* cash balances, there is a strong reason for not holding *excessive* balances—cash is a nonearning asset, so excessive cash balances simply lower the total asset turnover, thereby reducing both the rate of return on net worth and the value of the stock. Thus, firms are very much interested in establishing procedures for increasing the efficiency of their cash management; if they can make their cash work harder, they can reduce cash balances.

The Cash Budget

The most important tool in cash management is the *cash budget,* a statement showing the firm's projected cash inflows and outflows over some specified period of time. Cash budgets can be constructed on a monthly, a weekly, or even a daily basis. Table 8–1 shows a monthly cash budget covering the last six months of 1979 for the Dayton Printing Company, a leading producer of greeting cards.

Table 8–1
Dayton Printing Company: Worksheet and Cash Budget (Thousands of Dollars)

	May	June	July	Aug.	Sept.	Oct.	Nov.	Dec.	Jan.
Worksheet									
Sales (net of cash discounts)	$5,000	$5,000	$10,000	$15,000	$20,000	$10,000	$10,000	$5,000	$5,000
Collections									
During month of sale (20%)	1,000	1,000	2,000	3,000	4,000	2,000	2,000	1,000	
During first month after sale (70%)		3,500	3,500	7,000	10,500	14,000	7,000	7,000	
During second month after sale (10%)			500	500	1,000	1,500	2,000	1,000	
Total collections	$1,000	$4,500	$6,000	$10,500	$15,500	$17,500	$11,000	$9,000	
Purchases (70% of next month's sales)	$3,500	$7,000	$10,500	$14,000	$7,000	$7,000	$3,500	$3,500	
Payments (one-month lag)		$3,500	$7,000	$10,500	$14,000	$7,000	$7,000	$3,500	
Cash Budget									
(1) Collections			$6,000	$10,500	$15,500	$17,500	$11,000	$9,000	
(2) Payments									
(3) Purchases			$7,000	$10,500	$14,000	$7,000	$7,000	$3,500	
(4) Wages and salaries			750	1,000	1,250	750	750	500	
(5) Rent			250	250	250	250	250	250	
(6) Other expenses			100	150	200	100	100	50	
(7) Taxes					2,000			2,000	
(8) Payment for plant construction						5,000			
(9) Total payments			$ 8,100	$11,900	$17,700	$13,100	$ 8,100	$6,300	
(10) Net cash gain (loss) during month (Line 1 – Line 9)			($ 2,100)	($ 1,400)	($ 2,200)	$ 4,400	$ 2,900	$2,700	
(11) Cash at start of month if no borrowing is done			3,000	900	($ 500)	(2,700)	1,700	4,600	
(12) Cumulative cash (= cash at start plus gains or minus losses) (Line 10 + Line 11)			$ 900	($ 500)	($ 2,700)	$ 1,700	$ 4,600	$7,300	
(13) Deduct target level of cash			2,500	2,500	2,500	2,500	2,500	2,500	
(14) Total loans outstanding to maintain $2,500 cash balance			$ 1,600	$ 3,000	$ 5,200	$ 800			
(15) Surplus cash							$ 2,100	$4,800	

Note: 1. The amount shown on Line 11 for the first month, the $3,000 balance on July 1, is given. The values shown for each of the following months on Line 11 represent the "cumulative cash" as shown on Line 12 for the preceding month.

2. When the target cash balance of $2,500 (Line 13) is deducted from the cumulative cash balance (Line 12), if a negative figure results, it is shown on Line 14 as a required loan, while if a positive figure results, it is shown on Line 15 as surplus cash.

Dayton's birthday and get-well cards are sold year-round, but the bulk of the company's sales occurs during September, when retailers are stocking up for Christmas. All sales are made on terms that allow a cash discount for payments made within twenty days; if the discount is not taken, the full amount must be paid in forty days. However, like most other companies, Dayton finds that some of its customers delay payment up to ninety days. Experience shows that on 20 percent of the sales, payment is made during the month in which the sale is made; on 70 percent of the sales, payment is made during the second month after the sale; and on 10 percent of the sales, payment is made during the third month.

Rather than produce at a uniform rate throughout the year, Dayton prints cards immediately before they are required for delivery. Paper, ink, and other materials amount to 70 percent of sales and are bought the month before the company expects to sell the finished product. Its own purchase terms permit Dayton to delay payment on its purchases for one month. Accordingly, if July sales are forecast at $10 million, then purchases during June will amount to $7 million, and this amount will actually be paid in July.

Such other cash expenditures as wages and rent are given in the lower part of Table 8–1. The company must also make tax payments of $2 million on September 15 and on December 15, while payment for a new plant must be made in October. Assuming the company needs to keep a minimum cash balance of $2.5 million at all times, and that it has $3 million on July 1, what are Dayton's financial requirements for the period July through December?

The monthly cash requirements are worked out in Table 8–1. The top half of the table provides a worksheet for calculating collections on sales and payments on purchases. The first line in the worksheet gives the sales forecast for the period May through January; May and June sales are necessary to determine collections for July and August. Next, cash collections are given. The first line of this section shows that 20 percent of the sales during any given month are collected that month. The second line shows the collections on the prior month's sales: 70 percent of sales in the preceding month. The third line gives collections from sales two months earlier: 10 percent of sales in that month. The collections are summed to find the total cash receipts from sales during each month under consideration.

With the worksheet completed, the cash budget itself can be constructed. Receipts from collections are given on the top line. Next, payments during each month are summarized. The difference between cash receipts and cash payments is the net cash gain or loss during the month; for July there is a net cash loss of $2.1 million. The initial cash on hand at the beginning of the month is added to the net cash gain or loss during the month to obtain the cumulative cash that would be on hand if no financing were done; at the end of July, Dayton would have cumulative cash totaling $900,000.

The cumulative cash is next subtracted from the target cash balance, $2.5 million, to determine the firm's borrowing requirements or surplus cash, whichever the case may be. In July, Dayton expects to have cumulative cash as shown on Line 12 of $900,000. It has a target cash balance of $2.5 million. Thus, to maintain the target cash balance it must borrow $1.6 million by the end of July. Assuming that this amount is indeed borrowed, loans outstanding will total $1.6 million at the end of July.

This same procedure is used in the following months. Sales will expand seasonally in August. With the increased sales will come increased payments for purchases, wages, and other items. Receipts from sales will go up too, but the firm will still be left with a $1.4 million cash outflow during the month. The total financial requirements at the end of August will be $3 million, the cumulative cash plus the target cash balance. The $3 million is also equal to the $1.6 million needed at the end of July plus the $1.4 million cash deficit for August. Thus, loans outstanding will total $3 million at the end of August.

Sales peak in September, and the cash deficit during this month will amount to another $2.2 million. The total borrowing requirements through September will increase to $5.2 million. Sales, purchases, and payments for past purchases will fall markedly in October; collections will be the highest of any month because they reflect the high September sales. As a result, Dayton will enjoy a healthy $4.4 million cash surplus during October. This surplus can be used to pay off borrowings, so loans outstanding will decline by $4.4 million, to $800,000.

Dayton will have another cash surplus in November, which will permit it to eliminate completely the need for borrowing. In fact, the company is expected to have $2.1 million in surplus cash by the month's end, while another cash surplus in December will swell the extra cash to $4.8 million. With such a large amount of unneeded funds, Dayton's treasurer will doubtless want to invest in interest-bearing securities or put the funds to use in some other way.

Before concluding our discussion of the cash budget, we should make five additional points: (1) Our cash budget does not reflect interest on loans or income from the investment of surplus cash. This refinement could be added quite easily. (2) More important, if cash inflows and outflows are not uniform during the month, we could be seriously understating or overstating our financing requirements. For example, if all payments must be made on the fifth of each month, but collections come in uniformly throughout the month, then we would need to borrow much larger amounts than those shown in Table 8–1. In such a case, we would need to prepare cash budgets on a daily basis. (3) Since depreciation is a noncash charge, depreciation does not appear on the cash budget. (4) The cash budget represents a forecast, so all the values in the table are *expected* values. If actual sales, purchases, and so on are different from the forecasted levels, then our forecasted cash deficits and surpluses will also be incorrect. (5) Finally, we should note that the target cash balance would probably be adjusted over time, rising and falling with seasonal patterns and with longer-term changes in the scale of the firm's operations. Factors that influence the target cash balance are discussed in the next section.

Other Procedures for Increasing the Efficiency of Cash Management

While a carefully prepared cash budget is a necessary starting point, there are other elements in a good cash management program. For example, the $2.5 million minimum cash balance in the preceding example could probably be reduced if Dayton could predict its inflows and outflows more precisely. Most firms do not know exactly when bills will come in or when payments will be received, and transactions balances must be sufficient to allow for a random increase in bills requiring payment at a time when receipts lag below expectations. Although we do not consider them in this book, statistical procedures are available to help improve cash flow forecasts, and the better the cash flow forecast, the lower the minimum cash balance.

Synchronizing Cash Inflows and Outflows If you, as an individual, were to receive income on a daily basis instead of once a month, you could operate with a lower average checking account balance. If you could arrange to pay rent, tuition, and other charges on a daily basis, this would further reduce your required average cash balances. Exactly the same situation holds for business firms—by arranging things so that their cash receipts coincide with the timing of their cash outflows, firms can hold their transactions balances to a minimum. Recognizing this point, utility companies, oil companies, and others arrange to bill customers and to pay their own bills on a regular schedule throughout the month. In our cash budgeting example, if Dayton Printing could arrange a better synchronization of its cash inflows and outflows, it might be able to reduce somewhat its minimum cash balance, and therefore its required bank loans.

Speeding Collections of Checks Received and Slowing Collections of Checks Written Another important aspect of cash management deals with processing the checks a company writes and receives. It is obviously inefficient to put checks received in a drawer and deposit them every week or so; no well-run business would follow such a practice. Similarly, cash balances are drawn down unnecessarily if bills are paid earlier than required. In fact, efficient firms go to great lengths to speed up the processing of incoming checks, thus putting the funds to work faster, and they try to stretch their own payments out as long as possible.

When a customer writes and mails a check, this *does not* mean that the funds are immediately available to the receiving firm. Most of us have deposited a check in our account and then been told that we cannot write our own checks against this deposit until the check clears. Our bank must

(1) make sure that the check we deposited is good and (2) receive funds itself before releasing funds for us to spend.

As shown on the left side of Figure 8–1, quite a bit of time may be required for a firm to process incoming checks and obtain the use of the money. A check must first be delivered through the mails, then cleared through the banking system, before the money can be put to use. Checks received from customers in distant cities are especially subject to delays. First, possible mail delays can obviously cause problems. Second, clearing checks can also delay the effective use of funds received. Assume, for example, that we receive a check and deposit it in our bank. Our bank must present the check to the bank on which it was drawn. Only when this latter bank transfers funds to our bank are they available for us to use. Checks are generally cleared through the Federal Reserve System or through a clearinghouse set up by the banks in a particular city. Of course, if the check is drawn on the bank of deposit, that bank merely transfers funds by bookkeeping entries from one of its depositors to another. The length of time required for other checks to clear is a function of the distance between the payer's and the payee's banks; in the case of private clearinghouses, it can range from one to three days. The maximum time required for checks to clear through the Federal Reserve System is two days.

The right side of Figure 8–1 shows how the process can be speeded up. First, to reduce mail and clearing delays, a *lockbox plan* can be used. Suppose a New York firm makes sales to customers all across the country. It can arrange to have its customers send payments to post office boxes (lockboxes) in their own local areas. A local bank will pick up the checks, have them cleared in the local area, and then transfer the funds by wire to the company's New York bank. In this way, collection time can be reduced by one to five days. Examples of freeing funds in the amount of $5 million or more by this method are not uncommon.

Just as expediting the collection process conserves cash, slowing down disbursements accomplishes the same thing by keeping cash on hand for longer periods. One obviously could simply delay payments, but this involves equally obvious difficulties. Firms have, in the past, devised rather ingenious methods for "legitimately" lengthening the collection period on their own checks, ranging from maintaining deposits in distant banks to using slow, awkward payment procedures. Since such practices are usually recognized for what they are, there are severe limits to their use.

The most widely publicized of these procedures in recent years is the use of drafts. While a check is payable on demand, a draft must be transmitted to the issuer, who approves it and deposits funds to cover it, after which it can be collected. AT&T has used drafts. In handling its payrolls, for instance, AT&T can pay an employee by draft on Friday. The employee cashes the draft at a local bank, which sends it on to AT&T's New York bank. It may be Wednesday or Thursday before the draft arrives. The bank then sends it to the company's accounting department, which has until 3 P.M. that day to

Figure 8–1
Diagram of the Check Clearing Process

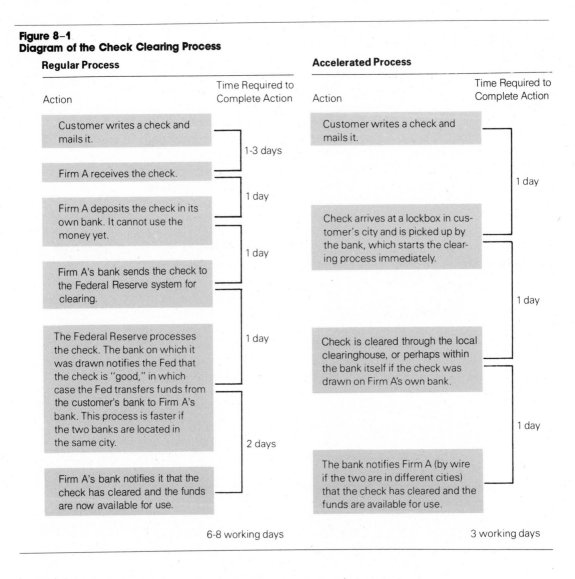

Regular Process

Action	Time Required to Complete Action
Customer writes a check and mails it.	1-3 days
Firm A receives the check.	
Firm A deposits the check in its own bank. It cannot use the money yet.	1 day
Firm A's bank sends the check to the Federal Reserve system for clearing.	1 day
The Federal Reserve processes the check. The bank on which it was drawn notifies the Fed that the check is "good," in which case the Fed transfers funds from the customer's bank to Firm A's bank. This process is faster if the two banks are located in the same city.	1 day
Firm A's bank notifies it that the check has cleared and the funds are now available for use.	2 days

6-8 working days

Accelerated Process

Action	Time Required to Complete Action
Customer writes a check and mails it.	1 day
Check arrives at a lockbox in customer's city and is picked up by the bank, which starts the clearing process immediately.	1 day
Check is cleared through the local clearinghouse, or perhaps within the bank itself if the check was drawn on Firm A's own bank.	1 day
The bank notifies Firm A (by wire if the two are in different cities) that the check has cleared and the funds are available for use.	

3 working days

inspect and approve it. Not until then does AT&T deposit funds in its bank to pay the draft. Many insurance companies also use drafts to pay claims.

Using Float Float is defined as the difference between the balance shown in a firm's (or an individual's) checkbook and the balance on the bank's books. Suppose a firm writes, on the average, checks in the amount of $5,000 each day. It takes about six days for these checks to clear and to be deducted from the firm's bank account. Thus, the firm's own checking records show a balance $30,000 smaller than the bank's records. If the firm receives checks in the amount of $5,000 daily but loses only four days while these checks are being deposited and cleared, its own books have a balance that is, because of this factor, $20,000 larger than the bank's balance. Thus the firm's net float—the difference between the $30,000 and the $20,000—is $10,000.

If a firm's own collection and clearing process is more efficient than that of the recipients of its checks—and this is generally true of larger, more efficient firms—then the firm could show a *negative* balance on its own records and a *positive* balance on the books of its bank. Some firms indicate that they *never* have true positive cash balances. One large manufacturer of construction equipment stated that, while its account according to its bank's records shows an average cash balance of about $2 million, its *actual* cash balance is *minus* $2 million; it has $4 million of net float. Obviously, the firm must be able to forecast its positive and negative clearings accurately in order to make such heavy use of float.

Matching the Costs and Benefits Associated with Cash Management

Although a number of procedures may be used to hold down cash balance requirements, implementing these procedures is not a costless operation. How far should a firm go in making its cash operations more efficient? As a general rule, the firm should incur these expenses so long as marginal returns exceed marginal expenses.

For example, suppose that by establishing a lockbox system and increasing the accuracy of cash inflow and outflow forecasts, a firm can reduce its investment in cash by $1 million without increasing the risk of running short of cash. Further, suppose the firm borrows at a cost of 12 percent. The steps taken have released $1 million, which can be used to reduce bank loans and thus save $120,000 per year. If the costs of the procedures necessary to release the $1 million are less than $120,000, the move is a good one; if the costs exceed $120,000, the greater efficiency is not worth the cost. It is clear that larger firms, with larger cash balances, can better afford to hire the personnel necessary to maintain tight control over their cash positions. Cash management is one element of business operations in which economies of scale are present.

Very clearly, the value of careful cash management depends upon the costs of funds invested in cash, which in turn depend upon the current rate of interest. In the late 1970s, with interest rates at historic highs, firms have been devoting more care than ever to cash management.

Compensating Balances

Earlier in the chapter we listed compensating balance requirements as one of the major determinants of cash balances. Banks provide services to firms—they clear checks, operate lockbox plans, supply credit information, and the like. These services cost the bank money, so the bank must be compensated for rendering them.

Banks earn most of their income by lending money at interest, and most of the funds they lend are obtained in the form of deposits. If a firm maintains a deposit account with an average balance of $100,000, and if the bank can lend these funds at a net return of $8,000, then the account is, in a sense, worth $8,000 to the bank. Thus, it is to the bank's advantage to provide services worth up to $8,000 to attract and hold the account.

Banks determine first the costs of the services rendered to their larger customers and then the average account balances necessary to provide enough income to compensate for these costs. Firms often maintain these compensating balances in order to avoid paying cash service charges to the bank.[2]

Compensating balances are also required by some bank loan agreements. During periods when the supply of credit is restricted and interest rates are high, banks frequently insist that borrowers maintain accounts that average some percentage of the loan amount as a condition for granting the loan; 15 percent is a typical figure. If the balance is larger than the firm would otherwise maintain, then the effective cost of the loan is increased; the excess balance presumably "compensates" the bank for making a loan at a rate below what it could earn on the funds if they were invested elsewhere.[3]

Compensating balances can be established (1) as an *absolute minimum,* say $100,000, below which the actual balance must never fall, or (2) as a *minimum average balance,* perhaps $100,000, over some period, generally a month. The absolute minimum is a much more restrictive requirement, because the total amount of cash held during the month must be above $100,000 by the amount of the transactions balances. The $100,000 in this case is "dead money" from the firm's standpoint. The minimum average balance, however, could fall to zero one day provided it was $200,000 some other day, with the average working out to $100,000. Thus, the $100,000 in this case is available for transactions.

Statistics on compensating balance requirements are not available, but average balances are typical and absolute minimums rare for business accounts. Discussions with bankers, however, indicate that absolute balance requirements are less rare during times of extremely tight money such as prevailed during 1979.

Overdraft Systems

Most countries outside the United States use *overdraft systems.* In such systems depositors write checks in excess of their actual balances, and the bank automatically extends loans to cover the shortages. The maximum amount of such loans must, of course, be established beforehand. Although

---

2 Compensating balance arrangements apply to individuals as well as to business firms. Thus, you might get "free" checking services if you maintain a minimum balance of $200, but be charged 10 cents per check if your balance falls below $200 during the month.

3 The interest rate effect of compensating balances is discussed further in Chapter 10.

statistics are not available on the usage of overdrafts in the United States, a number of firms have worked out informal, and in some cases formal, overdraft arrangements. (Also, both banks and credit card companies regularly establish "cash reserve" systems for individuals.) Thus, the use of overdrafts has been increasing in recent years, and if this trend continues, we can anticipate a further reduction of cash balances.

Establishing the Target Cash Balance

The firm's target cash balance is set as the larger of (1) its transactions balances plus precautionary balances or (2) its required compensating balances. Both the transactions balances and the precautionary balances depend upon the volume of business the firm does, the degree of uncertainty inherent in its forecasts of cash inflows and outflows, and its ability to borrow on short notice to meet cash shortfalls. Consider again the cash budget shown for Dayton Printing in Table 8–1. The target cash balance (or desired cash balance) is shown on Line 13 of the table. Other things held constant, the target cash balance would increase if Dayton expanded or decrease if Dayton contracted. Similarly, Dayton could afford to operate with a smaller target balance if it were more certain that inflows would come in as scheduled and that no unanticipated outflows such as those resulting from uninsured fire losses, lawsuits, and the like would occur. The higher the cash balance, the smaller the probability that reduced inflows or unexpected outflows will cause the firm to actually run out of cash.

Statistics are not available on whether transactions and precautionary balances or compensating balances actually control most firms' target cash balances, but compensating balance requirements do often dominate, especially during periods of high interest rates and tight money.[4]

Cash Management in the Multidivisional Firm

The concepts, techniques, and procedures described thus far in the chapter must be extended when applied to large, national firms. Such corporations have plants and sales offices all across the nation (or the world), and they deal with banks in all of their operating territories. These companies must maintain the required compensating balances in each of their banks, and

---

4 This point is underscored by an incident that occurred at a professional finance meeting. A professor presented a scholarly paper that used operations research techniques to determine "optimal cash balances" for a sample of firms. He then reported that actual cash balances of the firms greatly exceed "optimal" balances, suggesting inefficiency and the need for more refined techniques. The discussant of the paper made her comments short and sweet. She reported that she wrote and asked the sample firms why they had so much cash; they uniformly replied that their cash holdings were set by compensating balance requirements. The model was useful to determine the optimal cash balance in the absence of compensating balance requirements, but it was precisely those requirements that determined actual balances. Since the model did not include compensating balances as a determinant of cash balances, its usefulness is questionable.

they must be sure that no bank account becomes overdrawn. Cash inflows and outflows are subject to random fluctuations, so, in the absence of close control and coordination, there would be a tendency for some accounts to have shortages while excess balances existed in others. Thus, a sound cash management program for such a multibank corporation necessarily includes provisions for keeping strict account of the level of funds in each account and for shifting funds between accounts so as to minimize the total corporate cash balance. Mathematical models and electronic connections between a central computer and each branch location have been developed to help with such situations, but a discussion of these topics would go beyond the scope of this book.

MARKETABLE SECURITIES

Sizable holdings of such short-term marketable securities as U.S. Treasury bills (T-bills) or bank certificates of deposit (CDs) are often reported on financial statements. The reasons for such holdings, as well as the factors that influence the choice of securities held, are discussed in this section.

Reasons for Holding Marketable Securities

Marketable securities typically provide much lower yields than firms' operating assets; for example, International Business Machines (IBM) recently held a multibillion dollar portfolio of marketable securities that yielded about 8 percent, while its operating assets provided a return of about 18 percent. Why would a company such as IBM have such large holdings of low-yielding assets? There are two basic reasons for these holdings: first, they serve as a substitute for cash balances, and, second, they are used as a temporary investment. These points are considered below.

Marketable Securities as a Substitute for Cash Some firms hold portfolios of marketable securities in lieu of larger cash balances, liquidating part of the portfolio to increase the cash account when cash outflows exceed inflows. In such situations, the marketable securities could be a substitute for transactions balances, precautionary balances, speculative balances, or all three. In most cases, the securities are held primarily for precautionary purposes—most firms prefer to rely on bank credit to meet temporary transactions or speculative needs, but to hold some liquid assets to guard against a possible shortage of bank credit.

At the end of 1976, IBM had approximately $6 billion in marketable securities. This large liquid balance had been built up as a reserve for possible damage payments resulting from pending antitrust suits. When it became clear that IBM would win most of the suits, the liquidity need declined, and the company spent some of the funds on other assets, including repurchases of its own stock. This is a prime example of a firm's building up its precautionary balances to handle possible emergencies.

Marketable Securities Held as a Temporary Investment Whenever a firm has over 1 or 2 percent of its total assets invested in marketable securities, chances are good that these funds represent a strictly temporary investment. Such temporary investments generally occur in one of the three situations described below:

1. *When the firm must finance seasonal or cyclical operations.* Firms engaged in seasonal operations frequently have surplus cash flows during part of the year, deficit cash flows during other months. Such firms may purchase marketable securities during their surplus periods, then liquidate them when cash deficits occur. Other firms, particularly in capital goods industries, where fluctuations are violent, attempt to accumulate cash or near-cash securities during downturns in order to be ready to finance increases in assets when business returns to normal.
2. *When the firm must meet some known financial requirements.* If a major plant construction program is planned for the near future, or if a bond issue is about to mature, a firm may build up its marketable securities portfolio to provide the required funds. Furthermore, marketable securities holdings are frequently large immediately preceding quarterly corporate tax payment dates.
3. *When the firm has just sold long-term securities.* An expanding firm has to sell long-term securities (stocks or bonds) periodically. The funds from such sales can be invested in marketable securities, which can, in turn, be sold to provide funds as they are needed for permanent investments in operating assets.

Strategies Regarding Marketable Securities Holdings

Actually, each of the needs listed above can be met either by short-term loans or by holding marketable securities. Consider a firm such as Dayton Printing Company, which we discussed above, whose sales are growing over time but are fluctuating on a seasonal basis. As we saw from Dayton's cash budget (Table 8–1), the firm plans to borrow to meet seasonal needs. As an alternative financial strategy, Dayton could hold a portfolio of marketable securities, then liquidate these securities to meet its peak cash needs.

Figure 8–2 illustrates three alternative strategies for a firm such as Dayton. Under Plan A, Dayton would hold no marketable securities, relying

Figure 8–2
Alternative Strategies for Meeting Seasonal
Cash Needs

Plan A: Hold Zero
Marketable Securities

Plan B: Meet All
Seasonal Needs by Sale of
Marketable Securities

Plan C: Compromise—
Hold Some Marketable
Securities

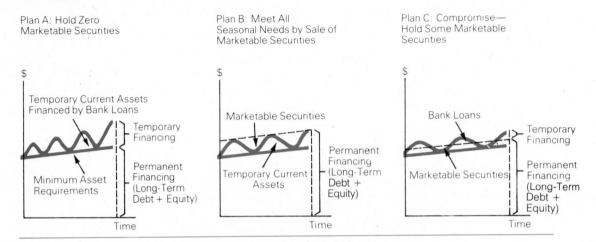

completely on bank loans to meet seasonal peaks. Under Plan B, Dayton
would stockpile marketable securities during slack periods, then sell these
securities to raise funds for peak needs. Plan C is a compromise; under this
alternative, the company would hold some securities, but not enough to
meet all of its peak needs. Dayton actually follows Plan C.

There are advantages and disadvantages to each of these strategies. Plan
A is clearly the most risky—the firm's current ratio is always lower than
under the other plans, indicating that it might encounter difficulties either in
borrowing the funds needed or in repaying the loan. On the other hand,
Plan A requires no holdings of low-yielding marketable securities, and this
will probably lead to a relatively high expected rate of return on both total
assets and net worth.

Exactly the same types of choices are involved with regard to meeting
such other known financial needs as plant construction, as well as in
deciding to issue long-term securities before or after the actual need for the
funds. Consolidated Edison, the electric utility serving New York City, can be
used to illustrate the issues involved in timing the sale of long-term
securities. Con Ed has a permanent, ongoing construction program,
generating a continuous need for new outside capital. As we shall see in
Chapters 13 and 14, there are substantial fixed costs involved in stock or
bond flotations, so these securities are issued infrequently and in large
amounts.

During the 1960s, Con Ed followed the practice of selling bonds and stock
before the capital was needed, investing the proceeds in marketable
securities, and then liquidating the securities to finance plant construction.
Plan A in Figure 8–3 illustrates this procedure.

Figure 8–3
Alternative Methods of Financing a Continuous
Construction Program

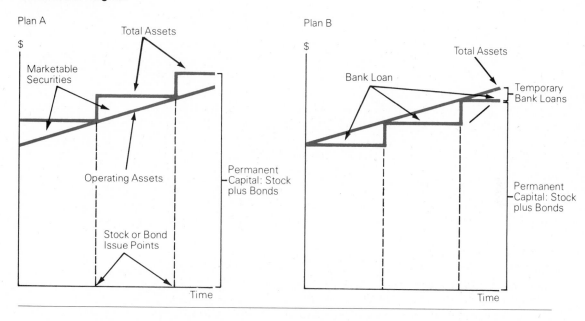

During the 1970s Con Ed encountered severe financial problems. It was forced to use up its liquid assets and to switch to its present policy of financing plant construction with short-term bank loans, then selling long-term securities to retire these loans when they have built up to some target level. This policy is illustrated by Plan B of Figure 8–3.

Plan A is the more conservative, less risky one. First, the company is minimizing its liquidity problems because it has no short-term debt hanging over its head. Second, it is sure of having the funds available to meet construction payments as they come due. On the other hand, firms generally have to pay higher interest rates when they borrow than the return they receive on marketable securities, so following the less risky strategy does have a cost. Again, we are faced with a risk-return tradeoff.

It is difficult to "prove" that one strategy is better than another. In principle, the practice of holding marketable securities reduces the expected rate of return, but it also reduces k_s, the required rate of return on the firm's stock. Although we can quantify the costs of following more conservative policies—this cost is the average percentage differential between the return received on marketable securities and the interest rate paid on the long-term debt—it is almost impossible to quantify the benefits of such a policy in terms of how much it reduces risk and how this risk reduction affects k_s. Accordingly, the basic policies with regard to securities holdings are generally set either on the basis of judgment or, as in the case of Con Ed, by circumstances beyond the company's control.

Factors Influencing the Choice of Securities

A wide variety of securities, differing in terms of default risk, interest risk, liquidity risk, and expected rate of return, are available. In this section, we first consider the characteristics of different securities, then show how the financial manager selects the specific instruments held in the marketable securities portfolio. These same characteristics are, incidentally, as important for individuals' investment decisions as for businesses' decisions.

Default Risk The risk that an issuer will be unable to make interest payments, or to repay the principal amount on schedule, is known as *default risk.* If the issuer is the U.S. Treasury, the default risk is negligible; thus, Treasury securities are regarded as being default-free. (Treasury securities are not completely free of risk; as we saw in Chapter 4, U.S. government bonds are subject to risk due to interest rate fluctuations, and they are also subject to loss of purchasing power due to inflation.) Corporate securities and bonds issued by state and local governments are subject to some degree of default risk. Several organizations (for example, Moody's Investment Services and Standard & Poor Corporation) "rate" bonds. They classify them on a scale from very high quality to highly speculative with a definite chance of going into default.[5] Ratings change from time to time. Thus, Penn Central's securities were given high ratings at one time, but the ratings were lowered as the company's financial position deteriorated.

Interest Rate Risk We saw in Chapter 4 that bond prices vary with changes in interest rates. Further, the prices of long-term bonds are much more sensitive to shifts in interest rates than are prices of short-term securities. Thus, if Dayton's treasurer purchased at par $1 million of twenty-five year U.S. Government bonds paying 5 percent interest, and interest rates rose to 9 percent, the market value of the bonds would fall from $1 million to approximately $607,000—a loss of about 40 percent. Had ninety day Treasury bills been held, the capital loss resulting from the change in interest rates would have been negligible.

Purchasing Power Risk Another type of risk is *purchasing power risk,* or the risk that inflation will reduce the purchasing power of a given sum of money. Purchasing power risk, which is important both to firms and to individual investors during times of inflation, is generally regarded to be lower on assets whose returns can be expected to rise during inflation than

5 Bond ratings are discussed in detail in Chapter 13.

on assets whose returns are fixed. Thus, real estate and common stocks are thought of as being better "hedges against inflation" than are bonds and other fixed income securities.

Liquidity (or Marketability) Risk An asset that can be sold on short notice for close to its quoted market price is defined as being highly liquid. If Dayton purchases $1 million of infrequently traded bonds of a relatively obscure company such as Bigham Pork Products, it will probably have to accept a price reduction to sell the bonds on short notice. On the other hand, if Dayton buys $1 million worth of U.S. Treasury bonds, or bonds issued by AT&T, General Motors, or Exxon, it will be able to dispose of them almost instantaneously at close to the quoted market price. These latter bonds are said to have very little *liquidity risk.*

Returns on Securities As we know from our earlier study of the security market line, the higher a security's risk, the higher the required return on the security. Thus corporate treasurers, like other investors, must make a tradeoff between risk and return when choosing investments for their marketable securities portfolios. Since the liquidity portfolio is generally held for a specific known need, or else for use in emergencies, the firm might be financially embarrassed should the portfolio decline in value. Further, most nonfinancial corporations do not have investment departments specializing in appraising securities and determining the probability of their going into default. Accordingly, the marketable securities portfolio is generally confined to highly liquid, short-term securities issued by either the U.S. government or the very strongest corporations. Given the purpose of the securities portfolio, treasurers are unwilling to sacrifice safety for higher rates of return.

The Term Structure of Interest Rates

To manage the marketable securities portfolio properly, and also to make proper decisions regarding how to finance asset acquisitions, it is important to have a good understanding of the relationship between the interest rates on long-term and short-term securities. In Chapter 4 we saw that long-term bonds are exposed to greater risks from changing interest rates than are short-term securities. Further, it seems natural to expect the risk of default to be higher on long-term than on short-term debt. For both these reasons we would expect to find higher risks, hence higher returns, on long-term than on short-term bonds. In fact, this condition does generally hold, but at times short-term securities provide higher yields than long-term bonds. In May 1979, for example, ninety day U.S. Treasury bills yielded 9.9 percent versus a yield of only 9.0 percent on long-term Treasury bonds.

The relationship between yields and maturities is called the *term structure of interest rates,* and graphs of this relationship are defined as *yield curves.*

Different yield curves exist at different points in time. The curves for Treasury securities in June 1977 and in May 1979 are shown in Figure 8–4.[6]

Figure 8–4
Yield Curves for U.S. Treasury Securities in 1977 and 1979

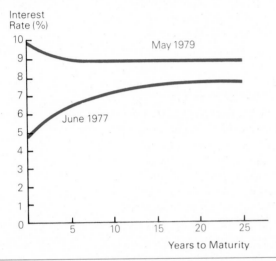

Note: These yield curves show the interest rate at a given date for U.S. Treasury securities of different maturities. Thus, on June 10, 1977, 30 day U.S. Treasury bills yielded 4.81 percent, one year certificates yielded 5.7 percent, five year notes yielded 6.8 percent, and so on. When the yield curve is upward sloping, investors obtain higher yields on bonds with long maturities, and conversely if the yield curve is sloping downward.

Whether long-term yields are above or below short-term yields (that is, whether the yield curve slopes up or down) depends on three factors: (1) risk preferences, (2) supply and demand conditions in long-term versus short-term markets, and (3) expectations about future interest rates. The effects of these three factors are explained below.

Risk Preferences It was noted above that long-term bond prices are especially sensitive to changes in interest rates, and that chances of default are higher on long-term than on short-term securities. Therefore, if long-term and short-term securities had identical yields, lenders would prefer to hold short-term issues. People holding long-term bonds would sell them to buy short-term bonds, and this would drive short-term prices up and yields

---

6 A yield curve is applicable only to securities of a given risk class. Figure 8–4 relates to default-free U.S. Treasury securities. If yield curves for the debt of A-rated corporations in June 1977 and May 1979 were also plotted on Figure 8–4, they would have shapes similar to the curves shown in the graph, but they would be higher, denoting a higher interest rate for every maturity.

down, and conversely for long-term bonds. Accordingly, lender pressure would cause short-term rates to be relatively low, long-term rates to be relatively high, and the yield curve to slope upward, other things held constant.

At the same time, borrowers generally prefer to issue long-term bonds, because then they will not have to worry about interest rates rising or about having to renew their loans frequently. Accordingly, borrowers are willing to pay more for long-term than for short-term credit, and this too causes the yield curve to slope upward. *Thus, both lenders' and borrowers' preferences tend to produce relatively low rates on short-term securities, high rates on long-term bonds, and an upward sloping yield curve.*

Supply-Demand Conditions Short-term debt capital is supplied by banks, while long-term debt is supplied mostly by pension funds and life insurance companies. At the same time, certain types of borrowers (home purchasers, as well as utilities, hospitals, and other organizations that have heavy fixed asset investments) are primarily interested in borrowing on a long-term basis, while other borrowers (individuals seeking consumer credit and business firms borrowing to finance inventories) are mainly interested in short-term credit. This suggests that the capital markets are *segmented.* Accordingly, if at a particular point in time demand is heavier in the short-term market, while capital is in more ample supply in the long-term market, this will tend to produce high short-term and low long-term rates, and a downward-sloping yield curve. At other times the situation could be reversed, with market supply-demand conditions leading to an upward sloping curve. Thus, supply-demand conditions, coupled with market segmentation, can produce either upward or downward sloping yield curves.

Expectations about Future Interest Rates The third factor affecting the yield curve is expectations about future interest rates. Suppose the yield curve is flat, or horizontal, with long- and short-term bonds providing identical yields—say, 8 percent. Now new statistics are reported, indicating an increase in the rate of inflation. You and everyone else think that the Federal Reserve will take action to combat inflation, and that this will result in higher future interest rates. If you had $1 million to invest, would you rather buy 8 percent, twenty year bonds or 8 percent bonds maturing in one month? Suppose you bought the twenty year bonds and interest rates rose to 10 percent. The value of the bonds would fall to $829,690.[7] Thus, you would incur a capital loss of $170,310 if you sold the bonds. If you did not sell, you would incur an opportunity loss of 2 percent, or $20,000, per year (with a present value of $170,310) by buying 8 percent bonds now rather than waiting until next month and buying 10 percent bonds.

---

7 Each bond originally sold at its $1,000 par value. The bond would fall in price to $80 (PVIFA 10%, 20 years) + $1,000 (PVIF 10%, 20 years) = $80 (8.5136) + $1,000 (0.1486) = $829.69. This assumes annual compounding.

On the other hand, if you invested the $1 million in the short-term bonds, you would earn 8 percent for one month, then still have the full $1 million to invest in bonds that would then yield 10 percent. Therefore, if interest rates were expected to rise, you and all other lenders would rather invest in short-term than in long-term bonds, as long as rates were the same on both types of bonds. Borrowers, meantime, would react in the opposite direction—they would want to borrow at 8 percent on a long-term basis to avoid paying the higher rates when they "rolled over," or renewed, their short-term loans. Thus, both lender and borrower pressures would rapidly produce a rising yield curve. *In general, other things held constant, the yield curve will be upward sloping if future rates are expected to rise, downward sloping if future rates are expected to fall, and flat if investors have no strong feelings about future changes in interest rates.*

You may also think of long-term rates as being an average (strictly speaking, a geometric average) of expected future short-term rates. For example, if the one year bill rate is 5 percent today, is expected to rise to 6 percent next year, and then is expected to go to 7 percent the following year, then the rate on three year bonds should be 6 percent—an investor could expect a 6 percent return by buying either a three year bond or a series of one year bills.

Empirical studies suggest that all three explanations of the slope of the yield curve—liquidity preference, market segmentation, and interest rate expectations—are valid, but at any given time one or the other factor dominates to actually determine the shape of the curve. Financial managers, and investors in general, must consider all three factors whenever they attempt to forecast future interest rates.

Securities Available for Investment of Surplus Cash

Table 8–2 provides a listing of the major types of investment securities available for investments, with yields as of June 10, 1977, and May 25, 1979. Depending on how long they will be held, the financial manager decides upon a suitable maturity pattern for the firm's holdings. Because their characteristics change with shifts in financial market conditions, it would be misleading to attempt to give detailed descriptions here.

SUMMARY

The first topic covered in this chapter was *cash management.* We saw that the key element in any cash management system is the *cash budget,* which is a forecast of cash inflows and outflows during a given planning period. The cash budget shows whether the firm can expect a cash deficit, in which case plans must be

Table 8–2
Securities Available for Investment
of Surplus Cash[a]

Type of Security	Typical Maturity at Time of Issue	Approximate Yields	
		June 10, 1977	May 25, 1979
U.S. Treasury bills	91 days–1 year	4.8%	9.9%
U.S. Treasury notes	3–5 years	6.8	9.1
U.S. Treasury bonds	Up to 20 years	7.6	9.0
Commercial paper[b]	Varies; up to 270 days	5.5	10.1
Negotiable certificates of deposit with U.S. banks (CDs)	1 year	6.0	9.9
Money market mutual funds[c]	Instant liquidity	5.1	9.8
Eurodollar bank time deposits	Varies; up to 6 months	6.1	10.7
Bonds of other corporations[d]	Varies; up to 30 years	8.2	9.7
State and local government bonds[e]	Varies; up to 30 years	5.7	7.5
Stocks of other corporations	Unlimited	Variable	Variable
Stock of the firm in question (treasury stock)	Unlimited	Variable	Variable

[a]U.S. agency notes and bonds are also available. These securities yield slightly more than U.S. Treasury securities. For example, on June 10, 1977, long-term agency bonds yielded about 7.8 percent versus 7.6 percent for Treasury bonds.

[b]Short-term notes issued by the strongest corporations. These securities are discussed further in Chapter 10.

[c]*Money market mutual funds* are mutual funds that hold only short-term securities such as treasury bills, CDs, and commercial paper. These funds provide instant liquidity, are safe, and are free from risk due to fluctuations in interest rates. They became popular in 1973, especially for individuals and smaller firms.

[d]The rate shown here is for Aaa bonds. Yields are higher on more risky corporate bonds.

[e]The yield shown here is for Aaa long-term municipal bonds. Interest on these bonds is exempt from federal income taxes; thus, the 1977 before-tax equivalent yield on a taxable bond for a taxpayer in the 50 percent bracket was 11.4 percent. (Before-tax equivalent yield = tax-free rate $\div$ (1 $-$ tax rate) = 5.7% $\div$ 0.5 = 11.4%.)

made to obtain external capital, or a cash surplus, in which case plans should be made to invest the available funds. We also discussed ways of speeding up cash flows by the use of *lockboxes,* what *float* is and how it can be used to hold down bank loans, and *compensating balances.*

Our study of marketable securities began with a discussion of why securities are held—primarily, they are held (1) as a reserve for future contingencies, (2) to meet seasonal needs, with holdings being built up during the slack season and then liquidated when cash requirements are high, (3) to meet known future cash requirements such as construction progress payments or taxes, and (4) immediately after the sale of long-term securities. Given the motives for holding them, treasurers generally do not want to gamble by holding risky securities— safety is the watchword, and rarely will a treasurer sacrifice safety for the higher yields offered on risky securities.

The final topic covered was the *term structure of interest rates,* or the relationship between securities' yields and maturities. Generally, short-term securities offer lower yields than long-term securities, but this is not always the case—if the current level of rates is high by historic standards and is expected to fall, then short rates may be higher than long rates.

Questions

8-1 What are the four principal reasons for holding cash? Can a firm estimate its target cash balance by summing the cash held to satisfy each of the four?

8-2 Explain how each of the following factors would probably affect a firm's target cash balance if all other factors are held constant.

   a. The firm institutes a new billing procedure which better synchronizes its cash inflows and outflows.

   b. The firm develops a new sales forecasting technique which improves its forecasts.

   c. The firm reduces its portfolio of U.S. Treasury bills.

   d. The firm arranges to use an overdraft system for its checking account.

   e. The firm borrows a large amount of money from its bank, and it also begins to write far more checks than it did in the past.

   f. Interest rates on Treasury bills rise from 5 percent to 10 percent.

8-3 In the cash budget shown in Table 8–1, is the projected maximum funds requirement of $5.2 million in September known with certainty, or should it be regarded as the expected value of a probability distribution? Consider how this peak would probably be affected by each of the following:

   a. A lengthening of the average collection period.

   b. An unanticipated decline in sales that occurred when sales were supposed to peak.

   c. A sharp drop in sales prices required to meet competition.

   d. A sharp increase in interest rates for a firm with a large amount of short-term debt outstanding.

8-4 Would a lockbox plan make more sense for a firm that makes sales all over the United States or for a firm with the same volume of business but concentrated in one city?

8-5 The yield curves shown in Figure 8–4 were constructed with data on the three U.S. Treasury securities shown in Table 8–2. In a recent *Wall Street Journal,* find yields on these same three types of securities today, and draw a third yield curve on Figure 8–4. Has the slope of the curve changed? Does its position indicate that most rates have risen or fallen?

8-6 What does the term *liquidity* mean? Which would be more important to a firm that held a portfolio of marketable securities as precautionary balances against the possibility of losing a major lawsuit—liquidity or rate of return? Explain.

8-7 Firm A's management is very conservative, while Firm B's managers are more aggressive. Is it true that, other things the same, Firm B would probably have larger holdings of marketable securities? Explain.

8-8 Is it true that *interest rate risk* refers to the risk that a firm will be unable to pay the interest on its bonds? Explain.

8-9 The curve describing the relationship between interest rates and term to maturity is known as the _____ curve. Other things held constant, how would each of the following factors affect the slope and the general position of this curve? Indicate by a (+) if it would lead to an increase in the curve, a (−) if it would cause the curve to shift downward, or a (0) if it would have no effect or an indeterminant effect on the slope or position of the curve.

	Effect on the Yield Curve	
	Slope	Position
a. Investors perceive the risk of default to increase on securities with longer maturities; that is, they become increasingly uncertain about the more distant future.	_____	_____
b. Future interest rates are expected to fall.	_____	_____
c. The Federal Reserve pumps a large amount of money into the banking system.	_____	_____
d. Business firms begin a massive inventory buildup.	_____	_____
e. An inexpensive method of harnessing solar power is developed; this development leads to a decline in the expected rate of inflation.	_____	_____

8-10 Corporate treasurers, when selecting securities for portfolio investments, must make a tradeoff between higher risk and higher returns. Is it true that most treasurers are willing to assume a fairly high exposure to risk to gain higher expected returns?

8-11 Assume that the yield curve is horizontal. Now you and other investors receive information that suggests the economy is headed into a recession. You and most other investors think that the Fed will soon relax credit and that this will lead to a decline in short-term interest rates. Over the long run (the next five, ten, or fifteen years) people expect a fairly high rate of inflation, and they expect that this will keep long-term rates fairly high. Explain what all of this will probably do to the yield curve. Use a graph to illustrate your answer.

Problems

8-1 The Edgar Products Company is setting up a new bank account with the First National Bank. Edgar plans to issue checks in the amount of $1 million each day and to deduct them from its own records at the close of business on the day they are written. On average, the bank will receive and clear (that is, deduct from the firm's bank balance) the checks at 5 P.M. the fourth day after they are written; for example, a check written on Monday will be cleared on Friday afternoon. The firm's agreement with the bank requires it to maintain a $750,000 average compensating balance; this is $250,000 greater than the cash balance the firm would otherwise have on deposit; that is, without the compensating balance, it would carry an average of $500,000.

a. Assuming that the firm makes deposits at 4 P.M. each day (and the bank includes the deposit in that day's transactions), how much must the firm deposit each day to maintain a sufficient balance on the day it opens the account, during the first four days after it opens the account, and once it reaches a "steady state"?

b. What ending daily balance should the firm try to maintain (1) on the bank's records and (2) on its own records?

c. Explain how net float can help increase the value of the firm's common stock.

8-2 Ed and Edna Starr recently leased space in the Southside Mall and opened a new business, Starr Jewelry, Inc. Business has been good, but the Starrs have frequently run out of cash. This has necessitated late payment on certain orders, and this, in turn, is beginning to cause a problem with suppliers. The Starrs plan to borrow from the bank to have cash ready as needed, but first they need a forecast of just how much they must borrow. Accordingly, they have asked you to prepare a cash budget for the critical period around Christmas, when needs will be especially high.

Sales are made on a *cash basis only*. Purchases must be paid for the following month. The Starrs pay themselves a salary of $1,200 per month, and the rent is $500 per month. In addition, the Starrs must make a property tax payment of $3,000 in December. The current cash on hand (on December 1) is $100, but the Starrs have agreed to maintain an average bank balance of $1,500—this is their target cash balance. (Disregard till cash, which is insignificant because everybody pays by check or credit card.)

The estimated sales and purchases for December, January, and February are shown below. Purchases during November amounted to $35,000.

	Sales	Purchases
December	$40,000	$10,000
January	10,000	10,000
February	15,000	10,000

a. Prepare a cash budget for December, January, and February.

b. Now suppose the Starrs were to start selling on a credit basis on December 1, giving customers thirty days to pay. All customers accept these terms, and all other facts in the problem are unchanged. What would the company's loan requirements be at the end of December in this case? (*Hint:* The calculations required to answer this question are minimal.)

8-3 The Addison Company is planning to request a line of credit from its bank.[8] The following sales forecasts have been made for 1980 and 1981:

May 1980	$ 750,000
June	750,000
July	1,500,000
August	2,250,000
September	3,000,000
October	1,500,000
November	1,500,000
December	375,000
January 1981	750,000

Collection estimates were obtained from the credit and collection department as follows: collected within the month of sale, 5 percent; collected the month following the sale, 80 percent; collected the second month following the sale, 15 percent. Payments for labor and raw materials are typically made during the month following the month in which these costs are incurred. Total labor and raw materials costs are estimated for each month as follows (payments are made the following month):

May 1980	$ 375,000
June	375,000
July	525,000
August	3,675,000
September	1,275,000
October	975,000
November	675,000
December	375,000

General and administrative salaries will amount to approximately $112,500 a month; lease payments under long-term lease contracts will be $37,500 a month; depreciation charges are $150,000 a month; miscellaneous expenses will be $11,500 a month; income tax payments of $262,500 will be due in both September and December; and a progress payment of $750,000 on a new research laboratory must be paid in October. Cash on hand on July 1 will amount to $550,000, and a minimum cash balance of $375,000 should be maintained throughout the cash budget period.

a. Prepare a monthly cash budget for the last six months of 1980.

b. Prepare an estimate of required financing (or excess funds) for each month during the period, that is, the amount of money that the Addison

8 A line of credit is an agreement that the bank will lend a specified sum of money to the company during a stated time period. Lines of credit are discussed extensively in Chapter 10. Also, note that this problem is adapted from *Cases in Managerial Finance,* 2d ed., Case 5.

Company will need to borrow (or will have available to invest) each month.

c. Suppose receipts from sales come in uniformly during the month; that is, cash payments come in 1/30th each day, but all outflows are paid on the fifth of the month. Would this have an effect on the cash budget; that is, would the cash budget you have prepared be valid under these assumptions? If not, what could be done to make a valid estimation of financing requirements?

d. Addison produces on a seasonal basis, just ahead of sales. Without making any calculations, discuss how the company's current ratio and debt ratio would vary during the year, assuming all financial requirements are met by short-term bank loans. Could changes in these ratios affect the firm's ability to obtain bank credit?

e. Now suppose a recession occurs, and sales fall below the forecast, or budgeted, levels. However, the firm continues production according to the indicated plans. Also, because of the recession, customers delay payments, so the lag between sales and collections lengthens. What would all this do to the realized cash surpluses and deficits, and to the external funds requirements?

f. If you prepared the cash budget in Part a correctly, you show a surplus of $426,000 at the end of July. Suggest some alternative investments for this money. Be sure to consider long-term bonds versus short-term debt instruments, and the appropriateness of investing in common stock.

g. Would your choice of securities in Part f be affected if the cash budget showed continuous cash surpluses versus alternating surpluses and deficits?

8-4 Suppose the interest rate on one year Treasury bills purchased today (1/1/80) is 12 percent. You and other investors anticipate that a recession is on the horizon and that the T-bill rate will fall to 10 percent next year (1/1/81) and to 8 percent the following year (1/1/82). Your best guess as to T-bill rates from 1/1/83 on is 9 percent, which is based on an expected long-term inflation rate of 7 percent and a 2 percent real risk-free interest rate. Assuming that the expectations theory holds exactly, what is the approximate equilibrium interest rate for (1) five year Treasury bonds and (2) ten year Treasury bonds?

9 ACCOUNTS RECEIVABLE AND INVENTORIES

In the last chapter we examined the firm's investment in cash and marketable securities. To complete our analysis of current assets, we now turn to accounts receivable and inventories. In 1979, the typical manufacturing firm had approximately 21 percent of its total assets invested in receivables, and another 21 percent in inventories. With such a large percentage of its funds tied up in these two accounts, the effectiveness with which they are managed is obviously important to a firm's profitability and risk, and thus to its stock price.

ACCOUNTS RECEIVABLE

Most firms sell on credit. When goods are shipped, inventories are reduced, and an *account receivable* is created.[1] Eventually, the customer will pay the account, at which time receivables will decline and cash will increase.

The total amount of accounts receivable outstanding at any given time is determined by two factors: (a) the volume of credit sales and (b) the average length of time between sales and collections. For example, suppose someone opens a store on January 1 and, starting the first day, makes sales of $100 each day. Customers are given ten days in which to pay. At the end of the first day, accounts receivable will be $100; they will rise to $200 by the end of the second day; and by January 10, they will have risen to 10 × $100 = $1,000. On January 11, another $100 will be added to receivables, but payments for sales made on January 1 will reduce receivables by $100,

---

1 Whenever goods are sold on credit, two accounts actually are created—an asset item entitled *accounts receivable* appears on the books of the selling firm, and a liability item called *accounts payable* appears on the books of the purchaser. At this point we are analyzing the transaction from the viewpoint of the seller, so we are concentrating on the variables under its control. We will examine the transaction from the viewpoint of the purchaser in Chapter 10, where we discuss accounts payable as a source of funds and consider the cost of these funds relative to the cost of funds obtained from other sources.

so total accounts receivable will remain constant at $1,000. In general, once the firm's operations are stable,

$$\text{Accounts receivable} = \text{Sales per day} \times \text{Length of collection period}$$
$$= \$100 \times 10 \text{ days} = \$1,000.$$

If either sales or the collection period changes, this change will be reflected in accounts receivable.

   Notice that the $1,000 investment in receivables must be financed. To illustrate, suppose that when our firm started on January 1, the owner had put up $100 as common stock and used this money to buy the goods sold the first day. Thus, the initial balance sheet would be as follows:

Inventory	$100	Common equity	$100
Total assets	$100	Total claims	$100

At the end of the day, the balance sheet would look like this:[2]

Accounts receivable	$100		
Inventory	0	Common equity	$100
Total assets	$100	Total claims	$100

In order to remain in business, the owner must replenish inventories. To do so requires that $100 of goods be purchased, and this requires $100. Assuming the owner borrows the $100 from the bank, the balance sheet at the start of the second day will be as follows:

Accounts receivable	$100	Notes payable to bank	$100
Inventories	100	Common equity	100
Total assets	$200	Total claims	$200

At the end of the day, the inventories will have been converted to receivables, and the firm will have to borrow another $100 to restock for the third day.

   This process will continue, provided the bank is willing to lend the necessary funds, until on the eleventh day the balance sheet reads as follows:

Accounts receivable	$1,000	Notes payable to bank	$1,000
Inventories	100	Common equity	100
Total assets	$1,100	Total claims	$1,100

2 Of course, a profit might have been earned on the sales, but it would, for a retail business, amount to only about 2 percent, or $2. Also, the firm would need other assets such as cash, fixed assets, and a permanent stock of inventory. We abstract from these details so that we may focus on receivables.

This balance sheet is in a "steady state" condition and will remain stable until the situation changes.

Now suppose sales doubled, to $200 per day. After a brief transition period (ten days), the balance sheet would be as follows:

Accounts receivable	$2,000	Notes payable to bank	$2,100
Inventories	200	Common equity	100
Total assets	$2,200	Total claims	$2,200

Or, if sales had remained constant at $100 per day but the collection period had doubled from ten to twenty days, the balance sheet would have changed as follows:

Accounts receivable	$2,000	Notes payable to bank	$2,000
Inventories	100	Common equity	100
Total assets	$2,100	Total claims	$2,100

These examples should make it clear (1) that accounts receivable depend jointly on the level of sales and the collection period, and (2) that any increase in receivables must be financed in some manner. We assumed bank financing, but other possibilities include the firm's buying on credit itself (in which case the claim would be represented by accounts payable rather than notes payable), selling bonds, or selling more common stock.[3] The question of the best method of financing accounts receivable (and other current assets) is considered in the next chapter. In the remainder of this one, we examine how the firm determines and attains the optimal level of receivables.

CREDIT POLICY

As noted above, accounts receivable are equal to (Sales per day) × (Collection period). Both of these factors are influenced by a set of controllable factors called the firm's *credit policy*. The four credit policy variables are

1. the *credit period,* which is the length of time for which credit is granted;
2. the *credit standards,* which refers to the minimum financial strength of acceptable credit customers;
3. the firm's *collection policy,* which is measured by its toughness or laxity in following up on slow-paying accounts; and
4. any *discounts* given for early payment.

3 In time, profits will presumably be earned and reinvested in the business, but, with normal profit margins, external funds will be needed to support rapid growth. This point was discussed in Chapter 7 in connection with the Arinson Supply Company. Also, as is shown later in this chapter, only the *incremental costs* tied up in receivables (and inventories) must be financed.

The credit manager has the responsibility for administering the credit policy. However, because of the pervasive importance of credit, the credit policy itself is established by the executive committee, which usually consists of the president and the vice-presidents in charge of finance, marketing, and production. If the credit policy is *eased* by lengthening the credit period, by relaxing credit standards, by following a less tough collection policy, or by offering cash discounts, then sales should increase: *Easing the credit policy stimulates sales.* However, if the credit policy is eased and sales do rise, then costs will also rise because more labor, more materials, and so on, will be required to produce more goods. Thus, the basic question that credit policy makers must answer is this: Will sales revenues rise more than costs, causing net income to increase, or will the increase in sales revenues be more than offset by higher costs?

The basic point of credit policy analysis is to provide an answer to the preceding question, and the basic approach employed is called *incremental analysis.* In incremental analysis, we attempt to determine the increase or decrease in both sales and costs associated with a given easing or tightening of the credit policy. The difference between incremental sales and incremental costs is defined as *incremental profit.* If the expected incremental profit is positive, then the proposed credit policy change is a good one.

Incremental analysis is not a difficult concept, but care must be taken to insure that all the relevant costs and benefits of a proposed change are considered. Generally, a credit policy change will affect these variables: (1) sales, (2) production costs associated with a higher or lower sales volume, (3) bad debt losses, (4) discount expenses, (5) the level of accounts receivable, hence the cost of the capital tied up in receivables, (6) the costs of administering the credit department, and (7) collection expenses. It is far from easy to estimate these factors. For example, to estimate the effect on sales of a given credit policy change requires a knowledge not only of how customers will respond but also of how the firm's competitors will react. Similarly, to estimate the effects on production costs involves a consideration of both variable costs per unit of output and the firm's capacity situation—incremental production costs will be far different if the firm is currently operating at full capacity than if excess capacity exists.

Credit Period

In this section, we examine the effects of changes in the credit period, while in the following three sections we consider credit standards, collection policy, and cash discounts. Throughout, we illustrate the situation with data on Judy-Rose Fashions, Inc. Judy-Rose currently sells on a cash only basis. Since it extends no credit, the company has no funds tied up in receivables, no bad debt losses, and no credit expenses of any kind. On the other hand, its sales volume is lower than it would be if credit terms were offered.

Judy-Rose is now considering extending credit on thirty day terms. Current sales are $100,000 per year, variable costs are 60 percent of sales, excessive productive capacity exists (so no new fixed costs will be incurred as a result of expanded sales), and the cost of new capital is 10 percent. Judy-Rose estimates that sales will increase to $150,000 per year if credit is extended.

We will need to set up some simple equations to analyze this credit policy change, so we begin by defining these terms and symbols:

S_0 = Judy-Rose's current sales = $100,000 per year.

ΔS = incremental sales = $50,000. Note that ΔS would be negative had Judy-Rose been selling on credit and then reduced the credit period.

V = variable costs as a percentage of sales = 60%. V includes the cost of administering the credit department and all other costs except bad debt losses and financing costs (interest charges) associated with carrying the investment in receivables. Costs of carrying inventories are included in V.

$1 - V = 1 - 0.6 = 0.4 = 40\%$ = contribution margin, or the percentage of each sales dollar that goes toward covering overhead and increasing profits.

k = the cost of financing the investment in receivables = 10%. k is the firm's cost of new capital when the capital is used to finance receivables.

ACP_0 = average collection period prior to a change in credit policy. Since Judy-Rose sold for cash only, $ACP_0 = 0$.

ACP_N = new average collection period after the credit policy change = 30 days. Here we assume that all customers pay on time, so ACP = specified credit period. Generally, some customers pay late, so as a general rule ACP > specified credit period.

Given this information, we can now calculate values for the following:

ΔI = incremental change in the level of the firm's investment in accounts receivable.

ΔP = incremental change in profits.

To begin, recognize that although easing credit by lengthening the credit period stimulates sales, there is a cost to tying up funds in receivables. The investment in receivables will increase for two reasons: (1) old customers will now take longer to pay, and (2) new sales will result in new receivables. The incremental investment in receivables (ΔI) is calculated as follows:

$$\Delta I = \begin{bmatrix} \text{Increased investment} \\ \text{in receivables associated} \\ \text{with original sales} \end{bmatrix} + \begin{bmatrix} \text{Investment in} \\ \text{receivables associated} \\ \text{with new sales} \end{bmatrix}$$

$$= \left[\begin{array}{c} \text{Change in} \\ \text{collection period} \end{array} \right] \left[\begin{array}{c} \text{Old sales} \\ \text{per day} \end{array} \right] + \left[V(\text{ACP}) \left(\begin{array}{c} \text{Incremental sales} \\ \text{per day} \end{array} \right) \right]$$

$$
\begin{aligned}
&= (\text{ACP}_N - \text{ACP}_0)(S_0/360) + [V(\text{ACP}_N)(\Delta S/360)] &&\text{(9–1)}\\
&= (30 - 0)(\$100,000/360) + 0.6[30(\$50,000/360)]\\
&= \$8,333 + \$2,500\\
&= \$10,833.
\end{aligned}
$$

Note that the increased investment in accounts receivable *(A/R)* associated with old sales is based on the full amount of the receivables; i.e., we do not multiply by *V* as we do for new sales. This difference reflects the facts (1) that the firm only invests its variable cost in *new* receivables but (2) that it would have collected the *full sales price* on the old receivables earlier had it not made the credit policy change. There is an *opportunity cost* associated with the $8,333 additional investment in *A/R* from old sales and a *direct financing cost* associated with the $2,500 investment in *A/R* from new sales.

Given this information, we may now determine the incremental profit, ΔP, associated with the proposed credit period change:

$$\Delta P = \left[\left(\begin{array}{c} \text{New} \\ \text{sales} \end{array} \right) \left(\begin{array}{c} \text{Contribution} \\ \text{margin} \end{array} \right) \right] - \left[\begin{array}{c} \text{Cost of carrying} \\ \text{new receivables} \end{array} \right]$$

$$
\begin{aligned}
&= \Delta S(1 - V) - k(\Delta I) &&\text{(9–2)}\\
&= \$50,000(0.4) - 0.10(\$10,833)\\
&= \$20,000 - \$1,083\\
&= \$18,917.
\end{aligned}
$$

Since pretax profits are expected to increase by $18,917, the credit policy change should be made.

Two simplifying assumptions which were made in our analysis should be noted: (1) we assumed that all customers paid on time (ACP = credit period), and (2) we assumed that no bad debt losses were incurred. The assumption of prompt payment can be relaxed quite easily—simply use the actual average collection period (say forty days) rather than the credit period in Equation 9–1 to calculate the investment in receivables, and then use this new (and higher) value of ΔI in Equation 9–2 to calculate ΔP. Thus, if $\text{ACP}_N = 40$ days, then

$$
\begin{aligned}
\Delta I &= [(40 - 0)(\$100,000/360)] + 0.6[40(\$50,000/360)]\\
&= \$11,111 + \$3,333 = \$14,444,
\end{aligned}
$$

and

$$
\begin{aligned}
\Delta P &= [\$50,000(0.4)] - [0.10(\$14,444)]\\
&= \$20,000 - \$1,444 = \$18,556.
\end{aligned}
$$

Incremental profits are reduced slightly, but they are still positive, so the credit policy should still be relaxed.

Bad debts can be handled equally easily. First, recognize that bad debts do not affect our calculation of the firm's incremental investment in receivables (Equation 9–1). However, notice that bad debts do reduce profits, so Equation 9–2 must be modified. Assuming that 5 percent of all sales after the change (S_N) end up as bad debt losses $(B_N = 5\% = 0.05)$, then we have

$$\Delta P = \left(\begin{array}{c} \text{New} \\ \text{sales} \end{array}\right)\left(\begin{array}{c} \text{Contribution} \\ \text{margin} \end{array}\right) - \left(\begin{array}{c} \text{Cost of carrying} \\ \text{receivables} \end{array}\right) - \left(\begin{array}{c} \text{Bad debt} \\ \text{losses} \end{array}\right)$$

$$= \Delta S(1 - V) - k(\Delta I) - B_N(S_N)$$
$$= \$50,000(0.4) - 0.10(\$14,444) - 0.05(\$150,000)$$
$$= \$20,000 - \$1,444 - \$7,500$$
$$= \$11,056.$$

Bad debts reduce the expected incremental profits, but ΔP is still positive, so the credit policy change still appears to be a good idea.[4]

Other factors could be introduced into the analysis. The company could consider a further easing of credit by extending the credit period to sixty days, or it could weigh the effects of shortening the period from thirty days to twenty days. The outcome of a sales expansion so great that fixed assets, hence higher fixed costs, had to be added could also be studied. Such additional factors complicate the analysis, but the basic principles are the same—just keep in mind that we are seeking to determine the *incremental sales revenues,* the *incremental costs,* and consequently the *incremental net income* associated with a given change in credit policy.

Credit Standards

The second element of the firm's credit policy relates to decisions about who will be granted credit. If the firm extended credit sales to only the strongest of customers, it would never have bad debt losses, nor would it incur much in the way of expenses for a credit department. On the other hand, it would probably be losing sales, and the profits that were foregone on these lost sales could be far larger than the costs that were avoided. Determining the optimal credit standards involves equating the incremental costs of credit to the incremental profits on the increased sales.

Incremental costs include production and selling costs plus those costs associated with the "quality" of the marginal accounts, or *credit quality costs.* These costs include (1) default, or bad debt losses, (2) higher investigation and collection costs, and (3) higher costs of capital tied up in the additional receivables that result when customers are less creditworthy,

---

4 If the company had been selling on credit initially and incurring bad debt losses, then we would have had to modify Equation 9–2 even further:

$$\Delta P = \Delta S(1 - V) - k(\Delta I) - \Delta(\text{Bad debt losses})$$
$$= \Delta S(1 - V) - k(\Delta I) - [\text{New bad debt losses} - \text{Old bad debt losses}]$$
$$= \Delta S(1 - V) - k(\Delta I) - [B_N S_N - B_0 S_0].$$

In our example, $B_0 S_0 = 0$ because $B_0 = 0$. Notice that B_N is the *average* credit loss percentage on total new sales. Bad debts may be higher for new customers attracted by the credit terms than for old customers who take advantage of them, but B_N is an average of these two groups.

pay their accounts more slowly, and so cause the average collection period to lengthen.

We have seen that a firm may change its credit standards either by *relaxing* them to increase sales or by *tightening* them to reduce both bad debt losses and slow-paying accounts. To illustrate the process, assume now that Judy-Rose Fashions currently sells on terms granting thirty days credit, written as "net 30," and that the following conditions hold:

$S_0 = \$150,000 =$ original sales per year.

$V = 60\% =$ variable cost percentage.

$1 - V = 40\% =$ contribution margin.

$k = 10\% =$ cost of capital.

$ACP_0 = 40$ days $=$ original average collection period (10 days late).

$B_0 = 5\% =$ original bad debt loss percentage.

Assume that excess capacity still exists and that management is considering relaxing its credit standards to permit sales to some new customers who did not qualify for credit under the old standards. However, bad debt losses will also rise, as will the average collection period, because weaker customers generally pay more slowly than strong ones. Should the change be made?

We begin the analysis by estimating incremental sales, the average collection period for the new customers (ACP_N), and the new bad debt loss percentage (B_N). Assume these values have been estimated as follows:

$\Delta S = \$50,000.$

$ACP_N = 60$ days.

$B_N = 15\%.$

Note that we are assuming no changes for the old customers—they continue with sales at the rate of $150,000 per year, $ACP_0 = 40$ days, and $B_0 = 5\%$.

With this information, we calculate the incremental investment in receivables as follows:

$$\Delta I = V(ACP_N)(\Delta S/360)$$
$$= 0.6(60)(\$50,000/360)$$
$$= \$5,000.$$

With ΔI calculated, we now find incremental profits:

$$\Delta P = \left(\begin{array}{c}\text{Increase in}\\\text{gross profits}\end{array}\right) - \left(\begin{array}{c}\text{Cost of carrying}\\\text{new receivables}\end{array}\right) - \left(\begin{array}{c}\text{Increased bad}\\\text{debt losses}\end{array}\right)$$

$$= (1 - V)(\Delta S) - k(\Delta I) - B_N(\Delta S)$$
$$= 0.4(\$50,000) - 0.10(\$5,000) - 0.15(\$50,000)$$
$$= \$20,000 - \$500 - \$7,500$$
$$= \$12,000.$$

Since profits are expected to increase, the analysis suggests that Judy-Rose should relax credit standards.

Measuring Credit Quality

A key element in setting credit standards relates to the factors that determine the likelihood that a given customer will pay slowly or even end up as a bad debt loss. This is called *measuring credit quality.* To begin the analysis, we need to define *credit quality.* Perhaps the best way is in terms of the probability of default. These probability estimates are, for the most part, subjective estimates, but credit evaluation is a well-established practice, and a good credit manager can make reasonably accurate judgments of the probability of default by different classes of customers. To evaluate credit risk, credit managers consider the five *C*'s of credit: character, capacity, capital, collateral, and conditions:

1. *Character* refers to the probability that customers will *try* to honor their obligations. This factor is of considerable importance, because every credit transaction implies a *promise* to pay. Will debtors make an honest effort to pay their debts, or are they likely to try to get away with something? Experienced credit managers frequently insist that the moral factor is the most important issue in a credit evaluation.
2. *Capacity* is a subjective judgment of customers' ability to pay. It is gauged by their past records, supplemented by physical observation of customers' plants or stores, and their business methods.
3. *Capital* is measured by the general financial position of firms as indicated by a financial ratio analysis, with special emphasis on the risk ratios—the debt/assets ratio, the current ratio, and the times interest earned ratio.
4. *Collateral* is represented by assets that customers may offer as security to obtain credit.
5. *Conditions* refers to the impact of general economic trends or to special developments in certain geographic regions or sectors of the economy that may affect customers' ability to meet their obligations.

The five *C*'s of credit represent the factors by which the credit risks are judged. Information on these items is obtained from the firm's previous experience with customers, supplemented by a well-developed system of information-gathering groups. Two major sources of external information are available. The first is the work of the *credit associations,* local groups which meet frequently and correspond with one another to exchange information on credit customers. These local groups have also banded together to create Credit Interchange, a system developed by the National Association of Credit Management for assembling and distributing information about debtors' past performances. The interchange reports show the paying records of different debtors, the industries from which they are buying, and the trading areas in which purchases are being made.

The second source of external information is the work of the credit-reporting agencies, which collect credit information and sell it for a fee; the best known of these agencies are Dun & Bradstreet (D&B) and TRW, Incorporated. D&B, TRW, and other agencies provide factual data that can be used in credit analysis; they also provide ratings similar to those available on corporate bonds.[5]

Modern credit managers practice "management by exception." Under such a system, customers are first classified into five or six categories according to degree of risk, and then the credit manager concentrates time and attention on the weakest customers. For example, the following classes might be established:

Risk Class	Percentage of Uncollectible Credit Sales	Percentage of Customers in This Class
1	0–$1/2$%	60%
2	$1/2$–2	20
3	2–5	10
4	5–10	5
5	Over 10	5

Firms in Class 1 might be extended credit automatically, and their credit status only reviewed once a year. Those in Class 2 might also receive credit (up to specified limits) automatically, but a ratio analysis of these firms' financial condition would be conducted more frequently (perhaps quarterly), and they would be moved down to Class 3 if their position deteriorated. Specific approvals might be required for credit sales to Classes 3 and 4, while sales to Class 5 might be on a COD (cash on delivery) basis only.

Managing such a system requires fast, accurate, up-to-date information, and to help get such information, the National Association of Credit Management (a group with 43,000 member firms) persuaded TRW, Inc., to develop a computer-based, fully automated data retrieval system. Such a system is now in existence, and teletype credit reports are available within minutes. While Dun & Bradstreet's reports are more complete, they come in more slowly, through the U.S. mail. A typical credit report would include the following pieces of information:

1. A summary balance sheet and income statement.
2. A number of key ratios, with trend information.
3. Information obtained from the firm's suppliers telling whether it has been paying promptly or slowly or has failed to make payments.

5 For additional information, see *Credit Management Handbook*, 2d ed., a publication of the National Association of Credit Management (Homewood, Ill.: Richard D. Irwin, 1965). Also, see Peter Nulty, "An Upstart Takes on Dun & Bradstreet," *Fortune*, April 9, 1979.

4. A verbal description of the physical condition of the firm's operations.
5. A verbal description of the backgrounds of the firm's owners, including any previous bankruptcies, lawsuits, and the like.
6. A summary rating, going from A+ for the best credits down to F for those who are most likely to default.

Although a great deal of credit information is available, it must still be processed in a judgmental manner. The data and information systems can assist in making better credit decisions, but, in the final analysis, credit decisions are really exercises in informed judgment.

Collection Policy

Collection policy refers to the procedures the firm follows to collect past-due accounts. For example, a letter may be sent to such accounts when the bill is ten days past due; a more severe letter, followed by a telephone call, may be used if payment is not received within thirty days; and the account may be turned over to a collection agency after ninety days.

The collection process can be expensive in terms of both out-of-pocket expenditures and lost goodwill, but at least some firmness is needed to prevent an undue lengthening in the collection period and to minimize outright losses. Again, a balance must be struck between the costs and benefits of different collection policies.

Changes in collection policy influence sales, the collection period, the bad debt loss percentage, and the percentage of customers who take discounts. Accordingly, the effects of a change in collection policy should be analyzed within the framework of the equations developed above. We shall not go through an analysis here, but the interested reader is referred to Appendix 9A of the second edition of *Financial Management*.

Cash Discounts

The last element in the credit policy decision, cash discounts for early payment, can also be analyzed through the use of our equation set. For example, Judy-Rose Fashions might decide to change its credit terms from thirty days (net 30) to allow a 2 percent discount if payment is received within ten days (stated "2/10, net 30"). This change should produce two benefits: (1) it would attract new customers who consider discounts a type of price reduction, and (2) the discounts would cause a reduction in the average collection period, since some old customers would pay more promptly in order to take advantage of the discount. Offsetting these benefits is the dollar cost of the discounts taken. The optimal discount is established at the point where the costs and benefits are exactly offsetting.[6]

---

6 Equations for the incremental investment in receivables and incremental profits, which incorporate discounts, can be found in Appendix 9A, *Financial Management*, 2d ed.

If sales are seasonal, a firm may use *seasonal dating* on discounts. For
example, Jenson, Inc., is a swimsuit manufacturer which sells on terms of
2/10, net 30, May 1 dating. This means that the effective invoice date is May
1, so the discount may be taken until May 10, or the full amount must be
paid on May 30, regardless of when the sale was made. If Jenson produces
throughout the year but retail sales of bathing suits are concentrated in the
spring and early summer, then offering seasonal datings may induce some
customers to stock up early, saving Jenson storage costs and also "nailing
down sales."

Simultaneous Changes in Policy Variables

The preceding discussion has considered the effects of changes in credit
policy one at a time. The firm could, of course, change several or all policy
variables simultaneously. An almost endless variety of equations could be
developed, depending on which policy variables are manipulated and on the
assumed effects on sales, discounts taken, the collection period, bad debt
costs, the existence of excess capacity, changes in credit department costs,
changes in the variable cost percentage, and so on. The analysis would get
"messy," and the incremental profit equation would be complex, but the
principles we have developed could be used to handle any type of policy
change.

Profit Potential in Carrying Accounts Receivable

Thus far we have emphasized the costs of carrying receivables. *However, if
it is possible to sell on credit and also to assess a carrying charge on the
receivables that are outstanding, then credit sales can actually be more
profitable than cash sales.*[7] This is especially true for consumer durables
(autos, appliances, clothing, and so on), but it is also true for certain types
of industrial equipment. Thus, the General Motors Acceptance Corporation
(GMAC) unit, which finances automobiles, is highly profitable, as is Sears
Roebuck's credit subsidiary. Some encyclopedia companies are even
reported to lose money on cash sales but to more than make up these
losses from carrying charges on their credit sales; obviously, such
companies would rather sell on credit than for cash!

The carrying charges on outstanding credit are generally about 18 percent
on an annual interest rate basis (1½% per month, so 1.5% × 12 = 18%).

---

7 Where companies do a large volume of sales financing, they typically set up subsidiary companies
called *captive finance companies* to do the actual financing. Thus, General Motors, Chrysler, and Ford
all have captive finance companies, as do Sears Roebuck and Montgomery Ward. The reason for this is
that consumer finance companies, because their assets are highly liquid, tend to use far more debt, and
especially short-term debt, than manufacturers or retailers. Thus, if GM did not use a captive finance
company, its balance sheet would show an exceptionally high debt ratio and a low current ratio. By
setting up GMAC as a separate but wholly owned corporation, GM avoids distorting its own balance
sheet, and this presumably helps it raise capital on more favorable terms.

Unless administrative expenses and bad debt losses are exceedingly high, having receivables outstanding that earn 18 percent is highly profitable.

How Effective Is the Firm's Credit Policy?

It is apparent from the preceding sections that the optimal credit policy, hence the optimal level of accounts receivable, depends on the firm's own unique operating conditions. Thus, a firm with excess capacity and low variable production costs should extend credit more liberally and carry a higher level of accounts receivable than a firm operating at full capacity. However, in spite of the individualized nature of the credit management process, it is still useful to analyze the effectiveness of the firm's credit policy in an overall, aggregate sense.

As we saw in connection with the du Pont analysis, an excessive investment in any asset account will lead to a low rate of return on net worth. For comparative purposes, we can examine the firm's accounts receivable turnover ratio (sales/receivables) both over time and against the industry average turnover, or we can focus on the average collection period as discussed in Chapter 6.

In Chapter 6 we saw that Carter Chemical Company's average collection period was forty-two days, compared to an industry average of thirty-six days. If Carter lowered its average collection period by six days to thirty-six days, this would mean a reduction of (6)($8,333,333) = $49,999,998 in the amount of capital tied up in receivables. If the cost of funds tied up in receivables is 10 percent, this would mean a savings of $5 million per year, other things held constant.

The average collection period can also be compared to Carter's credit terms. Carter typically sells on terms of 1/10, net 30, so its customers, on average, are not paying their bills on time: the forty-two day average collection period is greater than the thirty day credit period. Note, however, that some of the customers could be paying within ten days to take advantage of the discount, while others could be taking much longer than forty-two days to pay. To check against this possibility, we use the *aging schedule,* which breaks down accounts receivable according to how long they have been outstanding. Carter Chemical's aging schedule is shown below:

Age of Account (Days)	Percent of Total Value of Accounts Receivable
0–10	52%
11–30	20
31–45	13
46–60	4
Over 60	11
Total	100%

Most of the accounts pay on schedule or after only a slight delay, but a significant number are over one month past due. This indicates that even though the average collection period is close to the thirty day credit period, Carter has quite a bit of capital tied up in slow-paying accounts, some of which may eventually result in losses.

Management analyzes the firm's average collection period and its aging schedule in comparison with industry averages, recent trends, and the firm's credit terms to see how effectively the credit department is operating. If the average collection period is much longer than the terms of the sale, and if the aging schedule shows a significant percentage of past due accounts, then the credit standards may be too low, the credit manager may not be enforcing the standards closely enough, or the collection policy may be too lax. In any event, these tools are useful for reviewing the credit manager's performance.

Investors—both stockholders and bank loan officers—should pay close attention to accounts receivable management; otherwise, they could be misled by the current financial statements and later suffer serious losses on their investments. When a sale is made, the following events occur: (1) inventories are reduced by the cost of goods sold, (2) accounts receivable are increased by the sales price, and (3) the difference is recorded as a profit. If the sale is for cash, the profit is definitely earned, but if the sale is on credit, the profit is not actually earned unless and until the account is collected. Firms have been known to encourage "sales" to very weak customers in order to inflate reported profits. This could boost the stock price, at least until credit losses begin to lower earnings, at which time the stock price falls. An analysis along the lines suggested above would detect any such questionable practice, as well as any unconscious deterioration in the quality of accounts receivable. Such early detection could help both investors and bankers avoid losses.[8]

INVENTORY MANAGEMENT

Inventories, which may be classified as (1) *raw materials,* (2) *work-in-process,* and (3) *finished goods,* are an essential part of most business operations. Like accounts receivable, inventory levels depend heavily upon sales. However, whereas receivables build up *after* sales have been made, inventories must be acquired *ahead* of sales. This is a critical difference, and the necessity of forecasting sales before establishing target inventory levels makes inventory management a difficult task.

---

8 Accountants are increasingly interested in these matters. Investors have sued several of the Big Eight accounting firms for substantial damages where (1) profits were overstated and (2) it could be shown that the auditors should have conducted an analysis along the lines described here and then should have reported the results to stockholders on the audited financial statements.

Some examples of typical inventory decisions will make clear the types of issues involved.

1. *Retail clothing store.* Glamour Galore Boutique must order bathing suits for summer sales in January, and it must take delivery by April to be sure of having enough suits to meet the heavy May–June demand. Bathing suits come in many styles, colors, and sizes. If the buyer stocks incorrectly, either in total or in terms of the style-color-size distribution, then the store will have trouble. It will lose potential sales if it stocks too few suits, and it will be forced to mark them down and take losses if it stocks too many or the wrong types.

The effects of inventory changes on the balance sheet are important. For simplicity, assume that Glamour Galore has a $100 base stock of inventories, financed by common stock. Its initial balance sheet is as follows:

Inventories (base stock)	$100	Common stock	$100
Total assets	$100	Total claims	$100

Now it anticipates a seasonal increase in sales of $300 and takes on additional inventories in this amount, financing them with a bank loan:

Inventories	$400	Notes payable to bank	$300
		Common stock	100
Total assets	$400	Total claims	$400

If everything works out as planned, sales will occur, inventories will be converted to cash, the bank loan can be retired, and the company will have earned a profit. The balance sheet, after a successful season, might look like this:

Cash and marketable securities	$ 50	Notes payable to bank	$ 0
Inventories (base stock)	100	Common stock	100
		Retained earnings	50
Total assets	$150	Total claims	$150

The company is now in a highly liquid position and is ready to begin a new season.

Now suppose the season had not gone well. Sales were slow, and as fall approached the balance sheet looked like this:

Inventories	$300	Notes payable to bank	$200
		Common stock	100
Total assets	$300	Total claims	$300

Suppose the bank insists on repayment of its loan, and it wants cash, not bathing suits. But if the bathing suits did not sell well in the summer, how will out-of-style suits sell in the fall? Assume that Glamour Galore is forced to mark the suits down to half price in order to sell them to raise cash to repay the bank loan. The result will be:

Cash	$150	Notes payable to bank	$200
		Common equity	(50)
Total assets	$150	Total claims	$150

At this point, Glamour Galore goes bankrupt. The bank gets the $150 of cash and takes a $50 loss on its loan. The stockholders are wiped out, and the company goes out of business.

2. *Manufacturer.* Now consider a different type of situation, that of Whirlwind Corporation, a well-established appliance manufacturer whose inventory position is shown below:

Raw materials	$200
Work-in-process	200
Finished goods	600
	$1,000

Suppose Whirlwind anticipates that the economy is about to get much stronger and that the demand for appliances is likely to rise sharply. If it is to share in the expected boom, Whirlwind will have to increase production. This means it will have to increase inventories, and, since the inventory increase will precede sales, additional financing will be required. The details are not shown here, but some liability account, perhaps notes payable, would have to be increased in order to support the inventory buildup.

Proper inventory management requires close coordination among the sales, purchasing, production, and finance departments. The sales/marketing department is generally the first to spot changes in demand. These changes must be worked into the company's purchasing and manufacturing schedules, and the financial manager must arrange any financing that will be needed to support the inventory buildup.

Improper coordination among departments, poor sales forecasts, or both can lead to disaster. For example, Varner Corporation, a manufacturer of electronic components, was recently forced into bankruptcy because of a poor system of internal controls. The company set its production schedules for 1979 on the basis of 1978 sales. However, sales for several key items dropped sharply during the first half of 1979. Production schedules were not adjusted downward, so both inventories and bank debt built up. By the time the situation was properly assessed, inventories of now obsolete components had risen to over $10 million. The situation was like this:

Cash	$ 1		Accounts payable	$ 3
Receivables	8		Notes payable to bank	15
Inventories: good	6		Total current liabilities	$18
bad	10		Long-term debt	10
Total current assets	$25		Common equity	7
Fixed assets	10			
Total assets	$35		Total claims	$35

The bank insisted upon payment of the note. Varner simply could not generate the necessary cash, so it was forced into bankruptcy.[9]

Inventory Models

Inventories are obviously necessary, but it is equally obvious that a firm will suffer if it has too much or too little inventory. How can one determine the *optimal* inventory level? One commonly used approach to determining optimal levels is the *Economic Ordering Quantity (EOQ) Model,* which is described in this section.

We begin the EOQ analysis by noting that the inventory of any item consists of a *working stock* and a *safety stock.* The working stock depends on the pattern of inflows and outflows, while the safety stock is designed to guard against unexpectedly high demand, delays in receiving shipments, or both. In this section we first analyze optimal working balances, then go on to look at safety stocks.

Figure 9–1 illustrates the basic premise on which inventory theory is built. First, you should recognize that the average investment in inventories depends on how frequently orders are placed and the size of each order—if we order every day, average inventories will be much smaller than if we order once a year. Further, as Figure 9–1 shows, some of the firm's costs rise with larger orders: included here are warehousing costs, interest on funds tied up in inventory, insurance, and obsolescence. Other costs decline with larger orders and inventories: for example, lost profits on sales lost because of shortages and the cost of production interruptions caused by inadequate inventories. If these two curves are added, the sum represents the total cost of ordering and holding inventories. The point where the total cost curve is minimized represents the optimal order quantity, or the EOQ, and this, in turn, determines the optimal average inventory level.

It can be shown that, under certain reasonable assumptions, the order

9 As we shall see in Chapter 10, bank loans are generally written as 90 day notes. Thus, the loan must be repaid or renewed every 90 days. If the bank thinks the firm's situation has deteriorated, as Varner's had, it will refuse to renew. Then, if the firm cannot raise cash to repay the loan, it is bankrupt.

Figure 9–1
Determination of the Optimal Order Quantity

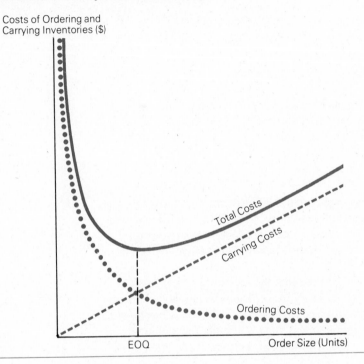

quantity that minimizes the total cost curve in Figure 9–1, or the EOQ, can
be found by use of this formula:[10]

$$EOQ = \sqrt{\frac{2FS}{CP}}. \qquad (9-3)$$

Here,

EOQ = the economic ordering quantity, or the optimum quantity to be
        ordered each time an order is placed.

F = fixed costs of placing and receiving an order.

S = annual sales in units.

C = carrying cost expressed as a percentage of inventory value.

P = purchase price per unit of inventory.

---

10 The EOQ model is derived in Appendix 9B of *Financial Management,* 2d ed. In essence, the fixed costs
   of ordering inventory (including production setup costs for a manufacturing operation) and of carrying it
   are expressed as a percentage of the dollar volume of inventory holdings. Next, these costs are added
   to form the total cost of ordering and carrying inventories. This total cost function is then differentiated,
   and the first derivative is set equal to zero to locate the minimum point on the total cost curve in Figure
   9–1. Equation 9–3 results from this operation.

The assumptions of the model, which will be relaxed shortly, include the following: (1) sales can be forecast perfectly, (2) sales are evenly distributed throughout the year, and (3) orders are received with no delays whatever.

To illustrate the EOQ model, consider the following data, supplied by Romantic Books, Inc., publisher of the classic novel, *Madame Boudoir:*

S = sales = 26,000 copies per year.

C = carrying cost = 20 percent of inventory value.[11]

P = purchase price per book to Romantic Books from a printing company = $6.1538 per copy. (The sales price is $9, but this is irrelevant for our purposes.)

F = fixed cost per order = $1,000. The bulk of this cost is the labor cost for setting the plates on the presses, as well as for setting up the binding equipment for the production run. The printer bills this cost separately from the $6.1538 cost per copy.

Substituting these data into Equation 9–3, we obtain

$$EOQ = \sqrt{\frac{2FS}{CP}}$$

$$= \sqrt{\frac{(2)(1,000)(26,000)}{(0.2)(6.1538)}}$$

$$= \sqrt{42,250,317}$$

$$= 6,500 \text{ copies.}$$

Average inventory holdings depend directly on the EOQ; this relationship is illustrated graphically in Figure 9–2. Immediately after an order is received, 6,500 copies are in stock. The usage rate, or sales rate, is 500 copies per week (26,000/52 weeks), so inventories are drawn down by this amount each week. Thus, the actual number of units held in inventory will vary from 6,500 books just after an order is received to zero just before an order arrives. On average, the number of units held will be 6,500/2 = 3,250 books. At a cost of $6.1538 per book, the average investment in inventories will be 3,250 × $6.1538 = $19,999.85 ≈ $20,000. If inventories are financed by bank loans, the loan will vary from a high of $40,000 to a low of $0.0, but the average amount outstanding over the course of a year will be $20,000.

Because a two week lead time is required for production and shipping, orders are placed when the stock falls to 1,000 copies, which is defined as the *order point.* Some procedure, perhaps computerized, should trigger an order when the stock hits this level. With a 6,500 beginning balance, a zero

11 In an unpublished study, the U.S. Department of Commerce estimated that, on the average, manufacturing firms have an annual cost of carrying inventories that equals 25 percent of original inventory cost. This percentage is broken down as follows: obsolescence, 8 percent; physical depreciation, 4 percent; interest, 9 percent; handling, 2.50 percent; property taxes, 0.50 percent; insurance, 0.25 percent; storage, 0.75 percent.

Figure 9–2
Inventory Position without Safety Stock

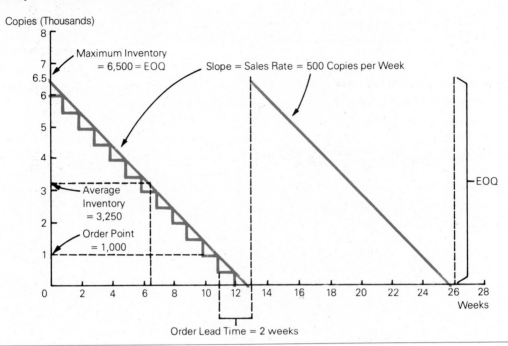

Order Lead Time = 2 weeks

ending balance, and a uniform sales rate, inventories will average one-half
the EOQ, or 3,250 copies, during the year.

Safety Stocks

If Romantic Books knew for certain that both the sales rate and the order
lead time would never vary, it could operate exactly as shown in Figure 9–2.
However, sales rates do change, and production and/or shipping delays are
frequently encountered; to guard against these events, the company will
carry additional inventories, or *safety stocks.*

The concept of a safety stock is illustrated in Figure 9–3. First, note that
the slope of the sales line measures the expected rate of sales. The
company *expects* sales of 500 copies per week, but let us assume a
maximum likely sales rate of twice this amount, or 1,000 copies each week.
It initially orders 7,500, the EOQ plus a safety stock of 1,000 copies.
Subsequently, it reorders the EOQ, 6,500 copies, whenever the inventory
level falls to 2,000 copies, the safety stock of 1,000 copies plus the 1,000

copies expected to be used while awaiting delivery of the order. Notice that the company could, over the two week delivery period, sell 1,000 copies a week, or double its normal expected sales. This maximum rate of sales is shown by the steeper dashed line in Figure 9–3. The condition that makes possible this higher maximum sales rate is the introduction of a safety stock of 1,000 copies.

Figure 9–3
Inventory Position with Safety Stock Included

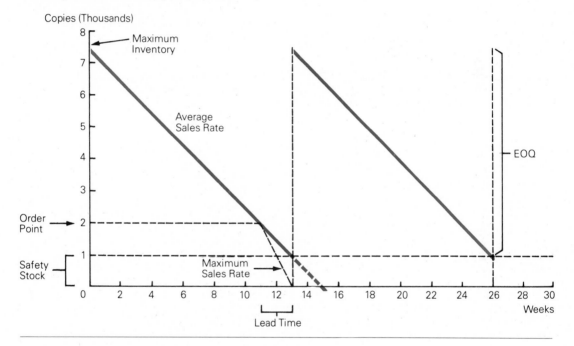

The safety stock is also useful to guard against delays in receiving orders. The expected delivery time is two weeks; however, with a 1,000 copy safety stock, the company could maintain sales at the expected rate of 500 copies per week for an additional two weeks if production or shipping delays held up an order.

The optimum safety stock varies from situation to situation, but, in general, it *increases* with (1) the uncertainty of demand forecasts, (2) the costs (in terms of lost sales and lost goodwill) that result from inventory shortages, and (3) the probability of delays in receiving shipments. The optimum safety stock *decreases* with the cost of carrying the extra inventory.[12]

Effects of Inflation on Inventory Management

Moderate inflation—say, 3 percent per year—can largely be ignored for purposes of inventory management, but the higher the rate of inflation, the more important it is to consider this factor. If the rate of inflation in the types of goods the firm stocks tends to be relatively constant, it can be dealt with quite easily—simply deduct the expected annual rate of inflation from the carrying cost percentage, *C,* in Equation 9–3, and use this modified version of the EOQ model to establish the working stock.

The reason for making this deduction is that inflation causes the value of the inventory to rise, thus offsetting somewhat the effects of depreciation and other carrying cost factors. Since *C* will now be smaller, the calculated EOQ, hence the average inventory, will increase. However, the higher the rate of inflation, the higher are interest rates, and this factor will increase *C,* thus lowering the EOQ and average inventories. On balance, there is no evidence that inflation either raises or lowers the optimal inventories of firms in the aggregate. Inflation should still be explicitly considered, however, for it will raise the individual firm's optimal holdings if the rate of inflation for its own inventories is above average (and is greater than the effects of inflation on interest rates), and vice versa.

SUMMARY

The typical manufacturing firm has about 42 percent of its assets invested in inventories and receivables, so the management of these assets is obviously important. The investment in receivables is dependent on the firm's *credit policy,* and the four credit policy variables are these: (1) the *credit standards,* or the financial strength customers must exhibit in order to be granted credit, (2) the *credit period,* or length of time for which credit is extended, (3) *cash discounts* designed to encourage rapid payment, and (4) *collection policy,* which helps

---

12 For a more detailed discussion of safety stocks, see Arthur Snyder, "Principles of Inventory Management," *Financial Executive,* April 1964, pp. 13–21. If we knew (1) the probability distribution of usage rates and (2) the probability distribution of order lead times, we could determine joint probabilities of stock-outs with various safety stock levels. With a safety stock of 1,000 copies, for example, the probability of a stock-out for *Madame Boudoir* might be 5 percent. If the safety stock is reduced to 500 copies, the stock-out probability might rise to 15 percent, while this probability might be reduced to 1 percent with a safety stock of 2,000 copies. If we had additional information on the precise cost of a stock-out, we could compare this with the cost of carrying larger safety stocks. The optimum safety stock is determined at the point where the marginal stock-out cost is equal to the marginal inventory carrying cost.

determine how long accounts remain outstanding. Credit policy has an important impact on the volume of sales, and the optimal credit policy involves a tradeoff between the costs inherent in various credit policies and the profits generated by higher sales. From a practical standpoint, it is impossible to determine the optimal credit policy in a mathematical sense—good credit management involves a blending of quantitative analysis and business judgment.

Inventory management centers around the balancing of a set of costs that increase with larger inventory holdings (storage costs, cost of capital, physical deterioration) and a set of costs that decline with larger holdings (ordering costs, lost sales, disruptions of production schedules). Inventory management has been quantified to a greater extent than most aspects of business. The EOQ model is one important part of most inventory systems. This model can be used to determine optimal order quantity, which, when combined with a specified safety stock, determines the average inventory level.

Questions

9-1 Is it true that when one firm sells to another on credit, the seller records the transaction as an account receivable while the buyer records it as an account payable, and that, disregarding discounts, the receivable typically exceeds the payable by the amount of profit on the sale?

9-2 What are the four elements in a firm's credit policy? To what extent can firms set their own credit policies as opposed to having to accept credit policies as dictated by "the competition"?

9-3 Suppose a firm makes a purchase and receives the shipment on February 1. The terms of trade as stated on the invoice read, "2/10, net 40, May 1 dating." What is the latest date on which payment can be made and the discount still be taken? What is the date on which payment must be made if the discount is not taken?

9-4 a. What is the "average collection period" for a firm whose sales are $2,880,000 per year and whose accounts receivable are $312,000? (Use 360 days per year.)

   b. Is it true that if this firm sells on terms of 3/10, net 40, its customers probably all pay on time?

9-5 Is it true that if a firm calculates its average collection period, it has no need for an aging schedule?

9-6 Firm A had no credit losses last year, but 1 percent of Firm B's accounts receivable proved to be uncollectible and resulted in losses. Should Firm B fire its credit manager and hire A's?

9-7 Indicate by a (+), (−), or (0) whether each of the following events would probably cause accounts receivable *(A/R),* sales, and profits to increase, decrease, or to be affected in an indeterminant manner:

	A/R	Sales	Profits
a. The firm tightens its credit standards.	_____	_____	_____
b. The terms of trade are changed from 2/10, net 30, to 3/10, net 30.	_____	_____	_____
c. The terms are changed from 2/10, net 30, to 3/10, net 40.	_____	_____	_____
d. The credit manager gets tough with past due accounts.	_____	_____	_____

9-8 If a firm calculates its optimal inventory of widgets to be 1,000 units when the general rate of inflation is 2 percent, is it true that the optimal inventory (in units) will almost certainly rise if the general rate of inflation climbs to 10 percent?

9-9 Indicate by a (+), (−), or (0) whether each of the following events would probably cause average annual inventories (the sum of the inventories held at the end of each month in the year divided by 12) to rise, fall, or change in an indeterminant manner:
   a. Our suppliers switch from delivering by train to air freight. _____
   b. We change from producing to meet seasonal sales to steady year-round production. Sales peak at Christmas. _____
   c. Competition in the markets in which we sell increases. _____
   d. The rate of general inflation increases. _____
   e. Interest rates rise; other things are constant. _____

Problems

9-1 A firm sells on terms of 2/10, net 30. Total sales for the year are $300,000. Forty percent of the customers pay on the tenth day and take discounts; the other 60 percent pay, on average, forty days after their purchases.
   a. What is the average collection period?
   b. What is the average investment in receivables?
   c. What would happen to the average investment in receivables if the firm toughened up on its collection policy, with the result that all nondiscount customers paid on the thirtieth day?

9-2 Callaway Electronics Company is considering changing its credit terms from 2/15, net 30, to 3/10, net 45. All of its sales are "credit sales," but 75 percent of the customers presently take the 2 percent cash discount; under the new terms this percentage is expected to decline to 65 percent. The average collection period is also expected to change under the new policy, from seventeen days at present to twenty days under the new plan. (*Note:* These averages are heavily weighted with customers who pay on the tenth day.)

   Expected sales, before discounts are deducted, are $600,000 with the present terms, but they will rise to $675,000 if the new terms are used. Assume that Callaway presently earns a 12 percent gross profit margin on sales, and that this margin will also apply after the change in credit policy. However, profits will be reduced somewhat if the new credit policy is put into effect because of additional credit-associated costs. Callaway has a 5 percent opportunity cost, or cost of capital, for any additional funds tied up in receivables. Calculate the following items:

a. The increase in gross profits before credit costs.

b. The cost of increasing the cash discount.

c. The increased cost of carrying receivables.

d. The net change in pretax profits.

9-3 The following relations for inventory costs have been established for the Lomer Fabricating Corporation:

1. Orders must be placed in multiples of 100 units.
2. Requirements for the year are 300,000 units.
3. The purchase price per unit is $3.
4. Carrying cost is 25 percent of the purchase price of goods.
5. Cost per order placed is $20.00.
6. Desired safety stock is 10,000 units; this amount is on hand initially.
7. Three days are required for delivery.

a. What is the EOQ?

b. How many orders should Lomer place each year?

c. At what inventory level should a reorder be made?

9-4 King Keg, Inc., distributes keg beer to bars and restaurants in the Columbia, Missouri, area. Mike Fazio, the owner-manager, is thinking of changing his credit terms from 2/15, net 30, to 3/15, net 45, in an effort to boost sales. Fazio's main concern is the effect the change will have on his profits and financing needs. Mike asks you to help him analyze the effects of the change.

Fazio's records are in terrible shape; he does not know exactly how many of his customers take the discount or when the others pay. He tells you, however, to assume that 60 percent of his accounts pay in fifteen days and take the discount, while the other 40 percent pay in thirty days.

a. Do Fazio's assumptions about his collections seem realistic to you?

b. Assuming Fazio's collection assumptions are correct, what is his average collection period? (*Hint:* Calculate a weighted average.)

c. Sales last year were 10,000 kegs at a price of $30 per keg. How much does Fazio have in outstanding receivables, assuming his collections data are correct? Use 360 days per year and disregard discounts in answering this question.

d. Fazio estimates that the change in credit policy will increase annual sales by 4,000 kegs, that 60 percent of his customers will continue to take discounts, and that the other customers will pay on time. Under these assumptions, what will happen to his average collection period and to his average accounts receivable?

e. Fazio buys kegs of beer for $20. He estimates that his inventory carrying costs are 20 percent and that his ordering costs are $200 per order. *Before* he changes his credit policy, what is (1) Fazio's EOQ, (2) the number of orders he should place each year, and (3) his average inventory balance assuming a zero safety stock?

f. Assume Fazio changes his credit policy, and sales increase according to his forecast. Calculate his new EOQ, number of orders, and average inventory balance.

g. Assume Fazio's general, administrative, and sales expenses (GA&S) amount to 20 percent of sales; that his income tax rate is 20 percent; and that he must borrow at a 10 percent interest rate the funds needed to carry his *added* receivables and inventory. (He currently has no debt outstanding.) Calculate his net income under the two credit policies. Use the income statement format shown below:

	Old	New
Gross sales		
Less discounts		
Net sales		
Cost of goods sold		
Gross profit		
GA&S		
Interest		
Net profit before taxes		
Taxes at 20%		
Net income after taxes		

h. Should Fazio change his credit policy? In answering this question, consider the reliability of the numerical answers you have developed and ways of improving the reliability factor.

10 FINANCING CURRENT ASSETS: SHORT-TERM CREDIT

As we noted in Chapter 8, working capital management involves decisions relating to current assets, including decisions about how these assets are to be financed. The primary purposes of this chapter are (1) to discuss alternative strategies for financing working capital and (2) to examine the types of short-term credit that are available. Decisions in these two areas will affect both the firm's riskiness and its expected rate of return, hence its market value.

ALTERNATIVE STRATEGIES FOR FINANCING WORKING CAPITAL

As defined in Chapter 8, the term *gross working capital* means total current assets, while *net working capital* means current assets minus current liabilities. The concept of working capital originated at a time when most industries were closely related to agriculture. Processors would buy crops in the fall, process them, sell the finished product, and end up just before the next harvest with relatively low inventories. Bank loans with maximum maturities of one year were used to finance both the purchase and the processing costs, and these loans were retired with the proceeds from the sale of the finished products.

This situation is depicted in Figure 10–1, where fixed assets are shown to be growing steadily over time, while current assets jump at harvest season, decline during the year, and end at zero just before the next crop is harvested. Short-term credit is used to finance current assets, and fixed assets are financed with long-term funds. Thus, the top segment of the graph deals with working capital.

The figure represents an idealized situation—actually, current assets build up gradually as crops are purchased and processed; inventories are drawn down less regularly; and ending inventory balances do not decline to zero. Nevertheless, the example does illustrate the general nature of the

Figure 10–1
Fixed and Current Assets and Their Financing

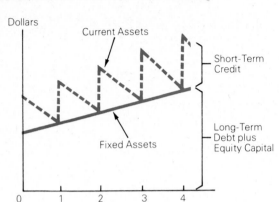

production and financing process, and working capital management consists of decisions relating to the top section of the graph—managing current assets and arranging the short-term credit used to finance them.

As the economy became less oriented toward agriculture, the production and financing cycles of "typical" businesses changed. Although seasonal patterns still existed, and business cycles also caused asset requirements to fluctuate, it became apparent that current assets rarely drop to zero. This realization led to the development of the idea of "permanent current assets," diagramed in Figure 10–2. As the figure is drawn, it maintains the

Figure 10–2
Fluctuating versus Permanent Assets;
Exactly Matching Maturities

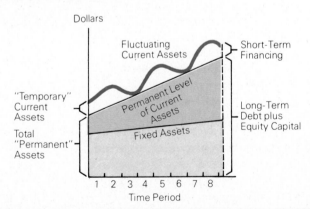

traditional notion that permanent assets should be financed with long-term capital, while temporary assets should be financed with short-term credit.

The matching of asset and liability maturities as shown in Figures 10–1 and 10–2 was considered to be desirable because it minimizes the risk that the firm may be unable to pay off its maturing obligations. To illustrate, suppose a firm borrows on a one year basis and uses the funds obtained to build and equip a plant. Cash flows from the plant (profits plus depreciation) would almost never be sufficient to pay off the loan at the end of only one year, so the loan must be renewed. If for some reason the lender refuses to renew the loan, then the firm has problems. Had the plant been financed with long-term debt, however, cash flows over a longer time frame would have been sufficient to retire the loan, and the problem of renewal would not have arisen.

At the limit, a firm could attempt to match the maturity structure of its assets and liabilities exactly. Inventory expected to be sold in a few weeks could be financed with a short-term bank loan; a machine expected to last for five years could be financed by a five year loan; a twenty year building could be financed by a twenty year mortgage bond; receivables expected to be collected in twenty days could be financed by a twenty day bank loan; and so forth. Actually, of course, uncertainty about the lives of assets prevents this exact maturity matching. For example, a firm may finance inventories with a thirty day loan, expecting to sell the inventories and use the cash generated to retire the loan. But if sales are slow, the cash will not be forthcoming, and the use of short-term credit may cause a problem.

Figure 10–2 above showed the situation for a firm that attempts to match asset and liability maturities. Such a policy could be followed, but firms may also follow other maturity-matching policies. Figure 10–3, for example, illustrates the situation for a firm that finances all of its fixed assets with

Figure 10–3
Fluctuating versus Permanent Assets

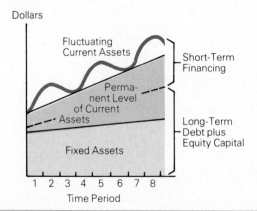

long-term capital but part of its permanent current assets with short-term credit.[1]

The dashed line could even have been drawn *below* the line designating fixed assets, indicating that all the current assets and part of the fixed assets are financed with short-term credit; this would be a highly aggressive, nonconservative position, and the firm would be very much subject to potential loan renewal problems. However, as we shall see in the next section and later in the chapter, short-term debt is often cheaper than long-term debt, so some firms may be willing to sacrifice safety for possibly higher profits.

Alternatively, as in Figure 10–4, the dashed line could be drawn *above* the

Figure 10–4
Fluctuating versus Permanent Assets and Liabilities

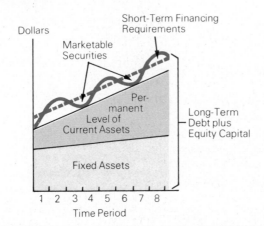

line designating permanent current assets, indicating that permanent capital is being used to meet seasonal demands. In this case, the firm uses a small amount of short-term credit to meet its peak requirements, but it also meets a part of its seasonal needs by "storing liquidity" in the form of marketable securities during the off-season. The humps above the dashed line represent short-term financing; the troughs below the dashed line represent short-term security holdings. This would represent a very safe, conservative position.

---

1 Firms generally have some short-term credit in the form of "spontaneous" funds—accounts payable and accruals (see Chapter 7). Used within limits, these constitute "free" capital, so virtually all firms employ at least some short-term credit at all times.

Advantages and Disadvantages of Short-Term Credit

Although using short-term debt is generally riskier than using long-term debt, short-term credit does have some offsetting advantages. The pros and cons of financing with short-term debt are considered in this section.

Flexibility If its needs for funds are seasonal or cyclical, a firm may not want to commit itself to long-term debt. Such debt can be repaid early, provided the loan agreement includes a prepayment provision, but, even so, prepayment penalties can be expensive. Accordingly, if a firm thinks its need for funds will diminish in the near future, it should choose short-term debt for the flexibility it provides.

Cost of Long-Term versus Short-Term Debt In Chapter 8 we saw that the yield curve is often upward-sloping, indicating that interest rates are lower on short-term than on long-term debt. When this situation exists, interest expense will be lower if the firm borrows on a short-term rather than a long-term basis.

Risk of Long-Term versus Short-Term Debt Even though short-term debt is generally less expensive than long-term debt, financing with short-term debt subjects the firm to more risk than does financing with long-term debt. This risk effect occurs for two reasons: (1) If a firm borrows on a long-term basis, its interest costs will be relatively stable over time, but if it borrows short-term, its interest expense will fluctuate widely, at times going quite high. For example, from 1977 to 1979, the short-term rate for large corporations more than doubled, going from 6.25 percent to 15 percent. (2) If a firm borrows heavily on a short-term basis, it may find itself unable to repay this debt, and it may be in such a weak financial position that the lender will not extend the loan; thus, the firm could be forced into bankruptcy.

A good example of the riskiness of short-term debt is provided by Transamerica Corporation, a major financial services company. Transamerica's chairman noted in a recent interview that the company was moving aggressively to reduce its dependency on short-term loans whose costs vary with short-term interest rates:

Mr. Beckett said Transamerica has reduced its variable-rate loans by about $450 million over the past two years. "We aren't going to go through the enormous increase in debt expense again that had such a serious impact [on earnings]," he said. The company's earnings fell sharply because money rates rose to records. "We were almost entirely in variable-rate debt," he said, but currently out of total debt of slightly more than $1 billion, "about 65% is fixed rate and 35% variable. We've come a long way and we'll keep plugging away at it," he added.

Transamerica's earnings were depressed by the increase in short-term rates, but other companies were even less fortunate—they simply could not pay the interest charges, and this forced them into bankruptcy.[2]

Statements about the flexibility, cost, and riskiness of short-term versus long-term credit depend, to a large extent, on the nature of the short-term credit that is actually used. To make these distinctions clear, the major types of short-term credit are discussed in the following sections.

ACCRUED WAGES AND TAXES

Firms generally pay employees on a weekly, biweekly, or monthly basis, so the balance sheet will typically show some accrued wages. Similarly, the firm's own estimated income taxes, social security and income taxes withheld from employee payrolls, and sales taxes collected by the firm are generally paid on a weekly, monthly, or quarterly basis, so the balance sheet will typically show some accrued taxes.

As we saw in Chapter 7, accruals increase spontaneously as a firm's operations expand. Further, this type of debt is "free" in the sense that no interest must be paid on funds raised through accruals. However, a firm cannot ordinarily control its accruals: payrolls and the timing of wage payments are set by economic forces and by industry custom, while tax payment dates are established by law. Thus, firms use all the accruals they can, but they have little control over the level of these accounts.

ACCOUNTS PAYABLE, OR "TRADE CREDIT"

Firms generally make purchases from other firms on credit, recording the debt as an *account payable*. Accounts payable, or *trade credit,* as it is commonly called, is the largest single category of short-term debt, representing about 40 percent of the current liabilities of nonfinancial corporations. This percentage is somewhat larger for smaller firms: because

---

2 Some academicians argue that while financial policy related to working capital affects a firm's *total risk,* it has a much smaller effect on *systematic or beta risk.* Hence, from its stockholders' point of view, the riskiness of a firm's working capital policy is not too important. Several comments are appropriate. First, it is difficult to prove this point one way or the other, but most authorities would probably argue that working capital policy *does* have a significant effect on beta risk. Second, by following a risky working capital policy, a firm can increase greatly the odds of bankruptcy or other types of financial distress, and this can lower its expected future profit stream at the same time that it raises the riskiness of the stream. This would have a double-barreled effect on the value of the firm.

small companies often do not qualify for financing from other sources, they rely rather heavily on trade credit.[3]

Trade credit is a "spontaneous" source of financing in that it arises from ordinary business transactions. For example, suppose a firm makes average purchases of $2,000 a day on terms of net 30. On the average it will owe thirty times $2,000, or $60,000, to its suppliers. If its sales, and consequently its purchases, were to double, then its accounts payable would also double to $120,000. The firm would have spontaneously generated an additional $60,000 of financing. Similarly, if the terms of credit were extended from thirty to forty days, accounts payable would expand from $60,000 to $80,000. Thus, lengthening the credit period, as well as expanding sales and purchases, generates additional financing.

The Cost of Trade Credit

As we saw in Chapter 9 in connection with accounts receivable management, firms that sell on credit have a *credit policy* that includes setting the *terms of credit.* For example, Carter Chemical Company's Textile Products division sells on terms of 2/10, net 30, meaning that a 2 percent discount is given if payment is made within ten days of the invoice date and that the full invoice amount is due and payable within thirty days if the discount is not taken.

Suppose Fall Mills, Inc., buys an average of $12 million of materials from Carter each year, less a 2 percent discount, or net purchases of $11,760,000/360 = $32,666.67 per day. For simplicity, suppose Carter Chemical is Fall Mills' only supplier. If Fall Mills takes the discount, paying at the end of the tenth day, its payables will average (10)($32,666.67) = $326,667; Fall Mills will, on average, be receiving $326,667 of credit from its only supplier, Carter Chemical Company.

Now suppose Fall Mills decides *not* to take the discount; what will happen? First, Fall Mills will begin paying invoices after thirty days, so its accounts payable will increase to (30)($32,666.67) = $980,000.[4] Carter Chemical will now be supplying Fall Mills with an *additional* $653,333 of credit. Fall Mills could use this additional credit to pay off bank loans, to

---

3 In a credit sale, the seller records the transaction as an *account receivable,* the buyer as an *account payable.* We examined accounts receivable as an asset investment in Chapter 9. Our focus in this chapter is on accounts payable, a liability item. We might also note that if a firm's accounts payable exceed its receivables, it is said to be *receiving net trade credit,* while if its receivables exceed its payables, it is *extending net trade credit.* Smaller firms frequently receive net credit; larger firms extend it.

4 A question arises: Will accounts payable reflect gross purchases or purchases net of discounts? Although generally accepted accounting practices permit either treatment on the grounds that the difference is not material, most accountants prefer recording both inventories and payables net of discounts, then reporting the higher payments that result from not taking discounts as an additional expense. *Thus, we show accounts payable net of discounts even when the company does not expect to take the discount.*

expand inventories, to add fixed assets, to build up its cash account, or even to increase its own accounts receivable.

Fall Mills' new credit from Carter Chemical has a cost—Fall Mills is foregoing a 2 percent discount on its $12 million of purchases, so its costs will rise by $240,000 per year. Dividing this $240,000 by the additional credit, we find the implicit percentage cost of the added trade credit as follows:

$$\text{Percentage cost} = \frac{\$240,000}{\$653,333} = 36.7\%.$$

Assuming that Fall Mills can borrow from its bank (or from other sources) at an interest rate of less than 36.7 percent, it should not expand its payables by foregoing discounts.

The following equation may be used to calculate the approximate percentage cost, on an annual basis, of not taking discounts:

$$\substack{\text{Percentage} \\ \text{cost}} = \frac{\text{Discount percent}}{100 - \left(\substack{\text{Discount} \\ \text{percent}}\right)} \times \frac{360}{\left(\substack{\text{Days credit} \\ \text{is} \\ \text{outstanding}}\right) - \left(\substack{\text{Discount} \\ \text{period}}\right)}. \quad (10\text{--}1)$$

The numerator of the first term, discount percent, is the cost per dollar of credit, while the denominator in this term (100 − discount percent) represents the funds made available by not taking the discount. The second term shows how many times each year this cost is incurred. To illustrate the equation, the cost of not taking a discount when the terms are 2/10, net 30, is computed as follows:[5]

$$\text{Cost} = \frac{2}{98} \times \frac{360}{20} = 0.0204 \times 18 = 0.367 = 36.7\%.$$

Notice also that the calculated cost can be reduced by paying late. Thus, if Fall Mills pays in sixty days rather than in the specified thirty, the credit period becomes 60 − 10 = 50, and the calculated cost becomes

$$\text{Cost} = \frac{2}{98} \times \frac{360}{50} = 0.0204 \times 7.2 = 0.147 = 14.7\%.$$

In periods of excess capacity, firms may be able to get away with late

---

5 In compound interest terms, the rate is even higher. As discussed in Chapter 3, if interest is earned and paid during the year, and if interest is earned on interest, then the effective annual rate is increased over the rate with annual compounding. In the case of trade discounts, the discount amounts to interest, and with terms of 2/10, net 30, we have 18 "interest periods" per year. The first term in our equation is (Discount percent)/(100 − Discount percent) = 0.02/(0.98) = 0.0204. This "interest rate" is "earned" 18 times each year, so the effective annual rate cost of trade credit is

$$\text{Percentage cost} = (1.0204)^{18} - 1.0 = 1.438 - 1.0 = 43.8\%.$$

Thus, the 36.7% cost calculated above understates the cost of trade credit in a compound interest sense.

payments, but they may also suffer a variety of problems associated with being a "slow payer" account. These problems are discussed later in the chapter.

The cost of additional trade credit resulting from not taking discounts can be worked out for other purchase terms. Some illustrative costs are shown below:

Credit Terms	Cost of Additional Credit If Cash Discount Not Taken
1/10, net 20	37%
1/10, net 30	18
2/10, net 20	73
3/15, net 45	37

As these figures show, the cost of not taking discounts can be substantial. Incidentally, throughout the chapter we assume that payments are made either on the *last day* for taking discounts or on the last day of the credit period unless otherwise noted. It would be foolish to pay, say, on the fifth or twentieth day if the credit terms were 2/10, net 30.

Effects of Trade Credit on the Financial Statements

A firm's policy with regard to taking or not taking discounts can have a significant effect on its financial statements. To illustrate, let us assume that Fall Mills is just beginning its operations. On the first day, it makes net purchases of $32,666.67. This amount is recorded on the balance sheet under accounts payable.[6] The second day it buys another $32,666.67. The first day's purchases are not yet paid for, so at the end of the second day accounts payable total $65,333.34. Accounts payable increase by another $32,666.67 the third day, to a total of $98,000, and after ten days accounts payable are up to $326,667.

If Fall Mills takes discounts, then on the eleventh day it will have to pay for the $32,666.67 of purchases made on day one, which will reduce accounts payable. However, it will buy another $32,666.67, which will increase payables. Thus, after the tenth day of operations, Fall Mills' balance sheet will level off, showing a balance of $326,667 in accounts payable, assuming the company pays on the tenth day in order to take discounts.

Now suppose Fall Mills decides not to take discounts. In this case, on the eleventh day it will add another $32,666.67 to payables, but it will not pay for the purchases made on the first day. Thus, the balance sheet figure for accounts payable will rise to 11 × $32,666.67 = $359,333.37. This buildup

---

6 Inventories also increase by $32,666.67, but we are not concerned with this account at this time.

will continue through the thirtieth day, at which point payables will total
30 × $32,666.67 = $980,000. On the thirty-first day, it will buy another
$32,667 of goods, which will increase accounts payable; but it will pay for
the purchases made the first day, which will reduce payables. Thus, the
balance sheet item "accounts payable" will stabilize at $980,000 after thirty
days, assuming Fall Mills does not take discounts.

Table 10–1 shows Fall Mills' balance sheet, after it reaches a steady state,
under the two trade credit policies. The assets are unchanged by this policy
decision, and we also assume that accruals and common equity are
unchanged. The differences show up in accounts payable and notes
payable; when Fall Mills elects to take discounts and thus gives up some of
the trade credit it otherwise could have obtained, it will have to raise
$653,333 from some other source. It could have sold more common stock,
or it could have used long-term bonds, but it chose to use bank credit,
which has a 10 percent cost and is reflected in notes payable.

Table 10–1
Fall Mills' Balance Sheet with Different Trade
Credit Policies

A. Do Not Take Discounts; Use Maximum Trade Credit

Cash	$ 500,000	Accounts payable	$ 980,000
Receivables	1,000,000	Notes payable	0
Inventories	2,000,000	Accruals	500,000
Fixed assets	2,980,000	Common equity	5,000,000
	$6,480,000		$6,480,000

B. Take Discounts; Borrow from Bank

Cash	$ 500,000	Accounts payable	$ 326,667
Receivables	1,000,000	Notes payable (10%)	653,333
Inventories	2,000,000	Accruals	500,000
Fixed assets	2,980,000	Common equity	5,000,000
	$6,480,000		$6,480,000

Table 10–2 shows Fall Mills' income statement under the two policies. If
the company does not take discounts, then its interest expense is zero, but
it will have a $240,000 expense for "discounts lost." On the other hand, if it
does take discounts, it incurs an interest expense of $65,333, but it also
avoids the cost of discounts lost. Since discounts lost exceed the interest
expense, the take-discounts policy results in the higher net income and,
thus, in a higher value of the stock.

Table 10–2
Fall Mills' Income Statement with Different
Trade Credit Policies

	Do Not Take Discounts	Take Discounts
Sales	$15,000,000	$15,000,000
Purchases	11,760,000	11,760,000
Labor and other costs	2,000,000	2,000,000
Interest	0	65,333
Discounts lost	240,000	0
Total costs	$14,000,000	$13,825,333
Net income before tax	1,000,000	1,174,667
Tax (40%)	400,000	469,867
Net income after tax	$ 600,000	$ 704,800

Components of Trade Credit: Free versus Costly

Based on the preceding discussion, trade credit can be divided into two components:

1. *Free trade credit,* which involves credit received during the discount period. For Fall Mills, this amounts to ten days of net purchases, or $326,667.[7]
2. *"Costly" trade credit,* which involves credit in excess of the free credit. This credit has an implicit cost equal to the foregone discounts. Fall Mills could obtain $653,333, or twenty days' net purchases, of such credit at a cost of approximately 37 percent.

Financial managers should always use the free component, but they should use the costly component only after analyzing the cost of this capital and determining that it is less than the cost of funds obtained from other sources. Under the terms of trade found in most industries, the costly component will involve a relatively high percentage cost, so stronger firms will avoid using it.

Another point which may be made about trade credit is that firms sometimes can and do deviate from the stated credit terms, thus altering the percentage cost figures cited above. To illustrate, a California manufacturing firm that buys on terms of 2/10, net 30, makes a practice of paying in fifteen days (rather than ten) and still taking discounts. Its treasurer simply waits

---

7 There is some question as to whether any credit is really "free," because the supplier will have a cost of carrying receivables which must be passed on to the customer in the form of higher prices. Still, where suppliers sell on standard terms such as 2/10, net 30, and where the base price cannot be negotiated downward for early payment, then for all intents and purposes the ten days of trade credit is indeed "free."

until fifteen days after receipt of the goods to pay, then writes a check for the invoiced amount less the 2 percent discount. The company's suppliers want its business, so they tolerate this practice. Similarly, a Wisconsin firm that also buys on terms of 2/10, net 30, does not take discounts, but it pays in sixty rather than in thirty days. As shown above, both practices reduce the cost of trade credit. Neither of these firms is "loved" by its suppliers, and neither could continue these practices in times when suppliers were operating at full capacity and had order backlogs, but these practices can and do reduce the costs of trade credit during times when suppliers have excess capacity.

SHORT-TERM BANK LOANS

Commercial banks, whose loans appear on firms' balance sheets as notes payable, are second in importance to trade credit as a source of short-term financing.[8] The banks' influence is actually greater than appears from the dollar amounts they lend, because banks provide *nonspontaneous* funds. As a firm's financing needs increase, it requests its bank to provide the additional funds. If the request is denied, often the firm is forced to slow down its rate of growth. Some features of bank loans are discussed below.

Maturity Although banks do make longer-term loans, *the bulk of their lending is on a short-term basis*—about two-thirds of all bank loans mature in a year or less. Bank loans to businesses are frequently written as ninety day notes, so the loan must be repaid or renewed at the end of ninety days. Of course, if a borrower's financial position has deteriorated, the bank may well refuse to renew the loan. This can mean serious trouble for the borrower.

Promissory Note When a bank loan is taken out, the agreement is executed by the signing of a promissory note. The note specifies (1) the amount borrowed; (2) the percentage interest rate; (3) the repayment schedule, which can involve either a lump sum or a series of installments; (4) any

---

8 There are two types of banks: (1) *Savings banks do not* make short-term loans to businesses. These banks accept mainly time deposits, and they invest heavily in residential mortgage loans. Savings banks are located principally in the Northeast and are very similar to savings and loan associations. (2) *Commercial banks do* accept demand deposits and *do* make short-term loans to both individuals and businesses. When the word "bank" is used in this book, it means a commercial bank unless otherwise specified. (There are also "investment banking houses," which are firms such as Merrill Lynch engaged in various aspects of the securities business. Investment bankers accept *no* regular deposits and make *no* regular loans. Investment bankers simply buy stocks and bonds issued by business firms for resale to investors. Investment banking is described in detail in Chapters 13 and 14.)

collateral that might be put up as security for the loan; and (5) any other terms and conditions to which the bank and the borrower may have agreed. When the note is signed, the bank credits the borrower's demand deposit with the amount of the loan. On the borrower's balance sheet, both cash and notes payable increase.

Compensating Balances In Chapter 8, compensating balances were discussed in connection with the firm's cash account. As noted there, banks typically require that a regular borrower maintain an average checking account balance of 10 to 20 percent of the face amount of the loan. These compensating balances raise the effective interest rate. For example, if a firm needs $80,000 to pay off outstanding obligations, but it must maintain a 20 percent compensating balance, then it must borrow $100,000 to obtain a usable $80,000. If the stated interest rate is 8 percent, the effective cost is actually 10 percent: $8,000 divided by $80,000 equals 10 percent.[9]

Line of Credit A line of credit is a formal or an informal understanding between the bank and the borrower indicating the maximum size loan the bank will allow the borrower. For example, on December 31 a bank loan officer may indicate to a financial manager that the bank regards the firm as being "good" for up to $80,000 for the forthcoming year. On January 10 the manager signs a promissory note for $15,000 for ninety days—this is called "taking down" $15,000 of the total line of credit. This amount is credited to the firm's checking account at the bank. Before repayment of the $15,000, the firm may borrow additional amounts up to a total outstanding at any one time of $80,000.

Revolving Credit Agreement A *revolving credit agreement* is a more formal line of credit arrangement often used by large firms. To illustrate, Carter Chemical negotiated a revolving credit agreement for $100 million with a group of banks. The banks were formally committed for four years to lend Carter up to $100 million if the funds were needed. Carter, in turn, paid a commitment fee of one-quarter of one percent on the unused balance of the commitment to compensate the banks for making the funds available. Thus, if Carter did not take down any of the $100 million commitment during a year, it would still be required to pay a $250,000 fee. If it borrowed $50 million, the unused portion of the line of credit would fall to $50 million, and the fee would fall to $125,000. Of course, interest also had to be paid on the amount of money Carter actually borrowed. As a general rule, the rate of

9 Note, however, that the compensating balance may be set as a minimum monthly *average;* if the firm would maintain this average anyway, the compensating balance requirement does not entail higher effective rates. Also, note that these *loan* compensating balances are added to any *service* compensating balances (discussed in Chapter 8) that the firm's bank may require.

interest on "revolvers" is pegged to the prime rate (see next section), so the cost of the loan varies over time as interest rates vary. Carter's rate was set at prime plus $1/2$ percent.

The Cost of Bank Loans

The cost of bank loans varies for different types of borrowers at a given point in time, and for all borrowers over time. Interest rates are higher for riskier borrowers. Rates are also higher on smaller loans because of the fixed costs of making and servicing loans. If the firm can qualify as a "prime risk" because of its size and financial strength, it can borrow at the *prime rate,* the lowest rate banks charge. Rates on other loans are scaled up from the prime rate.[10]

Bank rates vary widely over time depending on economic conditions and Federal Reserve policy. When the economy is weak, then (1) loan demand is usually slack and (2) the Fed also makes plenty of money available to the system. As a result, rates on all types of loans are relatively low. Conversely, when the economy is booming, loan demand is typically strong, and the Fed generally restricts the money supply—the result is high interest rates. As an indication of the kinds of fluctuations that can occur, the prime rate in 1974 varied from a low of $8^1/2$ percent to a high of 12 percent, and it rose to $15^3/4$ percent in November 1979. Interest rates on other bank loans vary more or less with the prime rate.

Interest rates on bank loans are calculated in three ways: as "simple" interest, as "discount" interest, and as "add-on" interest. These three methods are explained below.

Regular, or Simple, Interest Exactly the type of interest rate we discussed in Chapters 3 and 4 is involved in simple interest.[11] On the typical loan for $10,000 for one year at 9 percent, the borrower receives $10,000 now and repays $10,900 at the end of the year:

$$\text{Effective rate of interest} = \frac{\text{Interest}}{\text{Borrowed amount}} = \frac{\$900}{\$10,000} = 9\%. \qquad (10\text{--}2)$$

Discounted Interest If the bank deducts the interest in advance *(discounts the loan),* the effective rate of interest is increased. On the $10,000 loan for 9

---

10 Each bank sets its own prime rate, but, because of competitive forces, most banks' prime rates are identical. Further, most banks follow the rate set by the large New York City banks, and they, in turn, generally follow the rate set by Citibank, New York City's largest. Citibank sets the prime rate each week at 1¼ to 1½ percentage points above the average rate on large certificates of deposit (CDs) during the three weeks immediately preceding. CD rates represent the "price" of money in the open market, and they rise and fall with the supply and demand of money, so CD rates are "market-clearing" rates. By tying the prime rate to CD rates, the banking system insures that the prime rate will also be a market-clearing rate.

11 Years ago, the term *simple interest* meant that interest was not earned on interest, and it was distinguished from compound interest. Today, at least in banking, when people refer to simple interest they mean plain old compound interest.

percent, the discount is $900, and the borrower obtains the use of only $9,100. The effective rate of interest is 9.9 percent versus 9 percent on a simple interest loan:

$$\frac{\text{Effective rate}}{\text{of interest}} = \frac{\text{Interest}}{\text{Amount borrowed} - \text{Interest}}$$

$$= \frac{\$900}{\$9,100} = 9.9\%. \tag{10-3}$$

Installment Loans: Add-On Interest Banks (and other lenders) typically charge add-on interest on automobile and other types of installment loans for under about $10,000. The term *add-on* means that interest is calculated and added on to the funds received to determine the face amount of the note. To illustrate, suppose our $10,000 loan is to be repaid in twelve monthly installments. At a 9 percent add-on rate, the borrower pays a total interest charge of $900. Thus, the note signed is for $10,900. However, since the loan is paid off in installments, the borrower has the full $10,000 only during the first month, and by the last month eleven-twelfths of the loan will have been repaid. The borrower must pay $900 for the use of only about half the amount received, as the *average* amount of the original loan outstanding during the year is only about $5,000. Therefore, the effective rate on the loan is approximately 18 percent, calculated as follows:

$$\frac{\text{Approximate interest rate}}{\text{on installment loan}} = \frac{\text{Interest paid}}{\text{Loan amount} \div 2}$$

$$= \frac{\$900}{\$5,000} = 18\%. \tag{10-4}$$

The main point to note here is that interest is paid on the *original* amount of the loan, not on the amount actually outstanding (the declining balance), which causes the effective interest rate to be almost double the stated rate.[12]

---

12 This is only an approximation of the true rate of interest. To determine the precisely correct annual percentage rate (APR) on the loan, we proceed as follows:
   1. The total loan to be repaid is $10,000 plus $900 interest, which is added on to the amount borrowed, for a total of $10,900.
   2. The monthly payment is $10,900 ÷ 12 = $908.33.
   3. The bank is, in effect, buying a twelve period annuity of $908.33 for $10,000, so $10,000 is the PV of the annuity. Expressed in equation form,

$$PV = \$10,000 = \sum_{t=1}^{12} \$908.33 \left[\frac{1}{1+k_d}\right]^t. \tag{10-5}$$

   4. This equation can be solved for k_d, which is the rate per month. Here $k_d = 1.3513\%$.
   5. The APR is calculated as follows:

$$APR = (1 + k_d)^{12} - 1.0 = (1.013513)^{12} - 1.0 = 1.175 - 1.0 = 17.5 \text{ percent.}$$

   6. Under the truth-in-lending laws, banks, department stores, and other installment lenders are required to report the APR in boldface type on the face of all installment loan contracts. This is to prevent lenders from calling a loan with an effective rate of 17.5 percent a 9 percent loan.
   7. If an installment loan is paid off ahead of schedule, other complications arise. For a discussion of this point, see Dick Bonker, "The Rule of 78," *Journal of Finance*, June 1976, pp. 877–888.

Consumer Revolving Credit Credit card companies, department stores, and banks grant consumers lines of credit up to specified limits. Interest is calculated each month on the outstanding balance, and this interest is added to the previous balance. Frequently, the rate is set at 1½ percent per month, and the annual percentage rate (APR) is stated to be 12 × 1½ = 18%.[13]

Effective Interest Rates When Compensating Balances Apply

Compensating balances tend to raise the effective interest rate on bank loans. To illustrate this, suppose a firm needs $10,000 to pay for some equipment that it recently purchased. A bank offers to lend the company money at a 9 percent simple interest rate, but the company must maintain a compensating balance equal to 20 percent of the amount of the loan. If it did not take the loan, the firm would keep no deposits with the bank. What is the effective interest rate on the loan?

First, note that although the firm needs only $10,000, it must borrow $12,500, calculated as follows:[14]

$$\text{Amount of loan} = \frac{\text{Funds needed}}{1.0 - \text{Compensating balance percentage}}$$

$$= \frac{\$10,000}{0.8} = \$12,500. \qquad (10\text{–}6)$$

The interest paid will be (0.09)($12,500) = $1,125, but the firm will only get the use of $10,000. Therefore, the effective interest rate is

$$\frac{\text{Effective}}{\text{interest rate}} = \frac{\text{Interest paid}}{\text{Funds actually used}} = \frac{\$1,125}{\$10,000} = 0.1125 = 11.25\%.$$

In general, we can use this formula to find the effective interest rate when compensating balances apply:

$$\frac{\text{Effective}}{\text{interest rate}} = \frac{\text{Stated interest rate}}{1.0 - \text{Compensating balance fraction}}. \qquad (10\text{–}7)$$

In our example,

$$\frac{\text{Effective}}{\text{interest rate}} = \frac{9\%}{1 - 0.2} = \frac{9\%}{0.8} = 11.25\%.$$

---

13 Although the APR is said (legally, under the truth-in-lending laws) to be 18 percent, the "really true" rate in a compound interest sense is

$$(1.015)^{12} - 1.0 = 1.196 - 1.0 = 0.196 = 19.6\%.$$

14 The logic behind Equation 10–6 is explained below:

Amount of loan = Amount needed + Compensating balance
    = $10,000 + (0.2)(Amount of loan)
Amount of loan − 0.2(Amount of loan) = $10,000
Amount of loan (1− 0.2) = $10,000
Amount of loan = $10,000/0.8 = $12,500
    = (Funds needed)/(1 − Compensating balance).

The analysis can be extended to the case where compensating balances are required and the loan is based on discount interest:

$$\frac{\text{Effective}}{\text{interest rate}} = \frac{\text{Stated interest rate}}{(1.0) - \left(\begin{array}{c}\text{Compensating balance}\\\text{fraction}\end{array}\right) - \left(\begin{array}{c}\text{Stated interest}\\\text{rate}\end{array}\right)}.$$

For example, if we needed $10,000 and were offered a loan with a stated interest rate of 9 percent, discount interest, with a 20 percent compensating balance, the effective interest rate would be

$$\text{Effective interest rate} = \frac{9\%}{1.0 - 0.2 - 0.09} = \frac{9\%}{0.71} = 12.68\%.$$

The amount that we would need to borrow would be

$$\text{Amount borrowed} = \frac{\$10,000}{1.0 - 0.2 - 0.09} = \$14,084.51.$$

We would use this $14,084.51 as follows:

To make required payment	$10,000.00
Compensating balance (20% of $14,084.51)	2,816.90
Prepaid interest (9% of $14,084.51)	1,267.61
	$14,084.51

In our example, compensating balances and discount interest combined to push the effective rate of interest up from 9 percent to 12.68 percent. Note, however, that our analysis assumed that the compensating balance requirements forced the firm to increase its bank deposits. Had the company had transactions balances which could be used to supply all or part of the compensating balances, the effective interest rate would have been less than 12.68 percent.

Choosing a Bank

Individuals whose only contact with their bank is through the use of its checking services generally choose a bank for the convenience of its location and the competitive cost of its checking service. However, a business that borrows from banks must look at other criteria, and a potential borrower seeking banking relations should recognize that important differences exist among banks. Some of these differences are considered below.

1. Banks have different basic policies toward risk. Some banks are inclined to follow relatively conservative lending practices; others engage in what are properly termed "creative banking practices." These policies reflect partly

the personalities of officers of the bank and partly the characteristics of the bank's deposit liabilities. Thus, a bank with fluctuating deposit liabilities in a static community will tend to be a conservative lender, while a bank whose deposits are growing with little interruption may follow "liberal" credit policies. A large bank with broad diversification over geographical regions or among industries served can obtain the benefit of combining and averaging risks. Thus, marginal credit risks that might be unacceptable to a small bank or to a specialized unit bank can be pooled by a branch banking system to reduce the overall risks of a group of marginal accounts.

2. Some bank loan officers are active in providing counsel and in stimulating development loans with firms in their early and formative years. Certain banks have specialized departments to make loans to firms expected to grow and thus become more important customers. The personnel of these departments can provide much counseling to customers.

3. Banks differ in the extent to which they will support the activities of the borrower in bad times. This characteristic is referred to as the degree of *loyalty* of the banks. Some banks may put great pressure on a business to liquidate its loans when the firm's outlook becomes clouded, whereas others will stand by the firm and work diligently to help it get back on its feet. An especially dramatic illustration of this point was Bank of America's recent bail-out of Memorex Corporation. The bank could have forced Memorex into bankruptcy, but instead it loaned the company additional capital and helped it survive a bad period. Memorex's stock price subsequently rose on the New York Stock Exchange from $1.50 to $68, so Bank of America's help was indeed substantial.

4. Banks differ greatly in their degrees of loan specialization. Larger banks have separate departments specializing in different kinds of loans, for example, real estate loans, installment loans, and commercial loans. Within these broad categories there may be a specialization by line of business, such as steel, machinery, or textiles. The strengths of banks are also likely to reflect the nature of the business and the economic environment in which they operate. For example, Texas banks have become specialists in lending to oil companies, while many midwestern banks are agricultural specialists. A firm can obtain more creative cooperation and more active support by going to the bank that has the greatest experience and familiarity with its particular type of business. The financial manager should therefore choose a bank with care. A bank that is excellent for one firm may be unsatisfactory for another.

5. The size of a bank can be an important factor. Since the maximum loan a bank can make to any one customer is generally limited to 10 percent of capital accounts (capital stock plus retained earnings), it will generally not be appropriate for large firms to develop borrowing relationships with small banks.

COMMERCIAL PAPER

Commercial paper consists of unsecured promissory notes of large, strong firms and is sold primarily to other business firms, to insurance companies, to pension funds, and to banks. Although the amounts of commercial paper outstanding are much smaller than bank loans outstanding, this form of financing has grown rapidly in recent years.

Maturity and Cost

Maturities of commercial paper generally vary from two to six months, with an average of about five months.[15] The rates on commercial paper fluctuate with supply and demand conditions—they are determined in the market place and vary daily as conditions change. Typically, commercial paper rates range from $1^1/_4$ to $1^1/_2$ percentage points below rates on prime business loans. Also, since compensating balances are not required for commercial paper, the *effective* cost differential is still wider.[16]

Use

The use of commercial paper is restricted to a comparatively small number of concerns that are exceptionally good credit risks. Dealers prefer to handle the paper of concerns whose net worth is $10 million or more and whose annual borrowing exceeds $1 million.

Other Factors

One potential problem with commercial paper is that a debtor who is in temporary financial difficulty may receive little help, because commercial paper dealings are generally less personal than are bank relationships. Thus, banks are generally more able and willing to help a good customer weather a temporary storm than is a commercial paper dealer. On the other hand, using commercial paper permits a corporation to tap a wide range of credit sources, including banks outside its own area and industrial corporations across the country.

---

15 The maximum maturity without SEC registration is 270 days.
16 However, this factor is offset to some extent by the fact that firms issuing commercial paper are generally required by commercial paper dealers to have unused bank lines of credit to back up their outstanding commercial paper, and fees must be paid on these lines. In other words, to sell $1 million of commercial paper, a firm must have a line of credit available to pay off the paper when it matures, and commitment fees on this unused credit line (about ½ percent) increase the effective cost of the paper.

USE OF SECURITY IN SHORT-TERM FINANCING

Given a choice, it is ordinarily better to borrow on an unsecured basis, as the bookkeeping costs of secured loans are often high. However, weak firms may find (1) that they can borrow only if they put up some type of security to protect the lender, or (2) that by using some security they can borrow at a much lower rate.

Several different kinds of collateral can be employed—marketable stocks or bonds, land or buildings, equipment, inventory, and accounts receivable. Marketable securities make excellent collateral, but few firms hold portfolios of stocks and bonds. Similarly, real property (land and buildings) and equipment are good forms of collateral, but they are generally used as security for long-term loans. However, a great deal of secured short-term business borrowing involves the use of accounts receivable and inventories.

To understand the use of security, consider the case of a Gainesville hardware dealer who wanted to modernize and expand his store. He requested a $200,000 bank loan. After examining his business's financial statements, the bank indicated (1) that it would lend him a maximum of $100,000, and (2) that the interest rate would be 10 percent discount, or an effective rate of 11.11 percent. The owner had a substantial personal portfolio of stocks, so he offered to put up $300,000 of high quality stocks to support the $200,000 loan. The bank then granted the full $200,000 loan, and at a rate of only 8 percent simple interest. The store owner might also have used his inventories or receivables as security for the loan.

In the past, state laws varied greatly with regard to the use of security in financing. Today, however, all states except Louisiana operate under a *Uniform Commercial Code,* which standardizes and simplifies the procedure for establishing loan security. The heart of the Uniform Commercial Code is the *Security Agreement,* a standardized document, or form, on which the specific assets that are pledged are stated. The assets can be items of equipment, accounts receivable, or inventories. Procedures for financing under the Uniform Commercial Code are described in Appendix 10A.

SUMMARY

This chapter began with a discussion of the use of short-term or long-term debt to finance current assets. We saw that because short-term credit offers advantages of lower cost and greater flexibility, most firms use at least some current debt, in spite of the fact that short-term debt increases the firm's risk.

The chapter also examined the four major types of short-term credit available to a firm: (1) *accruals,* (2) *accounts payable, or "trade credit,"* (3) *bank loans,* and (4) *commercial paper.* Companies use accruals on a regular basis, but this usage is not subject to discretionary actions. The other types of credit are controllable, at least within limits.

Accounts payable may be divided into two components, *free trade credit* and *costly trade credit.* The cost of the latter is based on discounts lost, and it can be quite high. The financial manager should use all the free trade credit that is available, but costly trade credit should be used only if other credit is not available on better terms.

The third major source of short-term credit is the *commercial banking system.* Bank loans may be obtained as the need arises, or they may be obtained on a regular basis under a *line of credit.* There are three different kinds of interest charges on bank loans: (1) *simple interest,* (2) *discount interest,* and (3) *add-on interest* for installment loans. Banks often require borrowers to maintain *compensating balances;* if the required balance exceeds the balance the firm would otherwise maintain, compensating balances raise the effective cost of bank loans.

Commercial paper constitutes another important source of short-term credit, but it is available only to large, financially strong firms. Interest rates on commercial paper are generally below the prime bank rate, and the relative cost of paper is even lower when compensating balances on bank loans are considered. However, commercial paper does have disadvantages—if a firm that depends heavily on commercial paper experiences problems, its source of funds will immediately dry up. Commercial bankers are much more likely to help their customers ride out bad times.

Although we mentioned it only briefly in the chapter, short-term credit is often secured by inventories and accounts receivable. Techniques for using security to obtain short-term credit are discussed in the appendix to this chapter.

Questions

10-1 "Firms can control their accruals within fairly wide limits; depending on the cost of accruals, financing from this source will be increased or decreased." Discuss.

10-2 Is it true that both trade credit and accruals represent a spontaneous source of capital to finance growth? Explain.

10-3 Is it true that most firms are able to obtain some "free" trade credit, and that additional trade credit is often available, but at a cost? Explain.

10-4 Define each of the following terms:
   a. Promissory note.
   b. Compensating balance.
   c. Line of credit.
   d. Prime rate.
   e. Revolving credit agreement.
   f. Simple interest, discount interest, add-on interest, and APR.

10-5 What is commercial paper? Could Mamma and Pappa Gus's Corner Grocery borrow on commercial paper?

10-6 From the standpoint of the borrower, is long-term or short-term credit riskier? Explain.

10-7 If long-term credit exposes a borrower to less risk, why would people or firms borrow on a short-term basis?

10-8 Suppose that a firm can borrow at the prime rate and it can also sell commercial paper. (a) If the prime rate is 12 percent, what is a reasonable estimate for the cost of commercial paper? (b) If a substantial cost differential exists, why might a firm such as this one actually borrow from both markets?

Problems

10-1 Calculate the implicit cost of nonfree trade credit under the following terms, using Equation 10-1.
   a. 2/15, net 40.
   b. 3/10, net 20.
   c. 1/10, net 60.

10-2 a. If a firm buys under terms of 2/10, net 40, but actually pays after fifteen days and *still takes the discount,* what is the cost of its nonfree trade credit?
   b. Does it receive more or less trade credit than it would if it paid within ten days?

10-3 Suppose a firm makes purchases of $1,200,000 per year under terms of 2/10, net 30. It takes discounts.
   a. What is the average amount of its accounts payable, net of discounts? (Assume the $1.2 million purchases are net of discounts; that is, gross purchases are $1,224,490, discounts are $24,490, and net purchases are $1.2 million. Also, use 360 days in a year.)
   b. Is there a cost of the trade credit it uses?
   c. If it did not take discounts, what would its average payables be, and what would be the cost of this nonfree trade credit?

10-4 You plan to borrow $5,000 from the bank. The bank offers to lend you the money at an 8 percent interest rate on a one year loan. What is the true, or effective, rate of interest for (a) simple interest, (b) discount interest, and (c) add-on interest, if the loan is a twelve month installment loan?

10-5 Engineering Associates, Inc., (EA) projects an increase in sales from $1 million to $1.5 million, but the company needs an additional $300,000 of assets to support this expansion. The money can be obtained from the bank at an interest rate of 9 percent discount interest. Alternatively, EA can finance the expansion by no longer taking discounts, thus increasing accounts payable. EA purchases under terms of 2/10, net 30, but it can delay payment for an additional thirty days, paying in sixty days and thus becoming thirty days past due, without a penalty at this time.
   a. Based strictly on an interest rate comparison, how should EA finance its expansion? Show your work.

b. What additional qualitative factors should be considered in reaching a decision?

10-6 The Adcock Corporation had sales of $1.95 million last year and earned a 3 percent return, after taxes, on sales. Although its terms of purchase are thirty days, its accounts payable represent sixty days' purchases. The president of the company is seeking to increase the company's bank borrowings in order to become current (that is, have thirty days' payables outstanding) in meeting its trade obligations. The company's balance sheet is shown below:

a. How much bank financing is needed to eliminate past-due accounts payable?

b. Would you as a bank loan officer make the loan? Why?

Adcock Corporation Balance Sheet

Cash	$ 25,000	Accounts payable	$ 300,000
Accounts receivable	125,000	Bank loans	250,000
Inventory	650,000	Accruals	125,000
Current assets	$ 800,000	Current liabilities	$ 675,000
Land and buildings	250,000	Mortgage on real estate	250,000
Equipment	250,000	Common stock,	
		par 10 cents	125,000
		Retained earnings	250,000
		Total liabilities	
Total assets	$1,300,000	and net worth	$1,300,000

10-7 Parelli & Sons sells on terms of 2/10, net 40. Annual sales in 1979 were $4.6 million. Half of Parelli's customers pay on the tenth day and take discounts.

a. If accounts receivable in 1979 averaged $447,230, what is Parelli's average collection period *on nondiscount sales?*

b. What rate of return is Parelli earning on its nondiscount receivables, where this rate of return is defined to be equal to the cost of this trade credit to the nondiscount customers?

10-8 Swink & Daughter, Inc., has the following balance sheet:

Cash	$ 50,000	Accounts payable[a]	$ 500,000
Accounts receivable	450,000	Notes payable	50,000
Inventories	750,000	Accruals	50,000
Total current assets	$1,250,000	Total current liabilities	$ 600,000
		Long-term debt	150,000
Fixed assets	750,000	Common equity	1,250,000
		Total liabilities	
Total assets	$2,000,000	and equity	$2,000,000

[a]Stated net of discounts, even though discounts may not be taken.

Swink buys on terms of 1/10, net 30, but it has not been taking discounts and has actually been paying in seventy days rather than thirty days. Now

Swink's suppliers are threatening to stop shipments unless the company begins making prompt payments (that is, pays in thirty days or less). Swink can borrow on a one year note (call this a current liability) from its bank at a rate of 9 percent, discount interest, with a 20 percent compensating balance required. (All of the cash now on hand is needed for transactions; it cannot be used as part of the compensating balance.)

a. Determine what action Swink should take by (1) calculating the cost of nonfree trade credit, and (2) calculating the cost of the bank loan.

b. Based on your decision in Part a, construct a pro forma balance sheet. (*Hint:* You will need to include an account entitled "prepaid interest" under current assets.)

APPENDIX 10A   THE USE OF SECURITY IN SHORT-TERM FINANCING

Procedures under the Uniform Commercial Code for using accounts receivable and inventories as security for short-term credit are described in this appendix. As noted in Chapter 10, secured short-term loans involve quite a bit of paperwork and other administrative costs; hence, they are relatively expensive. However, this is often the only type of financing available to weaker firms.

FINANCING ACCOUNTS RECEIVABLE

Accounts receivable financing involves either the pledging of receivables or the selling of receivables (factoring). The *pledging of accounts receivable* is characterized by the fact that the lender not only has a claim against the receivables but also has recourse to the borrower (seller); if the person or the firm that bought the goods does not pay, the selling firm must take the loss. In other words, the risk of default on the accounts receivable pledged remains with the borrower. Also, the buyer of the goods is not ordinarily notified about the pledging of the receivables. The financial institution that lends on the security of accounts receivable is generally either a commercial bank or one of the large industrial finance companies.

Factoring, or *selling accounts receivable,* involves the purchase of accounts receivable by the lender without recourse to the borrower (seller). With factoring, the buyer of the goods is typically notified of the transfer and makes payment directly to the lender. Since the factoring firm assumes the risk of default on bad accounts, it must do the credit checking. Accordingly, factors provide not only money but also a credit department for the borrower. Incidentally, the same financial institutions that make loans against pledged receivables also serve as factors. Thus, depending on the circumstances and the wishes of the borrower, a financial institution will provide either form of receivables financing.

Procedure for Pledging Accounts Receivable

The financing of accounts receivable is initiated by a legally binding agreement between the seller of the goods and the financing institution. The agreement sets forth in detail the procedures to be followed and the legal obligations of both parties. Once the working relationship has been established, the seller periodically takes a batch of invoices to the financing institution. The lender reviews the invoices and makes credit appraisals of the buyers. Invoices of companies that do not meet the lender's credit standards are not accepted for pledging.

The financial institution seeks to protect itself at every phase of the operation. Selection of sound invoices is the essential first step in safeguarding the financial institution. If the buyer of the goods does not pay the invoice, the lender still has recourse against the seller of the goods. However, if many buyers default, the seller firm may be unable to meet its obligation to the financial institution. Additional protection is afforded the lender in that the loan will generally be for less than 100 percent of the pledged receivables; for example, the lender may advance the selling firm only 75 percent of the amount of the pledged receivables.

Procedure for Factoring Accounts Receivable

The procedure for factoring is somewhat different from that for pledging. Again, an agreement between the seller and the factor is made to specify legal obligations and procedural arrangements. When the seller receives an order from a buyer, a credit approval slip is written and immediately sent to the factoring company for a credit check. If the factor does not approve the sale, the seller generally refuses to fill the order. This procedure informs the seller, prior to the sale, about the buyer's creditworthiness and acceptability to the factor. If the sale is approved, shipment is made and the invoice is stamped to notify the buyer to make payment directly to the factoring company.

The factor performs three functions in carrying out the normal procedure as outlined above: (1) credit checking, (2) lending, and (3) risk bearing. The seller can select various combinations of these functions by changing provisions in the factoring agreement. For example, a small or a medium-sized firm can avoid establishing a credit department. The factor's service might well be less costly than a department that may have excess capacity for the firm's credit volume. At the same time, if the firm uses part of the time of a noncredit specialist to perform credit checking, then lack of education, training, and experience may result in excessive losses.

The seller may utilize the factor to perform the credit-checking and risk-taking functions but not the lending function. The following procedure is carried out on receipt of a $10,000 order. The factor checks and approves the invoices. The goods are shipped on terms of net 30. Payment is made to the factor, who remits to the seller. But assume that the factor has received only $5,000 by the end of the credit period. The $10,000 must still be remitted to the seller (less a fee, of course). If the remaining $5,000 is never paid, the factor sustains a $5,000 loss.

Now consider the more typical situation in which the factor performs a lending function by making payment in advance of collection. The goods are shipped and, even though payment is not due for thirty days, the factor immediately makes funds available to the seller. Suppose $10,000 of goods is shipped. The factoring commission for credit checking is 2½ percent of the invoice price, or $250, and the interest expense is computed at a 9 percent annual rate on the invoice balance, or $75.[1] The seller's accounting entry is as follows:

Cash	$9,175	
Interest expense	75	
Factoring commission	250	
Reserve due from factor on collection of account	500	
Accounts receivable		$10,000

The $500 due from factor on collection of account is a reserve established by the factor to cover disputes between sellers and buyers on damaged goods, goods returned by the buyers to the seller, and failure to make outright sale of goods. The reserve is paid to the selling firm when the factor collects on the account.

Factoring is normally a continuous process instead of the single cycle described above. The firm selling the goods receives orders; it transmits the purchase orders to the factor for approval; on approval, the goods are shipped; the factor advances the money to the seller; the buyers pay the factor when payment is due; and the factor periodically remits any excess reserve to the seller of the goods. Once a routine is established, a continuous circular flow of goods and funds takes place between the seller, the buyers of the goods, and the factor. Thus, once the factoring agreement is in force, funds from this source are *spontaneous*.

Cost of Receivables Financing

Accounts receivable pledging and factoring services are convenient and advantageous, but they can be costly. The credit-checking commission is 1 to 3

---

1 Since the interest is only for one month, we take one-twelfth of the stated rate, 9 percent, and multiply this by the $10,000 invoice price:

$$\frac{1}{12} \times 0.09 \times \$10,000 = \$75.$$

Note that the effective rate of interest is really above 9 percent, because a discounting procedure is used and the borrower does not get the full $10,000. In many instances, however, the factoring contract calls for interest to be computed on the invoice price *less* the factoring commission and the reserve account.

percent of the amount of invoices accepted by the factor. The cost of money is reflected in the interest rate (usually two to three percentage points over the prime rate) charged on the unpaid balance of the funds advanced by the factor. When risk to the factoring firm is excessive, it purchases the invoices (with or without recourse) at discounts from face value.

Evaluation of Receivables Financing

It cannot be said categorically that accounts receivable financing is always either a good or a poor method of raising funds for an individual business. Among the advantages is, first, the flexibility of this source of financing. As the firm's sales expand and more financing is needed, a larger volume of invoices is generated automatically. Because the dollar amounts of invoices vary directly with sales, the amount of readily available financing increases. Second, receivables or invoices provide security for a loan that a firm might otherwise be unable to obtain. Third, factoring provides the services of a credit department that might otherwise be available to the firm only under much more expensive conditions.

Accounts receivable financing also has disadvantages. First, when invoices are numerous and relatively small in dollar amount, the administrative costs involved may render this method of financing inconvenient and expensive. Second, the firm is using a highly liquid asset as security. For a long time, accounts receivable financing was frowned upon by most trade creditors. In fact, such financing was regarded as a confession of a firm's unsound financial position. It is no longer regarded in this light, and many sound firms engage in receivables pledging or factoring. However, the traditional attitude causes some trade creditors to refuse to sell on credit to a firm that is factoring or pledging its receivables, on the grounds that this practice removes one of the most liquid of the firm's assets and, accordingly, weakens the position of other creditors.

Future Use of Receivables Financing

We might make a prediction at this point: in the future, accounts receivable financing will increase in relative importance. Computer technology is rapidly advancing toward the point where credit records of individuals and firms can be kept in computer memory units. Systems have been devised so that a retailer can have a unit on hand that, when an individual's magnetic credit card is inserted into a box, gives a signal that the credit is "good" and that a bank is willing to "buy" the receivable created when the store completes the sale. The cost of handling invoices will be greatly reduced over present-day costs because the new systems will be so highly automated. This will make it possible to use accounts receivable financing for very small sales, and it will reduce the cost of all receivables financing. The net result will be a marked expansion of accounts receivable financing.

INVENTORY FINANCING

A rather large volume of credit is secured by business inventories. If a firm is a relatively good credit risk, the mere existence of the inventory may be a sufficient basis for receiving an unsecured loan. If the firm is a relatively poor risk, the lending institution may insist upon security, which often takes the form of a *blanket lien* against the inventory. Alternatively, *trust receipts* or *field warehouse receipts* can be used to secure the loan. These methods of using inventories as security are discussed below.

Blanket Inventory Lien

The blanket inventory lien gives the lending institution a lien against all inventories of the borrower. However, the borrower is free to sell inventories; thus the value of the collateral can be reduced.

Trust Receipts

Because of the weakness of the blanket lien for inventory financing, another kind of security is used—the trust receipt. A trust receipt is an instrument acknowledging that the borrower holds the goods in trust for the lender. When trust receipts are used, the borrowing firm, on receiving funds from the lender, conveys a trust receipt for the goods. The goods can be stored in a public warehouse or held on the premises of the borrower. The trust receipt states that the goods are held in trust for the lender or are segregated in the borrower's premises on behalf of the lender, and proceeds from the sale of goods held under trust receipts are transmitted to the lender at the end of each day. Automobile dealer financing is the best example of trust receipt financing.

One defect of trust receipt financing is the requirement that a trust receipt must be issued for specific goods. For example, if the security is bags of coffee beans, the trust receipts must indicate the bags by number. In order to validate its trust receipts, the lending institution would have to send someone to the premises of the borrower to see that the bag numbers are correctly listed. Furthermore, complex legal requirements of trust receipts require the attention of a bank officer. Problems are compounded if borrowers are widely separated geographically from the lender. To offset these inconveniences, *warehousing* has come into wide use as a method of securing loans with inventory.

Warehouse Financing

Like trust receipts, warehouse financing uses inventory as security. A *public warehouse* represents an independent third party engaged in the business of storing goods. Items which must age, such as tobacco and liquor, are often financed and stored in public warehouses. Sometimes a public warehouse is not practical because of the bulkiness of goods and the expense of transporting them to and from the borrower's premises. *Field warehouse* financing represents an economical method of inventory financing in which the warehouse is established at the place of the borrower. To provide inventory supervision, the lending institution employs a third party in the arrangement, the field warehousing company. This company acts as the control (or supervisory) agent for the lending institution.

Field warehousing is illustrated by a simple example. Suppose a potential borrower firm has stacked iron in an open yard on its premises. A field warehouse can be established if a field warehousing concern places a temporary fence around the iron and erects a sign stating: "This is a field warehouse supervised and conducted by the Smith Field Warehousing Corporation." These are minimal conditions, of course.

The example illustrates the two elements in the establishment of a warehouse: (1) public notification of the field warehouse arrangement and (2) supervision of the field warehouse by a custodian of the field warehouse concern. When the field warehousing operation is relatively small, the second condition is sometimes violated by hiring an employee of the borrower to supervise the inventory. This practice is viewed as undesirable by the lending institution, because there is no control over the collateral by a person independent of the borrowing concern.[2]

The field warehouse financing operation is described best by a specific illustration. Assume that a tomato cannery is interested in financing its operations by bank borrowing. The cannery has sufficient funds to finance 15 to 20 percent of its operations during the canning season. These funds are adequate to purchase and process an initial batch of tomatoes. As the cans are put into boxes and rolled into the storerooms, the cannery needs additional funds for both raw materials and labor. Because of the cannery's poor credit rating, the bank decides that a field warehousing operation is necessary to secure its loans.

The field warehouse is established, and the custodian notifies the lending institution of the description, by number, of the boxes of canned tomatoes in storage and under warehouse control. Thereupon, the lending institution establishes for the cannery a deposit on which it can draw. From this point on, the bank finances the operations. The cannery needs only enough cash to initiate the cycle. The farmers bring more tomatoes; the cannery processes them; the cans are boxed, and the boxes are put into the field warehouse; field warehouse receipts are drawn up and sent to the bank; the bank establishes further deposits for the cannery on the basis of the receipts; the cannery can draw on the deposits to continue the cycle.

---

2 This absence of independent control was the main cause of the breakdown that resulted in the huge losses connected with the loans to the Allied Crude Vegetable Oil Company. American Express Field Warehousing Company hired men from Allied's staff as custodians. Their dishonesty was not discovered because of another breakdown—the fact that the American Express touring inspector did not actually take a physical inventory of the warehouses. As a consequence, the swindle was not discovered until losses running into the hundreds of millions of dollars had been suffered. See N. C. Miller, *The Great Salad Oil Swindle* (Baltimore, Md.: Penguin Books, 1965), pp. 72–77.

Of course, the cannery's ultimate objective is to sell the canned tomatoes. As the cannery receives purchase orders, it transmits them to the bank, and the bank directs the custodian to release the inventories. It is agreed that, as remittances are received by the cannery, they will be turned over to the bank. These remittances by the cannery pay off the loans made by the bank.

Typically, a seasonal pattern exists. At the beginning of the tomato harvesting and canning season, the cannery's cash needs and loan requirements begin to rise and reach a maximum at the end of the canning season. It is hoped that, well before the new canning season begins, the cannery has sold a sufficient volume to have paid off the loan completely. If for some reason the cannery has had a bad year, the bank may carry it over another year to enable it to work off its inventory.

Acceptable Products In addition to canned foods, which account for about 17 percent of all field warehouse loans, many other product inventories provide a basis for field warehouse financing. Some of these are miscellaneous groceries, which represent about 13 percent; lumber products, about 10 percent; and coal and coke, about 6 percent. These products are relatively nonperishable and are sold in well-developed, organized markets. Nonperishability protects the lender if it should have to take over the security. For this reason, a bank would not make a field warehousing loan on perishables such as fresh fish. However, frozen fish, which can be stored for a long time, can be field warehoused. An organized market aids the lender in disposing of an inventory that it takes over. Banks are not interested in going into the canning or the fish business. They want to be able to dispose of an inventory with the expenditure of a minimum of time.

Cost of Financing The fixed costs of a field warehousing arrangement are relatively high; such financing is therefore not suitable for a very small firm. If a field warehouse company sets up the field warehouse itself, it will typically set a minimum charge of about $350 to $600 a year, plus about 1 to 2 percent of the amount of credit extended to the borrower. Furthermore, the financing institution will charge an interest rate of two to three percentage points over the prime rate. An efficient field warehousing operation requires a minimum inventory of about $500,000.

Appraisal The use of field warehouse financing as a source of funds for business firms has many advantages. First, the amount of funds available is flexible because the financing is tied to the growth of inventories, which in turn is related directly to financing needs. Second, the field warehousing arrangement increases the acceptability of inventories as loan collateral. Some inventories would not be accepted by a bank as security without a field warehousing arrangement. Third, the necessity for inventory control, safekeeping, and the use of specialists in warehousing has resulted in improved warehouse practices. The services of the field warehouse companies have often saved money for the firm in spite of the costs of financing mentioned above. The field warehouse company may suggest inventory practices which reduce the labor that the firm has to employ, and reduce inventory damage and loss as well. The major disadvantage of a field warehousing operation is the fixed cost element, which reduces the feasibility of this form of financing for small firms.

Problem

10A-1 The Fagan Company manufactures plastic toys. It buys raw materials, manufactures the toys in the spring and summer, and ships them to department stores and toy stores by late summer or early fall. Fagan factors its receivables. If it did not, Fagan's October 1979 balance sheet might appear as below:

Fagan Company: Pro Forma Balance Sheet, October 31, 1979

Cash	$ 40,000	Accounts payable	$1,200,000
Receivables	1,200,000	Notes payable	800,000
Inventory	800,000	Accruals	80,000
Total current assets	$2,040,000	Total current liabilities	$2,080,000
		Mortgages	200,000
		Common stock	400,000
Fixed assets	800,000	Retained earnings	160,000
Total assets	$2,840,000	Total claims	$2,840,000

Fagan provides advanced dating on its sales; thus, its receivables are not due for payment until January 31, 1980. Also, Fagan would have been overdue on some $800,000 of its accounts payable if the above situation had actually existed.

Fagan has an agreement with a finance company to factor the receivables for the period October 31 through January 31 of each selling season. The factoring company charges a flat commission of 2 percent, plus 6 percent a year interest on the outstanding balance; it deducts a reserve of 8 percent for returned and damaged materials. Interest and commission are paid in advance. No interest is charged on the reserved funds or on the commission.

a. Show the balance sheet of Fagan on October 31, 1979, giving effect to the purchase of all the receivables by the factoring company and the use of the funds to pay accounts payable.

b. If the $1.2 million is the average level of outstanding receivables, and if they turn over four times a year (hence the commission is paid four times a year), what are the total dollar costs of financing and the effective annual interest rate?

V CAPITAL BUDGETING: INVESTING IN FIXED ASSETS

Capital budgeting is an exceptionally important subject. By definition, "fixed assets" are those which last for a number of years, so investment decisions of this type affect the course of a business for years into the future. Chapter 11 describes the basics of capital budgeting, while Chapter 12 explores the subject in more depth and considers in detail how the riskiness of different projects is evaluated.

11 THE BASICS OF CAPITAL BUDGETING

In Part IV we analyzed decisions relating to current assets and current liabilities, or working capital management. Now we turn to investment decisions involving fixed assets, or the process of capital budgeting. The term *capital* refers to fixed assets used in production, while a *budget* is a plan detailing projected inflows and outflows during some future period. Thus, the *capital budget* outlines the planned expenditures on fixed assets, and *capital budgeting* is the whole process of analyzing projects and deciding whether they should be included in the capital budget.

Our treatment of capital budgeting is divided into two parts. First, Chapter 11 gives an overview of the process and explains the basic analysis necessary in capital budgeting. Then, in Chapter 12, we go on to consider the special case of replacement decisions as well as risk analysis in capital budgeting.

SIMILARITIES BETWEEN CAPITAL BUDGETING AND SECURITY VALUATION

Fixed assets are, by definition, expected to provide cash flows for some years into the future. Thus, the discounting process, which is largely ignored in current asset analysis, is of critical importance in capital budgeting. In fact, the capital budgeting process involves exactly the same six conceptual steps that are used in security analysis as described in Chapters 4 and 5:

1. First, management estimates the expected cash flows from a given project, including the value of the asset at a specified terminal date. This is similar to estimating future dividends and stock prices, as well as bond interest payments plus maturity values, in security analysis.
2. Next, the riskiness of projected cash flows must be estimated.
3. The firm then chooses an appropriate discount rate, called the *cost of capital,* at which these cash flows are to be discounted; this is equivalent to determining a required rate of return in security analysis.

4. The expected cash flows are then discounted and put on a present value basis to obtain an estimate of the asset's value to the firm.

5. This calculated value is next compared to the cost of the project; if the asset's present value exceeds its cost, the project should be accepted.

6. Finally, and very importantly, the effect of the capital budgeting process on the value of the firm is considered. If an individual investor identifies and invests in a security whose market price is less than its true value, then the value of the investor's portfolio will be increased. Similarly, if the firm identifies (or creates) investment opportunities with present values greater than their costs, the value of the firm will be increased. This increase in firm value, on a per share basis, will be reflected in the growth factor, g, that we discussed in Chapters 4 and 5. Thus, there is a very direct link between capital budgeting and stock values: The more effective the firm's capital budgeting procedures, the higher its growth rate, hence the higher the price of its stock.

IDEAS FOR CAPITAL PROJECTS

Even though the same concepts and mathematics are involved in both capital budgeting and security analysis, there are important differences in the collection and analysis of data for the two types of investments. A set of stocks and bonds exists in the securities market, and investors select a portfolio from this set. *However, capital projects are created by the firm.* For example, a salesperson may report that customers are asking for a particular product that the company does not now produce. The sales manager then discusses the idea with people in the marketing research group to determine whether a sizable market exists for the proposed product. If it appears likely that a market does exist, cost accountants and engineers will be brought in to estimate production costs. If this type of investigation suggests that the product can be produced and sold to yield a sufficient profit, then the project will be undertaken.

A firm's growth and development, even its ability to remain competitive and to survive, depend upon a constant flow of new investment ideas. Accordingly, a well-managed firm will go to great lengths to develop good capital budgeting proposals. For example, the executive vice-president of a major corporation indicated that his company takes the following steps to generate projects:

Our R & D department is constantly searching for new products, or for ways to improve existing products. In addition, our Executive Committee, which consists of senior executives in marketing, production, and finance, identifies the products and markets in which our company will compete, and the Committee sets long-run targets for each division. These targets, which are formalized in the

Corporation's strategic plan, provide a general guide to the operating executives who must meet them. These executives then seek new products, set expansion plans for existing products, and look for ways to reduce production and distribution costs. Since bonuses and promotions are based in large part on each unit's ability to meet or exceed its targets, these economic incentives encourage our operating executives to seek out profitable investment opportunities.

While our senior executives are judged and rewarded on the basis of how well their units perform, people further down the line are given bonuses for specific suggestions, including ideas that lead to profitable investments. Additionally, a percentage of our corporate profit is set aside for distribution to nonexecutive employees. Our objective is to encourage lower level workers to keep on the lookout for good ideas, including those that lead to capital investments.

If the firm has capable and imaginative executives and employees, and if its incentive system is working properly, many ideas for capital investment will be advanced. Since some ideas will be good ones while others will not, procedures must be established for screening projects. Steps in the screening process are discussed in the following sections.

PROJECT CLASSIFICATION

Analyzing capital expenditure proposals is not a costless operation—benefits can be gained from a careful analysis, but such an investigation does have a cost. For certain types of projects, a relatively refined analysis may be warranted; for others, cost/benefit studies may suggest that a simpler procedure should be used. Accordingly, firms frequently classify projects into the following categories:

1. *Replacement: Maintenance of Business.* Expenditures necessary to replace worn-out or damaged equipment are in this group. These expenditures need not be "in kind," but they do not increase capacity or alter production processes.
2. *Replacement: Cost Reduction.* Expenditures to replace serviceable, but obsolete, equipment fall into this category. The purpose of these expenditures is to lower the cost of labor, materials, or other items such as electricity.
3. *Expansion of Existing Products or Markets.* Expenditures to increase output of existing products, or to expand outlets or distribution facilities in markets now being served, are included here.
4. *Expansion into New Products or Markets.* These are expenditures necessary to produce a new product, or to expand into a geographic area not currently being served.
5. *Safety and/or Environmental Projects.* Expenditures necessary to comply

with government orders, labor agreements, or insurance policy terms are listed here. These expenditures are often called *mandatory investments,* or *non-revenue-producing projects.*

6. *Other.* This catch-all includes home office buildings, parking lots, and so on.

In general, relatively simple calculations and only a few supporting documents are required to support replacement decisions, especially maintenance-type investments in profitable plants. More detailed analysis is required for cost reduction replacements, for expansion of existing product lines, and for investments into new products or areas. Also, within each category, projects are broken down by their dollar costs: the larger the required investment, the more detailed the analysis and the higher the level of the officer who must authorize the expenditure. Thus, while a plant manager may be authorized to approve maintenance expenditures up to $10,000 on the basis of a relatively unsophisticated analysis, the full board of directors may have to approve decisions which involve either amounts over $1 million or expansions into new products or markets, and a very detailed, refined analysis will be required to support these decisions.

ESTIMATING THE CASH FLOWS

The most important, but also the most difficult, step in the analysis of a capital expenditure proposal is the estimation of the cash flows associated with the project—the outflows associated with building and equipping the new facility and the annual cash inflows the project will produce after it goes into operation. A great many variables are involved in the cash flow forecast, and many individuals and departments participate in developing them. We cannot in this book fully develop the techniques and methodologies used in cash flow analysis, but an examination of Tables 11–1 through 11–4 will give an idea of what is entailed. The example used is taken from the files of a major industrial firm, which we shall call Carter Chemical Company. Carter's cash flow analysis for the Compound X project is typical of that used in all types of businesses with sales in excess of about $10 million.[1]

Table 11–1 summarizes the investment outlay required for the project. A total of $5 million is necessary: $3.5 million for land, buildings, and

---

1 The company has eighteen printed forms upon which different types of information related to capital expenditures are submitted. Not all forms are used for every investment decision, but most are used for larger projects. For the illustrative case, fifteen forms were completed, in addition to a great many worksheets, letters, memos, and so on that were developed in the course of analyzing the project. Firms do not make $5 million expenditures on the basis of a casual analysis, at least not if they wish to survive.

Table 11–1
Carter Chemical Company: Estimated
Investment Requirements for Compound X

	1980	1981	1982	1983	Total
Immediate Investment					
(Supported by Engineering Estimate)					
Capital					
1. Land	$ 0	$ 0	$	$	$ 0
2. Land improvements	0	0			0
3. Buildings	475,000	511,000			986,000
4. Process equipment	1,000,000	1,702,000			2,702,000
5. Mobile equipment		75,000			75,000
Less: Investment tax credit	(102,570)	(160,430)			(263,000)
6. Subtotal	$1,372,430	$2,127,570			$3,500,000
Expenses					
7. Relocations	0	0			0
8. _____					
9. _____					
10. Subtotal	$	$	$	$	$
11. Total authorized	$1,372,430	$2,127,570			$3,500,000

	1980	1981	1982	1983	Total
Working Capital					
12. Accounts receivable	$	$ 742,500	$ 148,500	$ 99,000	$ 990,000
13. Raw materials inventory		157,500	31,500	21,000	210,000
14. Parts inventory		0	0	0	0
15. Goods in process		180,000	36,000	24,000	240,000
16. Finished materials inventory		202,500	40,500	27,000	270,000
17. Operating materials and supplies		112,500	22,500	15,000	150,000
18. Payables/accruals	( )	(270,000)	(54,000)	(36,000)	(360,000)
19. Net working capital	$	$1,125,000	$ 225,000	$ 150,000	$1,500,000
Total investment (lines 11 + 19)					$5,000,000

equipment, and $1.5 million for the net investment in working capital. These expenditures will be incurred over a four year period, from 1980 to 1983. The plant will be constructed and equipped in 1980 and 1981, while working capital will be built up during 1981, 1982, and 1983.

Table 11–2 shows a series of income statements detailing the expected cash flows during certain years of the project's projected fifteen year service life. Sales in both units and dollars are shown, after which the various types of expenses and taxes are deducted to produce the net income expected from the project as shown on the third line from the bottom. These incremental profits are *before* financing charges; the cost of the capital

Table 11–2
Carter Chemical Company: Cash Flow
Analysis for Compound X

Profit Center: Textile Products   Location: Raleigh, N.C.   Title: Plant to Manufacture Compound X

Estimated Profits and Cash Flows

	1981	1982	1983	1984		1994	1995
Quantity shipped, tons	75,000	90,000	100,000	100,000	Years	100,000	100,000
					1985		
Gross sales, dollars	$4,564,000	$5,477,000	$6,085,000	$6,085,000	through	$6,085,000	$6,085,000
Less: Freight	46,000	55,000	61,000	61,000	1993	61,000	61,000
Cash discounts	18,000	22,000	24,000	24,000	not	24,000	24,000
Total deductions	64,000	77,000	85,000	85,000	shown	85,000	85,000
Net sales	$4,500,000	$5,400,000	$6,000,000	$6,000,000	here	$6,000,000	$6,000,000
Cost of sales							
Variable	$2,340,000	$2,880,000	$3,240,000	$3,240,000		$3,240,000	$3,240,000
Fixed, excluding depreciation and depletion	360,000	360,000	360,000	360,000		360,000	360,000
Break-in costs	351,000	144,000	—	—		—	—
Total	3,051,000	3,384,000	3,600,000	3,600,000		3,600,000	3,600,000
Depreciation	437,550	408,380	379,210	350,040		58,290	29,120
Total cost of sales	$3,488,550	$3,792,380	$3,979,210	$3,950,040		$3,658,290	$3,629,120
Gross profit	$1,011,450	$1,607,620	$2,020,790	$2,049,960		$2,341,710	$2,370,880
Selling expenses	240,000	240,000	240,000	240,000		240,000	240,000
Advertising	130,000	105,000	90,000	90,000		90,000	90,000
Administrative	300,000	300,000	300,000	300,000		300,000	300,000
Provision for bad debts	26,825	31,325	34,325	34,325		34,325	34,325
Total: Selling, etc., costs	696,825	676,325	664,325	664,325		664,325	664,325
Net income before tax	314,625	931,295	1,356,465	1,385,635		1,677,385	1,706,555
State and federal income tax @ 48%	151,020	447,022	651,103	665,105		805,145	819,146
Net income	163,605	484,273	705,362	720,530		872,240	887,409
Add back depreciation	437,550	408,380	379,210	350,040		58,290	29,120
Net cash flow	$ 601,155	$ 892,653	$1,084,572	$1,070,570		$ 930,530	$ 916,529

Salvage value: buildings and machines = 0
Recovery of working capital = $1,500,000
Net cash flow, year 1995 = $2,416,529

used to finance the project is accounted for when the cash flows are discounted to find their present value.[2] Depreciation, which is not a cash outlay, is added to profits to produce the bottom-line figures, the net cash flows from the project.[3]

The new plant will go into service in 1981, and it is expected to generate a net cash flow of $601,155 in that year. Cash flows are expected to climb during the next two years, as the plant is broken in and the market is developed, but to decline thereafter because of rising taxes caused by declining deductions for depreciation.[4]

Table 11–3 lists the critical assumptions that were made in developing the cash flow estimates shown in Table 11–2. They are of key importance, for the most serious errors in capital budgeting are caused by incorrect assumptions about basic operating conditions. Mistakes in these basic assumptions will lead to incorrect cash flow forecasts and, consequently, to bad accept-reject decisions. For this reason, executives pay a great deal of attention to the basic assumptions used to generate expected cash flows.

Table 11–4 summarizes the analysis of the Compound X expenditure proposal; it provides information on the investment outlays, the projected cash flows from the project, and the expected profitability of the project (the "net present value" and "internal rate of return," which will be explained later in the chapter). Note also that the summary sheet has been reviewed by marketing, production, engineering, accounting, and industrial relations people at the profit center.[5] They must verify that they consider the cash flows, investment requirements, and so on to be reasonable estimates. If the project is undertaken and turns out to be unprofitable, these are the people who will be required to explain what went wrong, so they are careful in

---

2 The process of discounting a future cash flow has the effect of reducing it by an amount sufficient to cover the cost of the capital investment needed to produce the cash flow. Thus, if financing charges were included in the income statement given in Table 11–2 and the net cash flows were later discounted, we would be double counting the financing costs.

3 If the treatment of depreciation is not clear, recognize that net sales represent cash received, and that all items *except depreciation* represent cash outlays during the year. Thus, Carter expects to have net sales for cash of $4.5 million in 1981 and to incur *cash* costs for taxes and all costs shown *except* depreciation, so that $4.5 million cash from net sales, minus cash costs totaling $3,051,000 + $696,825 = $3,747,825, minus $151,020 income taxes, equals $601,155. The $601,155 cash flow is, of course, also equal to net income after tax plus depreciation.

4 Carter Chemical, like most firms, uses accelerated depreciation for tax calculations. This causes depreciation (a noncash charge) to be high early in the project's life, lower later on. The high initial depreciation results in lower taxes, hence in higher cash flows during the early years.

  Two other points are worth mentioning here. First, people sometimes ask, "What happens to the cash flows shown at the bottom of Table 11–2?" The answer is that they go into Carter Chemical's coffers for payment of interest and dividends, as well as for reinvestment in other projects. The second point has to do with the recovery of working capital. As we saw in Chapter 7, some amount of working capital (inventories, receivables, and cash transactions balances, less payables and accruals) must be held to support sales. In this case, the investment in net working capital is $1.5 million, and this investment must be maintained intact as long as operations continue. Thus, the $1.5 million working capital will be needed until the plant closes in 1995. During that year, as operations are closed down, inventories will be sold off and not replaced; receivables will be collected with no new ones created because sales will cease; and the cash balances to operate the plant will no longer be needed. Thus, during 1995 the $1.5 million of working capital will be recovered and, presumably, reinvested elsewhere in the company.

5 A *profit center* is an operating unit with responsibility for a given product line or geographic area. Carter Chemical has twelve profit centers, one of which is Textile Products.

Table 11–3
Carter Chemical Company: Key Assumptions
in the Cash Flow Analysis for Compound X

1. It is assumed that the annual sales volume will be 100,000 tons by the third year. This is 10 percent of projected industry sales. These estimates are based on (1) the results of a test marketing program for our new patented Compound X and (2) the market potential as projected for the next fifteen years by the Market Research Department.
2. The net sales price will be $60.00 per ton. This estimate is based on present competitive price levels as determined by the Marketing Department.
3. The assumed production rates, lost time, and labor crew requirements were estimated by the Production Department and are consistent with design speeds approved by the Engineering Department.
4. The assumed labor rates, fringe benefits, training, and availability are based on studies in the plant site area made by the Industrial Relations Department.
5. It is assumed that pollution control standards will not be increased.
6. Selling and advertising expenses, which were estimated by the Marketing Department, are based on other products sold to the textile industry.
7. The assumed percentages of general and administrative expenses are based on past experience.
8. Fuel costs are based on oil at $23 per barrel.
9. An inflation rate of 8 percent in labor and materials cost is expected. Sales prices will increase at this same rate.[a]
10. The $5 million of capital needed to undertake the project can be raised at an average cost (average of debt and equity) of 10 percent.

[a]Table 11–2 is, in effect, stated in 1980 dollars. In current dollars, sales and costs are both expected to rise by 8 percent per year.

---

making their estimates. Note also that the project is reviewed at the corporate level. Since this is a major project, its approval must go all the way up to the board of directors. Had this project involved only $5,000, it could have been approved at the profit center level, and no initials would appear in the section headed "Corporate—Reviews and Approvals."

METHODS USED TO EVALUATE PROPOSED PROJECTS

A number of different methods are used to rank projects and to decide whether or not they should be accepted for inclusion in the capital budget. Three of the most commonly used are these:[6]

1. *Payback (or Payback Period).* This is the number of years required to return the original investment.

---

6 A number of "average rate of return" methods have been discussed in the literature and used in practice. These methods are generally unsound and are rapidly being replaced by the methods considered here. Finally, a "benefit/cost" or "profitability index" method is sometimes used; this method is discussed in Appendix 11B.

Table 11–4
Carter Chemical Company:
Authorization for
Expenditure

Profit Center: Textile Products

Location: Raleigh, North Carolina

Title: Construct Plant to Manufacture Compound X

Authorization
Number: 550–0080–0001

Date: September 1979

Amount
Requested: $5,000,000

Description of Request—Summary:

Construction of a plant in Raleigh for the manufacture of 100,000 tons of Compound X annually. This new product, used in the dyeing process for textile fibers, will be shipped from Raleigh primarily to the Southeastern United States.

After Approval—Estimated Start Jan. 1980, Completion: Mar. 1981.

Benefits of Request—Summary:

The addition of Compound X to the existing products we sell to the textile industry will complete our product line and substantially improve our competitive position. The net present value ($2.3 million) is favorable, and the projected future product growth is large, so these returns could be bettered.

Classification of Project	Return on Investment		Predicted Performance— First 10 Years		
☒ New Business	Net present				
☐ Expansion—Existing Business	value: $2,303,000			Net	Net
☐ Cost Reduction	Internal Rate of Return:	17.0%	Year	Sales	Cash Flow
☐ Replacement			1981	4,500,000	601,155
☐ Quality	Payback		1982	5,400,000	892,653
☐ Safety/Environmental	(useful life 15 yrs.)	5.25 Yrs.	1983	6,000,000	1,084,572
☐ _____			1984	6,000,000	1,070,570
			1985	6,000,000	1,056,569
	Break-even percent		1986	6,000,000	1,042,567
	of capacity	46.2%	1987	6,000,000	1,028,565
			1988	6,000,000	1,014,564
			1989	6,000,000	1,000,543
			1990	6,000,000	986,551

Summary of Expenditures   Proposed Expenditures:

	1980	1981	1982–83	Total
Capital	$1,372,430	$2,127,570	—	$3,500,000
Working Funds	—	1,125,000	375,000	1,500,000
Total Investment	1,372,430	3,252,570	375,000	5,000,000

Profit Center — Reviews and Approvals

Marketing	10/15/79 Date	Industrial Relations	9/12/79 Date
Production	10/8/79 Date	Cost Accounting	10/18/79 Date
Engineering	9/12/79 Date	Chief Operations Officer	10/20/79 Date

Corporate — Reviews and Approvals

Tax	11/2/79 Date	Chief Financial Officer	11/20/79 Date
Legal	11/10/79 Date	President	11/25/79 Date
Director of Capital Budgeting	11/15/79 Date	Board of Directors	12/1/79 Date

2. *Net Present Value (NPV).* This is the present value of future cash flows, discounted at the appropriate cost of capital, minus the cost of the investment. The NPV (and also the IRR) method is called a *discounted cash flow (DCF)* method.
3. *Internal Rate of Return (IRR).* This is the discount rate that equates the present value of the future cash flows to the initial cost of the project. The IRR corresponds to the yield to maturity on a bond.

Future cash flows are, in all cases, defined as the net cash inflows from the investments. The nature and characteristics of these methods are illustrated and explained below, where we use the cash flow data shown in Table 11–5 for Projects S and L to illustrate each method. For now, we assume that the projects are equally risky. Note that cash flows consist of both profits and depreciation, not profits alone. Also, most projects require both fixed assets and an addition to net working capital as in the Compound X case; the investment outlay includes working capital.

Table 11–5
Cash Flows for Projects S and L (the Investment Outlay, or Initial Cost, is $1,000 for Each Project)

| Year | Net Cash Flow (= Profit after Taxes plus Depreciation) | |
	Project S	Project L
1	$ 500	$ 100
2	400	300
3	300	400
4	100	600
Total inflows	$1,300	$1,400

Payback Method

The payback period is defined as the number of years it takes a firm to recover its original investment from net cash flows. Since both projects cost $1,000, the payback period is 2⅓ years for Project S and 3⅓ years for Project L. If the firm were to require a payback of three years or less, Project S would be accepted, but Project L would be rejected. If the projects were *mutually exclusive,* S would be accepted over L because S has the shorter payback.[7] Thus, the payback method ranks S over L. Incidentally, the S

---

7 *Mutually exclusive* projects are alternative investments; if one project is taken on, the other must be rejected. For example, the installation of a conveyor belt system in a warehouse and the purchase of a fleet of fork trucks for the same warehouse would be mutually exclusive projects—accepting one implies rejection of the other. *Independent* projects are projects whose costs and revenues are independent of one another. For example, the Compound X project and the purchase of a corporate jet by Carter Chemical would represent independent projects.

stands for *short* and the L for *long:* Project S is a short-term project and L a long-term one in the sense that S's cash inflows tend to come sooner than L's.

Prior to the 1960s the payback was the most commonly used method for screening capital expenditure proposals. It is still widely used, but generally only for smaller replacement projects or as a risk indicator for larger projects. Some features of the payback, which indicate both its strengths and its weaknesses, are listed below:

1. *Ease of Calculation.* The payback is easy to calculate and apply. This was an important consideration in the precomputer, precalculator days.
2. *Ignores Returns beyond Payback Period.* One glaring weakness of the payback method is that it ignores returns beyond the payback period. Thus, Project L might have had a return of $1,000 in Year 5, but this fact would not influence either the payback or a payback ranking of Projects S and L. Ignoring returns in the distant future means that the payback method is biased against long-term projects.
3. *Ignores Time Value of Money.* The timing of cash flows is obviously important, yet the payback method ignores the time value of money. A dollar in Year 3 is given the same weight as a dollar in Year 1.

Net Present Value (NPV) Method

As the flaws in the payback method were recognized, people began to search for methods of evaluating projects that would recognize that a dollar received immediately is preferable to a dollar received at some future date. This led to the development of *discounted cash flow (DCF)* techniques to take account of the time value of money. One such DCF technique is called the *net present value method. To implement this approach, find the present value of the expected net cash flows of an investment, discounted at an appropriate percentage rate, and subtract from it the initial cost outlay of the project.* If its net present value is positive, the project should be accepted; if negative, it should be rejected. If two projects are mutually exclusive, the one with the higher net present value should be chosen.

The equation for the net present value (NPV) is

$$\text{NPV} = \sum_{t=1}^{n} \frac{R_t}{(1+k)^t} - C$$

$$= \left[\frac{R_1}{(1+k)^1} + \frac{R_2}{(1+k)^2} + \cdots + \frac{R_n}{(1+k)^n} \right] - C$$

$$= R_1(\text{PVIF}_{k,\,1}) + R_2(\text{PVIF}_{k,\,2}) + \cdots + R_n(\text{PVIF}_{k,\,n}) - C. \quad (11\text{--}1)$$

Here, R_1, R_2, and so forth represent the annual receipts, or net cash flows; k is the appropriate discount rate, or the project's cost of capital; C is the initial cost of the project; and n is the project's expected life.[8] The cost of capital, k, depends on the riskiness of the project, the level of interest rates in the economy, and several other factors. In this chapter we take k as a given, but it is discussed in detail in Chapter 16.

The net present values of Projects S and L are calculated in Table 11–6, using the procedures developed in Chapter 3. Assuming that they each have a 10 percent cost of capital, Project S has an NPV of $78.80, while L's NPV is $49.15. On this basis, both should be accepted if they are independent, but S should be the one chosen if they are mutually exclusive. The NPV for Carter Chemical's Compound X is calculated in Appendix A to this chapter.

The value of a firm is a composite of the values of its parts. Thus, when a firm takes on a project with a positive NPV, the value of the firm should increase by the amount of the NPV. In our example, the value of the firm increases by $78.80 if it takes on Project S, but by only $49.15 if it takes on Project L. *The increase in the value of the firm from its capital budget for the year is the sum of the NPVs of all accepted projects.* Viewed in this manner, it is easy to see why S, which adds $78.80 to the value of the firm,

Table 11–6
Calculating the Net Present Values (NPVs) of Projects S and L

Year	Project S Net Cash Flow	PVIF (10%)	PV of Cash Flow	Project L Net Cash Flow	PVIF (10%)	PV of Cash Flow
1	$500	0.9091	$ 454.55	$100	0.9091	$ 90.91
2	400	0.8264	330.56	300	0.8264	247.92
3	300	0.7513	225.39	400	0.7513	300.52
4	100	0.6830	68.30	600	0.6830	409.80
	PV of inflows		$1,078.80	PV of inflows		$1,049.15
	Less cost		−1,000.00	Less cost		−1,000.00
	$NPV_S =$		$ 78.80	$NPV_L =$		$ 49.15

8 If costs are spread over several years, this must be taken into account. Suppose, for example, that a firm bought land in 1980, erected a building in 1981, installed equipment in 1982, and started production in 1983. One could treat 1980 as the base year, comparing the present value of the costs as of 1980 to the present value of the benefit stream as of that same date.

Also, note that Equation 11–1 can be written as follows:

$$NPV = \sum_{t=0}^{n} \frac{R_t}{(1 + k)^t} \qquad (11–1a)$$

In this alternative format, R_0 is the initial investment, or cost, made at time $t = 0$, and it is *negative*.

The alternative format is especially useful for considering projects for which the investment costs are incurred over several years, as was true of Carter Chemical's Compound X project. Equation 11–1a is actually used, in Appendix 11A, to calculate Compound X's NPV.

is preferred to L, which adds only $49.15, and it is also easy to see the logic of the NPV approach.[9]

The Internal Rate of Return (IRR)

In Chapter 4 we examined procedures for finding the rate of return on a bond purchased and held as an investment. This rate of return is called the *yield to maturity,* and if a bond's yield exceeds its required rate of return, then it represents a good investment. Exactly the same concepts are employed in capital budgeting when the internal rate of return method is used.

The internal rate of return (IRR) is the discount rate that equates the present value of the expected future cash flows, or receipts, to the initial cost of the project. The equation for calculating this rate is

$$\sum_{t=1}^{n} \frac{R_t}{(1+r)^t} - C = 0$$

$$\frac{R_1}{(1+r)^1} + \frac{R_2}{(1+r)^2} + \cdots + \frac{R_n}{(1+r)^n} - C = 0$$

$$R_1(\text{PVIF}_{r,1}) + R_2(\text{PVIF}_{r,2}) + \cdots + R_n(\text{PVIF}_{r,n}) - C = 0. \qquad (11\text{--}2)$$

Here we know the value of C and also the values of $R_1, R_2, \ldots, R_n$, but we do not know the value of r. Thus, we have an equation with one unknown, and we can solve for the value of r. *Some value of r will cause the sum of the discounted receipts to equal the initial cost of the project, making the equation equal to zero: This value of r is defined as the internal rate of return.* In other words, the solution value of r is the IRR.

Notice that the internal rate of return formula, Equation 11–2, is simply the NPV formula, Equation 11–1, solved for the particular discount rate that causes the NPV to equal zero. Thus, the same basic equation is used for both methods, but in the NPV method the discount rate, k, is specified and the NPV is found, while in the IRR method the NPV is specified to equal zero and the value of r that forces the NPV to equal zero is found.[10]

The internal rate of return may be found in a number of ways. Several methods are discussed below.

---

9 One important point should be noted here: If a new product competes with one of the firm's existing products, then this fact must be considered when analyzing the new project. In essence, we must reduce the net cash flows of the new project by the amount that the cash flows from the old project will be reduced. Thus, we end up with net *incremental* cash flows from the new project—the amount by which the *firm's* cash flows will be increased if the project is accepted.

10 If costs are incurred over several years, Equation 11–2 must be modified in the same manner as the modified version of Equation 11–1, which is used to find the NPV (see Equation 11–1a in footnote 8). In fact, we can modify Equation 11–1a as follows: (1) set NPV = 0, and (2) replace k with r. Now solve for r; the solution value is the IRR. This equation, with the graphic method explained below, was used to determine the IRR for the Carter Chemical Compound X project, which was determined to be 17.0 percent.

Procedure 1: IRR with Constant Cash Inflows If the cash flows from a project are constant, or equal in each year, then the project's internal rate of return can be found by a relatively simple process. In essence, such a project is an annuity: the firm makes an outlay, *C,* and receives a stream of cash flow benefits, *R,* for a given number of years. The IRR for the project is found by applying Equation 3–5, discussed in Chapter 3.

To illustrate, suppose a project has a cost of $10,000 and is expected to produce cash flows of $1,627.45 a year for ten years. The cost of the project, $10,000, is the present value of an annuity of $1,627.45 a year for ten years, so applying Equation 3–5, we obtain

$$\frac{Cost}{R} = \frac{\$10,000}{\$1,627.45} = 6.1446 = PVIFA_{k, n}.$$

Looking up PVIFA in Table A–2 in Appendix A (at the end of the text) across the row for Year 10, we find it located under the 10 percent column. Accordingly, 10 percent is the project's IRR. In other words, 10 percent is the value of *r* that would force Equation 11–2 to zero when *R* is constant at $1,627.45 for ten years and *C* is $10,000. This procedure works only if the project has constant annual cash flows; if it does not, the IRR must be found by one of the methods discussed below.

Procedure 2: Trial and Error In the trial and error method, we first compute the present value of cash flows from an investment, using a somewhat arbitrarily selected discount rate. Since the cost of capital for most firms is in the range of 10 to 15 percent, it is to be hoped that projects will promise a return of at least 10 percent. Therefore, 10 percent is a good starting point for most problems.[11] Then we compare the present value so obtained with the investment's cost. Suppose the present value of the inflows is larger than the project's cost. What do we do now? We must *lower* the present value, and to do this we must *raise* the discount rate and go through the process again. Conversely, if the present value is lower than the cost, we lower the discount rate and repeat the process. We continue until the present value of the flows from the investment is approximately equal to the project's cost. *The discount rate that brings about this equality is defined as the internal rate of return.*[12]

This calculation process is illustrated in Table 11–7 for the same Projects S and L that we analyzed earlier. First, the 10 percent interest factors are obtained from Table A–1 in Appendix A, at the end of the text. These factors are then multiplied by the cash flows for the corresponding years, and the present values of the annual cash flows are placed in the appropriate columns. Next, the present values of the yearly cash flows are summed to

11 Another useful starting point is to obtain the arithmetic average of the cash flows, treat it as an annuity, and then find a "starting point discount rate" by the method outlined in Procedure 1.
12 In order to reduce the number of trials required to find the internal rate of return, it is important to minimize the error at each iteration. One reasonable approach is to make as good a first approximation as possible, then to "straddle" the internal rate of return by making fairly large changes in the discount rate early in the iterative process.

Table 11–7
Finding the Internal Rate of Return for Projects S and L

		Year	Cash Flows (R_t Values) S	Cash Flows (R_t Values) L
C = investment = $1,000.		1	$500	$100
		2	400	300
		3	300	400
		4	100	600
	Total receipts		$1,300	$1,400

		10%			15%	
		Present Value			Present Value	
Year	PVIF	PV_S	PV_L	PVIF	PV_S	PV_L
1	0.9091	$ 454.55	$ 90.91	0.8696	$ 434.80	$ 86.96
2	0.8264	330.56	247.92	0.7561	302.44	226.83
3	0.7513	225.39	300.52	0.6575	197.25	263.00
4	0.6830	68.30	409.80	0.5718	57.18	343.08
Present value		$1,078.80	$1,049.15		$ 991.67	$ 919.87
Less cost		1,000.00	1,000.00		1,000.00	1,000.00
Net present value		$ 78.80	$ 49.15		$ (8.33)	$ (80.13)

obtain the investment's total present value. Subtracting the cost of the project from this figure gives the net present value. Because the net present value of both investments is positive at the 10 percent rate, we increase the rate to 15 percent and try again. At this point the net present value of S is just below zero, which indicates that its internal rate of return is slightly less than 15 percent. L's net present value at 15 percent is well below zero, so its IRR is quite a bit less than 15 percent. These trials could be continued to obtain closer and closer approximations to the exact IRR, but, as noted below, procedures are available to speed up the process.

Procedure 3: Graphic Solution The third method for finding IRRs involves plotting curves that show the relationship between a project's NPV and the discount rate used to calculate the NPV. Such a curve is defined as the project's *net present value profile;* profiles for Projects L and S are shown in Figure 11–1. To construct the graph, we first note that at a zero discount rate, the NPV is simply the total undiscounted cash flows less the cost of the project; thus, at a zero discount rate NPV_S = $1,300 − $1,000 = $300, while

NPV_L = $400. These values are plotted as the vertical axis intercepts in Figure 11–1. Next, we calculate the project's NPVs at three discount rates, say 5, 10, and 15 percent, and plot these values. (Since we have already calculated NPVs at 10 percent and 15 percent, we may take these values from Table 11–7.) The four points plotted on our graph are these:

Discount Rate	NPV_S	NPV_L
0%	$300.00	$400.00
5	180.42	206.50
10	78.80	49.15
15	(8.33)	(80.13)

When we connect these points, we have the net present value profiles.[13]

Figure 11–1
Net Present Value Profiles: NPVs of Projects S and L at Different Discount Rates

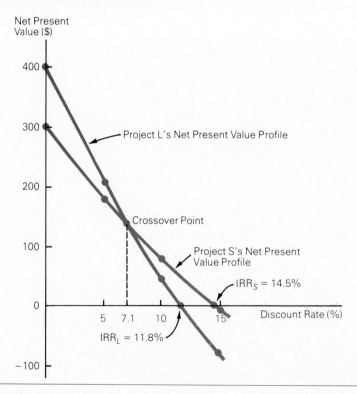

[13] Notice that the present value profiles are curved—they are *not* straight lines. Also, the NPVs approach the negative of the cost of the project as the discount rate increases without limit. The reason is that, at an infinitely high discount rate, the PV of the inflows would be zero, and NPV = 0 − Cost = −Cost. We should also note that under certain conditions the NPV profiles can cross the horizontal axis several times, or never cross it. This point is discussed in Appendix 11B.

Since the IRR is defined as the discount rate at which a project's NPV equals zero, *the point where its net present value profile crosses the horizontal axis indicates the project's internal rate of return.* Figure 11–1 shows that IRR_S is 14.5 percent, while IRR_L is 11.8 percent. With graph paper and a sharp pencil, the graphic method yields reasonably accurate results.[14]

Procedure 4: Computer Solutions Since the internal rates of return can be calculated by computers, many firms have computerized their capital budgeting processes and automatically generate IRRs, NPVs, and paybacks for all projects. Even some of the more powerful hand-held calculators are programmed to compute IRRs. Thus, business firms have no difficulty with the mechanical side of capital budgeting.

Rationale and Use of the IRR Method

What is so special about the particular discount rate that equates a project's cost with the present value of its receipts? To answer this question, let us first assume that our firm obtains $1,000 by borrowing from a bank at an interest rate of 14.5 percent to invest in Project S. Since the internal rate of return on this particular project was calculated to be 14.5 percent, the same as the cost of the bank loan, the firm can invest in the project, use the cash flows generated by the investment to pay off the principal and interest on the loan, and come out exactly even on the transaction. This point is demonstrated in the following tabulation, which shows that Project S provides cash flows that are just sufficient to pay 14.5 percent interest on the unpaid balance of a bank loan, retire the loan over the life of the project, and end up with a balance that differs from zero only by a rounding error of thirty-two cents:

Beginning Investment (1)	Cash Flow (2)	"Interest" or "Profit" at 14.5% (3) = 0.145 × (1)	Return of Capital (4) = (2) − (3)	Ending Balance (5) = (1) − (4)
$1,000.00	$500	$145.00	$355.00	$645.00
645.00	400	93.53	306.47	338.53
338.53	300	49.09	250.91	87.62
87.62	100	12.70	87.30	0.32

If the internal rate of return exceeds the cost of the funds used to finance the project, a surplus is left over after paying for the capital. This surplus accrues to the firm's stockholders, so taking on the project increases the

---

14 For all practical purposes, an IRR that is accurate to within about one-half percent is sufficient, given the inaccuracy of the cash flow estimates. The calculations may be carried out to several decimal places, but for most projects this is spurious accuracy.

value of the firm. If the internal rate of return is less than the cost of capital, taking on the project imposes a cost on existing stockholders, so in this case accepting the project would result in a reduction of value. It is this "breakeven" characteristic that makes us interested in the internal rate of return.[15]

Continuing with our example of Projects L and S, if the firm uses a cost of capital of 10 percent, the internal rate of return criterion indicates that if the projects are independent, both should be accepted—they both do better than "break even." If they are mutually exclusive, S ranks higher and should be accepted, while L should be rejected. If the cost of capital is 15 percent, both projects should be rejected.

NPV Rankings Depend on the Discount Rate

We saw in Figure 11–1 that each project's NPV declines as the discount rate increases. Notice in the figure that Project L has the higher NPV at low discount rates, while NPV_S is greater than NPV_L if the discount rate exceeds 7.1 percent. Notice also that Project L's NPV is "more sensitive" to changes in the discount rate than is NPV_S; that is, Project L's net present value profile has the steeper slope, indicating that a small change in k has a larger effect on NPV_L than on NPV_S.

To see why these relationships hold, recall first that the cash flows from S are received faster than those from L; in a payback sense, S is a short-term project, while L is a long-term project. This point is emphasized in Figure 11–2, which graphs the projects' cash flows over time.

Next, recall the equation for the NPV:

$$NPV = \frac{R_1}{(1 + k)^1} + \frac{R_2}{(1 + k)^2} + \frac{R_3}{(1 + k)^3} + \frac{R_4}{(1 + k)^4} - C.$$

Now notice that the denominators of the terms in this equation increase as k and t increase, and that the increase is exponential; that is, the effect of a higher k is more pronounced if t is larger. To understand this point more clearly, consider the following data:

PV of $100 due in 1 year, discounted at 5%	$95.24
PV of $100 due in 1 year, discounted at 10%	$90.91
Percentage decline in PV resulting from increased k	−4.5%
PV of $100 due in 10 years, discounted at 5%	$61.39
PV of $100 due in 10 years, discounted at 10%	$38.55
Percentage decline in PV resulting from increased k	−37.2%

---

15 This example illustrates the logic of the IRR method, but for technical correctness, the capital used to finance the project should be assumed to come from both debt and equity, not from debt alone. This point is discussed further in Chapter 16.

Figure 11-2
Timing of Cash Flows: Cash Flow Patterns for
Projects S and L

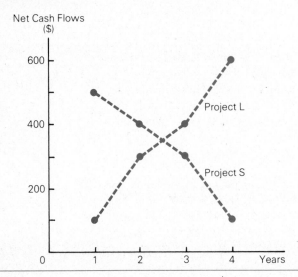

Thus, if a project has most of its cash flows coming in early years, its NPV will not be lowered very much if the discount rate increases, but a project whose cash flows come late will be severely penalized by high discount rates. Accordingly, Project L, which has its largest cash flows in the later years, looks relatively good when the discount rate is low but bad when high rates are used, while Project S, which has relatively rapid cash flows, receives a less adverse impact from high discount rates.[16]

Next, consider the economic implications of these mathematical relationships. A high cost of capital implies that the firm must pay dearly to obtain funds. Thus, projects with relatively fast paybacks will tend to look relatively good when the cost of capital is high, while long-term, slow-payback projects tend to look relatively good when the cost of capital is low. This fact has important economic implications. For example, it explains why utilities, housing, and other industries whose projects are long-lived are especially sensitive to interest rate levels. It also explains why firms tend to favor shorter-term, less capital-intensive projects over long-term projects when money costs are high.

---

16 The situation here is exactly like the one described for long- and short-term bonds in Figure 4-3, where we saw that the prices of long-term bonds are much more sensitive to interest rate changes than are short-term bond prices.

THE POST-AUDIT

The final aspect of the capital budgeting process is the *post-completion audit,* or *post-audit,* which involves (1) a comparison of actual results to those predicted in the request for funds, and (2) an explanation of observed differences. Carter Chemical, for example, requires that the operating divisions send a monthly report for the first six months after a project such as that for Compound X goes into operation, and a quarterly report thereafter until the project's results are up to expectations. From then on, reports on the operation are handled like those of other operations.

The post-audit has several purposes, including the following:

1. *Improve Forecasts.* When decision makers systematically compare their projections to actual outcomes, there is a tendency for estimates to improve. Conscious or unconscious biases are observed and eliminated; new forecasting methods are sought as the need for them becomes apparent; and people simply tend to do everything better, including forecasting, if they know that their actions are being monitored.

2. *Improve Operations.* Businesses are run by people, and people can perform at higher or lower levels of efficiency. When a divisional team has made a forecast about a new installation, its members are, in a sense, putting their reputations on the line. If Carter Chemical's executives forecast annual sales of 100,000 tons of Compound X, and a production cost of $45 per ton, then *because of the post-audit* these executives have every incentive to "make it happen." If costs are above predicted levels, sales below expectations, and so on, then executives in production, sales, and other areas will strive to improve operations and to bring results into line with forecasts.

The post-audit is not a simple process. First, we must recognize that each element of the cash flow forecast is subject to uncertainty, so a percentage of all projects undertaken by any reasonably venturesome firm will necessarily go awry. This fact must be considered when appraising the performances of the operating executives who submit capital expenditure requests. Second, projects sometimes fail to meet expectations for reasons beyond the control of the operating executives and for reasons that no one could realistically be expected to anticipate.[17] For example, the imposition of price controls in the early 1970s adversely affected many projects for which price increases had been projected, and the quadrupling of oil prices in the mid 1970s hurt others. Third, it is often difficult to separate the operating

---

17 Because of such uncertainties, many firms include in the "request for expenditure" package a list of key assumptions such as the one shown in Table 11–3. Top managers often have more information on national political and economic trends than do division managers, engineers, and lower-level people, and highlighting the key assumptions in a separate exhibit helps to better utilize top management's unique expertise.

results of one investment from those of a larger system. While the Compound X project stands alone and permits ready identification of costs and revenues, the actual cost savings that result from a replacement project may be very hard to measure. Fourth, if the post-audit process is not used with care, executives may be reluctant to suggest potentially profitable but risky projects. And fifth, the executives who were actually responsible for a given decision may have moved on by the time the results of the decision are known.

Because of these difficulties, some firms tend to play down the importance of the post-audit. However, observations of both businesses and governmental units suggest that the best-run and most successful organizations are the ones that put the greatest stress on post-audits. Accordingly, the post-audit is one of the most important elements in a good capital budgeting system.

OTHER ISSUES IN CAPITAL BUDGETING

Thus far, the chapter has outlined the basic procedures used by most firms when making decisions about investments in fixed assets. However, capital budgeting is a very complex subject, and we have by no means dealt with all the important issues. Some of the significant ones that have not been covered are listed below and discussed very briefly to provide an indication of the types of questions that can arise when one actually becomes involved in the capital budgeting process.

1. *Acceptable projects under NPV are also acceptable under IRR.* With projects of the type we have been discussing, the NPV will be positive if and only if the IRR is greater than the cost of capital. This can be seen in Figure 11–1. If the cost of capital is to the left of (smaller than) the project's IRR, then the NPV is greater than zero, while if the cost of capital is to the right of (higher than) the IRR, the project's NPV will be negative. Thus, any project acceptable by NPV will also be acceptable by the IRR method.

2. *Conflicts in project rankings occur under NPV and IRR.* Look again at Figure 11–1. Notice that if the cost of capital is lower than the crossover rate, 7.1 percent, the NPV method ranks Project L higher but the IRR method indicates that Project S is better. Thus, if L and S are mutually exclusive, then L will be chosen if the NPV method is used and the cost of capital is below the crossover rate, but S will be selected if the firm uses IRR. There will be no conflict if the cost of capital is above the crossover rate. The reasons for this potential conflict are discussed in Appendix 11B. The appendix also suggests that NPV is usually the better method and that conflicts should be resolved in favor of the project with the higher NPV.

3. *Growth is preferable to "expansion."* A firm's earnings per share, hence its dividends and stock price, can grow over time even if it invests in projects with zero (or even negative) NPVs. Recognize that a project's NPV will be negative if its IRR is less than the cost of capital. However, if the IRR is positive, and if the project is financed with retained earnings, then taking on the project will make some contribution to earnings, hence to earnings growth. This being the case, why not take on projects with zero or even negative NPVs, so long as the IRRs are positive? The reason has to do with stockholders' *opportunity costs,* or what stockholders could do with earnings if they were distributed rather than invested in projects which earn less than their cost of capital. This point is discussed further in Chapters 15 and 16, where true growth (NPV > 0) is compared to "expansion" (NPV ≤ 0). The conclusion reached there is that stockholders are served best by having the firm accept only projects with NPV > 0.

4. *Multiple IRRs may be found.* Under certain conditions, more than one value of r solves Equation 11–2. Thus, a project can have more than one IRR. The reason for this situation is also explained in Appendix 11B.

5. *The size of the capital budget can have an effect on the cost of capital.* Throughout this chapter, we have assumed that the firm's cost of capital is a given constant. However, as is shown in Appendix 11B, the size of the capital budget can influence the cost of capital, hence the acceptability of specific projects.

6. *Capital may be rationed.* Firms occasionally set limits on the amount of money they will spend on fixed assets; this is called *capital rationing.* Thus, it is conceivable that a firm may end up with more projects having acceptable NPVs or IRRs than it is willing to finance. This situation is also discussed in Appendix 11B.

7. *Project risk must be taken into account.* Thus far, we have abstracted from the riskiness of different projects. This subject is taken up in Chapter 12.

8. *The cost of capital is critical.* The cost of capital, which is the discount rate used in the NPV method and the cutoff rate in the IRR method, is difficult to estimate, yet vital to the capital budgeting process. Methods for estimating the cost of capital are discussed in Chapter 16.

9. *Inflation must be dealt with.* The best procedure is to estimate inflation rates for the product's sales price and also for each cost item, and then to let these rates be reflected in the cash flows as shown in Table 11–2 for Compound X. Inflation is discussed in Chapter 12.

SUMMARY

Capital budgeting is similar in principle to security valuation—future cash flows are estimated, risks are appraised and reflected in a cost of capital discount rate, all cash flows are put on a present value basis, and if a project's *net present value* (NPV) is positive, it is accepted. In outline form, the capital budgeting process centers around the following steps:

1. Ideas for projects are developed.
2. Projects are classified by type of investment: replacement, expansion of existing product lines, expansion into new markets, and "other."
3. The expected future cash flows from a project are estimated. This involves (a) estimating the investment outlay required for the project and (b) estimating the cash inflows over the project's projected life.
4. The riskiness inherent in the project is appraised. This important subject is taken up in Chapter 12.
5. The next step is to rank projects by their NPVs or IRRs, accepting those with NPV > 0 or IRR > the cost of capital.
6. The final step in a good capital budgeting system is the *post-audit,* which involves comparing actual to predicted results. Post-audits help get the best results from every accepted project; they also lead to improvements in the forecasting process and, hence, to better future capital budgeting decisions.

While this chapter has presented the basic elements of the capital budgeting process, there are many other aspects of this important topic. Some of the more technical ones are discussed in Appendix 11B, while others are taken up in Chapter 12.

Questions

11-1 How is a project classification scheme (for example, replacement, expansion into new markets, and so forth) used in the capital budgeting process?

11-2 a. Why is the investment tax credit subtracted from expenditures on fixed assets in the top section of Table 11–1?
   b. Why is working capital included in a capital budgeting analysis? Why are "payables/accruals" deducted from working capital? Would the working capital section of Table 11–1 need to be filled out if the project were for replacement rather than for expansion?

11-3 If Carter Chemical used straight line rather than sum-of-years' digits depreciation, how would this affect (a) the total amount of depreciation, net income, and net cash flows over the project's expected life, (b) the timing of depreciation, net income, and net cash flows, and (c) the project's payback and NPV?

11-4 Net cash flows rather than profits are listed in Table 11–4. What is the basis for this emphasis on cash flows as opposed to profits?

11-5 Explain why the NPV of a relatively long-term project, defined as one with a high percentage of its cash flows expected in distant future years, is more sensitive to changes in the cost of capital than is the NPV of a short-term project.

11-6 Explain why, if two mutually exclusive projects are being compared, the short-term project might have the higher ranking under the NPV criterion if the cost of capital is high, but the long-term project might be deemed better if the cost of capital is low. Would changes in the cost of capital ever cause a change in the IRR ranking of two such projects?

Problems

11-1 Project M has a cost of $1,000, and its expected net cash inflows are $263.80 per year for five years.
   a. What is the project's payback, to the closest year?
   b. The cost of capital is 8 percent. What is the project's NPV?
   c. What is the project's IRR? (*Hint:* Recognize that the project is an annuity.)

11-2 Project Z costs $10,000 and is expected to produce cash flows of $3,343.81 per year for five years.
   a. What is the project's payback?
   b. The cost of capital is 12 percent. What is its NPV?
   c. What is the project's IRR? (*Hint:* Recognize that the project is an annuity.)

11-3 Two projects each involve an investment of $9,000. Cash flows (after-tax profits plus depreciation) are $6,000 a year for two years for Project S and $2,400 a year for six years for Project L.
   a. Compute the net present value of each project if the firm's cost of capital is 0 percent and if it is 6 percent. NPVs for S at 10 percent and 20 percent, respectively, are $1,413 and $166.80, while NPVs for L at 10 percent and 20 percent are $1,452.72 and ($1,018.80).
   b. Graph the present value profiles of the two projects, putting NPV on the *Y* axis and the cost of capital on the *X* axis, and use the graph to estimate each project's IRR.
   c. Use a formula to calculate the internal rate of return for each project.
   d. If these projects were mutually exclusive, which one would you select, assuming a cost of capital of (1) 8 percent, (2) 10.3 percent, or (3) 12 percent? Explain. *Note:* In Chapter 12 we shall discuss "replacement chains," where projects such as these are extended out to common life. For this problem, assume that the operation will terminate at the end of the project's life, making replacement chain analysis unnecessary.

11-4 The net cash flows for Projects X and Y are shown below. Each project has a cost of $10,000, and the company uses a 10 percent cost of capital.

	Net Cash Flows	
Year	Project X	Project Y
1	$6,500	$3,500
2	3,000	3,500
3	3,000	3,500
4	1,000	3,500

   a. Calculate each project's payback.
   b. Calculate each project's NPV at the 10 percent cost of capital.

   c. Calculate each project's IRR. (*Hint:* Use the graphic method for Project X, and notice that Y is an annuity.)

   d. Should X and/or Y be accepted if they are independent projects?

   e. Which project should be accepted if they are mutually exclusive?

   f. How might a change in the cost of capital produce a conflict between NPV and IRR? At what values of k would this conflict exist?

11-5 The Bey Burger Company is considering two mutually exclusive investments. Project A has a cost of $20,000 and will produce after-tax net cash flows of $3,752.21 per year for ten years. Project B also has a cost of $20,000, and it is expected to produce cash flows of $5,880.72 per year for five years.

   a. Assuming that Bey's average cost of capital is 12 percent, and that these two projects are both of average risk, which, if either, should Bey accept? (See note to Problem 11–3.)

   b. Now assume that Bey's cost of capital rises to 14 percent. What is your decision now? (*Note:* $NPV_B = \$189.10$.)

   c. Suppose Bey's cost of capital falls to 10 percent. How does this affect your decision? (*Note:* $NPV_B = \$2,292.63$.)

   d. Graph the two projects' NPV profiles. (*Hint:* At a zero cost of capital, $NPV_A = \$17,522.10$ and $NPV_B = \$9,403.60$.)

   e. Explain why Project A's NPV profile declines more rapidly than that of Project B. Also, explain the economic logic of why A is better at a low cost of capital, while B is better at a high capital cost.

11-6 Rolling Wheels, Inc., is considering the installation of a new production line for its rapidly expanding skate division. The line will have a cost of $100,000 and will be depreciated toward a zero salvage value over a five year period. The following income statements are expected to apply to the machine for each of its five operating years:

	Year 1	Year 2	Year 3	Year 4	Year 5
Sales	$100,000	$100,000	$100,000	$100,000	$100,000
Costs other than depreciation	71,667	71,667	71,667	71,667	71,667
Depreciation	33,333		20,000		6,667
Total costs	105,000		91,667		78,334
Income before taxes	(5,000)		8,333		21,666
Taxes (credit)	(2,000)		3,333		8,666
Net income after taxes	(3,000)		5,000		13,000
Add back depreciation	33,333		20,000		6,667
Net cash flow	$30,333		$25,000		$19,667

The company's cost of capital is 15 percent, and its tax rate is 40 percent.

   a. Complete the table, assuming the company uses sum-of-years' digits depreciation, and then calculate the project's net present value. (See Appendix 2A for depreciation calculation.)

b. What would the NPV have been if the company had used straight line depreciation?

c. Suppose a 10 percent investment tax credit had been applicable. How would this have affected your NPV calculations?

11-7 The Scott Paper Company's director of capital budgeting is analyzing a proposal to build a pulp mill in northern Wisconsin. The following data have been developed thus far:

Land acquisition, cost incurred at start of Year 1 ($t = 0$)	$300,000
Plant construction, cost incurred at start of Year 2 ($t = 1$)	$700,000
Equipment purchase, cost incurred at start of Year 3 ($t = 2$)	$1,000,000
Net working capital, investment made at start of Year 4 ($t = 3$)	$400,000

A 10 percent investment tax credit is available on plant and equipment expenditures, but not on land costs. The credit is received at the beginning of the year in which the expenditure is made.

Operations will begin in Year 4 and will continue for ten years, through Year 13. Sales revenues and operating costs are assumed to come at the end of each year. Since the plant will be in operation for ten years, operating costs and revenues occur at the end of Years 4 through 13 ($t = 4$ to 13). The following additional assumptions are made:

1. The plant and equipment will be depreciated over a ten year life, starting in Year 4. The buildings and equipment will be worthless after ten years' use, but Scott expects to sell the land for $300,000 when the plant is closed down. Scott uses straight line depreciation.

2. Scott uses a cost of capital of 14 percent to evaluate projects such as this one.

3. Annual sales = 10,000 tons at $113.50 per ton. Annual sales revenues = $1,135,000.

4. Annual fixed operating costs *excluding* depreciation are $130,000.

5. Annual variable operating costs are $200,385, assuming the plant operates at full capacity.

6. Scott's marginal income tax rate is 48 percent.

   a. Calculate the project's NPV. Should Scott's management accept this project?

   b. Assuming constant sales prices and constant variable costs per unit, what will happen to the NPV if unit sales fall 10 percent below the forecast level?

APPENDIX 11A   CALCULATING THE NPV AND IRR FOR CARTER CHEMICAL'S COMPOUND X

Table 11A–1 gives a time line that shows the timing of cash flows for Project X. The cash flows in this table were taken from Tables 11–1, 11–2, and 11–4. The project's NPV is calculated to be $2,303,581.

To see this, refer back to Carter Chemical's Project X, Tables 11–1 and 11–2. Carter used January 1, 1980, as $t = 0$. Further, Carter assumed that all the investment outlays reported in Table 11–1 would be incurred at the *beginning* of each year but that the cash inflows reported in Table 11–2 would be received at the *end* of the year in question. Thus, R_0 = 1980 total expenditures = $- \$1,372,430$; R_1 = 1981 expenditures = $- \$2,127,570 - \$1,125,000 = - \$3,252,570$; R_2 = 1982 expenditures (incurred at the *beginning* of 1982) + 1981 inflows (assumed received at the *end* of 1981) = *minus* $225,000 *plus* $601,155 = $+ \$376,155$; R_3 = 1982 inflows $- \$150,000 = \$742,653$, etc.; down to R_{16} = 1995 inflows + return of working capital = $916,529 + $1,500,000 = $2,416,529. Inserting these values and $k = 10\%$ into Equation 11–1a, we obtain

$$\text{NPV} = -\frac{\$1,372,430}{(1.10)^0} - \frac{\$3,252,570}{(1.10)^1} + \frac{\$376,155}{(1.10)^2} + \cdots + \frac{\$2,416,529}{(1.10)^{16}}.$$

When the inflows for all the years were plugged in, the NPV was found to be $2,303,000. This may look like a formidable arithmetic problem, but with Carter's computerized capital budgeting system, it can be solved almost instantaneously. It is not even much work with a hand calculator.

Carter Chemical's capital budgeting process is computerized, so the company actually found IRR_X on the computer. However, one could check the computer solution by use of the graphic method described in Chapter 11. Simply find the NPV at discount rates of 0 percent, 10 percent (which is $2,303,000), 15 percent, and 20 percent; plot the NPVs against their respective discount rates; connect the points to obtain an NPV profile; and recognize that the discount rate shown as the horizontal axis intercept is the IRR. In this case, IRR_X is 17.0 percent.

APPENDIX 11B   OTHER ISSUES IN CAPITAL BUDGETING

This appendix addresses several important issues that were not covered in Chapter 11: (1) reasons for conflicts between NPV and IRR, (2) the problem of multiple rates of return if the IRR method is used, (3) the effect of the level of investment on the cost of capital, (4) capital rationing, and (5) the "profitability index" criterion.

Table 11A–1
Calculating the NPV for Project X

Year	1/1/80 t = 0	1/1/81 1	12/31/81 or 1/1/82 2	12/31/82 or 1/1/83 3	12/31/83 4	12/31/84 5	12/31/85 6	12/31/86 7	12/31/87 8	12/31/88 9
Net Cash Flow	(1,372,430)	(2,127,570) (1,125,000) (3,252,570)	601,155 (225,000) 376,155	892,653 (150,000) 742,653	1,084,572	1,070,570	1,056,569	1,042,567	1,028,565	1,014,564

Continuation of Time Line	12/31/89 10	12/31/90 11	12/31/91 12	12/31/92 13	12/31/93 14	12/31/94 15	12/31/95 16
	1,000,543	986,551	972,535	958,519	944,503	930,530	916,529 1,500,000 (Working Capital) 2,416,529

$$NPV = \sum_{t=0}^{16} \frac{\text{Net cash flow}_t}{(1 + k)^t} = \frac{-\$1,372,430}{(1.10)^0} + \frac{-\$3,252,570}{(1.10)^1} + \cdots + \frac{\$2,416,529}{(1.10)^{16}}$$

$$= -\$1,372,430 + (-\$3,252,570)(PVIF_{10\%, \, 1 \, yr.}) + \cdots + (\$2,416,529)(PVIF_{10\%, \, 16 \, yrs.})$$

$$= (1,372,430) + (2,956,586) + 310,704 + 557,732 + 740,763 + 664,824 + 595,905 + 534,837 + 480,340 + 430,175 +$$

$$386,210 + 345,293 + 310,239 + 277,971 + 248,404 + 222,397 + 526,803$$

$$= \$2,303,000.$$

CONFLICTS BETWEEN NPV AND IRR

There are two basic conditions under which the NPV and IRR may give different rankings: (1) *scale effects*—the cost of one project is larger than that of the other, and (2) *timing effects* —the timing of cash flows from the two projects differs, with one producing higher cash flows in the early years, and the other having larger cash flows in later years. Although scale and timing are the *conditions* that lead to conflicts, the basic *cause* of the conflicts is the fact that the use of the NPV and IRR methods requires us to make different implicit assumptions about the rate at which cash flows may be reinvested; that is, they involve different *reinvestment rate assumptions*. These points are analyzed in this section.

Scale Effects Suppose we are analyzing a plant modernization program, one element of which calls for choosing between a large project, Project A, which involves an investment of $1 million in a conveyor-belt system for handling goods in a storage warehouse, and a smaller project, Project B, which involves an expenditure of $300,000 to do the same thing by employing a fleet of fork trucks. The conveyor-belt system has lower operating costs, so its cash flows are larger. The net present values are found to be $200,000 for A and $100,000 for B. Using the NPV criterion, we would select Project A. However, suppose we compute the projects' IRRs and find $IRR_B > IRR_A$; this suggests that we should choose Project B.

Given this conflict, which project should be accepted? If we assume that the cost of capital is a constant, as is usually done whenever the NPV or IRR is used, then the answer is A, the project with the higher NPV. The differential between the initial outlays of the two projects ($700,000) can be looked upon as an investment itself, Project C. That is, Project A can be broken down into two components, one equal to Project B, the other a residual project equal to the hypothetical Project C. The hypothetical investment has a "cost" of $700,000 and a net present value equal to the differential between the NPVs of the first two projects, or $100,000. This is shown below:

Project	Cost	NPV
A	$1,000,000	$200,000
B	− 300,000	− 100,000
C	$ 700,000	$100,000

Since the hypothetical Project C has a positive net present value, it should be accepted. This amounts to accepting Project A.

To put it another way, Project A can be split into two components, one costing $300,000 and having a net present value of $100,000, the other costing $700,000 and having a net present value of $100,000. As each of the two components has a positive net present value, both should be accepted. But if Project B is accepted, the effect is to reject the second component of Project A, the hypothetical Project C. Since the IRR method selects Project B while the NPV method selects Project A, we conclude that the NPV method is preferable.[1]

Timing of Cash Flows Conflicts between the NPV and IRR methods can arise when two projects are of equal size but the time patterns of their cash flows differ. Projects L and S discussed in Chapter 11 have such a difference—refer back to Figure 11–2 for a graphic picture of the cash flows from the two projects. Also, recall that in Chapter 11 we showed that long-term projects such as L are severely penalized by high interest rates, while fast payback investments such as Project S are affected less severely by high discount rates. This causes Project L's NPV profile to decline more sharply than that of S, and we saw in Figure 11–1 that L's NPV profile crosses that of S at $k = 7.1\%$.

If the cost of capital exceeds 7.1 percent, then Project S is ranked higher by both the NPV and the IRR methods, so no conflict exists. However, if k is less than 7.1 percent, the NPV method ranks L higher, but the IRR method ranks S first. Thus, for projects that differ primarily in terms of the timing of their cash flows, whether or not an NPV versus IRR conflict occurs depends on whether the cost of capital is above or below the crossover rate. If the cost of capital exceeds the crossover rate, then no conflict exists, but if the cost of capital is less than the crossover rate, then a conflict does exist.

The Reinvestment Rate Assumption

One who uses the NPV method to compare projects implicitly assumes that the opportunity exists to reinvest the cash flows generated by a project at the cost of capital, while use of the IRR method implies the opportunity to reinvest at the IRR. The cash flows may actually be withdrawn and spent on beer and pizza, but the assumption of a reinvestment opportunity is still implicit in the calculations. To demonstrate this, consider the following steps:

Step 1. Notice that both the NPV and IRR methods involve the use of present value interest factors (PVIFs) in the solution process; for example, to determine the NPV, multiply a series of cash flows by appropriate PVIFs, sum these products, subtract the initial cost, and the result is the NPV. Thus, the NPV

---

1 The matter of project size can be considered in more dramatic terms: would a business that is able to raise all the capital it wants at a cost of 10 percent rather have a 100 percent rate of return on a $1 investment or a 50 percent return on a $1 million investment? The answer is obvious here, and the same principle applies in more realistic situations. Notice also that, under the assumption of unlimited capital at a constant cost, the existence of other projects is irrelevant to the choice between A and B. Any other projects that are "good" can be accepted and financed regardless of whether or not A or B is selected.

method involves using present value tables, and the same thing holds for finding the IRR.

Step 2. Refer back to Chapter 3, Table 3–1 and Equation 3–2, and notice how present value tables are constructed. *The present value of any future sum is defined as the beginning amount which, when compounded at a specified and constant interest rate, will grow to equal the future amount over the stated time period.* From Table 3–1 we can see that the present value of $127.63 due in five years, when discounted at 5 percent, is $100 because $100, when interest earned is reinvested and compounded at 5 percent for five years, will grow to $127.63. Thus, compounding and discounting are reciprocal relationships, and the *very construction of PV tables implies a reinvestment process.*

Step 3. Since both the NPV and IRR methods involve the use of compound interest tables, and since the very construction of these tables involves an assumed reinvestment process, the concept of reinvestment opportunities underlies the two methods.

Step 4. The implicitly assumed reinvestment rate used in the NPV method is the cost of capital, k; that used in the IRR method is r, which is the IRR in the solution process. These are the rates built into the PVIFs.

Suppose the cash flows from a project are not reinvested but are used for current consumption. No reinvestment is involved, yet an IRR for the project could still be calculated—does this show that the reinvestment assumption is not *always* implied in the IRR calculation? The answer is *no;* reinvestment itself is not necessarily assumed, but the *opportunity* for reinvestment *is* assumed. Because that assumption is made in the very construction of the PV tables, we simply could not define or interpret the concepts of NPV or IRR without it.

Terminal (or Future) Value

These concepts, and the impact of actual reinvestment rates on the choice of capital budgeting methods, can be made clear through the use of an example involving both *terminal value* (the value of an asset at the end of its life) and present value. Notice that the value of any asset, or a collection of assets such as a firm, can be estimated at any point in time. We are primarily interested in the value of the asset at the present time, or its present value, because this figure represents stockholders' wealth, which is what management seeks to maximize. However, the terminal value is useful for examining the difference between the NPV and the IRR.

Assume that a firm is considering the two alternative projects, X and Y, whose salient features are given in Table 11B–1. The cost of capital is assumed to be

Table 11B–1
Terminal Value Analysis of Projects X and Y

	Cost (1)	Year 1 (2)	Year 2 (3)	Year 3 (4)	Alternative Reinvestment Rates (%) (5)	Terminal Value at End of Year 3[a] (6)	Present Value of Terminal Value Discounted at 6% (7)	Net Present Value of Cash Flows Discounted at 6% (8)
		Cash Flows at End of						
Project X	$10,000	$5,000	$5,000	$ 5,000	6.0	$15,918	$13,365	$3,365
					10.0	16,550	13,895	
					18.3	17,912	15,040	
					20.0	18,200	15,281	
					23.4[b]	18,784	15,771	
Project Y	$10,000	0	0	$16,550	6.0	$16,550	$13,895	$3,895
					10.0	16,550	13,895	
					18.3[c]	16,550	13,895	
					20.0	16,550	13,895	
					23.4	16,550	13,895	

Note: NPV_X = $13,365 − $10,000 = $3,365 at k = 6%.
$\qquad NPV_Y$ = $13,895 − $10,000 = $3,895 at k = 6%.

[a]The terminal value for Project X is computed as follows:
(Annual cash flow) (FVIFA for 3 years at appropriate reinvestment rate).

$$[b] 23.4\% = IRR_X: \sum_{t=1}^{3} \frac{\$5,000}{(1.234)^t} - \$10,000 \approx 0.$$

$$[c] 18.3\% = IRR_Y: \frac{\$16,550}{(1.183)^3} - \$10,000 \approx 0.$$

6 percent. Both projects cost $10,000, but X provides cash flows every year while Y has no cash flows until Year 3. Because of these timing differences, the IRR and NPV methods give conflicting rankings: IRR_X = 23.4% > IRR_Y = 18.3%, but at the assumed 6 percent cost of capital NPV_Y = $3,895 > NPV_X = $3,365. Which of the two projects should be selected?

The proper choice depends upon investment opportunities during Years 2 and 3. Project Y has no intermediate cash flows, so its terminal value will be $16,550 regardless of reinvestment rates. However, the terminal values of Project X range from $15,918 to $18,784, depending on the reinvestment opportunity rate for cash flows during Years 2 and 3. Notice that *the projects' contribution to the value of the firm today is the present value of the terminal value, discounted at the stockholders' 6 percent assumed cost of capital.* The addition to the value of the firm is $13,895 if Project Y is chosen, but it will range from $13,365 to $15,771, depending on reinvestment opportunities, if Project X is selected. At a reinvestment rate of 10 percent, the two projects are approximately equal. If expected reinvestment rates exceed 10 percent, then management should choose Project X. If the expected reinvestment rate is less than 10 percent, Y is preferable. Thus, 10 percent corresponds to the crossover point in Figure 11–1.[2]

Which Reinvestment Rate Assumption Is Better?

We have seen that use of the NPV method implicitly assumes reinvestment, or at least the opportunity to reinvest, at the cost of capital, while the use of the IRR method assumes that the firm has the opportunity to reinvest a project's cash flows at the project's IRR. Which is the better assumption? Ordinarily, the NPV assumption of reinvestment at the cost of capital is the better one. This is demonstrated in the following sequence of events:

1. Assume that the firm's cost of capital is 10 percent. Management can obtain all the funds it wants at this rate. This condition is expected to hold in the future.
2. Projects are evaluated at $k = 10\%$. All the projects with NPV > 0 are accepted. Plenty of capital is available to finance these projects, both now and in the future.
3. As cash flows come in from past investments, what will be done with them? If the good projects have already been accepted, the only projects left will have NPV < 0, so the cash flows can only be paid out to investors or, more likely, be used as a substitute for outside capital that costs 10 percent. *Thus, since the cash flows are expected to save the firm 10 percent, this is their opportunity cost reinvestment rate.*
4. The IRR method implicitly assumes reinvestment at the internal rate of return itself. Under the assumptions of a constant expected future cost of capital and ready access to capital markets, this assumption is incorrect. The NPV's assumption of reinvestment at the cost of capital is a better one.

The above reasoning leads to the conclusion that the assumption of reinvestment at the cost of capital, which is implied in the case of the NPV method, is the better one. This, in turn, leads to a preference for the NPV method, at least for firms willing and able to obtain capital at a cost reasonably close to their current cost of capital. However, there are instances where the actual reinvestment rate may differ from the assumed cost of capital—the situation described in Table 11B–1 is one example. Here the best approach is either to redefine the cost of capital as the reinvestment rate or else to use the terminal value method.

---

2 It has been argued that the terminal value approach, where terminal values of projects at some horizon date are compared, would lead to better capital budgeting decisions, because this procedure would require the explicit consideration of reinvestment rates. While this may be true, (1) it is extremely difficult to estimate future reinvestment rates, and (2) as we show in the next section, the appropriate reinvestment rate for a firm that is willing to go into the capital markets to obtain capital is the marginal cost of capital. For these reasons, the terminal value and present value approaches will lead to identical decisions if consistent input data are used.

Redefining NPV and IRR: NPV* and IRR*

We can use the terminal value concept to redefine both the NPV and the IRR in the following manner:

$$NPV^* = \frac{\text{Terminal value}}{(1 + k)^n} - \text{Cost,}$$

and

$$IRR^* = \text{Solution value of } r \text{ in the equation}$$

$$\frac{\text{Terminal value}}{(1 + r)^n} - \text{Cost} = 0,$$

where the terminal value is based on the best available estimates of future reinvestment rates. In words, we can define NPV* (pronounced "NPV-star") as the present value of the terminal value, discounted at the cost of capital, minus the cost, and IRR* as the value of r that equates the present value of the terminal value to the cost of the project.

To calculate these modified NPVs and IRRs, we need to know the relevant terminal values, and in order to calculate terminal values, we need reinvestment rates. If the pattern of reinvestment rates is known, then we *should* calculate NPV* and IRR*—they are clearly more accurate measures of project profitability than the unmodified versions.

Suppose we have estimates of the appropriate reinvestment rates, calculate NPV* and IRR*, and find a conflict, perhaps because one project is larger than the other. Which project should be selected? *The answer is the one with the higher NPV*; in this case, the NPV method always makes the better choice.*

If the modified NPV method always makes unambiguously correct choices between mutually exclusive projects, why not use it instead of the "regular" NPV method? Actually, we would prefer to see it used, and we believe that firms would use it *if they had sufficiently reliable information about reinvestment rates to warrant this use.* However, we know of no firm currently using the modified NPV method.

Other Reasons for Preferring the NPV Method to the IRR Method

Conflicts do not always arise between NPV and IRR when mutually exclusive projects are being considered, but it should be apparent that such conflicts can easily exist. Thus, if one firm happens to be using the NPV method while another uses the IRR, they could make different choices when faced with identical decisions. It has been argued at several points that the NPV method is better. This contention is pursued further in this section.

Effect of the Cost of Capital A project's calculated IRR is not dependent on the firm's cost of capital. Thus, Project S has a higher IRR than Project L, and S will always be chosen, regardless of the cost of capital, if the firm uses the IRR method. The NPV, on the other hand, varies with the cost of capital. Thus, if money is tight and interest rates are high, Project L's NPV will be lower than that of Project S, and conversely if rates are low. This is a very reasonable and desirable feature, for it is entirely logical that projects with fast cash throw-offs would tend to be favored when money is tight and interest rates are high. On the other hand, it makes economic sense for longer-term projects to look relatively good when funds are readily available at a low cost. Thus, the fact that the NPV method takes account of the cost of capital, while the IRR method does not, gives an advantage to the NPV.

Multiple Internal Rates of Return Another problem with the IRR is the fact that under certain circumstances several different values of r can be used to solve Equation 11B–1:

$$0 = \frac{R_1}{(1 + r)^1} + \frac{R_2}{(1 + r)^2} + \cdots + \frac{R_n}{(1 + r)^n} - C. \qquad (11B–1)$$

Notice that this equation is a polynomial of degree n. Therefore there are n different roots, or solutions, to the equation. All except one of the roots either are imaginary numbers or are negative when investments are "normal"—a normal investment being one that has one or more outflows (costs) followed by a series of inflows (receipts)—so in the normal case only one positive value of r appears. If, however, a project calls for a large outflow either sometime during or at the end of its life, then it is a "nonnormal" project, and the possibility of multiple real roots arises.

To illustrate this problem, suppose the project calls for the expenditure of $1.6 million to develop a strip mine. The mine will produce a cash flow of $10 million at the end of Year 1. Then, at the end of Year 2, $10 million must be expended to restore the land to its original condition. Therefore, the project's cash flows are as follows:

Year end: 0   1   2

Cash flow: − $1.6 million   + $10 million   − $10 million.

These values can be substituted into Equation 11–1 to derive the NPV for the investment:

$$NPV = -\$1.6\,\text{million} + \frac{\$10\,\text{million}}{(1 + k)^1} - \frac{\$10\,\text{million}}{(1 + k)^2}.$$

$NPV = 0$ when $k = r = 25\%$ and also when $r = 400\%$, so the IRR of the investment is both 25 and 400 percent. This relationship is graphically depicted in Figure

11B–1. Note that no dilemma would arise if the NPV method were used; we would simply use Equation 11–1, find the NPV, and use this for ranking.[3]

**Figure 11B–1
Net Present Value as a
Function of Cost of Capital**

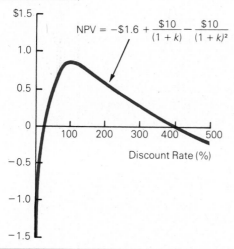

Net Present Value
(Millions of Dollars)

$$NPV = -\$1.6 + \frac{\$10}{(1 + k)} - \frac{\$10}{(1 + k)^2}$$

Discount Rate (%)

Another example of multiple internal rates of return occurred when a major California bank *borrowed* funds from an insurance company, then used these funds (plus an initial investment of its own) to buy a number of jet engines, which it then leased to a major airline. The bank expected to receive positive net cash flows (lease payments minus interest on the insurance company loan) for a number of years, then several large negative cash flows as it repaid the insurance company loan, and, finally, a large inflow from the sale of the engines when the lease expired.[4]

The bank discovered two IRRs and wondered which was correct. It could not ignore the IRR and use the NPV method, as the lease was already on the books; meanwhile, the bank's senior loan committee as well as the Federal Reserve

3 Does this analysis suggest that the firm should try to *raise* its cost of capital to about 100 percent in order to maximize the NPV of the project? Certainly not. As we shall see later in the book, the firm should seek to *minimize* its cost of capital—this will maximize the price of its stock. Taking actions to raise the cost of capital might make this particular project look good, but these actions would be terribly harmful to the firm's more numerous "normal" projects. Only if the firm's cost of capital is high, in spite of efforts to keep it down, will the illustrative project have a high NPV.

4 The situation described here is a *leveraged lease.* See Chapter 21 for more on leveraged leases, and the Omega Airlines Case in *Cases in Managerial Finance,* third edition, for a detailed discussion.

Bank examiners wanted to know the return on the lease. The bank's solution called for compounding the cash flows—both positive and negative—at an assumed reinvestment rate of 9 percent, its average return on loans, to arrive at a compounded terminal value for the operation. Then the interest rate that equated this terminal sum to the bank's initial cost was called the IRR, or the rate of return on the lease. This procedure satisfied both the loan committee and the bank examiners.[5]

THE EFFECT OF THE VOLUME OF EXPANSION ON THE COST OF CAPITAL

As we shall see in Chapter 16, a firm's cost of new capital will increase if it expands so rapidly that it must sell large amounts of securities, or borrow large sums from its banks, or both. Thus, if the firm that is analyzing Projects L and S in Figure 11–1 has relatively few good investment opportunities, it may require no external capital and have a cost of capital as low as 6 percent. In this case, the NPV method would select Project L. On the other hand, the firm might have many good investment opportunities, and to take them all would require not only heavy bank borrowing but also the sale of bonds and stock. This might push the cost of capital up to 10 percent, in which case Project S would have the higher NPV.

Figure 11B–2 illustrates the relationship between investment opportunities (the Investment Opportunity Schedule, or IOS curve), the marginal cost of capital, and the size of the total capital budget. Here we assume that the firm's treasurer first estimates the marginal cost of capital schedule—in effect, the treasurer tells the director of capital budgeting (DCB) that the cost of capital is 10 percent, provided the total capital budget does not exceed Q^* dollars. If the budget exceeds Q^*, then a higher cost of capital will exist. The DCB next estimates each project's IRR and graphs the projects in descending order as shown in Figure 11B–2. The height of each project represents its IRR, while the width of the lines represents the cost of each project. Thus, the DCB plots the investment required for each project against its IRR.[6]

The curve IOS_1 designates relatively good investment opportunities—quite a few investments are available with high expected rates of return. The firm would accept Projects A through G, thus raising and investing Q_2 dollars during the year. IOS_2, on the other hand, shows a situation where investment opportunities are generally poorer.

5 For additional insights into the multiple root problem, see James C. T. Mao, *Quantitative Analysis of Financial Decisions* (New York: Macmillan, 1969), Chapter 6.
6 The exact same graph could be developed by the NPV method. Here, the DCB would start with a high discount rate, say 25 percent, and determine how many projects had NPV > 0. None would, so the discount rate would be lowered. At 22 percent, Project A would have NPV just barely greater than zero, so A would be plotted on the graph. The process would be continued to develop the remainder of the IOS. The IOS is identical regardless of which method is used to calculate it.

It should be clear from Figure 11B–2 that if the IOS cuts the MCC to the left of Q^*, where the MCC is horizontal, then the director of capital budgeting does not need to worry about the effect of the aggregate capital budget on the value of the cost of capital. However, if the firm has many good investment opportunities, causing the IOS to cut the cost of capital curve to the right of Q^*, then the discount rate used in the project selection process must be estimated by finding the intersection of the cost of capital and IOS schedules. The exact procedure for determining this intersection is deferred to Chapter 16, where we discuss the derivation of the cost of capital schedule.

Figure 11B–2
Investment Opportunity Schedule (IOS) and
Marginal Cost of Capital (MCC)

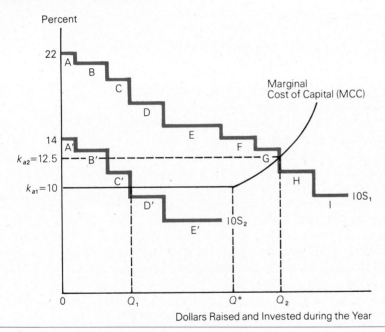

CAPITAL RATIONING

Ordinarily, firms operate as illustrated in Figure 11B–2; that is, they take on investments to the point where the marginal returns from investment are just equal to the estimated marginal cost of capital. For firms operating in this manner, the decision process is as described above—they make those investments having positive net present values, reject those whose net present values are negative, and choose between mutually exclusive investments on the basis of the higher net present value. However, a firm will occasionally set an absolute limit on the size of its capital budget that is less than the level of investment called for by the NPV or IRR criteria. This is called *capital rationing.*

The principal reason for such action is that some firms are reluctant to engage in external financing (borrowing, or selling stock). One management, recalling the plight of firms with substantial amounts of debt in the 1930s, may simply refuse to use debt. Another management, which has no objection to selling debt, may not want to sell equity capital for fear of losing some measure of voting control. Still others may refuse to use any form of outside financing, considering safety and control to be more important than additional profits. These are all cases of capital rationing, and they result in limiting the rate of expansion to a slower pace than would be dictated by "purely rational wealth-maximizing behavior."[7]

Project Selection under Capital Rationing

How should projects be selected under conditions of capital rationing? First, note that under conditions of true capital rationing, the firm's value is not being maximized—if management were maximizing, then it would move to the point where the marginal project's NPV was zero, and capital rationing as defined would not exist. So, if a firm uses capital rationing, it has ruled out value maximization. The firm may, however, want to maximize value *subject to the constraint that the capital ceiling not be exceeded.* Following constrained maximization behavior will, in general, result in a lower value than following unconstrained maximization, but some type of constrained maximization may produce reasonably satisfactory results. Linear programming is one method of constrained maximization that has been applied to capital rationing. Much work is going on in the area, and linear programming may, in the future, be widely applied in capital budgeting.

If a financial manager does face capital rationing, and if the constraint cannot be lifted, what can be done? The objective should be to select projects, subject

---

7 We should make three points here. First, we do *not* necessarily consider a decision to hold back on expansion irrational. If the owners of a firm have what they consider to be plenty of income and wealth, then it might be quite rational for them to "trim their sails," relax, and concentrate on enjoying what they have already earned rather than on earning still more. Such behavior would not, however, be appropriate for a publicly owned firm.

    The second point is that it is not correct to interpret as capital rationing a situation where the firm is willing to sell additional securities at the going market price but finds that it cannot because the market simply will not absorb more of its issues. Rather, such a situation indicates that the cost-of-capital curve is rising. If more acceptable investments are indicated than can be financed, then the cost of capital being used is too low and should be raised.

    Third, firms sometimes set a limit on capital expenditures, not because of a shortage of funds, but because of limitations on other resources, especially managerial talent. A firm might, for example, feel that its personnel development program is sufficient to handle an expansion of no more than 10 percent a year, then set a limit on the capital budget to insure that expansion is held to that rate. This is not capital rationing—rather, it involves a downward reevaluation of project returns if growth exceeds some limit; that is, expected rates of return are, after some point, a decreasing function of the level of expenditures.

to the capital rationing constraint, such that the sum of the projects' NPVs is maximized. Linear programming can be used, or, if not too many projects are involved, one can simply enumerate all the sets of projects that meet the budget constraint and then select the set with the largest total NPV.[8]

NPV VERSUS PROFITABILITY INDEX

The Profitability Index (PI), or the benefit/cost ratio as it is sometimes called, is defined as

$$PI = \frac{PV\ benefits}{Cost} = \frac{\sum_{t=1}^{n} \frac{R_t}{(1 + k)^t}}{Cost}.$$

The PI shows the *relative* profitability of any project, or the present value of benefits per dollar of cost.[9]

As was true in the NPV versus IRR comparison, the NPV and PI always make the same accept-reject decisions, but NPV and PI can give different project rankings, which presents problems when mutually exclusive projects are compared. In an earlier section we compared Project A, which calls for an investment of $1 million in a conveyor-belt system for handling goods in a storage warehouse, with Project B, which calls for an expenditure of $300,000 to do the same thing by employing a fleet of forklift trucks. The conveyor-belt system has lower operating costs, so its cash flows are larger; the net present values are found to be $200,000 for A and $100,000 for B. Using the NPV criterion, on the one hand, we would select Project A. On the other hand, if we compute the ratio of the present value of the returns on each project to its cost, we find A's ratio to be $1,200,000/$1,000,000 = 1.20 and B's ratio to be $400,000/$300,000 = 1.33. Thus, using the PI for our ranking, we would select Project B because it produces higher net returns per dollar invested.

Given this conflict, which project should be accepted? Alternatively stated: Is it better to use the net present value approach on an absolute basis (NPV) or on a relative basis (PI)? For a firm that seeks to maximize stockholders' wealth, the NPV method is better. Recall that the differential between the initial outlays of the two projects ($700,000) can be looked upon as an investment itself. Project A can be broken down into two projects, one equal to Project B and one a residual

8 For one interested in programming solutions to capital budgeting problems, a good starting point for further study is James C. T. Mao, *Quantitative Analysis of Financial Decisions* (New York: Macmillan, 1969).
9 If investment expenditures are incurred over several years, as they were in the Compound X example discussed in Chapter 11, then the denominator will be the present value of these outlays.

project equal to the hypothetical Project C. Since both Projects B and C contribute positively to the value of the firm, they should both be accepted. This amounts to accepting Project A, the one chosen by the NPV method. Thus, we conclude that the NPV method leads to better decisions than the PI method.

Questions

11B-1 In what sense is a reinvestment rate assumption embodied in NPV and IRR calculations? What is the implicitly assumed reinvestment rate of each method?

11B-2 "Assume that a firm has no mutually exclusive projects, only independent ones; that it does not face capital rationing; and that all of its projects are normal in the sense of having an outflow followed by a stream of inflows. Under these conditions, the NPV and IRR methods will always result in identical capital budgets." Discuss the statement.

11B-3 "If a project's IRR is greater than the cost of capital, its NPV will always be greater than zero, and accepting the project will *always* increase the firm's value. There is no class of investments where this is not true." Discuss the statement.

Problems

11B-1 Assume that a firm is set up with a total capital of $20,000. No additional funds can be brought into the firm, but cash flows can be reinvested in the business. Thus, a capital rationing constraint of $20,000 exists in Year 1, and later years' capital expenditures are limited to the available cash throwoff from this and succeeding investments.

The investors who set up the firm have a 10 percent cost of capital, and they have mutually agreed to terminate the firm at the end of three years. Therefore, the stockholders' welfare will be maximized by having the firm attain the highest possible future value. Two projects are available at $t = 0$. Each costs $20,000 and provides cash flows as follows:

Year	Project A	Project B
1	$10,000	$ 0
2	10,000	0
3	10,000	35,000

a. Calculate NPVs and IRRs for Project A. $NPV_B = \$6,296$, and $IRR_B = 20.5\%$. On the basis of these calculations, which project should be accepted?

b. Now calculate NPV* and IRR* for Project A, assuming cash flows are reinvested at 14 percent. $NPV^*_B = \$6,296$, and $IRR^*_B = 20.5\%$. On the basis of these calculations, which project should be accepted?

rate is 10 percent. An investment tax credit (ITC) of 10 percent of the purchase price can be used if the new machine is acquired. Working capital requirements will also increase by $1000. Should Carter buy the new machine?

Provided the annual cash flows are constant, as they are in this example, the worksheet presented in Table 12–1 can be used to analyze the project.[1] A description of the table is given on the next page.

Table 12–1
Worksheet for Replacement Analysis

	Amount before Tax (1)	Amount after Tax (2)	Year Event Occurs (3)	PV Factor at 10% (4)	PV (5)
Net outflows at the time the investment is made: $t = 0$					
1. Cost of new equipment	$12,000	$12,000	0	1.0	$12,000
2. Salvage value of old equipment	(1,000)	(1,000)	0	1.0	(1,000)
3. Tax effect of sale of old equipment	(4,000)	(1,840)	0	1.0	(1,840)
4. Increased working capital (if applicable)	1,000	1,000	0	1.0	1,000
5. Investment tax credit	(1,200)	(1,200)	0	1.0	(1,200)
6. Total initial outflows (PV of costs)					$ 8,960
Net inflows over the project's life: $t = 1$ to 10					
7. Decrease in costs	$ 3,000	$ 1,620	1–10	6.1446	$ 9,954
8. Depreciation on new machine	1,000	—	—	—	—
9. Depreciation on old machine	(500)	—	—	—	—
10. Net change in tax savings from depreciation	500	230	1–10	6.1446	1,413
11. Estimated salvage value of new machine	2,000	2,000	10	0.3855	771
12. Return of working capital (if applicable)	1,000	1,000	10	0.3855	386
13. Total PV of cash inflows					$12,524

14. NPV = PV of inflows − PV of costs = $12,524 − $8,960 = $3,564.

1 If the cash flows are not level over the project's life, then it will be necessary to calculate after-tax savings for each year. This requires that income statements such as the one for Compound X in Chapter 11, Table 11–2, be set up.

Line 1 The top section of the table, Lines 1 through 6, relates to cash flows which occur at (approximately) $t = 0$, the time the investment is made. Line 1 shows the purchase price of the machine, including any installation charges. No discounting is required, so the present value factor is 1.0.

Line 2 Here we show the price received for sale of old equipment. The parentheses denote that this amount is deducted when finding the net cash outflow at $t = 0$.

Line 3 Since the old equipment was sold at a loss, this reduces Carter's taxable income, hence its next quarterly income tax payment. The tax savings is equal to (loss $\times$ t) = ($4,000)(0.46) = $1,840. Here t is the tax rate. The Tax Code defines this loss as an operating loss, not a capital loss, because it reflects the fact that inadequate depreciation was taken on the old asset. If there had been a profit on the sale (that is, if the sales price had exceeded book value), Line 3 would have shown taxes *paid,* a positive cash outflow. In the actual case, the equipment was sold at a loss, so no taxes were paid. In effect, Carter receives a tax credit of $1,840.

Line 4 The investment in additional net working capital (current assets required less spontaneous accounts payable and accruals) is shown here. This investment will be recovered at the end of the project's life. No taxes are involved.

Line 5 The ITC is equal to 10 percent of the purchase price.

Line 6 Here we show the net cash outflow at the time the replacement is made. Carter writes a check for $12,000 to pay for the machine, and another $1,000 is invested in working capital, but these outlays are partially offset by the items on Lines 2, 3, and 5.

Line 7 The lower section of the table shows the *incremental future* cash flows, or benefits, that will result if the replacement is made. The first of these benefits is the reduction in operating costs shown in Column 1. This amount is multiplied by $(1 - t)$ to obtain the after-tax benefits: thus, $3,000(1 - 0.46) = $3,000(0.54) = $1,620. These benefits occur in Years 1–10, so the PV of this annuity is equal to $1,620(6.1446) = $9,954, the amount shown in the last column. Also, note that had the replacement resulted in an increase in sales in addition to the reduction in costs (if the new machine had been both larger and more efficient), then this amount would also be reported on Line 7. Alternatively, a separate line could be added. See Problem 12–4 for an example.

Lines 8, 9, and 10 Lines 8 and 9 show the depreciation on the new and old machines, while Line 10 shows both the net addition to depreciation and the tax savings from this additional depreciation. Depreciation is not in itself a cash inflow, but the increase in depreciation reduces Carter's taxes. The amount of the taxes saved by the increased depreciation is $500($t$) = $500(0.46) = 230; this figure is shown in Column 2. The savings occur in Years 1–10, and the present value of this ten year annuity is $230(6.1446) = $1,413, the amount shown in Line 10, Column 5.

Note that the relevant cash flow is the tax savings on the *net increase* in depreciation, not the depreciation on the new equipment. Replacement decisions are based on *incremental* cash flows. Since we lose $500 of depreciation if we replace the old machine, the incremental or additional depreciation is only $1,000 − $500 = $500.

Line 11 The estimated salvage value on the new machine at the end of its ten year life is $2,000. This is a return of capital, so no taxes are involved. The PV of the salvage value is $2,000(0.3855) = $771.

Line 12 An investment of $1,000 was made in net working capital at $t = 0$. This investment, like the salvage value, will be recovered when the project is terminated at the end of Year 10. Accounts receivable will be collected, inventories will be drawn down and not replaced, and the cash required to operate the facility will no longer be needed. The present value of the recovered working capital is $386.

Line 13 This line sums the PVs of the benefits.

Line 14 Here we calculate the net present value of the replacement project. The PV of the benefits exceeds the investment outlay, so the project has a positive NPV of $3,564. Therefore, the old machine should be replaced.[2]

RISK ANALYSIS IN CAPITAL BUDGETING

Risk analysis is important in all financial decisions, including those relating to capital budgeting. As we saw in Chapter 5, the higher the risk associated with an investment, the higher the rate of return needed to compensate investors for assuming the risk. Procedures for both measuring project risk and incorporating it into the accept-reject decision are covered in this section.

Actually, two separate and distinct types of risk have been identified in capital budgeting: (1) *beta risk,* which measures risk only from the standpoint of an investor who holds a highly diversified portfolio, and (2) *total,* or *corporate, risk* which looks at risk from other parties' viewpoints.

---

2 To simplify matters, we assumed that the replacement project has the same expected life as the years of usage remaining in the old machine. If this assumption is not correct, then it may be necessary to set up a series of replacement chains. This topic is covered in Appendix 12A.

Beta Risk

In Chapter 5 we developed the concept of the *beta coefficient,* which is an index of the riskiness of a particular stock relative to that of an average stock. As we saw, betas generally range from about 0.5 to about 1.5. Further, the beta of a portfolio of stocks is equal to the weighted average of the betas of the individual stocks in the portfolio, with the weights based on the number of dollars invested in each stock.

We also saw in Chapter 5 that the required rate of return on a company's stock (k) is equal to the riskless rate (R_F) plus a risk premium which is equal to the stock's beta coefficient (b) times the market risk premium ($k_M - R_F$):

$$k = R_F + b(k_M - R_F).$$

For example, consider the case of Erie Steel Company, an integrated producer operating in the Great Lakes region. Erie Steel's beta is 1.1, so if $R_F = 8\%$ and $k_M = 12\%$, then

$$k = 8\% + 1.1(4\%) = 12.4\%.$$

Stockholders are willing to have Erie invest their money if the company can earn 12.4 percent on this money. *Therefore, as a first approximation, Erie should invest in capital projects if and only if these projects have an expected return of 12.4 percent or more.*[3] In other words, Erie should use 12.4 percent as its discount rate to determine projects' NPVs or as the "hurdle rate" if the IRR method is used.

Suppose, however, that taking on a particular project will change Erie's beta coefficient. For example, the company might be considering the construction of a fleet of barges to haul iron ore, and barge operations might have betas of about 1.5. Since the corporation itself may be regarded as a "portfolio of assets," and since the beta of any portfolio is a weighted average of the betas of the individual assets, taking on the barge investment will cause the overall corporate beta to rise and to end up somewhere between the original beta of 1.1 and the barge division's beta of 1.5. The exact position will depend on the relative size of the investment in basic steel versus that in barges. If 80 percent of the total corporate funds were in basic steel and 20 percent were in barges, then the new beta would be $0.8(1.1) + 0.2(1.5) = 1.18$.

An increase in the beta coefficient will cause the stock price to decline *unless the increased beta is offset by a higher expected rate of return.* Specifically, the overall corporate cost of capital will rise to 12.72 percent:

$$k_{(new)} = 8\% + 1.18(4\%) = 12.72\%.$$

---

3 To simplify things somewhat, we assume at this point that the firm uses only equity capital. If debt is used, then the cost of capital used must be a weighted average of the cost of debt and equity. This point is discussed at length in Chapter 16.

Therefore, to keep the barge investment from lowering the value of the firm, Erie's expected overall rate of return must rise from 12.4 percent to 12.72 percent.

If investments in basic steel earn 12.4 percent, how much must the barge investment earn in order for the new overall rate of return to equal 12.72 percent? Let X be the required return on the barge investment, and then calculate the value of X as follows:

$$0.8(12.4\%) + 0.2(X) = 12.72\%$$
$$X = 14.0\%.$$

In summary, if Erie makes the barge investment, its beta will rise from 1.1 to 1.18; its overall required rate of return will rise from 12.4 percent to 12.72 percent; and it will achieve this new required rate if the barge investment earns 14 percent. If the barge investment has an expected return of more than 14 percent, taking it on will increase the value of Erie's stock. If the expected return is less than 14 percent, taking it on will decrease the stock's value. At an expected return of 14 percent, the barge project is a "breakeven" proposition in terms of its effect on the value of the stock.

This line of reasoning leads to the conclusion that, if the beta coefficient for each project could be determined, individual projects' costs of capital could be found as follows:

$$k_{(project)} = R_F + b_{(project)}(k_M - R_F).$$

Thus, for basic steel projects with $b = 1.1$, Erie should use 12.4 percent as the discount rate. The barge project should be evaluated at a 14 percent discount rate:

$$k_{(barge)} = 8\% + 1.5(4\%) = 8\% + 6\% = 14\%.$$

A low-risk project such as a new steel distribution center with a beta of only 0.5 would have a cost of capital of 10 percent:

$$k_{(center)} = 8\% + 0.5(4\%) = 10\%.$$

Figure 12–1 gives a graphic summary of these concepts as applied to Erie Steel. Note the following points:

1. The SML is the same as the Security Market Line developed in Chapter 5. It shows how investors are willing to make tradeoffs between risk as measured by beta and expected returns. The higher the risk, the higher the rate of return needed to compensate investors for bearing this risk, and the SML specifies the nature of this relationship.
2. Erie Steel initially had a beta of 1.1, so its required rate of return on average-risk investments is 12.4 percent.
3. High-risk investments like the barge line require higher rates of return, while low-risk investments like the distribution center have lower required rates of return. Note also that if Erie makes relatively large investments in

Figure 12–1
Using the Security Market Line Concept in
Capital Budgeting

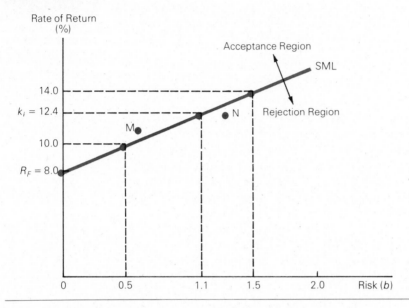

either high- or low-risk projects, as opposed to those with average risks,
both the corporate beta and the required rate of return on the common
stock (k_s) will change.

4. If the expected rate of return on a given capital project lies *above* the SML,
the expected rate of return on the project is more than enough to
compensate for its risk, so it should be accepted. Conversely, if the
project's rate of return lies *below* the SML, it should be rejected. Thus,
Project M in Figure 12–1 is acceptable, while Project N should be rejected.
N has a higher expected return than M, but the differential is not enough to
offset N's much higher risk.

Corporate Risk versus Beta Risk

A particular project might have highly uncertain returns, yet taking it on
might not affect the firm's beta coefficient at all. Recall that the beta
coefficient reflects only that part of an investor's risk which cannot be
eliminated by holding a large portfolio of stocks. Now suppose that 100
firms in the oil business each drill one wildcat well. Each company has
invested $1 million. If a firm strikes oil, then it will earn $1.4 million, while if
it hits a dry hole, it will suffer a $1 million loss and go bankrupt. The
probability of striking oil is 50 percent.

From the standpoint of the individual firms, this is a very risky business. Their expected rate of return is 20 percent, calculated as follows:

$$\frac{\text{Expected rate}}{\text{of return}} = \frac{\text{Expected profit}}{\text{Investment}} = \frac{0.5(-\$1\text{ million}) + 0.5(+\$1.4\text{ million})}{\$1\text{ million}}$$

$$= \frac{-\$500,000 + \$700,000}{\$1,000,000} = 20\%.$$

Note, however, that even though the expected return is 20 percent, there is a 50 percent probability of each firm's being wiped out.

Although the riskiness of each individual firm is high, if a stockholder constructs a portfolio consisting of a few shares of each of the 100 companies, the riskiness of this portfolio is not high at all. Some of the stocks will hit and do well, others will miss and go out of business, but the portfolio's return will be very close to the expected 20 percent. Therefore, since investors can diversify away the risks inherent in each of the individual companies, these risks are *not market-related;* that is, they do not affect the companies' beta coefficients.[4]

With this background, *we may define the corporate risk of a capital budgeting project as the probability that the project will incur losses which will, at a minimum, destabilize the corporation's earnings and, at the extreme, cause it to go bankrupt.* A project with a high degree of corporate risk will not necessarily affect the firm's beta to any great extent; our hypothetical example demonstrates this point. On the other hand, if the riskiness of a project is not diversifiable, then it may have a high degree of both corporate and beta risk. For example, suppose a firm decides to undertake a major expansion to build solar powered autos. The firm is not sure if its technology will work on a mass production basis, so there are great risks in the venture. Management also estimates that the project will have a higher probability of success if the economy is strong, for then people will have the money to spend on buying the new autos. This means that the plant will tend to do well when other companies are also doing well, and to do badly when they do badly, so the plant's beta coefficient will be high. A project like this will have a high degree of both corporate risk and beta risk.

Beta risk is obviously important because of beta's effect on the value of a firm's stock. At the same time, corporate risk is also important for two primary reasons:

1. Undiversified stockholders, including the owners of small businesses, are more concerned about corporate risk than about beta risk.
2. The firm's stability is important to its managers, workers, customers,

---

4 Note also that, if the 100 separate companies were merged, the combined company would not be very risky—it would drill lots of wells, losing on some and hitting on others, but it would earn a relatively steady profit.

suppliers, and creditors, and also to the community in which it operates. Firms that are in serious danger of bankruptcy, or even of suffering low profits and reduced output, have difficulty attracting and retaining good managers and workers. Also, both suppliers and customers will be reluctant to depend on the firm, and it will have difficulty borrowing money except at high interest rates. These factors will tend to reduce the firm's profitability, hence the price of its stock.

TECHNIQUES FOR MEASURING CORPORATE RISK

Measuring the risk inherent in capital projects is a difficult task. Studies suggest that corporations give less weight to beta than to corporate risk and that they consider beta risk only in terms of subjective evaluations, not by statistical and mathematical processes. Corporate risk, on the other hand, is given great weight in the capital budgeting process, and it is analyzed by both quantitative and qualitative methods. Some of these methods are discussed in this section.

The starting point for analyzing corporate risk involves determining the uncertainty inherent in a project's cash flows. This analysis can be handled in a number of ways, ranging from informal judgments to complex economic and statistical analyses involving large-scale computer models. To illustrate what is involved here, refer back to Carter Chemical's Compound X project as described in Chapter 11. Most of the elements in Table 11–2, which gave the income statement projections for Compound X, are subject to uncertainty. For example, sales for 1981 are projected at 75,000 tons to be sold at a net price of $60 per ton, or $4.5 million in total. However, unit sales will probably be somewhat higher or lower than 75,000 tons, and the sales price might be different from $60 per ton. *In effect, these estimates are expected values taken from probability distributions, as are all the other figures shown in Table 11–2.* The distributions could be relatively "tight," with small standard deviations, or they could be "flat," denoting a great deal of uncertainty about the variable in question. For example, the 75,000 ton sales estimate for 1981 could have come from a distribution like A, B, or C in Figure 12–2. The more peaked the distribution, the higher the probability that actual sales will be close to the predicted level, hence the smaller the risk of the project.[5]

Sensitivity Analysis

Intuitively, we know that every element in Table 11–2 represents an expected value taken from a distribution like one of those shown in Figure

---

5 For convenience, we frequently use distributions that are approximately normal. While the assumption of normality is often appropriate, at times a skewed distribution is more realistic.

Figure 12–2
Probability Distributions for Tons of
Compound X Sold in 1981

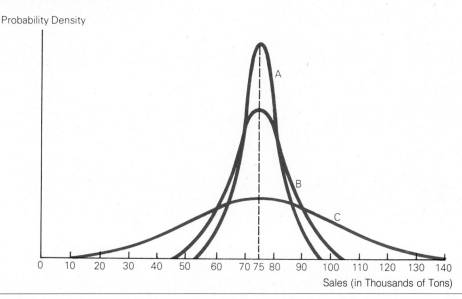

12–2. We also know that if a key input variable such as tons sold changes, so will the project's NPV. *Sensitivity analysis indicates exactly how much NPV will change in response to a given change in an input variable, other things held constant.* Sensitivity analysis is sometimes called "what if" analysis because it answers questions such as this: "What if sales are only 75,000 units rather than 100,000? What will then happen to NPV?"

Sensitivity analysis begins with a *base case* situation. To illustrate the procedure, we shall consider the data given in Table 12–2, where projected income statements for Project Y, a $100,000 plant with a five year expected life, are shown. The values for unit sales, sales price, fixed and variable costs, and construction costs are the *most likely,* or *base case,* values, and the resulting $13,970 NPV is called the *base case NPV.* Now we begin asking a series of "what if" questions: "What if output is 20 percent below the forecasted level?" "What if sales prices fall?" "What if the construction cost is $120,000 rather than the expected $100,000?" *Sensitivity analysis is designed to answer questions such as these.*

In a sensitivity analysis, we change each variable by specific percentages above and below the base case value, calculate new NPVs (holding other things constant), and then plot the NPVs against the variable in question. Figure 12–3 shows Project Y's sensitivity graphs for a number of the key input variables. The slopes of the lines show how sensitive NPV is to changes in each of the inputs: the steeper the slope, the more sensitive the NPV is to changes in the variable.

Table 12–2
Project Y: Data on Project and Base Case
Analysis

Project cost: $100,000 expenditure at $t = 0$.
Salvage value: $15,000.
Expected life: 5 years.
Depreciation method: Straight line. Annual depreciation $= (\$100,000 - \$15,000)/5$
$= \$17,000$.

Cost of capital: 10%.

Projected income statement, base case:

	Year 1	Year 2	Year 3	Year 4	Year 5
Sales (units)	3,000	3,000	3,000	3,000	3,000
Sales price	$75	$75	$75	$75	$75
Net sales	$225,000	$225,000	$225,000	$225,000	$225,000
Variable costs ($45.87/unit)	137,600	137,600	137,600	137,600	137,600
Fixed costs (except depreciation)	50,000	50,000	50,000	50,000	50,000
Depreciation	17,000	17,000	17,000	17,000	17,000
Total costs	$204,600	$204,600	$204,600	$204,600	$204,600
EBIT	$20,400	$20,400	$20,400	$20,400	$20,400
Federal and state taxes (48%)	9,792	9,792	9,792	9,792	9,792
Net income	$10,608	$10,608	$10,608	$10,608	$10,608
Add back: depreciation	17,000	17,000	17,000	17,000	17,000
salvage					15,000
Net cash flow	$27,608	$27,608	$27,608	$27,608	$42,608

NPV $= \$27,608 \ (\text{PVIFA}_{10\%,\ 5}) + \$15,000(\text{PVIF}_{10\%,\ 5}) - \$100,000$
$= \$27,608(3.7908) + \$15,000(0.6209) - \$100,000$
$= \$13,970$.

If we were comparing two projects, other things held constant, the one with the steeper sensitivity lines would be regarded as riskier—a relatively small misestimation of variables such as demand for the product would produce a large error in the project's projected NPV. Thus, sensitivity analysis provides useful insights into the relative riskiness of different projects. It is interesting—and it should be frightening to management—to note that even a small decline in tons sold or the sales price, or a small rise in the variable cost per unit, would cause the NPV to change from positive to negative. Project Y has quite a bit of corporate risk.

Figure 12-3
Sensitivity Analysis for Project Y

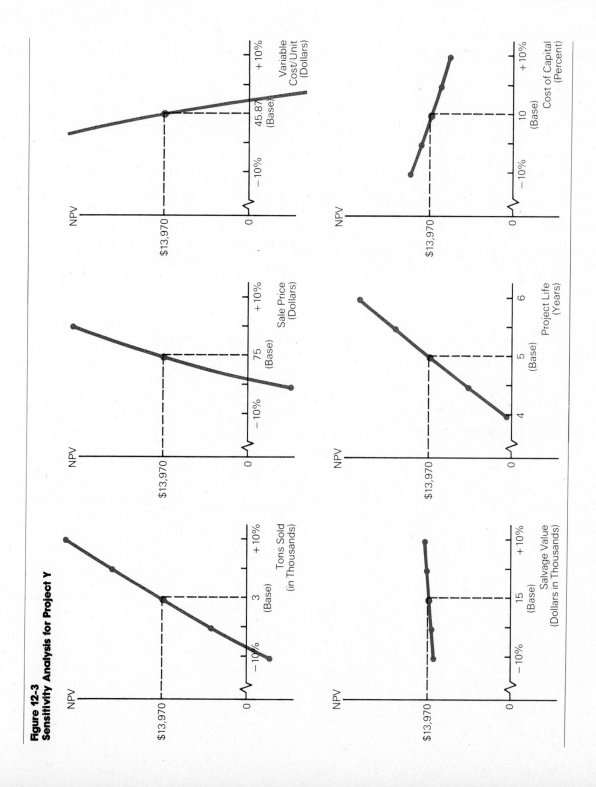

Computer Simulation[6]

Although sensitivity analysis is widely used in industry, it does have some severe limitations. Consider, for example, a proposed coal mine whose NPV is highly sensitive to changes in both output and sales prices. Still, if a utility company has contracted to buy most of the mine's output at a fixed price per ton, then the mine venture may not be very risky in spite of the steep sensitivity lines. *In general, a project's risk depends on both its sensitivity to changes in key variables and the range of likely values of these variables, i.e., the variables' probability distributions.*

Computer simulation provides a means of tying together sensitivities and probability distributions to quantify a project's risk. The first step in a computer simulation is to specify a probability distribution for each of the key variables in the analysis. To illustrate, suppose we have determined that the probability distribution of the future unit sales of Compound Y is represented by Columns 1 and 2 of Table 12–3.[7] The expected value of units sold is 3,000, but sales can range from 2,000 to 4,000 units. The third column of Table 12–3 gives a range of random numbers associated with each sales estimate. Computers have stored in them (or they can generate) random numbers such as those given in Table 12–4. Notice that in Column 2 of Table 12–3 there is a 5 percent probability of sales as low as 2,000 units; therefore, 5 digits (0, 1, 2, 3, and 4) are assigned to this output (see Column

---

Table 12–3
Probability Distribution for Units Sold of Compound Y

Units Sold (1)	Probability (2)	Random Numbers (3)
2,000	0.05	00–04
2,500	0.20	05–24
3,000	0.50	25–74
3,500	0.20	75–94
4,000	0.05	95–99
3,000 = Expected value		

---

6 The concept of simulation analysis in capital budgeting was first reported by D. B. Hertz, "Risk Analysis in Capital Investments," *Harvard Business Review* (January 1964).

7 Here we assume that sales are always in multiples of 500 and that there is no probability of sales below 2,000 or above 4,000 units. These simplifications are purely for illustrative purposes; actual simulation models need have no such restrictions. In fact, standard computer simulation software packages can very easily handle continuous normal distributions or distributions skewed in any manner. At the University of Florida we use a program called Interactive Financial Planning System (IFPS), which is available from Execucom Systems Corporation, Austin, Texas. IFPS is also used by several hundred large corporations and is on Control Data Corporation's time sharing system. One can learn to use this system (or others that are available) in a few days and then do the type of analysis described here very easily.

3 of Table 12–3). Twenty digits are assigned to an output of 2,500, and so on for the other possible outputs. If the distributions and associated random numbers have been specified for all the other key variables—sales price, unit variable costs, and construction costs, to name some—the computer simulation can begin. These are the steps involved:

1. The computer selects a random number for each uncertain variable (a different number for each variable). For example, it might select 44 for units sold; 17 for the sales price; and 16 for labor costs—these are the first three random numbers listed in Table 12–4.
2. Depending on the random number selected, a value is determined for each variable. The 44 associated with the units sold indicates in Table 12–3 that the appropriate number of units for use in the first run is 3,000. Had a 3 come up, then tons sold would have been 2,000, while if 99 had come up, then the designated tons sold would have been 4,000. Values for all the other variables are set in like manner.[8]
3. Once values have been established for all the variables, the computer generates a set of income statements and cash flows similar to the ones shown earlier in Table 12–2. (Table 12–2 is based on the expected values of the designated variables.) These cash flows are then discounted at the cost of capital (which may also be treated as a random variable); the value

Table 12–4
Illustrative Table of Two Digit Random Numbers

44	17	16	58	01	79	83	86	19	62	06	76	50	03	10
84	16	07	44	99	83	11	46	32	24	20	14	85	88	45
82	97	77	77	81	07	45	32	14	08	32	98	94	07	72
50	92	26	11	97	00	56	76	31	38	80	22	02	53	53
83	39	50	08	30	42	34	07	96	88	54	42	06	87	98
40	33	20	38	26	13	89	51	03	74	17	76	37	13	04
96	83	50	87	75	97	12	25	93	47	70	33	24	03	54
88	42	95	45	72	16	64	36	16	00	04	43	18	66	79
33	27	14	34	09	45	59	34	68	49	12	72	07	34	45
50	27	89	87	19	20	15	37	00	49	52	85	66	60	44

8 Simulation models can be programmed to assume either independence or dependence among variables. In this simple example, we assume independence; however, in many real simulations it is more realistic to assume dependence. Thus, it might be assumed that if demand is weak and the figure for tons sold is relatively low, then prices will also be weak. Similarly, the sales price in one year can be completely independent of or dependent on the price in the preceding year, or it can be somewhat correlated with the previous year's price. Simulation programs such as the one used at the University of Florida (IFPS) can handle these issues with ease, although decision makers often have trouble specifying exactly how the different variables are related to one another.

of the construction cost is subtracted; and the result is the net present value of the project on the computer's first run.

4. The NPV generated on Run 1 is stored, and the computer then goes on to Run 2. Here a different set of random numbers, hence cash flows, is used. The NPV generated in Run 2 is then stored, and the model proceeds on out to perhaps 500 runs. Modern computers can complete this operation almost instantaneously for a cost of less than two dollars.

5. The stored NPVs (all 500 of them) are then printed out in the form of a frequency distribution, together with the expected NPV and the standard deviation of this NPV.[9]

The simulation process is summarized in Figure 12–4. Here we see (in graph form) the probability distributions of the key variables, a listing of the steps in the simulation process, and the NPV distribution that results when Compound Y is subjected to simulation analysis.

The significant advantage of simulation is that it shows us the range of possible outcomes if the project is accepted, not just a point estimate of the NPV. The expected NPV can be used as a measure of the project's profitability, while the standard deviation of this NPV can be used to measure risk.

Limitations of Simulation Analysis

In spite of its obvious appeal, simulation analysis has not been as widely used in industry as one might think. Five major reasons for this lack of general acceptance are discussed below.

Cost versus Benefits One reason that simulation is not more widely used has to do with its cost in relation to the benefits of its use. Until quite recently, developing a simulation model was a major undertaking that required a good deal of high-powered programming talent and a lot of expensive computer time. This is no longer true. Simulation software, and computer hardware, have been developed to the point where cost is simply not a major consideration, at least for the larger firms.

Time Lag It generally takes a while for any new managerial technology to become widely accepted, and simulation analysis may be in this position. This point was made by several executives who reviewed this book.

Interdependencies among the Variables The simulation process described above assumes that the variables are independent of one another. However, it may very well be that such variables as unit sales and sales prices are correlated. If demand is weak, sales prices may also be

---

9 The programs give other information, such as IRR, σ_{IRR}, and payback. They also generate the data points required for a sensitivity analysis.

Figure 12–4
Illustration of Simulation Analysis

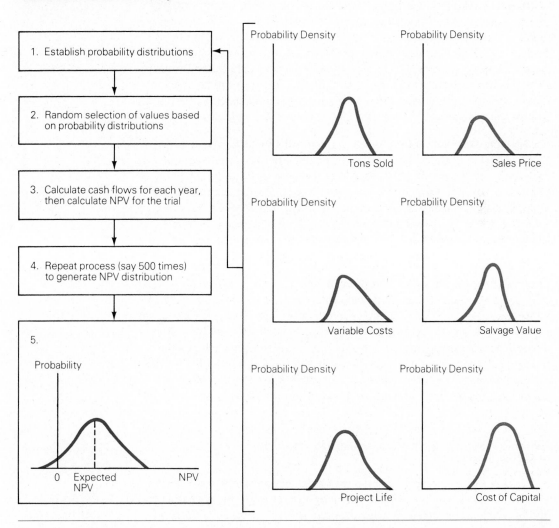

depressed. This suggests that if a low value of tons sold is selected, a low value for the sales price should be used.[10] Similarly, the simulation process described above assumes that the values of each variable, hence the bottom line cash flows, are independent over time. However, in many situations it seems more reasonable to assume that high sales in the early years imply

10 This statement implies a *downward shift* in the demand curve for the product. However, one can also visualize *movement along a demand curve,* which would imply that low sales prices would be associated with high demand.

market acceptance, hence high sales in future years, rather than intertemporal independence of sales.

It is easy enough to incorporate any type of correlation among variables that one desires into a simulation analysis. However, it is *not* easy to specify what the correlations should be. Indeed, people who have tried to obtain such relationships from the operating executives who must estimate them have eloquently emphasized the difficulties involved.[11] Clearly, the problem is not insurmountable, as the use of simulation is growing rapidly. However, it is important not to underestimate the difficulty of obtaining valid estimates of probability distributions and correlations among the variables.[12]

No Specific Decision Rule A fourth problem with simulation analysis is that, even when a simulation analysis has been completed, no clear-cut decision rule emerges. We end up with an expected NPV and a distribution about this expected value, but the analysis has no mechanism to indicate whether the profitability as measured by the expected NPV is sufficient to compensate for the risk as indicated by σ_{NPV}. This is in sharp contrast to the beta approach, where a project is specifically acceptable if its expected rate of return exceeds its beta-determined required rate of return.

Ignores Diversification The fifth problem with simulation is that it ignores the effects of diversification, both within the firm and by investors. Thus, an individual project may have highly uncertain returns, but if those returns are not correlated with the returns on the firm's other assets, then the project may not be risky in the sense of destabilizing the firm as a whole. Similarly, if a project's returns are not correlated with the stock market, even a project with highly variable returns might not be regarded as risky by well-diversified stockholders, who are concerned with *market risk,* not with *total risk.*

Scenario Analysis: Optimistic, Pessimistic, and Most Likely Outcomes

Because of the problems associated with simulation analysis, especially the problem of dealing with correlations among the variables, firms often use a shorter version of simulation called *scenario analysis.* Here the operating executives pick a "bad" set of circumstances (low unit sales, low sales price, high variable cost/unit, high construction cost, etc.) and a "good" set. Perhaps each set might be selected on the basis that the probability of each variable being as high or as low as the indicated value is no more than 25 percent. The NPV under the "bad" and "good" conditions would be calculated and compared to the most likely, or base case, NPV.

11 For an excellent discussion of this problem, see K. Larry Hastie, "One Businessman's View of Capital Budgeting," *Financial Management,* Winter 1974.
12 Some critics use the terms "GIGO" and "SWAG" to describe simulation analysis. These terms are defined in the glossary.

PORTFOLIO EFFECTS WITHIN THE FIRM

As we noted in Chapter 5, a security might be quite risky if held in isolation but not very risky if held as a part of a well-diversified portfolio. The same thing is true of capital budgeting—the returns on an individual project might be highly uncertain, but if the project is small relative to the total firm, and if its returns are not highly correlated with the firm's other assets, then the project may not be very risky in either the corporate or the beta sense.

Many firms do make serious efforts to diversify; often, this is a specific objective of the long-run strategic plan. For example, the oil companies have diversified into both nuclear energy and coal to broaden their operating bases, while real estate developers have diversified geographically to lessen the impact of a slowdown in one region. The major objective of such moves is to stabilize earnings, reduce corporate risk, and raise the value of the firm's stock.

RISK-ADJUSTED DISCOUNT RATES

Thus far we have seen that capital budgeting can affect a firm's beta risk, its corporate risk, or both. We have also seen that it is exceedingly difficult to quantify either effect—it is possible to reach the conclusion that one project is riskier than another (in either the beta or the corporate sense), but it is difficult to develop a really good index of project risk.

This lack of a precise measure of project risk makes it difficult to specify risk-adjusted rates of return, or costs of capital, with which to evaluate individual projects. As we shall see in Chapter 16, it is possible to estimate a firm's overall cost of capital reasonably accurately. Moreover, it is generally agreed that riskier projects should be evaluated with a higher cost of capital than the overall corporate cost, while a lower discount rate should be used for lower-risk projects. Unfortunately, there is no good way of specifying exactly *how much* higher or lower these discount rates should be—given the present state of the art, risk adjustments are necessarily judgmental and somewhat arbitrary.

In spite of the inexactness of the process, Carter Chemical classifies all projects into three categories: (1) low risk, (2) average risk, and (3) high risk. The company calculates its cost of capital as described in Chapter 16, then uses this discount rate for average projects, reduces it by one percentage point when evaluating low-risk projects, and raises it by two percentage points for high-risk projects. For example, if the corporate cost of capital is estimated to be 10 percent, then a 12 percent discount rate will be used for high-risk projects and a 9 percent rate for low-risk projects. Average-risk projects, which constitute about 80 percent of the capital budget, are evaluated at the 10 percent corporate cost of capital. This procedure is not very elegant, but it does at least recognize differential project riskiness, and the financial staff feels that these adjustments are in the right direction and result in better decisions than would be obtained if no adjustments at all were made.[13]

SUMMARY

This chapter has dealt with two important issues in capital budgeting—equipment replacement decisions and risk. The key to making good replacement decisions is to develop accurate estimates of *incremental* cash flows—how large an investment will the replacement entail, and what *net* savings will it produce? If the present value of the net savings exceeds the cost of the equipment, then the replacement should be undertaken.

Our analysis of risk has focused on two issues: (1) the effect of a given project on the firm's beta coefficient *(beta risk)* and (2) the project's effect on the probability of bankruptcy *(corporate risk)*. Both types of risk are important. Beta risk directly affects the value of the firm's stock. Corporate risk affects the financial strength of the firm, and this, in turn, influences its ability to use debt, to maintain smooth operations over time, and to avoid crises that might consume the energy of the firm's managers and disrupt its employees, customers, suppliers, and community.

Both measuring risk and incorporating it into capital budgeting decisions involve judgment. It is possible to use techniques such as simulation and sensitivity analysis, but the assessment of risk in capital budgeting nonetheless remains a judgmental process.

Questions

12-1 Look at Table 12–1, and answer these questions:
   a. Why are the salvage values shown on Lines 2 and 11 not reduced for taxes?
   b. Why is depreciation on the old machine deducted on Line 9?
   c. What would happen if the new machine permitted a *reduction* in working capital?
   d. Why are the cost savings on Line 7 reduced by multiplying the before-tax figure by $(1 - t)$, whereas the net depreciation figure on Line 10 is multiplied by t?

---

13 Firms often expand this type of analysis to include an analysis of *divisional risk*. For example, Carter might determine the beta coefficients for single-product firms which operate in each of its major product lines. Independent firms in the plastics business might have betas which average 1.2; industrial chemical firms might have betas of 1.1; consumer products firms might have betas of 0.90, and so on. This analysis might be used to raise or lower each division's cost of capital from the corporate average cost. Then, within each division, projects with higher or lower risk could be handled as described above.

12-2 In what sense do the key assumptions listed in Table 11–3 in Chapter 11 represent points on probability distributions? Would it be more important to conduct a sensitivity analysis on input variables with peaked or with flat distributions?

12-3 Differentiate between (a) simulation analysis, (b) optimistic–pessimistic–most likely analysis, and (c) sensitivity analysis. If AT&T were considering two investments, one calling for the expenditure of $100 million to develop a satellite communications system, and the other involving the expenditure of $5,000 for a new truck, on which one would the company be more likely to use simulation?

12-4 Distinguish between the beta risk and the corporate risk of a project being considered for inclusion in the capital budget. Which type do you feel should be given the greater weight in capital budgeting decisions?

Problems

12-1 The Bey Burger Company's average cost of capital is 10 percent. The company is choosing between two mutually exclusive projects. Project B is of average risk, it has a cost of $20,000, and it has expected cash flows of $5,880.72 per year for five years. Project A is of above average risk; and management estimates that its cost of capital is 12 percent. A also costs $20,000, and it is expected to provide cash flows of $3,752.21 per year for ten years. Each project will terminate at the end of its designated life.

   a. Calculate risk-adjusted NPVs for the two projects, and use these NPVs to choose between them. (*Note:* No new calculations are needed if you worked Problem 11–5 in Chapter 11.)

   b. Explain how you could find a risk-adjusted discount rate for Project A that would make its risk-adjusted NPV_A equal to NPV_B when B is evaluated at a 10 percent cost of capital.

12-2 The LeClair Company is considering the purchase of a new machine tool to replace an obsolete one. The machine being used for the operation has both a tax book value and a market value of zero; it is in good working order and will last, physically, for at least an additional fifteen years. The proposed machine will perform the operation so much more efficiently that LeClair's engineers estimate that labor, material, and other direct costs of the operation will be reduced by $4,500 a year if it is installed. The proposed machine costs $24,000 delivered and installed, and its economic life is estimated to be fifteen years with a zero salvage value. The company expects to earn 12 percent on its investment after taxes (12 percent is the firm's cost of capital). The tax rate is 60 percent, and the firm uses straight line depreciation. Should LeClair buy the new machine? The investment tax credit does not apply.

12-3 Seal-Best is contemplating replacing one of its bottling machines with a newer and more efficient machine. The old machine has a book value of $200,000 and a remaining useful life of five years. The firm does not expect to realize any return from scrapping the old machine in five years, but if it is sold now to another firm in the industry, Seal-Best would receive $120,000 for it.

The new machine has a purchase price of $440,000, an estimated useful life of five years, and an estimated salvage value of $40,000. A 10 percent investment tax credit is in effect. The new machine is expected to economize on electric power usage, labor, and repair costs, and also to reduce defective bottles; in total, an annual saving of $80,000 will be realized if the new machine is installed. (*Note:* To calculate depreciation, assume that the salvage value *is* deducted from cost to get the depreciable cost.) The company is in the 40 percent tax bracket, has a 10 percent cost of capital, and uses straight line depreciation.

a. Should Seal-Best purchase the new machine? Support your answer.
b. In general, how would each of the following factors affect the investment decision, and how would each be treated? (Give verbal answers.)
  (1) The expected life of the existing machine decreases.
  (2) Improvements in the equipment to be purchased are expected to occur each year, and the result will be to increase the returns or expected savings from new machines over the savings expected with this year's model for every year in the foreseeable future.

12-4 Block Printing Company has an opportunity to purchase a new, more efficient printing press, Model 1980, to replace two presses now in use, Models 1962 and 1977. Block's vice-president in charge of purchasing has reported that the new press, Model 1980, will cost $62,500. It has an expected eight year useful life and a salvage value of $6,500 based on figures approved by the IRS. However, since Model 1980 represents a new generation of presses, it is predicted that the press will actually be sold for $7,500 at the end of its useful life. Use straight line depreciation.

From an examination of the company's books, you have determined that Model 1962 has been fully depreciated, while Model 1977, which was purchased three years ago for $62,000, is being depreciated over an original eleven year period toward an estimated salvage value of $7,000. The demand in the market for these older presses is such that Model 1962 could be sold today for $3,000 and Model 1977 for $20,000.

If the Model 1980 printing press is purchased, Block will be able to *decrease* inventories by $7,000, and accounts payable will decline by $4,000 for the duration of Model 1980's useful life. Model 1980 will generate annual inflows of $10,833 before tax. You have been asked to calculate the NPV for this project. Block's income tax rate is 40%, the capital gains tax rate is 30%, and Model 1980 is eligible for a 10% investment tax credit. The company's cost of capital is 14 percent. (*Hint:* Remember to treat capital gains and capital losses separately—they should not be netted out. Also, remember that recaptured depreciation is taxed at regular income tax rates: only sums received from the sale of equipment in excess of the original depreciable cost are taxed as capital gains.)

APPENDIX 12A   COMPARING PROJECTS WITH UNEQUAL LIVES

To simplify matters, our example of replacement decisions assumed that the new machine had a life equal to the remaining life of the existing one. Suppose, however, that we must choose between two mutually exclusive replacement alternatives that have *different* lives. For example, Machine S has an expected life of ten years, while L has a fifteen year life. The most typical procedure for solving problems of this type is to set up a series of *replacement chains* extending out to the "common denominator" year, that is, the year in which both alternatives would require replacement. For Machines S and L this would be Year 30, so it would be necessary to compare a three chain cycle for S, the ten year machine, with a two chain cycle for L, the fifteen year project.

To illustrate both the replacement chain problem and its solution, suppose we are considering the replacement of a fully depreciated printing press with a new one. The plant in which the press is used is profitable and is expected to continue in operation for many years. The old press could continue to be used indefinitely, but it is not as efficient as the new ones. Two replacement machines are available. Press A has a cost of $36,100, will last for five years, and will produce after-tax incremental cash flows of $9,700 per year for five years. Press B has a cost of $57,500, will last for ten years, and will produce net cash flows of $9,500 per year. Both the costs and performances of Presses A and B have been constant in recent years and are expected to remain constant in the future. The company's cost of capital is 10 percent.

Should the old press be replaced, and if so, with A or B? To answer these questions, we first calculate A's NPV as follows:

$$\text{NPV}_A = \$9,700(3.7908) - \$36,100 = \$36,771 - \$36,100 = \$671.$$

B's NPV is:

$$\text{NPV}_B = \$9,500(6.1446) - \$57,500 = \$58,374 - \$57,500 = \$874.$$

These calculations suggest that the old press should indeed be replaced, and that Press B should be selected. However, the analysis is incomplete, and the decision to choose Press B is incorrect. If we choose Press A, we will have an opportunity to make a similar investment after five years, and this second investment will also be profitable. However, if we choose Press B, we will not have this second investment opportunity. Therefore, to make a proper comparison of Presses A and B, we must find the present value of Press A over a ten year period and compare it with Press B over the same ten years.

The NPV for Press B as calculated above is correct as it stands. For Press A, however, we must take three additional steps: (1) determine the NPV of the second Press A five years hence, (2) bring this NPV back to the present, and (3) sum these two component NPVs:

1. NPV_{A2} five years in future $= \$9,700(3.7908) - \$36,100 = \$671.$
2. PV of $\text{NPV}_{A2} = \$671(\text{PVIF}_{10\%,\ 5\ \text{years}}) = \$671(0.6209) = \$417.$
3. "True" $\text{NPV}_A = \$671 + \$417 = \$1,088.$

The sum $1,088, which is the "true" NPV of Press A, can then be compared with NPV_B. Since the value of the firm will increase by $1,088 if the old press is replaced by Press A versus only $874 for Press B, Press A should be selected.

Equivalent Annual Annuity Method

Although our simple example illustrates why a chain analysis is necessary if mutually exclusive projects have different lives, in practice the arithmetic is generally more complex. For example, Press A might have had a life of eight years versus an eleven year life for B. This would require an analysis over eighty-eight years, the lowest common denominator of the two presses' lives. In such a situation, it is often simpler to use another procedure, the *equivalent annual annuity* method. Here we find the present value of each project assuming continuous replacement chains on out to infinity. Three steps are involved:

1. Find each project's NPV over its original life. For the printing press example, we found $NPV_A = \$671$ and $NPV_B = \$874$.
2. Divide the original NPV of each project by the annuity factor for the project's original life to obtain the equivalent annual annuity:

$$\text{Equivalent annual annuity, Press A} = NPV_A/PVIFA_{10\%, \ 5 \text{ years}}$$
$$= \$671/3.7908$$
$$= \$177.01.$$

$$\text{Equivalent annual annuity, Press B} = \$874/6.1446$$
$$= \$142.24.$$

Press A, in effect, provides an annuity of $177.01 per year for five years—such an annuity would be worth exactly 3.7908($177.01) = $671—while Press B provides an equivalent annuity of $142.24.

3. Assuming infinite replacement, these equivalent annual annuities will continue on out to infinity; that is, they will constitute perpetuities. Recognizing (from Chapter 4) that the value of a perpetuity is $V = $ Annual receipt/k, we can find the net present values of the infinite annuities provided by Presses A and B:

$$NPV_A = \$177.01/0.10 = \$1,770.10.$$
$$NPV_B = \$142.24/0.10 = \$1,422.40.$$

Since the infinite horizon NPV of A exceeds that of B, Press A should be accepted. Therefore, the equivalent annual annuity method leads to the same decision rule as the simple chain method—accept Press A.

Computationally, the equivalent annual annuity method is often easier to apply than the chain method. However, the chain method is often easier to explain to decision makers, and it does not require the assumption of an infinite time horizon. Also, note that Step 3 above is not really necessary for making the decision—we could have just chosen the project with the larger annual annuity.

Implications for Nonreplacement Decisions

Once students become aware of the replacement chain problem, they often ask this question: "Shouldn't replacement chains, or common life analysis, be used for *all* capital budgeting analysis, not just for replacement decisions? For example, if we were analyzing one project with a five year life and another with a ten year life, shouldn't we put them on a common time basis?" The answer to this question is, "Not necessarily." For example, we could compare the NPV on Carter Chemical's fifteen year Compound X project with the NPV on a ten year project in the company's building supply division. There would be no need whatever to put the projects on a common life basis—each project should be accepted if its NPV is positive or rejected if its NPV is negative, and these decisions are independent of one another. On the other hand, suppose Carter has two alternative ways to produce Compound X. Method 1 involves a plant that could be operated for fifteen years, while Method 2 involves a plant with a five year life. Assuming the market demand for the product is expected to last for fifteen years, then Method 2 must be evaluated over three five year cycles when it is compared to Method 1. Otherwise, the analysis would be seriously biased against the plant with the shorter life.

As a general rule, (1) the replacement chain issue does not arise for independent projects, but (2) it can arise if mutually exclusive projects with different lives are being evaluated. However, it is not always appropriate to run the analysis out to a common denominator year—this depends on whether the operation will actually be continued. If the operation is likely to be continued, then the extension must be considered to avoid biasing the analysis against the project with the shorter life.

Inflation and Changing Equipment Performance

One weakness of our replacement analysis is the fact that we have ignored possible inflation in the purchase price of future equipment—if inflation is expected to continue, then replacement equipment will have a higher price, and this should be incorporated into the analysis. However, there may be an offset to inflation—future generations of equipment, like printing presses, may have better performance characteristics and cause additional cost reductions. The best way of handling these complications is to build inflation and possible efficiency gains directly into the cash flow estimates, and then use the replacement chain approach. The arithmetic is complicated, but the concepts are exactly the same as in our examples.

Problem

12A-1 Station WJXT is considering the replacement of its old, fully depreciated sound mixer. Two new models are available. Mixer X has a cost of

$108,300, a five year expected life, and after-tax cash flows (labor savings) of $29,100 per year. Mixer Y has a cost of $172,500, a ten year life, and after-tax cash flows of $31,700 per year. No new technological developments are expected, but mixer prices are falling because of competition from Japanese imports. In five years, mixer prices are expected to be only 75 percent of current prices. The cost of capital is 12 percent. If the replacement is to be made, it must be done now. Should WJXT replace the old mixer and, if so, with X or Y?

VI LONG-TERM FINANCING DECISIONS

A decision to increase assets means that the firm must also raise new capital. In Part VI we shall examine (1) the types of long-term capital available to the firm and (2) the analysis employed when choosing among these types. We begin in Chapters 13 and 14 by examining the characteristics of bonds, preferred stock, and common stock. Then, in Chapter 15, we consider the optimal mix of these securities, or the capital structure decision. Chapter 16 shows how the costs of different types of capital are combined to form the weighted average cost of capital used in capital budgeting. Finally, Chapter 17 shows how the firm's investment opportunities and supply of capital schedule interact to determine dividend policy.

13 LONG-TERM DEBT AND PREFERRED STOCK

Most firms find it both necessary and desirable to use long-term debt financing, and some also use preferred stock. There are many types of fixed-income securities: secured and unsecured, marketable and nonmarketable, convertible and nonconvertible, and so on. Different groups of investors favor different types of securities, and their tastes change over time. An astute financial manager knows how to "package" securities at a given point in time to make them most attractive to the most potential investors, thereby keeping the firm's cost of capital to a minimum. This chapter first discusses long-term securities in general, then analyzes the three most important types of *fixed-income securities*—term loans, bonds, and preferred stocks. Later chapters deal with other types of long-term capital, while the proper mix of securities is discussed in Chapters 15 and 16.

FUNDED DEBT

Funded debt is simply long-term debt. When a firm is said to be planning to "fund" its floating debt, it is planning to replace short-term debt with securities of longer maturity. Funding does not imply placing money with a trustee or other repository; it is simply part of the jargon of finance and means making debt long-term. Tampa Electric Company provides a good example of funding. This company has a continuous construction program. Typically, it uses short-term debt to finance construction expenditures. However, once short-term debt has built up to about $75 million, the company sells a stock or bond issue, uses the proceeds to pay off its bank loans, and starts the cycle again. The high flotation cost on a small security issue, discussed later in this chapter, makes this process desirable. (See Figure 8–3, Plan B, in Chapter 8 for a graphic view of the process of funding short-term debt.)

TERM LOANS

A *term loan* is a contract under which a borrower agrees to make payments of interest and principal, on specific dates, to a lender.[1] Term loans are usually negotiated directly between the borrowing firm and a financial institution—generally a bank, an insurance company, or a pension fund. Although the maturities of term loans vary from two to thirty years, most are for periods in the three to fifteen year range.

Advantages of Term Loans

Term loans have three major advantages over publicly issued securities— *speed, flexibility,* and *low issuance costs.* Because they are negotiated directly between the lender and the borrower, formal procedures are minimized. The key provisions of the loan can be worked out much more quickly, and with more flexibility, than can those for a public issue, and it is not necessary for a term loan to go through the Securities and Exchange Commission (SEC) registration process (see Appendix 13A). A further advantage of term loans over publicly held debt securities has to do with future flexibility: If a bond issue is held by many different bondholders, it is difficult to obtain permission to alter the terms of the agreement, even though new economic conditions may make such changes desirable. With a term loan, the borrower generally can sit down with the lender and work out modifications in the contract.

Amortization

Most term loans are *amortized,* or paid off, in equal installments over the life of the loan. (At this point, you should review the discussion of amortization in Chapter 3.) The purpose of amortization is to have the loan repaid gradually over its life rather than fall due all at once. Amortization forces the borrower to retire the loan slowly; this protects both the lender and the borrower against the possibility that the borrower will not make adequate provisions for its retirement during the life of the loan. Amortization is especially important whenever the loan is used to purchase a specific item of equipment; here the repayment schedule should be matched to the productive life of the equipment, with the payments being made from cash flows resulting from its use.

---

1 If the interest and maturity payments are not met on schedule, the issuing firm is said to have *defaulted* and can then be forced into *bankruptcy.* See Chapter 20 for a discussion of bankruptcy.

Interest Rate

The interest rate on a term loan can be either fixed for the life of the loan or variable. If it is fixed, the rate used will be close to the rate on long-term bonds for companies of equivalent risk. If the rate is variable, it is usually set at a certain number of percentage points over the prime rate. Thus, when the prime rate goes up or down, so does the rate on the outstanding balance of the term loan.

BONDS

A bond is a long-term contract under which a borrower agrees to make payments of interest and principal, on specific dates, to the holder of the bond. Bonds are generally issued with maturities of between twenty and thirty years. Although bonds are similar to term loans, a bond issue is generally advertised, offered to all investors (the "public"), and actually sold to many different investors. Indeed, thousands of individual and institutional investors may purchase bonds when a firm sells a bond issue, while there is generally only one lender in the case of a term loan.[2] With bonds, the interest rate is almost always fixed. There are a number of different types of bonds, the more important of which are discussed in this chapter.

Indenture and Trustee

An *indenture* is a legal document that spells out the rights of both the bondholders and the issuing corporation, and a *trustee* is an official (usually of a bank) who represents the bondholders and makes sure the terms of the indenture are carried out. The indenture may be several hundred pages in length, and it will cover such points as the conditions under which the issuer can pay off the bonds prior to maturity, the times interest earned ratio the issuer must maintain if it is to sell additional bonds, restrictions against the payment of dividends unless earnings meet certain specifications, and the like. The trustee monitors the situation and takes action on behalf of the bondholders in the event that the issuer violates any provision in the indenture.

The Securities and Exchange Commission (1) approves indentures and (2) makes sure that all indenture provisions are met before allowing a company to sell new securities to the public. Also, it should be noted that the indentures of most larger corporations were actually written back in the

2 However, for very large term loans, twenty or more financial institutions may form a syndicate to grant the credit. Also, it should be noted that a bond issue can be sold to one or a few lenders; in this case, the bond is said to be "privately placed." Companies that place bonds privately do so for the same reasons that they use term loans—speed, flexibility, and low issuance costs.

1930s or 1940s, and that many issues of new bonds, all covered by this same indenture, have been sold down through the years. The interest rates on the bonds and perhaps their maturities will change from issue to issue, but bondholders' protections as spelled out in the indenture will be the same for all bonds in the class.[3] Some of the more important provisions in most indentures are discussed in the following sections.

Mortgage Bonds

Under a mortgage bond, the corporation pledges certain real assets as security for the bond. To illustrate, suppose $10 million is required to purchase land and to build a plant. Bonds in the amount of $4 million, secured by a mortgage on the property, are issued. If the company defaults on the bonds (that is, if it does not pay interest or required payments on the principal on time), the bondholders can foreclose on the plant and sell it to satisfy their claims. (Procedures for foreclosure are discussed later in this chapter and also in Chapter 20.)

If our illustrative company chose to, it could issue *second mortgage bonds* secured by the same $10 million plant. In the event of liquidation, the holders of these second mortgage bonds would have a claim against the property only after the first mortgage bondholders had been paid off in full. Thus, second mortgages are sometimes called *junior mortgages* because they are junior in priority to the claims of senior mortgages, or *first mortgage bonds*.

The first mortgage indentures of most major corporations were written twenty, thirty, forty, or more years ago. These indentures are generally "open-ended," meaning that new bonds may be issued from time to time under the existing indenture. However, the amount of new bonds that can be issued is virtually always limited to a specified percentage of the firm's total "bondable property," which generally includes all plant and equipment. For example, Savannah Electric can issue first mortgage bonds in total up to 60 percent of its fixed assets. If fixed assets totaled $200 million, and if the company had $100 million of first mortgage bonds outstanding, then it could, by the property test, issue another $20 million of bonds (60% of $200 million = $120 million).

In 1979, Savannah Electric could not issue any new first mortgage bonds at all because of another indenture provision: its times interest earned ratio was below 2.5 times, the minimum coverage that must be attained prior to the sale of new bonds. Thus, Savannah Electric passed the property test but failed the coverage test; hence, it could not issue first mortgage bonds. Since first mortgage bonds carry lower rates of interest, this restriction is a costly one.

Savannah Electric's neighbor, Georgia Power Company, has more

---

3 A firm will have different indentures for each of the major classes of bonds described in this chapter.

flexibility under its indenture; its interest coverage requirement is only 2.0 times. In hearings before the Georgia Public Service Commission, it was suggested that Savannah Electric change its indenture coverage to 2.0 times so that it could issue more first mortgage bonds. This is simply not possible—the holders of the outstanding bonds would have to approve the change, and it is inconceivable that they would vote for a change that would seriously weaken their position!

Debentures

A debenture is an unsecured bond and, as such, provides no lien on specific property as security for the obligation. Debenture holders are, therefore, general creditors whose claims are protected by property not otherwise pledged. In practice, the use of debentures depends on the nature of the firm's assets and its general credit strength. If its credit position is exceptionally strong, the firm can issue debentures—it simply does not need specific security. American Telephone & Telegraph finances mainly through debentures; AT&T is such a strong corporation that it does not have to put up property as security for its debt issues. Debentures are also issued by companies in industries where it would not be practical to provide security through a mortgage on fixed assets. Examples of such industries are the large mail-order houses and the finance companies, which characteristically hold most of their assets in the form of inventory or receivables, neither of which is satisfactory security for a mortgage bond.

Subordinated Debentures

The term *subordinate* means "below," or "inferior." Thus, subordinated debt has claims on assets in the event of bankruptcy only after senior debt (usually mortgage bonds) has been paid off. Debentures may be subordinated to designated notes payable—usually bank loans—or to all other debt. In the event of liquidation or reorganization, holders of subordinated debentures cannot be paid until senior debt as named in the debentures' indenture has been paid. Precisely how subordination works, and how it strengthens the position of senior debt holders, is shown later in the chapter.

Other Types of Bonds

Several other types of bonds are used sufficiently often to warrant mention. First, *convertible bonds* are securities that are convertible into shares of common stock, at a fixed price, at the option of the bondholder; convertibles are discussed in detail in Chapter 22. *Income bonds* are bonds that pay interest only when the interest is earned. Thus, these securities cannot bankrupt a company, but from an investor's standpoint they are riskier than "regular" bonds. Another type of bond that has been discussed in the United States, but not yet used here, is the *indexed or purchasing power bond,* which is popular in Brazil, Israel, and a few other countries long plagued by inflation. The interest rate paid on these bonds is based on an inflation index such as the consumer price index; interest paid rises when the inflation rate rises, thus protecting the bondholders against inflation. Mexico is using bonds whose interest rate is pegged to the price of oil to finance the development of its huge petroleum reserves; these bonds will probably be even better than regular indexed bonds, as oil prices are rising faster than other prices.

Two similar types of bonds that have been used in recent years are *floating rate bonds* and *bonds that are redeemable at par at the option of the holder.* Ordinarily, a bond's coupon interest payment is fixed when it is issued and remains fixed for the life of the bond. Floating rate bonds, which have been used extensively by major banks, including Chase Manhattan and Citibank, have interest payments that move up or down (generally within limits) as interest rates in general shift. Thus, the investor's interest income will vary (as will the borrower's interest expense), but the market value of the bond will not fluctuate much.

Bonds that are redeemable at the holder's option also protect the holder against a rise in interest rates. If rates rise, fixed-rate bonds' prices decline. Should these redeemable bonds' prices go down due to rising rates, the holders would simply turn them in, receive the par value, and invest in new, high-rate bonds. Examples of such bonds include Transamerica's $50 million issue of twenty-five year, 8½ percent bonds sold in June 1976. The bonds are not callable by the company, and holders can turn them in for redemption at par on or after July 1984. If interest rates rise, holders will turn in the bonds and reinvest the proceeds at a higher rate. This feature enabled Transamerica to sell the bonds with an 8½ percent coupon at a time when other similarly rated bonds had yields of 8¾ percent.

Two more types of bonds that are being used increasingly are *development bonds* and *pollution control bonds.* State and local governments may set up *industrial development agencies* and *pollution control agencies.* These agencies are allowed, under certain circumstances, to sell *tax-exempt bonds,* making the proceeds available to corporations for specific uses deemed (by Congress) to be in the public interest. Thus, a Florida industrial development agency might sell bonds to provide funds for a paper company to build a plant in the West Florida area, where unemployment is high. Similarly, a Tampa pollution control agency might sell bonds to provide Tampa Electric Company or Tampa Steel with funds to be used to purchase pollution control equipment. In both cases, the income from the bonds would be tax exempt to the holders; hence, the bonds would sell at relatively low interest rates. Note, however, that these bonds are guaranteed by the corporation that will use the funds, not by a unit of government.

Coverage Ratios

One of the key elements in the analysis of corporate bonds is *coverage,* which measures a firm's ability to meet interest and principal payments and thus avoid default. The most commonly used coverage ratio is the *times interest earned* (TIE). This ratio is defined below and illustrated with data for Carter Chemical Company (see Chapter 6 for the basic data):

$$\text{Times interest earned} = \frac{\text{Earnings before interest and taxes (EBIT)}}{\text{Interest}} = \frac{\$266}{\$66}$$

$$= 4.03 \text{ for Carter Chemical.}$$

$$\text{Industry average} = 6 \text{ times.}$$

The times interest earned ratio (TIE) depends on the level of interest payments, which in turn depends on the percentage of total capital represented by debt. For example, if Carter had used twice as much debt (with a corresponding reduction in equity), and if the interest rate remained constant, then its interest charges would be $\$66 \times 2 = \$132$. EBIT is not affected by changes in capital structure, so the increased use of debt would lower Carter's TIE to 2.02:

$$\text{TIE} = \frac{\$266}{\$132} = 2.02 \text{ times.}$$

As we shall see in Chapter 15, the times interest earned ratio is given careful consideration when a firm establishes its target capital structure. The pro forma, or projected, TIE that would result under different financing plans is calculated, and care is taken to insure that the use of debt does not lower the TIE to an unacceptable level.

Another ratio that is often used to measure a company's ability to service its debt is the *fixed charge coverage ratio,* defined as follows:

$$\text{Fixed charge coverage ratio} = \frac{\text{EBIT} + \text{Lease payments}}{\text{Interest} + \left(\begin{array}{c}\text{Lease} \\ \text{payments}\end{array}\right) + \left(\dfrac{\text{Sinking fund payment}}{1 - \text{Tax rate}}\right)}$$

$$= \frac{\$266 + \$28}{\$66 + \$28 + [\$20/(1 - 0.4)]}$$

$$= 2.3 \text{ times for Carter Chemical.}$$

$$\text{Industry average} = 2.5 \text{ times.}$$

Sinking funds are discussed later in this chapter, but, in essence, a sinking fund payment goes toward the retirement of the bond. Since sinking fund payments are not tax deductions, whereas interest and lease payments are deductible, the sinking fund payment is divided by (1 − Tax rate) to find the before-tax income required to pay taxes and have enough left to make the sinking fund payment.

Treatment of Bonds in the Event of Bankruptcy

Although bankruptcy is discussed in detail in Chapter 20, it is nevertheless useful at this point to trace through the handling of bondholders' claims in the event a firm goes into bankruptcy and must be liquidated.[4] The three cases described in Table 13–1 illustrate how different classes of debt are treated in a bankruptcy liquidation.[5]

Bond Repayment Provisions

Sinking Fund A sinking fund is a provision that facilitates the orderly retirement of a bond issue (or, in some cases, an issue of preferred stock). Typically, the sinking fund provision requires the firm to retire a portion of the bond issue each year. On rare occasions, the firm is required to deposit money with a trustee, who invests the money and then uses the accumulated sum to retire the bonds when they mature. Sometimes the stipulated sinking fund payment is tied to sales or earnings of the current year, but usually it is a mandatory fixed amount. If it is mandatory, a failure to meet the sinking fund requirement causes the bond issue to be thrown into default, which may force the company into bankruptcy. Obviously, then, a sinking fund can constitute a dangerous cash drain on the firm.

In most cases the firm is given the right to handle the sinking fund in either of two ways:

1. It may call in for redemption a certain percentage of the bonds at a stipulated price each year—for example, 2 percent of the total original amount of the issue at a price of $1,000. The bonds are numbered serially, and the ones called for redemption are determined by a lottery.
2. It may buy the required amount of bonds on the open market.

The firm will take whichever action results in the greatest reduction of outstanding bonds for a given expenditure. Therefore, if interest rates have risen and bond prices have fallen, the company will elect to use the option of buying bonds at a discount in the open market.

It must be recognized that the sinking fund may at times work to the detriment of bondholders. If, for example, the bond carries a 9 percent interest rate, and if yields on similar securities are 6 percent, then the bond will sell above par. A sinking fund call at par would thus greatly disadvantage some bondholders.

On balance, securities that provide for a sinking fund and continuing

---

4 This company had no preferred stock outstanding, but suppose it had had $500 million of preferred and $500 million of common. In the first situation, the preferred would have been paid off in full, while the common would have been wiped out.

5 In this case, as in most where subordinated debentures are used, the debentures were issued as part of a "package deal." The banks agreed to supply credit in the form of notes payable *if and only if* the company would simultaneously issue debentures subordinated to the bank loans. The debentures' indenture stated that they were subordinated to the notes payable. The rate of interest on the debentures is, of course, higher than that on the bank debt because the debentures are riskier.

Table 13–1
Illustration of Bankruptcy: Payments to Senior
Debt, Other Debt, and Subordinated Debt
(Millions of Dollars)

I. A total of $1,500 is available to meet claims.

	Book Value of Claims (1)	Percent of Total Debt (2)	Initial Allocations (3)	Actual Payments after Subordination Adjustment (4)	Percent of Original Claims Satisfied (5)
Accounts payable	$ 60	6%	$ 60	$ 60	100%
Notes payable to bank	100	10	100	100	100
Taxes and accrued wages	140	14	140	140	100
Mortgage bonds	500	50	500	500	100
Subordinated debentures (subordinated to notes payable)	200	20	200	200	100
Total debt	$1,000	100%	$1,000	$1,000	100%
Common equity	1,000		500	500	50%
Total	$2,000		$1,500	$1,500	75%

All debts are satisfied, and $500 is left for common equity.

II. A total of $750, including $600 realized from sale of plant and equipment, is available to meet claims.

	Book Value of Claims (1)	Percent of Total Debt (2)	Initial Allocations (3)	Actual Payments after Subordination Adjustment (4)	Percent of Original Claims Satisfied (5)
Accounts payable	$ 60	6%	$ 18.33	$ 18.33	30.55%
Notes payable to bank	100	10	30.56	91.67	91.67
Taxes and accrued wages	140	14	140.00	140.00	100.00
Mortgage bonds	500	50	500.00	500.00	100.00
Subordinated debentures	200	20	61.11	0.00	0.00
Total debt	$1,000	100%	$750.00	$750.00	75.00%
Common equity	1,000				0.00
Total	$2,000				37.50%

Basis of allocation in Case II:

1. The mortgage bonds receive $500 of the $600 obtained from sale of property. This satisfies their claim in full, and $500 is recorded in Column 3. This leaves $750 − $500 = $250 available for other claims.
2. By law, wages have first claim on the remaining available funds, and taxes have second priority. Thus taxes and accrued wages receive $140. This amount is also

Table 13-1 (continued)

shown in Column 3. At this point $250 − $140 = $110 is still available for other creditors, called "general creditors."

3. The claims of general creditors total $360, consisting of the following: accounts payable, $60; notes payable, $100; subordinated debentures, $200. Since there is only $110 available to creditors with claims for $360, the general creditors receive $110/$360 = 0.3056 per dollar of debt, so the figures shown for these creditors in Column 3 are 0.3056 times the amounts shown in Column 1.

4. The debentures are subordinated to the notes payable. This means that the debenture holders must turn over monies initially allocated to them until either the notes payable have been satisfied or the funds allocated to the debentures have been exhausted. Thus, the entire $61.11 allocated to the debentures is reallocated to the notes payable. In Column 4, Actual Payments, the notes payable are shown to receive $30.56 + $61.11 = $91.67, while the debenture holders receive nothing.

III. A total of $750, including $400 realized from sale of plant and equipment, is available to meet claims.

	Book Value of Claims (1)	Percent of Total Debt (2)	Initial Allocations (3)	Actual Payments after Subordination Adjustment (4)	Percent of Original Claims Satisfied (5)
Accounts payable	$ 60	6%	$ 27.40	$ 27.40	45.65%
Notes payable to bank	100	10	45.65	100.00	100.00
Taxes and accrued wages	140	14	140.00	140.00	100.00
Mortgage bonds	500	50	400 + 45.65	445.65	89.13
Subordinated debentures	200	20	91.30	36.95	18.48
Total debt	$1,000	100%	$750.00	$750.00	75.00%
Common equity	1,000				0.00
Total	$2,000				37.50%

Basis of allocation in Case III:

1. Mortgage bonds receive $400. Since the mortgage claim was $500, there is a deficiency of $100. The mortgage bondholders are classified as general creditors in the amount of $100, and $350 is available for other claims.

2. Taxes and wages receive $140.

3. After payment of taxes and wages, and $400 to the mortgage bonds, there remains $750 − $140 − $400 = $210. There are claims of $460 (accounts payable, notes payable, $100 deficiency of mortgage bonds, and debentures) against this amount, so the general creditors will receive $210/$460 = 0.4565 per dollar of claims. Multiplying 0.4565 by the amounts shown in Column 1 for accounts payable, notes payable, and debentures produces the amounts for the initial allocation in Column 3. Taxes and wages receive their full $140, while the mortgage bonds are allocated $400 + 0.4565 ($100).

4. The subordinated debentures must remit sufficient funds to the notes payable to satisfy the notes. Thus $100 − $45.65 = $54.35 is transferred to notes payable. This completes the actual payments shown in Column 4.

redemption are likely to be offered initially on a lower yield basis than are securities without such a fund. Since sinking funds provide additional protection to investors, bond issues which have them are likely to sell initially at higher prices; hence, they have a lower cost of capital to the issuer.

Call Provision A call provision gives the issuing corporation the right to call the bond for redemption. If it is used, the call provision generally states that the company must pay an amount greater than the par value for the bond, with this additional sum being defined as the *call premium*. The call premium is typically set equal to one year's interest if the bond is called during the first year, with the premium declining at a constant rate each year thereafter. For example, the call premium on a $1,000 par value, twenty year, 8 percent bond would generally be $80 if it were called during the first year, $76 during the second year (calculated by reducing the $80, or 8 percent, premium by one-twentieth), and so on.

The call privilege is valuable to the firm but potentially detrimental to the investor, especially if the bond is issued in a period when interest rates are cyclically high. Accordingly, the interest rate on a new issue of callable bonds will exceed that on a new issue of noncallable bonds. For example, on May 24, 1979, Great Falls Power Company sold an issue of A-rated bonds to yield 10.375 percent. These bonds were callable immediately. On the same day, Midwest Electric sold an issue of A-rated bonds to yield 10.20 percent. Midwest's bonds were noncallable for ten years. (This is known as a *deferred call*.) Investors were apparently willing to accept a 0.175 percent lower interest rate on Midwest's bonds for the assurance that the relatively high (by historic standards) rate of interest would be earned for at least ten years. Great Falls, on the other hand, had to incur a 0.175 percent higher annual interest rate to obtain the option of calling the bonds in the event of a subsequent decline in interest rates. We discuss the analysis for determining when to call an issue in Appendix 13B.

Note that the call for refunding purposes is quite different from the call for sinking fund purposes. The call for sinking fund purposes generally has no call premium, but only a small percentage of the issue is callable each year.

Restrictive Covenants

A *restrictive covenant* is a provision in a bond indenture or term loan agreement that requires the issuer of the bond to meet certain stated conditions. Typical provisions include requirements that debt not exceed a specific percentage of total capital, that the current ratio be maintained above a specific level, that dividends not be paid on common stock unless earnings are maintained at a given level, and so on. Overall, these covenants are designed to insure, insofar as possible, that the firm does nothing to cause the bonds' quality to deteriorate after they are issued.

The trustee is responsible for making sure the covenants are not violated, or for taking appropriate action if a violation occurs. What constitutes "appropriate action" varies with the circumstances. It might be that to insist on immediate compliance would result in bankruptcy and possibly large losses on the bonds. In such a case the trustee may decide that the bondholders would be better served by giving the company a chance to work out its problems and thus avoid bankruptcy.

Bond Ratings

Since the early 1900s, bonds have been assigned quality ratings that reflect their probability of going into default. The two major rating agencies are Moody's Investors Service and Standard & Poor's Corporation (S&P). These agencies' rating designations are shown in Table 13–2.

Table 13–2
Comparison of Bond Ratings

	High Quality		Investment Grade		Substandard		Speculative
Moody's	Aaa	Aa	A	Baa	Ba	B	Caa to D
S&P	AAA	AA	A	BBB	BB	B	CCC to D

The triple A bonds are extremely safe, while the double A and single A bonds are also strong enough to be held in conservative portfolios.[6] The triple Bs are strong enough to be called "investment grade," and banks and other institutional investors are permitted by law to hold these bonds. Double B and lower bonds are speculations, with a significant probability of default; many financial institutions are prohibited from buying them.

Although the rating assignments are judgmental, they are based on both qualitative and quantitative factors, some of which are listed below:

1. Debt/assets ratio.
2. Times interest earned ratio.
3. Times fixed charges covered ratio.
4. Current ratio.
5. Mortgage provisions: Is the bond secured by a mortgage? If it is, and if the property has a high value in relation to the amount of bonded debt, the bond's rating is enhanced.
6. Subordination provisions: Is the bond subordinated to other debt? If so, it

---

6 In the discussion to follow, reference to the S&P code is intended to imply the Moody code as well. Thus, for example, *triple B bonds* means both BBB and Baa bonds; *double B bonds,* both BB and Ba bonds. Chairman Bobby Pafford of the Georgia Public Service Commission came up with a new rating just after Savannah Electric's bonds were downgraded from Baa to Ba: the rating BAD.

will be rated at least one notch below the rating it would have if it were not subordinated. Conversely, a bond with other debt subordinated to it will have a somewhat higher rating.

7. Guarantee provisions: Some bonds are guaranteed by other firms. If a weak company's debt is guaranteed by a strong company (usually the weak company's parent), then the bond will be given the strong company's rating.
8. Sinking fund: Does the bond have a sinking fund to insure systematic repayment? This feature is a plus factor to the rating agencies.
9. Maturity: Other things the same, a bond with a shorter maturity will be judged less risky than a longer-term bond, and this will be reflected in the rating.
10. Stability of sales and earnings.
11. Regulation: Is the company regulated, and could an adverse regulatory climate cause the company's economic position to decline? Regulation is especially important for utilities, airlines, railroads, and telephone companies.
12. Antitrust: Are any antitrust actions pending against the firm that could erode its position?
13. Overseas operations: What percentage of the firm's sales, assets, and profits are from overseas operations, and what is the political climate in the host countries?
14. Environmental factors: Is the firm likely to face heavy expenditures for pollution control equipment?
15. Pension liabilities: Does the firm have unfunded pension liabilities that could pose a future problem?
16. Labor unrest: Are there potential labor problems on the horizon that could weaken the firm's position?
17. Resource availability: Is the firm likely to face supply shortages that could force it to curtail operations?

Analysts at the rating agencies have consistently stated that no precise formula is used when setting a firm's rating—all the factors listed, plus others, are taken into account, but not in a mathematically precise manner. Statistical studies have borne out this contention; researchers who have tried to predict bond ratings on the basis of quantitative data have had only limited success, indicating that the agencies do indeed use a good deal of subjective judgment when establishing a firm's rating.[7]

Bond ratings are very important both to firms and to investors. First, a bond's rating is an indicator of its risk; hence, the rating has a direct, measurable influence on the bond's interest rate and the firm's cost of debt capital. Second, most bonds are purchased by institutional investors, not by individuals, and these institutions are generally restricted to investment-

---

7 See G. E. Pinches and K. A. Mingo, "A Multivariate Analysis of Industrial Bond Ratings," *Journal of Finance,* March 1973.

grade securities. Thus, if a firm's bonds fall below BBB, it will have a difficult time selling new bonds, as most of the potential purchasers will not be allowed to buy them.

Ratings also have an effect on the availability of debt capital. If an institutional investor buys BBB bonds and these bonds are subsequently downgraded to BB or lower, then (1) the institution's regulators will reprimand or perhaps impose restrictions on the institution if it continues to hold the bonds, but (2) since many other institutional investors cannot purchase the bonds, the institution that owns them will probably not be able to sell them except at a sizable loss. Because of this fear of downgrading, many institutions restrict their bond portfolios to at least A, or even AA, bonds. Some even confine purchases to AAA bonds. Thus, the lower a firm's bond rating, the smaller the group of available purchasers for its new issues.

As a result of their higher risk and more restricted market, lower-grade bonds have much higher required rates of return, k_d, than do high-grade bonds. Figure 13–1 illustrates this point—throughout the twenty-six years shown on the graph, U.S. Government bonds always have had the lowest yields, AAA have been next, and the BBB bonds have had the highest yields of the three types.

Figure 13–1 also shows that the gaps between yields on the three types of bonds vary over time; in other words, the cost differentials, or risk premiums, fluctuate from year to year.[8] This point is highlighted in Table 13–3, which gives the yields on the three types of bonds, and the risk premiums for AAA and BBB bonds, in June 1963 and again in June 1975. All the yields were higher in 1975, but risk premiums rose dramatically, causing an especially sharp increase in the rates on BBB bonds.

The Table 13–3 data are plotted in Figure 13–2 to show approximately what happened to risk premiums between 1963 and 1975.[9] First, the riskless

---

8 The term *risk premium* ought to reflect only the difference in expected (and required) returns between two securities that results from differences in their risk. However, the difference between *yields to maturity* on different types of bonds consists of (1) a risk premium; (2) a liquidity, or marketability, premium, which reflects the fact that U.S. Treasury bonds are more readily marketable than corporates; (3) a call premium, because most treasury bonds are not callable, while corporate bonds are; and (4) a default premium which reflects the probability of loss on the corporate bonds. As an example of the latter point, suppose the yield to maturity on a BBB bond is 10 percent versus 7 percent on government bonds, but there is a 0.5 percent probability of default loss on the corporate bond. In this case, the expected return on the BBB bond is 9.5 percent, and the risk premium is 2.5 percent, not the full 3 percentage point difference in yields to maturity. Therefore, the risk premiums given in Table 13–3 overstate somewhat the true (but unobservable) risk premiums.

9 The relationship graphed here is akin to the Security Market Line (SML) developed in Chapter 5, although bond ratings rather than beta coefficients are used to measure risk. A word about the scaling of the horizontal axis and about the placement of the points is in order. (1) We have shown a linear fit, although there is no theoretical reason to think that yields plotted against bond ratings are necessarily linear. (2) We have shown the interval on the horizontal axis between AAA and BBB to be equal to that between U.S. Government bonds and AAA, but this is an arbitrary scaling. (3) Finally, on a very accurate, large-scale graph it would be clear that the plotted points for the AAA and BBB bonds are not precisely on the straight lines shown in the graph; however, they are sufficiently close to warrant our analysis.

Attempts have been made to calculate beta coefficients for bonds and to plot bonds on the same Security Market Line that is used for common stocks. However, these results have not been successful—bonds do not plot on the same linear SML. See W. F. Sharpe, *Investments* (Englewood Cliffs, N.J.: Prentice-Hall, 1978), pp. 246–252.

Figure 13-1
Yields on U.S. Government Bonds, AAA
Corporates, and BBB Corporates, 1953-1979

Source: Federal Reserve Board, *Historical Chart Book,* 1979.

Table 13-3
Risk Premiums in 1963 and 1975

| | Long-Term Government Bonds (Risk-free) (1) | AAA Corporate Bonds (2) | BBB Corporate Bonds (3) | Risk Premiums | |
				AAA (4) = (2) − (1)	BBB (5) = (3) − (1)
June 1963	4.00%	4.23%	4.84%	0.23%	0.84%
June 1975	6.86	8.77	10.40	1.91	3.54

Source: Federal Reserve Bulletins, December 1963 and December 1975.

Figure 13–2
Relationship between Bond Ratings and Bond Yields, 1963 and 1975

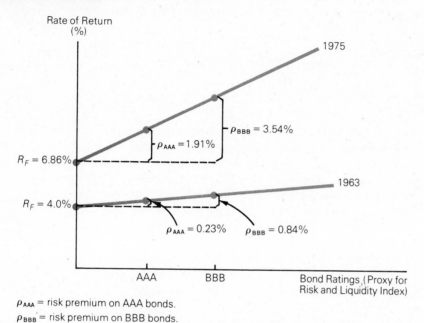

ρ_{AAA} = risk premium on AAA bonds.
ρ_{BBB} = risk premium on BBB bonds.

Source: Table 13–3.

rate, or vertical axis intercept, rose almost three percentage points—this reflected the increase in realized and anticipated inflation. Second, the slope of the line also rose sharply, indicating increased investor risk aversion.

Changes in Ratings

A change in a firm's bond rating will have a significant effect on its ability to borrow long-term capital, and on the cost of that capital. Rating agencies review outstanding bonds on a periodic basis, occasionally upgrading or downgrading a bond as a result of its issuer's changed circumstances. Also, an announcement of a new issue of bonds will trigger agency reviews and possibly lead to rating changes.[10]

If a firm's situation has deteriorated somewhat but its bonds have not been reviewed and downgraded, it may choose to use a term loan or short-term debt rather than finance through a public bond issue. This will perhaps postpone an agency review until the situation has improved. For example, a

---

10 Rating agencies do review ratings without being prompted by the company, but most reviews associated with new issues are actually requested by the company. The investment bankers will make this a condition of the offering.

number of public utilities delayed bond issues in 1974 and 1975, financing with short-term debt until rate increases could be obtained to raise interest coverage ratios to acceptable levels. After rate increases were put into effect, the companies sold bonds and used the proceeds to retire the excess short-term debt.

PREFERRED STOCK

Preferred stock is similar to bonds in some respects and similar to common stock in other ways. Preferred has a par value, usually either $25 or $100. The dividend is indicated either as a percentage of par, in dollars, or sometimes both ways. For example, Mississippi Power Company recently sold 150,000 shares of $100 par value preferred stock for a total of $15 million. This preferred had a stated dividend of $12 per share, so the preferred dividend yield was $12/$100 = 0.12, or 12 percent, at the time of issue. The dividend was set when the stock was issued—it will not be changed in the future. Therefore, if the market price of the stock changes from $100 after the issue date—as it certainly will—then the yield will go up or down. For example, if the market price rises to $120, the yield will fall to $12/$120 = 10 percent.

If the preferred dividend is not earned, the company does not have to pay it. However, most preferred issues are *cumulative,* meaning that the cumulative total of all unpaid preferred dividends must be paid before dividends can be paid on common stock. Unpaid preferred dividends are called *arrearages.*[11]

Even though nonpayment of preferred dividends will not bankrupt a company, corporations issue preferred with every intention of paying the dividends. Failure to pay the preferred dividend precludes payment of common dividends and, in addition, makes it virtually impossible for a firm to raise capital by selling bonds, more preferred, or common stock. However, having preferred stock outstanding does give a firm that experiences temporary problems a chance to overcome its difficulties; had bonds been used instead of preferred stock, the company might have been forced into bankruptcy. Thus, preferred stock is less risky than bonds from the viewpoint of the issuing corporation.

Investors, on the other hand, regard preferred stock as being riskier than bonds for two reasons: (1) preferred stockholders' claims are subordinated to bondholders' in the event of liquidation, and (2) bondholders are more likely to continue receiving income during hard times than are preferred

---

11 Dividends in arrears do not earn interest; thus, arrearages do not increase in a compound interest sense. They only grow from continued nonpayment of the preferred dividend.

stockholders. Accordingly, investors historically have required a higher rate of return on a given firm's preferred stock than on its bonds. However, the fact that preferred dividends are largely exempt from the corporate tax has made preferred stock attractive to corporate investors.[12] In recent years, high-grade preferred stock, on average, has sold on a lower yield basis than high-grade bonds. As an example, on March 27, 1973, AT&T sold a preferred issue that yielded 7.28 percent to an investor. On that same date, AT&T's bonds yielded 7.55 percent, or 0.27 percentage points *more* than its preferred. The tax treatment accounted for this differential; the after-tax yield to corporate investors was greater on the preferred stock than on the bonds.[13]

About half of all preferred stock issued in recent years is convertible into common stock. For example, a firm might issue preferred stock whereby one share of preferred could be converted into three shares of common, at the option of the preferred stockholder. Convertibles are discussed at length in Chapter 22.

Preferred stock generally has no maturity date; thus, preferred stock is similar to perpetual bonds. However, many preferred shares do have a sinking fund provision; if the sinking fund called for the retirement of 1 percent of the issue each year, the issue would "mature" in a maximum of 100 years. Also, many preferred issues are callable by the issuing corporation; this feature, if exercised, will limit the life of the preferred.

COST OF ISSUING SECURITIES

Table 13–4 gives an indication of the flotation costs associated with public issues of bonds, preferred stocks, and common stocks. As the table shows, costs as a percentage of the proceeds are higher for stocks than for bonds, and costs are higher for small than for large issues. The relationship between size of issue and flotation cost is due primarily to the existence of fixed costs—certain costs must be incurred regardless of the size of the issue, so the percentage flotation cost is quite high for small issues.

Data are not available on the costs involved in borrowing through term loans, but these costs are certainly lower than the costs of issuing bonds to the public.[14]

12 Recall from Chapter 2 that 85 percent of dividends received by one corporation from another corporation is exempt from corporate income taxes.

13 The after-tax yield on a 7.5 percent bond to a corporate investor paying a 48 percent marginal tax rate is $7.5(1 - t) = 7.5(0.52) = 3.9\%$. The after-tax yield on a 7.5 percent preferred stock is $7.5(0.85) + 7.5(0.15)(0.52) = 6.96\%$.

14 Additional material on the process of issuing securities to the public is contained in Appendix 13A and also in Chapter 14.

Table 13–4
Costs of Flotation, 1971–1972 (Costs Expressed as Percentage of Gross Proceeds)

Size of Issue (Millions of Dollars)	Debt			Preferred Stock			Common Stock		
	Underwriting Commission	Other Expenses	Total Costs	Underwriting Commission	Other Expenses	Total Costs	Underwriting Commission	Other Expenses	Total Costs
Under 0.5	—	—	—	—	—	—	13.3	10.4	23.7
0.5–0.9	9.9	3.4	13.3	—	—	—	12.6	8.3	20.9
1.0–1.9	—	—	—	8.3	3.5	11.8	11.0	5.9	16.9
2.0–4.9	4.0	2.2	6.2	—	—	—	8.6	3.8	12.4
5.0–9.9	2.4	0.8	3.2	1.9	0.7	2.6	6.3	1.9	8.1
10.0–19.9	1.2	0.7	1.9	1.4	0.4	1.8	5.1	0.9	5.9
20.0–49.9	1.0	0.4	1.4	1.4	0.3	1.7	4.1	0.5	4.6
50.0 and over	0.9	0.2	1.1	1.4	0.2	1.6	3.3	0.2	3.5

Source: Securities and Exchange Commission, *Cost of Flotation of Registered Equity Issues, 1971–1972* (Washington, D.C.: U.S. Government Printing Office, December 1974). Because of rounding errors, totals may not equal the sum of the parts. Preferred stocks were used infrequently, as were bond issues of under $2 million. Therefore (1) all bond issues of under $2 million were lumped together, and (2) blanks are shown for several preferred stock categories because no issues in those size ranges were reported.

RATIONALE FOR THE USE OF DIFFERENT TYPES OF SECURITIES

At this point, two questions are likely to come to mind: (1) Why are there so many different forms of long-term securities? (2) Why would anybody ever be willing to purchase subordinated bonds or income bonds? The answers to both questions may be made clear by reference to Figure 13–3, which depicts the now familiar risk-return tradeoff function drawn to show the risk and the expected returns for the various securities of the Longstreet Company. Longstreet's first mortgage bonds are slightly riskier than U.S. Treasury bonds and sell at a slightly higher expected return. The second mortgage bonds are even riskier and have a still higher expected return. Subordinated debentures, income bonds, and preferred stocks are all increasingly risky and have increasingly higher expected returns. Longstreet's common stock, the riskiest security the firm issues, has the highest expected return of any of its offerings.

Figure 13–3
Longstreet Company, Risk and Expected Returns on Different Classes of Securities

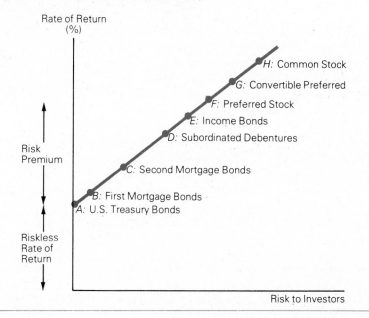

Why does Longstreet issue so many different classes of securities? Why not just offer one type of bond plus common stock? The answer lies in the fact that different investors have different risk-return tradeoff preferences; to appeal to the broadest possible market, Longstreet must offer securities that interest as many different investors as possible. Also, different types of securities are most appropriate at different points in time. Used wisely, a policy of selling differentiated securities to take advantage of market conditions can lower a firm's overall cost of capital below what it would be if it issued only one class of debt and common stock.

ADVANTAGES AND DISADVANTAGES OF BONDS AND PREFERRED STOCK

There are pros and cons to holding bonds and preferred stocks as investments, and also to their use as a means of financing by corporations. Some of these factors are considered below:

Income and Cost Are Limited Regardless of how profitable the company is or may become, bondholders and preferred stockholders receive only a fixed, limited income. This is an advantage from the firm's standpoint, as more of the operating income is available for the common stockholders, but it is a distinct disadvantage to the bondholders or preferred stockholders.

Control Typically, bondholders and preferred stockholders are not entitled to vote for directors—voting control lies in the hands of the common stockholders. Thus, when a firm is considering alternative means of financing, if the existing management group is concerned about losing voting control of the business, then selling bonds or preferred stock will have an advantage over financing with common stock. This point is covered in more detail in Chapter 14.

Taxes Bond interest is a deductible expense to the issuing firm, so for a firm in the 48 percent tax bracket, the federal government in effect pays 48 percent of the interest charges on debt. Thus, bonds have an advantage over common and preferred stock to a corporation planning to raise new capital. (This point was covered in Chapter 2 and will be examined again in Chapters 15 and 16.)

Risk To the corporation, bonds or term loans, especially those with sinking funds or amortization payments, entail significantly more risk than do preferred or common stocks. Further, the shorter the maturity, the greater the risk. However, from the investor's viewpoint, bonds (or term loans) are safer.

Flexibility The indenture provisions (restrictive covenants) on a long-term bond are generally much more stringent than they are either in a short-term credit agreement or for common or preferred stock. Hence, the firm may be subject to much more disturbing and crippling restrictions under a long-term debt arrangement than would be the case if it had borrowed on a short-term basis or had issued common or preferred stock.

Similarly, there is a limit on the extent to which funds can be raised through long-term debt. Generally accepted standards of financial policy dictate that the debt ratio must not exceed certain limits. When debt grows beyond these limits, its cost rises rapidly, or it may simply cease to be available.

Another significant point connected with flexibility relates to the ability to finance in times of economic stress. As a firm's fortunes deteriorate, it experiences greater difficulties in raising capital. Further, in such times investors are increasingly concerned with the security of their investments, and they may refuse to advance funds to the firm except on the basis of well-secured loans. A firm that finances with debt during good times to the point where its debt/assets ratio is at the upper limits for its industry simply may not be able to finance at all during times of stress. Thus, corporate treasurers like to maintain some "reserve borrowing capacity"; this restrains their use of debt financing.

These points are always considered by firms planning new security issues. However, we will defer further consideration of the pros and cons of alternative securities until we have analyzed in the next chapter the other principal type of long-term capital—common stock.

SUMMARY

This chapter described the characteristics, advantages, and disadvantages of the major types of long-term, fixed-income securities: *term loans, bonds,* and *preferred stocks.* The key difference between bonds and term loans is the fact that term loans are sold directly by a corporate borrower to between one and twenty lenders, while bonds are generally sold to many public investors through investment bankers. Preferred stocks are similar to bonds in that they offer a fixed return. However, preferred stock is less risky than bonds from the corporation's viewpoint because (1) the dividend does not have to be paid if it is not earned, and (2) nonpayment of preferred dividends will not bankrupt the firm. From the investors' standpoint, however, preferred stocks are riskier than bonds because (1) firms are more likely to omit preferred dividends than to fail to pay interest, and (2) bonds have priority over preferred stock in the event of bankruptcy.

Appendix A to this chapter describes the procedures involved in issuing bonds and preferred stocks, while Appendix B describes the analysis that a firm should undertake when deciding whether to call a bond for refunding prior to its maturity date. Other types of long-term securities, including common stock, leases, and convertible bonds, are described in later chapters, and in Chapters 15 and 16 we discuss the *optimal mix of securities,* or the *capital structure decision.*

Questions

13-1 This chapter is *descriptive;* it is designed to describe the key features and terms of the markets for long-term debt and preferred stock. Any investor, or anyone concerned with the financial operation of a business, should understand and be able to define the following terms. If you do not understand them, look them up in the chapter or the glossary.

    a. Bond

    b. Term loan

    c. Mortgage

    d. Debenture

    e. Convertible

    f. Subordinated debenture

    g. Income bond

    h. Development bond

    i. Pollution control bond

    j. Indenture

    k. Restrictive covenant

    l. Call provision

    m. Sinking fund

    n. Amortization schedule

    o. Funded debt

    p. Preferred stock arrearage

    q. Flotation costs

13-2 What effect would each of the following items have on the interest rate a firm must pay on a new issue of long-term debt? Indicate by a plus (+), minus (−), or zero (0) whether the factor will tend to raise, lower, or have an indeterminate effect on the firm's interest rate:

	Effect on Interest Rate
a. The firm uses bonds rather than a term loan.	_____
b. The firm uses nonsubordinated debentures rather than first mortgage bonds.	_____
c. The firm makes its bonds convertible into common stock.	_____
d. The firm makes its debentures subordinated to its bank debt. What will the effect be	
(1) on the debentures?	_____
(2) on the bank debt?	_____
(3) on the average total debt?	_____
e. The firm sells income bonds rather than debentures.	_____

    f. The firm must raise $100 million, all of which will be used to construct a new plant, and is debating the sale of mortgage bonds or debentures. If it decides to issue $50 million of each type, as opposed to $75 million of mortgage bonds and $25 million of debentures, how will this affect

(1) the debentures? _____

(2) the mortgage bonds? _____

(3) the average cost of the $100 million? _____

g. The firm is planning to raise $25 million of long-term capital. Its outstanding bonds yield 9 percent. If it sells preferred stock, how will this affect the yield on the outstanding debt? _____

h. The firm puts a call provision on its new issue of bonds. _____

i. The firm includes a sinking fund on its new issue of bonds. _____

j. The firm's bonds are downgraded from A to BBB. _____

13-3 Rank the following securities from lowest (1) to highest (10) in terms of their riskiness for an investor. All securities (except the government bond) are for a given firm. If you think two or more securities are equally risky, so indicate.

	Rank (10 = Highest Risk)
a. Income bond	_____
b. Subordinated debentures–noncallable	_____
c. First mortgage bond–no sinking fund	_____
d. Preferred stock	_____
e. Common stock	_____
f. U.S. Treasury bond	_____
g. First mortgage bond–with sinking fund	_____
h. Subordinated debentures–callable	_____
i. Amortized term loan	_____
j. Nonamortized term loan	_____

13-4 A sinking fund can be set up in one of two ways:

1. The corporation makes annual payments to the trustee, who invests the proceeds in securities (frequently government bonds) and uses the accumulated total to retire the bond issue at maturity.

2. The trustee uses the annual payments to retire a portion of the issue each year, either calling a given percentage of the issue by a lottery and paying a specified price per bond or buying bonds on the open market, whichever is cheaper.

Discuss the advantages and disadvantages of each procedure from the viewpoint of both the firm and the bondholders.

Problems

13-1 Suppose a firm is setting up an amortized term loan. What are the annual payments for a $2 million loan under the following terms:

a. 8 percent, five years?

b. 8 percent, ten years?

c. 10 percent, five years?

d. 10 percent, ten years?

13-2 Set up an amortization schedule for a $1 million, three year, 9 percent term loan.

13-3 A company borrows $1 million on a three year, 9 percent, partially amortized term loan. The annual payments are to be set so as to amortize $700,000 over the loan's three year life, plus pay interest on the $300,000 nonamortized portion of the loan.

   a. How large must each annual payment be? (*Hint:* Think of the loan as consisting of two loans, one fully amortized for $700,000 and one on which interest only is paid each year until the end of the third year.)

   b. Suppose the firm requested a $1 million, 9 percent, three year loan with payments of $250,000 per year (interest plus some principal repayment) for the first two years, with the remainder to be paid off at the end of the third year. How large must the final payment be?

13-4 The Florida Tile Company has the following balance sheet:

Current assets	$2,800	A/P	$ 600
Fixed assets	1,500	N/P (to bank)	300
		Accrued taxes	100
		Accrued wages	100
		Total current liabilities	$1,100
		First mortgage bonds	$ 500
		Second mortgage bonds	500
		Total mortgage bonds	$1,000
		Subordinated debentures	600
		Total debt	$2,700
		Preferred stock	200
		Common equity	1,400
Total assets	$4,300	Total claims	$4,300

The debentures are subordinated (only) to the notes payable. If Florida Tile goes bankrupt and is liquidated, how much will each class of investors receive if a total of $2,000 is received from sale of assets? Of this amount, $700 is derived from sale of the fixed assets, which were pledged as security for the first and second mortgage bonds, and $1,300 is from the sale of current assets. *Note:* Under the federal bankruptcy laws, $700 will be immediately allocated to the mortgage bonds, and $200 of the $1,300 from sale of current assets will be immediately allocated to accrued wages and taxes.

13-5 A firm has the following balance sheet:

Current assets	$1,500,000	Bank debt	$ 300,000
Fixed assets	1,500,000	Trade credit	600,000
		Subordinated debentures	600,000
		Total debt	$1,500,000
		Common equity	1,500,000
Total assets	$3,000,000	Total claims	$3,000,000

If the debentures are subordinated only to the bank debt, and the firm goes bankrupt, how much will each class of investors receive under each of the following conditions?

a. A total of $2 million is received from sale of assets.

b. A total of $1.5 million is received from sale of assets.

c. A total of $1 million is received from sale of assets.

d. A total of $500,000 is received from sale of assets.

e. What is the significance of these findings for the banks, the trade creditors, the debenture holders, and the common stockholders?

13-6 The Montreal Development Company has just issued a $100 million, ten year, 8 percent bond. A sinking fund will retire the issue over its life. Sinking fund payments are of equal amounts and will be made semiannually, and the proceeds will be used to retire bonds immediately. Bonds can be called at par for sinking fund purposes, or the funds paid into the sinking fund can be used to buy bonds in the open market.

a. How large must each semiannual sinking fund payment be? *Note:* You do *not* need to calculate a loan amortization payment; try $5 million, but explain *why* $5 million is the correct answer.

b. What will happen, under the conditions of the problem thus far, to the company's debt service requirements per year for this issue over time?

c. Now suppose that Montreal Development had set its sinking fund so that equal *annual* amounts, payable at the end of each year, were paid into a sinking fund trust held by a bank, with the proceeds being used to buy government bonds that pay 6 percent interest. The payments, plus accumulated interest, must total $100 million at the end of ten years, and the proceeds will be used to retire the bonds at that time. How large must the annual sinking fund payment now be?

d. What are the annual cash requirements to cover bond service costs under this procedure? *Note:* Under either procedure, interest must be paid on Montreal's outstanding bonds, but not on bonds that have been retired.

e. What would have to happen to interest rates to cause the company to buy bonds on the open market rather than call them under the original sinking fund plan?

13-7 In 1936 the Canadian government raised $55 million by issuing perpetual bonds at a 3 percent annual rate of interest. Unlike most bonds issued today, which have a specific maturity date, these perpetual bonds can remain outstanding forever; they are, in fact, perpetuities.

At the time of issue, the Canadian government stated that cash redemption was *possible* at face value ($100) on or after September 1966; in other words, the bonds were callable at par after September 1966. Believing that the bonds would in fact be called, many investors in the early 1960s purchased these bonds with expectations of receiving $100 in 1966 for each perpetual they held. In 1963 the bonds sold for $55, but a rush of buyers drove the price to just below the $100 par value by 1966. Prices fell dramatically, however, when the Canadian government announced that these perpetual bonds were indeed perpetual and would not be paid off. A new thirty year supply of coupons was sent to each bondholder, and the bonds' market price declined to $42 in December 1972.

Because of their severe losses, hundreds of Canadian bondholders have formed the Perpetual Bond Association to lobby for face value redemption of the bonds. Government officials in Ottawa insist that claims for face value payment are nonsense, that the bonds were clearly identified as perpetuals, and that they did not mature in 1966 or at any other time. One Ottawa official states, "Our job is to protect the taxpayer. Why should we pay $55 million for less than $25 million worth of bonds?"

a. Would it make sense for a business firm to issue bonds such as the Canadian bonds described above? Would it matter if the firm was a proprietorship or a corporation?

b. If the United States government today offered a five year bond, a fifty year bond, a "regular perpetuity," and a Canadian-type perpetuity, what do you think the relative order of interest rates would be; that is, rank the bonds from the one with the lowest to the one with the highest rate of interest. Explain your answer.

c. (1) Suppose that because of pressure by the Perpetual Bond Association, you believe that the Canadian government will redeem this particular perpetual bond issue in five years. Which course of action is more advantageous to you: (a) to sell your bonds today at $42 or (b) to wait five years and have them redeemed? Similar risk bonds earn 8 percent today, and interest rates are expected to remain at this level for the next five years.

   (2) If you have the opportunity to invest your money in bonds of similar risk, at what rate of return are you indifferent between selling your perpetuals today or having them redeemed in five years; that is, what is the expected yield to maturity on the Canadians? (*Hint:* You might want to consider the yield to maturity as being the IRR on the bonds and obtain a graphic solution to the IRR.)

d. Show, mathematically, the perpetuities' value if they yield 7.15 percent, pay $3 interest annually, and are considered as regular perpetuities. Show what would happen to the price of the bonds if the interest rate fell to 2 percent.

e. Are the Canadian bonds more likely to be valued as "regular perpetuities" if the going rate of interest is above or below 3 percent? Why?

f. Do you think the Canadian government would have taken the same action with regard to retiring the bonds if the interest rate had fallen rather than risen between 1936 and 1966?

g. Do you think the Canadian government was "fair" or "unfair" in its actions? Give pros and cons, and justify your reason for thinking that one outweighs the other.

APPENDIX 13A PROCEDURES FOR ISSUING LONG-TERM DEBT AND PREFERRED STOCK

Long-term investment capital is supplied primarily by individuals who spend less than they earn. Most of these savings reach business borrowers through a *financial intermediary,* often called an *institutional investor,* such as a life insurance company, mutual fund, pension fund, savings and loan association, or bank. In the institutional market, savers transmit funds to the institutional investors, who in turn buy business securities or make loans to business firms. As we shall see in Chapter 14, individual investors are very important in the stock market, but institutional investors dominate the market for long-term debt. In this appendix, we examine the process by which firms issue long-term debt and preferred stock.

DIRECT (OR PRIVATE) PLACEMENTS

One obvious method of selling long-term debt is for the issuing firm and a potential lender (or perhaps a syndicate of two to twenty lenders) to simply sit down and hammer out an agreement under which the lender (virtually always a bank, insurance company, or pension fund) will lend money to the company. Such loans are called *term loans,* or *direct placements.* In recent years about one-third of all long-term debt raised by corporations has been directly placed, although the percentage varies from year to year.

PUBLIC OFFERINGS BY INVESTMENT BANKERS

Most smaller ($10 million and less) long-term debt issues are privately placed, but if larger sums are involved, the amount of money may become too great for an individual institution or a small group of institutions to handle. Institutions seek wide diversification in their investment portfolios, so they are unwilling to purchase in its entirety a large issue such as the $1 billion debt issue IBM sold in October 1979. Thus, these larger issues are sold to "the public" by *investment bankers,* whose functions are described next.

Investment banking houses play two main roles in the security markets. First, they serve as intermediaries in the process of selling new securities—the investment bankers buy securities from the issuing firm and then sell them to ultimate purchasers. Second, investment banking houses help maintain a secondary market for securities after they have been issued—this is the *brokerage* side of investment banking. Thus, Merrill Lynch, Pierce, Fenner & Smith is an investment banking house which not only helps firms raise capital by issuing stocks and bonds, but also, through its brokerage operations, facilitates trading in these securities after their original issue. Since brokerage activities are concentrated primarily on common stocks rather than bonds, we shall defer analysis of that aspect of investment banking to Chapter 14.

STEPS IN ISSUING A BOND

The following steps are involved in long-term debt financing. Although the steps do indicate the *approximate* sequence of events, this sequencing is not exact. In certain circumstances several of the steps may be reversed, or they may occur simultaneously.[1]

Step 1 The *approximate* amount of funds to be raised must be determined. The final decision on the amount of money to be raised is often reached after consultation with investment bankers and lenders.

Step 2 Whether the funds are to be raised as a private placement or in a public offering must be decided. Often this decision will be reached after discussions with insurance companies and other institutional investors who make term loans, and also with the investment bankers who would handle a public offering. Direct placements can be obtained faster and with lower issuing costs, so if the interest rates and other terms are comparable, firms generally opt for direct placements. However, lower rates can sometimes be obtained on public offerings, especially if the issue is a large one, so treasurers must investigate carefully the pros and cons of private placements versus public offerings.

Step 3 If the issue is to be a public offering, the firm must choose an investment banker. If the firm is well known and has issued securities in the past, it probably already has established relations with an investment banking firm. If the firm is going public for the first time, it will "shop" for a banker; low cost as well as a reputation for good service are key characteristics the firm will seek.

Step 4 Once the investment banker has been selected, the issuing firm and the banker meet and settle the key features of the issue—the exact size, maturity, type of security to be offered, call feature, sinking fund, and, of course, the interest rate and the fees the investment banker will charge.

Step 5 The interest rate depends primarily on (1) the firm's financial strength and (2) the rate of interest on outstanding bonds comparable to this issue. The

---

1 The procedure described here relates to a *negotiated sale.* Alternatively, the firm could use a *competitive sale,* whereby it would simply inform all investment bankers that it wished to raise X of money by selling twenty year bonds and then let the bankers bid competitively for the issue. The firm would award the issue to the banker who offered the best terms, i.e., the lowest interest rate to the firm.

investment banker can judge the firm's strength, and if it has bonds outstanding already, the rating agencies will have assigned them a rating. The interest rate also depends on the detailed terms of a bond issue—the rate will be lower if the bond is not callable, if it has a sinking fund, if it includes a mortgage, and if it has strong covenants designed to protect the bondholders' interests.

Step 6 The issue can be sold either on an *underwritten* basis or on a *best efforts* basis. In an underwriting, the banker actually purchases the issue from the firm, then sells the bonds to permanent investors. There may be an interval of time between the purchase and the resale, during which interest rates may rise, causing bond values to drop. For example, in October 1979, IBM sold $1 billion of debt securities. Interest rates rose dramatically during the underwriting period, causing the bonds' prices to fall. The investment bankers handling the issue lost about $10 million, but IBM did not have to worry about the risk of market price fluctuations while the investment bankers were selling the bonds. IBM had received its money. Since the investment banking firms often underwrite, or guarantee, the sale of the issue, investment bankers are sometimes called *underwriters.*

On a *best efforts* sale, the investment banking house does not guarantee the sale of the issue—it merely agrees to use its best efforts to help the corporation sell the bonds. Best efforts arrangements are employed primarily in two situations: (1) where the firm is so strong and prices the issue so attractively that it does not feel the need for the banker's guarantee, and (2) where the issue is so "shaky" that the bankers refuse to guarantee its sale. Actually, best efforts arrangements are more common in stock than in bond flotations—most bonds are sold on an underwritten basis.

Step 7 The selling procedures must be worked out. On large public offerings ($20 million or more), the investment banker will generally work with other bankers in a *syndicate.* The banking house that does the direct negotiations with the issuing firm is called the *lead* or *managing underwriter,* and it manages the issue and coordinates the activities of the other investment bankers involved in the issue. On very large issues ($100 million or more), as many as 100 investment banking firms may be involved.

Step 8 The investment banker's compensation and other costs associated with the issue must be settled. Table 13–4 in the text gives an indication of the flotation costs associated with different types of securities.

Step 9 The investment bankers and the firm must clear the issue with the Securities and Exchange Commission (SEC), the government agency charged with making sure that investors are given valid information that is not misleading. A detailed report (the *registration statement*) must be filed with the SEC twenty days prior to the actual sale, and another report (the *prospectus*) must be made available to potential investors. These reports contain detailed financial information on the firm, indicate the key features of the issue, describe the firm's history and management, and indicate what the firm plans to do with the proceeds of the sale.

Step 10 The final phase of the operation is the actual sale of securities to the public. The investment bankers will have reached tentative agreements with at least some potential investors before the formal sale begins. The formal public offering is called "opening the books," an archaic term reflecting ancient customs of the investment banking trade. When the books are opened, the manager accepts subscriptions to the issue. If the demand is great, the books may be closed immediately and an announcement made that the issue is oversubscribed; the issue is said to "fly out the window." If the reception is weak, the books may remain open for an extended period. If the bankers completely misjudged the market, or if interest rates rose after the rate to the issuer had been settled, the bankers may have to cut the price of the bonds and take losses to move the issue. This happened with the IBM issue.

APPENDIX 13B   REFUNDING OPERATIONS

Suppose a company sells bonds or preferred stock at a time when interest rates are relatively high. Provided the issue is callable, as many are, the company can sell a new issue of low-yielding securities if and when interest rates drop and use the proceeds to retire the high-rate issue. This is called a *refunding operation.*

The decision to refund a security issue is analyzed in much the same manner as a capital budgeting expenditure. The costs of refunding—the "investment outlays"—are (1) the call premium paid for the privilege of calling the old issue and (2) the flotation costs incurred in selling the new issue. The annual receipts, in the capital budgeting sense, are the interest payments that are saved each year. For example, if interest expense on the old issue is $1 million while that on the new issue is $700,000, the $300,000 saving constitutes the annual benefits.

In analyzing the advantages of refunding, the net present value method is the recommended procedure—discount the future interest savings back to the present and compare the discounted value with the cash outlays associated with the refunding. *In the discounting process, the after-tax cost of the new debt, k_d, should be used as the discount factor.* The reason for this is that there is relatively little risk to the savings—their value is known with relative certainty, which is quite unlike the cash flows of most capital budgeting decisions. The following example illustrates the calculations needed in a refunding decision.

The Carter Chemical Company has outstanding a $60 million, twenty-five year bond issue, carrying an 8 percent interest rate. This issue, which was sold five years ago, had flotation costs of $3 million, which the firm is currently amortizing on a straight line basis over the life of the issue. The bond indenture carries a call provision making it possible for the company to retire the bonds by calling them in at a 6 percent call premium. Investment bankers have assured the company that it could sell an additional $60 to $70 million worth of twenty year bonds at an interest rate of 6 percent. To ensure that funds required to pay off the old debt will be available, the new bonds will be sold one month before the old issue is called, so for one month, interest must be paid on two issues. Predictions are that interest rates are unlikely to fall below 6 percent.[1] Flotation costs on the new issue will amount to $2.65 million. Carter's effective tax rate is 40 percent. Should the company refund the $60 million worth of bonds? The following steps outline the decision process, while Table 13B–1 summarizes the process in worksheet form.

Step 1 Determine the investment outlay required to refund the issue.

a. Call premium:

$$\text{Before tax: } 0.06 \times \$60,000,000 = \$3,600,000.$$

$$\text{After tax: } \$3,600,000(1 - t) = \$3,600,000(0.6)$$
$$= \$2,160,000.$$

---

1 The firm's management has estimated that interest rates will probably rise to center on 7 percent in the near future, with a standard deviation of ¾ percent. This implies that there is only a 9 percent chance (1.33 standard deviations from the mean) of future rates falling below 6 percent.

Although Carter must expend $3.6 million on the call premium, this is a deductible expense in the year the call is made. Since the company is in a 40 percent tax bracket, it saves $1.44 million in taxes. Therefore, the after-tax cost of the call is only $2,160,000.

b. Flotation costs on new issue:

Total flotation costs are $2.65 million. For tax purposes, flotation costs are amortized over the life of the new bond, or twenty years. Therefore, the annual tax deduction is

$$\frac{\$2,650,000}{20} = \$132,500.$$

Since Carter is in the 40 percent tax bracket, it has a tax saving of $132,500 times 0.4 = $53,000 a year for twenty years. This is an annuity of $53,000 for twenty years. The present value of this annuity, discounted at 3.6 percent, the after-tax cost of debt, is calculated as follows:[2]

$$\begin{aligned} \text{PV of tax saving} &= \text{PVIFA} \times \$53,000 \\ &= 14.085 \times \$53,000 \\ &= \$746,505. \end{aligned}$$

The net after-tax cost of new flotation costs is

New flotation costs	$2,650,000
PV of tax saving	−746,505
Net cost	$1,903,495

c. Flotation costs on old issue:

The old issue has an unamortized flotation cost of $2.4 million (20/25 × $3,000,000). This may be recognized immediately as an expense, thus creating an after-tax savings of $2,400,000(t) = $960,000. The firm will, however, lose a tax deduction of $120,000 a year for twenty years, or an after-tax benefit of $48,000 a year. The present value of this lost benefit, discounted at 3.6 percent, is

---

2 The cost of capital is developed in detail in Chapter 16. There we will see (1) that the cost of capital increases as the riskiness of the firm increases and (2) that there is a cost of debt, a cost of equity, and an "average cost of capital," which is a weighted average of the cost of debt and equity. Also, we will see that the relevant cost of debt is an *after-tax cost*, calculated as follows:

   After-tax cost of debt = (Interest rate)(1 − Tax rate) = (6%)(0.6) = 3.6%.

This calculation recognizes that interest is tax deductible, so the federal government, in effect, bears a portion of the cost of debt.

   Since a 3.6 percent interest rate is not in the tables, how do we obtain PVIFA for 3.6 percent for twenty years? One way would be to interpolate. Alternatively, we could use the equation

$$\text{PVIFA} = \sum_{t=1}^{n} \frac{1}{(1 + k)^t} = \frac{1 - \dfrac{1}{(1 + k)^n}}{k} = 14.085.$$

$$\text{PV of } \textit{lost} \text{ benefit} = \text{PVIFA} \times \$48,000$$
$$= 14.085 \times \$48,000$$
$$= \$676,080.$$

The net after-tax effect of old flotation costs is

Tax savings on old flotation costs	($960,000)
PV of lost benefits of old flotation costs	676,080
Net after-tax effect of old flotation costs	($283,920)

d. Additional interest:[3]

One month "extra" interest on old issue, after taxes, is

$$\text{Dollar amount} \times \text{¹/₁₂ of } 8\% \times (1 - \text{Tax rate}) = \text{Interest cost}$$
$$\$60,000,000 \times 0.0067 \times 0.6 = \$240,000.$$

e. Total after-tax investment:

The total investment outlay required to refund the bond issue, which will be financed by debt, is thus

Call premium	$2,160,000
Flotation cost, new	1,903,495
Flotation cost, old	(283,920)
Additional interest	240,000
Total investment	$4,019,575

Step 2 Calculate the annual savings.

a. Old bond interest, after tax:

$$\$60,000,000 \times 0.08 \times 0.6 = \$2,880,000$$

b. New bond interest, after tax:

$$\$60,000,000 \times 0.06 \times 0.6 = \$2,160,000$$

c. Savings $\qquad\qquad\qquad\qquad\qquad\qquad\;\; \$\;\,720,000$

Step 3 Find the present value of the savings.

a. Twenty year PVIFA at 3.6 percent = 14.085.

b. PV of $720,000 a year for twenty years:

$$14.085 \times \$720,000 = \$10,141,200.$$

---

3 If the proceeds from the new issue are invested in short-term securities for one month, as they typically will be, this reduces the effect of the "extra" interest.

Step 4 Conclusion: Since the present value of the receipts is $10,141,200, which exceeds the required investment of $4,019,575, the issue should be refunded.

Two other points are significant. First, since the $720,000 savings is an essentially riskless investment, its present value is found by discounting at the firm's least risky rate—its after-tax cost of debt. Second, since the refunding operation is advantageous to the firm, it must be disadvantageous to bondholders—they must give up their 8 percent bonds and reinvest in new ones yielding 6 percent. This points out the danger of the call provision to bondholders and explains why bonds without a call provision command higher prices than callable bonds.

Table 13B–1
Worksheet for the Bond Refunding Decision

	Amount before Tax	Amount after Tax	Year(s) Event Occurs	PV Factor at 3.6%	PV
Costs of Refunding at t = 0					
1. Call premium outflow	$3,600,000	$2,160,000	0	1.0	$2,160,000
2. Flotation cost on new issue	2,650,000	2,650,000	0	1.0	2,650,000
3. Tax savings on flotation cost amortization, new	(132,500)	(53,000)	1–20	14.085	(746,505)
4. Tax savings on old flotation cost expense	(2,400,000)	(960,000)	0	1.0	(960,000)
5. Tax benefits lost on old flotation cost	120,000	48,000	1–20	14.085	676,080
6. Extra interest on old issue	400,000	240,000	0	1.0	240,000
			Total after-tax investment = (PV of investment)		$4,019,575
Savings over the Life of the New Issue: t = 1 to 20					
7. Interest on old bond	$4,800,000	$2,880,000			
8. Interest on new bond	3,600,000	2,160,000			
Net savings on interest, after tax	$1,200,000	$ 720,000	1–20	14.085	$10,141,200

NPV = PV of interest savings − PV of investment.
= $10,141,200 − $4,019,575 = $6,121,625.

Problem

13B-1 The Wonder Corporation is considering whether to refund a $50 million, 11 percent coupon, twenty year bond issue which was sold five years ago. It is amortizing $2 million of flotation costs on the 11 percent bonds over the twenty year life of that issue. Wonder's investment bankers have indicated that the company could sell a new $50 million, fifteen year issue at an interest rate of 9³/₄ percent in today's market. Neither they nor Wonder's management sees much chance that interest rates will fall below 9³/₄ percent any time soon, but there is a chance that rates will increase.

A call premium of 5 percent would be required to retire the old bonds, and flotation costs on the new issue would amount to $3 million. Wonder's marginal tax rate is 40 percent. The new bonds would be issued one month before the old bonds were called, with the proceeds of the new issue being invested in short-term government securities with a 5 percent coupon during the interim period.

a. Calculate the NPV of the bond refunding. Should Wonder refund the old issue at this time? (*Hint:* the PVIFA of 5.85 percent for fifteen years is 9.8082.)

b. If the yield curve at this time were sharply downward sloping, how might this fact alter management's expectations about future interest rates and affect the decision to refund at this time?

14 COMMON STOCK

Common stock—or, for unincorporated businesses, the proprietors' or partners' capital—represents the ownership of the firm. In earlier chapters, we discussed the process by which stock prices are determined in the marketplace. Now we consider legal and accounting aspects of common stocks, the markets in which stock is traded, and the procedures involved when firms raise new capital by issuing additional shares of stock.

BALANCE SHEET ACCOUNTS AND DEFINITIONS

Legal and accounting terminology is vital to both investors and financial managers if they are to avoid misinterpretations and possibly costly mistakes, so we begin our analysis of common stocks with a discussion of accounting and legal issues. Consider first Table 14–1, which shows the "common stockholders' equity" section of Carter Chemical Company's balance sheet; these data are reproduced from Table 6–2 in Chapter 6. Carter's owners, its stockholders, have authorized management to issue a total of 60 million shares, and management has, thus far, actually issued (or sold) 50 million shares. Each share has a *par value* of $1; this is the minimum amount for which new shares can be issued.[1]

Carter Chemical is an old company, established in 1873. Its initial equity capital consisted of 5,000 shares sold at the $1 par value, so on its first

---

1 A stock's par value is an arbitrary value that indicates the minimum amount of money stockholders have put up, or that they must put up in the event of bankruptcy. Actually, the firm could legally sell new shares at below par, but any purchaser would be liable for the difference between the issue price and the par value in the event the company went bankrupt. Thus, if Carter sold an investor 10,000 shares at 40 cents per share, for $4,000, the investor would have to put up an additional $6,000 if the company should later go bankrupt. This contingent liability effectively precludes the sale of new common stock at prices below par.

Also, we should point out that firms are not required to establish a par value for their stocks. Thus, Carter could have elected to use "no par" stock, in which case the "common stock" and "additional paid-in capital" accounts could have been consolidated under one account called "common stock," which would show a balance of $150 million.

Table 14–1
Carter Chemical Company: Stockholders'
Equity Accounts, December 31, 1979

Common stock (60 million shares authorized, 50 million shares outstanding, $1 par)	$ 50,000,000
Additional paid-in capital	100,000,000
Retained earnings	750,000,000
Total common stockholders' equity (or common net worth)	$900,000,000

$$\text{Book value per share} = \frac{\text{Total common stockholders' equity}}{\text{Shares outstanding}}$$

$$= \frac{\$900,000,000}{50,000,000}$$

$$= \$18.$$

---

balance sheet the total stockholders' equity was $5,000. The additional paid-in capital and retained earnings accounts showed zero balances. Over the years, Carter retained earnings, and the firm issued new stock to raise capital from time to time. As we saw in Chapter 6, during 1979 Carter earned $120 million, paid $100 million in dividends, and retained $20 million. The $20 million was added to the $730 million accumulated retained earnings shown on the year-end 1978 balance sheet to produce the $750 million retained earnings at year-end 1979. Thus, since its inception in 1873, Carter has retained, or plowed back, a total of $750 million. This is money that belongs to the stockholders and that they could have received in the form of dividends. Instead, the stockholders chose to let management reinvest the $750 million in the business.

Now consider the $100 million additional paid-in capital. This account shows the difference between the stock's par value and what new stockholders paid when they bought newly issued shares. As noted above, Carter was formed in 1873 with 5,000 shares issued at the $1 par value; thus, the first balance sheet showed a zero balance for additional paid-in capital. By 1888, the company had demonstrated its profitability and was earning $0.50 per share. Further, it had built up the retained earnings account to a total of $10,000, so the total stockholders' equity was $5,000 of par value plus $10,000 of retained earnings = $15,000, and the book value per share was $15,000/5,000 shares = $3.00. Carter had also borrowed heavily, and in spite of its retained earnings, the company's debt ratio had built up to an unacceptable level, precluding further use of debt without an infusion of equity.

The company had profitable investment opportunities, so to take advantage of them, it decided to issue another 2,000 shares of stock. The market price at the time was $4 per share, which was eight times the 50 cent earnings per share (the price/earnings ratio was 8×). This $4 market value was also well in excess of the $1 par value, and also higher than the $3 book value per share, demonstrating that par value, book value, and market value are not directly related. Had the company lost money since its inception, it would have had *negative* retained earnings, the book value would have been below par, and the market price might well have been below book. After the 2,000 new shares had been sold to investors back in 1888, at a price of $4 per share, which was the market price then, Carter Chemical's partial balance sheet changed as shown below:

	Before Sale of Stock
Common stock (5,000 shares outstanding, $1 par)	$ 5,000
Additional paid-in capital	0
Retained earnings	10,000
Total stockholders' equity	$15,000
Book value per share = $15,000/5,000 =	$3.00

	After Sale of Stock
Common stock (7,000 shares outstanding, $1 par)	$ 7,000
Additional paid-in capital ($4 − $1) × 2,000 shares	6,000
Retained earnings	10,000
Total stockholders' equity	$23,000
Book value per share = $23,000/7,000 =	$3.29

Each share brought in $4, of which $1 represented the par value and $3 represented the excess of the sale price above par. Since 2,000 shares were involved, a total of $2,000 was added to common stock, while $6,000 was entered in additional paid-in capital. Notice also that book value per share rose from $3 to $3.29; whenever stock is sold at prices above book, the book value increases, and conversely if stock is sold below book.[2]

Similar transactions have taken place down through the years to produce

---

2 The effects on book value are not important for industrial firms, but they are *very* important for utility companies, whose allowable earnings per share are, in effect, determined by regulators as a percentage of book value. Thus, if a utility's stock is selling below book, and the company sells stock to raise new equity, this dilutes its book value and drives down its allowable earnings per share, which in turn drives down the market price. Most U.S. electric utilities' stocks sold below book in the 1970s. They needed to raise large amounts of capital. Although this capital could not all be raised as debt, selling stock at below book tended to depress the market value of the stock still further. At this writing, the situation is posing a real problem for utility managers, who see a need to raise more capital to build the plants necessary to provide electricity in the future, but who cannot raise capital without depressing the prices of their companies' stocks, to the detriment of their stockholders.

the current situation, as shown on Carter's latest balance sheet in Table 6–2.[3]

LEGAL RIGHTS AND PRIVILEGES OF THE COMMON STOCKHOLDERS

The common stockholders are the owners of the corporation, and as such they have certain rights and privileges. The most important of these are discussed in this section.

Control of the Firm

The stockholders have the right to elect the firm's directors, who in turn select the officers who manage the business. In a small firm, the major stockholder typically assumes the positions of president and chairman of the board of directors. In a large, publicly owned firm, the managers typically have some stock, but their personal holdings are insufficient to exercise voting control; thus, the management of a publicly owned firm can be removed by the stockholders if the stockholder group decides the management is not effective.

Various state and federal laws stipulate how stockholder control is to be exercised. First, corporations must hold an election of directors periodically, usually once a year, with the vote taken at the annual meeting. Frequently, one-third of the directors are elected each year for a three year term. Each share of stock has one vote; thus, the owner of 1,000 shares has 1,000 votes. Stockholders can appear at the annual meeting and vote in person, or they can transfer their right to vote to a second party by means of an instrument known as a *proxy.* Management always solicits stockholders' proxies and usually gets them. However, if earnings are poor and stockholders are dissatisfied, an outside group may solicit the proxies in an effort to overthrow management and take over control of the business. This is known as a *proxy fight.*

The question of control has become a central issue in finance in recent years. The frequency of proxy fights has increased, as have attempts by one corporation to take over another by purchasing a majority of the outstanding stock. This latter action, which is called a *takeover,* is discussed in detail in Chapter 19. Managers who do not have majority control of their firms' stocks (over 50 percent) are very much concerned about takeovers, and many of them are attempting to get stockholder approval for changes in their corporate charters that would make takeovers more difficult. For example, a number of companies tried in 1978 to get their stockholders to

---

3 Stock dividends, stock splits, and stock repurchases (the reverse of stock issues) also affect the capital accounts. However, we shall defer a discussion of these topics until Chapter 17.

agree (1) to elect only one-third of the directors each year (rather than to elect all directors each year) and (2) to require 75 percent of the stockholders (rather than 50 percent) to approve a merger. Managements seeking such changes generally indicate a fear of the firm's being picked up at a bargain price, but some stockholders wonder whether concern about their jobs might not be an even more important consideration.[4]

The Right to Purchase New Stock: The Preemptive Right

Common stockholders often have the right, called the *preemptive right,* to purchase any additional shares sold by the firm. In some states, the preemptive right is made a part of every corporate charter; in others, it is necessary to insert the preemptive right specifically into the charter.

The purpose of the preemptive right is twofold. First, it protects the power of control of present stockholders. If it were not for this safeguard, the management of a corporation under criticism from stockholders could prevent stockholders from removing it from office by issuing a large number of additional shares and purchasing these shares itself. Management would thereby secure control of the corporation to frustrate the will of the current stockholders.

The second, and by far the more important, protection that the preemptive right affords stockholders regards dilution of value. For example, assume that 1,000 shares of common stock, each with a price of $100, are outstanding, making the total market value of the firm $100,000. An additional 1,000 shares are sold at $50 a share, or for $50,000, thus raising the total market value of the firm to $150,000. When the total market value is divided by the new total shares outstanding, a value of $75 a share is obtained. Thus, selling common stock at below market value will dilute the price of the stock and will be detrimental to present stockholders and beneficial to those who purchase the new shares. The preemptive right prevents such occurrences.[5]

Types of Common Stock

Although most firms have only one type of common stock, in some instances special classifications of stock are created to meet the special needs of the company. Generally, when different types of stock are used, one type is designated *Class A,* the second *Class B,* and so on. Small, new companies seeking to acquire funds from outside sources sometimes use different types of common stock. For example, stock designated Class A may be sold to the public, pay a dividend, and have full voting rights. The stock designated Class B, however, may be retained by the organizers of the company, and the legal terms may state that dividends will not be paid on it

4 One frequently used voting procedure, *cumulative voting,* is discussed in Appendix 14A.
5 Procedures for issuing stock to existing stockholders, called a *rights offering,* are discussed in Appendix 14B.

until the company has established its earning power by building up retained earnings to a designated level. By the use of classified stock, the public can take a position in a conservatively financed growth company without sacrificing income. In situations such as this, the Class B stock is often called *founders' shares* and given *sole* voting rights for a number of years. This permits the organizers of the firm to maintain complete control of the operations in the crucial early stages of the firm's development. At the same time, other investors are protected against excessive withdrawals of funds by the original owners.

Savannah Electric provides an example of yet another type of classification. This company has Class A common that pays a $1.34 annual dividend versus $1.00 for the Class B common. If earnings increase and the dividend on the Class B stock is raised to a level above $1.34, the Class A stockholders can convert to Class B. Conversion from A to B will occur automatically in 1984 if voluntary conversion has not occurred earlier. The reason for selling the Class A was quite simple—while Savannah needed money badly in 1972, it could not sell debt because of indenture restrictions, it could not sell preferred stock because of other restrictions, and it could not sell "regular" common because the market would not absorb it without depressing the price very badly. The Class A common was the only feasible alternative.

Note that "Class A," "Class B," and so on have no standard meanings. First, most firms have no classified shares. Also, one firm may designate its Class B shares as founders' shares and its Class A shares as those sold to the public. Another firm can reverse these designations. Other firms, like Savannah Electric, can use the A and B designations for entirely different purposes.

THE MARKET FOR COMMON STOCK

Common stocks are bought by individual investors, by institutional investors (mutual funds, pension funds, insurance companies, university endowment funds, etc.), by foreign investors, and by corporate investors, including corporations formed specifically to invest in new, developing businesses.

Prior to the 1950s, the vast majority of the stock of U.S. corporations was owned by individual investors. More recently, there has been a tremendous change in the way people save that has greatly increased the proportion of stocks held by institutional investors, especially bank trust departments and insurance companies—both of which administer government and corporate pension funds—and mutual funds. Prior to 1950, relatively few corporations had pension plans, so people had to save for retirement on an individual basis. Now almost everyone is covered by a pension plan, and both employees and employers pay billions into these funds each year. Because much of this money has been invested in common stocks, today institutional investors own 33 percent of the stock of major U.S. corporations. However, since the institutional investors are more active in the market than are individual investors, they account for about 77 percent of the trading activity in the stock market.

The stocks of smaller companies are generally owned by their management groups—such companies are called *closely held corporations,* or *closed corporations.* Most of the stock of larger firms is owned by a large number of investors not actively involved with management—these companies are known as *publicly held corporations.* The managers of most publicly held firms own some shares but not the 50 percent plus necessary for absolute voting control, although in some instances the managements of public companies do have voting control.

Types of Stock Market Transactions

We can classify stock market transactions into three distinct categories:

1. *Trading in the outstanding shares of established, publicly owned companies: the secondary market.* Carter Chemical Company has 50 million shares of stock outstanding. If the owner of 100 shares sells this stock, the trade is said to have occurred in the *secondary market.* Thus, the market for outstanding shares, or *used shares,* is defined as the secondary market. The company receives no new money when sales occur in the secondary market.
2. *Additional shares sold by established, publicly owned companies: the primary market.* If Carter Chemical decides to sell an additional one million shares to raise new equity capital, this transaction is said to occur in the primary market.[6]
3. *New public offerings by privately held firms: the primary market.* In 1975 the Coors Brewing Company, which was owned by the Coors family at the time, decided to sell some stock to raise capital needed for a major expansion program.[7] This type of transaction is defined as *going public—* whenever stock in a closely held corporation is offered to the public for the first time, the company is said to be going public. The market for stock that has recently gone public is often called the *new issue market.*

Firms can go public without raising any additional capital. For example, in its early days the Ford Motor Company was owned exclusively by the Ford family. When Henry Ford died, he left a substantial part of his stock to the Ford Foundation. When the Foundation later sold some of this stock to the general public, the Ford Motor Company went public, even though the company raised no capital in the transaction.

---

6 Recall that Carter has 60 million shares authorized but only 50 million shares are outstanding. Thus the company has 10 million authorized but unissued shares. If it had no authorized but unissued shares, management could increase the authorized shares by obtaining stockholders' approval, which would generally be granted without any arguments.

7 The stock Coors offered to the public was designated Class B, and it was nonvoting. The Coors family retained the "founders' shares," called Class A stock, which carried full voting privileges.

Markets for Outstanding Shares: The Stock Exchanges

There are two basic types of security markets—the *organized exchanges,* typified by the New York Stock Exchange, and the less formal *over-the-counter markets.* Since the organized exchanges have actual physical market locations and are easier to describe and understand, we shall consider them first.

The organized security exchanges are tangible, physical entities. Each of the larger ones occupies its own building, has specifically designated members, and has an elected governing body—its board of governors. Members are said to have "seats" on the exchange, although everybody stands up. These seats, which are bought and sold, represent the right to trade on the exchange. In 1968, seats on the New York Stock Exchange (NYSE) sold at a record high of $515,000, but in 1979 they sold for as little as $40,000.

Most of the larger stock brokerage firms own seats on the exchanges and designate one or more of their officers as members. The exchanges are open daily, with the members meeting in a large room equipped with telephones and other electronic equipment that enable each brokerage house member to communicate with the firm's offices throughout the country.

Like other markets, security exchanges facilitate communication between buyers and sellers. For example, Merrill Lynch, Pierce, Fenner & Smith, Inc. (the largest brokerage firm), might receive an order in its Atlanta office from a customer who wants to buy 100 shares of General Motors stock. Simultaneously, a brokerage house in Denver might receive an order from a customer wishing to sell 100 shares of GM. Each broker communicates by wire with the firm's representative on the NYSE. Other brokers throughout the country are also communicating with their own exchange members. The exchange members with *sell orders* offer the shares for sale, and they are bid for by the members with *buy orders.* Thus, the exchanges operate as *auction markets.*[8]

Special procedures are available for handling large blocks of securities. For example, if General Motors, whose stock is already listed on the NYSE, plans to sell a new issue of stock, the exchange has facilities that make it easier for the market to absorb the new issue. Similarly, if a large mutual fund or pension fund wants to sell a large block of a listed stock, procedures are available that facilitate the sale without putting undue pressure on the stock price.

---

8 This discussion is highly simplified. The exchanges have members known as *specialists,* who facilitate the trading process by keeping an inventory of shares of the stocks in which they specialize. If a buy order comes in at a time when no sell order arrives, the specialist may sell off some inventory. Similarly, if a sell order comes in, the specialist will buy and add to inventory. The specialist sets a *bid price* (the price the specialist will pay for the stock) and an *asked price* (the price at which shares will be sold out of inventory). The bid and asked prices are set at levels designed to keep the inventory in balance. If many buy orders start coming in because of favorable developments, or sell orders because of unfavorable events, the specialist will raise or lower prices to keep supply and demand in balance.

Stock Market Reporting Securities traded on the organized security exchanges are called *listed securities.* (Other securities are known as *unlisted,* or *over-the-counter,* securities, and they are discussed later in this chapter.) Quite a lot of information is available dealing with transactions of both listed and unlisted securities, and the very existence of this information reduces the uncertainty inherent in security investments. We cannot delve deeply into the matter of financial reporting—this is more properly the field of investment analysis—but it is useful to explain the basics of the stock market reporting system.

Table 14–2 is a section of the stock market page taken from the *Wall Street Journal* for June 14, 1978, for stocks listed on the NYSE. Similar information is available on stocks listed on the other exchanges, and also on stocks traded over the counter. Stocks are listed alphabetically, from ACF Industries to Zurn Industries; the data in Table 14–2 were taken from the top of the page. The two columns on the left show the highest and lowest prices at which the stocks have sold during the year; ACF, the first company shown, has traded in the range from $38⅝ to $28⅞ (or from $38.625 to $28.875) during the past fifty-two weeks. The figure just to the right of the company's abbreviated name is the dividend expected for the year; ACF had a current indicated dividend rate of $2.10 per share and a dividend yield of 6 percent in 1978. Next comes the P/E ratio, followed by the volume of trading for the day; 17,300 shares of ACF stock were traded on June 14, 1978. Following the volume come the high and the low prices for the day, and then the closing price. On June 14, ACF traded as high as $35⅞ and as low as $34½, while the last trade was at $34¾. The last column gives the change from the closing price on the previous day. ACF was down

Table 14–2
Stock Market Transactions, June 14, 1978

52 Weeks High	Low	Stock	Div.	Yld %	P-E Ratio	Sales 100s	High	Low	Close	Net Chg.
38⅝	28⅞	ACF	2.10	6.0	9	173	35⅞	34½	34¾	− ⅝
21	15⅝	AMF	1.24	6.4	9	224	19⅝	19⅜	19½	− ⅛
15¾	9⅜	APL	1	7.5	9	×591	13¾	13¼	13¼	− ⅛
45	32⅜	ARA	1.45	3.4	10	38	42⅜	42	42⅜	+ ⅜
23⅜	17½	ASA	1	4.8	. .	475	20⅝	20⅛	20⅝	+ ⅜
12⅜	7¾	ATO	.40	3.4	7	168	12	11½	11⅝	− ⅜
35¾	29	AbbtLb	.72	2.1	16	796	34⅝	33¾	34	. . . .
20¾	11	AcmeC	.80	4.0	10	93	20	19¾	19⅞	. . . .
5½	2⅝	AdmDg	.04	.8	7	61	5⅛	5	5	− ⅛
13	11¼	AdaEx	1.11	9.1	. .	34	12¼	12	12¼	+ ¼
7½	3⅞	AdmMl	.20e	2.7	10	19	7⅜	7¼	7⅜	. . . .
25	12¼	Addrsg	.20	.8	. .	×150	24⅜	24⅛	24¼	. . . .
44⅛	31	AetnaLf	2.20	5.1	5	855	43⅝	42⅝	42⅞	− ½

⅝, or $0.625, so the previous close must have been $35⅜ (since $35⅜ − ⅝ = $34¾, the indicated closing price on June 14).

A set of footnotes always accompanies the stock market quotes, giving additional information about specific issues. Most of these notes refer to dividends, and they can best be understood after our discussion of this topic in Chapter 17, so we defer further comment on Table 14–2 until that chapter.[9]

Over-the-Counter Security Markets

In contrast to the organized security exchanges, the over-the-counter market is a nebulous, intangible organization. Perhaps an explanation of the term *over-the-counter* will help clarify exactly what this market is. The exchanges operate as auction markets—buy and sell orders come in more or less simultaneously, and the exchanges are used to match these orders. But if a stock is traded less frequently, perhaps because it is the stock of a new or a small firm, few buy and sell orders come in, and matching them within a reasonable length of time would be difficult. To avoid this problem, brokerage firms maintain an inventory of the stocks. They buy when individual investors wish to sell, and sell when investors want to buy. At one time the inventory of securities was kept in a safe, and when bought and sold, the stocks were literally passed over the counter.

Today, over-the-counter markets are defined as all facilities that provide for security transactions not conducted on the organized exchanges. These facilities consist primarily (1) of the relatively few dealers who hold inventories of over-the-counter securities and who are said to "make a market" in these securities and (2) of the thousands of brokers who act as agents in bringing these dealers together with investors. The dealers who make a market in a particular stock will, upon request, quote a price at which they are willing to buy the stock (the *bid* price) and a price at which they will sell shares (the *asked* price). The spread between bid and asked prices represents the dealer's mark-up, or profit.

In terms of numbers of issues, the majority of stocks are traded over the counter. However, because the stocks of larger companies are listed on the exchanges, it is estimated that two-thirds of the dollar volume of stock trading takes place on the exchanges. The situation is reversed in the bond market. Although the bonds of a number of the larger companies are listed on the NYSE bond list, over 95 percent of bond transactions take place in the over-the-counter market. The reason for this is that bonds typically are traded among the large financial institutions, for example, life insurance

---

9 We should note that some shares listed on the NYSE are also traded on one or more regional exchanges. The *Wall Street Journal* reports trades of NYSE stocks made not only on the NYSE itself but also on the regional exchanges. Thus, if ACF were listed on both the NYSE and the Midwest Exchange, the 17,300 shares traded could have represented 17,000 shares traded on the NYSE and 300 shares traded on the Midwest Exchange. Similarly, the high, low, and closing prices could represent trades on either the NYSE or the Midwest Exchange.

companies and pension funds, which deal in very large blocks of securities. It is relatively easy for the over-the-counter bond dealers to arrange the transfer of large blocks of bonds among the relatively few holders of the bonds. It would be impossible to conduct similar operations in the stock market among the literally millions of large and small stockholders.

Some Trends in Security Trading Procedures

From the NYSE's inception in the 1800s until the 1970s, the vast majority of all stock trading occurred on the Exchange and was conducted by member firms. The Exchange established a set of minimum brokerage commission rates, and no NYSE member firm could charge a commission lower than the set rate. This was a monopoly, pure and simple. Finally, in the 1970s, the SEC, with strong prodding from the Antitrust Division of the Justice Department, forced the NYSE to abandon its fixed commissions. Commissions declined dramatically, falling in some cases as much as 80 percent from former levels. These changes were a boon for the investing public, but not for the brokerage industry. A number of brokerage houses went bankrupt, and others were forced to merge with stronger firms. Many Wall Street experts predict that, once the dust settles, the number of brokerage houses will have declined from literally thousands in the 1960s to perhaps twenty large, strong, nationwide companies.

Decision to List Stock

The exchanges have certain requirements that firms must meet before their stocks can be listed. These requirements relate to size of company, number of years in business, earnings record, number of shares outstanding, total market value, and the like. In general, requirements become more stringent as we move from the regional exchanges toward the NYSE.

The firm itself makes the decision to seek to list or not to list its securities on an exchange. Typically, the stocks of new and small companies are traded over the counter—there is simply not enough activity to justify the use of an auction market for such stocks. As the company grows, establishes an earnings record, expands the number of shares outstanding, and increases its list of stockholders, it may decide to apply for listing on one of the regional exchanges. For example, a Chicago company might list on the Midwest Stock Exchange, or a West Coast company might list its stock on the Pacific Coast Exchange. As the company grows still more, and as its stock becomes distributed throughout the country, it may seek a listing on the American Stock Exchange, the smaller of the two national exchanges. Finally, if it becomes one of the nation's leading firms, it could switch to the Big Board, the New York Stock Exchange.

Assuming a company qualifies, many people believe that listing is beneficial both to it and to its stockholders. Listed companies receive a certain amount of free advertising and publicity, and their status as a listed company enhances their prestige and reputation. This may have a beneficial effect on the sales of the products of the firm, and it probably is advantageous in terms of lowering the required rate of return on the common stock. Investors respond favorably to increased information, increased liquidity, and increased prestige. By providing investors with these services in the form of listing their companies' stocks, financial managers may lower their firms' costs of capital.

ISSUING COMMON STOCK

Suppose a firm has analyzed its investment opportunities, concluded that its profitable investments exceed its internally generated funds, and decided to float a stock issue to raise the needed capital. In this section we trace through the procedures for marketing the issue.

Choosing an Investment Banker Most established firms will already have a working relationship with an investment banking firm. If not, or if the firm is not satisfied with the service it has been receiving, an underwriter must be selected.

Deciding Whether the Issue Should Be a Rights Offering If the firm's stockholders have the preemptive right, then the stock must be offered to the existing stockholders. Otherwise, the firm, in consultation with its bankers, must decide whether to offer the stock to existing stockholders or to the general public. The complex technical issues which are involved in this decision are discussed in Appendix 14B.

Registration with the SEC A registration statement must be filed with the SEC. This statement will be completed by the firm and its investment banker, with the aid of lawyers and accountants who specialize in security offerings. The statutes set a twenty day waiting period (which in practice may be shortened or lengthened by the SEC) during which time the SEC staff analyzes the registration statement to determine whether there are any omissions or misrepresentations of fact. The SEC may file exceptions to the registration statement or may ask for additional information from the issuing company or the underwriters during the examination period. During this period the investment bankers are not permitted to offer the securities for sale, although they may print preliminary prospectuses with all the customary information except the offering price.

Determining Flotation Costs The firm and its investment bankers must agree on the banker's compensation, or the flotation cost involved in issuing the stock. As shown in Table 13–4 in Chapter 13, the costs of issuing common stock generally range from 23.7 percent of the issue price on small issues to 3.5 percent on issues involving stock with a value of over $50 million. Since the figures in the table are *averages,* the extremes are even wider—cases of flotation costs of 25 percent have been observed on very small offerings.

Flotation costs to the firm consist of two elements—compensation to the investment banker plus legal, accounting, printing, and other out-of-pocket costs borne by the issuer. In addition, if a firm is small and is going public for the first time, the underwriters may accept warrants as part of their compensation. (Warrants are options to buy stock; they are discussed in Chapter 22.) Assuming warrants are not involved, the investment banker's compensation consists of the *spread* between the price the company is paid for the stock and the price at which the stock is sold to the public, called the *offering price.* Naturally, the company wants to receive the highest possible price for the stock, so it bargains with the banker over both the offering price and the spread. The higher the offering price and the lower the spread, the more the company receives per share of stock sold; and the more it receives per share, the fewer the number of shares required to raise a given amount of money.

Setting the Offering Price The offering price is not generally determined until the close of the registration period. There is no universally followed practice, but one common arrangement for a new issue of stock calls for the investment banker to buy the securities at a prescribed number of points below the closing price on the last day of registration. Suppose that in October 1979 the stock of Carter Chemical Company had a current price of $28.50 and that it had traded between $25 and $30 a share during the previous three months. Suppose further that Carter and its underwriter agreed that the investment banker would buy 10 million new shares at $1 below the closing price on the last day of registration. If the stock closed at $26 on the day the SEC released the issue, Carter would receive $25 a share. Typically, such agreements have an escape clause that provides for the contract to be voided if the price of the securities ends below some predetermined figure. In the illustrative case, this "upset" price might be set at $25 a share. Thus, if the closing price of the shares on the last day of registration had been $24.50, Carter would have had the option of withdrawing from the agreement.[10]

The investment banker will have an easier job if the issue is priced relatively low. The issuer of the securities naturally wants as high a price as possible. Some conflict of interest on price therefore arises between the investment banker and the issuer. If the issuer is financially sophisticated and makes comparisons with similar security issues, the investment banker will be forced to price close to the market.

---

10 The type of arrangement described above holds, of course, only for additional offerings of stock of firms whose old stock was previously traded. When a company goes public for the first time, the investment banker and the firm must negotiate a price.

The offering price may have to be set at a price substantially below the preoffering market price. Consider Figure 14–1, in which d_0 is the estimated market demand curve for Carter Chemical stock and S_0 is the number of shares outstanding. Initially, there are 50 million shares outstanding, and the equilibrium price of the stock is $28.50. As we saw in Chapter 5, this price is found in accordance with the following equation:

$$P_0 = \frac{D_1}{k_s - g} = \frac{\$2}{0.12 - 0.05} = \$28.57 \approx \$28.50.$$

Figure 14–1
Estimated Demand Curve for Carter Chemical
Company's Common Stock

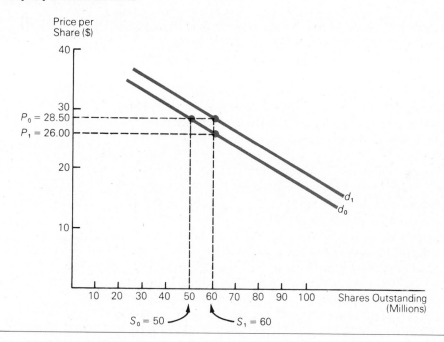

The values shown for D_1, k_s, and g are the *estimates of an average stockholder.* Some stockholders doubtlessly regard Carter as being less risky than others, hence assign it a lower value for k_s. Similarly, some stockholders will estimate the company's growth rate higher than others, so use $g > 5$ percent when calculating the stock's intrinsic value. Thus, there are some investors who think Carter's stock is worth more than $28.50 and others who think it is worth less, but the marginal investor thinks the stock is worth $28.50. Accordingly, this is its current price.

If Carter is to sell another 10 million shares of stock, it will have to either attract some investors who are apparently not willing to own the stock at the $28.50 price or else induce present stockholders to buy additional shares.

There are two ways this can be accomplished: (1) by reducing the price of the stock or (2) by "promoting" or "advertising" the company and thus shifting the demand curve to the right.[11] If the demand curve does not shift at all, we see from Figure 14–1 that the only way the 10 million additional shares could be sold would be by setting the offering price at $26 per share. However, if the investment bankers can promote the stock sufficiently to shift the demand curve out to d_1, then the offering price can be set equal to the current market price, $28.50.[12]

The extent to which the demand curve can be shifted depends primarily on two factors: (1) what investors think the company can do with the money brought in by the stock sale, and (2) how effectively the brokers promote the issue. If investors can be convinced that the new money will be invested in highly profitable projects that will substantially raise earnings and the earnings growth rate, then the shift will occur, and the stock price may even go above $28.50. Even if investors do not radically change their expectations about the company's fundamental factors, the fact that thousands of stockbrokers telephone their clients with suggestions that they consider purchasing Carter's stock may shift the demand curve. The extent to which this promotion campaign is successful in shifting the demand curve depends, of course, upon the effectiveness of the investment banking firm. Therefore, Carter's financial manager's perceptions about the effectiveness of different investment bankers will be an important factor in the choice of an underwriter.

One final point is that *if pressure from the new shares drives down the price of the stock, all shares outstanding—not just the new shares—are affected.* Thus, if Carter's stock should fall from $28.50 to $26 as a result of the financing, and if the price should remain at this new level, then the company would incur a loss of $2.50 on each of the 50 million shares previously outstanding, or a total market value loss of $125 million. In a sense, this loss could be called a *flotation cost,* as it is a cost associated with the new issue. However, most observers feel that even though pressure may drive stock prices down immediately after a new issue is announced, demand curves do shift over time, so Carter Chemical would not be likely to suffer a permanent loss anywhere close to $125 million on an issue such as this one.

The matter of flotation costs, including price pressure effects, is considered again in Chapter 16, where we calculate the marginal cost of capital and show how this cost is used in capital budgeting decisions.

---

11 It should be noted that investors can buy newly issued stock without paying normal brokerage commissions, and brokers are careful to point this out to potential purchasers. Thus, if an investor were to buy Carter stock at $28.50 in the regular market, the commission would be about 1 percent, or 28 cents per share. If the stock were purchased in an underwriting, this commission would be avoided.

It should also be noted that many academicians argue that the demand curve for a firm's stock is either horizontal or has only a slight downward slope. Most corporate treasurers, on the other hand, feel that there is a decided downward slope to the curve, especially if the sale occurs at a time when the stock is "out of favor" with the investing public. The controversy has not been resolved by empirical studies.

12 The supply curve is a vertical line, first at 50 million and then, after the new issue, at 60 million.

Formation of an Investment Banking Group Stocks are generally offered to the public the day after the issue is cleared by the SEC. Investors are required to pay for the stock within ten days, and the investment bankers must pay the issuing firm within four days of the time the offering officially begins. Typically, the bankers sell the stock within a day or two after the offering begins, but on occasion the bankers miscalculate, set the offering price too high, and are unable to move the issue. At still other times, the stock market declines during the offering period, forcing the bankers to reduce the price of the stock. In either instance, the firm receives the price that was agreed upon, and the bankers must absorb any losses that may be incurred.

Because they are exposed to large potential losses, investment bankers typically do not handle the purchase and distribution of issues singlehandedly unless the issue is a very small one. If the sum of money involved is large and the risk of price fluctuation is substantial, investment bankers form *underwriting syndicates* in an effort to minimize the amount of risk each one carries.

In addition to the underwriting syndicate, on larger offerings still more investment bankers are included in the *selling group,* which handles the distribution of securities to individual investors. The selling group includes dealers who take relatively small participations, or shares of the total issue, from the members of the underwriting syndicate. Thus, the underwriters act as wholesalers, while members of the selling group act as retailers. The number of houses in a selling group depends partly upon the size of the issue; for example, the one for Communications Satellite Corporation consisted of 385 members.

Maintenance of the Secondary Market In the case of a large, established firm such as Carter Chemical, the investment banking firm's job is finished once it has disposed of the stock and turned the net proceeds over to the issuing firm. However, in the case of a company going public for the first time, the investment banker is under some obligation to maintain a market in the shares after the issue has been completed. Such stocks are typically traded in the over-the-counter market, and the principal underwriter generally agrees to "make a market" in the stock so as to keep it reasonably liquid. The company wants a good market to exist for its stock, as do the stockholders. Therefore, if the banking house wants to do business with the company in the future, keep its own brokerage customers happy, and have future referral business, it will hold an inventory and help to maintain an active secondary market in the stock.

REGULATION OF SECURITY MARKETS

The operations of investment bankers, exchanges, and over-the-counter markets are regulated by the Securities and Exchange Commission (SEC) and, to a lesser extent, by each of the fifty states. Certain rules apply to new securities, while others apply to securities traded in the secondary markets:

1. *Elements in the regulation of new issues by the SEC:*
   a. The SEC has jurisdiction over all interstate offerings to the public in amounts of $500,000 or more.
   b. Securities must be registered at least twenty days before they are publicly offered. The registration statement provides financial, legal, and technical information about the company. A prospectus summarizes this information for use in selling the securities. SEC lawyers and accountants analyze both the registration statement and the prospectus, and if the information is inadequate or misleading, the SEC will delay or stop the public offering.
   c. After the registration has become effective, the securities may be offered if accompanied by the prospectus. Preliminary or "red herring" prospectuses may be distributed to potential buyers during the waiting period.
   d. If the registration statement or prospectus contains misrepresentations or omissions of material facts, any purchaser who suffers a loss may sue for damages. Severe penalties may be imposed on the issuer, its officers, directors, accountants, engineers, appraisers, underwriters, and all others who participated in the preparation of the registration statement.

2. *Elements in the regulation of outstanding securities:*
   a. The SEC regulates all national securities exchanges. Companies whose securities are listed on an exchange must file reports similar to registration statements with both the SEC and the stock exchange and must provide periodic reports as well.
   b. The SEC has control over corporate *insiders.* Officers, directors, and major stockholders of a corporation must file monthly reports of changes in their holdings of the stock of the corporation. Any short-term profits from such transactions are payable to the corporation.
   c. The SEC has the power to prohibit manipulation by such devices as pools (aggregations of funds used to affect prices artificially) or wash sales (sales between members of the same group to record artificial transaction prices).
   d. The SEC has control over the proxy machinery and practices.
   e. Control over the flow of credit into security transactions is exercised by the Board of Governors of the Federal Reserve System. The Fed exercises this control through the *margin requirements,* which stipulate the maximum percentage of the purchase price of a security that can be borrowed. If a great deal of margin borrowing has been going on, then a decline in stock prices can result in inadequate coverages, which forces the stockbrokers to issue "margin calls," requiring investors either to put up more money or to have their margined stock sold to pay off their loans. Such forced sales further depress the stock market and can set

off a downward spiral. To prevent this, the Fed controls the volume of margin borrowing.

3. *State regulations*

   a. States have some control over the issuance of new securities within their boundaries. This control is usually exercised by a "Corporation Commissioner" or similar official.

   b. State laws relating to security sales are called "Blue Sky Laws" because they were put into effect to keep unscrupulous promoters from selling securities that offered the blue sky but actually had little or no asset backing.

In general, government regulation of securities trading is designed to insure that investors receive information that is as accurate as possible, that no one artificially manipulates (that is, drives up or down) the market price of a given stock, and that corporate insiders do not take advantage of their position to profit in their companies' stocks at the expense of other stockholders. Neither the SEC nor the state regulators can prevent investors from making foolish decisions or from having "bad luck," but they can and do help investors obtain the best data possible for making sound investment decisions.

SUMMARY

Our discussions of common stock focused on these items: (1) the balance sheet treatment of common stock; (2) the legal rights of individual stockholders, especially their control of the firm; (3) the types of common stock that are in use (e.g., "founders' shares"); (4) the market for common stocks; (5) the steps that a firm must go through when issuing new shares; and (6) the government's regulation of security markets. Cumulative voting and the use of rights when selling new issues of common stock are discussed in the appendices. The chapter is more descriptive than analytical, but a knowledge of the issues discussed here is essential to an understanding of finance.

Questions

14-1 This chapter is descriptive; it is designed to describe the key features and terms of the markets for common stock. Any investor, or anyone concerned with the financial operations of a business, should understand and be able to define the following terms. If you do not know what each term means, look it up in the chapter or in the glossary.

   a. Net worth
   b. Common equity
   c. Paid-in capital
   d. Book value per share
   e. Proxy; proxy fight

    f.   Preemptive right

    g. Class A and Class B stock; founders' shares

    h. Closely held corporations versus publicly held corporations

    i.   Secondary market; primary market

    j.   Going public

    k. New issue market

    l.   The organized exchanges

    m. The over-the-counter market

    n. Listed stock

    o. Flotation costs

    p. Offering price; spread

    q. Market pressure

    r.   Shift in the stock demand curve

    s.   SEC

14-2 Examine Table 14–1. Suppose Carter sold 2 million new shares, with the company netting $25 per share. Construct a pro forma statement of the equity accounts to reflect this sale.

14-3 Is it true that the "flatter," or more nearly horizontal, the demand curve for a particular firm's stock, the more important the role of investment bankers when the company sells a new issue of stock?

14-4 Company A has assets of $20 million, net income after taxes of $1 million, manufactures widgets, and is publicly owned. Company B is identical to A in every respect except that B's stock is all owned by its founder. If each firm sells stock to the public to raise $5 million of new money for corporate purposes, which would probably have the higher flotation cost? Why?

14-5 Draw an SML graph. Put dots on the graph to show (approximately) where you think a particular company's (a) common stock and (b) bonds would lie. Now put on a dot to represent a riskier company's common stock.

Problem

14-1 The Callaway Company is a small jewelry manufacturer. The company has been successful and has grown. Now Callaway is planning to sell an issue of common stock to the public for the first time, and it faces the problem of setting an appropriate price on its common stock. The company and its investment bankers feel that the proper procedure is to select firms similar to it with publicly traded common stock and to make relevant comparisons.

    Several jewelry manufacturers are similar to Callaway with respect to product mix, size, asset composition, and debt/equity proportions. Of these, Sonnet and Mailers are most similar. Data are given on the next page.

    a. Assume that Callaway has 100 shares of stock outstanding. Use this information to calculate earnings per share (EPS), dividends per share (DPS), and book value per share for Callaway.

    b. Based on your answer to Part a, do you think Callaway's stock would sell at a price in the same "ballpark" as Sonnet's and Mailers's, i.e., sell in the range of $25 to $100 per share?

	Sonnet	Mailers	Callaway (Totals)
Earnings per share, 1980	$ 4.50	$ 7.50	$1,200,000
Average, 1974–1980	3.00	6.00	900,000
Price per share, 1980	36.00	75.00	—
Dividends per share, 1980	2.25	3.75	600,000
Average, 1974–1980	1.80	3.75	480,000
Book value per share	30.00	75.00	9,000,000
Market/book ratio	120%	100%	—

c. Assuming that Callaway's management can split the stock so that the 100 shares could be changed to 1,000 shares, 100,000 shares, or any other number, would such an action make sense in this case? Why?

d. Now assume that Callaway did split its stock and now has 400,000 shares. Calculate new values for EPS, DPS, and book value per share.

e. What can you say about the relative growth rates of the three companies?

f. What can you say about their dividend payout policies?

g. Return on equity (ROE) can be measured as EPS/book value per share, or as total earnings/total equity. Calculate ROEs for the three companies.

h. Calculate P/E ratios for Sonnet and Mailers.

i. Now determine a range of values for Callaway's stock, with 400,000 shares outstanding, by applying Sonnet's and Mailers's P/E ratios, price/dividends ratios, and price/book value ratios to your data for Callaway. For example, one possible price for Callaway's stock is (P/E Sonnet)(EPS Callaway) = (8) ($3) = $24 per share. Similar calculations would produce a range of prices based on both Sonnet and Mailers data.

j. At what price do you think Callaway's shares should be offered to the public? You will want to find the *equilibrium price,* i.e., a price that will be low enough to induce investors to buy the stock, but not so low that it will rise sharply immediately after it is issued. Think about relative growth rates, ROEs, dividend yields, and total returns ($k = D/P + g$). Also, as you think about the appropriate price, recognize that when Howard Hughes let the Hughes Tool Company go public in December 1972, different investment bankers proposed prices that ranged from $20 to $30 dollars per share. Hughes naturally accepted the $30 price, and the stock jumped to $40 almost immediately. Nobody's perfect!

k. Finally, would your recommended price be different if the offering were by the Callaway family, selling some of their 400,000 shares, or if it were new stock authorized by the company? For example, another 100,000 shares could be authorized, which when issued would bring the outstanding shares up to 500,000, with 400,000 shares owned by the Callaways and 100,000 shares held by the public. If the Callaways sell their own shares, they receive the proceeds as their own personal funds. If the company sells newly issued shares, the company receives the funds and presumably uses the money to expand the business. (*Hint:* Think about [1] the balance sheet position of the company after each of the two types of stock offerings, and [2] what the company will do with the capital raised if the company rather than the family sells the stock. There is no clear-cut answer to this question; your answer will depend on your assumptions.)

APPENDIX 14A   CUMULATIVE VOTING

Two methods of voting are employed to elect directors. Under one method, which is called *noncumulative voting,* each stockholder can vote for each directorship up for election. Thus, if you own 100 shares of stock and six directors are to be elected, you can cast 100 votes each for six different candidates. *Cumulative voting,* on the other hand, permits multiple votes for a single director. Thus, under a cumulative voting system, using our illustrative case, you could cast all of your 600 votes for *one* director. In other words, you can accumulate your votes and cast 600 votes for *one* director, instead of giving 100 votes to each of *six* directors. Cumulative voting is designed to enable a minority group of stockholders to obtain some voice in the control of the company by electing at least one director to the board.

The nature of cumulative voting is illustrated by use of the following formula:

$$N = \frac{d \times S}{D + 1}. \tag{14A-1}$$

N = number of shares required to elect a desired number of directors. If N solves to be a fraction, then round up, while if N is an integer, add 1.0.

d = number of directors stockholder desires to elect.

S = total number of shares of common stock outstanding and entitled to vote.[1]

D = total number of directors to be elected.

The formula may be made more meaningful by an example. The ABC company will elect six directors. There are fifteen candidates and 100,000 shares entitled to vote. If a group desires to elect two directors, how many shares must it have?

$$N = \frac{2 \times 100,000}{6 + 1} = 28,572. \tag{14A-2}$$

Observe the significance of the formula. Here, a minority group wishes to elect one-third of the board of directors. It can achieve its goal by owning less than one-third of the number of shares of stock.[2]

Alternatively, assuming that a group holds 40,000 shares of stock in this company (here N = 40,000), how many directors would it be possible for the group to elect, following the rigid assumptions of the formula? The formula can be used in its present form or can be solved for d and expressed as

$$d = \frac{N(D + 1)}{S}. \tag{14A-3}$$

Inserting the figures, the calculation would be

$$d = \frac{40,000 \times 7}{100,000} = 2.8. \tag{14A-4}$$

---

1 An alternative that may be agreed to by the contesting parties is to define S as the number of shares *voted,* not *authorized to vote.* This procedure, which in effect gives each group seeking to elect directors the same percentage of directors as their percentage of the voted stock, is frequently followed. When it is used, a group that seeks to gain control with a minimum investment must estimate the percentage of shares that will be voted and then obtain control of more than 50 percent of that number.

2 Note also that at least 14,286 shares must be controlled to elect one director. As far as electing a director goes, any number less than 14,286 constitutes a useless minority.

The 40,000 shares could elect two and eight-tenths directors. Since directors cannot exist as fractions, the group can elect only two directors.

As a practical matter, suppose that in the above situation the total number of shares is 100,000. Hence 60,000 shares remain in other hands. The voting of all the 60,000 shares may not be concentrated. Suppose the 60,000 shares (cumulatively, 360,000 votes) not held by our group are distributed equally among ten candidates, 36,000 votes in total for each candidate. If our group's 240,000 votes are distributed equally for each of six candidates, we could elect all six directors even though we do not have a majority of the stock.

Actually, it is difficult to make assumptions about how the opposition votes will be distributed. What is shown here is a good example of game theory. One rule in the theory of games is to assume that your opponents will do the worst they can do to you and to counter with actions to minimize the maximum loss. This is the kind of assumption followed in the formula. If your opposition concentrates its votes in the optimum manner, what is the best you can do to work in the direction of your goal? Other plausible assumptions can be substituted if there are sufficient facts to support alternative hypotheses about the behavior of the opponents.

APPENDIX 14B   THE USE OF RIGHTS IN FINANCING

If the preemptive right is contained in a particular firm's charter, then it must offer any new common stock to existing stockholders. If the charter does not prescribe a preemptive right, the firm has a choice of making the sale to its existing stockholders or to the public at large. If the sale is to the existing stockholders, the stock flotation is called a *rights offering.* Each stockholder is issued an option to buy a certain number of new shares, and the terms of the option are contained on a piece of paper called a *right.* Each stockholder receives one right for each share of stock held. The advantages and disadvantages of rights offerings are described in this appendix.

Several issues confront the financial manager who is deciding on the details of a rights offering. The various considerations can be made clear by the use of illustrative data on the Southeast Company, whose balance sheet and income statement are given in Table 14B–1.

Table 14B–1
Southeast Company: Financial Statements
before Rights Offering

Partial balance sheet (before sale of new stock)

	Total debt	$ 40,000,000
	Common stock	10,000,000
	Retained earnings	50,000,000
Total assets $100,000,000	Total liabilities and capital	$100,000,000

Partial income statement (before sale of new stock)

Earnings before interest and taxes	$20,000,000
Interest on debt	4,000,000
Income before taxes	16,000,000
Taxes (50% assumed)	8,000,000
Earnings after taxes	8,000,000
Earnings per share (1,000,000 shares)	$8
Market price of stock (price/earnings ratio of 12.5 assumed)	$100

Southeast earns $8 million after taxes and has 1 million shares outstanding, so earnings per share are $8. The stock sells at 12.5 times earnings, or for $100 a share. The company plans to raise $10 million of new equity funds through a rights offering and decides to sell the new stock to shareholders for $80 a share. The questions facing the financial manager are these:

1. How many rights will be required to purchase a share of the newly issued stock?

2. What is the value of each right?
3. What effect will the rights offering have on the price of the existing stock?

We will now analyze each of these questions.

Number of Rights Needed to Purchase a New Share

Southeast plans to raise $10 million in new equity funds and to sell the new stock at a price of $80 a share. Dividing the subscription price into the total funds to be raised gives the number of shares to be issued:

$$\text{Number of new shares} = \frac{\text{Funds to be raised}}{\text{Subscription price}} = \frac{\$10,000,000}{\$80}$$

$$= 125,000 \text{ shares.}$$

The next step is to divide the number of new shares into the number of previously outstanding shares to get the number of rights required to subscribe to one share of the new stock. Note that stockholders always get one right for each share of stock they own, so

$$\begin{array}{c}\text{Number of rights needed to} \\ \text{buy a share of the stock}\end{array} = \frac{\text{Old shares}}{\text{New shares}} = \frac{1,000,000}{125,000}$$

$$= 8 \text{ rights.}$$

Therefore, a stockholder will have to surrender eight rights plus $80 to receive one of the newly issued shares. Had the subscription price been set at $95 a share, 9.5 rights would have been required to subscribe to each new share; if the price had been set at $10 a share, only one right would have been needed.

Value of a Right

It is clearly worth something to be able to buy for less than $100 a share of stock selling for $100. The right provides this privilege, so the right must have a value. To see how the theoretical value of a right is established, we continue with the example of the Southeast Company, assuming that it will raise $10 million by selling 125,000 new shares at $80 a share.

First, notice that the *market value* of the old stock was $100 million: $100 a share times 1 million shares. (The book value is irrelevant.) When the firm sells the new stock, it brings in an additional $10 million. As a first approximation, we assume that the total market value of the common stock increases by exactly this $10 million. Actually, the market value of all the common stock will go up by more than $10 million if investors think the company will be able to invest these funds at a return substantially in excess of the cost of equity capital, but it will go up by less than $10 million if investors are doubtful of the company's ability to put the new funds to work profitably in the near future.

Under the assumption that market value exactly reflects the new funds brought in, the total market value of the common stock after the new issue will be $110 million. Dividing this new value by the new total number of shares outstanding, 1.125 million, we obtain a new market value of $97.78 a share. Therefore, we see that after the financing has been completed, the price of the common stock will have fallen from $100 to $97.78.

Since the rights give the stockholders the privilege of buying for only $80 a share of stock that will end up being worth $97.78, thus saving $17.78, is $17.78 the value of each right? The answer is *no,* because eight rights are required to buy one new share; we must divide $17.78 by 8 to get the value of each right. In the example, each right is worth $2.22.

Ex Rights

The Southeast Company's rights have a very definite value, and this value accrues to the holders of the common stock. What will be the price of the stock if it is traded during the offering period? This depends on who will receive the rights, the old owners or the new. The standard procedure calls for the company to set a "holder-of-record date," then for the stock to go *ex rights* four trading days prior to the holder-of-record date. If the stock is sold prior to the ex-rights date, it is sold "rights on"; that is, the new owner will receive the rights. If the stock is sold on or after the ex-rights date, the old owner will receive them. The exact time at which the stock goes ex rights is at the close of business (say 5 P.M.) on the fifth trading day before the holder-of-record date. The following tabulation indicates what is involved:

		Stock Price
Rights on	Nov. 9	$100.00
	Nov. 10	100.00
Ex-rights date:	Nov. 11	97.78
	Nov. 12	97.78
	Nov. 13	97.78
	Nov. 14	97.78
Holder-of-record date:	Nov. 15	97.78

On October 15, Southeast Company announced the terms of the new financing, stating that rights would be mailed out on December 1 to stockholders of record as of the close of business on November 15. Anyone buying the old stock on or before November 10 will receive the rights; anyone buying the stock on or after November 11 will *not* receive the rights. Thus, November 11 is the *ex-rights date;* before November 11 the stock sells *rights on.* In the case of Southeast Company, the *rights-on price* is $100, while the *ex-rights price* is $97.78.

Formula Value of a Right

Rights On Equations have been developed for determining the value of rights without going through all the procedures described above. While the stock is still selling rights on, the value at which the rights will sell when they are issued can be found by use of the following formula:

$$\text{Value of one right} = \frac{\text{Market value of stock, rights on} - \text{Subscription price}}{\text{Number of rights required to purchase one share} + 1}.$$

$$R = \frac{M_0 - S}{N + 1}. \qquad (14B-1)$$

Here,

M_0 = rights-on price of the stock.
S = subscription price.
N = number of rights required to purchase a new share of stock.
R = value of one right.

Substituting the appropriate values for the Southeast Company, we obtain

$$R = \frac{\$100 - \$80}{8 + 1} = \frac{\$20}{9} = \$2.22.$$

This agrees with the value of the rights we found by the long procedure.

Ex Rights Suppose you are a stockholder in the Southeast Company. When you return to the United States from a trip to Europe, you read about the rights offering in the newspaper. The stock is now selling ex rights for $97.78 a share. How can you calculate the theoretical value of a right? Simply by using the following formula, which follows the logic described in preceding sections:

$$\text{Value of one right} = \frac{\text{Market value of stock, ex rights} - \text{Subscription price}}{\text{Number of rights required to purchase one share}}.$$

$$R = \frac{M_e - S}{N}. \qquad (14B-2)$$

$$R = \frac{\$97.78 - \$80}{8} = \frac{\$17.78}{8} = \$2.22.$$

Here, M_e is the ex-rights price of the stock.[1]

Effects on Position of Stockholders

Stockholders have the choice of exercising their rights or selling them. Those who have sufficient funds and want to buy more shares of the company's stock will

---

[1] We developed Equation 14B–2 directly from the verbal explanation given in the section, "Value of a Right." Equation 14B–1 can then be derived from Equation 14B–2 as follows:

1. Note that

$$M_e = M_0 - R. \qquad (14B-3)$$

2. Substitute Equation 14B–3 into Equation 14B–2, obtaining

$$R = \frac{M_0 - R - S}{N}. \qquad (14B-4)$$

exercise their rights. Others can sell theirs. In either case, provided the formula value of the right holds true, the stockholder will neither benefit nor lose by the rights offering. This statement can be illustrated by the position of an individual stockholder in the Southeast Company.

Assume the stockholder had eight shares of stock before the rights offering. The eight shares each had a market value of $100 a share, so the stockholder had a total market value of $800 in the company's stock. If the rights are exercised, one additional share can be purchased at $80 a share, a new investment of $80. The total investment is now $880, and the investor owns nine shares of the company's stock, which, after the rights offering, has a value of $97.78 a share. The value of the stock is $880, exactly what is invested in it.

Alternatively, if the eight rights are sold at their value of $2.22 a right, the investor will receive $17.78, ending up with the original eight shares of stock plus $17.78 in cash. The original eight shares of stock now have a market price of $97.78 a share. This new $782.24 market value of the stock, plus the $17.78 in cash, is the same as the original $800 market value of the stock. From a purely mechanical or arithmetical standpoint, the stockholders neither benefit nor lose from the sale of additional shares of stock through rights. Of course, if they forget to either exercise or sell the rights, or if brokerage costs of selling their rights are excessive, then stockholders can suffer losses. However, in general, the issuing firm makes special efforts to minimize brokerage costs, and adequate time is given to enable the stockholders to take some action, so their losses are minimal.

Notice that after a rights offering, the price of the company's stock will be lower than it was prior to the offering. Stockholders have not suffered a loss, however, because they receive the value of the rights. Thus, the stock price decline is similar in nature to a *stock split,* a process described in some detail in Chapter 17. The larger the underpricing in the rights offering, the greater the stock split effect—that is, the lower the final stock price. Thus, if a company wants to lower its price by a substantial amount, it will set the subscription price well below the current market price. If it does not want to lower the price very much, it will set the subscription price just enough below the current price to ensure that the

---

Footnote 1 (continued)

3. Simplify Equation 14B–4 as follows, ending with Equation 14B–1.

$$R = \frac{M_0 - S}{N} - \frac{R}{N}$$

$$R + \frac{R}{N} = \frac{M_0 - S}{N}$$

$$R\left(\frac{N + 1}{N}\right) = \frac{M_0 - S}{N}$$

$$R = \frac{M_0 - S}{N} \cdot \frac{N}{N + 1}$$

$$R = \frac{M_0 - S}{N + 1}. \tag{14B–1}$$

This completes the derivation.

market price will remain above the subscription price during the offering period and thus cause the new shares to be purchased and the new funds to come into the corporation.

Problems

14B-1 The common stock of Irving Development Company is selling for $55 in the market. The stockholders are offered one new share at a subscription price of $25 for every five shares held. What is the value of each right?

14B-2 American Appliance Company's common stock is priced at $72 a share in the market. Notice is given that stockholders may purchase one new share at a price of $40 for every seven shares held. You hold 120 shares at the time of notice.
   a. At approximately what price will each right sell in the market?
   b. Why will this be the approximate price?
   c. What effect will the issuance of rights have on the original market price? Why?

14B-3 Jane Thompson has 300 shares of Piper Industries. The market price per share is $75. The company now offers stockholders one new share to be purchased at $60 for every four shares held.
   a. Determine the value of each right.
   b. Assume that Jane (1) uses 80 rights and sells the other 220, or (2) sells 300 rights at the market price you have calculated. Prepare a statement showing the changes in her position in each case.

15 THE TARGET CAPITAL STRUCTURE

This chapter considers the proper mix of securities: What proportions of short-term debt, long-term debt, and common equity should be used to finance a business? As we shall see, the firm analyzes a number of factors, then establishes a *target capital structure.* This target may change over time as conditions vary, but at any given moment the firm's management does have a specific capital structure in mind, and individual financing decisions should be consistent with this target. If the actual debt ratio is below the prescribed ratio, expansion capital will probably be raised by issuing debt, while stock will probably be sold if the debt ratio is above the target level.

Capital structure policy involves a choice between risk and expected returns. Using more debt raises the riskiness of the firm's earnings stream, but more debt generally means a higher expected rate of return. Higher risk tends to lower the stock's price, but a higher expected rate of return raises it. *The optimal capital structure strikes a balance between these risks and returns and thus maximizes the price of the stock.*

TYPES OF RISK

In Chapter 5, when we examined risk from the viewpoint of the individual investor, we distinguished between *market risk,* which is measured by the firm's beta coefficient, and *total risk,* which includes both the beta risk and an element of risk which can be eliminated by diversification. Then, in Chapter 12, we examined risk from the viewpoint of the corporation, and we considered how capital budgeting affects the riskiness of the firm. We again distinguished between *beta risk* (the effect of a project on the firm's beta) and *corporate risk* (the effect of the project on the firm's total risk).

Now we introduce two other dimensions of the risk picture: (1) *business risk,* or the riskiness of the firm's operations if it used no debt, and (2) *financial risk,* the additional risk borne by the common stockholders as a result of the firm's use of debt.[1] Conceptually, the firm has a certain amount of risk inherent in its operations—this is its business risk. When it uses debt, it partitions this risk and concentrates most of it on one class of investors—the common stockholders. However, the common stockholders are compensated by a higher expected return. One of the financial manager's primary tasks is to determine the optimal capital structure.

BUSINESS RISK

The single most important determinant of a firm's capital structure is its *business risk,* which is defined as the uncertainty inherent in projections of future *operating income,* or *earnings before interest and taxes (EBIT).* Figure 15–1 gives some clues about Carter Chemical's business risk. The top graph shows the trend in EBIT over the past eleven years; this gives both security analysts and Carter's management an idea of the degree to which EBIT has varied in the past and might vary in the future. The bottom graph shows a subjectively estimated probability distribution of Carter's EBIT for 1979. The estimate was made at the beginning of 1979, and the expected value of $275 million was read from the trend line in Figure 15–1a. As the graphs indicate, actual EBIT in 1979 fell below the expected value.

Carter's past fluctuations in EBIT were caused by many factors—booms and recessions in the national economy, successful new products introduced both by Carter and by its competitors, labor strikes, price controls, fires in Carter's major plants, and so on. Similar events will doubtless occur in the future, and when they do, EBIT will rise or fall. Further, there is always the possibility that a long-term disaster might strike, permanently depressing the company's earning power; for example, a competitor could introduce a new product that might permanently lower Carter's earnings.[2]

This element of uncertainty regarding Carter's future operating income is defined as the company's *basic business risk.* Business risk varies not only from industry to industry but also among firms in a given industry. Further, business risk can change over time. For example, the electric utilities were regarded for years as having little business risk, but a combination of events in the 1960s and 1970s altered the utilities' situation, produced sharp declines in their operating income, and greatly increased the industry's business risk. Now, food processors and grocery retailers are frequently given as examples of industries with low business risks, while cyclical manufacturing industries such as steel are regarded as having especially high business risks. Also, smaller companies, and those that are dependent

---

1 Using preferred stock also adds to financial risk.
2 Two examples of "safe" industries that turned out to be risky are the railroads just before automobiles, airplanes, and trucks took away most of their business, and Western Union just before telephones came on the scene. Numerous individual companies have been hurt, if not destroyed, by antitrust actions, fraud, or plain old bad management.

Figure 15-1
Carter Chemical Company: Trend in EBIT,
1969-1979, and Subjective Probability
Distribution of EBIT, 1979

(a) Trend in Earnings before Interest and Taxes (EBIT)

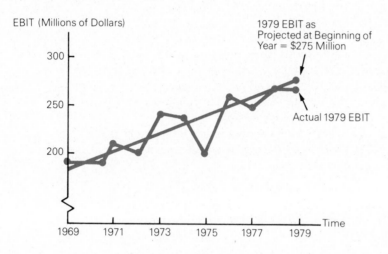

(b) Subjective Probability Distribution of EBIT

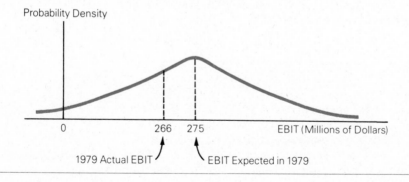

on a single product, are often regarded as having a high degree of business risk.[3]

Business risk depends on a number of factors, the more important of which include the following:

3 We have avoided any discussion of market versus company-specific risk in this section. We note now (1) that any action which increases business risk will generally increase a firm's beta coefficient but (2) that a part of business risk as we define it will generally be company-specific, hence subject to elimination by diversification by the firm's stockholders. This point is discussed at some length later in this chapter.

1. *Demand variability.* The more stable the demand for a firm's products, other things held constant, the lower its business risk.
2. *Sales price variability.* Firms whose products are sold in highly volatile markets are exposed to more business risk than similar firms whose output prices are more stable.
3. *Input price variability.* Firms whose input prices are highly uncertain are exposed to a high degree of business risk.
4. *Ability to adjust output prices for changes in input prices.* Some firms are better able to raise their own output prices when input costs rise than are others. The greater the ability to adjust output prices, the lower the degree of business risk, other things held constant. This factor has become increasingly important during the past few years because of inflation.
5. *The extent to which costs are fixed: operating leverage.* If a high percentage of a firm's costs are fixed, hence do not decline when demand falls off, then it is exposed to a relatively high degree of business risk. This point is discussed at length in the next section.

Each of these factors is determined partly by the firm's industry characteristics, but each of them is also controllable to some extent. For example, most firms can, through their marketing policies, take actions to stabilize both unit sales and sales prices. However, this stabilization may require firms to spend a great deal on advertising and/or price concessions in order to get their customers to commit to purchase fixed quantities at fixed prices in the future. Similarly, firms such as Carter Chemical may reduce the volatility of future input costs by negotiating long-term labor and materials supply contracts, but they may have to agree to pay prices above the current spot price level to obtain these contracts.[4]

OPERATING LEVERAGE

As was noted above, business risk depends in part on the extent to which a firm builds fixed costs into its operations—if fixed costs are high, even a small decline in sales can lead to a large decline in EBIT, so, other things held constant, the higher a firm's fixed costs, the greater its business risk. Higher fixed costs are generally associated with more highly automated, capital intensive firms and industries. Also, businesses that employ highly skilled workers who must be retained and paid even during business recessions have relatively high fixed costs.

If a high percentage of a firm's total costs are fixed costs, then the firm is said to have a high degree of operating leverage. In physics, leverage implies the use of a lever to raise a heavy object with a small force. In

---

4 For example, in the summer of 1977 utilities could buy coal in the spot market for about $20 per ton. Under a five year contract, coal cost about $40 per ton. Clearly, the price for reducing uncertainty was high!

politics, if people have leverage, their smallest word or action can accomplish a lot. *In business terminology, a high degree of operating leverage, other things held constant, implies that a relatively small change in sales results in a large change in operating income.*

Figure 15–2 illustrates the concept of operating leverage by comparing the results that a new firm can expect if it uses different degrees of leverage. Plan A calls for a relatively small amount of fixed charges—here the firm would not have much automated equipment, so its depreciation, maintenance, property taxes, and so on would be low. Note, however, that under Plan A the total cost line has a relatively steep slope, indicating that variable costs per unit are higher than they would be if the firm used more leverage. Plan B calls for a higher level of fixed costs. Here the firm uses automated equipment (with which one operator can turn out a few or many units at the same labor cost) to a much larger extent. The breakeven point is higher under Plan B: breakeven occurs at 40,000 units under Plan A versus 60,000 units under Plan B.[5]

How does operating leverage affect business risk? *Other things held constant, the higher a firm's operating leverage, the higher its business risk.* This point is demonstrated in Figure 15–3, where we show how probability distributions for EBIT under Plans A and B are developed.

The top section of Figure 15–3 gives the probability distribution of sales. This distribution depends on how demand for the product varies, not on whether the product is manufactured by Plan A or by Plan B. Therefore, the same sales probability distribution applies to both production plans, and expected sales are $220,000, but with a range from zero to about $500,000, under either plan.

We can use the information on the sales probability distribution, together with the operating profit (EBIT) at each sales level as shown in Column 4 of the tables in the lower part of Figure 15–2, to develop probability distributions for EBIT under Plans A and B. The calculations are shown in the footnote, with the resulting distributions shown in the lower part of Figure 15–3.[6] Plan B has a higher expected level of EBIT, but it also entails a much higher probability of large losses. Clearly, Plan B, the one with more

---

5 Algebraic procedures for determining breakeven points and for analyzing operating leverage are discussed in Appendix 15A.

6 The construction of the EBIT probability distributions in Figure 15–3 simply involves applying the sales probability distribution to the EBIT figures in the table contained in Figure 15–2. Exactly the same procedures as were discussed in Chapter 5 are involved. To illustrate, Figure 15–3 is a continuous version of the following discrete probability distribution for sales, hence EBIT:

Probability	Sales	$EBIT_A$	$EBIT_B$
0.05	$ 0	$−20.00	$−60.00
0.20	100	5.00	−10.00
0.50	220	35.00	50.00
0.20	325	61.25	102.50
0.05	500	105.00	190.00
Expected sales	$220		
Expected EBIT		$35.00	$50.00
Standard deviation		$26.72	$53.40

Figure 15-2
Illustration of Operating Leverage

Plan A

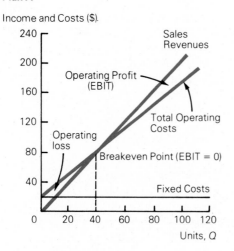

Selling price = $2.00
Fixed costs = $20,000
Variable costs = $1.50 Q

Plan B

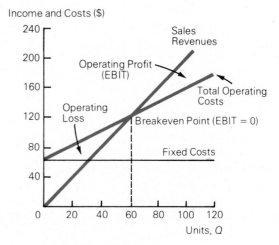

Selling price = $2.00
Fixed costs = $60,000
Variable costs = $1.00 Q

Units Sold, Q	Sales	Operating Costs	Operating Profit (EBIT)
20,000	$ 40,000	$ 50,000	−$ 10,000
40,000	80,000	80,000	0
60,000	120,000	110,000	10,000
80,000	160,000	140,000	20,000
100,000	200,000	170,000	30,000
110,000	220,000	185,000	35,000
120,000	240,000	200,000	40,000

Units Sold, Q	Sales	Operating Costs	Operating Profit (EBIT)
20,000	$ 40,000	$ 80,000	−$40,000
40,000	80,000	100,000	− 20,000
60,000	120,000	120,000	0
80,000	160,000	140,000	20,000
100,000	200,000	160,000	40,000
110,000	220,000	170,000	50,000
120,000	240,000	180,000	60,000

fixed costs and a higher degree of operating leverage, is riskier. *In general, holding other things constant, the higher the degree of operating leverage, the greater the degree of business risk as measured by variability of EBIT.*

To what extent can firms control their operating leverage? For the most part, operating leverage is determined by technology. Electric utilities, telephone companies, airlines, steel mills, and chemical companies simply *must* have heavy investments in fixed assets; this results in high fixed costs and operating leverage. Grocery stores, on the other hand, generally have

Figure 15–3
Analysis of Business Risk

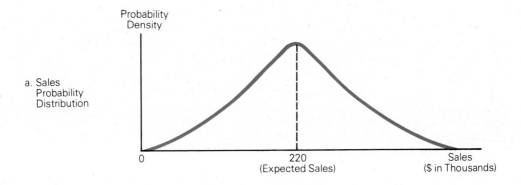

a. Sales Probability Distribution

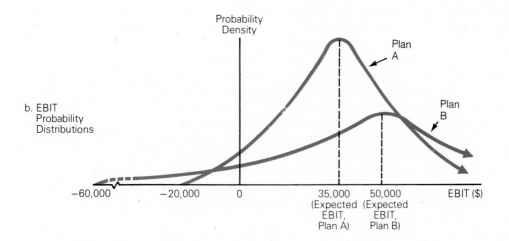

b. EBIT Probability Distributions

significantly lower fixed costs, hence lower operating leverage. Still, all firms have some control over their operating leverage. For example, an electric utility can expand its generating capacity by building either a nuclear reactor or a coal-fired plant. The nuclear generator would require a larger investment in fixed assets, which would involve higher fixed costs, but its variable operating costs would be relatively low. The coal plant, on the other hand, would require a smaller investment in fixed assets and would have lower fixed costs, but the variable costs (for coal) would be high. Thus, by its capital budgeting decisions a utility (or any other company) can influence its operating leverage, hence its basic business risk.

The concept of operating leverage was, in fact, originally developed for use in making capital budgeting decisions. Alternative methods for producing a given product often have different degrees of operating leverage, hence different breakeven points and different degrees of risk. Carter Chemical and other companies regularly undertake a type of breakeven analysis (the sensitivity analysis discussed in Chapter 12) as a part of their capital budgeting processes. Still, once a corporation's operating leverage has been established, the degree of this leverage influences its capital structure decisions. This point is covered next.

FINANCIAL LEVERAGE

Whereas operating leverage refers to the use of fixed operating costs, *financial leverage refers to the use of fixed income securities—debt and preferred stock.* In this section, we show how financial leverage affects a firm's expected earnings per share, the riskiness of these earnings, and consequently the price of the firm's stock. As we shall see, the value of a firm that has no debt first rises as it substitutes debt for equity, then hits a peak, and finally declines as the use of debt becomes excessive. The objective of our analysis is to determine the point at which value is maximized; this point is then used as the *target capital structure.*

We can illustrate the effects of financial leverage with the data for Firm B. As shown in Table 15–1, the company now has no debt. Should it continue the policy of using no debt, or should it start using financial leverage? And if it does decide to substitute debt for equity, how far should it go? As in all such decisions, *the correct answer is that it should choose the capital structure that maximizes the price of its stock.*

Since the price of a share of stock is the present value of the stock's expected future dividends, if the use of financial leverage is to affect the stock's price, it must do so by changing either the expected dividend stream or the required rate of return on equity (k_s), or both. We first consider the effect of capital structure on earnings and dividends; then we examine its effect on k_s.

Table 15–1
Data on Firm B

I. Balance Sheet on 12/31/79

Current assets	$100,000	Debt	$ 0
Net fixed assets	100,000	Common equity (10,000	
		shares outstanding)	200,000
Total assets	$200,000	Total claims	$200,000

II. Income Statement for 1979

Sales		$200,000
Fixed operating costs	$ 40,000	
Variable operating costs	120,000	160,000
Earnings before interest and taxes (EBIT)		$ 40,000
Interest		0
Taxable income		$ 40,000
Taxes (40%)		16,000
Net income after taxes		$ 24,000

III. Other Data

1. Earnings per share = EPS = $24,000/10,000 shares = $2.40.
2. Dividends per share = DPS = $24,000/10,000 shares = $2.40. (Thus Firm B pays all of its earnings out as dividends.)
3. Book value per share = $200,000/10,000 shares = $20.
4. Market price per share = P_0 = $20. Thus, the stock sells at its book value.
5. Price/earnings ratio = P/E = $20/$2.40 = 8.33 times.

The Effects of Financial Leverage on Expected EPS

Changes in the use of debt will cause changes in earnings per share (EPS), and consequently in the stock price. To understand the relationship between financial leverage and EPS, consider first Table 15–2, which shows how Firm B's cost of debt would vary if it used different percentages of debt in its capital structure. Naturally, the higher the percentage of debt, the riskier the debt, hence the higher the interest rate lenders will charge.

Table 15–2
Interest Rates for Firm B with Different
Debt/Assets Ratios

Amount Borrowed	Debt/Assets Ratio (Percent)[a]	Interest Rate, k_d, on All Debt (Percent)
$20,000	10%	8.0%
$40,000	20	8.3
$60,000	30	9.0
$80,000	40	10.0
$100,000	50	12.0
$120,000	60	15.0

[a]We assume that the firm must borrow in increments of $20,000. Also, we assume that Firm B is unable to borrow more than $120,000, or 60 percent of assets, because of restrictions in its corporate charter.

Table 15–3 shows how expected EPS varies with changes in financial leverage. The top third of the table shows EBIT at sales of $100,000, $200,000, and $300,000. EBIT is independent of financial leverage: EBIT does depend on operating leverage, but *EBIT does not depend on financial leverage.*[7]

The middle third of Table 15–3 goes on to show the situation if Firm B continues to use no debt. Net income after taxes is divided by the 10,000 shares outstanding to calculate EPS. If sales are as low as $100,000, EPS will be zero, but EPS will rise to $4.80 at sales of $300,000.

The EPS at each sales level is next multiplied by the probability of that sales level to calculate the expected EPS, which is $2.40 if Firm B uses no debt. We also calculate the standard deviation of EPS to get an idea of the firm's risk at a zero debt ratio: $\sigma_{EPS} = \$1.52$.[8]

The lower third of the table shows the financial results that would occur if the company financed with a debt/assets ratio of 50 percent. In this situation, $100,000 of the $200,000 total capital would be debt. The interest rate on the debt, 12 percent, is taken from Table 15–2. With $100,000 of 12 percent debt outstanding, the company's interest expense in Table 15–3 is $12,000 per year. This is a fixed cost, and it is deducted from EBIT as calculated in the top section. Next, taxes are taken out, to derive total net income. Then we calculate EPS = net income after taxes ÷ shares outstanding. With debt = 0, there are 10,000 shares outstanding. However, if half the equity is replaced by debt (debt = $100,000), then there will be only 5,000 shares outstanding, and we use this fact to determine the EPS figures that will result at each sales level. With a debt/assets ratio of 50 percent, EPS will be −$1.44 if sales are as low as $100,000; it will rise to $3.36 if sales are $200,000; and it will soar to $8.16 if sales are as high as $300,000.

The EPS distributions under the two financial structures are graphed in

---

7 If we were analyzing a firm with either more or less operating leverage, the top section of Table 15–3 would be quite different. The range of EBIT over the different sales levels would be smaller if a lower degree of operating leverage were used, but wider if more operating leverage were employed. Also, in the real world, capital structure *does* at times affect EBIT. First, if debt levels are excessive, the firm will probably not be able to finance at all if its earnings are low at a time when interest rates are high. This could lead to a stop-start construction program and/or to the necessity of passing up good investment opportunities. Second, a weak financial situation brought on by too much debt could cause a firm to lose contracts. For example, companies such as General Motors examine closely the financial strength of potential suppliers, and if they are so weak that they might not be able to deliver materials as called for in the contract, they simply will not get the business. Third, financially strong companies are able to bargain hard with unions as well as with other suppliers; weaker companies may have to give in simply because they do not have the financial resources to carry on the fight. And fourth, a company with so much debt that bankruptcy is a serious threat will have difficulty attracting and retaining managers and employees, or will have to pay them premium salaries. People value job security, and financially weak companies simply cannot provide such protection. For all these reasons, it is not totally correct to say that a firm's financial policy has no effect on its operating income.

8 See Chapter 5 for a review of procedures for calculating standard deviations. Also, it should be noted that it is sometimes useful to go one step further in this analysis and to calculate the *coefficient of variation,* which is the standard deviation of EPS divided by expected EPS:

$$\text{Coefficient of variation} = (\sigma_{EPS})/(\text{Expected EPS}) = \$1.52/\$2.40 = 0.63.$$

The advantage of the coefficient of variation is that it permits better comparisons when the mean values of EPS vary, as they do here in the 50 percent and zero debt situations. Still, for illustrative purposes we shall use standard deviations rather than coefficients of variation.

Table 15–3
Firm B: EPS with Different Amounts of Financial Leverage (Thousands of Dollars except per Share Figures)

Probability of indicated sales	0.2	0.6	0.2
Sales	$100.0	$200.0	$300.0
Fixed costs	40.0	40.0	40.0
Variable costs (60% of sales)	60.0	120.0	180.0
Total costs (except interest)	$100.0	$160.0	$220.0
Earnings before interest and taxes (EBIT)	$ 0.0	$ 40.0	$ 80.0

Debt/assets (D/A) = 0%

Less interest	0.0	0.0	0.0
Earnings before taxes	0.0	40.0	80.0
Taxes (40%)[a]	0.0	(16.0)	(32.0)
Net income after taxes	$ 0.0	$ 24.0	$ 48.0
Earnings per share on 10,000 shares (EPS)[b]	$ 0.0	$ 2.40	$ 4.80
Expected EPS		$ 2.40	
Standard deviation of EPS[c]		$ 1.52	

Debt/assets (D/A) = 50%

Less interest (0.12 × $100,000)	$ 12.0	$ 12.0	$ 12.0
Earnings before taxes	(12.0)	28.0	68.0
Taxes (40%)[a]	4.8	(11.2)	(27.2)
Net income after taxes	($ 7.2)	$ 16.8	$ 40.8
Earnings per share on 5,000 shares (EPS)[b]	($ 1.44)	$ 3.36	$ 8.16
Expected EPS		$ 3.36	
Standard deviation of EPS[c]		$ 3.04	

[a]Assumes tax credit on losses.
[b]The EPS figures can also be obtained using the following formula, where the numerator amounts to an income statement at a given sales level laid out horizontally:

$$EPS = \frac{(Sales - Fixed\ cost - Variable\ costs - Interest)(1 - Tax\ rate)}{Shares\ outstanding} = \frac{(EBIT - I)(1 - t)}{Shares\ outstanding}.$$

For example, at $S = \$200,000$,

$$EPS_{D/A\ =\ 0} = \frac{(\$200,000 - \$40,000 - \$120,000 - 0)(0.6)}{10,000} = \$2.40.$$

$$EPS_{D/A\ =\ 0.5} = \frac{(\$200,000 - \$40,000 - \$120,000 - \$12,000)(0.6)}{5,000} = \$3.36.$$

Since the equation is linear, the indifference level of sales, S_I, can be found by setting $EPS_{D/A\ =\ 0}$ equal to $EPS_{D/A\ =\ 0.5}$ and solving for S_I:

$$EPS_{D/A\ =\ 0} = \frac{(S_I - \$40,000 - 0.6S_I - 0)(0.6)}{10,000} = \frac{(S_I - \$40,000 - 0.6S_I - \$12,000)(0.6)}{5,000} = EPS_{D/A\ =\ 0.5}$$

$$S_I = \$160,000.$$

[c]The procedure for calculating the standard deviation is explained in Chapter 5.

Figure 15–4. Although expected EPS is much higher if financial leverage is employed, the graph makes it clear that the risk of low or even negative EPS is also higher if debt is used.

Figure 15–4
Firm B: Probability Distribution of EPS with
Different Amounts of Financial Leverage

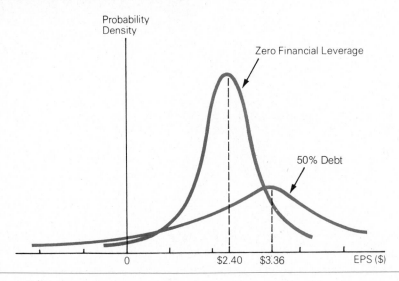

These relationships between expected EPS, risk, and financial leverage are extended in Table 15–4 and Figure 15–5. Here we see that expected EPS rises for a while as the use of debt increases—interest charges rise, but a smaller number of shares outstanding as debt is substituted for equity

---

Table 15–4
Firm B: Expected EPS and Standard Deviation
with Different Degrees of Financial Leverage[a]

Debt/Assets Ratio	Expected EPS	Standard Deviation of EPS
0%	$2.40	$1.52
10	2.56	1.69
20	2.75	1.90
30	2.97	2.17
40	3.20	2.53
50	3.36	3.04
60	3.30	3.79

[a]Values for D/A = 0 and 50 percent are taken from Table 15–3. Values at other D/A ratios are calculated similarly.

Figure 15–5
Firm B: Relationship between Expected EPS,
Risk, and Financial Leverage

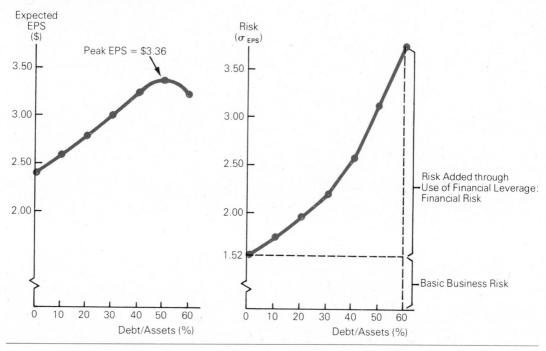

still causes EPS to increase. However, EPS peaks at a debt ratio of 50 percent. Beyond this ratio, interest rates rise so fast that EPS is depressed in spite of the falling number of shares outstanding. Risk, as measured by the standard deviation of EPS, rises continuously, and at an increasing rate, as debt is substituted for equity.

We see, then, that using leverage involves a risk-return tradeoff; higher leverage increases expected earnings per share (at least for a while), but it also increases the firm's risk. Exactly how this tradeoff should be resolved is discussed in the next section.

The Effect of Financial Leverage on Stock Prices

As we saw in the preceding section, Firm B's EPS is maximized at a debt/assets ratio of 50 percent. Does this mean that Firm B's optimal capital structure is 50 percent debt, 50 percent equity? Not necessarily. *The optimal capital structure is the one which maximizes the price of the firm's stock, and this may well call for a debt ratio different from the one which maximizes EPS.*

This statement is demonstrated in Table 15–5, which develops Firm B's estimated stock price at different debt/assets ratios. The data in Columns 1,

Table 15-5
Firm B: Stock Price Estimates with Different
Debt/Assets Ratios

Debt/ Assets (1)	k_d (2)	EPS (and DPS)[a] (3)	Estimated Beta (4)	$k_s = [R_F + b(k_M - R_F)]$[b] (5)	Implied Price[c] (6)	Resulting P/E Ratio (7)
0%	8.0%	$2.40	1.50	12.0%	$20.00	8.33
10	8.0	2.56	1.55	12.2	20.98	8.20
20	8.3	2.75	1.65	12.6	21.83	7.94
30	9.0	2.97	1.80	13.2	22.50	7.58
40	10.0	3.20	2.00	14.0	22.86	7.14
50	12.0	3.36	2.30	15.2	22.11	6.58
60	15.0	3.30	2.70	16.8	19.64	5.95

[a]We assume that Firm B pays all of its earnings out as dividends, hence EPS = DPS.
[b]We assume that $R_F = 6\%$ and $k_M = 10\%$. Therefore, at debt/assets equal zero, $k_s = 6\% + 1.5 (10\% - 6\%) = 6\% + 6\% = 12\%$. Other values of k_s are calculated similarly.
[c]Assuming all earnings are paid out as dividends, no retained earnings will be plowed back into the business, and growth in EPS and DPS will be zero. Hence, the zero growth stock price model developed in Chapter 4 can be used to estimate the price of Firm B's stock:

$$P_0 = \frac{DPS}{k_s}.$$

At debt/assets = 0,

$$P_0 = \frac{\$2.40}{0.12} = \$20.$$

Other prices were calculated similarly.

2, and 3 are taken from Tables 15-2 and 15-4. The beta coefficients shown in Column 4 were estimated. Recall from Chapter 5 that Stock B's beta measures its relative volatility as compared with an average stock. It has been demonstrated both theoretically and empirically that a firm's beta increases with its degree of financial leverage.[9] The exact nature of this relationship for a given firm is difficult to estimate, but the values given in Column 4 do show the approximate nature of the relationship.

Assuming that the riskless rate of return, R_F, is 6 percent and that the required return on an average stock, k_M, is 10 percent, we use the CAPM equation to develop the required rates of return for Firm B as shown in Column 5. Here we see that k_s is 12 percent if no financial leverage is used but that k_s rises to 16.8 percent if the company finances with 60 percent debt.

The zero growth stock valuation model developed in Chapter 4 is used, with the Column 3 values of DPS and the Column 5 values of k_s, to develop the implied stock prices shown in Column 6. Here we see that the expected stock price first rises with financial leverage, hits a peak of $22.86 at a debt/assets ratio of 40 percent, and then begins to decline. *Thus, Firm B's optimal capital structure calls for 40 percent debt.*

9 This point is discussed in detail in Chapters 15 and 16 of *Financial Management*, 2d ed.

The price/earnings ratios shown in Column 7 were calculated by dividing the implied price in Column 6 by the expected earnings given in Column 3. We use the pattern of P/E ratios as a check on the "reasonableness" of the other data. As a rule, P/E ratios do decline as the riskiness of a firm increases. Also, at the time the example was developed, the P/Es shown here were generally consistent with those of zero growth companies with varying amounts of financial leverage. Thus, the data in Column 7 reinforce our confidence that the implied prices shown in Column 6 are reasonable.

The EPS and stock price data in Table 15–5 are plotted in Figure 15–6. As the graph shows, the debt/assets ratio that maximizes Firm B's expected EPS is 50 percent, but the expected stock price is maximized with 40 percent debt. *Thus, the optimal capital structure calls for 40 percent debt, 60 percent equity.* Management should set its target capital structure at these ratios, and if the present ratios are off target, move toward the target when new security offerings are made.

TAXES, BANKRUPTCY COSTS, AND THE VALUE OF THE FIRM

Why does the expected stock price first rise as the firm begins to use financial leverage, then hit a peak, and finally decline when leverage becomes excessive? This pattern occurs primarily because of *corporate income taxes* and *bankruptcy costs.* Since interest on debt is tax deductible, the more debt a firm has, the greater the proportion of its operating income that flows through to investors, hence the higher the value of the firm. On the other hand, the larger the debt, the greater the risk of bankruptcy. At very high levels of debt, the odds are very great that bankruptcy will occur, and if this happens, lawyers may end up with almost as much of the firm's assets as do the investors.[10]

Figure 15–7 illustrates this concept. The left graph shows that, in the absence of bankruptcy costs, the price of the stock would increase continuously with the debt/assets ratio because of the tax shelter effect of interest. The middle graph shows that bankruptcy effects would cause the price of the stock to decrease with leverage if there were no corporate income taxes, or if interest payments were not deductible. The third graph combines the tax and bankruptcy effects. Here we see that the stock price peaks for Firm B at a debt/assets ratio of 40 percent, the same optimal structure we calculated earlier in the chapter.[11]

---

10 See Chapter 20 for a discussion of bankruptcy costs.
11 At 40 percent the absolute values of the slopes of the lines in the left and center graphs are equal, meaning that the marginal benefits of additional tax shelters are exactly offset by the marginal expected costs of bankruptcy. Actually, other costs besides bankruptcy expenses should be included in the center panel; for example, problems of retaining able workers and managers whose jobs are insecure, problems of obtaining favorable purchase or sales contracts if the firm might not be able to meet its contractual obligations, problems of getting loans from lenders who are penalized by regulators if their loan portfolios go sour, and so on. All of these factors are included in the term *bankruptcy costs.*

Figure 15–6
Firm B: Relationship between Debt/Assets
Ratio, EPS, and Estimated Stock Prices

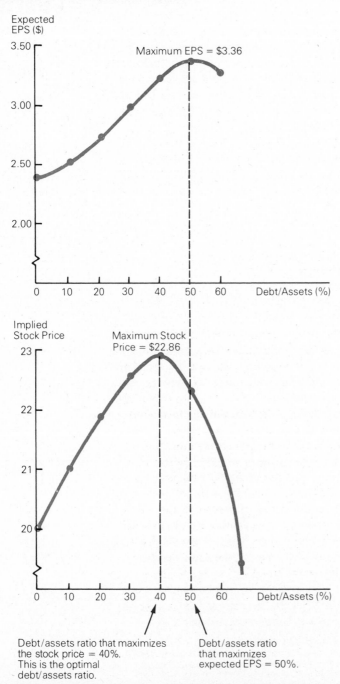

Figure 15–7
Firm B: Effects of Tax Deductions and
Bankruptcy Costs on Stock Value

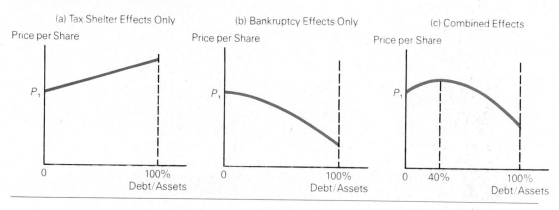

LIQUIDITY AND CASH FLOW ANALYSIS

There are some difficult problems with the type of analysis described above. Included are the following:

1. Because of the difficulties in determining exactly how P/E ratios and equity capitalization rates (k_s values) are affected by different degrees of financial leverage, management rarely, if ever, has sufficient confidence in this type of analysis to use it as the sole determinant of the target capital structure.
2. Many firms are not publicly owned. If the owners do not plan to ever have the firm go public, then potential market value data are irrelevant. However, an analysis based on implied market values for a privately owned firm is useful if the owner is interested in knowing how the market value of the firm would be affected by leverage should the decision be made to go public.
3. Even for publicly owned firms, the managers may be more or less "conservative" than the average stockholder, hence may set a somewhat different target capital structure than the one that would maximize the stock price. The managers of a publicly owned firm would never admit this, for unless they owned voting control, they would quickly be removed from office. However, in view of the uncertainties about what constitutes the value-maximizing structure, management could always say that the target capital structure employed is, in its judgment, the value-maximizing structure, and it would be difficult to prove otherwise.
4. Managers of large firms, especially those providing vital services such as electricity or telephones, have a responsibility to provide *continuous* service, so they must refrain from using leverage to the point where the

firm's long-run viability is endangered. Long-run viability may conflict with short-run stock price maximization.[12]

For all of these reasons, managers are very much concerned with the effects of financial leverage on the risk of bankruptcy, so an analysis of this factor is an important input in the capital structure decision. Accordingly, managements give considerable weight to such ratios as the *times interest earned ratio* (TIE). The lower this ratio, the higher the probability that a firm will default on its debt and be forced into bankruptcy.

Table 15–6 shows how Firm B's expected TIE ratio declines as the debt/assets ratio increases. When the debt/assets ratio is only 10 percent, the expected TIE is a high 25 times, but the interest coverage ratio declines rapidly as debt rises. Note, however, that these coverages are the expected values—the actual TIE will be higher if sales exceed the expected $200,000 level, but lower if sales fall below $200,000. The variability of the TIE ratios is highlighted in Figure 15–8, which shows the probability distributions of the ratios at debt/assets ratios of 40 percent and 60 percent. The expected TIE is much higher if only 40 percent debt is used. Even more important, with less debt there is a much lower probability of a TIE of less than 1.0, the level at which the firm is not earning enough to meet its required interest payment and is thus seriously exposed to the threat of bankruptcy.[13]

Table 15–6
Firm B: Expected Times Interest Earned Ratio at
Different Debt/Assets Ratios

Debt/Assets	TIE[a]
0%	Undefined
10	25.0
20	12.1
30	7.4
40	5.0
50	3.3
60	2.2

$^a\text{TIE} = \dfrac{\text{EBIT}}{\text{Interest}}.$

Example: Debt/Assets = 50%.

$\text{TIE} = \dfrac{\$40,000}{\$12,000} = 3.3.$

Data are from Tables 15–2 and 15–3.

---

12 Recognizing this fact, most public service commissions require utilities to obtain their approval before issuing long-term securities, and Congress has empowered the SEC to supervise the capital structures of public utility holding companies. However, in addition to concern over the firms' safety, which suggests low debt ratios, both managers and regulators recognize a need to keep all costs as low as possible, including the cost of capital. As we shall see in the next chapter, a firm's capital structure affects its cost of capital, so regulatory commissions and utility managers try to select capital structures that minimize the cost of capital, subject to the constraint that the firm's solvency is not endangered.

13 It should be noted that cash flows, which include depreciation, can be sufficient to cover required interest payments even though the TIE is less than 1.0. Thus, at least for a while, a firm can avoid bankruptcy even though its earnings are less than its interest charges.

Figure 15–8
Firm B: Probability Distributions of Times Interest
Earned Ratios with Different Capital Structures

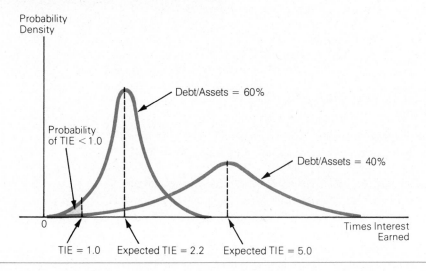

CAPITAL STRUCTURE AND MERGERS

One of the most exciting developments in the financial world during the 1970s was the high level of merger activity, especially takeovers. A *takeover* occurs when one firm buys out another over the opposition of the acquired firm's management. The acquired firm's stock is considered to be undervalued, so the acquiring firm will pay a premium of perhaps 50 percent to gain control. Mergers are discussed at length in Chapter 19, but it is useful to make these points now: (1) very often the acquiring firm issues debt and uses it to buy the target firm's stock; (2) this action effectively changes the enterprise's capital structure; and (3) the value enhancement resulting from the use of debt is apparently sufficient to cover the premium offered for the stock and still leave a profit for the acquiring company.

Recognizing the validity of the type of analysis described in this chapter literally led to the creation of companies whose major function was to acquire other companies as described above. The managers of these acquiring companies (often called "conglomerates") frequently made huge personal fortunes. Even shrewd individual investors, including a few professors, selected stock portfolios heavily weighted with prime acquisition targets and did well in the market. Of course, the managements of firms with low leverage ratios who did not want to be taken over could be expected to react by attempting to find their optimal debt levels and then issuing debt and repurchasing stock. Thereby, they would be raising the price of their stock and making their companies less attractive acquisition targets.

The game is far from over—indeed, it can never end, because economic shifts lead to continuing changes in optimal capital structures. This makes it especially important that the lessons to be learned from this chapter be thoroughly understood by everyone actively involved in financial management.

CHECKLIST OF FACTORS THAT INFLUENCE CAPITAL STRUCTURE DECISIONS

The factors listed and briefly discussed below all have an important, though hard to measure, bearing on the firm's choice of a target capital structure.

1. Sales Stability If its sales are relatively stable, a firm can safely take on more debt and incur higher fixed charges than can a company with unstable sales. Utility companies, because of their stable demand, have thus been able to undertake more debt financing than the average industrial firm.

2. Asset Structure Firms whose assets are suitable as security for loans tend to use debt rather heavily. Thus, real estate companies tend to be highly leveraged, while manufacturers with heavy investments in specialized machinery and work-in-process inventories employ less debt.

3. Operating Leverage Other things the same, a firm with less operating leverage is better able to employ financial leverage. Appendix 15A shows how operating and financial leverage interact to determine the overall impact of a decline in sales on operating income and net cash flows.

4. Growth Rate Other things the same, faster-growing firms must rely more heavily on external capital (see Chapter 7). Further, the flotation costs involved in selling common stock exceed those incurred when selling debt. Thus, to minimize financing costs, rapidly growing firms tend to use somewhat more debt than do slower-growth companies.

5. Profitability One often observes that firms with very high rates of return on investment use relatively little debt. Although there is no theoretical justification for this fact, the practical reason seems to be that very profitable firms such as IBM, 3M, and Xerox simply do not need to do much debt financing—their high profit margins enable them to do most of their financing with retained earnings.

6. Taxes Interest is a deductible expense, while dividends are not deductible. Hence, the higher a firm's corporate tax rate, the greater the advantage of using debt. This point is also discussed in more detail in Chapter 16.

7. Control The effect that debt or stock financing might have on a management's control position may influence its capital structure decision. If management has voting control (51 percent of the stock) but is not in a position to buy any more stock, debt may be the choice for new financings. On the other hand, a management group that is not concerned about voting control may decide to use equity rather than debt if the firm's financial situation is so weak that the use of debt might subject the firm to risk of default: if the firm goes into default, the managers will almost surely lose their jobs. However, if too little debt is used, management runs the risk of a takeover attempt; here some other company or management group tries to persuade stockholders to turn over control to the new group, which may plan to boost earnings by using financial leverage. In general, control considerations do not necessarily suggest the use of debt or equity, but if management is at all insecure, the effects of capital structure on control will certainly be taken into account.

8. Management Attitudes In the absence of proof that one capital structure will lead to higher stock prices than another, management can exercise its own judgment about a proper capital structure. Some managements tend to be more (or less) conservative than others, and thus use less (or more) debt than the average firm in their industry.

9. Lender and Rating Agency Attitudes Regardless of managers' own analyses of the proper leverage factors for their firms, there is no question but that lenders' and rating agencies' attitudes are frequently important determinants of financial structures. In the majority of cases, the corporation discusses its financial structure with lenders and rating agencies and gives much weight to their advice. But when management is so confident of the future that it seeks to use leverage beyond the norms for its industry, lenders may be unwilling to accept such debt increases or may do so only at a high price.

10. Market Conditions Conditions in the stock and bond markets undergo both long- and short-run changes, which can have an important bearing on a firm's optimal capital structure. For example, in 1974 after Consolidated Edison omitted its dividend for the first time in eighty years, there was simply no market for new issues of utility common stocks. Utilities that needed long-term capital were forced to go to the bond market. Actions such as this could represent either changes in their target capital structures or temporary departures from these targets, but the important point is that stock and bond market conditions at a point in time do influence the type of securities used for a given financing.

11. The Firm's Internal Conditions A firm's own internal conditions also have a bearing on its target capital structure. For example, suppose a firm has just successfully completed an R&D program and projects higher earnings in the immediate future. However, these new earnings are not yet anticipated by investors, hence are not reflected in the price of the stock. This company would not want to issue stock—it would prefer to finance with debt until the higher earnings materialize and are reflected in the stock price, at which time it might want to sell an issue of common stock, retire the debt, and return to its target capital structure.

VARIATIONS IN CAPITAL STRUCTURES AMONG FIRMS

As might be expected, wide variations in the use of financial leverage occur both among industries and among the individual firms in each industry. Table 15–7 illustrates this point. Retailers make heavy use of debt, especially short-term debt used to carry inventories. Manufacturing companies as a group use less debt, especially short-term debt. Within manufacturing, small firms with limited access to the stock market employ the most debt, and again the bulk of their liabilities are short-term. The data in the table are not broken down sufficiently to so indicate, but the majority of the debt shown for small manufacturers represents trade credit.

Table 15–7
Capital Components as a Percentage of Total
Capital, 1978

	Current Liabilities	Long-Term Debt	Total Liabilities	Equity
Retail trade	36%	20%	56%	44%
Manufacturing (all sizes)	23	23	46	54
Assets under $1 million	34	19	53	47
Assets over $1 billion	21	23	44	56
Selected manufacturing industries				
Aircraft	47	19	66	34
Electrical machinery	32	20	52	48
Steel	19	27	46	54
Drugs	17	20	37	63

Source: Federal Trade Commission, *Quarterly Financial Reports.*

Financing mixes also vary widely among manufacturing sectors. Aircraft companies are highly leveraged, borrowing heavily on a short-term basis to finance the construction of airplanes. Because of their long production cycle, aircraft manufacturers have large work-in-process inventories that must be financed. Aircraft manufacturers receive advances from their customers, and these advances are shown as current liabilities. Like the aircraft companies, manufacturers of electrical equipment also have long construction periods—for example, nuclear reactors take years to build— and short-term credit is often used to finance this construction. The drug companies, on the other hand, do not use much leverage. Their production period is short, and the uncertainties inherent in an industry that is both oriented toward research and development and exposed to lawsuits arising from adverse reactions to its products render the heavy use of leverage unwise.

SUMMARY

This chapter discussed the concepts of operating leverage, financial leverage, and target capital structure. *Operating leverage* refers to the use of fixed costs in operations, and it is related to the firm's production processes. The more operating leverage the firm has, the riskier are its securities, other things held constant.

Financial leverage refers to the use of debt in the capital structure—the more debt the firm employs, the higher its financial leverage. Financial leverage generally raises expected EPS, but it also increases the riskiness of the firm's securities. Because the risk of its stock and bonds increases as the debt/assets ratio rises, so do the interest rate on debt and the required rate of return on equity. Thus, leverage produces two opposing effects: higher EPS, which leads to a higher stock price, but increased riskiness, which depresses P_0. There is, however, a debt/assets ratio that strikes an optimal balance between these opposing effects; this ratio is called the *optimal capital structure,* and it is the one that maximizes the price of the firm's stock.

Although it is theoretically possible to determine the optimal capital structure, as a practical matter we cannot estimate this structure with precision. Accordingly, financial executives also analyze the effects of different capital structures on interest coverage ratios, which give clues about the probability of bankruptcy. Firms also tend to analyze such factors as sales stability, asset structure, and so on, and the final target capital structure is more judgmental than rigorously determined.

All of the concepts developed in this chapter are both used and extended in Chapters 16 and 17.

Questions

15-1 What is the uncertainty inherent in projections of future operating income called?

15-2 Firms with relatively high nonfinancial fixed costs are said to have a high degree of what?

15-3 "One type of leverage affects both EBIT and EPS. The other type affects only EPS." Explain what the statement means.

15-4 What is the relationship between *market* (or beta) risk and leverage?

15-5 Why is the following statement true? "Other things being the same, firms with relatively stable sales are able to incur relatively high debt ratios."

15-6 Why do public utility companies usually pursue a financial policy different from that of trade firms?

15-7 Some economists believe that swings in business cycles will not be as
wide in the future as they have been in the past. Assuming that they are
correct in their analysis, what effect might this added stability have on the
types of financing used by firms in the United States? Would your answer be
true for all firms?

15-8 Explain how tax effects and bankruptcy costs interact to determine a firm's
optimal capital structure.

15-9 Why is EBIT generally considered to be independent of financial leverage?
Why might EBIT actually be influenced by financial leverage at high debt
levels?

Problems

15-1 a. Given the graphs shown below, calculate the fixed costs, variable costs
per unit, and sales price for Firm A. Firm B's fixed costs are $120,000, its
variable costs per unit are $4, and its sales price is $8 per unit.

b. Which firm has the higher degree of operating leverage? Explain.

c. At what *sales level* do both firms earn the same profit?

Breakeven Charts for Problem 15–1

Firm A
Income and Costs
(Thousands of Dollars)

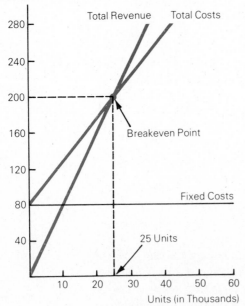

Firm B
Income and Costs
(Thousands of Dollars)

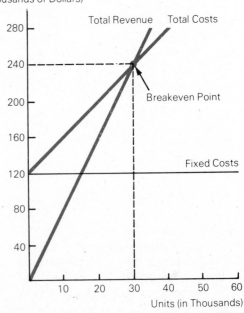

15-2 a. Given the following information, calculate the expected value for Firm C's EPS. EPS_A = $3.40, σ_A = $2.41; EPS_B = $2.80, σ_B = $1.97; and σ_C = $2.74.

	Probability				
	0.1	0.2	0.4	0.2	0.1
Firm A: EPS_A	($1.00)	$1.20	$3.40	$5.60	$7.80
Firm B: EPS_B	($0.80)	$1.00	$2.80	$4.60	$6.40
Firm C: EPS_C	($1.60)	$0.90	$3.40	$5.90	$8.40

b. Discuss the relative riskiness of the three firms' earnings.

15-3 Hank Bierman and Sid Smidt are planning to start a business to produce insulated window assemblies, utilizing a new process they recently patented. The enterprise is to be called B & S Window Company, and its initial plant will be located in upstate New York. As a result of optimistic reports by builders in the area, local banks and insurance companies are willing to supply the firm with debt capital on reasonably favorable terms. Stock can also be sold to local investors, so financing does not appear to be a problem.

Two production methods are available. Plan A calls for using a minimum amount of automated equipment, renting buildings, and purchasing—rather than manufacturing—major components. Under Plan A, fixed costs will be $1.8 million per year, while variable costs will be $70 per window assembly. Plan B calls for more operating leverage: fixed costs will be $4.8 million, but variable costs will be only $40 per unit. Regardless of which production process is used, the estimated sales price is $100 per unit. "Fixed costs" do not include any interest charges.

Bierman and Smidt are planning to promote their windows on the basis of fuel and air-conditioning cost savings. Although they will advertise for sales in the home improvement and renovation market, the major market will be to builders of new homes. Since new home starts are highly cyclical, sales will undoubtedly fluctuate widely. The two partners estimate that the following probability distribution of sales will apply, once the new firm is in full operation:

Probability	Sales in Units	Sales in Dollars
0.10	40,000	$ 4 million
0.15	80,000	$ 8 million
0.75	120,000[a]	$12 million

[a]The capacity limit is 120,000 under either production method.

a. Which production plan should Bierman and Smidt choose? To answer this question, calculate the breakeven point and expected EBIT under each plan, then analyze the riskiness of both A and B. Also, you should think about the probable amount of investment needed for each plan, as well as about the probable rate of return on this investment, in answering the question. Note, too, that the breakeven point can be determined graphically or by use of the equation

$$Q = \frac{F}{P - V},$$

where Q is the breakeven volume, F the fixed costs, and V the variable cost per unit. Finally, in answering this question you need only work with expected sales.

b. Regardless of your conclusion in Part a, assume that Bierman and Smidt decide on Plan B and that they require total capital of $10 million to put the plan into effect. Debt is available according to the following schedule (these rates apply to all the debt raised):

Amount Borrowed	Interest Rate
Up to $1 million	9.50%
$1.1 to $2 million	10.00
$2.1 to $3 million	10.75
$3.1 to $4 million	12.00
$4.1 to $5 million	15.00
$5.1 to $6 million	20.00
$6.1 to $7 million	27.00

Bierman and Smidt plan to invest their own funds in the new company, and also to sell stock to relatives, business associates, and employees. Some shares will also be offered to the public, so there will be a market price for the stock. Based on conversations with their investment bankers, they conclude that their firm's P/E ratio will depend on its debt/assets ratio. Specifically, they think the P/E ratio will vary with debt in accordance with the following schedule:

Debt/Assets	P/E
Up to 20%	10.00×
20.1 to 30%	9.75
30.1 to 40%	9.50
40.1 to 50%	9.00
50.1 to 60%	8.50
60.1 to 70%	7.50

If they want to maximize the price of their firm's stock, what capital structure should Bierman and Smidt choose? Use a 40 percent tax rate in your calculations. Also, assume that any funds not raised by debt will be obtained by selling common stock at a price of $10 per share. Hence, if they decide on a 50 percent debt ratio, they will raise $5 million as debt and $5 million as equity, selling 500,000 shares at $10 each. Disregard flotation costs in this problem. (*Hints:* [1] You can calculate expected sales and work only with this figure to generate expected EPS. [2] Rather than complete a table such as Table 15–3, you can use this equation to simplify calculations:

$$\text{EPS} = [(\text{EBIT} - \text{I})(1 - t)]/\text{Shares}.$$

[3] Note that this problem gives data on P/E ratios rather than on beta coefficients. Simply multiply calculated EPS values by the given P/E ratios to obtain the expected stock prices.)

c. At the expected sales level, and with your target debt/assets ratio, what is Bierman and Smidt's times interest earned ratio?

d. Suppose the debt is in the form of a five year term loan. What will be the annual amortization payment (interest plus principal)? Use this to calculate Bierman and Smidt's debt service coverage ratio. (The debt service ratio here is defined as EBIT/amortization payments. Also, PVIFA for 10.75 percent for five years = 3.719.)

e. What is Bierman and Smidt's expected rate of return on common equity?

f. Assume that Bierman and Smidt plan to pay out all earnings as dividends and thus to have a zero growth rate, and that investors are aware of this. What value of k_s is implied by the data you have been given?

g. Suppose this is *your* company and you plan to own 50 percent of the stock. Which capital structure would *you* choose? Would your choice be influenced by your other assets; that is, would it matter if your entire net worth were invested in this company versus a situation where you owned about $10 million of other securities?

APPENDIX 15A INTERRELATIONSHIP BETWEEN FINANCIAL AND OPERATING LEVERAGE

In our discussion of operating leverage in Chapter 15 we made no mention of financial leverage, and when we discussed financial leverage, the degree of operating leverage was assumed to be given. Actually, the two types of leverage are interrelated. For example, if Firm B could *reduce* its degree of operating leverage, then it could probably *increase* its use of financial leverage. On the other hand, if it decided to use more operating leverage, then its optimal capital structure would probably call for a lower debt ratio. Thus, there is a tradeoff between operating risk and financial risk.

The theory of finance has not been developed to the point where one can simultaneously determine the optimal levels of operating and financial leverage. However, we can get a better understanding of how operating and financial leverage interact through an analysis of the *degree of leverage*. The degree of operating leverage (DOL) is defined as the percentage change in operating profits associated with a given percentage change in sales volume, and Equation 15A–1 can be used to calculate the degree of operating leverage:[1]

$$\text{Degree of operating leverage at Point } Q = \frac{Q(P - V)}{Q(P - V) - F}. \qquad (15A-1)$$

$$\text{DOL} = \frac{S - VC}{S - VC - F}. \qquad (15A-1a)$$

Here Q is units of output, P is the average sales price per unit of output, V is the variable cost per unit, F is fixed operating costs, S is sales in dollars, and VC is total variable costs. Equation 15A–1a may also be thought of as the *contribution margin* divided by EBIT.

Applying Equation 15A–1a to data from Firm B at a sales level of $200,000 as shown in Table 15–3, we find its degree of operating leverage to be 2.0, so an X percent increase in sales will produce a 2 X percent increase in EBIT.

$$\text{DOL} = \frac{\$200,000 - \$120,000}{\$200,000 - \$120,000 - \$40,000}$$

$$= \frac{\$80,000}{\$40,000} = 2.0.$$

---

1 Equation 15A–1 is developed as follows. The change in output is defined as ΔQ. Fixed costs are constant, so the change in profits is $\Delta Q(P - V)$, where P is the price per unit and V the variable cost per unit. The initial profit is $Q(P - V) - F$, so the percentage change in profit is

$$\frac{\Delta Q(P - V)}{Q(P - V) - F}.$$

The percentage change in output is $\Delta Q/Q$, so the ratio of the change in profits to the change in output is

$$\text{DOL} = \frac{\dfrac{\Delta Q(P - V)}{Q(P - V) - F}}{\dfrac{\Delta Q}{Q}} = \frac{\Delta Q(P - V)}{Q(P - V) - F} \cdot \frac{Q}{\Delta Q} = \frac{Q(P - V)}{Q(P - V) - F}. \qquad (15A-1)$$

Operating leverage affects earnings before interest and taxes (EBIT), while financial leverage affects earnings after interest and taxes, or the earnings available to common stockholders. In terms of Table 15–3, operating leverage affects the top section of the table, financial leverage the lower sections. Thus, if Firm B had more operating leverage, its fixed costs would be higher than $40,000, its variable cost ratio would be lower than 60 percent of sales, and earnings before interest and taxes would vary with sales to a greater extent. Financial leverage takes over where operating leverage leaves off, further magnifying the effect on earnings per share of a change in the level of sales. For this reason, operating leverage is sometimes referred to as *first-stage leverage* and financial leverage as *second-stage leverage*.

DEGREE OF FINANCIAL LEVERAGE

The *degree of financial leverage* (DFL) is defined as the percentage change in earnings available to common stockholders that is associated with a given percentage change in earnings before interest and taxes (EBIT). An equation has been developed as an aid in calculating the degree of financial leverage for any given level of EBIT and interest charges, I:[2]

$$\text{Degree of financial leverage} = \frac{\text{EBIT}}{\text{EBIT} - I}. \qquad (15A-2)$$

---

2 The equation is developed as follows:

1. Notice that EBIT $= Q(P - V) - F$.

2. Earnings per share (EPS) $= \dfrac{(EBIT - I)(1 - t)}{N}$, where EBIT is earnings before interest and taxes, I is interest paid, t is the corporate tax rate, and N is the number of shares outstanding.

3. I is a constant, so ΔEPS, the change in EPS, is

$$\Delta EPS = \frac{\Delta EBIT(1 - t)}{N}.$$

4. The percentage change in EPS is the change in EPS over the original EPS, or

$$\frac{\dfrac{\Delta EBIT(1 - t)}{N}}{\dfrac{(EBIT - I)(1 - t)}{N}} = \frac{\Delta EBIT}{EBIT - I}.$$

5. The degree of financial leverage is the percentage change in EPS over the percentage change in EBIT, so

$$\text{Degree of financial leverage} = DFL = \frac{\dfrac{\Delta EBIT}{EBIT - I}}{\dfrac{\Delta EBIT}{EBIT}} = \frac{EBIT}{EBIT - I}.$$

6. This equation must be modified if the firm has preferred stock outstanding.

For Firm B at sales of $200,000 and an EBIT of $40,000, the degree of financial leverage with a 50 percent debt ratio is

$$\text{DFL at 50\% debt} = \frac{\$40,000}{\$40,000 - \$12,000}$$

$$= 1.43.$$

Therefore, a 100 percent increase in EBIT would result in a 100 (1.43) = 143 percent increase in earnings per share. If no debt were used, the degree of financial leverage would be 1.0, so a 100 percent increase in EBIT would produce a 100 percent increase in EPS. Table 15–3 confirms these statements.

COMBINING OPERATING AND FINANCIAL LEVERAGE

We have seen that operating leverage causes a change in sales volume to have a magnified effect on EBIT, and if financial leverage is superimposed on operating leverage, changes in EBIT will have a magnified effect on earnings per share. Therefore, if a firm uses a considerable amount of both operating leverage and financial leverage, even small changes in the level of sales will produce wide fluctuations in EPS.

Equation 15A–1 for the degree of operating leverage can be combined with Equation 15A–2 for financial leverage to show the total leveraging effect of a given change in sales on earnings per share:[3]

$$\text{Degree of total leverage (DTL)} = \frac{Q(P - V)}{Q(P - V) - F - I}.$$

$$\text{DTL} = \frac{S - VC}{S - VC - F - I}. \qquad (15A–3)$$

For Firm B at sales of $200,000, the degree of total leverage, using 50 percent debt, is

---

3 Equation 15A–3 is developed as follows:
  1. Recognize that EBIT = $Q(P - V) - F$, then rewrite Equation 15A–2 as follows:

$$\frac{\text{EBIT}}{\text{EBIT} - I} = \frac{Q(P - V) - F}{Q(P - V) - F - I} = \frac{S - VC - F}{S - VC - F - I}. \qquad (15A–2a)$$

  2. The degree of total leverage is equal to the degree of operating leverage times the degree of financial leverage, or Equation 15A–1 times Equation 15A–2a:

$$\text{Degree of total leverage} = (\text{Equation 15A–1})(\text{Equation 15A–2a})$$

$$\text{DTL} = \frac{Q(P - V)}{Q(P - V) - F} \cdot \frac{Q(P - V) - F}{Q(P - V) - F - I}$$

$$= \frac{Q(P - V)}{Q(P - V) - F - I} = \frac{S - VC}{S - VC - F - I}$$

$$= \text{DOL} \times \text{DFL}. \qquad (15A–3a)$$

$$\text{Degree of total leverage (DTL)} = \frac{\$200,000 - \$120,000}{\$200,000 - \$120,000 - \$40,000 - \$12,000}$$

$$= \frac{\$80,000}{\$28,000} = 2.86.$$

We can use the degree of total leverage (DTL) to find the new earnings per share (EPS_1) for a given percentage increase in sales (% Δ sales) as follows:

$$EPS_1 = EPS_0 + EPS_0[(DTL)(\% \ \Delta \ sales)]$$

$$= EPS_0[1.0 + (DTL)(\% \ \Delta \ sales)].$$

For example, a 50 percent increase in sales, from $200,000 to $300,000, would cause EPS_0 ($3.36 as shown in Table 15–3) to increase to $8.16.

$$EPS_1 = \$3.36[1.0 + (2.86)(0.50)]$$
$$= \$3.36[2.43]$$
$$= \$8.16.$$

This figure agrees with the one for EPS_1 worked out in Table 15–3.

The usefulness of the degree of leverage concept lies in the facts (1) that it enables us to specify the precise effect of a change in sales volume on earnings available to common stock and (2) that it permits us to show the interrelationship between operating and financial leverage. The concept can be used to show the owner or manager of a business, for example, that a decision to automate and to finance new equipment with bonds will result in a situation wherein a 10 percent decline in sales will produce a 50 percent decline in earnings, whereas a different operating and financial leverage package will be such that a 10 percent sales decline will cause earnings to decline by only 20 percent. Having the alternatives stated in this manner gives the decision maker a better idea of the ramifications of the possible actions.[4]

Question

15A–1 In public utility rate cases, a utility's riskiness is a key issue, as utilities are supposed to be allowed to earn the same rate of return on common equity as "unregulated firms of comparable risk." The difficulty is specifying in quantitative terms the riskiness of utilities and nonutilities. Do you see how the degree of leverage concepts (DOL, DFL, and DTL) might be used as indicators of risk in a rate case?

---

4 The concept is also useful for investors. If firms in an industry are classified as to their degrees of total leverage, an investor who is optimistic about prospects for the industry might favor those firms with high leverage, and vice versa if industry sales are expected to decline.

Problems

15A–1 a. Refer back to Chapter 15, Figure 15–2. Calculate the degree of
operating leverage for Plans A and B at sales of $120,000 and
$160,000. At sales of $80,000, DOL_A = undefined (or ∞) and DOL_B =
−2.0, while at sales of $240,000, DOL_A = 1.50 and DOL_B = 2.0.
   b. Is it true that the DOL is equal to approximately infinity just above the
breakeven point, implying that a very small increase in sales will
produce a huge percentage increase in EBIT, but that DOL declines
when calculated at higher levels of sales?
   c. Is it true for all sales levels where DOL > 0 for both plans that
DOL_B < DOL_A? Explain.
   d. Assume that Plans A and B can be financed in either of the two
following ways: (1) No debt; (2) $90,000 of debt at·10 percent.
Calculate the DFL for Plan A at sales of $120,000 and $160,000. The
DFLs for Plan B at these sales levels with debt are 0 and 1.82,
respectively.
   e. Calculate the degree of total leverage (DTL) under Plan A with debt
at sales of $120,000 and $160,000. The DTLs under Plan B at these
sales levels are −6.67 and 7.27, respectively.
   f. Several of the degree of leverage figures were negative; for example,
DTL_B at S = $120,000 in Part e was −6.67. Does a negative degree of
leverage imply that an increase in sales will *lower* profits?

15A–2 Varifixed Corporation will begin operations next year producing a single
product to be priced at $8 per unit. Varifixed has a choice of two methods
of production: Method A, with variable costs of $3 per unit and $400,000
of fixed costs, and Method B, with variable costs of $5 per unit and fixed
costs of $200,000. In anticipation of beginning operations, the firm has
acquired $1,000,000 in assets and has established a debt ratio of 30
percent. The current cost of debt (k_d) to Varifixed is 10 percent. Analysis
of the two methods requires the following calculations: (1) unit contribution
margins under each method, (2) breakeven points for each method, and
(3) level of sales in units at which the firm should be indifferent between
the two methods with respect to expected earnings.

The sales forecast for the coming year is 150,000 units. Under which
method would profits be most adversely affected if sales did not reach
expected levels? Given the present debt of the firm, which method would
produce the greatest percentage increase in earnings per share for a
given increase in EBIT? What is the maximum debt ratio under Method A
which would produce the same degree of total leverage as for Method B?
If the management of the firm is risk averse, which method of production
will most likely be selected? (*Hint:* Let DTL_A = DTL_B and then solve for I.)

16 THE COST OF CAPITAL

The cost of capital is critically important in finance. First, capital budgeting decisions have a major impact on the firm, and proper capital budgeting procedures require an estimate of the cost of capital. Second, many other types of decisions, including those related to leasing, to bond refunding, and to working capital policy require estimates of the cost of capital. Finally, maximizing the value of a firm requires that the costs of all inputs, including capital, be minimized, and to minimize the cost of capital we must be able to calculate it.[1]

The first task of this chapter is to explain the logic of the weighted average cost of capital. Next, we consider the costs of the major components of the capital structure. Third, the individual component costs are brought together to form a weighted average cost of capital. Finally, the relationship between capital budgeting and the cost of capital is discussed.

THE LOGIC OF THE WEIGHTED AVERAGE COST OF CAPITAL

Suppose a particular firm's cost of debt is estimated to be 8 percent, its cost of equity is estimated to be 12 percent, and the decision has been made to finance next year's projects by selling debt. The argument is sometimes made that the cost of capital for these projects is 8 percent, because debt will be used to finance them. However, this position is incorrect. To finance a particular set of projects with debt implies that the firm is also using up some of its potential for obtaining new low-cost debt in the future. As

---

1 The cost of capital is also vitally important in regulated industries, including electric, gas, telephone, railroad, airline, and trucking companies. In essence, regulatory commissions seek to measure a utility's cost of capital, then set prices so that the company will just earn this rate of return. If the estimate is too low, then the company will not be able to attract sufficient capital to meet long-run demands for service, and the public will suffer. If the estimate of capital costs is too high, customers will pay too much for service.

expansion occurs in subsequent years, at some point the firm will find it necessary to use additional equity financing to prevent the debt ratio from becoming too large.

To illustrate, suppose the firm borrows heavily at 8 percent during 1979, using up its debt capacity in the process, to finance projects yielding 9 percent. In 1980 it has projects available that yield 11 percent, well above the return on 1979 projects, but it cannot accept these new projects because they would have to be financed with 12 percent equity money. To avoid this problem, the firm should be viewed as an ongoing concern, and the cost of capital used in capital budgeting should be calculated as a weighted average, or composite, of the various types of funds it uses.

BASIC DEFINITIONS

Capital components are the items on the right-hand side of the balance sheet: various types of debt, preferred stock, and common equity. Any net increase in assets must be financed by an increase in one or more capital components.

Capital is a necessary factor of production, and like any other factor, it has a cost. The cost of each component is defined as the *component cost* of that particular type of capital. For example, if the firm can borrow money at 8 percent, the component cost of debt is defined as 8 percent. Throughout most of this chapter, we concentrate on debt, retained earnings, and new issues of common stock. These are the major capital structure components, and their component costs are identified by the following symbols:

k_d = interest rate on the firm's new debt = component cost of debt, before tax.

$k_d(1 - t)$ = component cost of debt, after tax, where t is the marginal tax rate. $k_d(1 - t)$ is the debt cost used to calculate the weighted average cost of capital.

k_s = component cost of retained earnings (or internal equity). This k_s is identical to the k_s developed in Chapter 5 and defined there as the required rate of return on common stock.

k_e = component cost of external capital obtained by issuing new common stock. As we shall see, it is necessary to distinguish between equity raised by retaining earnings versus that raised by selling new stock. This is why we distinguish between k_s and k_e.

k_a = an average, or composite, cost of capital. If a firm raises $1 of new capital to finance asset expansion, and if it is to keep its capital structure in balance (that is, if it is to keep the same percentage of debt and equity), then it will raise part of the dollar as debt and part as common equity (with equity coming either as retained earnings or from the sale of new common stock).[2]

These definitions and concepts are explained in detail in the remainder of this chapter.

COST OF DEBT

The component cost of debt used to calculate the weighted average cost of capital is the interest rate on debt, k_d, *multiplied by (1 − t), where t is the firm's tax rate:*[3]

$$\text{Component cost of debt} = k_d(1 - t). \qquad (16-1)$$

For example, if Firm B (the same company we analyzed in Chapter 15) can borrow at a rate of 10 percent, and if it has a tax rate of 40 percent, then its after-tax cost of debt is

$$k_d(1 - t) = 10\%(0.6) = 6.0\%.$$

The reason for making the tax adjustment is as follows. The value of the firm's stock, which we want to maximize, depends on *after-tax* income. Interest is a deductible expense. The effect of this is that the federal government pays part of the interest charges. Therefore, to put the costs of debt and equity on a comparable basis, we adjust the interest rate downward to take account of the preferential tax treatment of debt.

Note that the cost of debt is applicable to *new* debt, not to the interest on any old, previously outstanding debt. In other words, we are interested in the cost of new debt, or the *marginal* cost of debt. Our primary concern with the cost of capital is to use it in a decision-making process—the decision whether to obtain capital to make new investments. Whether the firm borrowed at high or low rates in the past is irrelevant for this purpose.[4]

---

2 Firms try to keep their debt and equity in balance, but they do not try to maintain any proportional relationship between the common stock and retained earnings accounts as shown on the balance sheet. Common equity is common equity, whether it is represented by common stock or by retained earnings.

   k_a also reflects the riskiness of the firm's various assets as discussed in Chapters 11 and 12. If a firm uses risk-adjusted discount rates for different capital projects, the average of these rates, weighted by the sizes of the various investments, should equal k_a.

   Finally, if the firm chooses to use preferred stock (although most firms do not), then the cost of preferred, k_p, must also be taken into account. This is discussed later.

3 Note that the cost of debt is considered in isolation. The impact of debt on the cost of equity, as well as on future increments of debt, is treated when the weighted cost of a combination of debt and equity is derived. Also, flotation costs, or the costs of selling the debt, are ignored. Flotation costs for debt issues are generally quite low; in fact, most debt is placed directly with banks, insurance companies, pension funds, and the like, and involves no flotation costs.

4 It should also be noted that the tax rate is zero for a firm with losses. Therefore, for a company that does not pay taxes the cost of debt is not reduced; that is, in Equation 16–1 the tax rate equals zero, so the after-tax cost of debt is equal to the interest rate.

COST OF RETAINED EARNINGS, k_s

The cost of debt is based on the interest rate investors require on debt issues, adjusted for taxes. *The cost of equity obtained by retaining earnings can be defined similarly; it is* k_s, *the rate of return stockholders require on the firm's common stock.*[5]

The required rate of return is equal to the riskless rate plus a risk premium: $k_s = R_F + \rho$. For stocks in equilibrium (which is the typical situation), the required rate of return is also equal to the expected rate of return, $\hat{k}_s$. In Chapters 4 and 5 we saw that the expected rate of return on a share of common stock depends, ultimately, on the dividends paid on the stock:

$$P_0 = \frac{D_1}{(1 + \hat{k}_s)} + \frac{D_2}{(1 + \hat{k}_s)^2} + \cdots. \tag{16-2}$$

Here P_0 is the current price of the stock; D_t is the dividend expected to be paid at the end of Year t; and $\hat{k}_s$ is the expected rate of return. If dividends are expected to grow at a constant rate, then, as we saw in Chapter 4, Equation 16–2 reduces to the following expression:

$$P_0 = \frac{D_1}{\hat{k}_s - g}. \tag{16-3}$$

We can solve for $\hat{k}_s$ to obtain the expected rate of return on common equity, which in equilibrium is also equal to the required rate of return:[6]

$$\hat{k}_s = \frac{D_1}{P_0} + \text{Expected } g. \tag{16-4}$$

Thus, investors expect to receive a dividend yield, D_1/P_0, plus a capital gain, g, for a total expected return of $\hat{k}_s$.

To illustrate, suppose Firm B in Chapter 15 has begun retaining some earnings rather than paying them all out as dividends. The stock is in equilibrium, and it still sells for $22.86, but the next expected dividend is $1.60, and the expected growth rate is now 7 percent. Firm B's expected and required rate of return, hence its cost of retained earnings, is

$$k_s = \hat{k}_s = \frac{\$1.60}{\$22.86} + 7\% = 7\% + 7\% = 14\%.$$

---

5 The term *retained earnings* can be interpreted to mean the balance sheet item "retained earnings," consisting of all the earnings retained in the business throughout its history, or it can mean the income statement item "additions to retained earnings." This latter definition is used in the present chapter: *"Retained earnings" for our purpose here refers to that part of current earnings which is not paid out in dividends but, rather, is retained and reinvested in the business.*

6 Note, however, that if a firm's growth rate is *not* expected to remain constant, then Equations 16–3 and 16–4 will not hold. In this case, it will be necessary to solve for k_s in the nonconstant growth formula developed in Chapter 4.

This is the minimum rate of return that management must be able to earn to justify retaining earnings and plowing them back into the business rather than paying them out to stockholders as dividends. Henceforth in this chapter we assume that equilibrium exists and use the terms k_s and $\hat{k}_s$ interchangeably.

The logic behind assigning a cost of capital to retained earnings involves the *opportunity cost principle.* The firm's after-tax earnings literally belong to the stockholders. Bondholders are compensated by interest payments, while earnings belong to the common stockholders and serve to ''pay the rent'' on stockholders' capital. Management may pay out earnings in the form of dividends, or earnings can be reinvested in the business. *If management decides to retain earnings, there is an opportunity cost involved—stockholders could have received the earnings as dividends and invested these funds in other stocks, in bonds, in real estate, or in anything else. Thus, the firm must earn on the retained earnings at least as much as stockholders themselves could earn in alternative investments of comparable risk.*

What rate of return do stockholders expect to earn on equivalent risk investments? The answer is k_s. Therefore, *if the firm cannot invest retained earnings and earn at least* k_s, *then it should pay these funds to its stockholders and let them invest directly in other assets that do provide this return.*[7]

COST OF NEWLY ISSUED COMMON STOCK, OR EXTERNAL EQUITY, k_e

The cost of new common stock, or external equity capital, k_e, *is higher than the cost of retained earnings,* k_s, *because of flotation costs involved in selling new common stock.* What rate of return must be earned on funds raised by selling stock in order to make this action worthwhile? To put it another way, what is the cost of new common stock?

For a firm with a constant growth rate, the answer is found by applying the following formula:

$$k_e = \frac{D_1}{P_0(1 - F)} + g. \qquad (16-5)$$

Here F is the percentage flotation cost incurred in selling the issue, so

---

7 One complexity in estimating the cost of retained earnings deals with the fact that dividends and capital gains are taxed differently. Retaining earnings rather than paying them out as dividends can convert ordinary income to capital gains. This point is discussed in Appendix 16A of *Financial Management,* 2d edition.

$P_0(1 - F)$ is the net price per share received by the company when it sells a new stock issue.[8]

For Firm B, whose flotation cost is 10 percent, the cost of new outside equity is computed as follows:

$$k_e = \frac{\$1.60}{\$22.86(1 - 0.10)} + 7\% = \frac{\$1.60}{\$20.57} + 7\%$$

$$= 7.8\% + 7\% = 14.8\%.$$

Investors require a return of $k_s = 14\%$ on Firm B's stock. However, because of flotation costs, the company must earn *more* than 14 percent on funds obtained by selling stock to provide this 14 percent. Specifically, if Firm B earns 14.8 percent on funds obtained from new common stock issues, then earnings per share will not fall below previously expected earnings; its expected dividend can be maintained; and as a result of all this, the price per share will not decline. If Firm B earns less than 14.8 percent, then earnings, dividends, and growth will fall below expectations, causing the price of the stock to decline. If it earns more, the price of the stock will rise.[9]

FINDING THE BASIC REQUIRED RATE OF RETURN ON COMMON EQUITY

It is obvious by now that the basic rate of return investors require on a firm's common equity, k_s, is a most important quantity. This required rate of return is the cost of retained earnings, and it forms the basis for the cost of

---

8 Equation 16–5 is derived as follows:
Step 1. The old stockholders expect the firm to pay a stream of dividends, D_t. This income stream will be derived from existing assets. New investors will likewise expect to receive the same stream of dividends, D_t. For new investors to obtain this stream *without impairing the D_t stream of the old investors*, the new funds obtained from the sale of stock must be invested at a return high enough to provide a dividend stream whose present value is equal to the price the firm receives:

$$P_n = \sum_{t=1}^{\infty} \frac{D_t}{(1 + k_e)^t}. \qquad (16\text{–}6)$$

Here P_n is the net price to the firm, and $P_n = P_0(1 - F)$; D_t is the dividend stream to new stockholders; and k_e is the cost of new outside equity.
Step 2. When growth is a constant, Equation 16–6 reduces to

$$P_n = P_0(1 - F) = \frac{D_1}{k_e - g}. \qquad (16\text{–}6a)$$

Step 3. Equation 16–6a may be solved for k_e:

$$k_e = \frac{D_1}{P_0(1 - F)} + g. \qquad (16\text{–}5)$$

9 On occasion, it may be useful to use another equation to calculate the cost of external equity:

$$k_e = \frac{\text{Dividend yield}}{(1 - F)} + g = \frac{D_1/P_0}{(1 - F)} + g. \qquad (16\text{–}5a)$$

Equation 16–5a is derived algebraically from 16–5, and it is useful when information on dividend yields, but not on dollar dividends and stock prices, is available.

capital obtained from new stock issues. How is this all-important quantity estimated? Several approaches may be used, including the following three.

The CAPM Approach

The Capital Asset Pricing Model (CAPM) as developed in Chapter 5 can be used to help estimate k_s. To use the CAPM, we proceed as follows:

Step 1. Estimate the riskless rate, R_F, generally taken to be either the U.S. Treasury bond rate or the thirty day Treasury bill rate.

Step 2. Estimate the stock's beta coefficient, b, and use this as an index of the stock's risk.

Step 3. Estimate the rate of return on "the market," or on an "average" stock. Designate this return k_M.

Step 4. Estimate the required rate of return on the firm's stock as follows:

$$k_s = R_F + b(k_M - R_F).$$

The value $(k_M - R_F)$ is the risk premium on the average stock, while b is an index of the particular stock's own risk.

To illustrate the CAPM approach, assume that $R_F = 6\%$, $k_M = 10\%$, and $b = 0.7$ for a given stock. The stock's k_s is calculated as follows:

$$k_s = 6 + 0.7(10 - 6) = 6 + 2.8 = 8.8\%.$$

Had b been 1.8, indicating that the stock was riskier than average, k_s would have been

$$k_s = 6 + 1.8(4) = 6 + 7.2 = 13.2\%.$$

It should be noted that while the CAPM approach appears to yield accurate, precise estimates of k_s, there are several problems with the approach. These problems were discussed in Chapter 5, so we shall not belabor the point here.

Bond Yield plus Risk Premium Approach

Although it is essentially an *ad hoc,* subjective procedure, analysts often estimate a firm's cost of common equity by adding a risk premium of about 4 percentage points to the interest rate on the firm's long-term debt. For example, if a firm's bonds yield 9 percent, then its cost of equity might be estimated as follows:

$$k_s = \text{Bond rate} + \text{Risk premium} = 9\% + 4\% = 13\%.$$

This risk premium is a judgmental estimate, so the estimated value of k_s is also judgmental.[10]

Dividend Yield plus Growth Rate (or DCF) Approach

We know that stocks are typically in equilibrium, with the expected rate of return equal to the required rate. If the firm is expected to grow at a constant rate, then we can estimate k_s by the discounted cash flow (DCF) formula as follows:

$$k_s = \frac{D_1}{P_0} + \text{Expected dividend growth rate.}$$

If past growth rates in earnings and dividends have been relatively stable, and if investors appear to be projecting a continuation of past trends, then g may be based on the firm's historic growth rate. *However, if the company's growth has been abnormally high or low, either because of its own unique situation or because of general economic conditions, then investors will not project the past growth rate into the future.* In this case, g must be estimated in some other manner. Security analysts regularly make earnings and dividends growth forecasts, looking at such factors as projected sales, profit margins, and competitive factors. Someone making a cost of capital estimate can obtain such analysts' forecasts and use them as a proxy for the growth expectations of investors in general, then combine g with the current dividend yield, and estimate k_s as follows:

$$k_s = \frac{D_1}{P_0} + \text{Growth rate as projected by security analysts.}$$

Again, note that this estimate of k_s is based upon the assumption that g is expected to remain constant in the future. If this assumption is not correct, then it will be necessary to solve for k_s in the nonconstant growth model developed in Chapter 4.[11]

In practical work, it is best to use all three methods, and then apply

---

10 Analysts who use this procedure often cite studies of historical returns on stocks and bonds and use the difference between the average yield (dividends plus capital gains) on stocks and the average yield on bonds as the risk premium of stocks over bonds. The most frequently cited study is R. G. Ibbotson and R. A. Sinquefield, "Stocks, Bonds, Bills, and Inflation: Year-By-Year Historical Returns (1926–1974)," *Journal of Business,* January 1976. The primary difficulties with using historical returns to estimate risk premiums are (1) historical returns differ depending on the beginning and ending dates used to estimate them, and (2) there is no reason to think that *past* differences in stock and bond yields exactly reflect *future* required risk premiums. As an alternative to historic data, forward-looking yield spreads have also been developed. For examples, see (1) B. G. Malkiel, "The Capital Formation Problem in the United States," *Journal of Finance,* May 1979, pp. 291–306, and (2) E. F. Brigham and D. K. Shome, "Risk Premiums on Common Stocks," paper presented at the Conference on Financial Management of Corporate Resource Allocations. Stichting Nijenrode, Breukelen, The Netherlands: The Netherlands School of Business, August 1979.

11 When the DCF method is used, we are implicitly assuming that the stock's price is in equilibrium, with $\hat{k}_s = D_1/P_0 + g = R_F + \text{Risk premium} = k_s$. Thus, the DCF and risk premium methods will, if all inputs are estimated correctly, produce identical cost of capital estimates. Also, as indicated above, growth rates may be estimated (1) by projecting past trends if there is reason to think these trends will continue or (2) by asking security analysts what growth rates they are projecting (or, alternatively, looking up projected growth rates in such publications as *Value Line,* a financial service subscribed to by many investors). A third method involves projecting the firm's dividend payout ratio and the

judgment when the methods produce different results. People experienced in estimating equity capital costs recognize that both careful analysis and some very fine judgments are required. *It would be nice to pretend that these judgments are unnecessary and to specify an easy, precise way of determining the exact cost of equity capital. Unfortunately, this is not possible. Finance is in large part a matter of judgment, and we simply must face this fact.*

COMBINING DEBT AND EQUITY: WEIGHTED AVERAGE, OR COMPOSITE, COST OF CAPITAL, k_a

In Chapter 15 we examined the effects of leverage on the cost of debt, on the cost of equity, and on the market price of a company's stock. We concluded that the optimal mix of securities, or the optimal capital structure, is the one that maximizes the price of the firm's stock, and that a rational firm would use this mix as its *target capital structure*. Further, we noted that the firm should raise new capital in proportion to its target capital structure in order to keep the capital structure on target over time.

The proportions of debt and equity in the target capital structure are used to help calculate the weighted average cost of capital. Firm B can again be used to illustrate the point. Assume that the company has a target capital structure calling for 40 percent debt and 60 percent equity. Other key data items are summarized below:

$P_0 = \$22.86$.

$D_0 = \$1.4953 = $ dividends per share in the *last* period. D_0 has already been paid, so someone purchasing this stock today would *not* receive D_0. Rather, he or she would receive D_1, the *next* dividend.

$g = 7\%$.

$$k_s = \frac{D_1}{P_0} + g = \frac{D_0(1 + g)}{P_0} + g = \frac{\$1.4953(1.07)}{\$22.86} + 0.07 = \frac{\$1.60}{\$22.86} + 0.07$$

$$= 0.07 + 0.07 = 0.14 = 14\%.$$

$k_d = 10\%$.

$t = 40\% = 0.4$.

$k_d(1 - t) = 10\%(0.6) = 6\%$.

Now suppose the company needs to raise $100. To keep its capital structure on target, it must obtain 0.4($100) = $40 as debt and 0.6($100) = $60 as equity. The weighted average cost of the $100 is calculated as follows:

Component	Weights	Component Cost	Product
Debt	0.4	6.0%	2.4%
Equity	0.6	14.0	8.4
		Weighted average cost = k_a =	10.8%

The calculations in the table can also be thought of in equation format:

$$k_a = \begin{pmatrix} \text{Fraction} \\ \text{of debt in} \\ \text{capital} \\ \text{structure} \end{pmatrix} \begin{pmatrix} \text{Interest} \\ \text{rate} \end{pmatrix} \begin{pmatrix} 1 - \text{Tax rate} \end{pmatrix} + \begin{pmatrix} \text{Fraction} \\ \text{of equity} \\ \text{in capital} \\ \text{structure} \end{pmatrix} \begin{pmatrix} \text{Cost of} \\ \text{equity} \end{pmatrix}$$

$$= w_d(k_d)(1 - t) + w_s(k_s)$$
$$= 0.4(10\%)(0.6) + 0.6(14\%) \tag{16-7}$$
$$= 2.4\% + 8.4\% = 10.8\%.$$

Using either method, we see that every dollar of new capital consists of forty cents of debt with an after-tax cost of 6 percent and sixty cents of equity with a cost of 14 percent. The average cost of the whole dollar is 10.8 percent.

Preferred Stock

Firm B does not use preferred stock. However, if it did, the cost of preferred would be included in the calculation of the composite cost of capital as follows:

1. Estimate the component cost of the preferred, k_p:

$$k_p = D_p/P_{np}.$$

Here D_p is the dividend that Firm B would have to pay on the preferred, and P_{np} is the net price per share the company would receive. If D_p = $2.75 and P_{np} = $25, then

$$k_p = \$2.75/\$25 = 0.11 = 11\%.$$

Since preferred dividends are not deductible, no tax adjustment is needed.

2. Determine the target capital structure percentages, or weights. We assume that Firm B has decided to use w_d = 35 percent debt, w_p = 10 percent preferred stock, and w_s = 55 percent common equity.

3. Combine the component costs with the capital structure weights to determine the weighted average cost of capital, using an expanded version of Equation 16-7. We assume that k_d = 10%, k_p = 11%, and k_s = 14%, so

$$k_a = w_d(k_d)(1 - t) + w_p k_p + w_s k_s$$
$$= 0.35(10\%)(0.6) + 0.10(11\%) + 0.55(14\%)$$
$$= 10.9\%.$$

Thus, if Firm B decided to use preferred stock in addition to debt and common stock, the average cost of each dollar raised would be 10.9 percent.[12]

Minimizing the Weighted Average Cost of Capital

A firm that seeks to maximize the price of its stock must also seek to minimize the costs of producing any given level of output. Thus, management should try to obtain its required capital at the lowest possible cost, and this amounts to minimizing its weighted average cost of capital.

Table 16–1, which again uses data developed for Firm B in Chapter 15, shows how the company's capital structure affects its weighted average cost of capital. At a zero debt ratio, all of Firm B's capital is common equity, so $k_a = k_s = 12\%$. When the company begins to use debt, the cost

Table 16–1
Calculation of Firm B's Average Cost of Capital,
k_a, **with Different Capital Structures**

Debt/ Assets Ratio	Before-Tax Cost of Debt, k_d	After-Tax Cost of Debt, $k_d(1 - t)$	Weight of Debt, w_d	Product: (3) × (4)	Cost of Equity, k_s	Weight of Equity, w_s	Product: (6) × (7)	Weighted Average Cost of Capital, $k_a =$ (5) + (8)	Stock Price from Table 15–5
(1)	(2)	(3)	(4)	(5)	(6)	(7)	(8)	(9)	(10)
0%	8.0%	4.80%	0.0	0.00%	12.0%	1.0	12.00%	12.00%	$20.00
10	8.0	4.80	0.1	0.48	12.2	0.9	10.98	11.46	20.98
20	8.3	4.98	0.2	1.00	12.6	0.8	10.08	11.08	21.83
30	9.0	5.40	0.3	1.62	13.2	0.7	9.24	10.86	22.50
40	10.0	6.00	0.4	2.40	14.0	0.6	8.40	10.80	22.86
50	12.0	7.20	0.5	3.60	15.2	0.5	7.60	11.20	22.11
60	15.0	9.00	0.6	5.40	16.8	0.4	6.72	12.12	19.64

Notes:
1. The marginal tax rate is 40 percent.
2. The before-tax cost of debt and the values for k_s are taken from Table 15–5 in Chapter 15.
3. The cost of capital is minimized, and the stock price is maximized, at a 40 percent debt/assets ratio.

12 As a general rule, if there are n types of capital, we may use this formula:

$$k_a = \sum_{i=1}^{n} w_i k_i. \qquad (16\text{–}7b)$$

Here the w_i's and the k_i's refer to the n types of capital, and the w_i's sum to 1.0. Equation 16–7b would be used if trade credit, short-term bank debt, commercial paper, and various types of long-term debt were to be included separately in the calculation of k_a.

of capital becomes a weighted average of the costs of debt and equity. As the use of debt increases, the weight of debt increases and that of equity decreases.

Notice that k_a declines until the debt/assets ratio hits 40 percent, at which point $k_a = 10.8$ percent. After this point, k_a begins to rise. Notice also that Firm B's stock price, taken from Table 15–5 and shown in Column 10 of Table 16–1, is maximized at the same 40 percent debt ratio that minimizes k_a. This illustrates a very important point—*the capital structure that minimizes a firm's weighted average cost of capital also maximizes the value of its stock.*

The values in Columns 3, 6, and 9 of Table 16–1 are plotted in Figure 16–1. This type of graph is used often in finance to show pictorially the relationship between each cost component—k_s, k_d, and k_a—and the debt/assets ratio.

Several additional points should be noted regarding Table 16–1 and Figure 16–1:

1. As indicated above, k_s cannot be measured with a high degree of precision. It is difficult to obtain an estimate of k_s for a given capital structure, and even more difficult to estimate the relationship between k_s and the debt/assets ratio. Thus, the data contained here should be taken as illustrative, not as representing precise estimates.

Figure 16–1
Relationship between Firm B's Capital Structure and Its Cost of Capital

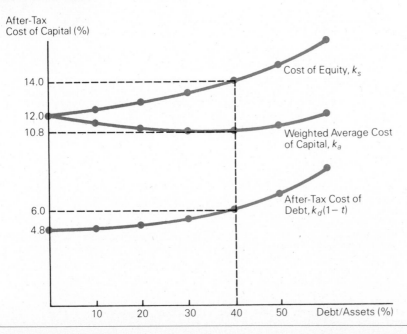

2. The costs of debt and equity do rise with increases in the debt ratio, and the weighted average cost of capital does first decline, then rise, as debt is added to the capital structure.

3. The average cost of capital curve seems to be shaped more like a *U* (or, really, like a shallow bowl) than like a *V* with a sharp, clearly defined minimum point. Thus, relatively small departures from the optimal capital structure will have no significant effect on the firm's cost of capital. For example, if Firm B used as little as 30 percent or as much as 50 percent debt, this would not have much effect on either its average cost of capital or its stock price. Further, a relatively flat average cost of capital curve gives financial managers flexibility in raising new capital—they can sell bonds one year, then stock the next, to take advantage of reduced flotation costs on larger offerings and also to take advantage of relatively favorable conditions in either stock or bond markets during a particular year.[13]

THE MARGINAL COST OF CAPITAL

The marginal cost of any item is the cost of another unit of that item; for example, the marginal cost of labor is defined as the cost of adding one additional worker. The marginal cost of labor might be $25 per person if ten workers are added, but $35 per person if the firm tries to hire 100 new

---

13 The weights used to calculate the average cost of capital should, in theory, be based on the market values of the capital components. This requires determining the market value of all debts (some of which may not be traded at all) and the market value of the common equity (number of shares times current price per share), and reconstructing a market value capital structure. To see what is involved here, consider a firm with assets and capital of $100, whose stock sells at a premium of 40 percent over its book value, and whose debt sells at its book value:

	Original Book Value Capital Structure		Original Market Value Capital Structure	
Debt	$ 50	50%	$ 50	42%
Common equity	50	50	70	58
	$100	100%	$120	100%

Suppose this firm plans to raise $50 of new capital. If it raises $25 of debt and $25 of equity, its book value capital structure will remain constant, but its market value percentages will change to 44 percent debt and 56 percent equity. Conversely, if it raises new capital so as to maintain its market value capital structure, that is, as $21 debt and $29 equity, then its book value structure will change to 47 percent debt, 53 percent equity.

Obviously, using different weights would produce a different calculated value for k_a, the average cost of capital. Even though it is theoretically better to use market value weights, most firms do, in fact, target on book value capital structures, and there seem to be three reasons for this choice: (1) market values fluctuate widely, and financial planning would be unstable if a market value target were used; (2) it is difficult if not impossible to specify a precise optimal capital structure anyway, whether it is measured in book or market terms; and (3) regardless of which choice is made with respect to the target capital structure, the book and market values of *marginal* capital will probably be approximately equal. Of course, if the *wrong* target capital structure is used as the target, the MCC will be higher than it needs to be; but with the present state of the art, it is almost impossible to *prove* that one capital structure is better than another, at least for capital structures over a fairly broad range, whether measured at book or at market. For an illustration of market value weights, see *Financial Management,* 2d edition, Chapter 16.

workers, because it would be harder to find that many people willing and able to do the work. The same concept applies to capital. As the firm tries to attract more new dollars, the cost of each dollar will, at some point, rise. *Thus, the marginal cost of capital is defined as the cost of obtaining another dollar of new capital.*

We can use Firm B to illustrate the marginal cost of capital concept. The company's capital structure is given below:[14]

Debt		$ 80,000	40%
Common equity			
Common stock	$ 6,000		
Retained			
earnings	114,000		
Total equity		120,000	60
Total capital		$200,000	100%

This actual capital structure is also the company's target structure, and, as we saw in the preceding section, at this level $k_d = 10$ percent, $k_s = 14$ percent, and $k_a = 10.8$ percent.

Since the firm's optimal capital structure calls for 40 percent debt and 60 percent equity, each new (or marginal) dollar will be raised as 40 cents of debt and 60 cents of equity. Otherwise, the capital structure will not stay on target. We also saw above that as long as it remains at its optimal capital

---

14 Firm B has only a negligible amount of payables and accruals, so these items were ignored. However, suppose the company had had $30,000 of payables/accruals in addition to $50,000 of interest-bearing debt. Payables/accruals could be handled in one of two ways:

1. Simply ignore these items on the grounds that, in the capital budgeting process, these spontaneously generated funds are netted out against the required investment outlay, then ignored in the cost of capital calculation. To illustrate, consider a retail firm thinking of opening a new store. According to customary practices, the firm should (1) estimate the required outlay, (2) estimate the net receipts (additions to profits) from the new store, (3) discount the estimated receipts at the cost of capital, and (4) accept the decision to open the new store only if the net present value of the expected revenue stream exceeds the investment outlay. The estimated accruals, trade payables, and other forms of credit that do not bear interest are deducted from the investment to determine the required outlay before making the calculation. This is exactly the procedure used by Carter Chemical and illustrated in Table 11–1, and it is what most companies actually do.

   For Firm B, we would have the following situation:

	Complete Capital Structure (1)	Relevant Capital Structure (2)	Percentage of Relevant Capital Structure (3)
Payables/accruals	$ 30,000	—	—
Debt (interest-bearing)	50,000	$ 50,000	29%
Equity	120,000	120,000	71
Total market value	$200,000	$170,000	100%

   The values in the third column would be used as the weights to determine the weighted average cost of capital. Payables/accruals are simply ignored.

2. Bring payables/accruals into the calculation directly. Accruals virtually always have a zero cost, as do payables for firms that take all discounts offered. If a firm has discounts available but does not take them, then it would be necessary to divide payables into "free" and "costly" components, and to determine an interest cost on the costly trade credit.

structure, Firm B's debt has an after-tax cost of 6 percent, its equity has a cost of 14 percent, and its weighted average cost of capital is 10.8 percent. Thus, each new dollar will be raised as 40 cents of debt and 60 cents of equity, and each dollar will have a weighted average cost of 10.8 percent.

The graph shown in Figure 16–2 is defined as Firm B's *marginal cost of capital schedule.* Here the dots represent dollars raised. Since each dollar of new capital has a cost of 10.8 percent, the marginal cost of capital (MCC) for Firm B is constant at 10.8 percent under the assumptions we have used thus far.

Figure 16–2
Marginal Cost of Capital Schedule (MCC) for Firm B

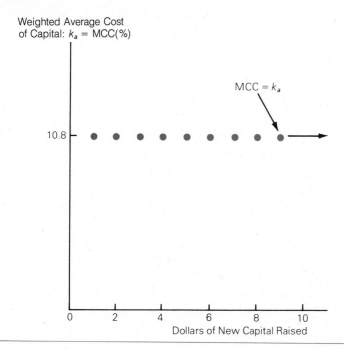

Firm B's MCC schedule in Figure 16–2 would be different (higher) if the company used any capital structure other than 40 percent debt, 60 percent equity. For example, as we saw in Table 16–1, k_a would be 11.08 percent if only 20 percent debt were used, so if the target debt ratio were set at 20 percent, the MCC would be a horizontal line at 11.08 percent. Similarly, the MCC would be a horizontal line at 12 percent if Firm B used all equity. *As a general rule, a different MCC schedule would exist for every possible capital structure; the optimal capital structure is the one that produces the lowest MCC schedule.*

Breaks, or Jumps, in the MCC Schedule

Could Firm B raise an unlimited amount of new capital at the 10.8 percent cost? The answer is no. As companies raise larger and larger sums during a given time period, the costs of both the debt and the equity components begin to rise, and as this occurs, the weighted average cost of new dollars also rises. Thus, just as corporations cannot hire unlimited numbers of workers at a constant wage, neither can they raise unlimited amounts of capital at a constant cost. At some point, the cost of each new dollar will increase above 10.8 percent.

Where will this point occur for Firm B? As a first step to determining this point, recognize that, although the company has total capital of $200,000, all of this capital was raised in the past, and all of it is invested in assets which are used in operations. Now suppose Firm B's capital budget calls for net expenditures of $50,000 during 1980. This new (or marginal) capital will presumably be raised so as to maintain the 40/60 debt/equity relationship. Therefore, the company will obtain the $50,000 as 0.4($50,000) = $20,000 of debt and 0.6($50,000) = $30,000 of equity. The new equity could come from two sources: *(1) that part of this year's profits which management decides to retain in the business rather than use for dividends (but not from earnings retained in the past) or (2) the sale of new common stock.*

The debt will have an interest rate of 10 percent, or an after-tax cost of 6 percent. The cost of equity will be k_s if the equity is obtained by retained earnings, but it will be k_e if the company must sell new common stock. Consider first the case where the new equity comes from retained earnings. Firm B's stock now sells for $22.86 per share; its last dividend (D_0) was $1.4953; its expected growth rate is 7 percent; and the next expected dividend is $1.60. Thus, the expected and required rate of return on common equity, k_s, is estimated to be 14 percent:

$$k_s = \frac{D_1}{P_0} + g = \frac{\$1.60}{\$22.86} + 7\% = 14\%.$$

If the company expands so rapidly that its retained earnings for the year are not sufficient to meet its needs for new equity, forcing it to sell new common stock, and if the flotation cost of new stock is 10 percent, then its cost of equity will rise to 14.8 percent (see Equation 16–5):

$$k_e = \frac{D_1}{P_0(1 - F)} + g = \frac{\$1.60}{\$22.86(0.9)} + 7\% = 14.8\%.$$

Firm B's weighted average cost of capital, using first new retained earnings (earnings retained this year, not in the past) and then new common stock, is shown in Table 16–2. We see that the weighted average cost of each dollar, or the marginal cost of capital, is 10.8 percent so long as retained earnings are used, but the average cost jumps to 11.3 percent as soon as the firm exhausts its retained earnings and is forced to sell new common stock.[15]

Table 16–2
Firm B's Marginal Cost of Capital Using (a) New Retained Earnings and (b) New Common Stock

a. MCC when equity is from new retained earnings

	Weight	Component Cost	Product
Debt	0.4	6.0%	2.4%
Equity	0.6	14.0	8.4
	1.0	MCC = k_a =	10.8%

b. MCC when equity is from sale of new common stock

	Weight	Component Cost	Product
Debt	0.4	6.0%	2.4%
Equity	0.6	14.8	8.9
	1.0	MCC = k_a =	11.3%

How much new capital can Firm B raise before it exhausts its retained earnings and is forced to sell new common stock; i.e., where will the breaking point occur? Assume that the company has total earnings of $16,800 for the year, and that it has a policy of paying out half of its earnings as dividends. Thus, the addition to retained earnings will be $8,400 during the year. How much *total financing,* debt plus this $8,400 of retained earnings, can be done before the retained earnings are exhausted and the firm is forced to sell new common stock? In effect, we are seeking some amount, *X,* which is defined as a *breaking point* and which represents the total financing that can be done before Firm B is forced to sell new common stock. We know that 60 percent of *X* will be the new retained earnings, which will amount to $8,400. Therefore

$$0.6X = \text{Retained earnings} = \$8,400.$$

Solving for *X,* we obtain

$$\text{Breaking point} = X = \frac{\text{Retained earnings}}{0.6} = \frac{\$8,400}{0.6} = \$14,000.$$

Thus, Firm B can raise $14,000, consisting of $8,400 of retained earnings

---

15 In Chapter 7 we examined the amount of external capital a firm would need to acquire the assets necessary to meet different growth rates in sales. At relatively low growth rates, expansion could be financed by spontaneously generated debt and retained earnings, but at higher growth rates, external capital was needed. A similar situation exists here—if an analysis like that in Chapter 7 indicated that Firm B would need no external equity, then its marginal cost of capital would be 10.8 percent. However, if its growth rate were so rapid as to require it to sell new common stock, then its marginal cost of capital would rise to 11.3 percent.

Figure 16–3
Marginal Cost of Capital Schedule for Firm B,
Using Both Retained Earnings and New
Common Equity

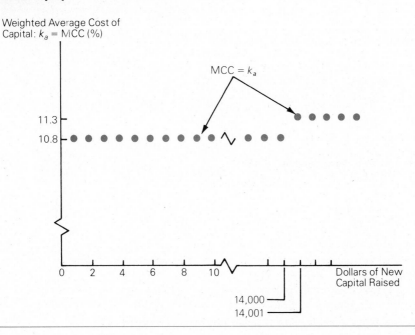

and $14,000 − $8,400 = $5,600 of new debt supported by these new retained earnings, without altering its capital structure:

40% = New debt supported by retained earnings	$ 5,600	
60% = Retained earnings	8,400	
Total expansion supported by retained earnings	$14,000	= Breaking point for retained earnings

Figure 16–3 graphs Firm B's marginal cost of capital schedule. Each dollar has a weighted average cost of 10.8 percent until the company has raised a total of $14,000. This $14,000 will consist of $5,600 of new debt with an after-tax cost of 6 percent and $8,400 of retained earnings with a cost of 14 percent. However, if Firm B raises $14,001, the last dollar will consist of 40 cents of debt and 60 cents of equity *obtained by selling new common equity at a cost of 14.8 percent,* so k_a = MCC rises from 10.8 percent to 11.3 percent, as calculated in Table 16–2.

Other Breaks in the MCC Schedule

There is a jump, or break, in Firm B's MCC schedule at $14,000 of new capital. Could there be other breaks in the schedule? Yes, there could be.

For example, suppose Firm B can obtain only $8,000 of debt at a 10 percent interest rate, with additional debt costing 12 percent. This will result in a second breaking point in the MCC schedule at the point where the $8,000 of 10 percent debt is exhausted. At what amount of *total financing* will the 10 percent debt be used up? If we let Y represent the total financing at this second breaking point, then

$$0.4Y = \$8,000,$$

and solving for Y, we obtain

$$Y = \frac{10\% \text{ debt}}{0.4} = \frac{\$8,000}{0.4} = \$20,000 = \text{Breaking point for debt.}$$

Thus, there will be another break in the MCC schedule after Firm B has raised a total of $20,000. As we saw above, up to $14,000 the MCC is 10.8 percent, while just beyond $14,000 the MCC rises to 11.3 percent. Now we see that the MCC rises again at $20,001, to 11.8 percent:

	Weight	Component Cost		Product
Debt	0.4	7.2[a]	=	2.9%
Equity	0.6	14.8	=	8.9
		k_a = MCC =		11.8%

[a]$12(1 - t) = 12(0.6) = 7.2\%.$

In other words, the next dollar beyond $20,000 will consist of 40 cents of 12 percent debt (7.2 percent after taxes) and 60 cents of new common stock (retained earnings were used up much earlier), and this marginal dollar will have an average cost of 11.8 percent.

The effect of this new MCC increase is shown in Figure 16–4. We now have two breaks, one caused by using up all the retained earnings and the other caused by using up all the 10 percent debt. With the two breaks, we have three different MCCs: MCC_1 = 10.8% for the first $14,000 of new capital; MCC_2 = 11.3% in the interval between $14,000 and $20,000; and MCC_3 = 11.8% for all new capital beyond $20,000.[16]

There could, of course, be still more breaking points—for example, debt costs could continue to rise, or the flotation costs on new common stock could increase above 10 percent as larger amounts of stock are sold. These changes would cause more breaks in the MCC. At the limit, we can even

---

16 When we use the term *weighted average cost of capital*, we are referring to k_a, which is the cost of one dollar raised partly as debt and partly as equity. One could also calculate the average cost of *all* capital the firm raises during a given year. For example, if Firm B raised $30,000, then the first $14,000 would have a cost of 10.8 percent, the next $6,000 would have a cost of 11.3 percent, and the last $10,000 would have a cost of 11.8 percent. The entire $30,000 would have a cost of

$$(14/30)(10.8\%) + (6/30)(11.3\%) + (10/30)(11.8\%) = 11.23\%.$$

This particular cost of capital should not be used for any financial decisions; it has no relevance in finance.

Figure 16–4
Marginal Cost of Capital Schedule for Firm B
Using Retained Earnings, New Common Stock,
and Higher-Cost Debt

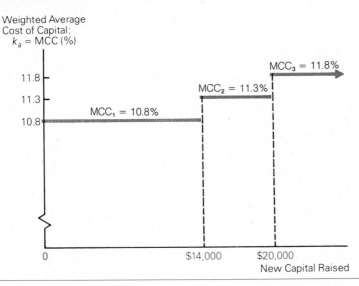

think of an MCC with so many breaking points that it rises almost
continuously beyond some given level of new financing. Such an MCC
schedule is shown in Figure 16–5.[17]

The easiest sequence for calculating MCC schedules is as follows:

1. Identify the points where breaks occur. A break will occur any time the cost
   of one of the capital components rises. (However, it is possible that two
   capital components could both increase at the same point.)
2. Determine the cost of capital for each component in the intervals between
   breaks.
3. Calculate the weighted averages of these costs; the weighted averages are
   the MCCs in each interval.

Notice that if there are *n* separate breaks, there will be *n* + 1 different
MCCs. For example, in Figure 16–4 we see two breaks and three different
MCCs.

Before closing this section, we should note again that a different MCC

---

17 The first breaking point is not necessarily the point where retained earnings are used up—it is possible
    that low-cost debt could be exhausted *before* retained earnings have been used up. For example, if
    Firm B had available only $5,000 of 10 percent debt, then Point Y would have occurred at $12,500:

$$Y = \frac{\$5,000}{0.4} = \$12,500.$$

This is well before the break for retained earnings, which occurs at $14,000.

Figure 16–5
Smoothed, or Continuous, Marginal Cost of
Capital Schedule

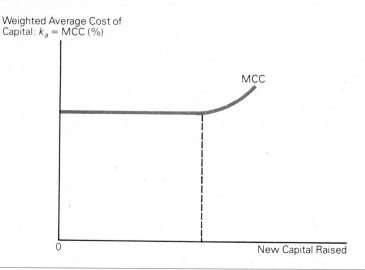

schedule would result if a different capital structure were used. The optimal
capital structure produces the lowest MCC.

COMBINING THE MCC AND THE INVESTMENT
OPPORTUNITY SCHEDULE (IOS)

Now that we have calculated the MCC schedule, we can use it to determine
the discount rate used in the capital budgeting process; *that is, we can use*
the MCC schedule to find the cost of capital for use in determining projects'
net present values (NPVs) as discussed in Chapter 11.

To understand how the MCC is used in capital budgeting, assume that
Firm B has three financial executives: a financial vice-president, a treasurer,
and a director of capital budgeting. The financial VP asks the treasurer to
develop the firm's MCC schedule, and the treasurer produces the schedule
shown earlier in Figure 16–4.

Next, the financial VP asks the director of capital budgeting (DCB) to
determine the dollar amounts of acceptable projects, using the IRR method
(or using the NPV method at a number of different discount rates). The DCB
has a listing of all the firm's potential projects, including the cost of each
project and its projected annual net cash inflows. This listing is shown in
Table 16–3. For example, Project A has a cost of $4,000 and is expected to
produce inflows of $1,082 per year for five years, while Project B, which has
a cost of $3,000, is expected to produce inflows of $657 per year for seven
years.

The DCB would first calculate each project's IRR as shown in the last column of Table 16–3, then plot the data given there as the Investment Opportunity Schedule (IOS) shown in Figure 16–6. The figure also reproduces Firm B's MCC schedule as developed by the treasurer and plotted in Figure 16–4. The IOS schedule shows how much money Firm B could profitably invest at different rates of return. If the cost of capital were *above* 13 percent, none of the available projects would have positive NPVs, hence none of them should be accepted. In this case, Firm B should simply not expand. If the cost of capital were 13 percent, Firm B should take on only Project D, and its capital budget would call for the company to raise and invest $7,000. If the cost of capital were 12.5 percent, the firm should take on Projects D and F, raising and investing a total of $12,000. Successively lower costs of capital call for larger and larger investment outlays.

Table 16–3
Potential Capital Budgeting Projects Available to Firm B

Project	Cost	Annual Inflows	Project Life (Years)	IRR, or Discount Rate at Which NPV = 0
A	$4,000	$1,082	5	11.0%
B	3,000	657	7	12.0
C	5,000	831	10	10.5
D	7,000	1,752	6	13.0
E	4,000	791	8	11.5
F	5,000	2,100	3	12.5

Just how far down its IOS curve should Firm B go? That is, which of its available projects should it accept? *The answer is that Firm B should accept the four projects (D, F, B, and E) which have rates of return in excess of the cost of the capital that would be used to finance them.* Projects A and C should be rejected, because they would have to be financed with capital that has a cost of 11.8 percent, and at that cost of capital, A and C (1) have negative NPVs and (2) have IRRs that are below their costs of capital. Therefore, Firm B's capital budget should total $19,000.[18]

---

18 People sometimes ask this question: "If we took Project A first, it would be acceptable, because its 11 percent return would exceed the 10.8 percent cost of money used to finance it. Why couldn't we do this?" The answer is that we are seeking, in effect, to maximize the *excess of returns over costs,* or the area that is above the MCC but below the IOS. We accomplish this by graphing (and accepting) the most profitable projects first.

　　Another question that sometimes arises is this: "What would happen if the MCC cut through one of the projects? For example, suppose the second breaking point in the MCC schedule had occurred at $18,000 rather than at $20,000, so that the MCC cut through Project E. Should we then accept Project E?" If Project E could be accepted in part, then we would take on only part of it. Otherwise, the answer would be determined by (1) finding the average cost of the funds needed to finance Project E (some of the money would cost 11.3 percent and some would cost 11.8 percent), and then (2) comparing the average cost of this money to the 11.5 percent return on the project. We should accept Project E if its return exceeds the average cost of the $4,000 needed to finance it.

Figure 16–6
Combining Firm B's MCC and IOS Curves to
Determine Its Optimal Capital Budget

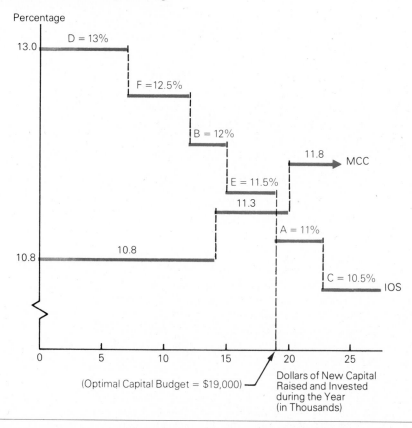

Now suppose we had the firm's expected investment opportunity schedule for the coming year as developed by the director of capital budgeting, as well as its MCC schedule as developed by the treasurer. These two schedules could be plotted on a graph like Figure 16–6, and the specific MCC where the IOS cuts the MCC schedule could be noted—in our example, the MCC is 11.3 percent at the intersection point. If the firm uses 11.3 percent to evaluate all projects, then Projects D, F, B, and E will be accepted, while A and C will be rejected. *Thus, the cost of capital used in the capital budgeting process as discussed in Chapter 11 is actually determined at the intersection of the IOS and MCC schedules. If this intersection rate is used, then the firm will make correct accept/reject decisions, and its level of financing and investment will be optimal. If it uses any other rate, its capital budgeting will not be optimal.*

We have, of course, abstracted from differential project riskiness in this chapter: implicitly, we have assumed that all projects are equally risky. As noted in Chapter 12, the cost of capital used to evaluate riskier projects should be adjusted upward, while a lower rate should be used for projects with below average risk. The MCC as determined in Figure 16–6 should be used to find the NPVs of new projects that are about as risky as the firm's existing assets. This cost of capital should be adjusted up or down to find NPVs for projects with higher or lower risk than the average project.[19]

SOME PROBLEM AREAS IN COST OF CAPITAL

A number of difficult issues relating to the cost of capital either have not been mentioned or else have been glossed over lightly thus far in the chapter. These topics are covered in advanced courses, but they deserve some mention now so that the reader may be alerted to potential dangers as well as provided with a preview of some of the matters dealt with in advanced finance courses.

1. The Effects of Personal Income Taxes Our discussion of the cost of capital dealt with corporate income taxes, but we abstracted from personal income taxes. When we use the equation $k_s = D_1/P_0 + g$, we often assume that investors are indifferent between dividend yield and capital gains. However, dividends are taxed at ordinary tax rates, whereas capital gains are taxed at a lower rate. Hence, investors may favor capital gains *(g)* more than dividend yield (D_1/P_0). This, in turn, might cause the differential between the cost of retained earnings *(k_s)* and new common stock *(k_e)* to be greater than can be accounted for by flotation costs alone. (See Appendix 16A of *Financial Management,* 2d edition.)

2. Depreciation-Generated Funds The largest single source of capital for many firms is depreciation, yet we did not discuss the cost of funds from this source. In brief, depreciation cash flows can either be reinvested or returned to investors—stockholders *and* creditors. The cost of depreciation-generated funds is approximately equal to the weighted average cost of capital in the interval where capital comes from retained earnings and low-cost debt. (See Appendix 16A of *Financial Management,* 2d edition.)

---

19 One way of handling project risk in Figure 16–6 is as follows:
  a. Determine the relative riskiness of each potential capital budgeting project.
  b. If a project is of average risk, use k_a = MCC to calculate its NPV. If the project is riskier than average, calculate its NPV at a higher risk-adjusted rate, say MCC_R = 1.2(MCC). If the project is less risky than average, use, say, MCC_L = 0.8(MCC).
  c. Now have the DCB assume some high MCC, say 25 percent, and calculate each project's risk-adjusted NPV. In this case, no project's NPV is positive. The DCB next shifts the assumed MCC to some lower level, say 24 percent, and repeats the process. When the assumed MCC is 13 percent, then Project D has NPV = 0, so it is accepted and plotted on the graph. (This assumes that D is of average risk; had D's risk been less than average, then it would have been acceptable at a higher MCC of 13%/0.8 = 16.25 percent. Had it been of above average risk, D would have been acceptable only at a corporate MCC of 13%/1.2 = 10.8 percent.
  d. As the assumed MCC is lowered, the different projects become acceptable and are plotted on the graph of Figure 16–6. Hence, we end up with a risk-adjusted IOS schedule. If this adjustment is not done, then it is possible that the IOS schedule will not show the various projects in proper perspective.

3. Deferred Taxes Most companies show, as a liability, an item called "deferred taxes." Deferred taxes arise principally from accelerated tax depreciation and delays in payments of regular taxes. Deferrals can constitute an important source of funds for many companies. Since deferred taxes are, in effect, an interest-free loan from the federal government, they have a zero cost. Many companies include deferred taxes in the weighted average cost of capital calculation but give it a zero cost. If deferred taxes are material for a given company, some care should be exercised in how this issue is handled.

4. Dynamic Considerations Capital budgeting and cost of capital estimates are a part of the *planning process*—they deal with ex ante, or estimated, data rather than ex post, or historical, data. Hence, we can be wrong about the location of the IOS and the MCC. For example, we can underestimate the MCC, hence accept projects that, with 20–20 foresight, we would have rejected. In a dynamic, changing world this is a real problem. Interest rates and money costs at the time plans are being laid and contracts to build plants are being let could be low, but six or eight months later money costs could have risen substantially. Thus, a project that formerly looked good could now look bad because we improperly estimated our MCC schedule.

5. Privately Owned Firms Our whole discussion of the cost of equity was related to publicly owned corporations, and we concentrated on the rate of return required by stockholders at large. There is a serious question as to how one should measure the cost of equity for a firm whose stock is not traded. Tax issues also become especially important in these cases. As a general rule, most authorities feel that the same principles of cost of capital estimation apply to both privately held and publicly owned firms, but the problems of obtaining input data are somewhat different.

6. Small Businesses Small businesses are generally privately owned, making it difficult to estimate their cost of equity, and they also often obtain debt from government sources (the Small Business Administration). However, the same theoretical principles apply to large and small firms.

7. Modigliani and Miller's Theory of Capital Structure and the Cost of Capital Franco Modigliani and Merton Miller (MM) are two well-known and highly regarded academicians who have done much important theoretical and empirical work on the cost of capital. MM have argued that k_a declines as the debt ratio increases because of the tax advantage of debt, and they specify precisely how this decline should occur. According to the strict MM theory, the optimal capital structure calls for the firm to use as much debt as it can get. Others have argued against the MM hypothesis, citing the rising costs of bankruptcy as the debt ratio increases. Most observers today feel that the relationship between k_a and the debt ratio has the approximate shape shown in Figure 16-1, although the optimal capital structure would vary among companies depending on their own unique circumstances.

8. Measurement Problems One cannot overemphasize the practical difficulties encountered in actually estimating the cost of equity. It is very difficult to obtain good input data for the CAPM, for g in the formula $k_s = D_1/P_0 + g$, and for the risk premium in the formula $k_s =$ bond yield plus risk premium.

9. Costs of Capital for Projects of Different Riskiness As noted in Chapter 12, a major difficulty arises when one attempts to assign different risk-adjusted discount rates to capital budgeting projects of differing degrees of riskiness.

10. Book Value Weights We have used book value capital structure weights throughout this chapter. This is consistent with what most firms actually do, but it is inconsistent with most of the theoretical finance literature. (See Chapters 15 and 16 of *Financial Management,* 2d edition, for a discussion.)

   Although the listing of problem areas appears formidable, the state of the art in cost of capital estimation is really not in bad shape. The procedures outlined in this chapter can be used to obtain cost of capital estimates that are sufficiently accurate for practical purposes, and the problems listed here are, in a sense, merely refinements. The refinements are not unimportant, but the problems we have identified certainly do not invalidate the usefulness of the procedures outlined in the chapter.

SUMMARY

This chapter showed how the MCC schedule is developed and then used in the capital budgeting process. We began by discussing the process of estimating the cost of each capital structure component. The *cost of debt* is simply $k_d(1 - t)$. The first increment of *common equity* is raised by *retaining earnings,* whose cost, k_s, may be estimated in one of three ways: (1) by the CAPM equation, $k_s = R_F + b(k_M - R_F)$; (2) by the dividend growth model, $k_s = D_1/P_0 + g$; or (3) by adding a risk premium of about 4 percent to the firm's cost of long-term debt. Once retained earnings have been exhausted, the firm must sell new common stock, or *external equity,* whose cost is $k_e = D_1/[P_0(1 - F)] + g$ in the case of a constant growth stock.

   The next task is to combine the component costs to form a *weighted average cost of capital,* k_a. The weights used to develop k_a should be based on the firm's target capital structure. If these weights are used, the stock price will be maximized and the cost of capital will simultaneously be minimized.

Capital typically has a higher cost if the firm expands beyond certain limits. This means that the MCC curve turns up beyond some point. We used the *breaking-point concept* to develop a step-function MCC schedule, which we then combined with the IOS schedule to determine both the optimal capital budget and the cost of capital that should be used in capital budgeting.

The concepts developed here are extended in Chapter 17, where we consider the optimal allocation of current earnings between dividends and retained earnings.

Questions

16-1 In what sense is the marginal cost of capital an average cost?

16-2 How would each of the following affect a firm's cost of debt, $k_d(1 - t)$; its cost of equity, k_s; and its average cost of capital, k_a? Indicate by a plus (+), a minus (−), or a zero (0) if the factor would raise, lower, or have an indeterminate effect on the items in question. Assume other things are held constant. Be prepared to justify your answer, but recognize that several of the parts probably have no single correct answer; these questions are to stimulate thought and discussion.

	Effect on		
	$k_d(1 - t)$	k_s	k_a
a. The corporate tax rate is lowered.	_____	_____	_____
b. The Federal Reserve tightens credit.	_____	_____	_____
c. The firm uses more debt; that is, it increases the debt/assets ratio.	_____	_____	_____
d. The dividend payout ratio is increased.	_____	_____	_____
e. The firm doubles the amount of capital it raises during the year.	_____	_____	_____
f. The firm expands into a risky new area.	_____	_____	_____
g. The firm increases its operating leverage.	_____	_____	_____
h. The firm merges with another firm whose earnings are countercyclical to those of the first firm and to the stock market.	_____	_____	_____
i. The stock market falls drastically, and our firm's stock falls along with the rest.	_____	_____	_____

	Effect on		
	$k_d(1-t)$	k_s	k_a
j. Investors become more risk averse.	_____	_____	_____
k. The firm is an electric utility with a large investment in nuclear plants. Several states propose a ban on nuclear power generation.	_____	_____	_____

16-3 The stock of XYZ Company is currently selling at its low for the year, but management feels that the stock price is only temporarily depressed because of investor pessimism. The firm's capital budget this year is so large that the use of new outside equity is contemplated. However, management does not want to sell new stock at the current low price and is therefore considering a departure from its "optimal" capital structure by borrowing the funds it would otherwise have raised in the equity markets. Does this seem to be a wise move?

16-4 Suppose a firm estimates its MCC and IOS schedules for the coming year and finds that they intersect at the point 10%, $10,000,000. What cost of capital should be used to evaluate average projects, high-risk projects, and low-risk projects?

16-5 The MCC and IOS schedules shown in Figure 16–6 could be thought of as "bands" rather than as lines to show that they are not known with certainty but, rather, are merely estimates of the true MCC and IOS schedules.

a. Do you think that the bands would be wider for the MCC or for the IOS schedule? In answering this question, visualize each point on the MCC and IOS schedules as being the expected value of a probability distribution.

b. For the IOS schedule, would the band, or confidence interval, associated with each project be identical? If not, what would this imply, and how might it affect the firm's capital budgeting analysis?

Problems

16-1 Calculate the after-tax cost of debt under each of the following conditions:
a. Interest rate, 10%; tax rate, 0%.
b. Interest rate, 10%; tax rate, 40%.
c. Interest rate, 10%; tax rate, 60%.

16-2 XYZ Company's last dividend per share was $1; that is, $D_0 = 1. The stock sells for $20 per share. The expected growth rate is 5 percent. Calculate XYZ's cost of capital from retained earnings.

16-3 The Dorfman Company's EPS in 1979 was $2. EPS in 1974 was $1.3612. The company pays out 40 percent of its earnings as dividends, and the stock sells for $21.60.

    a. Calculate the growth rate in earnings. (*Hint:* This is a *five* year growth period.)

    b. Calculate the *next* expected dividend per share, D_1. ($D_0 = 0.4(\$2) = \$0.80$.) Assume the past growth rate will continue.

    c. What is the cost of retained earnings, k_s, for the Dorfman Company?

16-4 Given the following data, and a tax rate of 40 percent, calculate the weighted cost of capital at each debt ratio and indicate the capital structure that minimizes the cost of capital.

Debt/Assets Ratio	k_d	k_s
0%	10 %	12 %
10	10	12
20	10.5	12.5
30	11	13
40	12	13.5
50	14	15.5
60	17	20

16-5 The Dorfman Company expects earnings of $10 million next year. Its dividend payout ratio is 40 percent, and its debt/assets ratio is 60 percent.

    a. What amount of retained earnings does Dorfman expect next year?

    b. At what amount of financing will there be a breaking point in the MCC schedule?

    c. If Dorfman can borrow $4 million at an interest rate of 8 percent, another $4 million at a rate of 9 percent, and additional debt at a rate of 10 percent, at what points will rising debt costs cause breaks in the MCC schedule?

16-6 The Dorfman Company's next expected dividend (D_1) is $0.864, its growth rate is 8 percent, and the stock now sells for $21.60. New stock can be sold at a price of $18.36.

    a. What is Dorfman's percentage flotation cost, F?

    b. What is Dorfman's cost of new common stock, k_e?

16-7 On January 1, the total assets of the Gould Company were $60 million. During the year, the company plans to raise and invest $30 million. The firm's present capital structure, shown below, is considered to be optimal. Assume that there is no short-term debt.

Debt	$30,000,000
Common equity	30,000,000
	$60,000,000

New bonds will have an 8 percent coupon rate and will be sold at par. Common stock, currently selling at $30 a share, can be sold to net the company $27 a share. Stockholders' required rate of return is estimated to be 12 percent, consisting of a dividend yield of 4 percent and an expected growth rate of 8 percent. (The next expected dividend is $1.20, so

$1.20/$30 = 4\%$.) Retained earnings for the year are estimated to be $3 million (ignore depreciation). The marginal corporate tax rate is 40 percent.

a. Assuming all asset expansion (gross expenditures for fixed assets plus related working capital) is included in the capital budget, what is the dollar amount of the capital budget? (Ignore depreciation.)

b. To maintain the present capital structure, how much of the capital budget must be financed by common equity?

c. How much of the new common equity funds needed must be generated internally? Externally?

d. Calculate the cost of each of the common equity components.

e. At what level of capital expenditures will there be a break in the MCC schedule?

f. Calculate the MCC (1) below and (2) above the break in the schedule.

g. Plot the MCC schedule. Also, draw in an IOS schedule that is consistent with both the MCC schedule and the projected capital budget. Any IOS schedule that is consistent will do.

16-8 The Collins Glass Company projects the following capital structure for December 31, 1980:

Debt		$12,000,000
Common stock	$ 6,000,000	
Retained earnings	$12,000,000	
Common equity		$18,000,000
Total capitalization		$30,000,000

Earnings per share have grown steadily over the last eight years, from $1 in 1972 to $2 in 1980. The investment community, expecting this growth to continue, applies a price/earnings ratio of 20 to yield a current market price of $40. The book value per share is also $40, and the total market value of the company is $30 million, the same as its accounting value. Collins's last annual dividend was $1.25, and it expects the dividend to grow at the same rate as earnings. Earnings are expected to grow at a 9 percent rate, so $D_1 = \$1.25(1.09) = \$1.3625$. The addition to retained earnings for 1980 is projected at $3 million; these funds will be available during the 1981 budget year. The corporate tax rate, including state income taxes, is 60 percent.

   Assuming that the capital structure relations set out above are maintained, new securities can be sold at the following costs:

Bonds: (1) Up to and including $3 million of new bonds, 8 percent yield to investor on all new bonds. (2) From $3.01 million to $6 million of new bonds, 8.5 percent yield to investor on this increment of bonds. (3) Over $6 million of new bonds, 10.5 percent yield to investor on this increment of bonds.

Common: (1) Up to $3 million of new outside common stock, $40 per share less $2 per share flotation cost ($F = 5\%$). (2) Over $3 million

of new outside common stock, $40 per share less $6 per share
flotation cost on this increment of new common ($F = 15\%$).

a. At what dollar amounts of new capital will breaks occur in the MCC
schedule? (*Hint:* There will be four breaks—one where retained
earnings are used up, two where interest rates rise, and one where stock
flotation costs increase.)

b. Calculate the MCC in the interval between each of these breaks, and
then plot the MCC schedule. *(Hint:* With *four* breaks, there will be five
intervals, hence five different MCCs.)

c. Discuss the breaking points in the MCC curve. What factors in the real
world would tend to make the MCC curve smooth?

d. Assume now that Collins has the following investment opportunities:

(1) It can invest up to $4 million at an 11 percent rate of return.

(2) It can invest an additional $12 million at a 10.2 percent rate of
return.

(3) It can invest still another $12 million at a 9.3 percent rate of return.
Thus, Collins's total *potential* budget is $28 million. Determine the size
of the company's optimal capital budget for the year.

16-9 The following tabulation gives earnings per share figures for Template
Manufacturing during the preceding ten years. The firm's common stock,
140,000 shares outstanding, is now selling for $50 a share, and the
expected dividend for the current year (1981) is 50 percent of the 1980
EPS. Investors expect past trends to continue, so g may be based on the
earnings growth rate.

Year	EPS
1971	$2.00
1972	2.16
1973	2.33
1974	2.52
1975	2.72
1976	2.94
1977	3.18
1978	3.43
1979	3.70
1980	4.00

The current interest rate on new debt is 8 percent. The firm's marginal tax
rate is 40 percent. The firm's capital structure, considered to be optimal, is
as follows:

Debt	$ 3,000,000
Common equity	7,000,000
	$10,000,000

a. Calculate the after-tax cost of new debt and of common equity,
assuming new equity comes only from retained earnings. Calculate the
cost of equity as $k_s = D_1/P_0 + g$.

    b. Find the marginal cost of capital, again assuming no new common stock is sold.

    c. How much can be spent for capital investments before external equity must be sold? (Assume that retained earnings available for 1981 investment are 50 percent of 1980 earnings. Obtain 1980 earnings by multiplying 1980 EPS by the shares outstanding.)

    d. What is the marginal cost of capital (cost of funds raised in excess of the amount calculated in Part c) if new common stock can be sold to the public at $50 a share to net the firm $45 a share? The cost of debt is constant.

    e. In the problem we assume that the capital structure is optimal. What would happen if the firm deviated from this capital structure? Use a graph to illustrate your answer. The graph should be "reasonable," but any reasonable set of curves will do.

16-10 Haslem Enterprises has the following capital structure, which it considers to be optimal under the present and forecasted conditions:

Debt (long-term only)	30%
Common equity	70
Total capital	100%

For the coming year, management expects to realize net earnings of $105,000. The past dividend policy of paying out 50 percent of earnings will continue. Present commitments from its banker will allow Haslem to borrow according to the following schedule:

Loan Amount	Interest Rate
$0 to $42,000	8%
$42,001 and above	12%

The company's tax rate is 40 percent, the current market price of its stock is $50 per share, its *last* dividend was $1.85 per share, and the expected growth rate is 8 percent. External equity (new common) can be sold at a flotation cost of 15 percent.

    The firm has the following investment opportunities for the next period:

Project	Cost	Annual Cash Flows	Project Life	IRR Schedule[a]
A	$ 75,000	$15,629	8 years	13.0
B	100,000	15,582	10 years	9.0
C	50,000	15,775	4 years	
D	25,000	14,792	2 years	12.0
E	50,000	12,858	6 years	

[a]Note: IRR schedule is *that discount rate* at which $NPV \approx 0$.

Management asks you to help determine what projects (if any) should be undertaken. You proceed with this analysis by answering the following questions as posed in a logical sequence:

a. How many breaks are there in the MCC schedule?
b. At what dollar amounts do the breaks occur, and what causes them?
c. What is the weighted average cost of capital, k_a, in each of the intervals between the breaks?
d. What are the IRR values for Projects C and E?
e. Graph the IOS and MCC schedules.
f. Which projects should Haslem's management accept?

17 DIVIDEND POLICY

Dividend policy involves the decision to pay out earnings or to retain them for reinvestment in the firm. Our basic stock price model, $P_0 = D_1/(k_s - g)$, shows that a policy of paying out more cash dividends will raise D_1, which will tend to increase the price of the stock. However, raising cash dividends means that less money is available for reinvestment, and plowing back less earnings into the business will lower the expected growth rate and depress the price of the stock. Thus, dividend policy has two opposing effects, and *the optimal policy is the one that strikes a balance between current dividends and future growth and thereby maximizes the price of the firm's stock.*

A number of factors influence dividend policy. Included are the differential tax rates on dividends and capital gains, the investment opportunities available to the firm, alternative sources of capital, and stockholders' preferences for current versus future income. The major goal of this chapter is to show how these and other factors interact to determine the optimal dividend policy.

THE RESIDUAL THEORY OF DIVIDENDS

In the preceding chapters on capital budgeting and the cost of capital, we indicated that, generally, the cost of capital and investment opportunity schedules must be combined before the cost of capital can be established. In other words, the optimum capital budget, the marginal cost of capital, and the marginal rate of return on investment are determined *simultaneously.* In this section we use this framework to develop what is called *the residual theory of dividends,* which states that a firm should follow these four steps: (1) determine the optimal capital budget; (2) determine the amount of equity needed to finance that budget; (3) use retained earnings to supply this equity to the extent possible; and (4) pay dividends only if more earnings are available than are needed to support the capital budget. The word *residual* implies "left over," and the residual theory states that dividends should be paid only out of leftover earnings.

The basis of the theory is that *investors prefer to have the firm retain and reinvest earnings rather than pay them out in dividends if the return on reinvested earnings exceeds the rate of return the investors could obtain on other investments of comparable risk.* If the corporation can reinvest retained earnings at a 20 percent rate of return, while the best rate stockholders can obtain if the earnings are passed on in the form of dividends is 12 percent, then stockholders would prefer to have the firm retain the profits.

We saw in Chapter 16 that the cost of retained earnings is an *opportunity cost* that reflects rates of return available to equity investors. If a firm's stockholders could buy other stocks of equal risk and obtain a 12 percent dividend-plus-capital-gain yield, then 12 percent is the firm's cost of retained earnings. The cost of new outside equity raised by selling common stock is higher because of the costs of floating the issue.

Most firms have a target capital structure that calls for at least some debt, so new financing is done partly with debt and partly with equity. As long as the firm finances at the optimum point, using the proper amounts of debt and equity, and provided it uses only internally generated equity (retained earnings), its marginal cost of each new dollar of capital will be minimized. Internally generated equity is available for financing a certain amount of new investment; beyond this amount, the firm must turn to more expensive new common stock. At the point where new stock must be sold, the cost of equity, and, consequently, the marginal cost of capital, rises.

These concepts, which were developed in Chapter 16, are illustrated in Figure 17–1 with data from the Erie Steel Company. Erie has a marginal cost of capital of 10 percent as long as retained earnings are available, but MCC begins to rise at the point where new stock must be sold. Erie has $60 million of earnings and a 40 percent optimum debt ratio. Provided it does

Figure 17–1
Marginal Cost of Capital

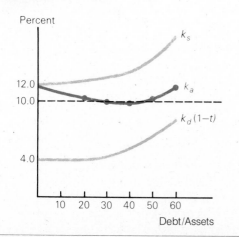

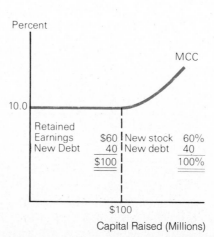

not pay cash dividends, Erie can make net investments (investments in addition to asset replacements financed from depreciation) of $100 million, consisting of $60 million from retained earnings plus $40 million of new debt supported by the retained earnings at a 10 percent marginal cost of capital. Therefore, its marginal cost of capital is constant at 10 percent up to $100 million of capital. Beyond $100 million, the marginal cost of capital rises as the firm begins to use more expensive new common stock. Of course, if Erie does not retain all of its earnings, the MCC will begin to rise before $100 million. For example, if Erie retained only $30 million, then the MCC would begin to rise at $30 million retained earnings + $20 million debt = $50 million.

Next, suppose Erie's director of capital budgeting constructs an investment opportunity schedule and plots it on a graph. The investment opportunity curves for three different years—one for a good year (IOS_G), one for a normal year (IOS_N), and one for a bad year (IOS_B)—are shown in Figure 17–2. IOS_G shows that Erie can invest more money, and at higher rates of return, than it can when the investment opportunities are as given by IOS_N and IOS_B.

Figure 17–2
Investment Opportunity (or IRR) Schedules

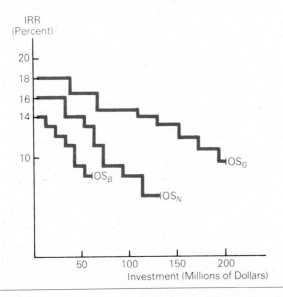

In Figure 17–3 we combine the investment opportunity schedules with the cost of capital schedule. The point where the IOS curve cuts the MCC curve defines the proper level of new investment. When investment opportunities are relatively bad (IOS_B), the optimum level of investment is $40 million; when opportunities are normal (IOS_N), $70 million should be invested; and

Figure 17-3
Interrelation among Cost of Capital,
Investment Opportunities, and New Investment

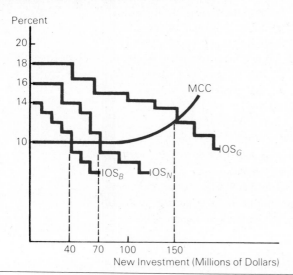

when opportunities are relatively good (IOS_G), Erie should make new investments in the amount of $150 million.

Consider the situation where IOS_G is the appropriate schedule. Erie has $60 million in earnings and a 40 percent target debt ratio. Thus, it can finance $100 million, consisting of $60 million of retained earnings plus $40 million of new debt, at a cost of 10 percent, if it retains all of its earnings. If it pays out part of the earnings in dividends, then it will have to begin using expensive new common stock earlier than need be, so the MCC curve will rise before it otherwise would. *This suggests that under the conditions of IOS_G, Erie should retain all of its earnings. According to the residual theory, its payout ratio should be zero.*

Under the conditions of IOS_N, however, Erie should invest only $70 million. How should this investment be financed? First, notice that if it retains the full amount of its earnings, $60 million, it will need to sell only $10 million of new debt. However, if Erie retains $60 million and sells only $10 million of new debt, it will move away from its target capital structure. To stay on target, Erie must finance 60 percent of the required $70 million by equity— retained earnings—and 40 percent by debt; this means retaining $42 million and selling $28 million of new debt. Since Erie retains only $42 million of its $60 million total earnings, it must distribute the residual, $18 million, to its stockholders. Thus, its optimal payout ratio is $18 million/$60 million = 30 percent.

Under the conditions of IOS_B, Erie should invest only $40 million. Because it has $60 million in earnings, it could finance the entire $40 million out of retained earnings and still have $20 million available for dividends.

Should this be done? Under our assumptions, this would not be a good decision, because Erie would move away from its optimal capital structure. To stay at the 40 percent target debt/assets ratio, Erie must retain $24 million of earnings and sell $16 million of debt. When the $24 million of retained earnings is subtracted from the $60 million total earnings, Erie is left with a residual of $36 million, the amount that should be paid out in dividends. Thus, the payout ratio as prescribed by the residual theory is 60 percent.

IS DIVIDEND POLICY REALLY RELEVANT?

It has been asserted that dividend policy has no effect either on the price of a firm's stock or on its cost of capital; that is, that dividend policy is irrelevant. The principal proponents of this view are Merton Miller and Franco Modigliani (MM).[1] MM prove their position in a theoretical sense, but only under the assumptions that (1) there are no personal or corporate income taxes and (2) there are no stock flotation costs. Since these assumptions are clearly not true, dividend policy may be and probably is relevant in the sense that it influences stock prices and the cost of capital.

However, MM's analysis does make it quite clear that the residual theory is only a starting point in establishing a dividend policy. Other factors must also be taken into account. Some of these factors are discussed in the next section.

FACTORS THAT INFLUENCE DIVIDEND POLICY

By definition, the optimal dividend policy is the one that maximizes the price of a firm's stock. Suppose Erie Steel has the cost of capital schedule shown in Figure 17–3, and IOS_N is the applicable set of investment opportunities. Under these conditions, the residual theory indicates that Erie should pay out 30 percent of its earnings. What would happen if Erie set a different dividend policy? How would this affect the price of the firm's stock?

Consider the options open to Erie. The firm could change its dividend policy by increasing or by decreasing the payout ratio, but either action would necessitate other changes in corporate policy. Thus, if Erie *raises* its dividends, it must do one of the following: (1) reduce its level of investment below $70 million, thereby foregoing profitable projects; (2) sell common stock to replace the retained earnings, thus incurring unnecessary flotation costs; or (3) replace the retained earnings with additional debt, thus moving away from the optimal capital structure. On the other hand, if Erie *reduces*

1 Merton H. Miller and Franco Modigliani, "Dividend Policy, Growth, and the Valuation of Shares," *Journal of Business* 34 (October 1961):411–433.

its dividends, it would also have to (1) increase its capital budget, which would involve accepting unprofitable projects, or (2) use the extra retained earnings as a substitute for new debt, which would cause a departure from the target capital structure.

It would therefore appear that the dividend policy as determined by the residual theory is the only dividend policy that will maximize the price of the firm's stock. However, a critical assumption is embodied in the residual theory—it assumes that k_s, the rate of return investors require on the stock, is not affected by the firm's dividend policy. In the case of Erie Steel, the residual theory implicitly assumes that so long as the company maintains its 40 percent debt ratio, k_s remains constant at 13.3 percent. This implies that investors are indifferent between dividends and capital gains, and that

$$k_s = D_1/P_0 + g = 13.3\%$$

for any combination of dividend yield and capital gains yield.

The question of whether or not dividend policy affects the cost of equity has been hotly debated in academic circles. Myron Gordon and John Lintner, on the one hand, have argued that k_s increases as the dividend payout ratio is reduced. They say, in effect, that investors value a dollar of expected dividends more highly than a dollar of expected capital gains.[2] Miller and Modigliani, on the other hand, have argued that k_s is independent of dividend policy, which implies that investors are indifferent between dividends and capital gains.[3]

Figure 17–4 presents two graphs which highlight the arguments. The left panel shows the Miller-Modigliani position. Here the company has $k_s = D_1/P_0 + g = 13.3\%$ for any dividend policy: The equilibrium return, k_s, is assumed to be a constant regardless of whether it comes entirely as dividend yield, entirely as expected capital gains, or as a combination of the two. Dividends may be less risky than expected capital gains, but capital gains are taxed at a lower rate, and MM assume that these two effects offset one another.

The right panel shows the Gordon-Lintner view. They argue that the risk effects more than offset the tax effects, so investors are willing to accept a lower total return *(k_s)* if it has a heavier dividend yield component. In other words, Gordon-Lintner assume that more than 1 percent of additional g is required to offset a 1 percent reduction of dividend yield.

Attempts have been made to test the MM and Gordon-Lintner hypotheses.[4] In theory, one could take a sample of companies which have different dividend policies, hence different dividend yield and growth rate components, and plot them on graphs such as those shown in Figure 17–4.

2 M. J. Gordon, "Optimal Investment and Financing Policy," *Journal of Finance* (May 1963), pp. 264–272; and J. Lintner, "Dividends, Earnings, Leverage, Stock Prices, and the Supply of Capital to Corporations," *Review of Economics and Statistics* (August 1962), pp. 243–269.
3 M. H. Miller and F. Modigliani, ibid.
4 See E. F. Brigham and M. J. Gordon, "Leverage, Dividend Policy, and the Cost of Capital," *Journal of Finance* (March 1968), pp. 85–104.

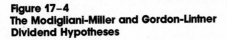

**Figure 17-4
The Modigliani-Miller and Gordon-Lintner
Dividend Hypotheses**

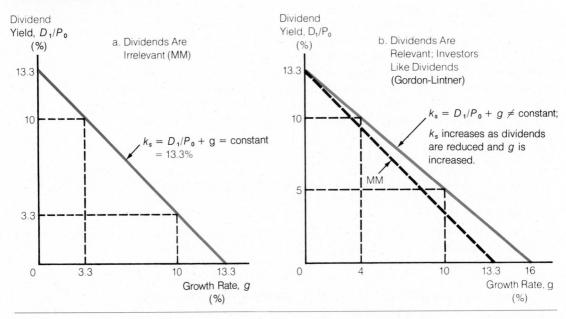

If the points all plotted on the line in the left graph so that the slope of the resulting regression line was −1.0, this would support the MM indifference hypothesis. If the points all plotted on the line in the right graph so that the slope was less negative than −1.0 (say −0.8), this would support the Gordon-Lintner hypothesis. In fact, when this is done with real companies, the slope of the regression line is found to be about −0.5. This seems to support Gordon-Lintner, but statistical difficulties prevent us from saying that this really *proves* that MM are wrong, and that dividend policy truly affects k_s. There are two basic problems here. First, for a valid statistical test, things other than dividend policy must be held constant; i.e., the sample companies must differ only with respect to their dividend policy. And second, we must be able to measure the expected growth rates for the sample firms with a high degree of accuracy. These conditions do not hold. We simply cannot find a set of publicly owned firms that differ only with respect to dividend policy, and we cannot get precise estimates of investors' expected growth rates. Therefore, we cannot determine empirically what effect, if any, dividend policy has on the cost of equity. However, the research that has been done does provide us with a good starting point for analyzing dividend policy decisions.

The factors which influence dividend policy may be grouped into four broad categories: (1) constraints on dividend payments, (2) investment opportunities, (3) availability and cost of alternative sources of capital, and

(4) effects of dividend policy on the required rate of return, k_s. Each of these categories has several subparts. They are all discussed below.

Constraints

1. Bond Indentures Debt contracts generally restrict dividend payment to earnings generated after the loan was granted. Also, debt contracts often stipulate that no dividends can be paid unless the current ratio, the times interest earned ratio, and other safety ratios exceed stated minimums.

2. Impairment of Capital Rule Dividend payments cannot exceed the balance sheet item "retained earnings." This is a legal restriction called "the impairment of capital rule," and it is designed to protect creditors. ("Liquidating dividends" can be paid out of capital, but they must be indicated as such, and they must not reduce capital below limits stated in the debt contract.)

3. Availability of Cash Cash dividends can only be paid with cash. Thus, a shortage of cash in the bank can restrict dividend payments. However, unused borrowing capacity can offset this factor.

4. Penalty Tax on Improperly Accumulated Earnings To prevent wealthy individuals from using corporations to avoid personal taxes, the tax code provides for a special surtax on improperly accumulated income (see Chapter 2). Thus, if the IRS can demonstrate that the dividend payout ratio is being deliberately held down to help stockholders avoid personal taxes, the firm is subject to heavy penalties.

Investment Opportunities

5. Location of the IOS Schedule If the relevant IOS schedule in Figure 17–3 is far to the right, this will tend to produce a low payout, and conversely if the IOS is far to the left. Also, the steeper the slope of the IOS, the more important it is to use the payout prescribed by the residual theory.

6. Possibility of Accelerating or Delaying Projects If the firm can accelerate or postpone projects, this will permit more flexibility in its dividend policy.

Alternative Sources of Capital

7. Cost of Selling New Stock If a firm wishes to finance a given level of investment, it can obtain equity by retaining earnings or by selling new common stock. If flotation costs are high, k_e will be well above k_s, making it much better to finance through retention versus sale of new common stock (see Chapter 16). If flotation costs are low, then dividend policy will be less important. Flotation costs must include underwriting costs and underpricing caused by a downward sloping demand curve for new stock (see Chapter 14). Flotation costs differ among firms (for example, they are higher for small firms). Hence, the importance of dividend policy and the optimal policy varies among firms.

8. Control If management is concerned about maintaining control, it may be reluctant to sell new stock, hence may retain more earnings than it otherwise would. This factor is most important for small, closely held firms.

9. Capital Structure Flexibility A firm can finance a given level of investment with debt or equity. As we saw above, if stock flotation costs are low, dividend policy is less important because equity can be raised by retaining earnings or by selling new stock. A similar situation holds for debt policy. If the firm is willing to adjust its debt ratio, it can maintain a constant dollar dividend by using a variable debt ratio. The shape of the average cost of capital curve (left panel in Figure 17–1) determines the practical extent to which the debt ratio can be varied. If the average cost of capital curve is relatively flat over a wide range, then dividend policy is less critical than it is if the curve has a distinct minimum. MM argue that the cost curve is flat, and this is one reason they think that dividend policy is irrelevant.

Effects of Dividend Policy on k_s

10. Capital Gains Tax Rate Dividends are taxed at federal rates up to 70 percent, plus additional state taxes. The tax on capital gains is generally limited to 28 percent. This makes wealthy investors tend to prefer capital gains to dividends. To the extent that this factor is important, k_s will be smaller the lower the payout, other things held constant. If k_s does vary with the dividend payout, then the MCC curves in Figures 17–1 and 17–3 are not constant as shown, but vary depending on the payout. This could invalidate the residual theory and require more complex decision rules. In general, the optimal payout would be *lower* than that suggested by the simple residual theory.

Large, publicly owned firms have stockholders whose tax brackets range from zero (for some retirees and institutional investors such as pension funds) to about 80 percent (for wealthy individuals). This makes it difficult to accommodate all stockholders and thus creates a problem—for which group of stockholders should dividend policy be set? To the extent that stockholders can shift their investments among firms, a firm can set any specific policy, then have stockholders who do not like this policy sell to other investors who do. Thus, the firm will attract a certain *clientele* of stockholders. However, switching may be inefficient because of
(1) brokerage costs, (2) the possibility that selling stockholders must pay

capital gains taxes, and (3) a possible shortage of investors who like the firm's newly stated dividend policy.

11. Stockholders' Desire for Current versus Future Income Some stockholders desire current income; retired individuals and university endowment funds are examples. Other stockholders have no need for current investment income and simply reinvest any dividends received, after first paying income taxes on the dividend income. If the firm retains and reinvests income, rather than paying dividends, those stockholders who need current income will be disadvantaged. They will presumably receive capital gains, but they will be forced to sell off some of their shares to obtain cash. This will involve brokerage costs, which are relatively high unless large sums are involved. Also, some institutional investors (or trustees for individuals) may be precluded from selling stock and then "spending capital." Stockholders who are saving rather than spending dividends will, of course, have to incur brokerage costs to reinvest their dividends. (However, as noted in a later section, many firms today have automatic dividend reinvestment plans which minimize the expense of reinvestment.)

Investors can, of course, switch companies if they own stock in a firm whose dividend policy differs from the policies they desire—this is another example of the "clientele effect." However, there are costs associated with such changes (brokerage and capital gains taxes), and there may be a shortage of investors to replace those seeking to switch, in which case the stock price may fall and remain low.

12. Risk of Dividends versus Risk of Capital Gains It has been argued by Gordon that investors regard returns coming in the form of dividends as being less risky than capital gains returns. Others disagree. If someone receives dividends, then turns around and reinvests them in the same firm or one of similar risk, there would appear to be little difference in risk between this operation and having the company retain and reinvest the earnings in the first place. This question has been subjected to statistical studies, but without conclusive results.

13. Information Content of Dividends It has been observed that an increase in the dividend (for example, the annual dividend per share is raised from $2 to $2.50) is often accompanied by an increase in the price of the stock, while a dividend cut generally leads to a stock price decline. This suggests to some that investors like dividends more than capital gains. However, MM argue differently. They state that corporations are always reluctant to cut dividends, so firms do not raise dividends unless they anticipate higher, or at least stable, earnings in the future. Thus, a dividend increase is a signal to investors that the firm's management forecasts good future earnings. Conversely, a dividend reduction signals that management is forecasting poor earnings in the future. Thus, MM state that a change in dividend policy is not important in the sense of showing that investors prefer dividends to retained earnings; the fact that price changes follow dividend actions simply indicates to them that there is an important *information content* in dividend announcements. Like most other aspects of dividend policy, empirical studies on this topic have been inconclusive. There clearly is some information content in dividend announcements, but it may or may not be the complete explanation for the stock price changes that follow increases or decreases in dividends.

14. Legal Listing New York and certain other important states have a list of stocks of good, solid companies which can be purchased by certain fiduciary institutions—this is called the "legal list." Institutional investors not subject to the legal list still consider it and often refuse to buy stocks that are not included. Being on the legal list increases the demand for a firm's stock, so companies like to be on it. Since one criterion for inclusion on the legal list is the absence of dividend reductions, companies try very hard to maintain stable dividend policies.

The fourteen points discussed above are considered by financial executives when they are establishing their firms' dividend policies, but the only real generalizations we can make are these:

1. The optimal dividend policy for a firm is influenced by many factors. Some suggest a higher payout than would be called for by the residual theory, while others suggest a lower optimal payout.
2. Much research has been done on dividend policy, but many points are still unresolved. Researchers are far from being able to specify a precise model for establishing corporate dividend policy.

Although no one has been able to construct a usable model for finding an optimal dividend policy, the residual theory does at least provide a good starting point, and we do have a checklist of factors to consider before finalizing the dividend policy. Later in the chapter we shall return to the process of establishing a dividend policy, but first we must take up three other components of dividend policy—actual payment procedures, stock splits, and stock dividends.

DIVIDEND PAYMENT PROCEDURES

Corporations tend to use one of three major dividend payment procedures. These alternatives are discussed in this section.

Constant, or Steadily Increasing, Dividend per Share Some firms set a specific annual dividend per share and then maintain it, increasing the annual dividend only if it seems clear that future earnings will be sufficient to allow the dividend to be maintained. A corollary of the policy is this rule: *Avoid ever reducing the annual dividend.* The fact that most corporations do in fact follow, or attempt to follow, such a policy lends support to the information content hypothesis of Modigliani and Miller (Factor 13 in the preceding section).

A stable payment policy is illustrated in Figure 17–5 with data for the Walter Watch Company over a thirty year period. Initially, earnings were $2 and dividends were $1 a share, so the payout ratio was 50 percent. Earnings rose for four years, while dividends remained constant; thus, the payout ratio fell during this period. During 1955 and 1956, earnings fell substantially; however, the dividend was maintained and the payout rose above the 50 percent target. During the period between 1956 and 1960, earnings experienced a sustained rise. Dividends were held constant for a time, while management sought to determine whether the earnings increase would be permanent. By 1961, it was apparent that the earnings gain would be maintained, so dividends were raised in three steps to reestablish the 50 percent target payout. During 1965, a strike caused earnings to fall below the regular dividend. Expecting the earnings decline to be temporary, management maintained the dividend. Earnings fluctuated on a fairly high plateau from 1966 through 1972, during which time dividends remained constant. A new increase in earnings permitted management to raise the dividend in 1973 to reestablish the 50 percent payout ratio.

Figure 17–5
Walter Watch Company: Dividends and Earnings over Time

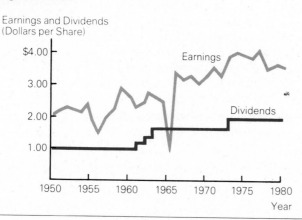

A variant of this policy is the "stable growth rate" policy. Here the firm sets a target growth rate for dividends, say 6 percent per year, and strives to increase dividends by this amount each year. Obviously, earnings must be growing at a reasonably steady rate for this policy to be feasible.

There are several rationales for these policies. First, given the existence of the "information content" idea, a fluctuating payment policy might lead to fluctuating stock prices, which in turn could lead to a high k_s. Second, stockholders who use dividends for current consumption want to be able to count on receiving dividends on a regular basis, so irregular dividends might lower demand for the stock. Third, a stable dividend policy is most consistent with the requirements for legal listing. Fourth, even though the optimal payout (in the residual theory sense) might vary somewhat from year to year, delaying some investment projects, departing from the target capital structure during a particular year, or even selling common stock might all be preferable to cutting the dividend or reducing its growth rate. Finally, setting a steady dividend growth rate will confirm investors' estimates of the g-factor and thus enhance the price of the stock; that is, investors will think of the stock as a "growth stock."

Constant Payout Ratio A very few firms follow a policy of paying out a constant percentage of earnings. Earnings will surely fluctuate, so following this policy necessarily means that the dollar amount of dividends will fluctuate. For reasons discussed in the preceding section, this policy is not likely to maximize a firm's stock price. However, before its bankruptcy, Penn Central Railroad did follow the policy of paying out one-half its earnings: "A dollar for the stockholders and a dollar for the company," as one director put it. Logic like this could drive any company to bankruptcy!

Low Regular Dividend plus Extras The low regular dividend plus a year-end extra is a compromise between the first two policies. It gives the firm flexibility, but it leaves investors somewhat uncertain about what their dividend will be. Still, if a firm's earnings and cash flows are quite volatile, using extra dividends may well be its best choice. The directors can set a relatively low regular dividend—low enough that it can be maintained even in low-profit years or in years when a considerable amount of reinvestment is needed—and then supplement it with an extra dividend in years when excess funds are available. General Motors, whose earnings fluctuate widely from year to year, has long followed the practice of supplementing its regular dividend with an extra dividend paid at the end of the year, when its profits and investment requirements are known.

The Actual Payment

Dividends are normally paid quarterly. For example, AT&T paid dividends of $5.00 during 1979, $1.25 each quarter. In common financial language, we say that AT&T's *regular quarterly dividend* is $1.25, or that its *regular annual dividend* is $5.00. The actual payment procedure is as follows:

1. *Declaration date.* The directors meet, say on November 15, and declare the regular dividend. On this date, the directors issue a statement similar to the

following: "On November 15, 1979, the directors of the XYZ Company met and declared the regular quarterly dividend of 50 cents a share, plus an extra dividend of $1.00 a share, payable to holders of record on December 15, payment to be made on January 2, 1980."

2. *Holder-of-record date.* At the close of business on the *holder-of-record date,* December 15, the company closes its stock transfer books and makes up a list of the shareholders as of that date. If XYZ Company is notified of the sale and transfer of some stock before 5 P.M. on December 15, the new owner receives the dividend. However, if notification is received on or after December 16, the old stockholder gets the dividend check.

3. *Ex dividend date.* Suppose Jean B buys 100 shares of stock from John S on December 13. Will the company be notified of the transfer in time to list B as the new owner and, thus, pay the dividend to her? To avoid conflict, the stock brokerage business has set up a convention of declaring that the right to the dividend remains with the stock until four days prior to the holder-of-record date; on the fourth day before the record date, the right to the dividend no longer goes with the shares. The date when the right to the dividend leaves the stock is called the *ex dividend date.* In this case, the ex dividend date is four days prior to December 15, or December 11:

Dec. 10
Ex dividend date: Dec. 11
Dec. 12
Dec. 13
Dec. 14
Holder-of-record date: Dec. 15

Therefore, if B is to receive the dividend, she must buy the stock by December 10. If she buys it on December 11 or later, S will receive the dividend.

The total dividend, regular plus extra, amounts to $1.50, so the ex dividend date is important. Barring fluctuations in the stock market, we would normally expect the price of a stock to drop by approximately the amount of the dividend on the ex dividend date.

4. *Payment date.* The company actually mails the checks to the holders of record on January 2, the payment date.

Dividend Reinvestment Plans[5]

During the mid-1970s most of the larger companies instituted *Dividend Reinvestment Plans,* or DRPs, whereby stockholders can automatically reinvest dividends received in the stock of the paying corporation. *There are*

---

5 See R. H. Pettway and R. P. Malone, "Automatic Dividend Reinvestment Plans," *Financial Management* (Winter 1973), pp. 11–18, for an excellent discussion of the topic.

two types of DRPs: one involves only stock that is already outstanding, while the other involves newly issued stock. In either case, the stockholder must pay income taxes on the amount of the dividends, even though stock rather than cash is received.

Under the first type of plan, the stockholder elects either to continue receiving dividend checks or to have the dividend used to buy more stock in the corporation. If the stockholder elects reinvestment, a bank (Citibank of New York is the leader), acting as trustee, takes the total funds available for reinvestment (less a fee), purchases the corporation's stock on the open market, and allocates the shares purchased to the participating stockholders' accounts on a *pro rata* basis. The transactions costs of buying shares (brokerage costs) are low because of volume purchases, so these plans benefit small stockholders who do not need cash dividends for current consumption.

The other type of DRP provides for dividends to be invested in *newly issued stock; hence, these plans raise new capital for the firm.* AT&T, Union Carbide, and many other companies had such plans in effect in 1979, using them to raise substantial amounts of new equity capital. No fees are charged to stockholders, and many companies offer stock at a discount below the actual market price. The companies absorb these costs as a tradeoff against flotation costs that would be incurred on stock sold through investment bankers rather than through the dividend reinvestment plans. Discussions with corporate treasurers suggest that many other companies are seriously considering establishing or switching to new-stock DRPs.[6]

STOCK REPURCHASES

As an alternative to cash dividends, a firm may distribute income to stockholders by *repurchasing its own stock.* For example, IBM recently bought back $713 million of its own shares. The principal advantages of this type of distribution are (1) it avoids the high personal tax rate on cash dividends; and (2) it permits those stockholders who want cash to acquire it by selling some of their shares back to the firm, while stockholders who do not want cash may simply keep their shares. Since fewer shares will be outstanding after the repurchase, earnings per share and consequently the price of the remaining shares should increase.

The principal disadvantages of repurchases are (1) they are usually done on an irregular basis, so a stockholder cannot depend on income from this source; and (2) if regular repurchases were made, there is a good chance

---

6 One interesting aspect of DRPs is that they are forcing corporations to reexamine their basic dividend policies. A high participation rate in a DRP suggests that stockholders might be better off if the firm simply reduced cash dividends, as this would save stockholders some personal income taxes. Quite a few firms are surveying their stockholders to learn more about their preferences and to find out how they would react to a change in dividend policy. A more rational approach to basic dividend policy decisions may emerge from this research.

that the Internal Revenue Service (or Congress) would rule that the repurchases were simply a tax avoidance scheme and would assess penalty tax rates. Stock repurchase operations are discussed in more detail in Appendix 17A.

STOCK DIVIDENDS AND STOCK SPLITS

Another aspect of dividend policy is the concept of stock dividends and stock splits. The rationale for stock dividends and splits can best be explained through an example; we use Carter Chemical Company to illustrate.

As Carter Chemical continues to grow and to retain earnings, its book value per share will also grow. More important, earnings per share and the market price per share will rise. Suppose only a few thousand shares were outstanding. After some years of growth, each share would have a very high EPS and DPS. If a "normal" P/E ratio were applied to the stock, the derived market price might be so high that few people could afford to buy even one share. This would limit demand for the stock, thus keeping the total market value of the firm below what it would be if more shares, at lower prices, were outstanding.

Although there is little empirical evidence to support the contention, there is nevertheless a widespread belief in financial circles that an *optimal price range* exists for stocks. *Optimal* means that, if the price is in this range, the price/earnings ratio will be maximized. Many observers, including Carter Chemical's management, feel that the best range for most stocks is from $20 to $80 per share. Accordingly, if at some future point the price of Carter's stock rose to $80, management would probably declare a *two-for-one stock split,* thus doubling the number of shares outstanding, halving the earnings and dividends per share, and thereby lowering the price of the stock. Each stockholder would have more shares, but each share would be worth less. If the post-split price were $40, Carter's stockholders would be exactly as well off as they were before the split. If the price of the stock were to stabilize above $40, stockholders would be better off. Stock splits can be of any size. For example, the stock could be split two-for-one, three-for-one, 1.5-for-one, or in any other way.[7]

Stock dividends are similar to stock splits in that they divide the pie into smaller slices without affecting the fundamental position of the company. On a 5 percent stock dividend, the holder of 100 shares would receive an additional five shares (without cost); on a 20 percent stock dividend, the same holder would receive twenty new shares; and so on. Again, the total

---

7 *Reverse splits,* which reduce the shares outstanding, can even be used; for example, a company whose stock sells for $5 might employ a one-for-five reverse split, exchanging one new share for five old shares and raising the value of the shares to about $25, which is within the "acceptable" range.

number of shares is increased, so earnings, dividends, and the price per share all decline.

If a firm wants to reduce the price of its stock, should a stock split or a stock dividend be used? Stock splits are generally used after a sharp price run-up, when a large price reduction is sought. Stock dividends are frequently used on a regular annual basis to keep the stock price more or less constrained. For example, if a firm's earnings and dividends are growing at about 10 percent per year, the price would tend to go up at about that same rate, and it would soon be outside the desired trading range. A 10 percent annual stock dividend would maintain the stock price within the optimal trading range.

Although the economic effects of stock splits and dividends are virtually identical, accountants treat them somewhat differently. On a two-for-one split, the shares outstanding are doubled, and the stock's par value is halved. This treatment is shown in Table 17-1, Section 2, for Carter Chemical, using a pro forma 1985 balance sheet. With a stock dividend, the par value is not reduced, but an accounting entry is made transferring capital from retained earnings to common stock and to paid-in capital. The transfer from retained earnings is calculated as follows:

**Table 17-1
Carter Chemical Company: Stockholders'
Equity Accounts, Pro Forma 12/31/1985**

1. **Before a stock split or a stock dividend:**

Common stock (60 million shares authorized, 50 million outstanding, $1 par)	$ 50,000,000
Additional paid-in capital	100,000,000
Retained earnings	1,850,000,000
Total common stockholders' equity	$2,000,000,000

2. **After a two-for-one stock split:**

Common stock (120 million shares authorized, 100 million outstanding, $0.50 par)	$ 50,000,000
Additional paid-in capital	100,000,000
Retained earnings	1,850,000,000
Total common stockholders' equity	$2,000,000,000

3. **After a 20 percent stock dividend:**

Common stock (60 million shares authorized, 60 million outstanding, $1 par)[a]	$ 60,000,000
Additional paid-in capital[b]	890,000,000
Retained earnings[b]	1,050,000,000
Total common stockholders' equity	$2,000,000,000

[a]Shares outstanding are increased by 20 percent, from 50 million to 60 million.
[b]A transfer equal to the market value of the new shares is made from retained earnings to additional paid-in capital and common stock:

$$\text{Transfer} = (50 \text{ million shares})(0.2)(\$80) = \$800 \text{ million.}$$

$$\begin{pmatrix} \text{Dollars} \\ \text{transferred from} \\ \text{retained} \\ \text{earnings} \end{pmatrix} = \begin{pmatrix} \text{Number} \\ \text{of shares} \\ \text{outstanding} \end{pmatrix} \begin{pmatrix} \text{Percentage} \\ \text{of the} \\ \text{stock dividend} \end{pmatrix} \begin{pmatrix} \text{Market} \\ \text{price of} \\ \text{the stock} \end{pmatrix}.$$

For example, if Carter Chemical, selling at $80, declared a 20 percent stock dividend, the transfer would be

$$\text{Dollars transferred} = (50 \text{ million})(0.2)(\$80) = \$800{,}000{,}000.$$

As shown in Section 3 of Table 17–1, of this $800 million transfer, $10 million is recorded in common stock and $790 million in additional paid-in capital. Retained earnings are reduced to $1.05 billion.[8]

Price Effects

Several empirical studies have examined the effects of stock splits and stock dividends on stock prices.[9] The findings of the Barker study are presented in Table 17–2. When stock dividends were associated with a cash dividend increase, the value of the company's stock six months after the ex dividend date had risen by 8 percent. On the other hand, where stock dividends were not accompanied by cash dividend increases, stock values fell by 12 percent, which approximated the percentage of the average stock dividend.

Table 17–2
Price Effects of Stock Dividends

	Price at Selected Dates (in Percentages)		
	Six Months prior to Ex Dividend Date	At Ex Dividend Date	Six Months after Ex Dividend Date
Cash dividend increase	100	109	108
No cash dividend increase	100	99	88

These data seem to suggest that stock dividends are seen for what they are—simply additional pieces of paper—and that they do not represent true income. When they are accompanied by higher earnings and cash dividends, investors bid up the value of the stock. However, when stock dividends are not accompanied by increases in earnings and cash dividends, the dilution

8 Note that Carter could not pay a stock dividend that exceeded 46.25 percent; a stock dividend of that percentage would exhaust the retained earnings. Thus, a firm's ability to declare stock dividends is constrained by the amount of its retained earnings.
9 C. A. Barker, "Evaluation of Stock Dividends," *Harvard Business Review* 36 (July–August 1958): 99–114. Barker's study has been replicated several times in recent years, and his results are still valid—they have withstood the test of time. Another excellent study, using an entirely different methodology yet reaching similar conclusions, is that of E. Fama, L. Fisher, M. C. Jensen, and R. Roll, "The Adjustment of Stock Prices to New Information," *International Economic Review* (February 1969), pp. 1–21.

of earnings and dividends per share causes the price of the stock to drop by about the same percentage as the stock dividend. The fundamental determinants of price are the underlying earnings and dividends per share.

ESTABLISHING A DIVIDEND POLICY: SOME ILLUSTRATIONS

Many factors interact to determine a firm's optimal dividend policy. Moreover, since these interactions are too complex to permit the development of a rigorous model for use as a guide to dividend policy, firms are forced to consider their dividend policies in a relatively subjective manner. Some illustrations of how dividend policies are actually set are given below.

Erie Steel Company

Erie analyzed its situation in terms of the residual theory as shown in Figure 17–3. The residual theory suggested a dividend of $1.80 per share during 1980, or a 30 percent payout ratio. Erie's stock is widely held, and a number of tax-exempt institutions are important stockholders. A questionnaire to its stockholders revealed no strong preferences for dividends versus capital gains. Erie's long-range planning group projected a cost of capital and a set of investment opportunities during the next three to five years that are similar to those shown for this year.

Based on this information, Erie's treasurer recommended to the board of directors that it establish a dividend of $1.80 for 1980, payable 45 cents quarterly. The 1979 dividend was $1.70, so the $1.80 represents an increase of about 6 percent. The treasurer also reported to the board that, in the event of an unforeseen earnings downturn, the company could obtain additional debt to meet its capital expenditure requirements. The board accepted the treasurer's recommendation and in December of 1979 declared a dividend of 45 cents per share, payable January 15, 1980. The board also announced its intention of maintaining this dividend for the balance of 1980.

Watkins Electronics

Watkins Electronics has a "residual theory position" that resembles IOS_G in Figure 17–3. This suggests that no dividend be paid. Watkins has, in fact, paid no dividend since its inception in 1962, even though it has been continuously profitable and earnings have recently been growing at a 25 percent rate. Informal conversations with the firm's major stockholders, all of whom are in high tax brackets, suggest that they neither expect nor want dividends—they would prefer to have the firm retain earnings, have good earnings growth, and provide capital gains which are taxed at relatively low rates. The stock now sells for $106 per share. Watkins's treasurer recommended a three-for-one split, no cash dividend, and a future policy of declaring an annual stock dividend geared to earnings for the year. The board of directors concurred.

Midwest Electric Company

Midwest Electric has an acute need for new equity capital. The company has a major expansion program underway and absolutely must come up with the money to meet construction payments. The debt ratio is high, and if the times interest earned ratio falls any lower (1) the company's bonds will be downgraded, and (2) it will be barred by bond indenture provisions from further debt issues. These facts suggest a cut in dividends from the $2.50 per share paid last year. However, the treasurer knows that many of the stockholders rely on dividends for current living expenses, so if dividends are cut, these stockholders may be forced to sell, thus driving down the price of the stock. This would be especially bad in view of the treasurer's forecast that there will be a need to sell new common stock during the coming year. (New outside equity would be needed even if the company totally eliminated the dividend.) The treasurer is aware that many other utilities face a similar problem. Some have cut their dividends, and their stock prices invariably have fallen by amounts ranging from 30 to 70 percent.

Midwest's earnings were forecast to increase from $3.33 to $3.50. The treasurer recommended that the dividend be raised from $2.50 to $2.70, with the dividend increase being announced a few weeks before the company floated a new stock issue. The hope was that this action would cause the price of the stock to increase, after which the company could sell a new issue of common stock at a better price.

North American Oil (NAO)

NAO's 1979 dividend was $2.45 per share, up from $2.30 in 1978. Both dividend figures represented about 50 percent of earnings, and this payout was consistent with a residual theory analysis. The company's growth rate in EPS and DPS had been in the 5 to 10 percent range during the past few years, and management had projected a continuation of this trend. The financial vice-president foresaw a cash flow problem in 1980—earnings were projected to increase in line with the historical average, but an especially large number of good investment opportunities (along with some unprofitable, but required, pollution control expenditures) were expected. A preliminary analysis using the residual theory suggested that the dividend in 1980 should be cut back sharply, if not eliminated.

The financial vice-president quickly rejected this cutback, recommending instead a 6 percent *increase* in the dividend, to $2.60. He noted that the company could easily borrow funds during the coming year to meet its capital requirements. The debt ratio would rise somewhat above the target, but the firm's average cost of capital curve is relatively flat, and cash flows from the 1980 investments should permit a reduction in the debt ratio over the next few years. The vice-president felt that it was more important to maintain the steady growth in dividends than to adhere strictly to the target debt ratio.

SUMMARY

Dividend policy involves the decision to pay out earnings or to retain them for reinvestment in the firm. Any change in dividend policy has both favorable and unfavorable effects on the price of the firm's stock. Higher dividends mean higher cash flows to investors, which is good, but lower future growth, which is bad. The optimal dividend policy balances these opposing forces and maximizes the price of the stock.

We identified a number of factors that bear on dividend policy, including these: legal constraints such as bond indenture provisions, the firm's investment opportunities, the availability and cost of funds from other sources (new stock and debt), tax rates, stockholders' desire for current income, and the "information effect" of dividend changes. Because of the large number of factors that bear on dividend policy, and also because the relative importance of these factors changes over time and across companies, it is impossible to develop a precise, generalized model for use in establishing dividend policy. Firms can, however, consider the *residual theory model,* along with other factors, in reaching a judgment as to the most appropriate dividend policy.

Firms tend to use one of three payment policies: (1) a stable or continuously increasing dollar dividend per share; (2) a low regular dividend plus extras that depend on annual earnings; and (3) a constant payout ratio, which will cause the dollar dividend to fluctuate. Most firms follow the first policy, a few use the second, and almost none use the third. Also, we noted that many firms today are using dividend reinvestment plans to help stockholders reinvest dividends at minimal brokerage costs, and some firms use stock repurchase plans in lieu of more cash dividends.

Stock splits and stock dividends were also discussed. Our conclusion was that these actions may be beneficial if the firm's stock price is quite high, but otherwise they have little effect on the value of the firm.

Questions

17-1 As an investor, would you rather invest in a firm that has a policy of maintaining (a) a constant payout ratio, (b) a constant dollar dividend per share, or (c) a constant regular quarterly dividend plus a year-end extra when earnings are sufficiently high or corporate investment needs are sufficiently low? Explain your answer.

17-2 How would each of the following changes probably affect aggregate (that is, the averages for all corporations) payout ratios? Explain your answers.

a. An increase in the personal income tax rate.

b. A liberalization in depreciation policies for federal income tax purposes.

c. A rise in interest rates.

d. An increase in corporate profits.

e. A decline in investment opportunities.

17-3 Discuss the pros and cons of having the directors formally announce what a firm's dividend policy will be in the future.

17-4 Most firms would like to have their stock selling at a high P/E ratio and also have an extensive public ownership (many different shareholders). Explain how stock dividends or stock splits may be compatible with these aims.

17-5 What is the difference between a stock dividend and a stock split? As a stockholder, would you prefer to see your company declare a 100 percent stock dividend or a two-for-one split? Assume that either action is feasible.

17-6 "The cost of retained earnings is less than the cost of new outside equity capital. Consequently, it is totally irrational for a firm to sell a new issue of stock and to pay dividends during the same year." Discuss this statement.

17-7 Would it ever be rational for a firm to borrow money in order to pay dividends? Explain.

17-8 Union representatives have presented arguments similar to the following: "Corporations such as General Foods retain about one-half their profits for financing needs. If they financed by selling stock instead of by retaining earnings, they could cut prices substantially and still earn enough to pay the same dividend to their shareholders. Therefore, their profits are too high." Evaluate this statement.

17-9 "Executive salaries have been shown to be more closely correlated to the size of the firm than to its profitability. If a firm's board of directors is controlled by management instead of by outside directors, this might result in the firm's retaining more earnings than can be justified from the stockholders' point of view." Discuss the statement, being sure (a) to use Figure 17–3 in your answer and (b) to explain the implied relationship between dividend policy and stock prices.

Problems

17-1 Barter Corporation declares a 4 percent stock dividend and a cash dividend of $0.40 per share. The cash dividend is paid on old shares *plus* shares received in the stock dividend. Construct a pro forma balance sheet giving effect to these actions; use one new balance sheet that incorporates both actions. The stock sells for $25 per share. A condensed version of the Barter Corporation's balance sheet as of December 31, 1979, before the dividends, is given below:

Cash	$ 50,000,000	Debt	$1,000,000,000
Other assets	1,950,000,000	Common stock	
		(60 million shares authorized, 50	
		million shares outstanding, $1 par)	50,000,000
		Paid-in capital	200,000,000
		Retained earnings	750,000,000
	$2,000,000,000		$2,000,000,000

17-2 Hazard Tobacco Company has for many years enjoyed a moderate but stable growth in sales and earnings. However, cigarette consumption and, consequently, Hazard's sales have been falling off recently, partly because of a national awareness of the dangers of smoking to health. Anticipating further declines in tobacco sales for the future, Hazard's management hopes eventually to move almost entirely out of the tobacco business and, instead, to develop a new, diversified product line in growth-oriented industries.

Hazard has been especially interested in the prospects for pollution-control devices—its research department has already done much work on problems of filtering smoke. Right now, the company estimates that an investment of $24 million is necessary to purchase new facilities and begin operations on these products, but the investment could return about 18 percent within a short time. Other investment opportunities total $9.6 million and are expected to return about 12 percent.

The company has been paying a $2.40 dividend on its 6 million shares outstanding. The announced dividend policy has been to maintain a stable dollar dividend, raising it only when it appears that earnings have reached a new, permanently higher level. The directors might, however, change this policy if reasons for doing so are compelling. Total earnings for the year are $22.8 million, common stock is currently selling for $45, and the firm's current leverage ratio (debt/assets ratio) is 45 percent. Current costs of various forms of financing are listed below:

New bonds, 7%
New common stock sold at $45 to yield the firm $41
Investors' required rate of return on equity, 9%
Tax rate, 50%

a. Calculate the marginal cost of capital above and below the point of exhaustion of retained earnings for Hazard, both with and without the dividend.
b. How large should Hazard's capital budget be for the year?
c. What is an appropriate dividend policy for Hazard? How should the capital budget be financed?
d. How might risk factors influence Hazard's cost of capital, capital structure, and dividend policy?
e. What assumptions, if any, do your answers to the above make about investors' preference for dividends versus capital gains, that is, investors' preferences regarding the D_1/P_0 and g components of k?

APPENDIX 17A   STOCK REPURCHASES AS AN ALTERNATIVE TO DIVIDENDS

Treasury stock is the name given to common stock that has been repurchased by the issuing firm, and the acquisition of treasury stock represents an alternative to the payment of dividends. If some of the outstanding stock is repurchased, fewer shares will remain outstanding; and, assuming the repurchase does not adversely affect the firm's earnings, the earnings per share of the remaining shares will increase. This increase in earnings per share should result in a higher market price per share, so capital gains will have been substituted for dividends.

Many companies have been repurchasing their stock in recent years. Most repurchases amount to a few million dollars, but in 1977 IBM, in the largest repurchase on record, bought 2,546,000 of its shares at a price of $280 per share, or $713 million in total. In another large repurchase, Gulf Oil bought back $338 million of its stock.

The effects of a repurchase are illustrated by American Development Corporation (ADC), which earned $4.4 million in 1978. Of this amount, 50 percent, or $2.2 million, had been allocated for distribution to common shareholders. There were 1,100,000 shares outstanding, and the market price was $20 a share. ADC could use the $2.2 million to repurchase 100,000 of its shares through a tender offer for $22 a share, or it could pay a cash dividend of $2 a share.[1]

The effect of the repurchase on the EPS and market price per share of the remaining stock can be determined in the following way:

1. Current EPS $= \dfrac{\text{Total earnings}}{\text{Number of shares}} = \dfrac{\$4.4 \text{ million}}{1.1 \text{ million}} = \$4 \text{ per share.}$

2. Current P/E ratio $= \dfrac{\$20}{\$4} = 5\times.$

3. EPS after repurchase of 100,000 shares $= \dfrac{\$4.4 \text{ million}}{1 \text{ million}} = \$4.40 \text{ per share.}$

4. Expected market price after repurchase $= (\text{P/E})(\text{EPS}) = (5)(\$4.40) = \$22 \text{ per share.}$

It should be noticed from this example that investors would receive benefits of $2 a share in any case, either in the form of a $2 cash dividend or a $2 increase in stock price. This result occurs because we assumed (1) that shares could be repurchased at exactly $22 a share and (2) that the P/E ratio would remain constant. If shares could be bought for less than $22, the operation would be even better for *remaining* stockholders, but the reverse would hold if ADC paid more than $22 a share. Furthermore, the P/E ratio might change as a result of the

---

[1] Stock repurchases are commonly made in three ways. First, a publicly owned firm can simply buy its own stock through a broker on the open market. Second, it can issue a *tender* under which it permits stockholders to send in (that is, "tender") their shares to the firm in exchange for a specified price per share. When tender offers are made, the firm generally indicates that it will buy up to a specified number of shares within a specified time period (usually about two weeks); if more shares are tendered than the company wishes to purchase, then purchases are made on a *pro rata* basis. Finally, the firm can purchase a block of shares from one large holder on a negotiated basis. If the latter procedure is employed, care must be taken to insure that this one stockholder does not receive preferential treatment not available to other stockholders.

repurchase operation, rising if investors viewed it favorably, falling if they viewed it unfavorably. Some factors that might affect P/E ratios are considered next.

Advantages of Repurchases from the Stockholder's Viewpoint

1. Profits earned on repurchases are taxed at the capital gains rate, whereas a dividend distribution would be taxed at the stockholder's marginal tax rate. This is significant. For example, it has been estimated that, on the average, stockholders pay a tax of about 45 percent on marginal income. Since the capital gains tax rate is generally only one-half the ordinary tax rate, the typical shareholder clearly benefits, other things the same, if the distribution is in the form of a stock repurchase rather than a dividend.
2. The stockholder has a choice—to sell or not to sell. On the other hand, with a dividend, one must accept the payment and pay the tax.
3. A qualitative advantage advanced by market practitioners is that repurchase can often remove a large block of stock overhanging the market.

Advantages of Repurchases from Management's Viewpoint

1. Studies have shown that dividends are "sticky" in the short run because managements are reluctant to raise dividends if the new dividend cannot be maintained in the future—managements dislike cutting cash dividends. Hence, if the excess cash flow is thought to be only *temporary,* management may prefer to "conceal" the distribution in the form of share repurchases rather than to declare a cash dividend they believe cannot be maintained.
2. Repurchased stock can be used for acquisitions or released when stock options are exercised. Discussions with financial managers indicate that it is frequently more convenient and less expensive to use repurchased stock than newly issued stock for these purposes, and also when convertibles are converted or warrants exercised.
3. If directors have large holdings themselves, they may have especially strong preferences for repurchases rather than dividend payments because of the tax factor.
4. Repurchases can be used to effect large-scale changes in capital structure. For example, at one time American Standard had virtually no long-term debt outstanding. The company decided that its optimal capital structure called for the use of considerably more debt, but even if it financed *only* with debt it would have taken years to get the debt ratio up to the newly defined optimal level. What could the company do? It sold long-term debt and used the proceeds to repurchase its common stock, thus producing an instantaneous change in its capital structure.
5. Treasury stock can be resold in the open market if the firm needs additional funds.[2]

---

2 Another interesting use of stock repurchases was Standard Products' strategy of repurchasing its own stock to thwart an attempted takeover. Defiance Industries, Inc., attempted to acquire a controlling interest in Standard Products through a tender offer of $15 a share. Standard's management countered with a tender offer of its own at $17.25 a share, financed by $1.725 million in internal funds and by $3.525 million in long-term debt. This kept stockholders from accepting the outside tender offer and enabled Standard Products' management to retain control.

Disadvantages of Repurchases from the Stockholder's Viewpoint

1. Stockholders may not be indifferent between dividends and capital gains, and the price of the stock might benefit more from cash dividends than from repurchases. Cash dividends are generally thought of as being relatively dependable, but repurchases are not. Further, if a firm announced a regular, dependable repurchase program, the improper accumulation tax discussed below would probably become more of a threat.
2. The *selling* stockholders may not be fully aware of all the implications of a repurchase or may not have all pertinent information about the corporation's present and future activities. For this reason, firms generally announce a repurchase program before embarking on it.
3. The corporation may pay too high a price for the repurchased stock, to the disadvantage of remaining stockholders. If the shares are inactive, and if the firm seeks to acquire a relatively large amount of its stock, the price may be bid above a maintainable price and then fall after the firm ceases its repurchase operations.

Disadvantages of Repurchases from Management's Viewpoint

1. Studies have shown that firms which repurchase substantial amounts of stock often have poorer growth rates and fewer good investment opportunities than ones that do not. Thus, some people feel that announcing a repurchase program is like announcing that management cannot locate good investment projects. One could argue that instituting a repurchase program should be regarded in the same manner as announcing a higher dividend payout, but if repurchases are regarded as indicating especially unfavorable growth opportunities, then repurchases can have an adverse impact on the firm's image, and also on the price of its stock.
2. Repurchases might involve some risk from a legal standpoint. If the Internal Revenue Service can establish that the repurchases are primarily for the avoidance of taxes on dividends, then penalties may be imposed on the firm under the improper accumulation of earnings provision of the Tax Code. Actions have been brought against privately held companies under Section 531, but we know of no case where such an action has been brought against a publicly owned firm, even though some firms have retired over one-half of their outstanding stock. Also, the SEC may raise serious questions if it appears that the firm may be manipulating the price of its shares.

Conclusion on Stock Repurchases

When all the pros and cons on stock repurchases are totaled, where do we stand? The conclusions may be summarized as follows:

1. Repurchases on a regular, systematic, dependable basis, like quarterly dividends, are not feasible because of uncertainties about the tax treatment of such a program and uncertainties about such things as the market price of the shares, how many shares would be tendered, and so forth.

2. However, repurchases do offer some significant advantages over dividends, so this procedure should be given careful consideration on the basis of the firm's own unique situation.
3. Repurchases can be especially valuable to make a significant shift in the capital structure within a short period.

Problem

17A-1 Gemstone, Inc., has earnings this year of $16.5 million, 50 percent of which is required to take advantage of the firm's excellent investment opportunities. The firm has 206,250 shares outstanding, selling currently at $320 a share. Greg Beaumont, a major stockholder (18,750 shares), has expressed displeasure with a great deal of managerial policy. Management has approached him with the prospect of selling his holdings back to the firm, and he has expressed a willingness to do this at a price of $320 a share. Assuming that the market uses a constant P/E ratio of 4 in valuing the stock, should the firm buy Beaumont's shares? Assume that dividends will not be paid on Beaumont's shares if repurchased. (*Hint:* Calculate the ex dividend price of the stock with and without the repurchase, and add to these values the dividends received to determine the remaining stockholders' value per share.)

VII SPECIAL TOPICS IN FINANCIAL MANAGEMENT

Parts I through VI developed the basic framework of financial management. However, we have deferred several important topics that can best be analyzed on an integrated basis using the analytical tools developed in Chapters 1 through 17. Chapter 18 covers multinational finance; Chapter 19 deals with mergers; Chapter 20 takes up bankruptcy and reorganization; Chapter 21 examines leasing; Chapter 22 covers warrants, convertibles, and options; and Chapter 23 focuses on the financial problems of small businesses.

18 MULTINATIONAL FINANCE

Almost 25 percent of U.S. manufacturing firms' assets are located abroad, and a similar percentage of their income is derived from foreign sources. Further, international investment is growing more rapidly than domestic investment for American firms in the aggregate. This growth, which is highlighted in the left panel of Figure 18–1, has been caused primarily by the high rates of return available on foreign investments, especially in developing nations, as shown in the right panel.

A firm that operates in two or more nations is defined as a *multinational corporation*. Such a company has a base corporation in one country (the *parent company*) and operates branches and subsidiaries throughout the world. Its shares are normally owned mostly, if not entirely, by residents of the parent company's country. Although there has been much talk recently in the United States about foreigners, especially those from the OPEC countries, buying control of U.S. real estate and corporations, the fact of the matter is that multinational companies based in the U.S. invest far more money abroad than do those based in any other country in the world. In fact, the United States has more assets abroad than do Britain, Japan, West Germany, Canada, and Switzerland combined. General Electric has television assembly plants in Mexico, South Korea, and Singapore; IBM has computer hardware manufacturing and servicing subsidiaries in many parts of Europe and the Far East; Caterpillar produces tractors and farm equipment in the Middle East, Europe, the Far East, and Africa. American executives increasingly travel and live abroad, and American multinational corporations have come to exert significant economic and political influence in many parts of the world.[1]

Companies actually move into multinational operations for a number of specific reasons. First, a good many firms started their international operations because

This chapter was written by Professor Hai Hong of the Graduate School of Management, Northwestern University.

1 Some of the political influence of multinational corporations is of dubious desirability and has aroused Congressional disapproval. Examples include the ITT affair in Chile, as well as the Lockheed scandals in Japan and the Netherlands.

Figure 18–1
Overseas Investment by U.S. Corporations and
Rates of Return on This Investment in Different
Countries

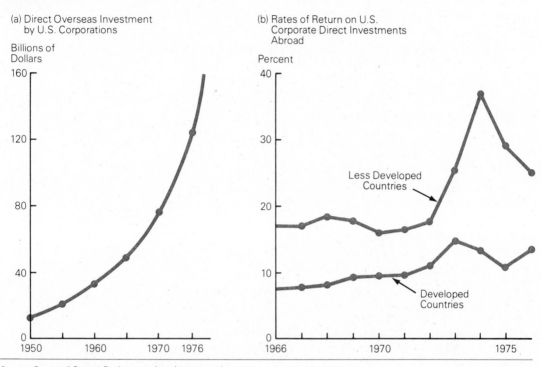

(a) Direct Overseas Investment
    by U.S. Corporations

(b) Rates of Return on U.S.
    Corporate Direct Investments
    Abroad

Source: *Survey of Current Business,* various issues.

raw materials were located abroad; this is true of oil, mining, and some food
processing companies. Other firms expanded overseas in order to obtain an outlet
for their finished products. Frequently, such firms first set up sales offices, then
develop manufacturing plants when it becomes clear that the market will support
such plants. Still other firms have moved their manufacturing facilities overseas in
order to take advantage of low production costs in cheap labor areas; the
electronics and textile companies are examples which spring immediately to
mind. Finally, the banks, accounting firms, and other service corporations have
expanded overseas both to better serve their primary customers and to take
advantage of profitable new investment opportunities.

The study of multinational finance takes traditional managerial finance as its
starting point, then builds on the models of capital budgeting, cost of capital, and
working capital management discussed earlier in this book. However, multinational
financial management must also take into account international differences in
financial markets and institutions. Accordingly, this chapter is divided into four
major sections: (1) foreign exchange rates and the international monetary system,
(2) procedures for analyzing foreign investments, (3) the financial management of
foreign assets, and (4) international capital markets.

EXCHANGE RATES AND THE INTERNATIONAL MONETARY SYSTEM

An *exchange rate* designates the number of units of a given currency that can be purchased for one unit of another currency. Exchange rates for the leading trading partners of the United States appear in the *Wall Street Journal* each day. See, for example, the rates given on March 24, 1978, as shown in Table 18–1.

Table 18–1
Illustrative Exchange Rates, March 24, 1978

	U.S. Dollars Required to Buy One Unit of Foreign Currency (1)	Number of Units of Foreign Currency per U.S. Dollar (2)
British pound	$1.8750	0.5333
Canadian dollar	0.8868	1.1277
Dutch guilder	0.4583	2.1820
French franc	0.2145	4.6620
Greek drachma	0.0282	35.4610
Indian rupee	0.1225	8.1633
Italian lira	0.001171	853.9710
Japanese yen	0.004388	227.8943
Mexican peso	0.0440	22.7273
Norwegian krone	0.1870	5.3476
Saudi Arabian riyal	0.2895	3.4542
Singapore dollar	0.4329	2.3100
Spanish peseta	0.0125	80.0000
Swedish krona	0.2172	4.6041
Swiss franc	0.5265	1.8993
Venezuelan bolivar	0.2332	4.2882
West German mark	0.4912	2.0358

Note: Column 2 equals 1.0 divided by Column 1.
Source: *Wall Street Journal,* March 24, 1978.

Recent History of the World Monetary System

From the end of World War II until August 1971, the world was on a *fixed exchange rate system* administered by the International Monetary Fund (IMF). Under this system, the U.S. dollar was linked to gold ($35 per ounce), and other currencies were then tied to the dollar. Exchange rates between other currencies and the dollar were controlled within narrow limits. For example, in 1964 the British pound was fixed at 2.80 dollars for one pound, with a one percent permissible fluctuation about this rate:

	Value of the Pound (Exchange Rate in Dollars per Pound)
Upper Limit (+1%)	2.828
Official Rate	2.800
Lower Limit (−1%)	2.772

Fluctuations occurred because of changes in the supply of and demand for pounds. The demand for pounds tends to increase whenever Britain's exports exceed its imports—people in other nations become net buyers of pounds to pay for British goods. This strong demand, in turn, tends to drive up the value of British pounds relative to other currencies—more dollars will be paid for each pound. Under the fixed exchange rate system, this increase in value was, of course, subject to the one percent upper limit.[2]

The demand for a currency, hence exchange rate fluctuations, also depends on capital movements. For example, suppose interest rates in Britain were higher than those in the United States. Americans would buy pounds with dollars, then use these pounds to purchase British securities. This would tend to drive up the price of pounds.[3]

Finally, there are always international speculators (who include the Arab money managers and the Swiss, as well as the treasurers of major U.S. corporations) who buy pounds whenever they expect the value of the pound to rise relative to other currencies.

Prior to 1972, these fluctuations were kept within the narrow one percent limit by regular intervention of the British government in the market. When the value of the pound was falling, the Bank of England would step in and buy pounds, offering gold or foreign currencies in exchange. This would push up the pound rate. Conversely, when the pound rate was too high, the Bank of England would sell pounds.

With the approval of the IMF, a country could *devalue* its currency if it experienced difficulty over a long period in preventing its exchange rate from falling below the lower limit, and if it was running out of the gold and other currencies necessary to buy its own currency and thus prop up its price. For just these reasons, the British pound was devalued from $2.80 per pound to $2.50 per pound in 1967. Conversely, a nation with an export surplus and a strong currency might *revalue* its currency upwards, as West Germany did in 1961 and again in 1969.

Today's Floating Exchange Rate System

Devaluations and revaluations occurred only rarely before 1971. They were usually accompanied by severe international financial repercussions, partly because nations tended to postpone these needed measures until economic pressures had built up to explosive proportions. For this and other reasons,

2 For example, the dollar value of the pound might move up from $2.800 to $2.828. This increase in the value of the pound would mean that British goods would now be more expensive in export markets. For example, a box of candy costing one pound in England would rise in price in the U.S. from $2.80 to $2.828. Conversely, U.S. goods would be cheaper in England. For example, the British could now buy goods worth $2.828 for one pound, whereas before the exchange rate change, one pound would only buy merchandise worth $2.80. These price changes would, of course, tend to *reduce* British exports and *increase* imports, and this, in turn, would lower the exchange rate because people in other nations would be buying fewer pounds to pay for English goods.
3 Such capital flows would also tend to drive down British interest rates. If rates were high in the first place because of efforts by the British monetary authorities to curb inflation, then the international currency flows would have helped thwart that effort. This is one of the reasons why domestic and international economics are so closely linked.

the old international monetary system came to a dramatic close in the early 1970s, when the U.S. dollar, the foundation upon which all other currencies were anchored, was cut loose from gold and, in effect, allowed to "float."

Under a system of *floating exchange rates,* currency prices are allowed to seek their own levels without much governmental intervention. The present world monetary system is known as a *managed floating system:* major world currency rates move (float) with market forces, unrestricted by any internationally agreed on limits. However, the central bank of each country does intervene in the foreign exchange market, buying and selling its currency to smooth out exchange rate fluctuations to some extent. Each central bank also tries to keep its average exchange rate at a level deemed desirable by its government's economic policy. This is important, because exchange rates have a profound effect on the levels of imports and exports, which in turn influence the level of domestic employment.

Figure 18–2 shows how German marks, Japanese yen, and British pounds moved in comparison to the dollar from 1960 through 1978. Until 1971, when the fixed rate system was terminated, rates were quite stable. The pound's fluctuations against the dollar were too small to even show up on the graph prior to 1967, when a devaluation occurred. The mark was revaluated upward in 1961 and again in 1969. The yen was stable until 1971, when the dollar was allowed to float. While the pound has continued to slip, the mark and the yen have appreciated dramatically against the dollar since 1971. The root cause of these divergent trends has been the relative strengths of the British, German, and Japanese economies versus that of the United States, and the relative inflation rates in the four countries. This point is discussed in detail in a later section.

Trading in Foreign Exchange

Importers, exporters, and tourists, as well as governments, buy and sell currencies in the foreign exchange market. For example, when a U.S. trader imports automobiles from West Germany, payment will probably be made in German marks. The importer buys marks (through its bank) in the foreign exchange market, much as one buys common stocks on the New York Stock Exchange or pork bellies on the Chicago Mercantile Exchange. However, while stock and commodity exchanges have organized trading floors, the foreign exchange market consists of a network of brokers and banks based in New York, London, Tokyo, and other financial centers. Most buy and sell orders are conducted by cablegram and telephone.[4]

Spot Rates and Forward Rates

The exchange rates shown in Table 18–1 are known as *spot rates,* which means the rate paid for delivery of the currency "on the spot" or, really, two

---

4 For a more detailed account of foreign exchange trading and money market instruments for financing foreign trade, see R. Rodriguez and E. Carter, *International Financial Management* (Englewood Cliffs, New Jersey: Prentice-Hall, 1976), Chapters 5 and 6.

Figure 18–2
Changes in the Value of Marks, Yen, and
Pounds versus the Dollar, 1960–1978

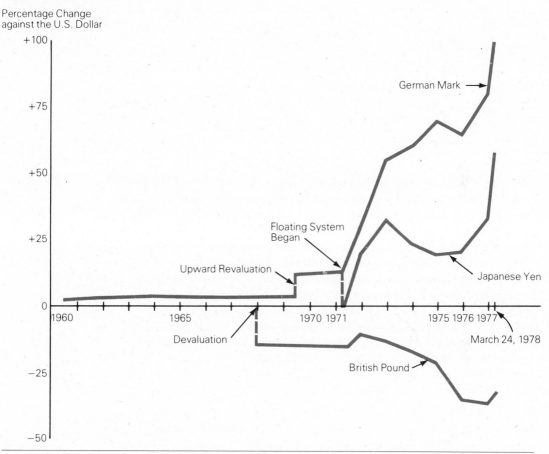

Source: *International Financial Statistics*, various issues.

days after the day of the trade. For most of the world's major currencies, it is also possible to buy (or sell) currency for delivery at some agreed on future date, usually 30, 90, or 180 days from the day the transaction is negotiated. This rate is known as the *forward exchange rate.* Forward rates are exactly analogous to futures prices on commodity exchanges, where contracts are drawn up for wheat or corn to be delivered at agreed on prices at some future date.

When the forward rate is above the current spot rate, the forward rate is said to be at a *premium;* conversely, when the forward rate is below the spot rate, it is said to be at a *discount.* Table 18–2 shows forward rates for British pounds and Swiss francs on March 24, 1978, along with spot rates from Table 18–1, which have been included for comparison. Note that forward

British pounds sell at a discount whereas forward Swiss francs sell at a premium. The reason for this divergence will be explained shortly.

Table 18–2
Illustrative Spot and Forward Exchange Rates,
March 24, 1978

	British Pounds	Swiss Francs
Spot Rate	$1.8750	$0.5265
30 Day Forward	1.8748	0.5295
90 Day Forward	1.8742	0.5365
180 Day Forward	1.8726	0.5450

Source: *Wall Street Journal,* March 24, 1978.

Why do individuals and corporations buy or sell forward currencies? The main reason is that forward markets provide protection against future changes in exchange rates. For example, suppose that on March 24, 1978, a U.S. jeweler buys watches from a Swiss manufacturer for one million Swiss francs. Payment is to be made in Swiss francs ninety days after the goods are shipped, or on June 23, so the Swiss firm is extending trade credit for ninety days. The Swiss franc has been strong recently, and the U.S. firm is afraid that the trend will continue. If the franc appreciates rapidly, more dollars will be required to buy the million francs, and the profits on the watches will be lost. Still, the U.S. firm does not want to forego the trade credit, so it protects itself by buying one million ninety day forward francs for $0.5365 × 1,000,000, or $536,500. When payment comes due on June 23, regardless of the spot rate on this day, the U.S. firm can obtain the needed Swiss francs at the agreed on price. The U.S. firm is said to have *covered its trade payments.*[5]

Inflation, Interest Rates, and Exchange Rates

Relative inflation rates, or the rates of inflation in foreign countries compared to that at home, have many implications for multinational financial decisions. Obviously, relative inflation rates will greatly influence production costs at home and those abroad. Equally important, relative inflation rates have a dominant influence not only on relative interest rates but also on exchange rates. Both relative interest rates and exchange rates influence the methods chosen by multinational corporations for financing their foreign investments, and both of these factors have a major impact on the profitability of foreign investments.

5 This example was first worked out in the summer of 1977, then updated in March 1978. At the earlier exchange rate, the watches had a dollar cost of $402,000. Nine months later, this cost had risen to $536,500, or by 33.5 percent, strictly because of the declining value of the dollar. These increases were being matched in other European countries, making European goods and services, including vacations, increasingly expensive for Americans. Conversely, American goods and services were becoming cheaper for Europeans.

The currencies of countries with higher inflation rates than that of the U.S. tend to depreciate against the dollar. Some countries where this is the case are Britain, Italy, Mexico, and all the South American nations. On the other hand, the currencies of countries such as West Germany, Switzerland, and Japan, which have had less inflation than the U.S., have appreciated relative to the dollar. *In fact, a foreign currency will, on average, depreciate at a percentage rate approximately equal to the amount by which its inflation rate exceeds our own.*[6]

Relative inflation rates are also reflected in interest rates. The interest rate in any country is largely determined by its inflation rate; this point was made in Chapters 2 and 5. Therefore, countries currently experiencing higher rates of inflation than the U.S. also tend to have higher interest rates, while the reverse is true for countries with lower inflation rates.

It is tempting for the treasurer of a multinational corporation to borrow in countries with the lowest interest rates. However, this is not always the best strategy. For example, suppose interest rates in West Germany are lower than those in the U.S. because of Germany's lower inflation rate. A U.S. multinational firm could save interest by borrowing in Germany, but the German exchange rate can be expected to appreciate in the future, causing annual interest and principal payments on this debt to cost an increasing number of dollars over time. Thus, the lower interest rate could be more than offset by losses from currency appreciation. Similarly, one should not expect multinational corporations to avoid borrowing in a country like Brazil where interest rates are very high—future depreciation of the Brazilian cruzeiro might well make such borrowing relatively inexpensive.

PROCEDURES FOR ANALYZING POTENTIAL FOREIGN INVESTMENTS

Although the same basic principles of investment analysis apply to both foreign and domestic operations, there are some key differences. First, *the cash flow analysis is much more complex for overseas investments.* Most multinational firms set up a separate subsidiary in each foreign country in which they operate. *The relevant cash flows are the dividends and royalties repatriated by each subsidiary to the parent company. These cash flows must be converted to the currency of the parent company and thus are subject to future exchange rate changes.*

Dividends and royalties are normally taxed by both foreign and domestic governments. Furthermore, a foreign government may restrict the amount and nature of the cash flows that may be *repatriated* to the parent company.

---

6 This is known as the Purchasing Power Parity Theorem. Some recent studies have shown that this theorem holds quite well over the long run (five years or more), but over the short run the relationship is much less accurate. This is because factors other than inflation are also important in the short run, especially the activities of the national governments in trying to support their exchange rates at some desired levels. Some evidence on this is given in R. Aliber and C. Stickney, "Accounting Exposures of Foreign Exchange: The Long and the Short of It," *Accounting Review* (January 1975), pp. 44–57.

For example, some governments place a ceiling, stated as a percentage of the company's net worth, on the amount of cash dividends that may be paid by a subsidiary to its parent company. Such restrictions are normally intended to force multinational firms to reinvest earnings in the foreign country, although they are sometimes imposed to prevent large currency outflows which might destabilize exchange rates. Finally, depreciation cash flows of the subsidiary are usually not directly available to the parent company, since they are not part of the earnings from which dividends are paid. This can be an important consideration, as we shall see later in the chapter.

In addition to the complexities of the cash flow analysis, *the cost of capital may be higher for a foreign project than for an equivalent domestic project because foreign projects may be riskier.* This higher risk could arise from two primary sources: (1) exchange risk and (2) sovereign risk.

Exchange risk refers to the fact that exchange rates fluctuate. This increases the inherent uncertainty about cash flows to the parent. In other words, foreign projects have an added risk element relating to what the basic cash flows will be worth in the parent company's home currency. As we shall see later, it is generally possible to "hedge" against exchange rate fluctuations, but it may not be possible to hedge completely.

Sovereign risk refers both to the possibility of expropriation and to unanticipated restrictions of cash flows to the parent company, such as tighter controls on repatriation of dividends or higher taxes. The risk of expropriation of U.S. assets abroad is small in traditionally friendly and stable countries such as Britain or Switzerland. However, in the East European countries and in most parts of the developing world of Latin America, Africa, and the Far East, the risk may be substantial. Recent expropriations include those of ITT and Anaconda Copper in Chile, Gulf Oil in Bolivia, Occidental Petroleum in Libya, International Petroleum in Peru, and many companies in Cuba and in Iran.

The combined impact of exchange and sovereign risks, as well as such "regular" risk factors as the stability and predictability of product markets, labor supplies, and governmental regulations, can be summarized as the "investment climate" of a foreign country. A recent survey of the investment climates in countries all over the world, which appeared in a leading Japanese business journal, is shown in Table 18–3. The countries are rated in descending order from AAA to B, in much the same way that Moody's rates corporate bonds for risk of default. These ratings, or other procedures as established by an individual multinational corporation, may be used as a basis for estimating the costs of capital for capital budgeting purposes in each country in which the firm operates.

An Illustration of Multinational Capital Budgeting

The principles of capital budgeting in a multinational setting can be illustrated by International Electronics Corporation's analysis of a proposed

Table 18–3
The Risks of Foreign Investments in
Various Countries

	Sociopolitical and Investment Climate	Risk Rating
West Germany	94	AAA
United States	95	AAA
Canada	91	AA
France	90	AA
Australia	83	AA
Sweden	90	AA
Netherlands	90	AA
Saudi Arabia	83	AA
Belgium	94	A
Spain	83	A
Britain	87	A
New Zealand	83	A
Italy	78	A
Singapore	80	BBB
Portugal	79	BBB
Brazil	77	BBB
Mexico	76	BBB
Malaysia	64	BBB
Indonesia	65	BBB
Philippines	68	BBB
Argentina	70	BB
Chile	79	BB
Kenya	72	BB
Pakistan	63	BB
South Korea	54	BB
Peru	60	BB
Thailand	54	BB
Egypt	30	BB
India	23	B

Source: *Nikkei Business,* reprinted in the *Far Eastern Economic Review,* March 18, 1977, p. 88. Iran was listed as an A-rated country in 1977; its rating recently has been lowered greatly.

plant in Bratina to assemble television sets for sale in Bratina and other South American countries. If the plant is built, a new subsidiary will be incorporated in Bratina. It will be financed only with common stock, all of which will be owned by the parent company.

The cost of capital used to analyze the plant was established by the methods described in Chapter 16 and is assumed to be 15 percent. Bratina has a 20 percent corporate income tax, and there is no withholding tax on dividends paid.

While there is no restriction on dividend repatriation, depreciation cash flows may not be repatriated except when the company is liquidated or sold. The investment, to be made in January 1980, consists almost entirely of plant and equipment, and the cost will be 50 million Bratinian cruzes. Because of the nature of the television industry and the Bratinian market, IEC bases its analysis on a time horizon of only five years. At the end of the five years (in 1984), it is assumed that the operation will have a terminal value of 25 million cruzes. Table 18–4 summarizes the projected income statements.

The parent corporation receives a *tax credit* from the U.S. government for taxes paid by its subsidiary to the foreign government. The amount of the credit depends on the dividend payout ratio of the subsidiary. With a 100 percent payout, which the Bratinian subsidiary has used, the parent corporation pays the difference between the U.S. tax rate (assumed to be 50 percent) and the Bratinian tax rate of 20 percent. Thus, the U.S. tax each year amounts to an additional 30 percent of the net income for that year. For example, in the 1980 column of Table 18–4 we see that if the subsidiary earned 15 million cruzes, it would pay a Bratinian tax of 20 percent, or 3 million cruzes, and a U.S. tax of 50 − 20 = 30 percent, or 4.5 million cruzes.[7]

Table 18–4
Projected Cash Flows, 1980–1984 (Millions of Bratinian Cruzes)

	1980	1981	1982	1983	1984
Revenues	50.0	55.0	60.0	65.0	70.0
Operating cost	30.0	30.0	35.0	35.0	40.0
Depreciation	5.0	5.0	5.0	5.0	5.0
Income	15.0	20.0	20.0	25.0	25.0
Bratinian tax	3.0	4.0	4.0	5.0	5.0
Net income	12.0	16.0	16.0	20.0	20.0
Dividends repatriated	12.0	16.0	16.0	20.0	20.0
U.S. tax	4.5	6.0	6.0	7.5	7.5
After-tax dividend	7.5	10.0	10.0	12.5	12.5

Since the cash flows from depreciation cannot be repatriated until the company is liquidated at the end of 1984, they will be invested in Bratinian government bonds to earn tax-exempt interest at the rate of 8 percent. The accumulated and interest-compounded depreciation cash flow at the termination of the project is shown in Table 18–5.

7 Often a foreign subsidiary will not pay out all of its income, but will retain a portion of it for new investments. Also, the foreign government may levy a withholding tax on repatriated dividends. The U.S. tax computation is somewhat more complicated then. The following formula may be used in this more general case. Net U.S. tax = $pE[t_{us} - t_F - (1 - t_F)t_D]$. Here, p is the foreign subsidiary's dividend payout ratio; E is the gross foreign income before taxes; t_F and t_{us} are the foreign and U.S. income tax rates; and t_D is the foreign withholding tax rate on repatriated dividends (Bratina has no such withholding tax). Note that U.S. taxes are collected only on the portion of income that is repatriated. (If payout, $p_{,} = 0$, no U.S. taxes are paid.) This works as an incentive for multinational corporations to reinvest earnings for the growth of the foreign subsidiary. It also explains why U.S. oil companies and other multinationals often have very low U.S. taxes in relation to reported income.

If the net tax computed from the above formula is negative, this deficit can be used to offset U.S. taxes on income from other foreign subsidiaries in any part of the world. For a more detailed explanation of multinational taxation, see the U.S. Tax Reform Act of 1976, or Price Waterhouse, *U.S. Corporations Doing Business Abroad* (New York: Price Waterhouse, 1976).

Table 18–5
Depreciation Cash Flows

Year of Depreciation	Amount (Millions of Cruzes)	Future Value Interest Factor at 8 percent	Terminal Value in 1984 (Millions of Cruzes)
1980	5.0	1.3605	6.802
1981	5.0	1.2597	6.299
1982	5.0	1.1664	5.832
1983	5.0	1.0800	5.400
1984	5.0	1.0000	5.000
		Total	29.333

The next steps in the analysis are: (1) to convert the annual cash flows from cruzes to dollars and (2) to find the net present value of the project. These steps are shown in Table 18–6. Column 1 gives the annual cash flows in cruzes. In 1980 through 1983, dividends represent the only cash flow, but the 1984 cash flow of 66.833 million cruzes consists of dividends (12.5 million cruzes), the estimated sale price of the fixed assets (25 million cruzes), and the interest-accumulated depreciation cash flows (29.333 million cruzes).

Table 18–6
Cash Flows to Parent Company and the Parent's NPV

	Cash Flows (Millions of Cruzes) (1)	Exchange Rate (2)	Cash Flows (Millions of Dollars) (3)	PVIF at 15 Percent (4)	PV of Cash Flows (Millions of Dollars) (5)
1980	7.500	5.00	$ 1.500	0.8696	$ 1.304
1981	10.000	5.25	1.905	0.7561	1.440
1982	10.000	5.51	1.815	0.6575	1.193
1983	12.500	5.79	2.159	0.5718	1.235
1984	66.833	6.08	10.992	0.4972	5.465
				Total	$10.637
		Less initial investment of 50 million cruzes at 5 cruzes per dollar			(10.000)
				NPV of project =	$ 0.637

The estimated exchange rates are shown in Column 2. The current rate, five cruzes to the dollar, is expected to hold during 1980, but the cruze is expected to depreciate thereafter at a rate of 5 percent per year.

Dividing the cash flows in cruzes (Column 1) by the exchange rates (Column 2) gives the expected cash flows in dollars as shown in Column 3. The dollar cash flows are converted to a present value basis in Column 5, and the sum of the annual PV cash flows is $10.637 million. By subtracting the initial cost of the project, $10 million, from the PV of the inflows, we obtain the project's NPV, $0.637 million. Since it is positive, the project should be accepted.[8]

Strategic Considerations in Analyzing Foreign Investments

Although we have emphasized the financial aspects of foreign investments, nonfinancial or *strategic* considerations often dominate the decision. For example, if Ford were to set up production in Peru, General Motors might feel compelled to do the same in order not to lose its position in the South American automobile market. Because of many unknown economic factors in foreign investment, top management may not trust the "numbers" and may decide that it simply cannot sit idly by while a major competitor expands and preempts a potentially important market. Under these circumstances, financial analysis is used only as a rough screening device to eliminate ventures that are obviously unprofitable.[9]

The political ramifications of foreign investment are another strategic consideration. In recent years, labor unions have increasingly opposed U.S. multinational investments abroad. The unions and their supporters in Congress claim that such investments "export" U.S. jobs and capital—U.S. citizens lose jobs to foreigners who work for U.S. subsidiaries abroad, and the outflow of U.S. dollars to finance the investments tends to weaken the dollar in foreign exchange markets. Regardless of the merits of such criticisms, a multinational corporation's management must weigh carefully the investment benefits to the company versus possible reprisals against domestic operations by labor unions or unfriendly politicians.[10]

Sources of Funds for Foreign Investments

In the preceding example, we assumed that the foreign subsidiary would obtain all of its capital as common equity supplied by the parent. Several other sources of funds exist, including (1) sale of common stock to local residents, (2) borrowing from local residents, and (3) borrowing in world financial markets.

Selling common stock to residents of foreign countries has both advantages and disadvantages. For example, it can result in loss of control

8 The project's IRR is 16.9 percent, which exceeds the 15 percent cost of capital, so the IRR criterion also indicates acceptance.
9 See A. Yair, "The Foreign Investment Decision Process" (Boston: Harvard Business School, Division of Research, 1966); and A. Stonehill and L. Nathanson, "Capital Budgeting and the Multinational Corporation." *California Management Review,* Summer 1968. An excellent survey of motives for foreign investments may be found in G. Ragazzi, "Theories of the Determinants of Foreign Investments," *IMF Staff Papers,* March 1966.
10 The Burke-Hartke Bill (1972) threatened to remove tax credits for U.S. multinational corporations and to limit the flow of investment funds abroad. For an interesting debate on the economic issues, see "The Foreign Trade and Investment Act of 1972: Three Points of View," *Columbia Journal of World Business,* March–April 1972.

of the subsidiary if the parent company owns less than 50 percent of the shares. Some countries require majority ownership by local residents. This allows the country to have some control over major decisions made by corporations operating within its boundaries, and it also enables the country to retain part of the company's profits. However, this is not necessarily bad from the point of view of the multinational corporation—local participation may be a desirable feature in countries with less stable governments, since it provides an incentive for the local residents to exert pressure against the threat of expropriation or other interference. Similar protection is obtained by borrowing funds in the subsidiary's country. If the subsidiary company is highly leveraged, using debt from local sources, expropriation will result in only minimal losses to the parent.

Aside from protecting against expropriation, borrowing locally may be advantageous if local sources of funds in the foreign country offer attractive interest rates. In comparing foreign and domestic interest rates, however, one must be careful to take into account expected future changes in the exchange rate. As was pointed out earlier, a country with interest rates lower than those in the United States has a currency that is likely to appreciate, causing the number of dollars required to meet interest and principal payments to increase over time and to offset the lower foreign interest rate.

The decision to use local or parent country financing necessarily depends in part on projections of future trends in foreign exchange rates. Because such projections are not always accurate, using foreign debt may be riskier than using domestic debt. With the growth of multinational corporations and the uncertainties of world inflation and floating rates, corporate treasurers are making increasing use of expertise offered by commercial bankers, who make such projections and advise firms on the best way to meet their foreign currency requirements. It should come as no surprise to learn that the international divisions have been some of the fastest-growing departments of the larger banks in recent years.

MANAGEMENT OF FOREIGN ASSETS

The *Wall Street Journal* recently reported that TRW, a major aerospace and electronics conglomerate, was losing $300,000 in earnings every time the German mark moved up one percent against the dollar. This happened because TRW's West German subsidiary had about $30 million worth of debt denominated in marks. Since the interest and principal on the debt had to be paid in marks, a one percent appreciation of the mark meant that, in terms of U.S. dollars, the company had to pay more dollars to buy the marks needed to service the debt. For example, the average exchange rate of marks for dollars was 0.416 dollars per mark in November, but it had appreciated to 0.423 dollars per mark by December. The mark debt account of TRW would therefore appear as follows:

Month	Mark Rate ($/Mark)	Debt in Marks	Debt in Dollars
November	0.416	72,115,384	$30,000,000
December	0.423	72,115,384	30,504,807
	Increase in dollar value of debt		$ 504,807

The increase in the dollar equivalent of foreign debt is reported as an *income loss item* under accounting standards introduced in 1976 by the Financial Accounting Standards Board (FASB #8). Such a loss is known as a *translation loss,* since it arises from "translating" financial statements from a foreign currency to U.S. dollars.[11]

Had TRW held only *monetary assets* (defined as cash, marketable securities, and accounts receivable) denominated in marks, its position would have been reversed: an appreciation of the mark would have produced a translation gain, while a depreciation would have led to losses. Had TRW both held monetary assets and owed money denominated in marks, then the difference between these two items would be its *net monetary position.* The net position indicates whether or not the company will have a translation gain or loss as a result of exchange rate fluctuations, that is, whether the company has exchange rate loss *exposure.*

Companies such as TRW operate on a worldwide basis, and they have positive net monetary positions in some countries and negative positions in others. Thus, TRW might have translation losses in Germany but translation gains in other countries, and its consolidated, or corporate, position could show either a gain or a loss. *Under FASB #8, the net corporate translation gain or loss must be reported through the income statement each quarter.* For firms with large foreign operations, translation losses can significantly lower earnings per share and thus have an adverse effect on stock prices. Therefore, multinational corporations have devised a number of ways to minimize the likelihood of translation losses. These techniques are discussed below.

Foreign Exchange Exposure

As noted above, an exposure to losses due to changing exchange rates is called *foreign exchange exposure.* It exists whenever the amounts of monetary assets and liabilities denominated in each foreign currency are not in exact balance. Monetary instruments like TRW's debt are obviously exposed, as are monetary assets such as cash held as marks. *Nonmonetary assets* can also be exposed. For example, if the French subsidiary of Goodyear carries an inventory of tires in Paris, the dollar value of these tires could change if the French franc is depreciated. The actual change in the tires' value will depend on where they are sold and on the contracts

11 Note, however, that if the German mark had depreciated against the dollar, TRW would have made a *translation gain.*

governing these sales. If all the tires are to be shipped to the United States at a predetermined dollar price, then a French devaluation will cause no loss in real value. But if the tires are to be sold to French consumers at a fixed French franc price, the dollar value of the inventory will fall. If the sales price is not fixed, and if the weakening of the franc results in a rise in French consumer prices, then the tires may be sold at franc prices high enough to produce the same number of dollars as was anticipated before the devaluation. We see, then, that the effect of depreciation on the dollar value of nonmonetary assets is difficult to determine.

If a multinational firm's income is to be reported properly to investors, the effects of changes in the value of assets and liabilities must be analyzed properly. Yet, since it is extremely difficult to determine the effects of changes in currency values on assets such as tires, finding the proper reporting method is a complex, difficult task.

FASB #8

Before FASB #8 was introduced by the accounting profession in 1976, multinational corporations accounted for their translation gains and losses in a variety of ways, often in the manner that best helped them present a good profit picture. FASB #8 has now standardized accounting practices as follows:

1. All *monetary assets and liabilities,* including accounts payable and accounts receivable, must be translated at the exchange rate that prevails at the end of the reporting period, which is called the *current rate.* Thus, even for a stable firm, the reported value of these items changes each quarter if exchange rates fluctuate, causing fluctuations in reported earnings unless the net monetary position is zero.
2. All *inventories* must be translated at the exchange rate that prevailed at the time the goods were placed in inventory, which is called the *historic rate.*
3. All *fixed assets* must be translated at *historic rates.*
4. *Sales revenues* are translated at *current rates.* Therefore, if the value of the foreign currency (say francs) appreciates, a given volume of franc sales will have a higher dollar translation value. However, the inventories sold to produce those sales are translated at the lower historic rate. Thus, the result in this instance would be high reported profits generated by the exchange rate change.

Many multinational corporations complain that reporting translation gains and losses in this manner makes their earnings volatile and subject to the vagaries of exchange rate fluctuations. Exchange rates may rise one quarter, then fall the next, and the corporation's income will rise and fall in concert, even though sales and other fundamental aspects of the operation may have been stable. FASB #8 is especially troublesome for a company like W. R. Grace, whose foreign subsidiaries (1) finance their inventories with local short-term debt and (2) have very little long-term debt. The company has argued that its exposure in current assets (inventories) approximately cancels out its exposure in current liabilities (debt). Therefore, it has no net *economic exposure,* and its *real economic income* is insensitive to exchange rate changes. However, under FASB #8 a depreciation in a foreign currency requires Grace's subsidiary in the foreign country to report a translation gain on debt in the quarter in which currency depreciation occurs. Then, in subsequent quarters when goods produced that quarter are sold, the recorded cost of goods sold is translated at the higher historic rate, and the subsidiary's profits shrink. Thus, because under FASB #8 sales are translated into dollars at the current rate while costs of goods sold are translated at the historic rate, large swings in reported income can occur which will make the company look less stable than it really is.[12]

Hedging Exposures

Suppose the financial manager of a multinational corporation has an estimate of the firm's exchange exposure in each country in which it operates. What actions can be taken to reduce the exposure? Consider our previous example of TRW's debt of 72 million German marks. If the financial manager fears an appreciation of the mark, all of TRW's German debt could be retired and replaced by borrowing in U.S. dollars. However, this would be desirable only if dollar funds are available at acceptable interest rates. Alternatively, the financial manager could use *forward contracts* in the foreign exchange market.

In November, the spot rate on marks was 0.4160 dollars per mark, and the thirty day forward rate was 0.4180 dollars per mark. To see how forward contracts can be used to protect against exchange rate risk, suppose that in late November TRW's financial manager is worried about the mark appreciating by December 31. TRW could enter into a contract to buy marks on December 31 at the forward price, 0.4180 dollars per mark. Suppose that by December 31 the spot price had risen to 0.4230. TRW could buy marks at the contractual price of 0.4180, sell them at the higher spot price of 0.4230, and earn a profit of $360,577:

On December 31 the forward contract becomes due. Buy 72,115,384 marks at the agreed upon price of $0.4180/mark.	$30,144,230
Sell 72,115,384 marks at the spot price of $0.4230/mark.	30,504,807
Profit in dollars	$ 360,577

12 The W. R. Grace Co. case is discussed in L. Snyder, "Have the Accountants Really Hurt the Multinationals?" *Fortune,* February 1977. A good summary of the arguments for and against FASB #8 is in J. Burns, *Accounting Standards and International Finance* (Washington, D.C.: American Enterprise Institute for Public Policy Research, 1976). A recent study of seventy multinational companies shows that the effect of FASB #8 on corporate earnings may not have been as severe as many companies claim. See R. Rodriguez, "FASB #8: What Has It Done to Us?" *Financial Analysts' Journal* (March–April 1977), pp. 40–47.

This profit would largely offset the $504,807 increase in TRW's German debt as previously computed. The difference of $144,230 is TRW's *hedging cost.*[13]

A number of other methods of hedging against exchange losses on different types of liabilities and assets are available, but to discuss them would go well beyond the scope of this book.[14] The important points, for our purpose, are: (1) fluctuating exchange rates can cause earnings fluctuations for multinational corporations, but (2) for a price, the financial manager can buy protection against this risk in the form of various types of hedges. In a world of floating exchange rates, managing assets and liabilities located all across the globe presents quite a challenge. The financial manager at corporate headquarters must not only anticipate currency realignments in each country, but also coordinate hedging strategies in all these countries.

INTERNATIONAL CAPITAL MARKETS

Direct foreign investment by U.S. multinational corporations is one way for Americans to invest in world markets. Another way is to purchase stocks, bonds, or various money market instruments issued in foreign countries. U.S. citizens actually do invest substantial amounts in the stocks and bonds of large corporations in Europe, and to a lesser extent in the Far East and South America. They also buy securities issued by foreign governments. Such investments in foreign capital markets are known as *portfolio investments* (and distinguished from *direct investments* by U.S. corporations in physical assets).

Eurodollars

Whenever a U.S. dollar is placed in a time deposit in a European bank, including a European branch of a U.S. bank, a *Eurodollar* is created. For example, Eurodollars would be created if a French wine exporter received a $100,000 payment (in dollars) for a shipment to the United States and then deposited the check in a Paris bank's time deposit (rather than exchanging the dollars for francs). Eurodollars are also created when a U.S. resident places dollar time deposits in any commercial bank located in Europe.

Eurodollars can be used to conduct transactions throughout Europe—

---

13 Note that this hedging cost is independent of the spot price on December 31. To illustrate this, suppose the spot rate had been much higher, say $0.600/mark. By going through the same calculations as before, we can readily show that the increase in TRW's German debt would have been $13,269,230 and its profit from the forward mark transaction $13,125,000. This again implies a hedging cost of $144,230. For this cost, the financial manager has protected the company completely against all possible appreciation of the mark between November 30 and December 31. The company is said to be in a *fully hedged position* in the German mark over this period. In general, the hedging cost is given by this formula: (Forward price − Spot price) × (Amount of debt). Check to see that this formula gives a cost of $144,230.

14 For a professional account of various strategies, see A. R. Prindl, *Foreign Exchange Risk* (New York: Wiley, 1976); and D. Eiteman and A. Stonehill, *Multinational Business Finance* (Reading, Mass.: Addison-Wesley, 1973), Chapter 11.

indeed, throughout the world. American firms, including banks, borrow in the Eurodollar market, as do the Japanese, South Americans, and Africans. The French wine exporter and thousands of other firms have Eurodollar deposits which they can use to conduct business. It is estimated that the total quantity of Eurodollars in 1978 approximated $200 billion, but no one knows the exact figure.[15]

Eurodollar Interest Rates

Eurodollars are always held in interest-bearing accounts. Thus, the French wine exporting firm would receive interest on its deposit balances. The interest rate paid on these deposits depends (1) on the bank's lending rate, as the interest a bank earns on loans determines its willingness and ability to pay interest on deposits, and (2) on rates of return available on U.S. money market instruments, for if rates in the U.S. are above Eurodollar deposit rates, these funds will be sent back and invested in the U.S., while if Eurodollar deposit rates are significantly above U.S. rates, more dollars will be sent to Europe, and this inflow will drive rates there down.[16]

International Bond Markets

The Eurodollar market is essentially a short-term market—most loans and deposits are for less than one year. However, there are also two important types of international bond markets: foreign bonds and Eurobonds. *Foreign bonds* are bonds sold by a foreign borrower but denominated in the currency of the country in which the issue is sold. Examples would include a U.S. firm selling a bond denominated in Swiss francs in Switzerland, or a Canadian government bond denominated in dollars floated in the U.S. The term *Eurobonds* is used to designate any bond sold in some country *other than* the one in whose currency the bond is denominated. Examples would include a Canadian firm's issue of dollar bonds sold in Europe through an international underwriting syndicate, a Ford Motor Company issue denominated in dollars and sold in West Germany, or a German firm's sale of mark bonds in Switzerland.

Over half of all Eurobonds are denominated in dollars; bonds in German

---

15 It should be noted that today U.S. dollar deposits in any part of the world outside the U.S. are called Eurodollars. It is also interesting to note that Eurodollars were first created by the Russians in Paris in the 1940s. The Russians wanted to use dollars to conduct trade with parties who did not want to be paid in Russian currency. At the same time, the Russians did not want to leave dollar balances in U.S. banks for fear these balances would be taken over and used to pay off defaulted Czarist bonds. Thus, they decided to purchase dollars, leave them on deposit in a Paris bank, and use them to conduct trade.

The idea of Eurodollars expanded rapidly thereafter. The dollar was, at that time, a strong and stable currency, which made it ideal for international trade. Gold had been used earlier to settle international balances, but it's much simpler to make electronic transfers of bank accounts than to ship gold bullion.

16 In November 1979 Eurodollar deposit rates were approximately one percentage point above domestic rates on bank time deposits of the same maturity: 13.5 percent for one month CDs versus 14.5 percent on Eurodollar deposits.

marks and Dutch guilders account for most of the rest. Although centered in Europe, Eurobonds are truly international. Their underwriting syndicates include investment bankers from all parts of the world, and the bonds are sold to investors not only in Europe but also in such faraway places as Bahrain and Singapore. Thus, multinational corporations, together with international financial institutions and national governments, play an important role in mobilizing capital in all parts of the world to finance production and economic growth. For better or for worse, this has resulted in great interdependence among world economies.

SUMMARY

As the world economy becomes more integrated, the role of multinational firms is ever increasing, and new companies are joining the ranks of the multinationals every day. Although the same basic principles of financial management apply to multinational corporations as to domestic ones, the financial manager of a multinational firm faces a much more complex task. The primary problem, from a financial standpoint, is the fact that cash flows must cross national boundaries. These flows may be constrained in various ways, and, equally important, their value in dollars may rise or fall depending on exchange rate fluctuations. This means that the multinational manager must be constantly aware of the many complex interactions among national economies and the effects of these interactions on multinational operations.

World capital markets allow people from different countries to invest in the productive resources of other countries. Americans buy the stocks and bonds of foreign corporations, and foreigners in turn buy American securities. This means that more efficient investments are possible for everyone due to the diversification opportunities offered through these markets.

Because of the central role of the U.S. dollar in international commerce, large markets have developed for U.S. dollar deposits (Eurodollars) and dollar-denominated bonds (Eurobonds) in Europe and Asia. These markets represent important sources of capital for multinational corporations.

Financial management in a multinational firm is both important and challenging. The risks of international operations are high, but so are the potential rewards. In a world economy that grows more interdependent each year, the multinational manager can look forward to an ever expanding role in corporate decision making.

Questions

18-1 Under the fixed exchange rate system, what was the currency against which all other currency values were defined?

18-2 Exchange rates fluctuate under both the fixed exchange rate and floating exchange rate systems. What, then, is the difference between the two systems?

18-3 If the French franc depreciates against the U.S. dollar, can a dollar buy more or fewer French francs as a result?

18-4 If the United States imports more goods from abroad than it exports, foreigners will tend to have a surplus of U.S. dollars. What will this do to the value of the dollar with respect to foreign currencies? What is the corresponding effect on Arab investments in the U.S.?

18-5 Why do U.S. corporations build manufacturing plants abroad when they can build them at home?

18-6 Most firms require higher rates of return on foreign projects than on identical projects located at home. Why?

18-7 What is a Eurodollar? If a French citizen deposits $10,000 in Chase Manhattan Bank in New York, have Eurodollars been created? What if the deposit is made in Barclay's Bank in London? Chase Manhattan's Paris branch?

18-8 How has FASB #8 created troublesome problems for corporate treasurers? If you were the treasurer of a multinational corporation, would you prefer the world to be on a fixed exchange rate system or a floating system?

Problems

18-1 British pounds currently sell for U.S. $1.70 per pound. What should dollars sell for in pounds per dollar?

18-2 Suppose one French franc can be purchased in the foreign exchange market for twenty cents today. If the franc appreciates 10 percent tomorrow against the dollar, how many francs will a dollar buy tomorrow?

18-3 After all foreign and U.S. taxes, a United States corporation expects to receive two pounds of dividends per share from a British subsidiary this year. The exchange rate at the end of the year is expected to be $1.80 per pound, and the pound is expected to depreciate 5 percent against the dollar each year for an indefinite period. The dividend (in pounds) is expected to grow at 10 percent a year indefinitely. The parent U.S. corporation owns 10 million shares of the subsidiary. What is the present value of its equity ownership of the subsidiary? Assume a cost of equity capital of 12 percent for the subsidiary.

18-4 You are the financial vice-president of International Widgets, Inc., headquartered in Miami, Florida. All shareholders of International Widgets live in the United States. Earlier this month you obtained a loan of 10 million Canadian dollars from a bank in Toronto to finance the construction of a new plant in Montreal. At the time the loan was received, the exchange rate was 98 U.S. cents to the Canadian dollar. By the end of the month, it has unexpectedly dropped to 94 cents. Has your company made a gain or loss as a result, and by how much?

18-5 The Smith-Capone Corporation of Chicago manufactures office machines for the world market. In early 1980, the company's board of directors requests the international planning department of the company to evaluate a proposal for setting up a wholly owned subsidiary in Paralivia, a country of

50 million people in South America. The subsidiary will make typewriters for the Paralivian market. Paralivia is a rapidly developing country which has effectively invested its rich oil revenues to support a growing industrial economy. Currently, it imports all of its typewriters from abroad, and Smith-Capone is expected to capture a large portion of this market.

Political sentiment in Paralivia regarding foreign investments has been somewhat lukewarm because such investments have overtones of foreign economic control. The government recently passed a law requiring all foreign investments to pass to local ownership after six years or less. Paralivia recently adopted a parliamentary system of government after twenty years of military dictatorship under General Francisco, but the transition of power was peaceful. Mr. Gordon Lidder, chairman of the board of Smith-Capone, has expressed concern about the stability of the new government, but "usually reliable" CIA sources indicate that the government has popular support and is unlikely to be toppled for at least five to ten years.

The following financial information on the proposed project is available:

Paralivian Currency: Because the inflation rate in Paralivia is about 5 percent higher than that in the United States, the Paralivian *ringo* is expected to depreciate relative to the dollar by about 5 percent a year. In 1981, when the investment will be made, the exchange rate is expected to be 2.00 ringos per dollar.

Investment: The estimated investment to be made in 1981 is 60 million ringos in inventory, plant, and equipment. The parent corporation, Smith-Capone, will provide all the capital in the form of equity in the subsidiary. The project will begin to generate earnings in 1982. At the end of six years (1987) all plant and equipment will be sold to the Paralivian government for 20 million ringos. This amount of money, plus all accumulated cash, will be repatriated as a liquidating dividend.

Repatriation: Only dividends may be repatriated by the subsidiary to the parent company. Cash flows from depreciation may not be repatriated except as part of the liquidating dividend in 1987. However, these cash flows can, in the meantime, be invested in local money market instruments to yield a 15 percent tax-free return.

Taxes: The Paralivian corporate income tax rate is 25 percent. There is also a 10 percent withholding tax on dividends. The United States tax rate is 50 percent on the gross earnings of the foreign subsidiary. However, the parent company gets a tax credit for taxes already paid to foreign governments. In the case of the liquidating dividend, the tax treatment is quite different. The Paralivian government will not tax this dividend. Smith-Capone has obtained a ruling from the Internal Revenue Service of the United States that the liquidating dividend will not be taxed by the U.S. government either.

Cost of Capital: Based on the sovereign and exchange risk characteristics of Paralivia, Smith-Capone gives Paralivia a BB rating and requires a rate of return of 20 percent on equity.

Projected Demand, Costs, and Exchange Rates:

Year	Demand for Typewriters (Thousands)	Price (Ringos)	Unit Variable Operating Cost (Ringos)	Exchange Rate (Ringos per Dollar)
1982	50	1,000	400	2.1
1983	55	1,000	420	2.2
1984	60	1,100	440	2.3
1985	70	1,100	460	2.4
1986	80	1,200	490	2.5
1987	90	1,200	540	2.6

Fixed Cost: Depreciation expense is 10 million ringos per year. Consider this to be the only fixed cost of the project.

Use the information given above to answer the following questions:

a. Excluding the liquidating dividend, estimate the after-tax dividend received by the parent company each year.

b. Estimate the liquidating dividend, remembering that blocked depreciation flows are reinvested at 15 percent.

c. What is your recommendation for the project? (Consider its NPV and specify any other relevant considerations.)

19 MERGERS

Most corporate growth occurs through *internal expansion,* which takes place when the firm's existing divisions grow through normal capital budgeting activities. However, the most dramatic growth, and often the largest increases in firms' stock prices, are the result of *mergers,* the subject of this chapter.[1]

ECONOMIC IMPLICATIONS OF MERGERS

The primary motivation for mergers is to increase the value of the combined enterprise. If Companies A and B merge to form Company C, and if C's value exceeds that of A and B taken separately, then *synergy* is said to exist. Such a merger is beneficial to both A's and B's stockholders.[2] Synergistic effects can arise from three sources: (1) *operating economies* resulting from economies of scale in production or distribution; (2) *financial economies,* including either a higher P/E ratio, a lower cost of debt, or a greater debt capacity; and (3) *increased market power* due to reduced competition. Operating and financial economies are socially desirable, but mergers that reduce competition are both undesirable and illegal.[3]

When two firms begin merger negotiations, or when one firm begins thinking about acquiring another, one of the first considerations is antitrust:

---

1 As we use the term, *merger* means any combination that forms one economic unit from two or more previous ones. For legal purposes there are distinctions between the various ways these combinations can occur, but our emphasis is on fundamental business and financial aspects of mergers or acquisitions.

2 If synergy exists, then the whole is greater than the sum of the parts. Synergy is also called the "2 plus 2 equals 5 effect." The distribution of the synergistic gain between A's and B's stockholders is determined by negotiation. This point is discussed later in the chapter.

3 In the 1880s and 1890s, many mergers occurred in the United States, and some of them were rather obviously directed toward gaining market power rather than increasing operating efficiency. As a result, Congress passed a series of acts designed to insure that mergers are not used as a method of reducing competition. The principal acts include the Sherman Act (1890), the Clayton Act (1914), and the Celler Act (1950). These acts make it illegal for firms to combine in any manner if the combination tends to lessen competition. The acts are administered by the Antitrust Division of the Justice Department and by the Federal Trade Commission.

Is the Justice Department likely to try to block the merger, and would it be able to do so? If the answer to either part of this question is yes, then chances are high that the merger will be aborted because of the legal expenses involved in fighting the Justice Department.

TYPES OF MERGERS

Economists classify mergers into four groups: (1) horizontal, (2) vertical, (3) congeneric, and (4) conglomerate. A *horizontal merger* occurs when, for example, one widget manufacturer acquires another, or one retail food chain merges with a second—that is, when one firm combines with another in its same line of business. An example of a *vertical merger* is a steel producer's acquisition of an iron or coal mining firm (a "downstream" merger), or an oil producer's acquisition of a petrochemical company (an "upstream" merger). Congeneric means "allied in nature or action"; hence, a *congeneric merger* involves related enterprises, but not producers of the same product (horizontal) or firms in a producer-supplier relationship (vertical). Examples of congeneric mergers include banks' acquisitions of leasing companies, as well as insurance companies' takeovers of mutual fund management companies. *Conglomerate mergers* occur when unrelated enterprises combine; Mobil Oil's acquisition of Montgomery Ward illustrates a conglomerate merger.

Operating economies (and also anticompetitive effects) are at least partially dependent on the type of merger involved. Vertical and horizontal mergers generally provide the greatest operating benefits, but they are also the ones most likely to be attacked by the Justice Department. In any event, it is useful to think of these economic classifications when analyzing the feasibility of a prospective merger.

PROCEDURES FOR COMBINING FIRMS

In the vast majority of merger situations, one firm (generally the smaller of the two) is acquired by another company. Occasionally the acquired firm will initiate the action, but it is much more common for a firm to seek acquisitions than to seek to be acquired.[4] Following convention, we shall call a company that seeks to acquire another the *acquiring company* and the one which it seeks to acquire the *target company*.

Once an acquiring company has identified a possible acquisition, it must establish a suitable price, or range of prices, that it is willing to pay. With

---

4 However, if a firm is in financial difficulty, if the managers are old and do not feel that suitable replacements are on hand, or if the firm needs the support (often the capital) of a larger company, then it may seek to be acquired.

this in mind, the acquiring firm's managers must decide how to approach the target company's managers. If the acquiring firm has reason to believe the target company's management will approve the merger, then it will simply propose a merger and, hopefully, work out some suitable terms. Then the two management groups will issue statements to their stockholders recommending that they approve the merger. Assuming that the stockholders do approve, the acquiring firm will simply buy the target company's shares from its stockholders, paying for them either with its own shares (in which case the target company's stockholders become stockholders of the acquiring company) or with cash. Situations in which the terms of the merger are approved by both management groups are called *friendly mergers.*

Under other circumstances, the target company's management may resist the merger. Perhaps it feels that the price offered for the stock is too low, or perhaps the target firm's management simply wants to maintain its independence. In either case, the target firm's management is said to be *hostile,* and the acquiring firm must make a direct appeal to the target firm's stockholders. In hostile mergers, the acquiring company generally makes a *tender offer,* in which it asks the stockholders of the firm it is seeking to control to submit, or "tender," their shares in exchange for a specified price. The price is generally stated as so many dollars per share of the stock to be acquired, although it can be stated in terms of shares of stock in the acquiring firm. The tender offer is a direct appeal to stockholders, so it need not be approved by the management of the target firm. Tender offers are not new, but the frequency of their use has increased greatly in recent years.[5]

Tenneco's acquisition of Kern County Land Company can be used to illustrate how a tender offer works. Kern was a relatively old, conservatively managed company whose assets consisted largely of oil properties and agricultural land, together with some manufacturing subsidiaries. Many informed investors believed that Kern's assets had a potential long-run value in excess of its current market price. Occidental Petroleum, a relatively aggressive company, made an investigation of Kern's assets and decided to make a cash tender offer for the stock. At that time, Kern's market price on the New York Stock Exchange was about $60 a share, while the price Occidental decided to offer Kern's stockholders was $83.50 a share. According to Kern's management, Occidental's executives got in touch with them over the weekend and stated that a tender offer would be made the following Monday.

Because Occidental's published statements indicated that it felt Kern's low market value was partly the result of an unimaginative management, Kern's executives could anticipate being fired if Occidental's takeover bid was successful. Naturally, they resisted it. Kern's president wrote a letter to the stockholders condemning the merger; the letter was also published as an

---

5 Tender offers can be friendly, with the target firm's management recommending that stockholders go ahead and tender their stock.

advertisement in the *Wall Street Journal.* His position was that Kern's stock was worth more than Occidental Petroleum had offered, and that stockholders should not sell out for $83.50.

How would Kern's stockholders react to these statements? In the first place, the stock had been selling at about $60 a share, and they were now offered $83.50 cash per share. With this differential, stockholders would certainly accept the offer unless Kern's management could do something to keep the price above $83.50. What Kern did was to obtain "marriage proposals" from a number of other companies. Kern's management reported to the newspapers—while Occidental's tender offer was still outstanding—that it had received a substantial number of proposals calling for the purchase of Kern's stock at prices substantially in excess of $83.50. This kept stockholders from tendering to Occidental.

The offer Kern's management finally recommended—and presumably the one giving Kern's stockholders the highest price—was from Tenneco Corporation. Tenneco offered one share of convertible preferred stock worth about $105 for each share of Kern's stock. Further, since the merger involved an exchange of stock rather than cash, Kern's stockholders would not have to pay capital gains tax on this stock at the time of the exchange. (Had they accepted Occidental's offer, the difference between $83.50 and the cost of their stock when they purchased it would have been taxable income.) Also, according to newspaper reports, Tenneco planned to keep Kern's existing management after the merger was completed.

FINANCIAL ANALYSIS OF A PROPOSED MERGER

In theory, merger analysis is quite simple. The acquiring firm simply performs a capital budgeting analysis to determine whether the present value of the expected future income from the merger exceeds the price paid for the target company. The target company's stockholders, on the other hand, should accept the proposal if the price offered exceeds the present value of the firm's expected future cash flows, assuming that it operates independently. However, some difficult issues are involved: (1) it is necessary for the acquiring company to estimate the cash flow benefits that will be obtained from the acquisition; (2) it is necessary to determine what effect, if any, the merger will have on the required rate of return on equity; and (3) having estimated the benefits of the merger, it is necessary for the acquiring and target firms' managers and stockholders to bargain over how to share these benefits.

Operating Mergers versus Financial Mergers

From the standpoint of financial analysis, there are two basic types of mergers:

1. *Operating mergers,* in which the operations of two companies are integrated with the expectation of obtaining synergistic effects.

2. *Pure financial mergers,* in which the merged companies will not be operated as a single unit and from which no operating economies are expected.

Of course, mergers may actually combine these two features.

The primary benefit from an *operating* merger is higher expected total profits. For example, the combined company may be able to reduce overheads and thereby raise profits. The expected benefits of *financial* mergers are more varied. In one case, the target company may have no financial leverage, so the acquiring firm may plan to buy the company, pay for it by issuing debt, and gain market value from the capital structure change. In another instance, one of the firms may be so small that its stock is illiquid, its k_s value high, and its P/E ratio low. In such a case, the stock will have a low value, and it may represent a bargain purchase for the acquirer. In still other instances, one firm may have excessive liquidity, large annual cash flows, and unused debt capacity, while another firm may need financial resources to take advantage of growth opportunities. Control Data's merger with Commercial Credit is a case in point. Control Data needed capital to compete with IBM, while Commercial Credit had large cash reserves and marketable securities that could be converted to cash. Finally, a significant number of mergers are of the "failing firm" or "shotgun marriage" variety designed primarily to avoid the "transactions costs" of bankruptcy. A good example of a failing firm merger was the 1978 merger of Jones & Laughlin and Youngstown Sheet and Tube, two of the top ten steel producers, who were given approval by the Justice Department to combine and form the fourth largest U.S. steel company.

Estimating Future Operating Income

In a pure financial merger, the postmerger cash flows are simply the sum of the expected cash flows of the two companies if they operated independently. However, if the two firms' operations are to be integrated, then good projected cash flow statements, which are absolutely essential to sound merger decisions, will be difficult to construct.

The basic rationale for any operating merger is synergy. Del Monte Corporation provides a good example of a series of well thought out, successful operating mergers. Del Monte successfully merged and integrated numerous small canning companies into a very efficient, highly profitable organization. It used standardized production techniques to increase the efficiency of all its plants, a national brand name and national advertising to develop customer loyalty, a consolidated distribution system, and a centralized purchasing office that obtained substantial discounts from volume purchases. Because of these economies, Del Monte became perhaps the most efficient and profitable canning company, and its merger activities helped make possible the size that produced these economies. Consumers also benefited, because Del Monte's efficiency enabled the company to sell high quality products at relatively low prices.

An example of poor pro forma analysis that resulted in a disastrous merger is the consolidation of the Pennsylvania and New York Central Railroads. The premerger analysis was highly misleading. It failed to reveal the fact that certain key elements in the two rail systems were incompatible and hence could not be meshed together. Rather than gaining synergistic benefits, the combined system actually incurred additional overhead costs that helped lead to its bankruptcy.

It is impossible to generalize further about the construction of pro forma statements except to say that, in planning operating mergers, the development of these statements is *the single most important aspect* of the merger analysis.[6]

Postmerger Market Values

Once the postmerger income statement has been estimated, the next step is to project the postmerger market price of the acquiring firm's stock. This, in turn, involves two steps: (1) estimating postmerger earnings per share and (2) estimating the postmerger price/earnings ratio. Since earnings per share depend on the terms of the merger (how much the acquiring firm pays for the acquired company), this topic is examined next.

Terms of the Merger

The terms of a merger include two important elements. (1) Who will control the combined enterprise? (2) How much will the acquiring firm pay for the acquired company?

Postmerger Control The employment/control situation is of vital interest when a small, owner-managed firm sells out to a larger concern. The owner-manager may be anxious to retain a high position and also be concerned about keeping operating control of the organization after the merger. Thus, these points are likely to be stressed during the merger negotiations.[7] When a publicly owned firm, not controlled by its managers, is merged into another company, the acquired firm's management also is worried about its

---

6 It should be noted that firms heavily engaged in mergers have "acquisition departments" whose functions include (1) seeking suitable merger candidates and (2) taking over and integrating acquired firms into the parent corporation. The first step involves developing both pro forma statements and a plan for making the projections materialize. The second step involves (1) streamlining operations of the acquired firm, if necessary, and (2) instituting a system of controls that will permit the parent to effectively manage the new division and to coordinate its operation with those of other units.

7 The acquiring firm may also be concerned about this point, especially if the acquired firm's management is quite good. A condition of the merger may be that the management team agree to stay on for a period such as five years after the merger, and, further, that they agree not to start a new, competing business. Also, the price paid may be contingent on the acquired firm's performance subsequent to the merger. For example, when International Holdings acquired Walker Products, the price set was 100,000 shares of International Holdings stock at the time the deal was closed plus an additional 10,000 shares each year for the next three years *provided Walker Products earned at least $500,000 during each of these years*. Since Walker's managers owned the stock and would receive the bonus, they had incentive to stay on and to help the firm meet its targets.

postmerger position. If the acquiring firm agrees to keep the old management, then management may be willing to support the merger and recommend its acceptance to the stockholders. If the old management is to be removed, then it will probably resist the merger, as Kern's management did in the example described earlier in the chapter.

The Price Paid The second key element in a merger is the price to be paid for the acquired company—the cash or shares of stock to be given in exchange for the firm. If the merger is to be for cash, the analysis is similar to a regular capital budgeting analysis: the incremental earnings are estimated; a discount rate is applied to find the present value of these earnings; and, if the present value of the future incremental earnings exceeds the price paid for the acquired firm, then the merger is approved. If, because of operating economies or financial considerations, the acquired firm is worth more to the acquiring firm than its market value as a separate entity, then the merger is feasible. Obviously, the acquiring firm tries to buy at as low a price as possible, while the acquired firm tries to sell out at the highest possible price. The final price is determined by negotiations, with the side that negotiates better capturing most of the incremental value. *The larger the synergistic benefits, the more room there is for bargaining and the higher the probability that the merger will actually be consummated.*[8]

If the merger calls for an exchange of stock, then the key issue is the *exchange ratio (ER), which is the number of shares the acquiring firm gives for each of the acquired firm's shares.* For example, when Emhart Industries acquired USM, 1.125 shares of Emhart were exchanged for each USM share; thus, the exchange ratio was 1.125. The three factors that have the greatest influence on the exchange ratio—current earnings, projected future earnings, and market prices—are discussed next.

Earnings per Share Suppose the acquiring company (Firm A) earns $4.53 per share, while the target company (Firm T) has EPS = $3.49, and the companies are equally risky. On the basis of relative earnings, the exchange ratio would be set at $3.49/$4.53 = 0.77. This means that 77 shares of Firm A's stock would be exchanged for every 100 shares of Firm T's stock. An exchange on this basis would leave each stockholder's postmerger earnings unchanged. For example, the holder of 100 shares of T would receive 77 shares of A. The premerger earnings would have been $100 \times \$3.49 = \$349$, while the postmerger earnings would be $77 \times \$4.53 = \$349$.

Projected Future Earnings The above situation would be appropriate if (1) there were no synergistic effects, and (2) the firms had identical growth rates. However, when the merger is expected to produce higher earnings, or when

---

8 It has been estimated that, of all merger negotiations seriously begun, only about one-third actually result in merger.

the firms' EPS growth rates differ, it is more appropriate to set the exchange ratio on the basis of *expected future EPS rather than historic EPS.*

First, consider the same case with no synergy, but with the additional information that Firm A has been growing and is expected to continue to grow at a 6 percent rate, while T's growth rate is 4 percent. On the basis of the latest reported earnings, the exchange ratio would be $3.49/$4.53 = 0.77. However, on the basis of next year's projected earnings, the ratio would be $3.49(1.04)/$4.53(1.06) = $3.63/$4.80 = 0.756. Further, on the basis of earnings five years hence, the exchange ratio would be $4.25/$6.06 = 0.701. Thus, a problem exists—on the basis of future earnings, the exchange ratio varies depending on how far into the future earnings are projected.

When possible synergistic effects are considered, it becomes even more difficult to use current earnings as a basis for the exchange ratio. Suppose, for example, that Firm A's EPS = $4.53, Firm T's EPS = $3.49, and no growth is expected. If the merger terms are based on relative EPS, then, as we have seen, the ratio will be set at 0.77, and both firms' stockholders will have the same postmerger earnings. Thus, EPS for Firm A, the surviving company, will remain at $4.53. However, let us assume that synergistic effects are present, and on the basis of a 0.77 exchange ratio, A's postmerger EPS will rise to $6. This will benefit both T's and A's stockholders—the holder of 100 shares of T will now have earnings of 77 × $6 = $462 versus $349 before the merger, while a 100 share owner of A will have 100 × $6 = $600 versus $453 without the merger.

Accordingly, if synergy is anticipated, then A can realistically pay more for T than 0.77 shares, while T's stockholders can accept less than 0.77 shares and still come out ahead. To calculate this "breakeven exchange ratio" from Firm A's standpoint, we apply the following formula:

$$ER_A = \frac{TE - EPS_A(N_A)}{EPS_A(N_T)} \qquad (19\text{--}1)$$

where ER_A is the maximum exchange ratio which will prevent dilution of Firm A's EPS; TE equals the consolidated total earnings (A's old earnings + T's old earnings + synergistic earnings); EPS_A is A's old EPS; N_A is the number of shares of A's stock outstanding before the merger; and N_T is the number of shares of T's stock outstanding before the merger.[9]

Suppose the following data exist:

$$N_T = 300 \text{ shares,}$$
$$N_A = 1{,}000 \text{ shares (before the merger),}$$
$$EPS_A = \$4.53, \text{ and}$$
$$TE = \$4{,}530 + \$1{,}047 + \$2{,}000 = \$7{,}577.$$

---

9 Equation 19–1 is developed by finding the *ER* that keeps A's new EPS equal to its old EPS:

$$\text{New EPS} = \text{Old EPS} = \frac{TE}{N_A + N_T(ER)}.$$

Solving for *ER* produces Equation 19–1, with EPS_A being equal to A's old EPS.

The $2,000 included in TE represents synergistic earnings. Substituting into Equation 19–1, we obtain

$$ER_A = \frac{\$7,577 - \$4.53(1,000)}{\$4.53(300)} = \frac{\$3,047}{\$1,359} = 2.24 \text{ shares.}$$

Thus, A can give as many as 2.24 of its shares for each share of T without causing a dilution in its EPS:

$$\text{Old EPS} = \$4.53.$$

$$\text{New EPS} = \frac{\$7,577}{1,000 + 300(2.24)} = \frac{\$7,577}{1,672} = \$4.53.$$

Any lower exchange ratio will increase A's EPS.

A similar analysis can be conducted from the standpoint of T's stockholders to determine just how low the exchange ratio can be set without diluting T's stockholders' earnings. This minimum ratio is equal to the following:[10]

$$ER_T = \frac{EPS_T N_A}{TE - N_T EPS_T}. \tag{19-2}$$

Substituting into Equation 19–2, we find the minimum ratio acceptable to T's stockholders to be 0.534:

$$ER_T = \frac{\$3.49(1,000)}{\$7,577 - 300(\$3.49)} = \frac{\$3,490}{\$6,530} = 0.534.$$

If this ratio is used, A's postmerger EPS will be

$$EPS_A = \frac{TE}{N_A + ER(N_T)} = \frac{\$7,577}{1,000 + 160} = \$6.53.$$

The holder of 100 old shares of T would have had total earnings of $100 \times \$3.49 = \$349$. After the merger, if the exchange ratio is set at 0.534, the total earnings still will be $349: 53.4 shares $\times$ \$6.53 = \$349$.

We see, then, that if no basic growth is expected, but synergy is present, our hypothetical merger should have an exchange ratio in the range of 0.53 to 2.24. The greater the synergistic effects, the wider the range of the exchange ratio. Obviously, the acquiring firm will want to set the exchange ratio as low as possible, while the target firm will want to use the upper end of the range. The actual exchange ratio will be determined by the bargaining process, but with such a wide range as this one, the merger will almost certainly take place.

---

10 Equation 19–2 is developed as follows: We are seeking to set Old EPS_T = New EPS_T. New EPS_T = new EPS_A (ER), so $EPS_A = EPS_T/ER$, where EPS_A is the new, *post-merger* EPS. Footnote 9 also gave an equation for EPS_A, and we can set these two equations equal to one another:

$$EPS_A = \frac{EPS_T}{ER} = \frac{TE}{N_A + N_T ER}.$$

We can now solve for *ER:*

$$ER_T = \frac{EPS_T N_A}{TE - N_T EPS_T}. \tag{19-2}$$

Market Values Current and future earnings, risk, growth rates, potential synergistic effects, and a host of other factors are embodied in a firm's market price, so in many respects relative market prices represent the best basis for setting exchange ratios. Suppose, for example, that Firm A sells for $40 per share, while T's current price is $30. On the basis of market values, the exchange ratio would be set at $30/$40 = 0.75.

If no synergistic effects are likely, or if T's synergistic value to potential acquiring firms has already been accounted for in its price, then the actual exchange ratio will probably be based on relative market values. However, if T's price reflects only its "stand alone" value, but it could enjoy substantially higher profits if combined with another company, then the actual exchange ratio could be set well above the market value ratio.

Illustration of a Merger Analysis

To illustrate how a merger might be analyzed, consider the proposed merger between Consolidated Enterprises and Target Technology, Inc. Consolidated Enterprises has been growing at a rate of about 5 percent per year, while Target Technology's past and projected future growth rate is 20 percent. Consolidated's total after-tax earnings are $50 million, or $4 for each of its 12.5 million shares; Target's latest earnings were $3 million, or $2 for each of its 1.5 million shares. Consolidated pays a $2 dividend, while Target pays $1 per share. Consolidated's current market price is $30 per share, and Target's is $20 per share.

When they began considering a possible merger, Consolidated's analysts first assumed that no synergistic effects would occur but that the combined companies would grow at a 5.85 percent rate, calculated as follows:[11]

	Total Earnings	Percentage Weights	Growth Rate	Product
Consolidated Enterprises	$50,000,000	0.9434	5%	4.717%
Target Technology	3,000,000	0.0566	20	1.132
	$53,000,000	1.0000		
Weighted average growth rate				5.849%

Next, the Consolidated analysts considered possible exchange ratios (ER). On the basis of current earnings, ER = $2/$4 = 0.5 shares of Consolidated given up for each share of Target Technology. On the basis of future earnings, the ratio would increase; for example, if earnings projected out five years were used, then the exchange ratio would be about 1.0:

---

11 Notice that, if the merger were analyzed next year, Target Technology's weight would be larger, hence the weighted average rate would be increased. In fact, if the growth rates of the two components were maintained after the merger, the growth rate of the combined enterprise would change each year, rising from 5.85 percent the first year and approaching 20 percent as the number of years since the merger increased. Target Technology could not, however, maintain a 20 percent growth rate indefinitely; if it did, it would eventually surpass the Gross National Product!

$$ER = (1.20)^5(\$2)/(1.05)^5(\$4)$$
$$= 2.4883(\$2)/1.2763(\$4)$$
$$= \$4.98/\$5.11 = 0.975 \approx 1.0.$$

On the basis of relative market prices, the exchange ratio would be set at $20/$30 = 0.667, and EPS would be $53/(12.5 + 0.667 × 1.5) = $3.93.

The Consolidated analysts then projected earnings per share for each of the next five years under the alternative exchange ratios. This projection was made by first estimating total corporate earnings of the combined firm for each year, then dividing by the number of shares outstanding, which differs depending on the exchange ratio used. Figure 19–1 gives a plot of Consolidated's EPS assuming no merger and also assuming a merger based on current market prices. As the graph shows, Consolidated's EPS would decline immediately after the merger, assuming no synergy and a 0.667 exchange ratio, but in the future EPS would grow more rapidly than it would have without the merger.

Figure 19–1
EPS Projections for Consolidated Enterprises

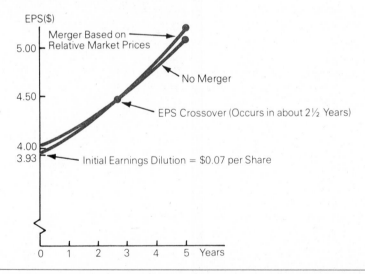

Using other exchange ratios, other earnings growth rates, and synergistic effects, we could derive many other EPS patterns. Because so many factors are involved, it is difficult to generalize about postmerger earnings per share. However, one important generalization should be made: *If a firm with a high P/E ratio buys a firm with a lower P/E ratio, and the exchange ratio is based on current market prices, then the acquiring firm will obtain an immediate increase in EPS. Conversely, if a low P/E ratio company buys a high P/E firm, there will be an immediate dilution in EPS.* This point is borne out by the Consolidated-Target merger analysis. Consolidated had a lower P/E ratio ($30/$4 = 7.5 ×) than Target Technology ($20/$2 = 10 ×), and this relationship led to the initial dilution in Consolidated's EPS as shown in Figure 19–1.[12] *In effect, Consolidated diluted its current EPS in order to obtain a higher future EPS growth rate.*

Target Technology's stockholders will have a higher level of current earnings at the market value exchange ratio.

Old earnings per 100 shares owned:	$100 × \$2 = \$200.$
New earnings per 100 shares formerly owned:	$100(0.667)(\$3.93) = \$262.$

They will, of course, be giving up some of their future growth opportunities.

Operating Synergy The analysis thus far is all based on the assumption of no operating synergies. However, Consolidated and Target Technology may complement one another. For example, Target's metallurgical scientists may be able to improve Consolidated's product line, or Consolidated's unused plant may be utilized by Target Technology. If synergy does occur, it could partially or completely offset the initial dilution and also result in an increase in the postmerger growth rate.

The Postmerger Market Price: Estimating a P/E Ratio After developing estimates of the postmerger EPS, the next task is to estimate a P/E ratio and then to apply this P/E ratio to the earnings estimate to obtain a *predicted postmerger market price.* The postmerger P/E ratio will reflect investors' estimates of the merged company's risk and growth prospects. If investors feel that Consolidated and Target Technology, as a combined enterprise, will be less risky because of diversification effects, then the P/E ratio may rise. Similarly, if investors think that the postmerger growth rate will be more reflective of Target Technology's situation, this too will enhance the P/E ratio.

The resulting P/E ratio might be the same as Consolidated's old ratio, 7.5 times. If this ratio is applied to an EPS of $3.93, the resulting price is $29.48. In this case, Consolidated's postmerger price would have declined from the old $30 level. On the other hand, if investors applied Target Technology's P/E of 10 to the combined company, then the postmerger stock price would be $39.30.

Several points should be clear from this brief discussion. First, Consolidated should acquire Target Technology if and only if the acquisition will raise Consolidated's stock price. Second, the postmerger price will reflect both the final EPS, which will depend on the exchange ratio and on possible synergistic effects, and the final P/E ratio, which will depend on investors' appraisal of the combined firm's risk and growth prospects. If a

---

12 The extent of this earnings dilution or increase depends on the size of the target company relative to that of the acquiring firm—the larger the target, the greater the earnings increase or decrease.

firm's analysts are good at estimating these factors, they will have a record of good acquisitions; otherwise, their merger program will not be successful.

EFFECTS OF ACCOUNTING PRACTICES ON REPORTED PROFITS

Although a detailed discussion of accounting is best left to accounting courses, at least some mention should be made of alternative accounting treatments of merged firms and their effects on reported profits. Mergers are handled in either of two basic ways: (1) as a *pooling of interests* or (2) as a *purchase.* The method used can have a significant effect on the postmerger reported profits, and this, in turn, can influence the desirability of the merger.

Pooling of Interests

In a pooling of interests, the consolidated balance sheet is constructed by simply adding together the balance sheets of the merged companies. Table 19–1 shows the essential elements of the consolidated balance sheet after Firms A and B have merged under a pooling of interests. This final balance sheet holds, regardless of how many shares Firm A gave up to acquire Firm B.

Table 19–1
Pooling of Interests Accounting

	Firm A	Firm B	Merged Firm: A
Current assets	$ 50	$25	$ 75
Fixed assets	50	25	75
Total assets	$100	$50	$150
Debt	$ 40	$20	$ 60
Common equity	60	30	90
Total liabilities and net worth	$100	$50	$150

Purchase Accounting

Under purchase accounting, the acquiring firm is assumed to have "bought" the acquired company much as it would buy any capital asset, paying for it with cash, debt, or stock of the acquiring company. If the price paid is exactly equal to the net asset value (total assets minus liabilities), then the consolidated balance sheet is similar to that under pooling. Otherwise, there is an important difference. If the price paid exceeds the net asset value, then assets are increased to reflect the price actually paid, while if the price paid is less than the net asset value, then assets are written down when preparing the consolidated balance sheet.

Table 19–2
Purchase Accounting

| | Firm A (1) | Firm B (2) | Firm A after the Merger[a] | | |
			$20 Paid (3)	$30 Paid (4)	$50 Paid (5)
Current assets	$ 50	$25	$ 75	$ 75	$ 80
Fixed assets	50	25	65[b]	75	80
Goodwill	0	0	0	0	10[d]
	$100	$50	$140	$150	$170
Debt	$ 40	$20	$ 60	$ 60	$ 60
Equity	60	30	80[c]	90	110[e]
	$100	$50	$140	$150	$170

[a]The price paid is the *net* asset value, that is, total assets minus debt.
[b]Assume Firm B's fixed assets are written down to $15 before constructing the consolidated balance sheet.
[c]Firm B's common equity is reduced by $10 prior to consolidation to reflect the fixed asset write-off.
[d]"Goodwill" refers to the excess paid for a firm over and above the appraised value of the physical assets purchased. Goodwill represents payment both for intangibles such as patents and also for "organization value" that might arise from having an effective sales force.
[e]Firm B's equity is increased prior to consolidation to reflect the above-book purchase price.

Table 19–2 illustrates purchase accounting, using the same data as for the pooled companies. Note that Firm B's net asset value is $30, which is also its reported common equity value. This $30 could reflect the correct market value (which is determined by the firm's earning power), but it could also be more or less than the true value. Three situations are considered. First, in Column 3 we assume that Firm A gives cash or stock worth $20 for Firm B. Thus, B was apparently overvalued, and A pays less than B's net asset value. The overvaluation could be in fixed or current assets; we assume that fixed assets are overvalued. Accordingly, we write down both B's fixed assets and its common equity by $10 before constructing the consolidated balance sheet shown in Column 3. Next, in Column 4 we assume that A pays exactly its net asset value for B. In this case, pooling and purchase accounting would produce identical balance sheets. Finally, in Column 5 we assume that A pays more than net asset value for B: $50 is paid for $30 of net assets. This excess is partly attributed to undervalued assets (land, buildings, and machinery, and also inventories worth more because of inflation); to reflect this fact, current and fixed assets are each increased by $5. In addition, we assume that $10 of the $20 excess is due to a superior sales organization, or some other intangible factor, and post this excess as "goodwill." B's common equity is correspondingly increased by $20, and this is reflected in the consolidated common equity account.

Income Statement Effects

There can be a significant difference in reported profits under the two accounting methods. If asset values are increased, this must be reflected in higher depreciation charges (and also in a higher cost of goods sold if inventories were written up). This reduces reported profits. Also, goodwill represents the excess paid for a firm over its net asset value. This excess, in turn, is paid because of the acquired firm's superior earning power, which will, presumably, be eroded over time as patents expire, as new firms enter the industry, and so on. Thus, the accountants (in Accounting Principles Board Opinion #17) require that goodwill be written off, or "depreciated," with the writeoff period corresponding to the expected life of the superior earning power but in no case exceeding forty years.

Goodwill is certainly not a trivial issue. For example, Philip Morris, Inc., recently acquired Seven-Up for a price of $520 million; approximately $390 million of this represented goodwill. Table 19–3 illustrates the effects of goodwill writeoff by showing the income statements for Firms A and B before the merger and for Firm A after the merger. For the purchase, we assume that A purchased B for $50, creating $10 of goodwill and $10 of higher physical asset value. Further, we assume that this $20 will be written off over ten years.[13] As Column 4 indicates, writing off goodwill and higher asset values under purchase accounting causes reported profits to be lower than under pooling.

The writeoff of goodwill is also reflected in earnings per share. In our hypothetical merger, we assume that nine shares exist in the consolidated firm. (Six of these shares went to A's stockholders, three to B's.) Under pooling, EPS = $2, while under purchase, EPS = $1.83. Further, the greater the amount of goodwill, the larger the writeoff and the more significant the dilution in reported earnings per share. This fact causes managers to prefer pooling to purchase accounting.

Requirements for Pooling

Six conditions must be met before the pooling method may be used:

1. The acquired firm's stockholders must maintain an ownership position in the surviving firm.
2. The basis of accounting for the assets of the acquired entity must remain unchanged.
3. Only independent interests may be combined; each entity must have had

---

13 The writeoff of goodwill is not a deduction for income tax purposes, but the other excess writeoffs are deductible. Also, "negative goodwill" is eliminated at the time of the merger, so negative goodwill cannot be used to increase reported profits in later years.

Table 19-3
Income Effects of Pooling versus Purchase Accounting

	Premerger		Postmerger: Firm A	
	Firm A (1)	Firm B (2)	Pooling (3)	Purchase (4)
Sales	$100	$50	$150	$150
Operating costs	72	36	108	109[a]
Operating income	$ 28	$14	$ 42	$ 41
Interest (10%)	4	2	6	6
Taxable income	$ 24	$12	$ 36	$ 35
Taxes (50%)	12	6	18	17.5
Earnings after tax	$ 12	$ 6	$ 18	$ 17.5
Goodwill writeoff	0	0	0	1[b]
Net income	$ 12	$ 6	$ 18	$ 16.5
EPS[c]	$ 2	$ 2	$ 2	$ 1.83

[a] Operating costs are $1 higher than they otherwise would be to reflect the higher reported costs caused by the physical asset markup at the time of purchase.
[b] $10 of increased goodwill ÷ 10 years = $1 writeoff per year.
[c] Firm A had six shares and Firm B three shares before the merger. A gives one of its shares for each of B's, so A has nine shares outstanding after the merger.

autonomy for two years prior to the initiation of the plan to combine, and no more than 10 percent ownership of voting common stock may be held as intercorporate investments.
4. The combination must be effected in a single transaction; contingent payouts are not permitted in poolings, but they may be used in purchases.
5. The acquiring corporation may issue only common stock identical to its outstanding voting common stock in exchange for substantially all the voting common stock of the other company; "substantially" is defined as 90 percent.
6. The combined entity cannot dispose of a significant portion of the assets of the combined companies for two years after the merger.

If all of these conditions are met, then the combination is, in a sense, a "merger among equals," and a pooling of interests has occurred. In contrast, a purchase involves (1) new owners, (2) an appraisal of the acquired firm's physical assets with a restatement of the balance sheet to reflect these values, and (3) the possible creation of goodwill.[14]

HOLDING COMPANIES

Holding companies date from 1889, when New Jersey became the first state to pass a law permitting corporations to be formed for the sole purpose of owning the

14 See APB Opinions 16 and 17.

stocks of other companies. Many of the advantages and disadvantages of holding companies are identical to the advantages and disadvantages of large-scale operations already discussed in connection with mergers and consolidations. Whether a company is organized on a divisional basis or with the divisions kept as separate companies does not affect the basic reasons for conducting a large-scale, multiproduct, multiplant operation. However, the holding company form of large-scale operations has some different advantages and disadvantages from those of completely integrated divisionalized operations.

Advantages of Holding Companies

Control with Fractional Ownership Through a holding company operation, a firm may buy 5, 10, or 50 percent of the stock of another corporation. Such fractional ownership may be sufficient to give the acquiring company effective working control or substantial influence over the operations of the company in which it has acquired stock ownership. Working control is often considered to entail more than 25 percent of the common stock, but it can be as low as 10 percent if the stock is widely distributed. One financier says that the attitude of management is more important than the number of shares owned, adding that "if they think you can control the company, then you do." In addition, control on a very slim margin can be held through friendship with large stockholders outside the holding company group.

Isolation of Risks Because the various operating companies in a holding company system are separate legal entities, the obligations of any one unit are separate from those of the other units. Catastrophic losses incurred by one unit of the holding company system are therefore not transmitted as claims on the assets of the other units.

Although this is the customary generalization of the nature of a holding company system, it is not completely valid. First, the parent company may feel obligated to make good on the subsidiary's debts, even though it is not legally bound to do so, in order to keep its good name and thus retain customers. Examples of this would include American Express's payment of over $100 million in connection with the salad oil swindle of the 1960s and United California Bank's coverage of its Swiss affiliate's multimillion dollar losses on cocoa futures in the 1970s. Second, a parent company may feel obligated to supply capital to an affiliate in order to protect its initial investment; General Public Utilities' continued support of its affiliate's Three Mile Island nuclear plant is an example. And, third, when lending to one of the units of a holding company system, an astute loan officer may require a guarantee or a claim on the assets of the parent or of other elements in the holding company system. To some degree, therefore, the assets in the various elements of a holding company are joined.

Disadvantages of Holding Companies

Partial Multiple Taxation Provided the holding company owns at least 80 percent of a subsidiary's voting stock, the Internal Revenue Service permits the filing of consolidated returns, in which case dividends received by the parent are not taxed. However, if less than 80 percent of the stock is owned, returns may not be consolidated, but 85 percent of the dividends received by the holding company may be deducted. With a tax rate of 46 percent, this means that the effective tax rate on intercorporate dividends is 6.9 percent. This partial double taxation somewhat offsets the benefits of holding company control with limited ownership, but whether the penalty of 6.9 percent of dividends received is sufficient to offset other possible advantages is a matter that must be decided in individual situations.

Ease of Enforced Dissolution It is relatively easy for the U.S. Department of Justice to require dissolution by disposal of stock ownership of a holding company operation it finds unacceptable. For instance, du Pont was required to dispose of its 23 percent stock interest in General Motors Corporation, acquired in the early 1920s. Because there was no fusion between the corporations, there were no difficulties, from an operating standpoint, in requiring the separation of the two companies. However, if complete amalgamation had taken place, it would have been much more difficult to break up the company after so many years, and the likelihood of forced divestiture would have been reduced.

Leverage in Holding Companies

The holding company vehicle has been used to obtain huge degrees of financial leverage. In the 1920s, several tiers of holding companies were established in the electric utility and other industries. In those days, an operating company might have $100 million of assets, financed by $50 million of debt and $50 million of equity. A first-tier holding company might own the stock (its only asset) and be financed with $25 million of debt and $25 million of equity. A second-tier holding company, which owned the stock of the first-tier company, might be financed with $12.5 million of debt and $12.5 million of equity. The system could be extended, but with only two holding companies, we see that $100 million of operating assets are controlled at the top by $12.5 million of equity, and that these assets must provide enough cash income to support $87.5 million of debt. *This holding company system is highly leveraged, even though the individual components only have 50 percent debt/asset ratios.* Because of this *consolidated leverage,* even a small decline in profits at the operating company level could bring the whole system down like a house of cards.[15]

---

15 Excessive leverage through holding companies caused problems for the electric utilities during the 1930s. Accordingly, Congress passed a law regulating utility holding companies and specifically forbidding them from issuing debt for the purpose of buying the stock of operating electric utilities. The same situation does not exist in the telephone industry. Therefore, telephone holding companies (such as AT&T) can and do sell bonds and use the proceeds to buy stock in operating companies. The purpose is to obtain capital at the lowest overall cost.

SUMMARY

A merger involves the consolidation of two or more firms. Mergers can provide economic benefits through economies of scale, but they also have the potential for reducing competition, and for this reason they are carefully regulated by governmental agencies.

In most mergers, one company (the *acquiring firm*) initiates action to take over another (the *target firm*). The acquiring company must analyze the situation and determine the value of the target company. Often there will be *operating economies,* or *synergistic benefits,* which will raise the earnings of the combined enterprise over the sum of the earnings of the two separate companies. In this circumstance, the merger is potentially beneficial to both sets of stockholders, but the two firms' managers and stockholders must agree as to how the net benefits will be shared. This all boils down to how much the acquiring company is willing to pay, either in cash or in shares of its own stock, for the target company. There are various methods for determining an appropriate price.

In a merger, one firm disappears. However, an alternative is for one firm to buy all or a majority of the common stock of another and to run the acquired firm as an operating subsidiary. When this occurs, the acquiring firm is said to be a *holding company.* Holding company operations have both advantages and disadvantages. The major advantage is the fact that control can often be obtained for a smaller cash outlay. The disadvantages include tax penalties and the fact of incomplete ownership.

Questions

19-1 Define the following terms:
   a. Synergy
   b. Tender offer
   c. Exchange ratio
   d. Holding company
   e. Operating company
   f. Purchase versus pooling

19-2 Four economic classifications of mergers are (a) horizontal, (b) vertical, (c) conglomerate, and (d) congeneric. Explain what each of these terms means, and explain their importance in merger analysis with regard to (1) the likelihood of Justice Department intervention and (2) possibilities for operating synergy.

19-3 Firm A wants to acquire Firm B. Firm B's management thinks the merger is a good idea. Might a tender offer be used?

19-4 Distinguish between operating mergers and pure financial mergers.

19-5 In late 1968 the SEC and the New York Stock Exchange each issued sets of rulings on disclosure of information which, in effect, required that firms disclose that they have entered into merger discussions as soon as they start such discussions. Since the previous procedure had been to delay disclosure until it was evident that there was a reasonably good expectation the merger under discussion would actually go through (and not to bring the matter up at all if the merger died in the early stages), it can safely be predicted that, in a statistical sense, a larger percentage of prospective mergers will be "abandoned" in the future than in the past.

a. Why do you think the new rulings were put into effect?

b. Will the new rulings have any adverse effects? Why?

19-6 Suppose that AT&T's twenty-one operating subsidiaries such as Pacific Telephone and Southern Bell all had preferred stock, bonds, and publicly owned common stock outstanding. (Actually, some have preferred outstanding; all issue bonds; and AT&T owns 100 percent of the common stock of sixteen operating telephone subsidiaries and a large fraction of that of the others.) AT&T's major asset is its stock in the operating telephone companies, but the parent company does own in its own right certain long distance telephone equipment.

Given this information, assume that you are required to write a report on the relative riskiness of investments in the common, preferred, and bonds both of AT&T itself (the parent) and of the operating subsidiaries.

19-7 Philip Morris, Inc., recently acquired Seven-Up Corporation for $520 million. Seven-Up had a book value of equity of $130 million. Do you think Philip Morris's management would prefer to treat the merger as a pooling or as a purchase? Would your reaction be the same if the book value had been $520 million and the price paid $130 million?

19-8 Two large, publicly owned firms are contemplating a merger. No operating synergy is expected, but returns on the two firms are not perfectly positively correlated, so σ_{EBIT} would be reduced for the combined corporation. One group of consultants argues that this risk reduction is sufficient grounds for the merger. Another group thinks that this type of risk reduction is irrelevant because stockholders could already hold the stock of both companies and thus gain the risk reduction benefits of merger. Whose position is correct?

Problems

19-1 The Hilltop Hotels are negotiating a merger with the Doze Inn Motel chain. Consider the following table:

	EPS	D_0	g	P_0	Number of Common Shares
Hilltop	$3.00	$1.50	8%	$53.55	5 million
Doze Inn	1.00	0.90	3	11.61	1 million

Establish the appropriate exchange ratio

a. based on current EPS.

b. based on EPS in five years.

c. based on current market values.

d to maintain Hilltop's current EPS.

e. to maintain Doze Inn's current EPS.

Note: for Parts d and e, assume that incremental earnings attributable to synergy equal $2 million.

19-2 Morris Sisters' Cafeterias hopes to acquire Davidson's Cafeterias through a merger. Davidson's management will consider the offer only if the price is high and management can stay on in its present capacity.

Morris Sisters' expects to gain operating efficiency from the merger through purchasing, advertising, and distribution economies. It estimates that if the two chains had been operating jointly during the year that just ended, earnings would have totaled $21 million.

a. Using the table below, calculate exchange ratios based on: (1) market values, (2) most recent earnings per share, (3) a comparison of Morris Sisters' most recent EPS and the expected postmerger EPS, and (4) a comparison of Davidson's most recent earnings with its expected postmerger earnings.

	EPS	DPS	g	P_0	Number of Shares
Morris Sisters'	$2.50	$2.00	6%	$40	6 million
Davidson's	1.80	0.90	2	18	2 million

b. Irrespective of your answers to Part a, assume that Morris Sisters' agrees to a one-for-one exchange of shares. Calculate the expected postmerger EPS.

c. Assume a postmerger P/E of 15. Now calculate the expected postmerger market price and compare it to next year's expected price without a merger. Should Morris Sisters' acquire Davidson's?

19-3 Beti's Boutique wishes to acquire Jan's Jeans for $250,000. Beti expects the incremental earnings to be $45,000 for ten years. She has also calculated her marginal cost of capital for this investment to be 12 percent. Conduct a capital budgeting analysis for Beti to determine whether or not she should purchase Jan's shop.

19-4 Southern Bakery is being acquired by the Royal Crumb Cookie Company. Their premerger balance sheets are as follows:

Southern Bakery

Current assets	$ 750	Debt	$ 875
Fixed assets	1,125	Common equity	1,000
		Total liabilities and	
Total assets	$1,875	net worth	$1,875

Royal Crumb Cookie Company

Current assets	$1,500	Debt	$2,000
Fixed assets	1,625	Common equity	1,125
		Total liabilities and	
Total assets	$3,125	net worth	$3,125

a. Construct the postmerger balance sheet for Royal Crumb Cookie Company assuming the acquisition is a pooling of interests.

b. Assume the merger in Part a was a purchase rather than a pooling of interests. Royal Crumb bought Southern for $2,000. Now construct the postmerger balance sheet.

c. Southern Bakery's and Royal Crumb's premerger income statements are shown below. Calculate postmerger net income and EPS for both purchase and pooling. Assume a one-for-one stock exchange was made and that goodwill will be written off over a twenty-five year expected life.

	Southern	Royal Crumb
Sales	$750	$1,300
Operating costs	488	830
Operating income	$262	$ 470
Interest	100	200
Taxable income	$162	$ 270
Taxes	81	135
Earnings after taxes	$ 81	$ 135
Goodwill writeoff	0	0
Net income	$ 81	$ 135
Common shares	60	100
EPS	$1.35	$ 1.35

APPENDIX 19A   USING MERGERS TO CREATE AN ILLUSION OF GROWTH

As noted in Chapter 19, if a company with a high P/E ratio buys a firm with a lower P/E, then an increase in the acquiring firm's EPS results from the merger. If a firm carries out a series of such mergers, this activity will produce a pattern of rising earnings per share, even though no real growth in operating income exists. This illusion of growth, in turn, can lead to an overvaluation of the firm's stock, and this overvaluation may continue so long as the firm continues to buy low P/E companies.

This point is illustrated by the data in Table 19A–1. In Section 1, we see that Firm A experienced a 20 percent growth rate in after-tax earnings from 1977 to 1979. However, its growth period is over, and, without mergers, total income would level out at $10 million and EPS at $1. Investors, however, do not know that Firm A's growth is over, so the stock has a P/E of 16 and is priced at $16 per share.

In 1980, A merges with B, a no-growth company that earns $1 per share and sells for $8, or 8 times earnings. The exchange ratio is based on relative market price, so $ER = \$8/\$16 = 0.5$. Therefore, A gives up 0.5 shares for each of B's 5 million shares, or 2.5 million shares in total. This produces the following 1980 EPS for the now enlarged Firm A:

$$EPS = \frac{A's\ earnings\ +\ B's\ earnings}{A's\ shares\ +\ Shares\ given\ for\ B}$$

$$= \frac{\$10,000,000\ +\ \$5,000,000}{10,000,000\ +\ 2,500,000}$$

$$= \$1.20.$$

Thus, A's earnings per share for 1980 increase by 20 percent over 1979 EPS. Without the merger, EPS would have been $1, with zero growth.

Because A's 20 percent historic EPS growth rate was maintained, the P/E remains at 16 times. Now, in 1981, A buys C, another no-growth company similar to B except that C is 50 percent larger than B. Working through the arithmetic, we see that, because of the merger, A's 1981 EPS rises to $1.44, so the 20 percent growth rate is again maintained. Although there is no real growth in any of the companies—operating earnings are flat—the fact that A started off with a high P/E ratio and then bought a series of low P/E ratio companies has produced growth in its EPS. Note, however, that A must buy increasingly larger firms to maintain this growth.

Now suppose the merger string is broken at some point—for example, the Justice Department might block a particular merger. (As the mergers get larger, there is increasing danger of Justice Department intervention.) A's EPS growth rate would fall to zero, and analysts would examine the company closely. This would probably cause the P/E ratio to decline, and if the P/E ratio dropped back to 8×, the norm for a no-growth company, then A could no longer play the merger game to obtain growth in EPS, and A's 1982 stock price would fall from $27.68 to $1.73 × 8 = $13.84.

Table 19A–1
Merger Analysis: Growth Illusion

1. Net Income after Taxes of Firms A, B, C, and D:

	A	B	C	D	Consolidated
1977	$ 6,944,444	$5,000,000	$7,500,000	$11,250,000	$30,694,444
1978	8,333,333	5,000,000	7,500,000	11,250,000	32,083,333
1979	10,000,000	5,000,000	7,500,000	11,250,000	33,750,000
1980	10,000,000	5,000,000	7,500,000	11,250,000	33,750,000
1981	10,000,000	5,000,000	7,500,000	11,250,000	33,750,000
1982	10,000,000	5,000,000	7,500,000	11,250,000	33,750,000

2. Assumptions and Basic Premerger Data
   a. P/E ratios: A's P/E = 16.
      Other firms' P/Es = 8.
   b. Exchange ratio *(ER):* Based on market values.
   c. Shares of acquired companies: Equal to earnings.
   d. Other companies' EPS = $1.
   e. Other companies' prices = $8.

3. Earnings per Share and Price Calculations
   a. *1980: Merge with B.*
      P_A = $16 = 16 × $1.
      P_B = $8 = 8 × $1.
      ER = $8/$16 = 0.5.
      Δ shares = 0.5(5 million) = 2.5 million.
      New EPS = ($10 + $5)/(10 + 2.5) = $1.20.
      New price = $1.20 × 16 = $19.20.
   b. *1981: Merge with C.*
      P_A = $19.20.
      P_C = $8.
      ER = 0.4167.
      Δ shares = 0.4167(7.5 million) = 3.125 million.
      New EPS = ($10 + $5 + $7.5)/(12.5 + 3.125) = $22.5/15.625 = $1.44.
      New price = $23.04.
   c. *1982: Merge with D.*
      P_A = $23.04.
      P_D = $8.
      ER = 0.3472.
      Δ shares = 0.3472(11.25 million) = 3.906 million.
      New EPS = ($10 + $5 + $7.5 + $11.25)/(15.625 + 3.906) = $33.75/19.531 = $1.73.
      New price = $27.68.

4. Calculated Earnings per Share for Firm A:

	A	B	C	D	Consolidated
1977	$0.69	$1.00	$1.00	$1.00	$1.57
1978	0.83	1.00	1.00	1.00	1.64
1979	1.00	1.00	1.00	1.00	1.73
1980	EPS$_A$ = $1.20		1.00	1.00	1.73
1981		EPS$_A$ = $1.44		1.00	1.73
1982			EPS$_A$ = $1.73		

5. Growth rate in EPS for A only: $1.73/$0.69 = 2.5072 = FVIF for 20%.
   Growth rate in consolidated EPS: $1.73/$1.57 = 1.1019 = FVIF for 2%.

Exactly this kind of thing happened during the conglomerate boom of the 1960s, and it has also occurred, though on a smaller scale, in the 1970s. In a very real sense, the growth obtained is illusory—it is not the kind of real growth that can be sustained. Buying stock in a firm that is using mergers to report growing EPS is very much like buying a chain letter; it can work out okay, but you had better know what you are doing, and you had better get in and out before the bubble bursts!

20 BANKRUPTCY AND REORGANIZATION

Thus far, the text has dealt with issues faced by growing, successful enterprises. However, many firms encounter financial difficulties, and some actually fail. An understanding of business failures, their causes, and their possible remedies is important to financial managers of successful as well as potentially unsuccessful firms, for the managers of the successful firms must know their rights and how to enforce them. There are several instances in which the failure of another firm affects a successful one: (1) sales and profits are lost when a major customer fails; (2) the flow of incoming materials is interrupted when a supplier fails; and (3) an increased share of the market becomes available when a competitor fails. At the same time, the financial manager of a failing firm must know how to ward off total collapse and thereby minimize losses. Such an ability often means the difference between loss of the firm versus rehabilitation and eventual success.

FAILURE

Failure can be defined in several ways, depending on the problems involved or the situation facing the firm. To distinguish among them, it is necessary to define the following terms:

Economic Failure Failure in an economic sense signifies that a firm's revenues do not cover its total costs, including its cost of capital.

Business Failure This term is used by Dun & Bradstreet, which is the major compiler of failure statistics, to include any business that has terminated with a resultant loss to creditors.[1]

This chapter was coauthored by Arthur L. Herrmann of the University of Hartford.

1 Dun & Bradstreet, Inc., *The Failure Record*. This publication is updated annually.

Technical Insolvency A firm can be considered technically insolvent if it cannot meet its current obligations as they fall due. Technical insolvency denotes a lack of liquidity and may be only temporary.

Insolvency in Bankruptcy A firm is insolvent in bankruptcy when its total liabilities exceed the fair valuation of its assets. This is usually a more serious condition than technical insolvency, and it often leads to liquidation of the firm.

Bankruptcy This is a legal term. Although many people use the term *bankrupt* to refer to any firm that has "failed," a firm is not legally bankrupt unless it has failed according to criteria established by the Federal Bankruptcy Act and has been adjudged bankrupt by a federal court. Bankruptcy is a legal procedure, carried out under special courts of law, for liquidating or reorganizing a business. It can be either *voluntary,* in which case the debtor petitions the court, or *involuntary,* in which case the creditors petition the court and prove that the debtor is not paying debts as they mature.

CAUSES OF FAILURE

The causes of financial failure are numerous, and they vary from situation to situation. However, it is useful to isolate the major underlying causes in order to avoid them if possible, or to correct them in the event a reorganization is necessary. A recent Dun & Bradstreet compilation assigned percentage values to these causes as follows:

Cause of Failure	Percentage of Total
Neglect	2.0
Fraud	1.5
Disaster	0.9
Management incompetence	93.1
Unknown	2.5
	100.00

Management incompetence includes the effects of recessions and unfavorable industry trends. This placement is logical, since managements should plan ahead and be prepared for both booms and recessions. Financial difficulties are usually the result of a series of errors, misjudgments, and interrelated weaknesses that can be attributed directly or indirectly to management, and signs of potential financial distress are often evident before the firm actually fails. Research to isolate and identify the causes of business failure, and thus to predict or prevent it, is extremely important. [2] A number of financial remedies are available to management when it becomes aware of the imminence or occurrence of insolvency. These remedies are described later in this chapter.

THE FAILURE RECORD

How widespread is business failure in the United States? In Table 20–1 we see that a fairly large number of businesses fail each year, although the failures in any one year are not a large percentage of the total business population. In 1977, for example, there were 7,919 business failures (as defined by Dun & Bradstreet), but this was only 0.28 percent of all business firms. It is interesting to note that while the failure rate per 10,000 businesses fluctuates with the economy, the average liability per failure has tended to increase over time. This is due both to increased price levels and to an increase in the number of multimillion dollar bankruptcies in recent years (see Table 20–2).

Table 20–1
Historical Failure Rate: Experience of United States Businesses

Years	Number of Failures	Average Failure Rate (per 10,000 Concerns)	Average Liability per Failure
1857–1968 (average per year)	11,233	87	$ 28,292
1900–1968 (average per year)	13,659	70	32,889
1946–1968 (average per year)	11,089	42	61,101
1959–1969 (average per year)	13,881	54	84,724
1970	10,748	44	175,638
1971	10,326	42	185,641
1972	9,566	38	209,099
1973	9,345	36	245,912
1974	9,915	38	307,937
1975	11,432	42	383,152
1976	9,628	35	312,762
1977	7,919	28	390,872
1978	6,619	24	355,946
1979 (estimated)	7,122	26	375,000

Sources: Edward I. Altman, *Corporate Bankruptcy in America* (Lexington, Mass.: Heath Lexington Books, 1972); Dun & Bradstreet, *The Failure Record* (1973); and *The Monthly Failure Report* (May 1976); U.S. Department of Commerce, *Survey of Current Business* (August 1979).

---

2 Much of the current academic work in this area is based on writings by Edward I. Altman: *Corporate Bankruptcy in America* (Lexington, Mass.: Heath Lexington Books, 1972) and "Financial Ratios, Discriminant Analysis, and the Prediction of Corporate Bankruptcy," *Journal of Finance* 23 (September 1968): 589–609. See Appendix A to Chapter 6 of *Financial Management,* 2d ed., for further discussion of Altman's work.

Table 20–2
The Ten Biggest Bankruptcies

	Liabilities	Date
Penn Central	$3.3 billion	June 1970
W. T. Grant	$1 billion	Oct. 1975
W. Judd Kassuba and related and controlled businesses	$420 million	Dec. 1973
Investors Funding	$379 million	Oct. 1974
U.S. Financial Services	$300 million	July 1973
Equity Funding	$200 million	April 1973
Interstate Dept. Stores	$195.6 million	May 1974
Fidelity Mortgage Investors	$182.4 million	Jan. 1975
Daylins Dept. Stores	$155.2 million	Feb. 1975
Chicago, Rock Island & Pacific	$97.8 million	March 1975

Source: *New York Times,* October 12, 1975, Section 3, p. 16.

While bankruptcy is more frequent among smaller firms, it is clear from Table 20–2 that large firms are not immune to bankruptcy. These data actually understate the financial problems among larger firms because, as Altman notes, mergers or governmental intervention are generally used as an alternative to outright bankruptcy except in cases of fraud or where the failing company is too large to be absorbed by another firm. The decision to give federal aid to Chrysler is one excellent illustration. Also, in recent years the Federal Home Loan Bank System has arranged the absorption of several very large "problem" savings and loan associations by sound institutions, and the federal banking authorities have done the same thing for banks. Several United States government agencies, principally the Defense Department, were able to "bail out" Lockheed when it otherwise would have failed, and the "shotgun marriage" of Douglas Aircraft and McDonnell was designed to prevent Douglas's failure. Merrill Lynch took over Goodbody & Company, which would otherwise have gone bankrupt and would have frozen the accounts of its 225,000 customers while the bankruptcy settlement was worked out. This would have panicked investors across the country, so the New York Stock Exchange member firms put up $30 million as an inducement to get Merrill Lynch to keep Goodbody from folding. Similar instances could be cited in other industries.

Why do government and industry seek to avoid bankruptcy among larger firms? There are many reasons. In the case of the financial institutions, the main one is to prevent an erosion of confidence. With Lockheed and Douglas, the Defense Department wanted not only to maintain viable suppliers but also to avoid disrupting local communities. Even when "the public interest" is not at stake, the fact that bankruptcy is a very expensive process gives private industry strong incentives to avoid out-and-out bankruptcy. The costs and complexities of bankruptcy are discussed in subsequent sections of this chapter, but first some less formal and less expensive remedies and legal actions are examined.

EXTENSION AND COMPOSITION

In the case of a fundamentally sound company whose financial difficulties appear to be temporary, the creditors generally prefer to work directly with the company and help it recover and reestablish itself on a sound financial basis. Such voluntary plans usually involve *extension,* which postpones the date of required payment of past-due obligations, and *composition,* by which the creditors voluntarily *reduce* their claims on the debtor. Both procedures are designed to keep the debtor in business and to avoid court costs. Although creditors do not obtain immediate payment and may still suffer losses, they often recover more money, and sooner, than if one of the formal procedures had been followed. Also, chances are good that a customer will be preserved.

The start of an extension or a composition is a meeting between the failing firm and its creditors. The creditors appoint a committee consisting of four or five of the largest creditors, plus one or two of the smaller ones. This meeting is typically arranged and conducted by an adjustment bureau associated with the local credit managers' association.[3] Once the decision has been reached that the case can be worked out, the bureau assigns investigators to make an exhaustive report. Then the bureau and the creditors' committee use the facts of the report to formulate a plan for adjustment of claims. Another meeting between the debtor and the creditors is then held in an attempt to work out an extension or a composition, or a combination of the two. Several meetings may be required to reach final agreements.

At least three conditions are usually necessary to make an extension or a composition feasible: (1) the debtor must be a good moral risk, (2) the debtor must show an ability to make a recovery, and (3) general business conditions must be favorable to recovery.

Creditors prefer *extension* because it provides for payment in full. The debtor buys current purchases on a cash basis and pays off the past balance over an extended time. In some cases, creditors may agree not only to extend the time of payment but also to subordinate existing claims to vendors extending new credit during the period of the extension. The creditors must have faith that the debtor will solve its problems.

In a *composition,* a reduced cash settlement is made. Creditors receive in cash from the debtor a uniform percentage of the amounts owed them. The cash received, which may be as low as ten cents on the dollar, is taken as full settlement of the debt. Bargaining will take place between the debtor and the creditors over the savings that result from avoiding costs associated with the bankruptcy: costs of administration, legal fees, investigators, and so

---

3 There is a nationwide group called the National Association of Credit Management, which consists of bankers and industrial companies' credit managers. This group sponsors research on credit policy and problems, conducts seminars on credit management, and operates local chapters in cities throughout the nation. These local chapters frequently operate adjustment bureaus.

on. In addition to escaping such costs, the debtor gains in that the stigma of bankruptcy may be avoided; as a result, the debtor may be induced to part with most of the savings that result from avoiding a formal bankruptcy.

Often the bargaining process will result in a compromise involving both an extension and a composition. For example, the settlement may provide for a cash payment of 25 percent of the debt immediately, plus six future installments of 10 percent each, for a total payment of 85 percent. Installment payments are usually evidenced by notes, and creditors will also seek protective controls.

These voluntary settlements are informal and simple. They are also relatively inexpensive because investigating, legal, and administrative expenses are held to a minimum. Thus, voluntary procedures result in the largest return to creditors. In addition, the almost-bankrupt business may be saved to continue as a future customer. One possible disadvantage is that the debtor is left to manage the business. This situation may result in an erosion of assets, but there are numerous controls available to protect the creditors. It should also be noted that small creditors may play a nuisance role by insisting on payment in full. As a consequence, settlements typically provide for payment in full for claims under $50 or $100. If a composition is involved and all claims under $50 are paid, all creditors will receive a base of $50 plus the agreed upon percentage for the balance of their claims.

REORGANIZATION

If the situation is such that informal procedures are not feasible, then it may become necessary to use more formal procedures. The first of these is a *reorganization,* which is a court-approved attempt to keep a company alive by changing its capital structure. It is like composition or extension, but the legal formalities are much more involved. Regardless of the legal procedure followed, reorganization processes have certain features in common.

1. The firm is insolvent either because it is unable to meet cash obligations as they come due (technical insolvency) or because claims on the firm exceed its assets (insolvency in bankruptcy). Hence, some modifications in the nature or amount of the firm's obligations must be made—fixed charges must be reduced. The procedure may include scaling down interest charges or converting short-term debt into long-term debt, and it often involves converting debt into common stock.
2. New funds must be raised for working capital and for property rehabilitation, because firms in financial trouble almost always let their properties run down, and they generally deplete their liquid assets.
3. The operating and managerial causes of the difficulty must be discovered and eliminated.

The procedures involved in a reorganization are highly legalistic and are, in fact, thoroughly understood only by attorneys who specialize in bankruptcy and reorganization. However, there are certain general principles of which all financial managers should be aware. As noted above, a reorganization requires a scaling down of claims, and in any reorganization two conditions must be met: (1) the scaling down must be fair to all parties, and (2) there must be a reasonably high probability of successful rehabilitation and profitable future operations. These are the standards of *fairness* and *feasibility,* which are analyzed further later in the chapter.

FEDERAL BANKRUPTCY LAWS

Bankruptcy proceedings begin when a debtor is unable to meet scheduled payments to creditors, and these central issues arise:

1. Is the inability to meet scheduled debt payments a temporary problem of technical insolvency or is it a permanent problem caused by asset values falling below debt obligations?
2. If basic long-run asset values have truly declined, then economic losses have occurred. In this event, who shall bear the losses? Two theories exist: (1) the *absolute priority doctrine,* which states that claims must be paid in strict accordance with the priority of each claim, regardless of the consequence to other claimants, and (2) the *relative priority doctrine,* which is more flexible and which gives a more balanced consideration to all claimants.
3. Is the company "worth more dead than alive," i.e., would the business be more valuable if it were maintained and continued in operation or if it were liquidated and sold off in pieces? Under the absolute priority doctrine, liquidations are more likely because this generally permits senior creditors to be paid off sooner, but often at the expense of junior creditors and stockholders. Under the relative priority doctrine, senior creditors are more likely to be required to wait for payment in order to increase the chances of providing some value to junior creditors and stockholders.
4. Who should control the firm while it is being liquidated or rehabilitated? The existing management may be left in control, or a *trustee* may be placed in charge of operations.

These are the issues that are addressed in the federal bankruptcy statutes.

Our bankruptcy laws were first enacted in 1898, were modified substantially in 1938, and then were changed radically in the Bankruptcy Reform Act of 1978. The 1978 act was designed primarily to streamline and speed up proceedings, and it also represented a shift from the absolute priority doctrine toward the relative priority doctrine. (These doctrines should be thought of as a continuum, not as absolute points. The new law represents a movement along the continuum, not a jump from one polar position to the other.) During the 1970s, as bankruptcies became larger and more complex, it was simply taking too long to conclude bankruptcy proceedings, so Congress acted to speed things up.

The new bankruptcy law consists of eight odd-numbered chapters. (The even numbers were eliminated by Congress in the rewrite.) Chapters 1, 3, and 5 contain general provisions applicable to the other chapters. Chapter 7 governs liquidations; Chapter 9 provides for financially distressed municipalities; Chapter 11 is the business reorganization chapter; Chapter 13 covers the adjustment of debts for "individuals with regular income"; and Chapter 15 sets up a system of trustees who help administer the new act. All bankruptcy cases filed after October 1, 1979, are governed by this new code.

Prior to passage of the new bankruptcy act, reorganizations in bankruptcy were of two types: either Chapter XI proceedings, which were voluntary reorganizations originated by the existing management, or Chapter X proceedings, which were involuntary, were originated by creditors, and called for a court-appointed trustee to restructure completely the finances of the firm or else to liquidate it. Long, drawn-out court fights occurred over whether the proceedings should be under Chapter X or Chapter XI.

The new bankruptcy code combines the old Chapters X and XI into a single procedure (the new Chapter 11) which is more flexible and which provides more scope for informal negotiations between a company and its creditors and stockholders. Under the new act, a case is started by the filing of a petition with the bankruptcy court. The petition may be either voluntary or involuntary; that is, it may be filed either by the firm's management or by its creditors. A committee of unsecured creditors is then appointed by the court to negotiate with management for a reorganization, which may include the restructuring of debt and other claims against the firm. A trustee may be appointed by the court if it is in the best interests of the creditors and stockholders; otherwise, the existing management may stay in office. Under the new Chapter 11, if no fair and feasible reorganization can be worked out, the firm will be liquidated under the procedures spelled out in Chapter 7 of the act.

FINANCIAL DECISIONS IN REORGANIZATION

When a business becomes insolvent, a decision must be made whether to dissolve the firm through *liquidation* or to keep it alive through *reorganization.* Fundamentally, this decision depends on a determination of the value of the firm if it were rehabilitated versus the value of the assets if they were sold off individually. The procedure that promises higher returns to the creditors and owners will be adopted. Often the greater indicated value of the firm in reorganization, compared with its value in liquidation, is used to force a compromise agreement among the claimants in a reorganization, even when each group feels that its relative position has not been treated fairly in the reorganization plan. Both the SEC and the courts are called upon to determine the *fairness* and the *feasibility* of proposed plans of reorganization.

Standards of Fairness

The basic doctrine of fairness states that claims must be recognized in the
order of their legal and contractual priority. Carrying out this concept of
fairness in a reorganization involves the following steps:

1. Future sales must be estimated.
2. Operating conditions must be analyzed so that the future earnings on sales
   can be predicted.
3. The capitalization rate to be applied to these future earnings must be
   determined.
4. This capitalization rate must be applied to the estimated future earnings to
   obtain an indicated value for the company.
5. Provision for distribution to the claimants must then be made.

   The meaning and content of these procedures may best be set out by the
use of an example of reorganization involving the Edison Paper Corporation.
Table 20–3 gives Edison's balance sheet as of March 31, 1980. The
company had been suffering losses running to $2.5 million a year, and, as
will be made clear below, the asset values in the March 31, 1980, balance
sheet are overstated. Since the firm was insolvent, it filed a petition for
reorganization, under Chapter 11 of the Bankruptcy Act, with a federal
court. The court, in accordance with the law, appointed a disinterested
trustee. On June 13, 1980, the trustee filed with the court a plan of
reorganization, which was subsequently analyzed by the SEC.
   The trustee found that the company could not be internally reorganized
and concluded that the only feasible program would be to combine Edison

---

Table 20–3
Edison Paper Corporation: Balance Sheet,
March 31, 1980 (Millions of Dollars)

Assets

Current assets	$ 3.50
Net property	12.50
Miscellaneous	0.70
Total assets	$16.70

Liabilities and capital

Accounts payable	$ 1.00
Taxes	0.25
Notes payable	0.25
Other current liabilities	1.75
7½% first-mortgage bonds, due 1995	6.00
9% subordinated debentures, due 1990	7.00
Common stock ($1 par)	1.00
Paid-in capital	3.45
Retained earnings	(4.00)
Total liabilities and capital	$16.70

---

with an established producer of paper containers and wrappers. Accordingly, the trustee solicited the interest of a number of paper companies. Late in July 1980 National Paper Company showed an interest in Edison. On August 3, 1980, National made a formal proposal to take over Edison's $6 million of $7\frac{1}{2}$ percent first-mortgage bonds, to pay the $250,000 taxes owed by Edison, and to pay 40,000 shares of National Paper common stock to the company. Since the stock had a market price of $75 a share, the value of the stock was equivalent to $3 million. Thus, National Paper was offering $3 million, plus the $6 million loan takeover and the $250,000 taxes—a total of $9.25 million on assets that had a net book value of $16.7 million.

Trustees's Plan The trustee's plan, based on 40,000 shares at $75 equaling $3 million, is shown in Table 20–4. As in all Chapter 11 plans, the secured creditors' claims are paid in full (in this case the mortgage bonds are taken over by National Paper). However, the total claims of the unsecured creditors equal $10 million, with only $3 million available. Thus, each claimant would be entitled to receive 30 percent before the adjustment for subordination. Before this adjustment, holders of notes payable would receive 30 percent of their $250,000 claim, or $75,000. However, the debentures are subordinated to the notes payable, so an additional $175,000 must be transferred to notes payable from the subordinated debentures. In the last column of Table 20–4 the dollar claims of each class of debt are restated in terms of the number of shares of National Paper common stock received by each class of unsecured creditors.

Table 20–4
Edison Paper Corporation: Trustee's Plan

Prior Claims	Amount	Receives
Taxes	$ 250,000	Cash paid by National Paper
Mortgage bonds, $7\frac{1}{2}$%, 1995	6,000,000	Bonds assumed by National Paper

Trustee's plans for remainder of claims:
Valuation based on 40,000 shares at $75 equals $3 million, or 30 percent of $10 million liabilities.

Other Claims	Original Amount	30% x Amount. of Claim	Claim after Subordination	Number of Shares of Common Stock
Notes payable	$ 250,000	$ 75,000	$ 250,000	3,333
General unsecured creditors	2,750,000	825,000	825,000	11,000
Subordinated debentures	7,000,000	2,100,000	1,925,000	25,667
	$10,000,000	$3,000,000	$3,000,000	40,000

The Securities and Exchange Commission evaluated the proposal from
the standpoint of fairness. The SEC began by estimating the value of Edison
Paper (Table 20–5). After a survey and discussion with various experts, it
arrived at estimated sales of $25 million a year. It further estimated that the
profit margin on sales would equal 6 percent, thus giving indicated future
earnings of $1.5 million a year.

Table 20–5
Edison Paper Corporation: SEC Evaluation

Estimated sales of Edison Paper Corporation	$25,000,000	per year
Earnings at 6 percent of sales	1,500,000	
Value with P/E ratio of 8 times earnings	12,000,000	
Mortgage bonds assumed	6,000,000	
Net value	$ 6,000,000	

Claims	Amount	Claim	Claim after Subordination
Taxes	$ 250,000	$ 250,000	$ 250,000
Notes payable	250,000	143,750	250,000[a]
General unsecured creditors	2,750,000	1,581,250	1,581,250
Subordinated debentures (subordinate to notes payable)	7,000,000	4,025,000	3,918,750[a]
Totals	$10,250,000	$6,000,000	$6,000,000
Total available	$ 6,000,000		
Percentage of claims[b]	57.5%		

[a]Notes payable must be satisfied before subordinated debentures receive anything.
[b]($6,000,000 − $250,000)/($10,250,000 − $250,000).

The SEC analyzed price/earnings ratios for comparable paper companies
and arrived at 8 times future earnings for a capitalization factor. Multiplying
8 by $1.5 million gave an indicated total value of the company of $12 million.
Since the mortgage bonds assumed by National Paper totaled $6 million, a
net value of $6 million was left for the other claims. This value is double that
of the 40,000 shares of National Paper stock offered for the remainder of the
company. Because the SEC felt that the value of these claims was $6 million
rather than $3 million, it concluded that the trustee's plan for reorganization
did not meet the test of fairness. Note that under both the trustee's plan and
the SEC plan, the holders of common stock were to receive nothing, which
is one of the risks of ownership, while the holders of the first-mortgage
bonds were to be paid in full.

National Paper was told of the SEC's conclusions and asked to increase
the number of shares it offered. National refused, and no other paper
company offered to acquire Edison. Because no better alternative offer could

be obtained, and the only alternative to the trustee's plan was liquidation, National Paper's proposal was accepted despite the SEC's disagreement with the valuation.

Standard of Feasibility

The primary test of feasibility in a reorganization is whether the fixed charges after reorganization will be adequately covered by earnings. Adequate coverage generally requires an improvement in earnings or a reduction of fixed charges, or both. Among the actions that must generally be taken are the following:

1. Debt maturities are usually lengthened, and some debt is usually converted into equity.
2. When the quality of management has been substandard and inadequate for the task, a new team must be given control of the company.
3. If inventories have become obsolete or depleted, they must be replaced.
4. Sometimes the plant and the equipment must be modernized before the firm can operate and compete successfully on a cost basis.
5. Reorganization may also require an improvement in production, marketing, advertising, and other functions.
6. It is sometimes necessary to develop new products or markets to enable the firm to move from areas where economic trends are poor into areas with more potential for growth or at least stability.

To illustrate how the feasibility tests are applied, let us refer again to the Edison Paper Corporation example. The SEC observed that in the reorganization National Paper Company would take over the properties of the Edison Paper Corporation. It judged that the direction and aid of National Paper would remedy the production deficiencies that had troubled Edison Paper. Whereas the debt/assets ratio of Edison Paper had become unbalanced, National Paper went into the purchase with only a moderate amount of debt. After consolidation, National Paper's total debt would be approximately $17.5 million versus total assets of more than $63 million, or a very reasonable debt ratio of about 27 percent.

National Paper's net income before interest and taxes had been running at a level of approximately $15 million. The interest on its long-term debt would be $1.5 million and, taking short-term borrowings into account, would total a maximum of $2 million a year. The $15 million profit before interest and taxes would therefore provide a 7.5 times coverage of fixed charges; this exceeds the norm of 5 times for the industry.

Notice that the question of feasibility would have been irrelevant (from the standpoint of the SEC) if National Paper had offered $3 million in cash rather than in stock, and had offered to pay off the bonds rather than take them over. It is the SEC's function to protect the interests of Edison Paper's creditors. Since they are being forced to take common stock in another firm, the SEC must look into the feasibility of the transaction. If National Paper had made a cash offer, however, the feasibility of its own operation after the transaction was completed would have been none of the SEC's concern.

LIQUIDATION PROCEDURES

Liquidation can occur in two ways: (1) through an *assignment,* which is a liquidation procedure that does not go through the courts, or (2) through a formal *bankruptcy* carried out under the jurisdiction of a special court. Liquidation should occur when the business is worth more dead than alive, or when the possibilities of restoring profitability are so remote that the creditors run a high risk of loss if operations are continued.

Assignment

Assignment is an informal procedure for liquidating debts, and it usually yields creditors a larger amount than they would receive in a formal bankruptcy. An assignment calls for title to the debtor's assets to be transferred to a third person, known as an *assignee* or *trustee.* The assignee is instructed to liquidate the assets through a private sale or a public auction, and then to distribute the proceeds among the creditors on a pro rata basis. The assignment does not automatically discharge the debtor's obligations. However, the debtor may write on the check to each creditor the requisite legal language to make endorsement of the check acknowledgment of full settlement of the claim.

Assignment has some advantages over bankruptcy through the courts, which involves more time, legal formality, and expense. The assignee has more flexibility in disposing of property than does a bankruptcy trustee. Action can be taken sooner, before the inventory becomes obsolete or the machinery rusts, and, since the assignee is often familiar with the channels of trade in the debtor's business, better results may be achieved. However, an assignment does not automatically result in a full and legal discharge of all the debtor's liabilities, nor does it protect the creditors against fraud. Both of these problems can be overcome by formal bankruptcy proceedings, which are discussed in the following section.

LIQUIDATION IN BANKRUPTCY

The Federal Bankruptcy Act serves three important functions during a liquidation: (1) It provides safeguards against fraud by the debtor. (2) It provides for an equitable distribution of the debtor's assets among the creditors. (3) It allows insolvent debtors to discharge all their obligations and to start new businesses unhampered by a burden of prior debt. However, liquidation is time-consuming, it can be costly, and it results in the loss of the business.

Priority of Claims on Distribution of Proceeds in a Bankruptcy

The order of priority of claims in bankruptcy under Chapter 7 of the 1978 act is as follows:

1. *Secured creditors, from the proceeds of the sale of specific property pledged for a lien or a mortgage.* If the proceeds from the sale of property do not fully satisfy the secured creditors' claims, the remaining balance is treated as a general creditor claim. See Item 8 below.[4]
2. *Trustee's costs to administer and operate the bankrupt estate.*
3. *Expenses incurred after an involuntary case has begun but before a trustee is appointed.*
4. *Wages due workers if earned within three months prior to the filing of the petition in bankruptcy.* The amount of wages is not to exceed $2,000 per person.
5. *Claims for unpaid contributions to employee benefit plans.* These claims, plus wages in Item 4, are not to exceed the $2,000 per wage-earner limit.
6. *Unsecured claims for customer deposits, not to exceed a maximum of $900 per individual.*
7. *Taxes due the United States, state, county, and any other government agency.*
8. *General or unsecured creditors.* Trade credit, unsecured loans, the unsatisfied portion of secured loans, and debenture bonds are classed as general creditors. Holders of subordinated debt also fall into this category, but they must turn over required amounts to the holders of senior debt.
9. *Preferred stock.*
10. *Common stock.*

To illustrate how this priority of claims works out, consider the balance sheet of Wallace, Inc., shown in Table 20–6. Assets total $90 million. The claims are indicated on the right-hand side of the balance sheet. Note that the debentures are subordinated to the notes payable to banks.

Now assume that the assets are sold. The assets as reported in the balance sheet in Table 20–6 are greatly overstated—they are, in fact, worth

---

4 When a firm or individual who goes bankrupt has a bank loan, the bank will attach any deposit balances and use them to offset the loan balances. This is called, in legal terms, "the right of offset." The loan agreement may stipulate that the bank has a first-priority claim against any deposits. If so, the deposits are used to offset all or part of the bank loan. In this case, the banks will not have to share the deposits with other creditors. Compensating balances are often designated as being security against a loan. If the bank has no explicit claim against deposits, the bank will attach the deposits and hold them for the general body of creditors, including the bank itself. Without an explicit statement in the loan agreement, the bank does not receive preferential treatment with regard to attached deposits.

Table 20–6
Wallace, Inc.: Balance Sheet

Current assets	$80,000,000	Accounts payable	$20,000,000
Net property	10,000,000	Notes payable	
		(due bank)	10,000,000
		Accrued wages,	
		1,400 at $500	700,000
		U.S. taxes	1,000,000
		State and local taxes	300,000
		Current debt	$32,000,000
		First mortgage	$ 6,000,000
		Second mortgage	1,000,000
		Subordinated	
		debentures[a]	8,000,000
		Long-term debt	$15,000,000
		Preferred stock	2,000,000
		Common stock	26,000,000
		Paid-in capital	4,000,000
		Retained earnings	11,000,000
		Total equity	$43,000,000
Total assets	$90,000,000	Total claims	$90,000,000

[a]Subordinated to $10 million notes payable to the First National Bank.

less than half of the $90 million at which they are carried. The following amounts are realized on liquidation:

Current assets	$28,000,000
Net property	5,000,000
Total receipts	$33,000,000

The order of priority for payment of claims is shown in Table 20–7. The first mortgage is paid from the net proceeds of $5 million from the sale of fixed property, leaving $28 million available to other creditors. Next come the fees and expenses of administration, which are typically about 20 percent of gross proceeds; in this example they are assumed to be $6 million. Next in priority are wages due workers, which total $700,000. The total amount of taxes to be paid is $1.3 million. Thus far, the total of claims paid from the $33 million is $13 million, leaving $20 million for the general creditors.

The claims of the general creditors total $40 million. Since $20 million is available, claimants would each receive 50 percent of their claims before the subordination adjustment. This adjustment requires that the subordinated debentures turn over to the notes payable all amounts received until the notes are satisfied. In this situation, the claim of the notes payable is $10 million, but only $5 million is available; the deficiency is therefore $5 million.

Table 20–7
Wallace, Inc.: Order of Priority of Claims

Distribution of Proceeds on Liquidation:

1. Proceeds of sale of assets	$33,000,000
2. First mortgage, paid from sale of net property	5,000,000
3. Fees and expenses of administration of bankruptcy	6,000,000
4. Wages due workers earned three months prior to filing of bankruptcy petition	700,000
5. Taxes	1,300,000
6. Available to general creditors	$20,000,000

Claims of General Creditors	Claim (1)	Application of 50 Percent (2)	After Subordination Adjustment (3)	Percentage of Original Claims Received (4)
Unsatisfied portion of first mortgage	$ 1,000,000	$ 500,000	$ 500,000	92
Unsatisfied portion of second mortgage	1,000,000	500,000	500,000	50
Notes payable	10,000,000	5,000,000	9,000,000	90
Accounts payable	20,000,000	10,000,000	10,000,000	50
Subordinated debentures	8,000,000	4,000,000	0	0
	$40,000,000	$20,000,000	$20,000,000	56

Notes:

1. Column 1 is the claim of each class of creditor. Total claims equal $40 million.

2. From line 6 in the upper section of the table we see that $20 million is available. This sum, divided by the $40 million of claims, indicates that general creditors will receive 50 percent of their claims. This is shown in Column 2.

3. The debentures are subordinated to the notes payable. Four million dollars is transferred from debentures to notes payable in Column 3.

4. Column 4 shows the results of dividing the Column 3 figure by the original amount given in Table 20–6, except for the first mortgage, where $5 million paid on sale of property is included. The 56 percent total figure includes the first mortgage transactions; that is, ($20,000,000 + $5,000,000) ÷ ($40,000,000 + $5,000,000) = 56%.

After transfer by the subordinated debentures of $4 million, there remains a deficiency of $1 million, which will be unsatisfied.

Note that 90 percent of the bank claim is satisfied, whereas only 50 percent of other unsecured claims will be satisfied. These figures illustrate the usefulness of the subordination provision to the security to which the subordination is made. Since no other funds remain, the claims of the holders of preferred and common stocks are completely wiped out.

Studies of the proceeds in bankruptcy liquidations reveal that unsecured creditors receive, on the average, about 15 cents on the dollar, while common stockholders generally receive nothing.[5]

SUMMARY

The major cause of business failure is incompetent management. Bad managers should, of course, be removed as promptly as possible, but if failure has occurred, a number of remedies are open to the interested parties.

The first question to be answered is whether the firm is better off "dead or alive"—whether it should be liquidated and sold off piecemeal or be rehabilitated. Assuming the decision is made that the firm should survive, it must be put through what is called a *reorganization.* Legal procedures are always costly, especially in the case of a business failure. Therefore, if it is at all possible, both the debtor and the creditors are better off if matters can be handled on an informal basis rather than through the courts. The informal procedures used in reorganization are (1) *extension,* which postpones the date of settlement, and (2) *composition,* which reduces the amount owed.

If voluntary settlement through extension or composition is not possible, the matter is thrown into the courts. If the court decides on reorganization rather than liquidation, it will appoint a trustee (1) to control the firm going through reorganization and (2) to prepare a formal plan for reorganization. The plan, which for large firms must be reviewed by the SEC, must meet the standards of *fairness* to all parties and be *feasible* in the sense that the reorganized enterprise will stand a good chance of surviving instead of being thrown back into the bankruptcy courts.

The application of standards of fairness and feasibility developed in this chapter can help determine the probable success of a particular plan for reorganization. The concept of fairness involves the estimation of sales and earnings and the application of a capitalization rate to earnings to determine the appropriate distribution to each claimant.

The feasibility test examines the ability of the new enterprise to carry the fixed charges resulting from the reorganization plan. The quality of management and

---

5 Pension plan liabilities may also have a bearing on bankruptcy settlements. Pension plans are of two types, *funded* and *unfunded*. Under a funded plan, the firm makes cash payments to an insurance company or to a trustee (generally a bank), who then uses these funds (and interest earned on them) to pay retirees' pensions. Under an unfunded plan, the firm is obligated to make payments to retirees, but it does not provide cash in advance. Most plans are actually partially funded—some money has been paid in advance, but not enough to provide full pension benefits to all employees.

If a firm goes bankrupt, the funded part of the pension plan remains intact and is available for retirees, but what about the unfunded amount? Do employees have a claim against the firm's assets for unfunded pension liabilities? Prior to 1974, employees had no explicit claim, but under the Employees' Retirement Income Security Act of 1974, up to 30 percent of the equity (common and preferred) is earmarked for employees' pension plans. This means, in effect, that the funded portion of a bankrupt firm's pension plan is secured but that the unfunded portion ranks with the stockholders and behind the creditors. Thus, if the proceeds from a liquidation were just sufficient to cover debts, neither stockholders nor unfunded pensioners would receive anything. If funds remained after payment of debts, 30 percent would be allocated to the pension plan.

the company's assets must be assured. Production and marketing may also require improvement.

Finally, where liquidation is regarded as the only solution to the debtor's insolvency, the creditors should adopt procedures that will net them the largest recovery. *Assignment* of the debtor's property is the cheaper and the faster procedure. Furthermore, there is more flexibility in disposing of the debtor's property and thus providing larger returns. *Bankruptcy* provides formal procedures for liquidation to safeguard the debtor's property from fraud. It also provides equitable distribution to the creditors. Nonetheless, it is a long and cumbersome process, and unless the trustee is closely supervised by the creditors, the debtor's property may be poorly managed during bankruptcy proceedings. The debtor does, however, obtain a full legal release from liability.

Questions

20-1 "A certain number of business failures is a healthy sign. If there are no failures, this is an indication (a) that entrepreneurs are overly cautious, hence not as inventive and as willing to take risks as a healthy, growing economy requires, (b) that competition is not functioning to weed out inefficient producers, or (c) that both situations exist." Discuss this statement.

20-2 How could financial analysis be used to forecast the probability of a given firm's failure? Assuming that such analysis is properly applied, could it always predict failure?

20-3 Why do creditors usually accept a plan for financial rehabilitation rather than demand liquidation of the business?

20-4 Would it be possible to form a profitable company by merging two companies, both of which are business failures? Explain.

20-5 Distinguish between a reorganization and a bankruptcy.

20-6 Would it be a sound rule to liquidate whenever the liquidation value is above the value of the corporation as a going concern? Discuss.

20-7 Why do liquidations usually result in losses for the creditors or the owners, or both? Would partial liquidation or liquidation over a period limit their losses? Explain.

20-8 Are liquidations likely to be more common for public utility, railroad, or industrial corporations? Why?

Problems

20-1 The financial statements of the Johnston Publishing Company for 1979 are shown below. A recapitalization plan is proposed in which each share of the $6 preferred will be exchanged for one share of $2.40 preferred (stated value, $37.50) plus one 8 percent subordinated income debenture (stated principal, $75). The $10.50 preferred would be retired from cash.
  a. Show the pro forma balance sheet (in millions of dollars) giving effect to the recapitalization and showing the new preferred at its stated value and the common stock at its par value.

b. Present the pro forma income statement (in millions of dollars carried to two decimal places).
c. How much does the firm increase income available to common stock by the recapitalization?
d. How much larger are the required pretax earnings after the recapitalization compared to the situation before the change? Required earnings are the amount that is just enough to meet fixed charges (debenture interest and/or preferred dividends).

**Johnston Publishing Company: Balance Sheet,
December 31, 1979 (Millions of Dollars)**

Current assets	$120	Current liabilities	$ 42
Investments	48	Advance payments for	
Net fixed assets	153	subscriptions	78
Goodwill	15	Reserves	6
		$6 preferred stock, $112.50 par (1,200,000 shares)	135
		$10.50 preferred stock, no par (60,000 shares, callable at $150)	9
		Common stock, par value of $1.50 (6,000,000 shares outstanding)	9
		Retained earnings	57
Total assets	$336	Total claims	$336

**Johnston Publishing Company: Consolidated
Statement of Income and Expense, Year
Ended December 31, 1979 (Millions of Dollars)**

Operating income		$540.0
Operating expense		516.0
Net operating income		$ 24.0
Other income		3.0
Other expense		0.0
Earnings before income tax		$ 27.0
Income tax at 50 percent		13.5
Income after taxes		$ 13.5
Dividends on $6 prior preferred stock	$7.2	
Dividends on $10.50 preferred stock	0.6	7.8
Income available for common stock		$ 5.7

---

e. How is the debt/assets ratio affected by the recapitalization? (Debt includes advances for subscriptions.)

  f. Would you vote for the recapitalization if you were a holder of the $6 prior preferred stock?

20-2 At the time it defaulted, Precision Glass had net current assets valued on its books at $20 million and net fixed assets valued at $25 million. At the time of final settlement its debts were as follows:

Current liabilities	$12 million
First-mortgage bonds	10 million
Second-mortgage bonds	5 million
Debenture bonds	4 million

  None of the current liabilities have preferences in liquidation as provided for in the bankruptcy laws, and none have been secured by pledge of assets.

  Assume that the amount shown for each of the four classes of liabilities includes all unpaid interest to the date of settlement. The fixed assets were pledged as security for the first-mortgage bonds and repledged for the second-mortgage bonds. Determine the appropriate distribution of the proceeds of liquidation under the following conditions:

  a. Liquidation of current assets realizes $18 million, and $7 million is obtained from fixed assets.

  b. Liquidation of current assets realizes $9 million, and $4 million is obtained from fixed assets.

21 LEASING

Firms generally own fixed assets and report them on their balance sheets, but it is the *use* of buildings and equipment that is important, not their ownership *per se*. One way of obtaining the use of facilities and equipment is to buy them, but an alternative is to lease them. Prior to the 1950s, leasing was generally associated with real estate—land and buildings. Today, however, it is possible to lease virtually any kind of fixed asset, and in 1979 about 20 percent of all new capital equipment acquired by businesses was financed through a lease arrangement.

Conceptually, as we show in this chapter, leasing is quite similar to borrowing, so leasing provides financial leverage. In effect, a lease is a type of debt.[1] Leasing takes several different forms, the three most important of which are (1) *sale and leaseback* arrangements, (2) *service leases,* and (3) straight *financial or capital leases.*

SALE AND LEASEBACK

Under a sale and leaseback arrangement, a firm owning land, buildings, or equipment sells the property to a financial institution and simultaneously executes an agreement to lease the property back for a specified period under specific terms. The financial institution could be an insurance company, a commercial bank, a specialized leasing company, or an individual investor. The lease is an alternative to a mortgage.

Note that the seller, or *lessee,* immediately receives the purchase price put up by the buyer, or *lessor.* At the same time, the seller-lessee retains the use of the property. This parallel to borrowing is carried over to the lease payment schedule. Under a mortgage loan arrangement, the financial institution would receive a series of equal payments just sufficient to

---

1 Some instructors will prefer to cover this chapter immediately after Chapter 13, which deals with long-term debt. If this is done, it will be necessary to discuss separately the after-tax cost of debt.

amortize the loan and to provide the lender with a specified rate of return on investment. Under a sale and leaseback arrangement, the lease payments are set up in exactly the same manner—the payments are sufficient to return the full purchase price to the investor, plus a stated return on the investment.

SERVICE LEASES

Service leases, sometimes called operating leases, provide for both *financing* and *maintenance.* IBM is one of the pioneers of the service lease contract. Computers and office copying machines, together with automobiles and trucks, are the primary types of equipment involved in service leases. These leases ordinarily call for the lessor to maintain and service the leased equipment, and the cost of the maintenance is built into the lease payments.

Another important characteristic of service leases is the fact that they are frequently *not fully amortized.* In other words, the payments required under the lease contract are not sufficient to recover the full cost of the equipment. However, the lease contract is written for a period considerably less than the expected life of the leased equipment, and the lessor expects to recover all costs either in subsequent renewal payments or through disposal of the leased equipment.

A final feature of service leases is that they frequently contain a *cancellation clause* giving the lessee the right to cancel the lease and return the equipment before the expiration of the basic lease agreement. This is an important consideration to the lessee, for it means that the equipment can be returned if it is rendered obsolete by technological developments or is simply no longer needed.

FINANCIAL, OR CAPITAL, LEASES

A financial lease, sometimes called a capital lease, is one that (1) does *not* provide for maintenance service, (2) is *not* cancellable, and (3) *is* fully amortized (that is, the lessor receives rental payments equal to the full price of the leased equipment). The typical arrangement involves the following steps:

Step 1 The firm that will use the equipment (the lessee) selects the specific items it requires and negotiates the price and delivery terms with the manufacturer.

Step 2 The user firm then arranges with a bank or a leasing company (the lessor) to buy the equipment from the manufacturer or the distributor. When the equipment is purchased, the user firm simultaneously executes an agreement to lease the equipment from the financial institution. The terms of the lease call for full amortization of the financial institution's investment, plus a rate of return on the unamortized balance close to the percentage rate the lessee would have to pay on a secured term loan. For example, if the lessee would have to pay 10 percent for a term loan, then a rate of about 10 percent would be built into the lease contract. The lessee is generally given an option to renew the lease at a reduced rental on expiration of the basic lease. However, the basic lease usually cannot be canceled unless the financial institution is completely paid off. Also, the lessee generally pays the property taxes and insurance on the leased property. Since the lessor receives a return *after,* or *net of,* these payments, this type of lease is often called a "net, net" lease.

Financial leases are almost the same as sale and leaseback arrangements, the major difference being that the leased equipment is new and the lessor buys it from a manufacturer or a distributor instead of from the user-lessee. A sale and leaseback may, then, be thought of as a special type of financial lease. Both sale and leaseback arrangements and financial leases are analyzed in the same manner.

INTERNAL REVENUE SERVICE REQUIREMENTS FOR A LEASE

The full amount of the annual lease payment is a deductible expense for income tax purposes *provided the Internal Revenue Service agrees that a particular contract is a genuine lease and not simply an installment loan called a lease.* This makes it important that a lease contract be written in a form acceptable to the Internal Revenue Service. The following are the major factors that are examined to determine whether a given contract is likely to be classified as a bona fide lease transaction from the standpoint of the IRS:

1. The term, or years involved in the lease, must be less than 75 percent of the life of the asset; otherwise the lease is likely to be regarded as a sale for tax purposes.
2. The rent must provide a reasonable rate of return to the lessor in relation to rates of return on loans.
3. The renewal option must be bona fide, and this requirement can best be met by giving the lessee the first option to meet an equal bona fide outside offer.
4. There should be no repurchase option; if there is, the lessee should merely be given parity with an equal outside offer.

The reason for the IRS's concern about these factors is that without restrictions a company could set up a "lease" transaction calling for very rapid payments, *which would be tax deductions.* The effect would be to depreciate the equipment over a much shorter period than its useful life. For example, if a $200,000 printing press with a twenty year life were leased for three years, then purchased under a purchase option for $1 or renewed for $1 a year, this would have the same cash flow effect as depreciating the press in three years rather than over twenty years.

EFFECTS OF LEASING ON A FIRM'S BALANCE SHEET

Leasing is often called "off balance sheet" financing, because, under certain conditions, neither the leased assets nor the liabilities under lease contracts appear on a firm's balance sheet. This point is illustrated in Table 21–1 by the balance sheets of two hypothetical firms, A and B. Initially, the balance sheets of both firms are identical, and they both have debt ratios of 50 percent. Next, they each decide to acquire assets costing $100. Firm A borrows $100 to make the purchase, so both an asset and a liability go on its balance sheet, and its debt ratio is increased to 75 percent. Firm B leases the equipment. The lease may call for fixed charges as high as or even higher than the loan, and the obligations assumed under the lease can be equally or more dangerous from the standpoint of financial analysis, but the firm's debt ratio will remain at 50 percent.

Table 21–1
Balance Sheet Effects of Leasing

	Before Asset Increase				After Asset Increase						
	Firms A and B				Firm A, Which Borrows and Buys				Firm B, Which Leases		
		Debt	$ 50			Debt	$150			Debt	$ 50
Total		Equity	50	Total		Equity	50	Total		Equity	50
assets	$100		$100	assets	$200		$200	assets	$100		$100

To correct this problem, the Financial Accounting Standards Board issued FASB #13, which requires that, for an unqualified audit report, firms entering into financial (or capital) leases must restate their balance sheets to report the leased asset under fixed assets and the present value of the future lease payments as a debt.[2] This process is called *capitalizing the lease,* and its net effect is to cause Firms A and B to have similar balance sheets, both of which will, in essence, resemble the one shown for Firm A.

2 FASB #13, *Accounting for Leases* (November 1976). This document spells out in detail the conditions under which the lease must be capitalized and the procedures for capitalizing it.

EVALUATING LEASE PROPOSALS

In the typical case, the events leading to a lease arrangement follow the sequence described below. There is a great deal of uncertainty regarding the theoretically correct way to evaluate lease versus purchase decisions, and some very complex decision models have been developed to aid in the analysis. However, the simple analysis given here is accurate enough for most decisions.

1. The firm decides to acquire a particular building or piece of equipment; this decision is based on regular capital budgeting procedures. The decision to acquire the machine is not at issue in the typical lease analysis—this decision was made previously as part of the capital budgeting process. In a lease analysis, we are concerned simply with whether to obtain the use of the machine by lease or by purchase. However, if the effective cost of the lease is substantially lower than the cost of debt—and, as explained later in this chapter, this could occur for a number of reasons, including the ability to obtain more debt financing if leasing is employed—then the cost of capital used in capital budgeting would have to be recalculated and, perhaps, projects formerly deemed unacceptable might become acceptable.
2. Once the firm has decided to acquire the asset, the next question is how to finance its acquisition. Well-run businesses do not have excess cash lying around, so new assets must be financed in some manner.
3. Funds to purchase the asset could be obtained by borrowing or by selling stock, or the asset could be leased.

As indicated at the beginning of this chapter, a lease is comparable to a loan in the sense that the firm is required to make a specified series of payments and that failure to meet these payments can result in bankruptcy. Thus, the most appropriate comparison is between lease financing and debt financing. The lease versus borrow-and-purchase analysis is illustrated with data on the Carter Chemical Company. The following conditions are assumed:

1. Carter plans to acquire equipment with a cost of $10,715,000, delivered and installed.
2. An investment tax credit of $715,000, which is approximately $6\frac{2}{3}$ percent, applies. Thus, the net financing required if Carter borrows and buys is $10 million.
3. Carter can borrow the required $10 million on a 10 percent loan to be amortized over five years. Therefore, the loan will call for payments of $2,637,965.60 per year, calculated as follows:

$$\text{Payment} = \frac{\$10,000,000}{\text{PVIFA}_{(10\%,\ 5\ \text{years})}} = \frac{\$10,000,000}{3.7908} = \$2,637,965.60.$$

4. The equipment will definitely be used for five years, at which time its

estimated salvage value is $715,000. If the operation is profitable, Carter will continue to use the equipment. If not, the equipment will be sold, presumably at its estimated salvage value.

5. Carter can lease the equipment for five years at a rental charge of $2,791,670 per year, but the lessor will own it at the expiration of the lease. (The lease payment schedule is established by the potential lessor, and Carter can accept it, reject it, or negotiate.) If Carter plans to continue using the equipment, a purchase arrangement will have to be negotiated with the lessor. We assume that Carter will be able to buy the equipment at its estimated salvage value, $715,000.

6. The lease contract calls for the lessor to maintain the equipment. If Carter borrows and buys, it will have to bear the cost of maintenance, which will be performed by the equipment manufacturer at a contracted cost of $500,000 per year.

7. Carter uses the sum-of-years'-digits depreciation method, and for this analysis we assume that its effective tax rate is 40 percent.

Table 21–2 shows the steps involved in the analysis. Columns 2 through 10 are devoted to the costs of borrowing and buying. Within this set, Columns 2 through 5 give the loan amortization schedule; Column 6 shows the maintenance expense; and Column 7 gives depreciation charges. Tax-deductible expenses—interest, maintenance, and depreciation—are summed and shown in Column 8, while Column 9 gives the taxes saved because Carter has these deductions. Column 10 summarizes the preceding columns and gives the annual net cash outflows Carter will incur if it borrows and buys the equipment.

The lease payments are $2,791,670 per year; this rate, which includes maintenance, was established by the prospective lessor and offered to Carter Chemical. If Carter accepts the lease, the full $2,791,670 will be a deductible expense, so the after-tax cost of the lease will be calculated as follows:

$$
\begin{aligned}
\text{After-tax cost} &= \text{Lease payment} - \text{Tax savings} \\
&= \text{Lease payment} - (\text{Tax rate})(\text{Lease payment}) \\
&= \text{Lease payment}\,(1 - \text{Tax rate}) \\
&= \$2{,}791{,}670(1 - 0.4) \\
&= \$1{,}675{,}000.
\end{aligned}
$$

This amount is shown in Column 11, Years 1 through 5.

Notice the last entry in Column 11, the $715 shown under Year 5. This represents the $715,000 expected Year 5 purchase price. We include this amount as a cost of leasing on the assumption that Carter Chemical will want to continue the operation and thus will be forced to purchase the equipment from the lessor. If we assume that the operation will not be continued, then we would put the $715 into Column 10 as an inflow; that is, it would have a minus sign.

**Table 21–2
Carter Chemical Company: Lease versus Purchase Analysis (Thousands of Dollars)**

	Applicable to Net Cost of Owning									Applicable to Lease	Comparative Costs		
	Loan Amortization Schedule												
Year (1)	Total Payment (2)	Interest (3)	Amortization Payment (4)	Remaining Balance (5)	Maintenance Cost (6)	Depreciation (7)	Tax-Deductible Expense = 3 + 6 + 7 (8)	Tax Savings = (0.4)(8)ᵃ (9)	Cash Outflow If Owned = 2 + 6 − 9 (10)	Lease Cost after Tax = (1 − 0.4) (Lease cost) (11)	PVIFs for 6% (12)	Present Value of the Cost of Owning = 10 × 12 (13)ᵃ	Present Value of the Cost of Leasing = 11 × 12 (14)ᵃ
1	$ 2,638	$1,000	$ 1,638	$8,362	$500	$ 3,333	$4,833	$1,933	$1,205	$1,675	0.9434	$1,137	$1,580
2	2,638	836	1,802	6,560	500	2,667	4,003	1,601	1,537	1,675	0.8900	1,368	1,491
3	2,638	656	1,982	4,578	500	2,000	3,156	1,262	1,876	1,675	0.8396	1,575	1,406
4	2,638	458	2,180	2,398	500	1,333	2,291	916	2,222	1,675	0.7921	1,760	1,327
5	2,638	240	2,398	0	500	667	1,407	563	2,575	1,675	0.7473	1,924	1,252
5ᵇ										715	0.7473		534
	$13,190	$3,190	$10,000			$10,000						$7,764	$7,590

Net advantage to leasing = $7,764 − $7,590 = $174

ᵃFigures in Columns 9, 13, and 14 are rounded to the nearest thousand dollars.
ᵇTwo lines are shown for Year 5 in order to account for the salvage value, $715,000.

Notes:
1. The net advantage to leasing could be calculated by subtracting Column 11 from Column 10, then discounting these differences. This procedure is more efficient, hence preferable in actual practice, but the procedure used here is better for explanatory purposes.
2. Leases often involve payments at the *beginning* of the period rather than at the end. Also, a "down payment" may be required under either the lease or the loan. In either event, it would be necessary to set up a "0" year to show payments made at time zero.

The next step is to compare the net cost of owning with the net cost of leasing. However, we must first put the annual cash flows of leasing and borrowing on a common basis. This requires converting them to present values, which brings up the question of the proper rate at which to discount the costs. In Chapter 5, we saw that the riskier the cash flow, the higher the discount rate used to find present values. This same principle was observed in our discussion of capital budgeting, and it also applies in lease analysis. Just how risky are the cash flows under consideration here? Most of them are relatively certain, at least compared to the types of cash flow estimates that were developed in capital budgeting. For example, the loan payment schedule is set by contract, as is the lease payment schedule. The depreciation expenses are also established and not subject to change, and the $500,000 annual maintenance cost is fixed by contract as well. The tax savings are somewhat uncertain, but they will be as projected so long as Carter's effective tax rate remains at 40 percent. The residual value is the least certain of the cash flows, but even here Carter's management is fairly certain it will want to acquire the property, hence will incur the $715,000 outlay in Year 5.

Since the cash flows under the lease and under the borrow-and-purchase alternatives are both relatively certain, they should be discounted at a relatively low rate. Most analysts recommend that the company's cost of debt be used, and this rate seems reasonable in this instance. Further, since all the cash flows are on an after-tax basis, *the after-tax cost of debt, which is 6 percent, should be used.*[3] Accordingly, we multiply the cash outflows in Columns 10 and 11 by the 6 percent PVIFs given in Column 12. The resulting present values are shown in Columns 13 and 14; when these columns are summed, we have the net present values of the costs of owning and leasing. The financing method that produces the smaller present value of cost is the one that should be selected. The example shown in Table 21–2 indicates that leasing has the advantage over buying: the present value of the cost of leasing is $174,000 less than that of buying. In this instance, it is to Carter Chemical's advantage to lease.

---

3 The matter of the appropriate discount for use in lease versus purchase analysis is highly controversial. The two extremes in the discount rate controversy are (1) discount at the firm's weighted average cost of capital and (2) discount at the after-tax cost of debt. One good rule to follow is this: Discount the cash flow streams at *both* the average cost of capital and the after-tax cost of debt. Generally, both rates will produce the same conclusion regarding the lease versus borrow alternatives. If conflicts arise, this indicates that the present value costs of borrowing are quite close to those of leasing, so it probably does not make much difference which alternative is selected.

It should also be mentioned that one can (1) assign a discount rate to each individual cash flow component (the columns in Table 21–2), (2) find the present value of each of the cash flow components (the PV of each column, discounted at its own rate), and (3) sum these PVs to determine the net advantage or disadvantage to leasing. One problem that arises if this procedure is followed is that, if higher discount rates are used for riskier (uncertain) components, then the greater the uncertainty about some future *outflow* such as maintenance, the lower the PV of this cost. This seems unreasonable—the greater the uncertainty about a future cost, the more a risk-averse investor should worry about it. For this reason, plus the facts (1) that it is hard to determine separate discount rates for the Table 21–2 columns and (2) that the columns are not independent of one another, most analysts use only one discount rate for all the cash flow components.

FACTORS THAT AFFECT LEASING DECISIONS

The basic method of analysis set forth in Table 21–2 is sufficient to handle most situations. However, certain factors warrant additional comment.

Estimated Residual Value

It is important to note that the lessor owns the property at the expiration of a lease. The value of the property at the end of the lease is called its *residual value.* Superficially, it would appear that where residual values are large, owning would have an advantage over leasing. However, this apparent advantage of owning is subject to substantial qualification. If residual values are large, as they will be for certain types of equipment and also if land is involved, competition between leasing companies and other financial sources, as well as competition among leasing companies themselves, will force leasing rates down to the point where potential residual values are fully recognized in the lease contract rates. Thus, the existence of residual values on equipment is not likely to result in materially lower costs of owning.

Increased Credit Availability

Leasing is sometimes said to have an advantage for firms seeking the maximum degree of financial leverage. First, it is frequently stated that firms can obtain more money for longer terms under a lease arrangement than under a secured loan agreement for the purchase of a specific piece of equipment. Second, since some leases do not appear on the balance sheet, lease financing has been said to give the firm a stronger appearance in a *superficial* credit analysis and thus to permit the firm to use more leverage than it could use if it did not lease.

There is probably some truth to these claims for smaller firms. However, now that large firms are required to capitalize major leases and report them on their balance sheets, this point is of questionable validity for them.

Investment Tax Credit and Accelerated Depreciation

The investment tax credit, discussed in Chapter 2, can be taken only if the firm's profits and taxes exceed a certain level. If a firm is unprofitable, or if it is expanding so rapidly and generating such large tax credits that it cannot use them all, then it may be worthwhile for it to enter a lease arrangement. Here the lessor (a bank or leasing company, or a wealthy individual) will take the credit and give the lessee a corresponding reduction in lease charges. Railroads and airlines have been large users of leasing for this reason in recent years, as have industrial companies faced with particular situations. Anaconda, for example, recently financed most of the cost of a $138 million aluminum plant through a lease arrangement. Anaconda had suffered a $356 million tax loss when Chile expropriated its copper mining properties, and the carry-forward of this loss would hold taxes down for years. Thus, Anaconda could not use the tax credit associated with the new plant. By entering a lease arrangement, Anaconda was able to pass the tax credit on to the lessors, who in turn gave Anaconda lower lease payments than would have existed under a loan arrangement. Anaconda's financial staff estimated that financial charges over the life of the plant would be $74 million less under the lease arrangement than under a borrow-and-buy plan.

Accelerated depreciation has the same type of effect as the tax credit. A firm that is suffering losses and not paying taxes cannot benefit from accelerated depreciation on new equipment. However, if the equipment is sold to a lessor who is in a high tax bracket, then the tax advantage of accelerated depreciation can be captured, and part of it can be returned to the lessee in the form of lower rental payments.

Tax considerations—the investment tax credit and accelerated depreciation—are probably the dominant motives behind most financial leases that are written today.

LEVERAGED LEASES

Historically, only two parties have been involved in lease transactions—the lessor, who puts up the money, and the lessee. In recent years, however, a new type of lease, the *leveraged lease,* has come into widespread use. Under a leveraged lease, the lessor arranges to borrow part of the required funds. The Anaconda lease described above was set up as a leveraged lease. A group of banks and an auto company provided about $38 million of equity and were the owner-lessors. These owner-lessors borrowed the balance of the required funds from Prudential, Metropolitan, and Aetna— large insurance companies. The banks and the auto company received not only the investment tax credit but also the tax shelter associated with accelerated depreciation on the plant. However, they also had to bear the risk that Anaconda would default on the lease payments, as the equity holders of the lease are required to guarantee repayment of the debt portion.

Such leveraged leases, often with wealthy individuals who seek tax shelters acting as owner-lessors, are an important part of the financial scene today. Incidentally, whether or not a lease is leveraged is not important to the lessee; from the lessee's standpoint, the method of analyzing a proposed lease is unaffected by whether or not the lessor borrows part of the required capital.

ANALYSIS OF A LEASE FROM
THE LESSOR'S VIEWPOINT

Thus far we have considered leasing from the lessee's viewpoint. It is also useful to analyze the transaction as the lessor sees it: Is the lease a good investment for the financial institution or the individual who must put up the money? The potential lessor obviously needs this information, and it is also useful for the prospective lessee to know how profitable the lease is to the lessor: Lease terms can often be negotiated, so it helps to have an idea of the other party's position.

The lessor's analysis involves (1) determining the net cash outlay, which is usually the invoice price of the leased equipment less any investment tax credit; (2) determining the annual cash inflows, which consist of the lease payments minus both income taxes and the lessor's maintenance expense; (3) estimating the *residual value* of the property when the lease expires; and (4) determining whether the present value of the inflows exceeds the lessor's net cost of buying the equipment.

To illustrate the lessor's analysis, we assume the same facts as for the Carter Chemical lease. Further, we assume: (1) The potential lessor is a wealthy individual whose current income is in the form of interest, and whose marginal federal plus state income tax rate, t_i, is 70 percent. (2) The investor can buy bonds that have a 10 percent yield to maturity, providing an after-tax yield of $(10\%)(1 - t_i) = (10\%)(0.3) = 3\%$. This is the after-tax return the investor will obtain if the lease investment is not made. (3) The bonds the investor would buy are about as risky as the cash flows expected under the lease. (4) The investor will, under the lease, receive the same investment tax credit as Carter Chemical; the same depreciation schedule will also be applicable.

The lease analysis from the investor's standpoint is developed in Table 21–3. Here we see that the lease as an investment has a net present value of $305,000: on a present value basis, the investor who invests in the lease rather than in the 10 percent bonds is better off by this amount. This indicates that the investor should be willing to write the lease. We also show in the table that the lease provides the investor with an after-tax rate of return of 4.19 percent versus an after-tax return of 3 percent on alternative investments; thus, the IRR method of analysis confirms that the investor should write the lease. Since we saw earlier that the lease is also advantageous to Carter Chemical, the transaction should be completed.[4]

The example in Table 21–3 is not set up as a leveraged lease. However, it would be possible for the lessor to borrow all or part of the required $10 million, making the transaction a leveraged lease. In this event, it would be necessary to add a set of columns to Table 21–3 to show the loan

---

4 Another point that should be noted here relates to the investment tax credit. Under 1979 IRS regulations, an individual investor may not take the credit if the lease is written for more than one-half the economic life of the equipment. Also, the tax credit can either be taken by the lessor or be passed back to the lessee. These points are ignored in the example.

Table 21–3
Lease Analysis from Lessor's Viewpoint
(Thousands of Dollars)

Year (1)	Lease Payment (2)	Maintenance Expense (3)	Depreciation (4)	Taxes = $(2 - 3 - 4)t_i$ (5)	Net Cash Flow = $(2 - 3 - 5)$ (6)	PVIFs at 3 Percent (7)	PV of After-Tax Cash Flows (8)
1	$ 2,791.67	$ 500	$ 3,333	($ 729)	$ 3,021	0.9709	$ 2,933
2	2,791.67	500	2,667	(263)	2,555	0.9426	2,408
3	2,791.67	500	2,000	204	2,088	0.9151	1,911
4	2,791.67	500	1,333	671	1,621	0.8885	1,440
5	2,791.67	500	667	1,137	1,155	0.8626	996
5	⎯⎯	⎯⎯	⎯⎯	⎯⎯	715	0.8626	617
	$13,958.35	$2,500	$10,000	$1,020	$11,155		$10,305

Less cost   10,000

NPV of the lease investment = $ 305

Notes:
1. The investment tax credit is deducted from the equipment purchase price to produce the "cost" of $10,000,000 shown in Column 8.
2. We could calculate the rate of return (IRR) on the lease; this simply involves solving for r in the following equation:

$$NPV = O = \sum_{t=1}^{5} \frac{\text{Net cash flows under lease plan}}{(1 + r)^t} - \$10,000,000.$$

The cash flows are taken from Column 6 in Table 21–3, and the solution value of r is 4.19 percent. Thus, the lease has an after-tax rate of return to this 70 percent tax rate investor of 4.19 percent, which exceeds the 3 percent after-tax return on 10 percent loans (or bonds). So, using either the IRR or the NPV method, the lease would appear to be a good investment.

amortization schedule. The interest component of this schedule would represent another tax deduction, while the loan repayments would constitute an additional cash outlay. The "initial cost" would also be reduced by the amount of the loan. With these changes made, a new NPV and IRR could be calculated and used to evaluate whether or not the lease represents a good investment.

Typically, leveraged leases provide the lessor with much higher expected rates of return (IRRs) and higher NPVs per dollar of invested capital than unleveraged leases. However, the riskiness of such leases is also much higher, for the lessor must still pay back the borrowed portion of the funds even if the lessee fails to meet the specified lease payments. Since leveraged leases are a relatively new development, no standard methodology has been developed for analyzing them in a risk-return framework. However, sophisticated lessors are now developing simulations similar to those described in Chapter 12 for use in analyzing the riskiness inherent in a lease transaction. Then, given the apparent riskiness of the lease investment, the lessor can decide whether the returns built into the contract are sufficient to compensate for the risk involved.

SUMMARY

This chapter analyzed the three major types of leases: (1) *service leases,* (2) *sale and leaseback plans,* and (3) *financial leases for new assets.* Service, or operating, leases provide both for the financing of an asset and for its maintenance, while both sale and leaseback plans and regular financial leases provide only financing and are alternatives to debt financing.

Financial leases (and sale and leaseback plans) are evaluated by a cash flow analysis. We start with the assumption that an asset will be acquired, and that the acquisition will be financed either by debt or by a lease. Next, we develop the annual net cash outflows associated with each financing plan. Finally, we discount the two sets of outflows at the company's after-tax cost of debt and choose the alternative with the lower present value of costs.

Leasing sometimes represents "off balance sheet" financing, which permits firms to obtain more financial leverage if they employ leasing than if they use straight debt. This was formerly cited as a major reason for leasing. However, today taxes are the primary reason for the growth of financial leasing. Leasing permits the tax shelters (deductible expenses and the ITC) to be transferred from the user of an asset to the supplier of capital, and if these parties are in different tax brackets, both can benefit from the lease arrangement.

Questions

21-1 Distinguish between service leases and financial leases. Would you be more likely to find a service lease employed for a fleet of trucks or for a manufacturing plant?

21-2 Would you be more likely to find that lessees are in high or low income tax brackets as compared to lessors?

21-3 Commercial banks moved heavily into equipment leasing during the early 1970s, acting as lessors. One major reason for this invasion of the leasing industry was to gain the benefits of accelerated depreciation and the investment tax credit on lease equipment. During this same period, commercial banks were investing heavily in municipal securities, and they were also making loans to real estate investment trusts (REITs). In 1974 and 1975, these REITs got into such serious difficulty that many banks suffered large losses on their REIT loans. Explain how its investments in municipal bonds and REITs could reduce a bank's willingness to act as a lessor.

21-4 One alleged advantage of leasing voiced in the past is that it kept liabilities off the balance sheet, thus making it possible for a firm to obtain more leverage than it otherwise could have. This raised the question of whether or not both the lease obligation and the asset involved should be capitalized and shown on the balance sheet. Discuss the pros and cons of capitalizing leases and the related assets.

21-5 Suppose there were no IRS restrictions on what constituted a valid lease. Explain, in a manner that a legislator might understand, why some restrictions should be imposed.

21-6 What is a leveraged lease? What are the advantages and disadvantages of such leases from the standpoint of (a) the lessee, (b) the equity investor in the lease, and (c) the supplier of the debt capital?

Problems

21-1 University Leasing, Inc., which specializes in business financing in the Minneapolis–St. Paul area, is setting up a financial lease with Memorial Stadium, Inc. The lease will cover ice machines, pizza ovens, popcorn poppers, and cola dispensers which have a total cost of $200,000. The lease runs for five years. What is the annual lease payment based on a 9 percent interest rate? (Nine percent is simply the rate used to establish the lease payments. It is not the rate of return to the lessor.)

21-2 Two furniture manufacturing companies, Henri-Don and Roy Hill, began operations with identical balance sheets. A year later, both required additional manufacturing capacity at a cost of $50,000. Henri-Don obtained a five year, $50,000 loan at an 8 percent interest rate from its bank. Roy Hill, on the other hand, decided to lease the required $50,000 capacity from Furniture Financers for five years at 8 percent. The balance sheet for each company, before the asset increases, is shown below:

		Debt	$ 50,000
		Equity	100,000
Total assets	$150,000	Total	$150,000

a. Show the balance sheets for both firms after the asset increase, and calculate each firm's debt ratio.

b. Show how Roy Hill's balance sheet would look immediately after the financing if it capitalized the lease.

21-3 Green Gardens, a manufacturer of lawn care and gardening products, has decided to expand production of its gardening tools division. The equipment necessary for expanded production can be either purchased or leased. The purchase plan requires Green Gardens to obtain a loan of $100,000 at a 10 percent interest rate, the loan to be amortized in level payments over a five year period. The lease provides $100,000 worth of equipment for five years, with the payment ($25,046) based upon an 8 percent interest rate. If the equipment is acquired through the borrow-and-purchase arrangement, maintenance costs of $4,000 per year must be borne by Green Gardens. However, the lessor will assume these costs if Green Gardens decides to lease. As a proprietorship, Green Gardens is taxed at Joe Green's personal income tax rate of 20 percent.

The equipment will be depreciated by the sum-of-years'-digits method, and it is expected to have a $25,000 salvage value after five years. It is assumed that Green Gardens will purchase the equipment at the expiration of the lease for $25,000. The lessor is Rachel Walsh, the famous actress,

whose marginal income is taxed at a 70 percent rate. She could invest the
$100,000 in taxable investments with risk similar to the lease yielding 10
percent before tax. The same depreciation schedule would apply for either
Miss Walsh or Mr. Green.

   a. Develop an exhibit analyzing Green Gardens' lease versus purchase
      alternatives following the format of Table 21–2. (Use PVIFA = 3.7908 to
      calculate the loan payment, and round to the nearest dollar.)
   b. Suppose a 5 percent investment tax credit applies, but because of his
      low taxes and investment tax credits on other investments, Mr. Green
      cannot use the investment tax credit, although Miss Walsh can use it.
      How could this fact affect Mr. Green's cost analysis? No calculations are
      necessary.

21-4 Minute-Ma'am operates a chain of retail grocery stores in the Southeast. In a
      move to increase distribution efficiency, the company has decided to
      modernize its warehouse facilities and equipment. Additional warehouse
      space will be rented, but the equipment—delivery trucks, fork lifts, and the
      like—must be financed. The equipment will cost a total of $10,000,000 and
      will be depreciated on a straight line basis over a five year expected life.
      The salvage value of the equipment is estimated to be $500,000, and the
      marginal tax rate is 40 percent. The cost of maintaining the equipment will
      average $20,000 per year over the five year period.

      One method of financing the equipment, Plan A, calls for a five year, 10
      percent, amortized term loan, to be secured by the equipment itself. Plan B
      calls for Minute-Ma'am to purchase the equipment, then sell it and lease it
      back over a five year period to yield the lessor 9 percent before taxes on
      his investment. The lessor is a wealthy investor whose income is derived
      primarily from interest and dividends; his marginal tax rate is 60 percent,
      and his before-tax return on capital averages 7½ percent on investments
      similar in risk and maturity to the lease. Thus, 7½ percent is the before-tax
      rate the investor could expect to earn if he simply maintained his existing
      investment portfolio. The lease would be written on a "net, net, net" basis,
      which means that all operating expenses, including maintenance, property
      taxes, and insurance, would be paid by the lessee, Minute-Ma'am. The
      investor would use the same depreciation schedule as would Minute-Ma'am.

   a. Calculate the net advantage to leasing for Minute-Ma'am. Remember to
      include the tax-adjusted maintenance cost as an outflow to the lessee.
   b. Would this be a good investment from the lessor's standpoint? Would the
      internal rate of return on the lease investment exceed the expected return
      on the investor's existing portfolio?
   c. Discuss the matter of discount rates used to evaluate the lease from the
      lessee's standpoint. Just how sensitive is the outcome of the analysis to
      the discount rate used; that is, in this instance, is the discount rate
      selected likely to have a material bearing on the lease versus borrow-
      and-purchase decision?

22 WARRANTS, CONVERTIBLES, AND OPTIONS

When we discussed long-term financing in Part VI, we concentrated on common stock, preferred stock, and various types of debt.[1] In this chapter, we see how the use of warrants and convertibles can make a company's securities attractive to an even broader range of investors, thereby increasing the supply of capital and decreasing its cost. Reducing the cost of capital will, of course, help to maximize the value of the firm's stock. Warrants and convertibles are rapidly gaining popularity, so a knowledge of these instruments is especially important today. We also examine briefly the rapidly growing options market, which is attractive to many investors.

WARRANTS

A warrant is an option to buy a stated number of shares of stock at a specified price. Generally, warrants are distributed with debt, and they are used to induce investors to buy a firm's long-term debt at a lower interest rate than would otherwise be required. For example, when Trans Pacific Airlines (TPA) wanted to sell $50 million of 20 year bonds in 1973, the company's investment bankers informed the financial vice-president that the bonds would be difficult to sell and that an interest rate of 14 percent would be required. However, as an alternative, the bankers suggested that investors might be willing to buy the bonds at a rate as low as $10\frac{3}{8}$ percent if the company would offer thirty warrants with each $1,000 bond, each warrant entitling the holder to buy one share of common stock at a price of $22 per share. The stock was selling for $20 per share at the time. The warrants would expire in 1983 if not exercised previously.

Why would investors be willing to buy Trans Pacific's bonds at a yield of only $10\frac{3}{8}$ percent just because warrants were also offered as part of the

---

1 If the instructor desires, this chapter may be covered immediately after Chapter 14, "Common Stock."

package? To answer this question, we must first see how warrants are valued in the market.

Formula Value of a Warrant

Warrants have both an "exercise," or "formula," value, which is equal to the value of the warrant if it were exercised today, and an actual price that is determined in the marketplace. The formula value is found by use of the following equation:

$$\begin{matrix} \text{Formula,} \\ \text{or exercise,} = \\ \text{value} \end{matrix} \left(\begin{matrix} \text{Market price} \\ \text{of common} \\ \text{stock} \end{matrix} - \begin{matrix} \text{Option} \\ \text{price} \end{matrix} \right) \times \left(\begin{matrix} \text{Number of shares} \\ \text{each warrant entitles} \\ \text{owner to purchase} \end{matrix} \right).$$

For instance, a TPA warrant entitles the holder to purchase one share of common stock at $22 a share. If the market price of the common stock rose to $64.50, the formula value of the warrant would be

$$(\$64.50 - \$22) \times 1.0 = \$42.50.$$

The formula gives a negative value when the stock is selling for less than the option price. For example, if TPA stock is selling for $20, the formula value of the warrants is minus $2.

Actual Price of a Warrant

Generally, warrants actually sell at prices above their formula values. When TPA stock sold for $20, the warrants had a formula value of minus $2 but were selling at a price of $8. This represented a premium of $10 above the formula value.

TPA stock rose substantially after the bonds with warrants were issued in 1973. A set of TPA stock prices, together with actual and formula warrant values, is given in Table 22–1 and plotted in Figure 22–1. At any stock price below $22, the formula value of the warrants is negative; beyond $22, each $1 increase in the price of the stock brings with it a $1 increase in the formula value of the warrants. The actual market price of the warrants lies above the formula value at each price of the common stock. Notice, however, that the premium of market price over formula value declines as the price of the common stock increases. For example, when the common stock sold for $22 and the warrants had a zero formula value, their actual price, and the premium, was $9. As the price of the stock rises, the *formula value* of the warrants matches the increase dollar for dollar, but for a while the *market price* of the warrants climbs less rapidly and the premium declines. The premium is $9 when the stock sells for $22 a share, but it declines to $1 by the time the stock price has risen to $75 a share. Beyond this point the premium seems virtually to disappear.

Why does this pattern exist? Why should the warrant ever sell for more than its formula value, and why does the premium decline as the price of the

Table 22–1
Formula and Actual Values of TPA Warrants at
Different Market Prices of Common Stock

Price of Stock	Formula Value	Actual Warrant Price	Premium
$ 20.00	$ − 2.00	$ 8.00	$10.00
22.00	0.00	9.00	9.00
23.00	1.00	9.75	8.75
24.00	2.00	10.50	8.50
33.67	11.67	17.37	5.70
52.00	30.00	32.00	2.00
75.00	53.00	54.00	1.00
100.00	78.00	78.50	0.50
150.00	128.00	Not available	—

stock increases? The answer lies in the speculative appeal of warrants—
they enable a person to gain a high degree of personal leverage when
buying securities. To illustrate, suppose TPA warrants sold for exactly their
formula value. Now suppose you are thinking of investing in the company's
common stock at a time when it is selling for $25 a share. If you buy a share
and the price rises to $50 in a year, you have made a 100 percent capital
gain. However, had you bought the warrants at their formula value ($3 when
the stock sells for $25), your capital gain would have been $25 on a $3
investment, or 833 percent. At the same time, your total loss potential with

Figure 22–1
Formula and Actual Values of TPA Warrants
at Different Common Stock Prices

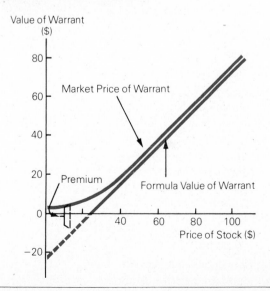

the warrant is only $3, while the potential loss from the purchase of the stock is $25. The huge capital gains potential, combined with the loss limitation, is clearly worth something—the exact amount it is worth to investors is the amount of the premium.

But why does the premium decline as the price of the stock rises? The answer is that both the leverage effect and the loss protection feature decline at high stock prices. For example, if you are thinking of buying the stock at $75 a share, the formula value of the warrants is $53. If the stock price doubles to $150, the formula value of TPA warrants goes from $53 to $128. The percentage capital gain on the stock is still 100 percent, but the percentage gain on the warrant is now only 142 percent versus 833 percent in the earlier case. Moreover, notice that the loss potential on the warrant is much greater when the warrant is selling at high prices. These two factors, the declining leverage impact and the increasing danger of losses, explain why the premium diminishes as the price of the common stock rises.

Initial Price of Bond with Warrants

Notice that the TPA bonds, if issued as straight debt, would have carried a 14 percent interest rate. However, with warrants attached, the bonds could be sold to yield $10^3/8$ percent. Notice also that with the stock selling at $20 per share, each of the 30 warrants attached to each bond sold for $8, making the warrants that come with each bond worth $240.

Someone buying the bonds at their $1,000 initial offering price would be receiving a package consisting of a $10^3/8$, 20 year bond and 30 warrants worth $240. Since the going interest rate on bonds as risky as those of TPA is 14 percent, we can find the straight-debt value of the bonds as follows:

$$\text{Value} = \sum_{t=1}^{20} \frac{\$103.75}{(1.14)^t} + \frac{\$1,000}{(1.14)^{20}}$$

$$= \$103.75(\text{PVIFA}_{14\%,\ 20}) + \$1,000(\text{PVIF}_{14\%,\ 20})$$

$$= \$103.75(6.6231) + \$1,000(0.0728)$$

$$= \$687.15 + \$72.80 = \$759.95.$$

Thus, a person buying the bonds in the initial underwriting would pay $1,000 and receive in exchange a straight bond worth about $760 plus warrants worth about $240:

$$\begin{matrix} \text{Price paid} \\ \text{for bond} \\ \text{with warrants} \end{matrix} = \begin{matrix} \text{Straight-debt} \\ \text{value of} \\ \text{bond} \end{matrix} + \begin{matrix} \text{Value of} \\ \text{warrants} \end{matrix}$$

$$= \$760 + \$240$$

$$= \$1,000.$$

Use of Warrants in Financing

In the past, warrants have generally been used by small, rapidly growing firms as "sweeteners" when selling either debt or preferred stocks. Such firms are frequently regarded by investors as being highly risky. Their bonds could be sold only if they were willing to pay extremely high rates of interest and to accept very restrictive indenture provisions. To avoid this, firms such as Trans Pacific often offered warrants along with the bonds. In the early 1970s, however, AT&T raised $1.57 billion by selling bonds with warrants. This was the largest financing of any type ever undertaken by a business firm, and it marked the first use ever of warrants by a large, strong corporation.[2]

Getting warrants along with bonds enables investors to share in the company's growth, if it does in fact grow and prosper; therefore, investors are willing to accept a lower bond interest rate and less restrictive indenture provisions. A bond with warrants has some characteristics of debt and some characteristics of equity. It is a hybrid security that provides the financial manager with an opportunity to expand the firm's mix of securities, appealing to a broader group of investors, and, thus, possibly lowering the firm's cost of capital.

Warrants can also bring in additional funds. The option price is generally set at from 10 to 20 percent above the market price of the stock at the time of the bond issue. If the firm does grow and prosper, and if its stock price rises above the option price at which shares may be purchased, warrant holders will surrender their warrants and buy stock at the stated price. There are several reasons for this. (1) Warrant holders will *surely* surrender warrants and buy stock if the warrants are about to expire with the market price of the stock above the option price. (2) Warrant holders will tend to surrender *voluntarily* and buy if the company raises the dividend on the common stock by a sufficient amount. No dividend is earned on the warrant, so it provides no current income. However, if the common stock pays a high dividend, it provides an attractive dividend yield. This induces warrant holders to exercise their option to buy the stock. (3) Warrants sometimes have *stepped-up option prices,* which prod owners into exercising them. For example, the Williamson Scientific Company has warrants outstanding with an option price of $25 until December 31, 1981, at which time the option price rises to $30. If the price of the common stock is over $25 just before December 31, 1981, many warrant holders will exercise their options before the stepped-up price takes effect.

Virtually all warrants today are *detachable.* Thus, after a bond with attached warrants is sold, the warrants can be detached and traded separately from the bond. Further, when these warrants are exercised, the bond issue remains outstanding, so the warrants bring in additional funds to the firm.

One desirable feature of warrants is that they generally bring in funds only

2 It is also interesting to note that before the AT&T issue, the New York Stock Exchange had a policy against listing warrants. The NYSE's stated policy was that warrants could not be listed because they were "speculative" instruments rather than "investment" securities. When AT&T issued warrants, however, the Exchange changed its policy and agreed to list warrants that met certain specifications. Many other warrants have since been listed.

when they are needed. If the company grows, it will probably need new
equity capital. At the same time, growth will cause the price of the stock to
rise, the warrants to be exercised, and the firm to obtain additional cash. If
the company is not successful and cannot profitably employ additional
money, the price of its stock will probably not rise sufficiently to induce
exercise of the options.

CONVERTIBLES

Convertible securities are bonds or preferred stocks that can be exchanged
for common stock at the option of the holder and under specified terms and
conditions. Unlike the exercise of warrants, which brings in additional funds
to the firm, converting a bond does not bring in additional capital: debt on
the balance sheet is simply replaced by common stock. Of course, this
reduction of the debt ratio will make it easier to obtain additional debt
capital, but this is a separate action.

One of the most important provisions of a convertible bond is the number
of shares of stock a bondholder receives upon conversion, defined as the
conversion ratio, R. Related to the conversion ratio is the *conversion price,*
P_c, which is the effective price paid for the common stock when
conversion occurs. The relationship between the conversion ratio and the
conversion price is illustrated by the Adams Electric Company's convertible
debentures, issued at their $1,000 par value in 1978. At any time prior to
maturity on July 1, 1998, a debenture holder can turn in a bond and receive
in its place twenty shares of common stock; therefore, $R = 20$. The bond
has a par value of $1,000, so the holder is giving up this amount upon
conversion. Dividing the $1,000 par value by the twenty shares received gives
a conversion price of $50 a share:

$$\text{Conversion price} = P_c = \frac{\text{Par value of bond}}{\text{Shares received}},$$

or

$$P_c = \frac{\$1,000}{R} = \frac{\$1,000}{20} = \$50.$$

Therefore,

$$R = \frac{\$1,000}{P_c} = \frac{\$1,000}{\$50} = 20 \text{ shares.}$$

Once R is set, this establishes the value of P_c, and vice versa.

Like warrant option prices, the conversion price is characteristically set at
from 10 to 20 percent above the prevailing market price of the common
stock at the time the convertible issue is sold. Exactly how the conversion

price is established can best be understood after examining some of the reasons firms use convertibles.[3]

Advantages of Convertibles

Convertibles offer advantages to corporations as well as to individual investors by functioning in the following two ways:

1. *As a "sweetener" when selling debt.* A company can sell debt with lower interest rates and less restrictive covenants by giving investors a chance to share in potential capital gains. Convertibles, like bonds with warrants, offer this possibility.

2. *To sell common stock at prices higher than those currently prevailing.* Many companies actually want to sell common stock, not debt, but feel that the price of their stock is temporarily depressed. Management may know, for example, that earnings are depressed because of a strike but think that they will snap back during the next year and pull the price of the stock up with them. To sell stock now would require giving up more shares to raise a given amount of money than management thinks is necessary. However, setting the conversion price 10 to 20 percent above the present market price of the stock will require giving up 10 to 20 percent fewer shares when the bonds are converted than would be required if stock were sold directly.

Notice, however, that management is counting on the stock's price rising above the conversion price to make the bonds attractive in conversion. If the stock price does not rise and conversion does not occur, then the company is saddled with debt.

How can the company be sure that conversion will occur when the price of the stock rises above the conversion price? Typically, convertibles contain a call provision that enables the issuing firm to force bondholders to convert. Suppose the conversion price is $50, the conversion ratio is 20, the

---

3 Generally, the conversion price and ratio are fixed for the life of the bond, although sometimes a stepped-up conversion price is used. Litton Industries' convertible debentures, for example, were convertible into 12.5 shares until 1972; they can be exchanged into 11.76 shares from 1972 until 1982, and 11.11 shares from 1982 until they mature in 1987. The conversion price thus started at $80, rose to $85, then will go to $90. Litton's convertibles, like most, are callable at the option of the company.

   Another factor that may cause a change in the conversion price and ratio is a standard feature of almost all convertibles—the clause protecting the convertible against dilution from stock splits, stock dividends, and the sale of common stock at prices below the conversion price. The typical provision states that if common stock is sold at a price below the conversion price, then the conversion price must be lowered (and the conversion ratio raised) to the price at which the new stock was issued. Also, if the stock is split, or if a stock dividend is declared, the conversion price must be lowered by the percentage amount of the stock dividend or split. For example, if Adams Electric were to have a two-for-one stock split, the conversion ratio would automatically be adjusted to 40 and the conversion price lowered to $25. If this protection were not contained in the contract, a company could completely thwart conversion by the use of stock splits and dividends. Warrants are similarly protected against dilution.

   The standard protection against dilution from selling new stock at prices below the conversion price can, however, get a company into trouble. For example, Litton Industries' stock fell to $11 in 1978. Thus, Litton would have to give the bondholders a tremendous advantage by lowering the conversion price from $85 to $11 if it wanted to sell new common stock. Problems such as this must be kept in mind by firms considering the use of convertibles or bonds with warrants.

market price of the common stock has risen to $60, and the call price on the convertible bond is $1,050. If the company calls the bond, bondholders can either convert into common stock with a market value of $1,200 or allow the company to redeem the bond for $1,050. Naturally, bondholders prefer $1,200 to $1,050, so conversion occurs. The call provision therefore gives the company a means of forcing conversion, provided the market price of the stock is greater than the conversion price.

Disadvantages of Convertibles

From the standpoint of the issuer, convertibles have two important disadvantages. (1) Although the convertible bond does give the issuer the opportunity to sell common stock at a price 10 to 20 percent higher than the price at which it could otherwise be sold, if the common stock greatly increases in price, the issuing firm may find that it would have been better off if it had waited and simply sold the common stock. (2) If the company truly wants to raise equity capital, and if the price of the stock does not rise sufficiently after the bond is issued, then the company is stuck with debt. This debt will, however, have a low interest rate.

Model of a Convertible Bond[4]

Figure 22–2 gives a graph that shows how investors tend to view convertible securities. A firm issues twenty year convertible bonds at a price of $1,000 per bond; this $1,000 is also the maturity (and par) value. The bonds pay a 4 percent annual coupon interest rate, or $40 per year, and each bond may be converted into twenty shares of stock. The stock now sells at $45 per share, and this price is expected to grow at a rate of 4 percent per year. If the bonds had not been made convertible, they would have had a yield of 4.5 percent, given their riskiness and the yields on other bonds.

The graph shows what investors *expect* to happen over time.

1. The horizontal line at $1,000 represents the par (and maturity) value. Also, $1,000 is the price at which the bond is initially offered to the public.

2. $1,040 is the initial call price on the bond. The call price declines over time and is $1,000 just prior to maturity.

3. The value of the convertible as a "straight," nonconvertible bond is $935. Since the bond has a 4 percent coupon rate, and since the yield on a nonconvertible bond of similar risk was stated to be $4\frac{1}{2}$ percent, the "straight bond" value of the convertible must be less than par. It is actually

$$V_B = \sum_{t=1}^{20} \frac{\$40}{(1.045)^t} + \frac{\$1,000}{(1.045)^{20}} = \$935.$$

---

4 This section may be omitted without loss of continuity. Also, the interested reader is referred to Appendix 22A of *Financial Management*, 2d edition, for a detailed explanation of the model.

Figure 22–2
Model of a Convertible Bond

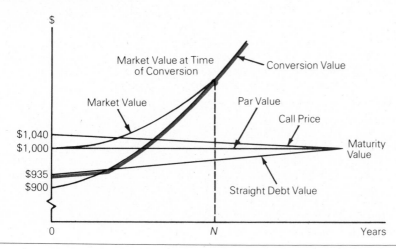

Note, however, that the bond's straight debt value must be $1,000 just prior to maturity, so the bond value rises over time. (See Figure 4–1.)

4. The $900 represents the bond's initial *conversion value,* or the value of the stock the investor would receive if the bond were converted at $t = 0$: Conversion value = $45 × 20 shares = $900. Since the stock price is expected to grow at a 4 percent rate, the conversion value of the bond will rise over time. For example, in Year 5 it will be $45(1.04)^5(20) = $1,095.

5. The actual market price of the bond must always be equal to or greater than the higher of its straight debt value or its conversion value. If the market price were below the straight bond value, people who wanted bonds would recognize it as a bargain and buy it as a bond. If the market price were below the conversion value, people would buy the bond, convert it to stock, and sell the stock at a profit. Therefore, the higher of the bond value and conversion value curves in the graph represents a "floor price" for the bond.

6. In fact, the bond's market value will typically exceed its floor value. It will exceed the straight bond value because the conversion possibility is worth something—a 4 percent bond with conversion possibilities is worth more than a 4 percent bond without this option. The actual price will typically exceed the conversion value because holding the convertible is safer than holding the common stock—the stock can fall to zero, but the convertible bond will not fall below its straight bond value. We cannot say exactly where the market value line will lie, but it will be above the "floor" set by the straight bond and conversion value lines.

7. At some point, the market value line will hit the conversion value line. First, the stock will pay higher and higher dividends as the years go by, but

the interest payments on the convertible are fixed. Thus, at some point rising dividends will push against fixed interest payments and cause investors to want to convert. Second, the market value of the bond cannot get very far above both the conversion value and the call price without exposing investors to the danger of a call. For example, suppose the market value was $1,200, the conversion value was $1,100, the call price was $1,030, and you had just bought ten bonds for $12,000. Now suppose the company called the bonds. You just lost $100 per bond, or $1,000! Recognizing this danger, investors simply will not pay much of a premium over the higher of the call or the conversion value.

8. The Point N represents the year when investors expect conversion to occur, either voluntarily because of rising dividends or because the company calls the convertibles to strengthen its balance sheet by substituting equity for debt.

9. An investor can find the expected rate of return on the bond, k_c, which is an "internal rate of return," as follows:

$$\$1,000 = \sum_{t=1}^{N} \frac{\$40}{(1 + k_c)^t} + \frac{\text{Expected market value at time of conversion}}{(1 + k_c)^N} .$$

If we assume that $N = 8$, then k_c turns out to be between 6 and 7 percent. (Plug in PVIFA and PVIF factors for these percentages and eight years to confirm this; the exact rate is 6.3 percent.)

10. The yield on its convertibles (k_c) should lie between a company's cost of straight debt (k_d) and its cost of common stock (k_s) because convertibles are more risky than debt (returns depend partly on what the stock does) but less risky than the stock. Investment bankers use the type of model described here, plus a knowledge of the market, to set the terms (conversion ratio and coupon interest rate) so that the bond will just "clear the market" at its $1,000 offering price.

This has been a very sketchy overview of the reasoning involved in convertible bond analysis. As noted earlier, the interested reader is referred to Appendix 22A of the second edition of *Financial Management*.

DECISIONS ON USE OF WARRANTS AND CONVERTIBLES

The Winchester Company, an electronic circuit and component manufacturer with assets of $60 million, illustrates a typical case in which convertibles proved useful. Winchester's profits had been depressed as a result of its heavy expenditures on research and development for a new product. This situation held down the growth rate of earnings and dividends; the price-earnings ratio was only 18 times, as compared with an industry average of 22. At the current $2 earnings per share and P/E of 18, the stock was selling for $36 a share. The Winchester family owned 70 percent of the 1.5 million shares outstanding, or 1.05 million shares. It wanted to retain majority control but could not buy more stock.

The heavy R&D expenditures had resulted in the development of a new type of printed circuit that management believed would be highly profitable. Twenty-five million dollars was needed to build and equip new production facilities, but profits were not expected to flow into the company for some eighteen months after construction on the new plant was started. Winchester's debt amounted to $27 million, or 45 percent of assets, well above the 25 percent industry average. Its debt indenture provisions restricted the company from selling additional debt unless the new debt was subordinated to outstanding debt.

Investment bankers informed J. H. Winchester, Jr., the financial vice-president, that subordinated debentures could not be sold at any reasonable interest rate unless they were convertible or had warrants attached. Convertibles or bonds with warrants could be sold with a 5 percent coupon interest rate if the conversion price or warrant option price was set at 15 percent above the market price of $36, or at $41 a share. Alternatively, the investment bankers were willing to buy convertibles or bonds with warrants at a $5^{1}/_{2}$ percent interest rate and a 20 percent conversion premium, or a conversion (or exercise) price of $43.50. If the company wanted to sell common stock directly, it could net $33 a share.

Which of the alternatives should Winchester have chosen? First, note that if common stock were used, the company would have to sell 757,576 shares ($25 million divided by $33). Combined with the 450,000 shares already held outside the family, this amounts to approximately 1.2 million shares versus the Winchester holdings of 1.05 million. Thus the family would lose majority control if common stock were sold.

If the 5 percent convertibles or bonds with warrants were used and the bonds were converted or the warrants exercised, 609,756 new shares would be added. Combined with the old 450,000, the outside interest would then be 1,059,756, so again the Winchester family would lose majority control. However, if the $5^{1}/_{2}$ percent convertibles or bonds with warrants were used, then after conversion or exercise only 574,713 new shares would be created. In this case, the family would have 1,050,000 shares versus 1,024,713 for outsiders; absolute control would be maintained.

In addition to assuring control, using the convertibles or warrants would also benefit earnings per share in the long run—the total number of shares would be less because fewer new shares would be issued to get the $25 million, so earnings per share would be higher. Before conversion or exercise, however, the firm would have a considerable amount of debt outstanding. Adding $25 million would raise the total debt to $52 million against new total assets of $85 million, so the debt ratio would be over 61 percent versus the 25 percent industry average. This could be dangerous. If delays were encountered in bringing the new plant into production, if demand failed to meet expectations, if the company experienced a strike, if the economy went into a recession—if any of these things occurred—the company would be extremely vulnerable because of the high debt ratio.

In the present case, the decision was made to sell the $5\frac{1}{2}$ percent convertible debentures. Two years later, earnings climbed to $3 a share, the P/E ratio to 20, and the price of the stock to $60. The bonds were called, but, of course, conversion occurred. After conversion, debt amounted to approximately $27.5 million against total assets of $87.5 million (some earnings had been retained), so the debt ratio was down to a more reasonable 31 percent.

Convertibles were chosen rather than bonds with warrants for the following reason. If a firm has a high debt ratio and its near-term prospects are favorable, it can anticipate a rise in the price of its stock and thus be able to call the bonds and force conversion. Warrants, on the other hand, have a stated life, and even though the price of the firm's stock rises, the warrants may not be exercised until near their expiration date. If, subsequent to the favorable period (during which convertibles could have been called), the firm encounters less favorable developments and the price of its stock falls, the warrants may lose their value and may never be exercised. The heavy debt burden will then become aggravated. Therefore, the use of convertibles gives the firm greater control over the timing of future capital structure changes. This factor is of particular importance to the firm if its debt ratio is already high in relation to the risks of its line of business.

REPORTING EARNINGS IF WARRANTS OR CONVERTIBLES ARE OUTSTANDING

If warrants or convertibles are outstanding, a firm could theoretically report earnings per share in three ways:

1. *Simple EPS,* where earnings available to common stockholders are divided by the average number of shares actually outstanding during the period.
2. *Primary EPS,* where earnings available are divided by the average number of shares that would have been outstanding if warrants and convertibles "likely to be converted in the near future" had actually been exercised or converted. The accountants have a formula which basically compares the conversion or option price with the actual market value of the stock to determine the likelihood of conversion, and they also add interest on the convertible bonds back into earnings.
3. *Fully diluted EPS,* which is similar to primary EPS except that *all* warrants and convertibles are assumed to be exercised or converted, regardless of the likelihood of exercise or conversion.

Simple EPS is virtually never reported by firms which have warrants or convertibles likely to be exercised or converted—the SEC requires that primary and fully diluted earnings be shown. For firms with large amounts of option securities outstanding, there can be a substantial difference between the two EPS figures. The purpose of the provision is, of course, to give investors a more accurate picture of the firm's true profit position.

OPTIONS

An option is a contract which gives its holder the right to buy (or sell) an asset at some predetermined price within a specified period of time. Thus, a warrant is an option, as are the stock options that corporations give their key executives as an incentive-based form of compensation. In the cases of both warrants and executive stock options, the options are created by the company and given up in exchange for something of value to the firm (low interest rate debt or better executive performance).

However, in recent years a new and rapidly growing market has developed —options created by individuals as opposed to issuing corporations. For example, if someone owned 100 shares of IBM stock, which in July 1979 sold for $73\frac{1}{2}$, that stockholder could give (or sell) to someone else the right to buy the 100 shares at any time during the next six months at a price of, say, $80 per share. (The $80 is called the "striking price.") Such options are actually offered, and they are traded on a number of stock exchanges, the Chicago Board Options Exchange (CBOE) being the oldest and largest. On July 10, 1979, IBM six month, $80 options sold on the CBOE for $2.625. Thus, for $2.625 \times 100 = $262.50 you could buy an option giving you the right to purchase 100 shares of IBM at a price of $80 per share anytime during the next six months. If the stock price stayed below $80 during that period, you would lose your $262.50, but if it rose to $150, then your $262.50 investment would have grown to ($150 − $80)(100) = $7,000! That translates into a very healthy rate of return. Incidentally, if the stock did go up, you would probably not actually buy the stock—the writer of the option would just pay you your profit.

An option to *buy* stock such as we have just described is termed a *call option*. One can also buy an option to *sell* stock—these are called *put options*. For example, suppose you think that IBM's price is going to decline from its current level of $73.50 sometime during the next six months. For $7.25 you could buy a six month put option giving you the right to sell one share (which you would not necessarily own) at a price of $70 ($70 is the striking price). If you bought a 100 share contract for $725 and IBM fell to $40, you would make ($70 − $40)(100) = $3,000.

Options trading is probably the "hottest" financial activity in the U.S. today. The leverage involved makes it possible for speculators with just a few dollars to make a fortune almost overnight. Also, investors with sizable portfolios can sell options on their stocks and make the value of the option (less brokerage commissions) even if the stock's price remains constant.[5]

---

5 An investor who sells options against stock held in a portfolio is said to be selling *covered options*. Options sold without the stock to back them up are called *naked options*.

Still, perhaps those who have profited most from the development of options trading are security brokers, who earn commission income on such trades.[6]

Corporations such as IBM on whose stock options are written have nothing to do with the options market. The corporations do not raise money in the options market or have any direct transactions in it. Option holders do not vote for corporate directors (unless they exercise their options to purchase the stock, which few actually do). There have been studies by the SEC and others as to whether options trading stabilizes or destabilizes the stock market, and whether it helps or hinders corporations seeking to raise new capital. The studies have not been conclusive one way or the other. In any event, options trading is here to stay, and many regard it as the most exciting game in town.[7]

SUMMARY

Both warrants and convertibles are forms of options used to finance business firms. The use of such long-term options is encouraged by an economic environment in which either recessions or booms can occur. The senior position of the securities protects against recessions, while the option feature offers the opportunity for participation in rising stock markets.

Both convertibles and warrants are used as "sweeteners." The option privileges they grant may make it possible for small companies to sell debt or preferred stock that otherwise could not be sold. For large companies, the "sweeteners" result in lower costs of the securities sold.

The conversion of bonds by their holders does not provide additional funds to the company. The exercise of warrants does provide such funds. The conversion of securities results in reduced debt ratios. The exercise of warrants also strengthens the equity position, but it still leaves the debt or preferred stock on the balance sheet. A firm with a high debt ratio should probably choose to use convertibles rather than senior securities carrying warrants. A firm with a moderate or low debt ratio may choose to employ warrants.

In the past, larger and stronger firms tended to favor convertibles over bonds with warrants, so most warrants have been issued by smaller, weaker concerns. AT&T's use of warrants in its $1.57 billion financing has caused other large firms to reexamine their positions on warrants, and warrants have come into increasing use since that time.

Partly because of investors' interest in warrants and convertibles, a new market

---

6 On a sparkling, sunny day sometime back, a famous stockbroker took a client to the New York Yacht Club for lunch. The broker pointed out one trim yacht and said it belonged to Broker A, nodded toward the one moored next to it, which was even longer, and said it belonged to Broker B, and so on. When he had finished, his guest turned to him and asked plaintively, "But where are the *clients'* yachts?"

7 Formal, mathematical models have been developed to aid in the valuation of options. See F. Black and M. Scholes, "The Pricing of Options and Corporate Liabilities," *Journal of Political Economy* (May–June 1973), pp. 637–654. Also, see J. F. Weston and E. F. Brigham, *Managerial Finance*, 6th ed., pp. 610–623, for a simplified explanation of the Black-Scholes model.

in pure options was developed during the 1970s. Option contracts are created by investors, not by the firms whose securities are involved in option contracts. The corporations themselves do not raise capital from the sale of these options and, in fact, have no direct involvement with this market.

Questions

22-1 Why do warrants typically sell at prices higher than their formula values?

22-2 What effect does the trend in stock prices (subsequent to issue) have on a firm's ability to raise funds (1) through convertibles and (2) through warrants?

22-3 If a firm expects to have additional financial requirements in the future, would you recommend that it use convertibles or bonds with warrants? What factors would influence your decision?

22-4 How does a firm's dividend policy affect each of the following?
   a. The value of long-term warrants.
   b. The likelihood that convertible bonds will be converted.
   c. The likelihood that warrants will be exercised.

22-5 Evaluate the following statement: "Issuing convertible securities represents a means by which a firm can sell common stock at a price above the existing market."

22-6 Why do corporations often sell convertibles on a rights basis?

Problems

22-1 a. Coit Industries, Inc., has warrants outstanding that permit the holders to purchase one share of stock per warrant at a price of $25. Calculate the formula value of Coit's warrants if the common sells at each of the following prices: (1) $20, (2) $25, (3) $30, (4) $100.

   b. At what approximate price do you think the warrants would actually sell under each condition indicated above? What premium is implied in your price? Your answer is a guess, but your prices and premiums should bear reasonable relationships to one another.

   c. How would each of the following affect your estimates of the warrant's prices and premiums in Part b?
      (1) The life of the warrant.
      (2) Expected variability (σ_p) in the stock's price.
      (3) The expected growth rate in the stock's EPS.
      (4) The company announces a change in dividend policy: Whereas it formerly paid no dividends, henceforth it will pay out *all* earnings as dividends.

   d. Assume Coit's stock now sells for $20 per share. The company wants to sell some 25 year, annual interest, $1,000 par value bonds. Each bond will have attached 50 warrants, each exercisable into one share of stock at an exercise price of $25. Coit's straight bonds yield 12 percent. Regardless of your answer to Part b above, assume that the warrants will have a market value of $3 when the stock sells at $20.
      What coupon interest rate, and dollar coupon, must the company set on

the bonds-with-warrants if they are to clear the market? Round to the nearest dollar or percentage point.

22-2 The Valley Forge Foundry was planning to finance an expansion in the summer of 1978. The principal executives of the company were agreed that an industrial company such as theirs should finance growth by means of common stock rather than by debt. However, they felt that the price of the company's common stock did not reflect its true worth, so they decided to sell a convertible security. They considered a convertible debenture but feared the burden of fixed interest charges if the common stock did not rise in price to make conversion attractive. They decided on an issue of convertible preferred stock, which would pay a dividend of $2.10 per share.

The common stock was selling at $42 a share at the time. Management projected earnings for 1978 at $3 a share and expected a future growth rate of 10 percent a year in 1978 and beyond. It was agreed by the investment bankers and the management that the common stock would sell at 19 times earnings, the current price/earnings ratio.

a. What conversion price should be set by the issuer? The conversion ratio will be 1.0; that is, each share of convertible preferred can be converted into one share of common. Therefore, the convertible's par value (and also the issue price) will equal the conversion price as a percentage over the current market price of the common. Your answer will be a guess, but make it a reasonable one.

b. Should the preferred stock include a call provision? Why?

22-3 In June 1976, U.S. Steel sold $400 million of convertible bonds, the largest issue on record. The bonds had a twenty-five year maturity, a $5^3/4$ percent coupon rate, and were sold at their $1,000 par value. The conversion price was set at $62.75 against a current price of $55 per share of common. The bonds were subordinated debentures, and they were given an A rating; straight nonconvertible debentures of the same quality yielded about $8^3/4$ percent at the time.

a. Calculate the premium on the bonds, i.e., the percentage excess of the conversion price over the current stock price.

b. What is U.S. Steel's annual interest savings on the convertible issue versus a straight debt issue?

c. Look up U.S. Steel's current stock price in the paper. Based on this price, do you think it likely that the bonds would have been converted? (Calculate the value of the stock one would receive by converting a bond.)

d. The bonds originally sold for $1,000. If interest rates on A-rated bonds had remained constant at $8^3/4$ percent, what do you think would have happened to the price of the convertible bonds? (*Note:* Bond prices are quoted daily in the *Wall Street Journal* as well as in major newspapers, so you can look up the price of U.S. Steel's bonds to check your answer.)

e. Now suppose the price of U.S. Steel's common stock had fallen from $55 on the day the bonds were issued to $20 at present. (At the time this problem was written, that is exactly what had happened.) Suppose also that the rate of interest had fallen from $8^3/4$ to $5^3/4$ percent. (This had not happened when the problem was being written—the interest rate on A bonds was about 11 percent.) Under these conditions, what do you think would have happened to the price of the bonds?

f. Set up a graphic model to illustrate how investors must have felt about the U.S. Steel convertibles in 1976. How well were these expectations realized?

22-4 The Dirk Manufacturing Company has grown rapidly during the past five years. Recently its commercial bank urged the company to consider increasing permanent financing. Its bank loan under a line of credit has risen to $250,000, carrying 8 percent interest. Dirk has been thirty to sixty days late in paying trade creditors.

Discussions with an investment banker have resulted in the decision to raise $500,000 at this time. Investment bankers have assured Dirk that the following alternatives are feasible (flotation costs will be ignored):

Alternative 1. Sell common stock at $8.

Alternative 2. Sell convertible bonds at an 8 percent coupon, convertible into 100 shares of common stock for each $1,000 bond (that is, the conversion price is $10 per share).

Alternative 3. Sell debentures at an 8 percent coupon, each $1,000 bond carrying 100 warrants to buy common stock at $10.

Tom O'Brien, the president, owns 80 percent of the common stock of Dirk Manufacturing Company and wishes to maintain control of the company. One hundred thousand shares are outstanding. Additional information is given below.

Dirk Manufacturing Company: Balance Sheet

	Current liabilities	$400,000
	Common stock, par $1.00	100,000
	Retained earnings	50,000
Total assets $550,000	Total claims	$550,000

Dirk Manufacturing Company: Income Statement

Sales	$1,100,000
All costs except interest	990,000
Gross profit	$ 110,000
Interest	20,000
Profit before taxes	$ 90,000
Taxes at 50%	45,000
Profits after taxes	$ 45,000
Shares	100,000
Earnings per share	$0.45
Price-earnings ratio	19×
Market price of stock	$8.55

a. Show the new balance sheet under each alternative. For Alternatives 2 and 3, show the balance sheet after conversion of the debentures or exercise of the warrants. Assume that one-half of the funds raised will be used to pay off the bank loan and one-half to increase total assets.

b. Show O'Brien's control position under each alternative, assuming that he does not purchase additional shares.

c. What is the effect on earnings per share of each alternative, if it is assumed that profits before interest and taxes will be 20 percent of total assets?

d. What will be the debt ratio under each alternative?

e. Which of the three alternatives would you recommend to O'Brien, and why?

23 SMALL BUSINESS FINANCE

The same general principles of financial management apply to both large and small firms. However, small firms do face problems that are somewhat different from those confronting larger businesses, and the goals of a small firm are likely to be oriented more toward the aspirations of an individual entrepreneur rather than toward investors in general. Also, the characteristics of the money and capital markets create problems for small firms, and a special governmental agency, the U.S. Small Business Administration, exists to help small firms with their financing problems. This chapter presents some of the key factors in small business finance.

LIFE CYCLE OF THE FIRM

The life cycle of an industry or firm is often depicted as an S-shaped curve, as shown in Figure 23–1. The four stages in the life cycle are described as follows:

Figure 23–1
Hypothetical Life Cycle of a Typical Firm

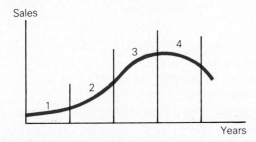

1. *Experimentation period.* Sales and profits grow slowly following the introduction of a new product or firm.
2. *Exploitation period.* The firm enjoys rapid growth of sales, high profitability, and acceptance of the product.
3. *Maturity.* The rate of growth of sales begins to slow down; growth is dependent in large part on replacement demand.
4. *Decline.* The firm faces new competitive products, technological and managerial obsolescence, and saturation of demand for its goods.

Although it is an oversimplification, Figure 23–1 provides a useful framework for analysis. The situation represented by the four stage life cycle concept is based on a number of assumptions. For example, it assumes competent management in the growth periods and a lack of management foresight prior to the decline phase. Obviously, one of management's primary goals is to prolong Stage 2 and to completely forestall Stage 4, and a great many firms are apparently successful in this endeavor. We shall discuss other aspects of the firm's life cycle later, giving special attention to the types of financing employed at each stage.

TRADITIONAL SMALL BUSINESS INDUSTRIES

Some firms are small because the nature of the industry dictates that small enterprises are more efficient than large ones, while other firms are small primarily because they are new companies—either new entrants to established industries or new enterprises in developing industries. These two types of small firms face fundamentally different situations, and they have vastly different problems and opportunities. Traditional small businesses are discussed in the remainder of this section, while those with growth potential are discussed later in the chapter.

Characteristics of Traditional Small Firms

The industries or segments of industries in which small businesses predominate exhibit three common characteristics: (1) a localized market, (2) low capital requirements, and (3) relatively simple technology. Because these characteristics lead to heavy dependence on one person, problems often arise:

1. The key individual may not possess the full range of managerial skills required: the owner may be good in sales but be unable to handle employees well, to keep adequate accounting records, to maintain financial control systems, or to deal adequately with other administrative tasks.
2. In a small business run by one key person, the control system tends to be informal, direct, and personal. If the business grows, the span of responsibilities may become excessive for the entrepreneur.

3. Because of the owner's preoccupation with the pressing problems of day-to-day operations, planning for the future is often inadequate. Therefore, changes in the economic environment or competitive shifts can have severe impacts on the firm.

4. A relatively high degree of managerial training, experience, and breadth are necessary, yet often lacking: preoccupied with the present, the characteristic small-firm entrepreneur simply does not plan for management succession. As was noted in Chapter 20, Dun & Bradstreet data on business failures indicate that more failures are caused by the lack of competent management than by any other factor.

Profitability of Small Firms

Most studies show that running a small business is anything but a picnic. Owners often put in sixty or more hours per week, have all of their capital tied up in a risky business, face nerve-racking problems, and earn less than the minimum wage for their efforts.

In the face of such discouraging statistics, why do people open their own businesses? The reasons vary. One is the hope that they will beat the odds and be successful—any community, large or small, has a group of very successful small business people who, while perhaps not millionaires, can afford $100,000 homes, country clubs, and trips to Europe, not to mention sending their children to college in style. A second reason is the freedom to make their own decisions, even if the price of this freedom is high. Third, they may not regard the time spent working in their own firms as drudgery; there is a wide variety of tasks to be performed in running a small enterprise, and the work can be both interesting and challenging.

Financing the Traditional Small Firm

The typical small business, even the successful one, cannot look to the general capital markets for funds. If the firm owns any real estate, it may be able to obtain a mortgage from a bank or a savings and loan. Equipment may perhaps either be purchased under a term loan or be leased. After the business has survived for a few years, bank financing may be available on a seasonal basis, but not for permanent growth capital. Trade credit will typically represent the bulk of outside financing available to the firm.

Financial ratio analysis will be of major and overriding importance to the small firm. Such analysis, on a regular basis, is essential to ascertain whether the firm is operating efficiently. Whereas a larger, stronger firm may have the financial strength to fall below its industry standards and still recover, the small firm has a smaller margin for error. Thus, anyone running a small firm is well advised to look at trends in its financial ratios and to compare them with industry standards.

Working capital management is also of overwhelming importance for most small firms. Because the amount of funds available is limited, liquidity is crucial. Trade credit appears to be an easy way of obtaining funds, yet even trade credit is obtained on terms that generally call for payment within thirty days. Since inventories typically represent a large percentage of total assets, a small firm's inventory policy must also be stressed. Large firms usually offer credit, so to meet competition, small firms may also have to extend credit. The large firm is likely to have an established credit department, but how does the small firm evaluate credit risks? What volume of accounts receivable can be built up without endangering both the solvency and the liquidity of the business? These are critical questions for the manager of a small business.

Current liability management is also important for the small firm. Although trade credit is relatively easy to obtain, it is often very costly. If discounts are available but not taken, the effective interest rate on such credit can be extremely high—as we know, not taking discounts on terms of 2/10, net 30 implies a 36 percent interest rate. Also, there is a temptation to be consistently slow in making payments, but this involves dangers: suppliers may refuse to extend any credit whatever, or they may quote higher prices.

In summary, three areas of finance are of the utmost importance to firms in traditional small business industries. *First,* the proprietor must rely on internal financing (retained earnings) to a greater extent than would the management of a larger firm. *Second,* the proprietor must be a jack-of-all-trades and master of *all* if the business is to survive in the long run. *Third,* working capital management is critical to the small entrepreneur; if a breakdown occurs here, the firm will not remain solvent, and it will go out of business.

Franchising

Many traditional small businesses are today moving toward franchise operations. Examples include McDonald's, Burger King, Midas Mufflers, Mr. Transmission, Hilton Hotels, Holiday Inn, and thousands more. Franchising represents a device whereby the training and experience required for a particular line of business is supplied to the proprietor on a rental contract basis. Sometimes the franchise also includes the use of a valuable name developed through national advertising and uniform standards (McDonald's), or of a special service (Holiday Inn's reservation service). Or, through bulk buying, the franchisor may be able to sell supplies to the franchisee at lower costs than would otherwise be available.

The typical arrangement calls for the franchisee (1) to construct a facility that meets the franchisor's specifications, (2) to pay the franchisor a one-time fee of, say, $10,000 for a license to operate in a given territory, (3) to send personnel to one of the franchisor's established locations for pre-opening training, and (4) to pay the franchisor a continuing fee of, say, 2 percent of sales revenues for continuing support. Each franchisee must also agree to operate in accordance with specified procedures and to permit regular inspections, for the maintenance of high, uniform standards is essential to the entire operation—one rotten franchise can spoil the whole barrel.

Most newly organized franchise operations require their franchisees to put up a substantial amount of "front money," mainly for buildings, inventory, and other start-up costs. Indeed, one reason for franchising rather than simply opening branch facilities is that there are much lower capital requirements for the parent organization, as capital is supplied by many individual entrepreneurs. However, once the franchisor becomes established and has developed lines of credit, the franchise-granting firm may reverse the process and supply capital to new operators (who are often promising but dollar-poor employees of existing franchisees).

Franchising can be very profitable to both the franchisor and the franchisees. It can project the franchisor from just another small business into a huge, national corporation, and it can give the franchisees a huge advantage over their competitors—how would you like to be the owner-operator of Ma & Pa's Motel and see the Holiday Inn construction crew pull up across the street? On the other hand, as many erstwhile franchise operators know, obtaining a franchise is not necessarily the road to riches—in many such arrangements, the owner of the franchised operation may be required to pay an excessive price for the trademark, specialty inputs, supplies, and managerial advice. As in most other aspects of business, franchising decisions should be based on a careful analysis of all the facts.

THE SMALL FIRM WITH GROWTH POTENTIAL

The second broad category of small business is the new firm with potential for substantial growth. Typically, such a firm has developed a new product or an innovative way of providing an old service: the electronics industry is a good example of the former, while franchised hamburgers and other food operations illustrate the latter. In this section, we discuss the financial aspects of such firms from inception until the business has matured enough to go public. The significant financial aspects of each stage of the life cycle will be set out as a guide to the establishment and development of the new small business enterprise.

Stage 1: Experimentation Period

As indicated above and shown in Figure 23–1, the first stage of a firm's life cycle involves experimentation and simply getting itself firmly entrenched. During this period, management must lay the foundation for future growth, realizing that growth occurs either because the firm can increase its share of the market or because of industry expansion. Market share expansion is difficult due to the reaction of existing firms, and even if the industry is growing, management must recognize that every product and industry has a life cycle. Hence, supernormal growth, whatever its cause, will continue for only a finite period.

Particularly in new industries, it is important that the firm identify the techniques needed to succeed in its line of business. When the auto industry was maturing, dealership organizations and the availability of repair parts and service were the critical factors to the success of individual firms. In the computer industry, a backup of software, marketing, and maintenance personnel was vital.

Like the owner of a firm in a traditional small business, a growth company entrepreneur must have a knowledge not only of products and markets, but also of the standard administrative tools essential for effective management in any line of business. Financial planning and control processes are especially important. Financial ratio analysis should be used to develop standards for determining the broad outlines of the balance sheet and the income statement, as well as for guidelines to help identify developing problem areas.

Planning for growth is especially important. Initially, such planning will emphasize the expansion of existing operations; later in the firm's life cycle, it must consider possible movement into new product lines. A basic decision that must be made, whatever type of expansion occurs, is to choose between using more or less highly automated productive processes. Standard breakeven analysis can be employed to measure how changing sales levels will affect the firm's risk and return characteristics.

Stage 2: Exploitation and Rapid Growth Period

After its inception, a successful firm with growth potential will enter Stage 2 of its financial cycle. Here, the firm has achieved initial success—it is growing rapidly and is reasonably profitable. Cash flows and working capital management have become increasingly important. Also, at this stage the firm will have an extraordinary need for additional outside financing; as we saw in Chapter 7, the need for external funds is a function of the firm's growth rate, so in Stage 2 large amounts of external funds are required. This necessitates good financial planning, for otherwise a shortage of capital may throttle the firm's growth opportunities.

Firms in Stage 2 have an especially difficult time obtaining equity capital. These firms are not large enough to go public, and relatively little is known about them. They are typically entering new areas about which little information is available. There may be great potential, but large risks are also involved, and for every glowing success story there are many instances of failure. Further, even after an innovative growth firm has been established, there are continued pressures because of the financial problems noted above. Also, demonstrated success will stimulate imitators, so growth projections must take into account the influx of new firms and the likelihood of a declining market share and increased competitive pressures. Furthermore, high profits may lead to excessive expansion, which will be followed by excess capacity, which in turn will cause problems for every firm in the industry. For all these reasons, the small, rapidly growing firm faces a precarious existence, even when the product market opportunities upon which it was conceived are sound.

The combination of high risks and profit potential inherent in Stage 2 firms has led to the development of *venture capital suppliers*—wealthy individuals, partnerships, or corporations whose business is supplying risk capital to small growth companies. When a new business makes an application for financial assistance from a venture capital firm, it receives a rigorous examination. Some development companies use their own staffs for this investigation, while others depend on a board of advisers acting in the capacity of consultants. A high percentage of applications is rejected, but if the application is approved, funds are provided. Venture capital companies generally take an equity position in the firms they finance, but they may also extend debt capital. However, when loans are made, they generally involve convertibles or warrants, or are tied in with the purchase of stock by the investment company.

Venture capital companies perform a continuing and active role in the enterprise. Typically, they do not insist on voting control, but they usually have at least one member on the board of directors of the new enterprise. The matter of control has *not* been one of the crucial considerations in investment companies' decisions to invest—indeed, if the management of a small business is not sufficiently strong to make sound decisions, the venture capital firm is not likely to be interested in the first place. However, the investment company does want to maintain continuous contact, to provide management counsel, and to monitor the progress of its investment.

Another distinctive contribution of the venture capital firm stems from its ownership by wealthy individuals. (Laurance Rockefeller, for example, is a leading venture capitalist.) For tax reasons, such people are interested in receiving their income in the form of capital gains rather than dividend income. They are, therefore, in a position to take larger risks. If they lose on the venture, the net after-tax loss is only a portion of the investment, since they are in a high personal income tax bracket. For example, a $100,000 loss "costs" only $25,000 for an investor who is in the 75 percent state-plus-federal tax bracket.[1] Their gains, if any, are in the form of capital gains and therefore are taxed at a rate lower than the rate on ordinary personal income. Thus, for the wealthy individual, investments in small businesses are attractive.

Another source of venture capital has been developed in recent years—large, well-established business firms. A number of large corporations have invested both money and various types of know-how to start or to help develop small business firms. The owner of the small firm is usually a specialist, frequently a technical person who needs both money and help

1 Special tax provisions make it possible to offset more than the regular amount of ordinary income by capital losses if the losses are on small businesses as defined by the tax code.

with administrative services such as accounting, finance, production, and marketing. The small firm's owner contributes entrepreneurship, special talents, a taste for risk taking, and "the willingness to work eighteen hours a day for peanuts." A number of major corporations have found that there is a mutual advantage in this form of venture capital investment.

Another important source of venture capital financing for small business is the Small Business Investment Company (SBIC). To assist small companies in overcoming their very real disadvantages in the capital markets, in 1958 Congress passed the Small Business Investment Company Act, which empowered the Small Business Administration (SBA) to license and regulate SBICs and to provide them with financial assistance. A minimum of $150,000 in private capital is required for the licensing of an SBIC, and this amount can be doubled by selling subordinated debentures to the SBA (at interest rates generally below those prevailing in the market).

In their operations, SBICs have followed two policies similar to those of investment development or venture capital companies: (1) Their investments are generally made by the purchase of convertible securities or bonds with warrants, thus giving the SBICs a residual equity position in the companies to which funds are provided. (2) SBICs emphasize management counsel, for which a fee is charged.[2]

Going Public

If the firm's Stage 2 growth continues long enough, it will experience increasing pressures to add large amounts of equity capital, and its owners may desire to establish a market for their own personal stock holdings. At this point, a full assessment of the critical step in a firm's life—that of "going public"—must be made.

Going public leads to four fundamental changes: (1) The firm moves from informal, personal control to a system of formal controls, and the need for financial techniques such as ratio analysis and the du Pont system of financial control greatly increases. (2) Information must be reported on a timely basis to the outside investors, even though the founders may continue to have majority control. (3) The firm must have a breadth of management in all areas if it is to operate its expanded business effectively. (4) The publicly owned firm typically draws on a board of directors to help formulate sound plans and policies; the board should include representatives of the public owners and other external interest groups to aid the management group in carrying out its broader responsibilities.

The valuation process is particularly important at the time the firm goes public: at what price will stock be sold to new outside investors? In analyzing the investment value of the small and growing firm, some

2 The larger SBICs have staffs similar to those of holding companies or conglomerates; these staffs provide assistance, for a fee, to the firms in which the SBICs have invested.

significant differences in capital costs between large and small firms should be noted:

1. It is especially difficult to obtain reliable estimates of the cost of equity capital for small, privately owned firms.
2. Because of the risks involved, the required rate of return tends to be high for small firms. However, portfolio effects from a pooling of risks can reduce this factor somewhat for publicly owned small firms.
3. Tax considerations are generally quite important for privately owned companies that are large enough to consider going public, as the owner-managers are probably in the top personal tax brackets. This factor can cause the effective after-tax cost of retained earnings to be considerably lower than the after-tax cost of new outside equity.[3]
4. Flotation costs for new security issues, especially new stock issues, are much higher for small than for large firms. This factor, as well as Item 3 above, causes the marginal cost of capital curve for small firms to rise rapidly once retained earnings have been exhausted.

The timing of the decision to go public is also especially important because small firms are more affected by variations in money market conditions than larger companies. During periods of tight money and high interest rates, financial institutions, especially commercial banks, find that the quantity of funds demanded exceeds the supply available at legally permissible rates. One important method employed to ration credit is to raise credit standards. During tight money periods, both a stronger balance sheet record and a longer and more stable record of profitability are required in order to qualify for bank credit. Since financial ratios for small and growing firms tend to be less strong, such firms bear the brunt of credit restraint. Obviously, the small firm that goes public and raises equity capital before a money squeeze occurs is in a better position to ride out a tight money period. This firm has already raised some of its needed capital, and its equity cushion enables it to present a stronger picture to the banks, thus helping it to obtain additional capital in the form of debt.

SMALL BUSINESS ADMINISTRATION

It is clear that small firms face difficulties in obtaining capital, and in recognition of this fact, the federal government set up the Small Business Administration (SBA).[4] The SBA operates a number of different programs. One was discussed above in connection with the formation and growth of SBICs. Another, the Business Loan Program, provides funds for

---

3 See Appendix A to Chapter 16 of *Financial Management*, 2d edition.
4 The SBA also helps small companies obtain a fair share of government contracts, and it administers training programs of various types designed to help small entrepreneurs.

construction, machinery, equipment, and working capital.[5] Loans under this program, which are available only when small businesses are unable to obtain funds on reasonable terms from private sources, are of two types: (1) direct loans and (2) participation loans. In a *direct loan,* the SBA simply makes a loan to a small business borrower. In a *participation loan,* the SBA lends part of the funds, while a bank or other private lending institution advances the balance. Under a participation loan, a portion of the funds advanced by the private party may be guaranteed by the SBA. The maximum amount the SBA may lend to any borrower is $350,000; this maximum applies to either a direct loan or the SBA's portion of a participation loan.

Since SBA loans or guarantees are advantageous to the business recipient, the definition of what constitutes a small business is important. Actually, the definition varies somewhat depending on the industry. Any manufacturing concern is defined as small if it employs fewer than 250 people, while it is defined as large if it employs more than 1,000 people. Within this range, the SBA has different standards for different industries. A wholesale firm is classified as small if its annual sales are $5 million or less. Most retail businesses and service firms are defined as small if their total annual receipts are less than $1 million.[6]

FINANCING PATTERNS

The key factors in small business financing are summarized briefly in Table 23–1, which sets forth the financing patterns at the firm's four stages of development. In its formative stage, the new small firm must rely most heavily on personal savings, trade credit, and government agencies. During its period of rapid growth, internal financing will become an important source for meeting its financing requirements, although continued reliance will be placed on trade credit. At this stage, its record of accomplishment also makes it possible to obtain bank credit to finance seasonal needs, and if the loan can be paid off on an amortized basis over two or three years, the firm may qualify for a term loan as well. If it has the potential for really strong growth, the firm may also be able to attract equity from a venture capital company.

---

5 In addition to the Business Loan Program, the SBA administers a number of other programs, including the following: (1) Equal Opportunity Loan Program, designed specifically for disadvantaged persons who wish to start or expand an existing business; (2) Development Company Loan Program, which is used to help attract businesses to geographic areas in need of economic stimulation; (3) Displaced Business Loan Program, designed to help small businesses that are forced to relocate because of urban renewal or similar events; (4) Disaster Loan Program, designed to aid both businesses and homeowners who suffer losses as a consequence of some natural disaster; (5) Lease Guarantee Program, designed to help small businesses obtain rental space in the commercial real estate market; (6) Revolving Line-of-Credit Program, designed to aid small building contractors; (7) Surety Bonding Program, designed to aid small business people who must post performance bonds when seeking contracts; and (8) Minority Enterprise SBIC Program, designed to stimulate SBICs whose clients are minority-owned firms.

6 A great deal of additional information on the SBA and its various programs may be obtained directly from the Small Business Administration, Washington, D.C., or from regional SBA offices.

**Table 23–1
Financing Patterns at Four Stages of a
Firm's Development**

Stage	Financing Pattern
1. Formation	Personal savings, trade credit, government agencies
2. Rapid growth	Internal financing, trade credit, bank credit, venture capital
3. Growth to maturity	Going public, money and capital markets
4. Maturity and industry decline	Internal financing, share repurchase, diversification, mergers

A particularly successful firm may reach Stage 3, where going public becomes feasible. This leads to access to the broader money and capital markets, and it represents a true coming-of-age for the small firm. Even at this point, however, the firm must look ahead, analyzing its products and their prospects. Because every product has a life cycle, the firm must be aware that without the continuous development of new products, growth will cease, and eventually the firm will decline. Accordingly, as Stage 4 approaches, the firm must plan for the possibility of share repurchases, mergers, or other long-term strategies. The best time to look ahead and plan for this is while the firm has energy, momentum, and a high price-earnings ratio, as it will during Stage 3.

SUMMARY

Our coverage of small business finance has focused on the formation and growth of the small firm, and on some of the special problems it faces in raising capital. We have not considered in detail the areas of working capital management, capital budgeting, leverage, or many other important topics. This omission is deliberate—these topics were all covered earlier in the book, and the principles and methods already discussed are applicable to large and small firms alike. Of course, there are economies of scale in the use of some of the more sophisticated techniques, hence it may not pay to apply them in a small firm. Also, there is less need for certain types of financial controls in the small firm—the owner-manager simply does not need to worry about the formal ways to insure coordination between different parts of the firm that are essential in a large, multiproduct, multiplant corporation. On the other hand, the small firm has less room for error, and the manager must have a broader range of expertise than any single executive in a large corporation.

Questions

23-1 Identify the four stages in a typical firm's life cycle, and describe the major sources of capital for firms in each stage.

23-2 What is a venture capital firm?

23-3 What tax provisions make investing in small business especially desirable for investors in high tax brackets?

23-4 Assume that your family owns a successful campground located close to a major interstate highway. You are considering affiliating with one of the national campground franchise organizations such as KOA. Discuss the pros and cons of such an affiliation. Might it be feasible for you to franchise others?

23-5 Would you expect the dividend policy of a "typical" small firm to be the same or different from that of a "typical" large firm? Explain.

23-6 Would you expect to find greater use of operating leverage in large or small firms? Explain.

Problem

23-1 Contact a small firm in your city. Identify the firm's strengths and weaknesses through a ratio analysis. Then report how the various topics covered in the book might be used to help the firm operate with maximum efficiency.

Other Exercises for Chapter 23

The following problems can be used to advantage with Chapter 23: 7-1, 7-2, 8-3, 9-4, 10-6, 10-8, 10A-1, and 14-1. Also, these cases from Brigham et al., *Cases in Managerial Finance* (1980 edition) are especially recommended: Rio Wood Products, Component Controls Corporation, and Cromwell Courts.

APPENDIX A

Table A-1 Present Value of $1: $PVIF_{k,n} = 1/(1 + k)^n$

Period	1%	2%	3%	4%	5%	6%	7%	8%	9%	10%
1	.9901	.9804	.9709	.9615	.9524	.9434	.9346	.9259	.9174	.9091
2	.9803	.9612	.9426	.9246	.9070	.8900	.8734	.8573	.8417	.8264
3	.9706	.9423	.9151	.8890	.8638	.8396	.8163	.7938	.7722	.7513
4	.9610	.9238	.8885	.8548	.8227	.7921	.7629	.7350	.7084	.6830
5	.9515	.9057	.8626	.8219	.7835	.7473	.7130	.6806	.6499	.6209
6	.9420	.8880	.8375	.7903	.7462	.7050	.6663	.6302	.5963	.5645
7	.9327	.8706	.8131	.7599	.7107	.6651	.6227	.5835	.5470	.5132
8	.9235	.8535	.7894	.7307	.6768	.6274	.5820	.5403	.5019	.4665
9	.9143	.8368	.7664	.7026	.6446	.5919	.5439	.5002	.4604	.4241
10	.9053	.8203	.7441	.6756	.6139	.5584	.5083	.4632	.4224	.3855
11	.8963	.8043	.7224	.6496	.5847	.5268	.4751	.4289	.3875	.3505
12	.8874	.7885	.7014	.6246	.5568	.4970	.4440	.3971	.3555	.3186
13	.8787	.7730	.6810	.6006	.5303	.4688	.4150	.3677	.3262	.2897
14	.8700	.7579	.6611	.5775	.5051	.4423	.3878	.3405	.2992	.2633
15	.8613	.7430	.6419	.5553	.4810	.4173	.3624	.3152	.2745	.2394
16	.8528	.7284	.6232	.5339	.4581	.3936	.3387	.2919	.2519	.2176
17	.8444	.7142	.6050	.5134	.4363	.3714	.3166	.2703	.2311	.1978
18	.8360	.7002	.5874	.4936	.4155	.3503	.2959	.2502	.2120	.1799
19	.8277	.6864	.5703	.4746	.3957	.3305	.2765	.2317	.1945	.1635
20	.8195	.6730	.5537	.4564	.3769	.3118	.2584	.2145	.1784	.1486
21	.8114	.6598	.5375	.4388	.3589	.2942	.2415	.1987	.1637	.1351
22	.8034	.6468	.5219	.4220	.3418	.2775	.2257	.1839	.1502	.1228
23	.7954	.6342	.5067	.4057	.3256	.2618	.2109	.1703	.1378	.1117
24	.7876	.6217	.4919	.3901	.3101	.2470	.1971	.1577	.1264	.1015
25	.7798	.6095	.4776	.3751	.2953	.2330	.1842	.1460	.1160	.0923
26	.7720	.5976	.4637	.3607	.2812	.2198	.1722	.1352	.1064	.0839
27	.7644	.5859	.4502	.3468	.2678	.2074	.1609	.1252	.0976	.0763
28	.7568	.5744	.4371	.3335	.2551	.1956	.1504	.1159	.0895	.0693
29	.7493	.5631	.4243	.3207	.2429	.1846	.1406	.1073	.0822	.0630
30	.7419	.5521	.4120	.3083	.2314	.1741	.1314	.0994	.0754	.0573
35	.7059	.5000	.3554	.2534	.1813	.1301	.0937	.0676	.0490	.0356
40	.6717	.4529	.3066	.2083	.1420	.0972	.0668	.0460	.0318	.0221
45	.6391	.4102	.2644	.1712	.1113	.0727	.0476	.0313	.0207	.0137
50	.6080	.3715	.2281	.1407	.0872	.0543	.0339	.0213	.0134	.0085
55	.5785	.3365	.1968	.1157	.0683	.0406	.0242	.0145	.0087	.0053

Table A–1 (continued)

Period	12%	14%	15%	16%	18%	20%	24%	28%	32%	36%
1	.8929	.8772	.8696	.8621	.8475	.8333	.8065	.7813	.7576	.7353
2	.7972	.7695	.7561	.7432	.7182	.6944	.6504	.6104	.5739	.5407
3	.7118	.6750	.6575	.6407	.6086	.5787	.5245	.4768	.4348	.3975
4	.6355	.5921	.5718	.5523	.5158	.4823	.4230	.3725	.3294	.2923
5	.5674	.5194	.4972	.4761	.4371	.4019	.3411	.2910	.2495	.2149
6	.5066	.4556	.4323	.4104	.3704	.3349	.2751	.2274	.1890	.1580
7	.4523	.3996	.3759	.3538	.3139	.2791	.2218	.1776	.1432	.1162
8	.4039	.3506	.3269	.3050	.2660	.2326	.1789	.1388	.1085	.0854
9	.3606	.3075	.2843	.2630	.2255	.1938	.1443	.1084	.0822	.0628
10	.3220	.2697	.2472	.2267	.1911	.1615	.1164	.0847	.0623	.0462
11	.2875	.2366	.2149	.1954	.1619	.1346	.0938	.0662	.0472	.0340
12	.2567	.2076	.1869	.1685	.1372	.1122	.0757	.0517	.0357	.0250
13	.2292	.1821	.1625	.1452	.1163	.0935	.0610	.0404	.0271	.0184
14	.2046	.1597	.1413	.1252	.0985	.0779	.0492	.0316	.0205	.0135
15	.1827	.1401	.1229	.1079	.0835	.0649	.0397	.0247	.0155	.0099
16	.1631	.1229	.1069	.0930	.0708	.0541	.0320	.0193	.0118	.0073
17	.1456	.1078	.0929	.0802	.0600	.0451	.0258	.0150	.0089	.0054
18	.1300	.0946	.0808	.0691	.0508	.0376	.0208	.0118	.0068	.0039
19	.1161	.0829	.0703	.0596	.0431	.0313	.0168	.0092	.0051	.0029
20	:1037	.0728	.0611	.0514	.0365	.0261	.0135	.0072	.0039	.0021
21	.0926	.0638	.0531	.0443	.0309	.0217	.0109	.0056	.0029	.0016
22	.0826	.0560	.0462	.0382	.0262	.0181	.0088	.0044	.0022	.0012
23	.0738	.0491	.0402	.0329	.0222	.0151	.0071	.0034	.0017	.0008
24	.0659	.0431	.0349	.0284	.0188	.0126	.0057	.0027	.0013	.0006
25	.0588	.0378	.0304	.0245	.0160	.0105	.0046	.0021	.0010	.0005
26	.0525	.0331	.0264	.0211	.0135	.0087	.0037	.0016	.0007	.0003
27	.0469	.0291	.0230	.0182	.0115	.0073	.0030	.0013	.0006	.0002
28	.0419	.0255	.0200	.0157	.0097	.0061	.0024	.0010	.0004	.0002
29	.0374	.0224	.0174	.0135	.0082	.0051	.0020	.0008	.0003	.0001
30	.0334	.0196	.0151	.0116	.0070	.0042	.0016	.0006	.0002	.0001
35	.0189	.0102	.0075	.0055	.0030	.0017	.0005	.0002	.0001	*
40	.0107	.0053	.0037	.0026	.0013	.0007	.0002	.0001	*	*
45	.0061	.0027	.0019	.0013	.0006	.0003	.0001	*	*	*
50	.0035	.0014	.0009	.0006	.0003	.0001	*	*	*	*
55	.0020	.0007	.0005	.0003	.0001	*	*	*	*	*

*The factor is zero to four decimal places.

Table A–2 **Present Value of an Annuity of $1 per Period for n Periods:** $PVIFA_{k,n} = \displaystyle\sum_{t=1}^{n} \dfrac{1}{(1+k)^t}$

$$= \dfrac{1 - \dfrac{1}{(1+k)^n}}{k}$$

Number of Payments	1%	2%	3%	4%	5%	6%	7%	8%	9%
1	0.9901	0.9804	0.9709	0.9615	0.9524	0.9434	0.9346	0.9259	0.9174
2	1.9704	1.9416	1.9135	1.8861	1.8594	1.8334	1.8080	1.7833	1.7591
3	2.9410	2.9839	2.8286	2.7751	2.7232	2.6730	2.6243	2.5771	2.5313
4	3.9020	3.8077	3.7171	3.6299	3.5460	3.4651	3.3872	3.3121	3.2397
5	4.8534	4.7135	4.5797	4.4518	4.3295	4.2124	4.1002	3.9927	3.8897
6	5.7955	5.6014	5.4172	5.2421	5.0757	4.9173	4.7665	4.6229	4.4859
7	6.7282	6.4720	6.2303	6.0021	5.7864	5.5824	5.3893	5.2064	5.0330
8	7.6517	7.3255	7.0197	6.7327	6.4632	6.2098	5.9713	5.7466	5.5348
9	8.5660	8.1622	7.7861	7.4353	7.1078	6.8017	6.5152	6.2469	5.9952
10	9.4713	8.9826	8.5302	8.1109	7.7217	7.3601	7.0236	6.7101	6.4177
11	10.3676	9.7868	9.2526	8.7605	8.3064	7.8869	7.4987	7.1390	6.8052
12	11.2551	10.5753	9.9540	9.3851	8.8633	8.3838	7.9427	7.5361	7.1607
13	12.1337	11.3484	10.6350	9.9856	9.3936	8.8527	8.3577	7.9038	7.4869
14	13.0037	12.1062	11.2961	10.5631	9.8986	9.2950	8.7455	8.2442	7.7862
15	13.8651	12.8493	11.9379	11.1184	10.3797	9.7122	9.1079	8.5595	8.0607
16	14.7179	13.5777	12.5611	11.6523	10.8378	10.1059	9.4466	8.8514	8.3126
17	15.5623	14.2919	13.1661	12.1657	11.2741	10.4773	9.7632	9.1216	8.5436
18	16.3983	14.9920	13.7535	12.6593	11.6896	10.8276	10.0591	9.3719	8.7556
19	17.2260	15.6785	14.3238	13.1339	12.0853	11.1581	10.3356	9.6036	8.9501
20	18.0456	16.3514	14.8775	13.5903	12.4622	11.4699	10.5940	9.8181	9.1285
21	18.8570	17.0112	15.4150	14.0292	12.8212	11.7641	10.8355	10.0168	9.2922
22	19.6604	17.6580	15.9369	14.4511	13.1630	12.0416	11.0612	10.2007	9.4424
23	20.4558	18.2922	16.4436	14.8568	13.4886	12.3034	11.2722	10.3711	9.5802
24	21.2434	18.9139	16.9355	15.2470	13.7986	12.5504	11.4693	10.5288	9.7066
25	22.0232	19.5235	17.4131	15.6221	14.0939	12.7834	11.6536	10.6748	9.8226
26	22.7952	20.1210	17.8768	15.9828	14.3752	13.0032	11.8258	10.8100	9.9290
27	23.5596	20.7069	18.3270	16.3296	14.6430	13.2105	11.9867	10.9352	10.0266
28	24.3164	21.2813	18.7641	16.6631	14.8981	13.4062	12.1371	11.0511	10.1161
29	25.0658	21.8444	19.1885	16.9837	15.1411	13.5907	12.2777	11.1584	10.1983
30	25.8077	22.3965	19.6004	17.2920	15.3725	13.7648	12.4090	11.2578	10.2737
35	29.4086	24.9986	21.4872	18.6646	16.3742	14.4982	12.9477	11.6546	10.5668
40	32.8347	27.3555	23.1148	19.7928	17.1591	15.0463	13.3317	11.9246	10.7574
45	36.0945	29.4902	24.5187	20.7200	17.7741	15.4558	13.6055	12.1084	10.8812
50	39.1961	31.4236	25.7298	21.4822	18.2559	15.7619	13.8007	12.2335	10.9617
55	42.1472	33.1748	26.7744	22.1086	18.6335	15.9905	13.9399	12.3186	11.0140

Table A–2   (continued)

Number of Payments	10%	12%	14%	15%	16%	18%	20%	24%	28%	32%
1	0.9091	0.8929	0.8772	0.8696	0.8621	0.8475	0.8333	0.8065	0.7813	0.7576
2	1.7355	1.6901	1.6467	1.6257	1.6052	1.5656	1.5278	1.4568	1.3916	1.3315
3	2.4869	2.4018	2.3216	2.2832	2.2459	2.1743	2.1065	1.9813	1.8684	1.7663
4	3.1699	3.0373	2.9137	2.8550	2.7982	2.6901	2.5887	2.4043	2.2410	2.0957
5	3.7908	3.6048	3.4331	3.3522	3.2743	3.1272	2.9906	2.7454	2.5320	2.3452
6	4.3553	4.1114	3.8887	3.7845	3.6847	3.4976	3.3255	3.0205	2.7594	2.5342
7	4.8684	4.5638	4.2883	4.1604	4.0386	3.8115	3.6046	3.2423	2.9370	2.6775
8	5.3349	4.9676	4.6389	4.4873	4.3436	4.0776	3.8372	3.4212	3.0758	2.7860
9	5.7590	5.3282	4.9464	4.7716	4.6065	4.3030	4.0310	3.5655	3.1842	2.8681
10	6.1446	5.6502	5.2161	5.0188	4.8332	4.4941	4.1925	3.6819	3.2689	2.9304
11	6.4951	5.9377	5.4527	5.2337	5.0286	4.6560	4.3271	3.7757	3.3351	2.9776
12	6.8137	6.1944	5.6603	5.4206	5.1971	4.7932	4.4392	3.8514	3.3868	3.0133
13	7.1034	6.4235	5.8424	5.5831	5.3423	4.9095	4.5327	3.9124	3.4272	3.0404
14	7.3667	6.6282	6.0021	5.7245	5.4675	5.0081	4.6106	3.9616	3.4587	3.0609
15	7.6061	6.8109	6.1422	5.8474	5.5755	5.0916	4.6755	4.0013	3.4834	3.0764
16	7.8237	6.9740	6.2651	5.9542	5.6685	5.1624	4.7296	4.0333	3.5026	3.0882
17	8.0216	7.1196	6.3729	6.0472	5.7487	5.2223	4.7746	4.0591	3.5177	3.0971
18	8.2014	7.2497	6.4674	6.1280	5.8178	5.2732	4.8122	4.0799	3.5294	3.1039
19	8.3649	7.3658	6.5504	6.1982	5.8775	5.3162	4.8435	4.0967	3.5386	3.1090
20	8.5136	7.4694	6.6231	6.2593	5.9288	5.3527	4.8696	4.1103	3.5458	3.1129
21	8.6487	7.5620	6.6870	6.3125	5.9731	5.3837	4.8913	4.1212	3.5514	3.1158
22	8.7715	7.6446	6.7429	6.3587	6.0113	5.4099	4.9094	4.1300	3.5558	3.1180
23	8.8832	7.7184	6.7921	6.3988	6.0442	5.4321	4.9245	4.1371	3.5592	3.1197
24	8.9847	7.7843	6.8351	6.4338	6.0726	5.4510	4.9371	4.1428	3.5619	3.1210
25	9.0770	7.8431	6.8729	6.4642	6.0971	5.4669	4.9476	4.1474	3.5640	3.1220
26	9.1609	7.8957	6.9061	6.4906	6.1182	5.4804	4.9563	4.1511	3.5656	3.1227
27	9.2372	7.9426	6.9352	6.5135	6.1364	5.4919	4.9636	4.1542	3.5669	3.1233
28	9.3066	7.9844	6.9607	6.5335	6.1520	5.5016	4.9697	4.1566	3.5679	3.1237
29	9.3696	8.0218	6.9830	6.5509	6.1656	5.5098	4.9747	4.1585	3.5687	3.1240
30	9.4269	8.0552	7.0027	6.5660	6.1772	5.5168	4.9789	4.1601	3.5693	3.1242
35	9.6442	8.1755	7.0700	6.6166	6.2153	5.5386	4.9915	4.1644	3.5708	3.1248
40	9.7791	8.2438	7.1050	6.6418	6.2335	5.5482	4.9966	4.1659	3.5712	3.1250
45	9.8628	8.2825	7.1232	6.6543	6.2421	5.5523	4.9986	4.1664	3.5714	3.1250
50	9.9148	8.3045	7.1327	6.6605	6.2463	5.5541	4.9995	4.1666	3.5714	3.1250
55	9.9471	8.3170	7.1376	6.6636	6.2482	5.5549	4.9998	4.1666	3.5714	3.1250

Table A–3   Future Value of \$1 at the End of n Periods: $\text{FVIF}_{k,n} = (1 + k)^n$

Period	1%	2%	3%	4%	5%	6%	7%	8%	9%	10%
1	1.0100	1.0200	1.0300	1.0400	1.0500	1.0600	1.0700	1.0800	1.0900	1.1000
2	1.0201	1.0404	1.0609	1.0816	1.1025	1.1236	1.1449	1.1664	1.1881	1.2100
3	1.0303	1.0612	1.0927	1.1249	1.1576	1.1910	1.2250	1.2597	1.2950	1.3310
4	1.0406	1.0824	1.1255	1.1699	1.2155	1.2625	1.3108	1.3605	1.4116	1.4641
5	1.0510	1.1041	1.1593	1.2167	1.2763	1.3382	1.4026	1.4693	1.5386	1.6105
6	1.0615	1.1262	1.1941	1.2653	1.3401	1.4185	1.5007	1.5869	1.6771	1.7716
7	1.0721	1.1487	1.2299	1.3159	1.4071	1.5036	1.6058	1.7138	1.8280	1.9487
8	1.0829	1.1717	1.2668	1.3686	1.4775	1.5938	1.7182	1.8509	1.9926	2.1436
9	1.0937	1.1951	1.3048	1.4233	1.5513	1.6895	1.8385	1.9990	2.1719	2.3579
10	1.1046	1.2190	1.3439	1.4802	1.6289	1.7908	1.9672	2.1589	2.3674	2.5937
11	1.1157	1.2434	1.3842	1.5395	1.7103	1.8983	2.1049	2.3316	2.5804	2.8531
12	1.1268	1.2682	1.4258	1.6010	1.7959	2.0122	2.2522	2.5182	2.8127	3.1384
13	1.1381	1.2936	1.4685	1.6651	1.8856	2.1329	2.4098	2.7196	3.0658	3.4523
14	1.1495	1.3195	1.5126	1.7317	1.9799	2.2609	2.5785	2.9372	3.3417	3.7975
15	1.1610	1.3459	1.5580	1.8009	2.0789	2.3966	2.7590	3.1722	3.6425	4.1772
16	1.1726	1.3728	1.6047	1.8730	2.1829	2.5404	2.9522	3.4259	3.9703	4.5950
17	1.1843	1.4002	1.6528	1.9479	2.2920	2.6928	3.1588	3.7000	4.3276	5.0545
18	1.1961	1.4282	1.7024	2.0258	2.4066	2.8543	3.3799	3.9960	4.7171	5.5599
19	1.2081	1.4568	1.7535	2.1068	2.5270	3.0256	3.6165	4.3157	5.1417	6.1159
20	1.2202	1.4859	1.8061	2.1911	2.6533	3.2071	3.8697	4.6610	5.6044	6.7275
21	1.2324	1.5157	1.8603	2.2788	2.7860	3.3996	4.1406	5.0338	6.1088	7.4002
22	1.2447	1.5460	1.9161	2.3699	2.9253	3.6035	4.4304	5.4365	6.6586	8.1403
23	1.2572	1.5769	1.9736	2.4647	3.0715	3.8197	4.7405	5.8715	7.2579	8.9543
24	1.2697	1.6084	2.0328	2.5633	3.2251	4.0489	5.0724	6.3412	7.9111	9.8497
25	1.2824	1.6406	2.0938	2.6658	3.3864	4.2919	5.4274	6.8485	8.6231	10.834
26	1.2953	1.6734	2.1566	2.7725	3.5557	4.5494	5.8074	7.3964	9.3992	11.918
27	1.3082	1.7069	2.2213	2.8834	3.7335	4.8223	6.2139	7.9881	10.245	13.110
28	1.3213	1.7410	2.2879	2.9987	3.9201	5.1117	6.6488	8.6271	11.167	14.421
29	1.3345	1.7758	2.3566	3.1187	4.1161	5.4184	7.1143	9.3173	12.172	15.863
30	1.3478	1.8114	2.4273	3.2434	4.3219	5.7435	7.6123	10.062	13.267	17.449
40	1.4889	2.2080	3.2620	4.8010	7.0400	10.285	14.974	21.724	31.409	45.259
50	1.6446	2.6916	4.3839	7.1067	11.467	18.420	29.457	46.901	74.357	117.39
60	1.8167	3.2810	5.8916	10.519	18.679	32.987	57.946	101.25	176.03	304.48

Table A–3 **(continued)**

Period	12%	14%	15%	16%	18%	20%	24%	28%	32%	36%
1	1.1200	1.1400	1.1500	1.1600	1.1800	1.2000	1.2400	1.2800	1.3200	1.3600
2	1.2544	1.2996	1.3225	1.3456	1.3924	1.4400	1.5376	1.6384	1.7424	1.8496
3	1.4049	1.4815	1.5209	1.5609	1.6430	1.7280	1.9066	2.0972	2.3000	2.5155
4	1.5735	1.6890	1.7490	1.8106	1.9388	2.0736	2.3642	2.6844	3.0360	3.4210
5	1.7623	1.9254	2.0114	2.1003	2.2878	2.4883	2.9316	3.4360	4.0075	4.6526
6	1.9738	2.1950	2.3131	2.4364	2.6996	2.9860	3.6352	4.3980	5.2899	6.3275
7	2.2107	2.5023	2.6600	2.8262	3.1855	3.5832	4.5077	5.6295	6.9826	8.6054
8	2.4760	2.8526	3.0590	3.2784	3.7589	4.2998	5.5895	7.2058	9.2170	11.703
9	2.7731	3.2519	3.5179	3.8030	4.4355	5.1598	6.9310	9.2234	12.166	15.916
10	3.1058	3.7072	4.0456	4.4114	5.2338	6.1917	8.5944	11.805	16.059	21.646
11	3.4785	4.2262	4.6524	5.1173	6.1759	7.4301	10.657	15.111	21.198	29.439
12	3.8960	4.8179	5.3502	5.9360	7.2876	8.9161	13.214	19.342	27.982	40.037
13	4.3635	5.4924	6.1528	6.8858	8.5994	10.699	16.386	24.758	36.937	54.451
14	4.8871	6.2613	7.0757	7.9875	10.147	12.839	20.319	31.691	48.756	74.053
15	5.4736	7.1379	8.1371	9.2655	11.973	15.407	25.195	40.564	64.358	100.71
16	6.1304	8.1372	9.3576	10.748	14.129	18.488	31.242	51.923	84.953	136.96
17	6.8660	9.2765	10.761	12.467	16.672	22.186	38.740	66.461	112.13	186.27
18	7.6900	10.575	12.375	14.462	19.673	26.623	48.038	85.070	148.02	253.33
19	8.6128	12.055	14.231	16.776	23.214	31.948	59.567	108.89	195.39	344.53
20	9.6463	13.743	16.366	19.460	27.393	38.337	73.864	139.37	257.91	468.57
21	10.803	15.667	18.821	22.574	32.323	46.005	91.591	178.40	340.44	637.26
22	12.100	17.861	21.644	26.186	38.142	55.206	113.57	228.35	449.39	866.67
23	13.552	20.361	24.891	30.376	45.007	66.247	140.83	292.30	593.19	1178.6
24	15.178	23.212	28.625	35.236	53.108	79.496	174.63	374.14	783.02	1602.9
25	17.000	26.461	32.918	40.874	62.668	95.396	216.54	478.90	1033.5	2180.0
26	19.040	30.166	37.856	47.414	73.948	114.47	268.51	612.99	1364.3	2964.9
27	21.324	34.389	43.535	55.000	87.259	137.37	332.95	784.63	1800.9	4032.2
28	23.883	39.204	50.065	63.800	102.96	164.84	412.86	1004.3	2377.2	5483.8
29	26.749	44.693	57.575	74.008	121.50	197.81	511.95	1285.5	3137.9	7458.0
30	29.959	50.950	66.211	85.849	143.37	237.37	634.81	1645.5	4142.0	10143.
40	93.050	188.88	267.86	378.72	750.37	1469.7	5455.9	19426.	66520.	*
50	289.00	700.23	1083.6	1670.7	3927.3	9100.4	46890.	*	*	*
60	897.59	2595.9	4383.9	7370.1	20555.	56347.	*	*	*	*

*FVIF > 99,999.

Table A–4 Sum of an Annuity of $1 per Period for _n_ Periods: $FVIFA_{k,n} = \sum\limits_{t=1}^{n} (1 + k)^{n-t}$

$$= \frac{(1 + k)^n - 1}{k}$$

Number of Periods	1%	2%	3%	4%	5%	6%	7%	8%	9%	10%
1	1.0000	1.0000	1.0000	1.0000	1.0000	1.0000	1.0000	1.0000	1.0000	1.0000
2	2.0100	2.0200	2.0300	2.0400	2.0500	2.0600	2.0700	2.0800	2.0900	2.1000
3	3.0301	3.0604	3.0909	3.1216	3.1525	3.1836	3.2149	3.2464	3.2781	3.3100
4	4.0604	4.1216	4.1836	4.2465	4.3101	4.3746	4.4399	4.5061	4.5731	4.6410
5	5.1010	5.2040	5.3091	5.4163	5.5256	5.6371	5.7507	5.8666	5.9847	6.1051
6	6.1520	6.3081	6.4684	6.6330	6.8019	6.9753	7.1533	7.3359	7.5233	7.7156
7	7.2135	7.4343	7.6625	7.8983	8.1420	8.3938	8.6540	8.9228	9.2004	9.4872
8	8.2857	8.5830	8.8923	9.2142	9.5491	9.8975	10.259	10.636	11.028	11.435
9	9.3685	9.7546	10.159	10.582	11.026	11.491	11.978	12.487	13.021	13.579
10	10.462	10.949	11.463	12.006	12.577	13.180	13.816	14.486	15.192	15.937
11	11.566	12.168	12.807	13.486	14.206	14.971	15.783	16.645	17.560	18.531
12	12.682	13.412	14.192	15.025	15.917	16.869	17.888	18.977	20.140	21.384
13	13.809	14.680	15.617	16.626	17.713	18.882	20.140	21.495	22.953	24.522
14	14.947	15.973	17.086	18.291	19.598	21.015	22.550	24.214	26.019	27.975
15	16.096	17.293	18.598	20.023	21.578	23.276	25.129	27.152	29.360	31.772
16	17.257	18.639	20.156	21.824	23.657	25.672	27.888	30.324	33.003	35.949
17	18.430	20.012	21.761	23.697	25.840	28.212	30.840	33.750	36.973	40.544
18	19.614	21.412	23.414	25.645	28.132	30.905	33.999	37.450	41.301	45.599
19	20.810	22.840	25.116	27.671	30.539	33.760	37.379	41.446	46.018	51.159
20	22.019	24.297	26.870	29.778	33.066	36.785	40.995	45.762	51.160	57.275
21	23.239	25.783	28.676	31.969	35.719	39.992	44.865	50.422	56.764	64.002
22	24.471	27.299	30.536	34.248	38.505	43.392	49.005	55.456	62.873	71.402
23	25.716	28.845	32.452	36.617	41.430	46.995	53.436	60.893	69.531	79.543
24	26.973	30.421	34.426	39.082	44.502	50.815	58.176	66.764	76.789	88.497
25	28.243	32.030	36.459	41.645	47.727	54.864	63.249	73.105	84.700	98.347
26	29.525	33.670	38.553	44.311	51.113	59.156	68.676	79.954	93.323	109.18
27	30.820	35.344	40.709	47.084	54.669	63.705	74.483	87.350	102.72	121.09
28	32.129	37.051	42.930	49.967	58.402	68.528	80.697	95.338	112.96	134.20
29	33.450	38.792	45.218	52.966	62.322	73.639	87.346	103.96	124.13	148.63
30	34.784	40.568	47.575	56.084	66.438	79.058	94.460	113.28	136.30	164.49
40	48.886	60.402	75.401	95.025	120.79	154.76	199.63	259.05	337.88	442.59
50	64.463	84.579	112.79	152.66	209.34	290.33	406.52	573.76	815.08	1163.9
60	81.669	114.05	163.05	237.99	353.58	533.12	813.52	1253.2	1944.7	3034.8

Table A–4 (continued)

Number of Periods	12%	14%	15%	16%	18%	20%	24%	28%	32%	36%
1	1.0000	1.0000	1.0000	1.0000	1.0000	1.0000	1.0000	1.0000	1.0000	1.0000
2	2.1200	2.1400	2.1500	2.1600	2.1800	2.2000	2.2400	2.2800	2.3200	2.3600
3	3.3744	3.4396	3.4725	3.5056	3.5724	3.6400	3.7776	3.9184	4.0624	4.2096
4	4.7793	4.9211	4.9934	5.0665	5.2154	5.3680	5.6842	6.0156	6.3624	6.7251
5	6.3528	6.6101	6.7424	6.8771	7.1542	7.4416	8.0484	8.6999	9.3983	10.146
6	8.1152	8.5355	8.7537	8.9775	9.4420	9.9299	10.980	12.135	13.405	14.798
7	10.089	10.730	11.066	11.413	12.141	12.915	14.615	16.533	18.695	21.126
8	12.299	13.232	13.726	14.240	15.327	16.499	19.122	22.163	25.678	29.731
9	14.775	16.085	16.785	17.518	19.085	20.798	24.712	29.369	34.895	41.435
10	17.548	19.337	20.303	21.321	23.521	25.958	31.643	38.592	47.061	57.351
11	20.654	23.044	24.349	25.732	28.755	32.150	40.237	50.398	63.121	78.998
12	24.133	27.270	29.001	30.850	34.931	39.580	50.894	65.510	84.320	108.43
13	28.029	32.088	34.351	36.786	42.218	48.496	64.109	84.852	112.30	148.47
14	32.392	37.581	40.504	43.672	50.818	59.195	80.496	109.61	149.23	202.92
15	37.279	43.842	47.580	51.659	60.965	72.035	100.81	141.30	197.99	276.97
16	42.753	50.980	55.717	60.925	72.939	87.442	126.01	181.86	262.35	377.69
17	48.883	59.117	65.075	71.673	87.068	105.93	157.25	233.79	347.30	514.66
18	55.749	68.394	75.836	84.140	103.74	128.11	195.99	300.25	459.44	700.93
19	63.439	78.969	88.211	98.603	123.41	154.74	244.03	385.32	607.47	954.27
20	72.052	91.024	102.44	115.37	146.62	186.68	303.60	494.21	802.86	1298.8
21	81.698	104.76	118.81	134.84	174.02	225.02	377.46	633.59	1060.7	1767.3
22	92.502	120.43	137.63	157.41	206.34	271.03	469.05	811.99	1401.2	2404.6
23	104.60	138.29	159.27	183.60	244.48	326.23	582.62	1040.3	1850.6	3271.3
24	118.15	158.65	184.16	213.97	289.49	392.48	723.46	1332.6	2443.8	4449.9
25	133.33	181.87	212.79	249.21	342.60	471.98	898.09	1706.8	3226.8	6052.9
26	150.33	208.33	245.71	290.08	405.27	567.37	1114.6	2185.7	4260.4	8233.0
27	169.37	238.49	283.56	337.50	479.22	681.85	1383.1	2798.7	5624.7	11197.9
28	190.69	272.88	327.10	392.50	566.48	819.22	1716.0	3583.3	7425.6	15230.2
29	214.58	312.09	377.16	456.30	669.44	984.06	2128.9	4587.6	9802.9	20714.1
30	241.33	356.78	434.74	530.31	790.94	1181.8	2640.9	5873.2	12940.	28172.2
40	767.09	1342.0	1779.0	2360.7	4163.2	7343.8	22728.	69377.	*	*
50	2400.0	4994.5	7217.7	10435.	21813.	45497.	*	*	*	*
60	7471.6	18535.	29219.	46057.	*	*	*	*	*	*

*FVIFA > 99,999.

APPENDIX B

ANSWERS TO SELECTED END-OF-CHAPTER PROBLEMS

We present here some of the intermediate steps and final answers to selected end-of-chapter problems. These are provided to aid the student in determining whether he or she is on the right track in the solution process. The primary limitation of this approach is that some of the problems may have *more than one* correct solution, depending upon which of several equally appropriate assumptions are made in the solution. Furthermore, there are often differences in answers due to rounding errors and/or other computational considerations. Many of the problems involve some verbal discussion as well as numerical calculations. This verbal material is *not* presented here.

Chapter 2	Background Information: Forms of Organization, Capital Markets, and Taxes
2–1	$31,350.
2–2	a. $26,750; b. $4,600; c. $690.

Chapter 3	The Time Value of Money
3–3	a. 7 years.
3–4	a. $1,593.74.
3–5	a. $614.46.
3–8	Approximately 15%.
3–10	c. 5%.
3–14	9%.
3–15	a. $17,730.
3–16	b. $136.86; d. $112.68.
3–17	a. $73.07.
3–21	a. $98,657; b. $2,920.
3–22	$2,827.

Chapter 4	Stock and Bond Values
4–1	a–1. $1,294.41; a–3. $887.02; b–2. $1,009.14.
4–3	a. $1,116.52; b. $898.90.

4–4	a. D_3 = \$2.32; b. PV = \$5.48; d. \$42.01.
4–5	b. 5%.
4–6	a–1. \$4.75.
4–7	c. \$805.94; f–1. 5.23%; Capital gains 1969 to 1986 = 1.77%.
4–8	\$21.43.

Chapter 5 Risk and Rates of Return

5–1	a. $\hat{k}_B$ = 12%.
5–2	a. k_A = 13.60%.
5–5	a. old P_0 = \$49.20.
5–6	a. k_D = 5.0%; b. P_C = \$32.61.
5–7	a. k_i = 5% + b_i (5%); c. k_D = 17.5%.

Chapter 6 Analysis of Financial Statements

6–1	ROE = 4.8%; ROA = 3%; Total asset utilization = 1.43.
6–2	ROE = 7.1%; ROA = 5%; Total asset utilization = 1.77.
6–3	a. Total sources = \$117 million; b. Net increase in working capital = \$12 million.
6–5	a. EPS growth = 6% to 7% depending on procedure used.

Chapter 7 Financial Forecasting

7–1	b. \$1,790,000.
7–2	a. \$5,398,750; c. Current ratio = 1.88 times; d–1. −\$2,250,000.
7–3	b. \$720,000.
7–4	a. Total assets = \$78,480,000; c. Total assets = \$86,976,000.

Chapter 8 Cash and Marketable Securities

| 8–1 | b. \$750,000; −\$3,250,000. |
| 8–3 | a. Surplus in July: \$426,000; loan in September: \$759,500. |

Chapter 9 Accounts Receivable and Inventories

9–1	a. 28 days; c. \$18,333.26.
9–2	a. \$9,000; d. \$4,404.
9–3	a. 4,000 units; c. 12,500.
9–4	b. 21 days; d. 27 days; e. EOQ = 1,000 units; avg. inv. = \$10,000.

Chapter 10 Financing Current Assets: Short-Term Credit

10–1	a. 29.4%.
10–2	a. 29.4%.
10–3	a. \$33,333; c. 36.73%.
10–4	b. 8.7%; c. 12%, or 14.5%, or 16%, depending on procedure.
10–6	a. \$150,000.
10–7	a. 60 days; b. 14.69%.
10–8	a–1. 18.18%; a–2. 12.68%.
10A–1	b. Total costs = \$160,800; 15.12%.

Chapter 11   The Basics of Capital Budgeting

11-1   c. IRR = 10%.
11-2   b. NPV = $2,053.77.
11-3   c. IRR_S = 21.525%.
11-4   a. X = $2^1/_6$ years;   c. IRR_Y = 15%.
11-5   a. NPV_A = $1,200.74.
11-7   a. PV of Inflows = $1,760,434; NPV = $72,718.   b. *New Net* Cash
         Flow = $451,400; new NPV = −$98,427.

Chapter 12   Other Topics in Capital Budgeting

12-1   b. k_A = 10.8%.
12-2   NPV = −$5,202.
12-3   a. PV of Outflows = $244,000; NPV = $23,447.
12-4   PV of Inflows = $35,302; NPV = $14,652.

Chapter 13   Long-Term Debt and Preferred Stock

13-1   a. $500,914.17.
13-2   R = $395,053.92, I_1 = $90,000, I_2 = $62,545.15.
13-5   a. 100%, 100%, 100%, 33%;   d. 100%, 33%, 0%, 0%.
13-6   c. $7,586,793.
13-7   c-1. $80.04;   c-2. 24%;   d. $41.96; $150.

Chapter 14   Common Stock

14-1   j. $22.50 to $30.00.
14B-1 $5.00.
14B-3   a. $3.00.

Chapter 15   The Target Capital Structure

15-1   c. $400,000.
15-3   b. D/A = 30%.
15A-1   e. CLE_A = 30, CLE_A = 3.64.

Chapter 16   The Cost of Capital

16-1   b. 6%.
16-3   b. D_1 = $0.864.
16-4   For D/A = 20%, k_a = 11.26%.
16-5   b. Breaking point = $15 million.
16-6   a. F = 15%.
16-7   c. $12 million;   d. k_e = 12.4%;   f. MCC below break = 8.40%.
16-8   b. MCC_1 = 8.73%.
16-9   a. k_s = 12%;   d. MCC = 10.15%.
16-10   c. MCC_1 = 9.84%;   d. IRR_c ≈ 10%.

Chapter 17   Dividend Policy

17-1   Total Assets = $1,979,200,000.
17-2   a. 6.53%, 6.82%;   b. $33.6 million.

Chapter 18 Multinational Finance

18-1   0.5882 pounds per dollar.
18-3   Total value of equity = $514.29 million.
18-5   a. NPV of regular dollar dividends = $21.59 million;
        b. Liquidating dividend (total value) = 107.54 million ringos.

Chapter 19 Mergers

19-1   c. ER ≈ 0.2168;   e. TE = $18 million, ER ≈ 0.2941.
19-2   b. EPS = $2.625;   c. $39.375.

Chapter 20 Bankruptcy and Reorganization

20-1   a. Total assets = $327 million;   e. D/A (before) = 35.7%, D/A
        (after) = 64.2%.

Chapter 21 Leasing

21-3   Annual payment = $26,380 (Borrow and Buy), Annual payment =
        $25,046 (Lease); NAL = $3,170.

Chapter 22 Warrants, Convertibles, and Options

22-1   a. P_s = $30, FV = $5;   b. P_s = $20, Warrant = $2, Premium = $7.
22-2   a. $46.20 to $50.40.
22-4   a. Alternative #1: Total assets = $800,000;   b. Percent of
        ownership, Plan #2 = 53%;   c. EPS, Plan #3 = $0.73;   d. D/A
        ratio, Plan #1 = 19%.

GLOSSARY

Absolute Priority Doctrine. In bankruptcy proceedings, the doctrine that states that claims must be paid in strict accordance with the priority of each claim, regardless of the consequence to other claimants.

Accelerated Depreciation. Depreciation methods that write off the cost of an asset at a faster rate than the write-off under the straight line method. The three principal methods of accelerated depreciation are: (1) sum-of-years'-digits, (2) double declining balance, and (3) units of production.

Accruals. Continually recurring short-term liabilities. Examples are accrued wages, accrued taxes, and accrued interest.

Add-on Interest. Interest calculated and added to funds received to determine the face amount of the note.

Aging Schedule. A report showing how long accounts receivable have been outstanding. It gives the percent of receivables not past due and the percent past due by, for example, one month, two months, or other periods.

Amortization Schedule. A schedule that shows precisely how a loan will be repaid. The schedule gives the required payment on each specific date and a breakdown of the payment showing how much of it constitutes interest and how much constitutes repayment of principal.

Amortize. To liquidate on an installment basis; an amortized loan is one in which the principal amount of the loan is repaid in installments during the life of the loan.

Annual Percentage Rate (APR). The effective annual rate of interest being charged on a credit agreement. The APR may differ from the stated rate.

Annual Report. A report, issued annually by corporations to their stockholders, which contains basic financial statements as well as management's opinion of the past year's operations and prospects for the future.

Annuity. A series of payments of a fixed amount for a specified number of years.

Annuity, Deferred. A series of payments of a fixed amount for a specified number of periods where the payments occur at the end of the period.

Annuity Due. A series of payments of a fixed amount for a specified number of periods where the payments occur at the beginning of the period.

Arrearage. Overdue payment; frequently, an omitted dividend on preferred stock.

Asked Price. The price at which a dealer or specialist in securities will sell shares of stock out of inventory.

Assignment. A relatively inexpensive way of liquidating a failing firm that does not involve going through the courts.

Automatic Dividend Reinvestment (ADR). An arrangement whereby stockholders automatically reinvest their dividends in the stock of the paying corporation.

Average Collection Period. Accounts receivable divided by credit sales per day. It represents the average length of time a firm must wait after making a sale before receiving cash.

Balloon Payment. When a debt is not fully amortized, the final payment that is larger than the preceding payments.

Bankruptcy. A legal procedure for formally liquidating a business, carried out under the jurisdiction of courts of law.

Bankruptcy Reform Act of 1978. Legislation enacted to speed up and streamline bankruptcy proceedings. This law represents a shift to a relative priority doctrine of creditors' claims.

Beta Coefficient. A measurement of the extent to which the returns on a given stock move with the stock market.

Beta Risk. Risk of a firm measured from the standpoint of an investor who holds a highly diversified portfolio.

Bid Price. The price a dealer or specialist in securities will pay for a stock.

Blue Sky Laws. State laws that prevent the sale of securities that have little or no asset backing.

Bond. A long-term debt instrument.

Book Value. The accounting value of an asset. The book value of a share of common stock is equal to the net worth (common stock plus retained earnings) of the corporation divided by the number of shares of stock outstanding.

Breakeven Analysis. An analytical technique for studying the relationships among fixed cost, variable cost, and profits. A breakeven *chart* graphically depicts the nature of breakeven analysis. The breakeven *point* represents the volume of sales at which total costs equal total revenues (that is, profits equal zero).

Business Failure. Condition when a business has terminated with a loss to creditors.

Business Risk. The basic risk inherent in a firm's operations. Business risk plus financial risk resulting from the use of debt equals total corporate risk.

Call. (1) An option to buy (or "call") a share of stock at a specified price within a specified period. (2) The process of redeeming a bond or preferred stock issue before its normal maturity.

Call Premium. The amount in excess of par value that a company must pay when it calls a security.

Call Price. The price that must be paid when a security is called. The call price is equal to the par value plus the call premium.

Call Privilege. A provision incorporated into a bond or a share of preferred stock that gives the issuer the right to redeem (call) the security at a specified price.

Call Provision. A provision in a bond contract that gives the issuer the right to redeem the bonds under specified terms prior to the normal maturity date.

Capital Asset. An asset with a life of more than one year that is not bought and sold in the ordinary course of business.

Capital Asset Pricing Model (CAPM). A model based on the proposition that any stock's required rate of return is equal to the riskless rate of return plus its risk premium.

Capital Budgeting. The process of planning expenditures on assets whose returns are expected to extend beyond one year.

Capital Gains. Profits on the sale of capital assets held for one year or more.

Capital Gains Yield. In any year, the capital gains yield is equal to the capital gain during the year divided by the beginning price.

Capital Intensity. The amount of assets required to finance each dollar of sales.

Capital Losses. Losses on the sale of capital assets.

Capital Market Line. A graphical representation of the relationship between risk and the required rate of return.

Capital Rationing. A situation where a constraint is placed on the total size of the capital investment during a particular period.

Capital Structure. The percentage of each type of capital used by the firm—debt, preferred stock, and net worth. (Net worth consists of capital, paid-in capital, and retained earnings.)

Capitalization Rate. A discount rate used to find the present value of a series of future cash receipts. Sometimes called *discount rate.*

Carry-back; Carry-forward. For income tax purposes, losses that can be carried backward or forward to reduce federal income taxes.

Cash Budget. A schedule showing cash flows (receipts, disbursements, and net cash) for a firm over a specified period.

Characteristic Line. A linear least squares regression line that shows the relationship between an individual security's return and returns on "the market." The slope of the characteristic line is the beta coefficient.

Charter. A formal legal document which describes the scope and nature of a corporation and defines the rights and duties of its stockholders and managers.

Chattel Mortgage. A mortgage on personal property (not real estate). A mortgage on equipment would be a chattel mortgage.

Closely Held Corporation. A corporation that is not publicly owned; a corporation owned by a few individuals who are typically associated with the management of the firm. Also called a *closed corporation.*

Coefficient of Variation. Standard deviation divided by the mean.

Collateral. Assets that are used to secure a loan.

Commercial Paper. Unsecured, short-term promissory notes of large firms, usually issued in denominations of $1 million or more. The rate of interest on commercial paper is typically somewhat below the prime rate of interest.

Commitment Fee. The fee paid to a lender for a formal line of credit.

Company Specific Risk. That part of a security's risk associated with random events; such risk can be eliminated by proper diversification.

Compensating Balance. A required minimum checking account balance that a firm must maintain with a commercial bank. The balance is generally equal to 15 to 20 percent of the amount of loans outstanding. Compensating balances can raise the effective rate of interest on bank loans.

Composite Cost of Capital. A weighted average of the component costs of debt, preferred stock, and common equity. Also called the "weighted average cost of capital," it reflects the cost of each additional dollar raised, not the average cost of all capital the firm has raised throughout its history.

Composition. An informal method of reorganization in which creditors voluntarily reduce their claims on the debtor firm.

Compound Interest. An interest rate that is applicable when interest in succeeding periods is earned not only on the initial principal but also on the accumulated interest of prior periods.

Compounding. The arithmetic process of determining the final value of a payment or series of payments when compound interest is applied.

Conditional Sales Contract. A method of financing new equipment by paying it off in installments over a one-to-five-year period. The seller retains title to the equipment until payment has been completed.

Congeneric Merger. A merger between firms in the same general industry, where the merger partners are neither customers nor suppliers of one another. The term was first used in connection with mergers between financial institutions, as, for example, when a bank holding company acquired a mortgage service company or a leasing company.

Conglomerate Merger. A merger between companies in different industries. If a grocery chain acquired a steel company, then a conglomerate corporation would result.

Consolidated Tax Return. An income tax return that combines the income statements of several affiliated firms.

Continuous Compounding (Discounting). As opposed to discrete compounding, a situation where interest is added continuously rather than at discrete points in time.

Conversion Price. The effective price paid for common stock when the stock is obtained by converting either convertible preferred stocks or convertible bonds. For example, if a $1,000 bond is convertible into twenty shares of stock, the conversion price is $50 (= $1,000/20).

Conversion Ratio or Conversion Rate. The number of shares of common stock that may be obtained by converting a convertible bond or share of convertible preferred stock.

Convertibles. Securities (generally bonds or preferred stocks) that are exchangeable at the option of the holder for common stock of the issuing firm.

Correlation Coefficient. A measurement of the degree of relationship between two variables.

Cost of Capital. The discount rate that should be used in the capital budgeting process.

Coupon Rate. The stated rate of interest on a bond.

Covenant. Detailed clause in loan agreements, designed to protect lenders. It includes such items as limits on total indebtedness, restrictions on dividends, minimum current ratio, and similar provisions.

Covered Options. Options sold by an investor against stock held in a portfolio.

Cumulative Dividends. A protective feature on preferred stock that requires all past preferred dividends to be paid before any common dividends are paid.

Current Ratio. Current assets divided by current liabilities. This ratio indicates the extent to which the claims of short-term creditors are covered by assets expected to be converted to cash in the near future.

Cut-off Point. In the capital budgeting process, the minimum rate of return on acceptable investment opportunities.

Debenture. A long-term debt instrument that is not secured by a mortgage on specific property.

Debt Ratio. Total debt divided by total assets.

Default. The failure to fulfill a contract; generally, the failure to pay interest or principal on debt obligations.

Default Risk. Risk that an issuer of securities will not be able to make interest payments or repay the principal amount on schedule.

Degree of Leverage. The percentage increase in profits resulting from a given percentage increase in sales. The degree of leverage may be calculated for financial leverage, operating leverage, or both combined.

Devaluation. The process of reducing the value of a country's currency stated in terms of other currencies; for example, the British pound might be devalued from $2.30 for one pound to $2.00 for one pound.

Development Bond. Bond sold by a government agency to raise funds to be used for economic development in a specific geographic region. Typically, a corporation agrees to build a plant in a local area, and the area's development agency sells tax exempt bonds, uses the proceeds to build the plant to the company's specifications, leases the plant to the company, and uses the lease payments to service the bond.

Discount Rate. The interest rate used in the

discounting process; sometimes called *capitalization rate.*

Discounted Cash Flow Techniques. Methods of ranking investment proposals, including (1) internal rate of return method, (2) net present value method, and (3) profitability index or benefit/cost ratio.

Discounting. The process of finding the present value of a series of future cash flows. Discounting is the reverse of compounding.

Discounting of Accounts Receivable. Short-term financing where accounts receivable are used to secure the loan. The lender does not *buy* the accounts receivable but simply uses them as collateral for the loan. Also called *pledging of accounts receivable.*

Dividend Yield. The ratio of the current dividend to the current price of a share of stock.

du Pont System. A system of analysis designed to show the relationships among return on investment, asset turnover, and the profit margin.

EBIT. Abbreviation for *earnings before interest and taxes.*

Economic Failure. Condition that exists when a firm's revenues do not cover its total costs, including its cost of capital.

Economic Ordering Quantity (EOQ). The optimum (least cost) quantity of merchandise which should be ordered.

Efficient Market Hypothesis. The hypothesis that securities are typically in equilibrium—that they are fairly priced in the sense that the price reflects all available information on the security.

Efficient Portfolio. The portfolio of securities that provides the highest possible expected return for any degree of risk or the lowest degree of risk for any expected return.

EPS. Abbreviation for *earnings per share.*

Equilibrium. A situation in which there is no systematic tendency for change. If a security is in equilibrium, then there is no pressure for its price to change.

Equity. The net worth of a business, consisting of capital stock, capital (or paid-in) surplus, earned surplus (or retained earnings), and, occasionally, certain net worth reserves. *Common equity* is that part of the total net worth belonging to the common stockholders. *Total equity* includes preferred stockholders. The terms *common stock, net worth,* and *common equity* are frequently used interchangeably.

Equivalent Annual Annuity. The NPV of a project over its original life divided by the annuity factor for the original life. The equivalent annual annuity provides a means to compare mutually exclusive projects of unequal lives.

Eurobond. A bond sold in a country other than the one in whose currency the bond is denominated.

Eurodollar. A United States dollar on deposit in a foreign bank—generally, but not necessarily, a European bank.

Ex Ante. Before the fact. Opposite of ex post.

Ex Dividend Date. The date on which the right to the current dividend no longer accompanies a stock. (For listed stock, the ex dividend date is four working days prior to the date of record.)

Ex Post. After the fact. Opposite of ex ante.

Ex Rights. The date on which stock purchase rights are no longer transferred to the purchaser of the stock.

Exchange Rate. The number of units of a given currency that can be purchased for one unit of another currency.

Exchange Ratio. In mergers, the number of shares the acquiring firm must give for each of the acquired firm's shares.

Excise Tax. A tax on the manufacture, sale, or consumption of specified commodities.

Exercise Price. The price that must be paid for a share of common stock when it is bought by exercising a warrant.

Expected Return. The rate of return a firm expects to realize from an investment. The expected return is the mean value of the probability distribution of possible returns.

Expected Value. The weighted average of all possible outcomes, where the weights are the probabilities of all expected outcomes.

Extension. An informal method of reorganization in which the creditors voluntarily postpone the date of required payment on past-due obligations.

External Funds. Funds acquired through borrowing or by selling new common or preferred stock.

Factoring. A method of financing accounts receivable under which a firm sells its accounts receivable (generally without recourse) to a financial institution (the "factor").

Feasible Set. Hypothetical set of all possible portfolios; also known as *attainable set*.

Federal Reserve System. The central banking system in the United States.

Field Warehousing. A method of financing inventories in which a "warehouse" is established at the place of business of the borrowing firm.

Financial Institutions. Establishments that handle monetary affairs, including insurance companies, commercial banks, savings and loans, leasing companies, and institutional investors.

Financial Lease. A lease that does not provide for maintenance services, is not cancellable, and is fully amortized over its life.

Financial Leverage. The ratio of total debt to total assets. There are other measures of financial leverage, especially ones that relate cash inflows to required cash outflows. In this book, either the debt/total asset ratio or the debt/total market value ratio is generally used to measure leverage.

Financial Risk. The portion of total corporate risk over and above basic business risk that results from using debt.

Financial Structure. The entire right-hand side of the balance sheet—the way a firm is financed.

Fixed Charges. Costs that do not vary with the level of output, especially fixed financial costs

such as interest, lease payments, and sinking fund payments.

Fixed Exchange Rate System. World monetary system in existence prior to 1971 under which the value of the U.S. dollar was tied to gold and the values of the other currencies were pegged to the U.S. dollar.

Float. The amount of funds tied up in checks that have been written but are still in process and have not yet been collected.

Floating Exchange Rates. Exchange rates not fixed by government policy ("pegged") but instead allowed to "float" up or down in accordance with supply and demand. When market forces are allowed to function, exchange rates are said to be floating.

Flotation Cost. The cost of issuing new stocks or bonds.

Foreign Bond. A bond sold by a foreign borrower but denominated in the currency of the country in which it is sold.

Foreign Exchange Exposure. Exposure to losses due to fluctuating exchange rates.

Forward Exchange Rate. An agreed upon price at which two currencies are to be exchanged at some future date.

Founders' Shares. Classified stock that has sole voting rights and restricted dividends. Owned by the firm's founders.

Franchise. A device for small business whereby training, experience, and perhaps a valuable name or supplies are provided for a proprietor on a rental contract basis.

Fully Diluted EPS. Earnings available to common stockholders divided by the average number of shares which would have been outstanding if all warrants and convertibles had been exercised or converted, regardless of the likelihood of their exercise or conversion.

Funded Debt. Long-term debt.

Funding. The process of replacing short-term debt with long-term securities (stocks or bonds).

Future Value. The amount to which a payment or series of payments will grow by a given future date when compounded by a given interest rate.

FV. Abbreviation for *future value*. FVIF = future value interest factor.

GIGO. One of the fundamental laws of computer science, it stands for "Garbage In, Garbage Out." The term has now been broadened and applied to all aspects of financial analysis. *See* the SWAG method for obtaining inputs to a GIGO system.

Going Public. The sale of stock by a closely held corporation (or its principal stockholders) to the public at large.

Goodwill. Intangible assets of a firm established by the excess of the price paid for the going concern over its book value.

Hedging. Process of protecting oneself against loss due to uncertainty.

Historic Rate of Return. Dividend yield plus capital gain or minus capital loss that actually occurred for a given stock in a given year.

Holder of Record Date. The date on which registered security owners are entitled to receive the forthcoming cash or stock dividend.

Holding Company. A corporation operated for the purpose of owning the common stocks of other corporations.

Horizontal Merger. The combination of two firms which produce the same type of goods or service, for example, the merger between two shoe retailing chains or two shoe manufacturers.

Hurdle Rate. In capital budgeting, the minimum acceptable rate of return on a project. If the expected rate of return is below the hurdle rate, the project is not accepted. The hurdle rate should be the marginal cost of capital.

Impairment of Capital. Legal restriction to protect creditors. It limits dividend payments to retained earnings.

Improper Accumulation. Earnings retained by a business for the purpose of enabling stockholders to avoid personal income taxes.

Income Bond. A bond that pays interest only if the current interest is earned.

Incremental Cash Flow. Net cash flow attributable to an investment project.

Incremental Cost of Capital. The average cost of the increment of capital raised during a given year.

Indenture. A formal agreement between the issuer of a bond and the bondholders.

Inflation Premium. A premium for anticipated or expected inflation that investors add to the pure rate of return.

Insolvency. The inability to meet maturing debt obligations.

Interest Factor (IF). Numbers found in compound interest and annuity tables. Usually called FVIF or PVIF.

Interest Rate Risk. Risk to which investors are exposed due to changing interest rates.

Internal Financing. Funds made available for capital budgeting and working capital expansion through the normal operations of the firm. Internal financing is approximately equal to retained earnings plus depreciation.

Internal Rate of Return (IRR). The rate of return on an asset investment, calculated by finding the discount rate that equates the present value of future cash flows to the cost of the investment.

Intrinsic Value. The value which, in the mind of the analyst, is justified by the facts. It is often used to distinguish between the "true value" of an asset (the intrinsic value) and the asset's current market price.

Investment Banker. One who underwrites and distributes new investment securities; more broadly, one who helps business firms obtain financing.

Investment Opportunity Schedule (IOS). A listing, or graph, of the firm's investment opportunities ranked in order of the projects' rates of return.

Investment Tax Credit. A specified percentage of the dollar amount of new investments in each of certain categories of assets which business firms can deduct as a credit against their income taxes.

Legal List. A list of securities in which mutual savings banks, pension funds, insurance companies, and other fiduciary institutions are permitted to invest.

Leverage Factor. The ratio of debt to total assets.

Leveraged Lease. Lease under which the lessor arranges to borrow a portion of the required funds.

Lien. A lender's claim on assets that are pledged for a loan.

Line of Credit. An arrangement whereby a financial institution (bank or insurance company) commits itself to lend up to a specified maximum amount of funds during a specified period. Sometimes the interest rate on the loan is specified; at other times, it is not. Sometimes a commitment fee is imposed for obtaining the line of credit.

Liquidation. Dissolving of a firm through the sale of its assets.

Liquidity. Reference to a firm's cash and marketable securities position and to its ability to meet maturing obligations. For an individual asset, it is the ability to sell the asset at a reasonable price on short notice.

Listed Securities. Securities traded on an organized security exchange.

Lockbox Plan. A procedure used to speed up collections and to reduce float.

Margin—Profit on Sales. The *profit margin* is the percentage of profit after tax to sales.

Margin—Securities Business. The buying of stocks or bonds on credit, known as *buying on margin*.

Marginal Cost. The cost of an additional unit. The marginal cost of capital is the cost of an additional dollar of new funds.

Marginal Efficiency of Capital. A schedule showing the internal rate of return on investment opportunities.

Marginal Revenue. The additional gross revenue produced by selling one additional unit of output.

Marginal Tax Rate. The tax rate applicable to the last unit of income.

Market Risk. The part of a security's risk that cannot be eliminated by diversification. It is measured by the beta coefficient.

Merger. Any combination that forms one company from two or more previously existing companies.

Money Market. Financial market in which funds are borrowed or lent for short periods. (The money market is distinguished from the capital market, which is the market for long-term funds.)

Mortgage. A pledge of designated property as security for a loan.

Multiple Discriminant Analysis (MDA). A statistical technique similar to regression analysis that can be used to evaluate financial ratios.

Naked Options. Options sold by an investor without any stock to back them up.

Net Present Value (NPV) Method. A method of ranking investment proposals. The NPV is equal to the present value of future returns, discounted at the marginal cost of capital, minus the present value of the cost of the investment.

Net Worth. The capital and surplus of a firm—capital stock, capital surplus (paid-in capital), earned surplus (retained earnings), and, occasionally, certain reserves. For some purposes, preferred stock is included; generally, *net worth* refers only to the common stockholders' position.

New Issue Market. The market that consists of stocks of companies that have just gone public.

Nominal Interest Rate. The contracted, or stated, interest rate, undeflated for price level changes.

Objective Probability Distribution. Probability distribution determined by statistical procedures.

Offering Price. Price at which common stock is sold to the public.

Operating Company. A subsidiary of a holding company.

Operating Leverage. The extent to which fixed costs are used in a firm's operation. Breakeven analysis is used to measure the extent to which operating leverage is employed.

Operating Merger. A merger in which the operations of two companies are integrated with the expectation of achieving synergistic benefits.

Opportunity Cost. The rate of return on the best *alternative* investment available—the highest return that will *not* be earned if the funds are invested in a particular project. For example, the opportunity cost of *not* investing in bond A yielding 8 percent might be 7.99 percent, which could be earned on bond B.

Option. A contract giving the holder the right to buy or sell an asset at some predetermined price within a specified period of time.

Ordinary Income. Income from the normal operations of a firm but specifically excluding income from the sale of capital assets.

Organized Security Exchanges. Formal organizations having tangible, physical locations and conducting auction markets in designated ("listed") investment securities. The New York Stock Exchange is an organized security exchange.

Overdraft System. A system where a depositor may write checks in excess of the balance, with the bank automatically extending a loan to cover the shortage.

Over-the-Counter Market. All facilities that provide for trading in unlisted securities—those not listed on organized exchanges. The over-the-counter market is typically viewed as a "telephone market," since most business is conducted by telephone.

Paid-in Capital. The funds a corporation receives in excess of the par value of its stock when it sells stock. Paid-in capital can also be increased when a company declares a stock dividend. Often called *additional paid-in capital*.

Par Value. The nominal or face value of a stock or bond.

Payback Period. The length of time required for the net revenues of an investment to return the cost of the investment.

Payout Ratio. The percentage of earnings paid out in the form of dividends.

Pegging. A market stabilization action taken by the manager of an underwriting group during the offering of new securities. Pegging is done by continually placing orders to buy at a specified price in the market.

Percentage of Sales Method. Method of forecasting financial requirements by expressing various balance sheet items as a percentage of sales, then using these percentages with expected future sales to construct *pro forma* balance sheets.

Perpetuity. A stream of equal future payments expected to continue forever.

Pledging of Accounts Receivable. Short-term borrowing from financial institutions where the loan is secured by accounts receivable. The lender may physically take the accounts receivable but typically has recourse to the borrower. Also called *Discounting of accounts receivable.*

Pollution Control Bond. Bonds similar to development bonds but whose proceeds are used by a company to purchase pollution abatement equipment. *See also* Development Bond.

Pooling of Interest. An accounting method for combining the financial statements of two firms that merge. Under the pooling-of-interest procedure, the assets of the merged firms are simply added to form the balance sheet of the surviving corporation. This method is different from the "purchase" method, where goodwill is put on the balance sheet to reflect a premium (or discount) paid in excess of book value.

Portfolio Effect. The extent to which the variation in returns on a combination of assets (a "portfolio") is less than the sum of the variations of the individual assets.

Portfolio Theory. Theory that deals with the selection of optimal portfolios—portfolios that provide the highest possible return for any specified degree of risk.

Post-audit. A comparison of the actual and expected results for a given capital project.

Precautionary Balance. Cash balance held in reserve for random, unforeseen fluctuations in inflows and outflows.

Preemptive Right. A provision contained in the corporate charter and bylaws that gives holders of common stock the right to purchase on a pro rata basis new issues of common stock (or securities convertible into common stock).

Preferred Stock. Long-term equity security paying a fixed dividend.

Present Value (PV). The value today of a future payment, or stream of payments, discounted at the appropriate discount rate.

Pressure. The effect on the price of a stock when a company sells a substantial block of new stock. The sale tends to depress somewhat the price of outstanding shares.

Price/Earnings (P/E) Ratio. The ratio of price to earnings, which shows the dollar amount investors will pay for $1 of current earnings. Faster growing or less risky firms typically have higher P/E ratios than either slower growing or riskier firms.

Primary EPS. Earnings available to common stockholders divided by the average number of shares that would have been outstanding if warrants and convertibles likely to be converted in the near future had actually been exercised or converted.

Prime Rate. The lowest rate of interest commercial banks charge very large, strong corporations.

Pro Forma. A financial statement that shows how an actual statement will look if certain specified assumptions are realized. *Pro forma* statements may be either future or past projections. A backward *pro forma* statement may be used when two firms are planning to merge and want to show what their consolidated financial statements would have looked like if they had been merged in preceding years.

Probability Distribution. Listing of all possible outcomes or events, with a probability (the chance of the event's occurrence) assigned to each outcome.

Profit Center. A unit of a large, decentralized firm that has its own investments and for which a rate of return on investment can be calculated.

Profit Margin. The ratio of profits after taxes to sales.

Profitability Index (PI). The present value of future returns divided by the present value of the investment outlay.

Progressive Tax. A tax that requires a higher percentage payment on higher incomes. The personal income tax in the United States, which is at a rate of 14 percent on the lowest increments of income to 70 percent on the highest increments, is progressive.

Prospectus. A document issued for the purpose of describing a new security issue. The Securities and Exchange Commission (SEC) examines prospectuses to insure that statements contained in them are not false or misleading.

Proxy. A document giving one person the authority or power to act for another. Typically, the authority in question is the power to vote shares of common stock.

Purchase. In mergers, the situation where a large firm acquires a smaller one.

Purchasing Power Risk. Risk that inflation will reduce the purchasing power of a given sum of money.

Put. An option to sell a specific security at a specified price within a designated period. Opposite of a call.

Quick Ratio. Current assets minus inventory, divided by current liabilities. Sometimes called *acid test.*

Rate of Return. The internal rate of return on an investment.

Recourse Arrangement. A term used in connection with accounts receivable financing. A firm may sell its accounts receivable to a financial institution under a recourse agreement. If the accounts receivable cannot be collected, the selling firm must repurchase them from the financial institution.

Rediscount Rate. The rate of interest at which a bank may borrow from a Federal Reserve Bank.

Refunding. Sale of new debt securities to replace an old debt issue.

Registration Statement. Statement of facts filed with the SEC about a company planning to issue securities.

Regression Analysis. A statistical procedure for predicting the value of one variable (dependent variable) on the basis of knowledge about one or more other variables (independent variables).

Reinvestment Rate. The rate of return at which cash flows from an investment are reinvested. The reinvestment rate may or may not be constant from year to year.

Relative Priority Doctrine. In bankruptcy proceedings, a flexible approach to the priority of creditors' claims, one giving balanced consideration to all claimants.

Reorganization. The situation where the assets of a financially troubled firm are restated to reflect their current market value and the firm's financial structure is restated to reflect any changes on the asset side of the statement. Under a reorganization the firm continues in existence, whereas under bankruptcy the firm is liquidated and ceases to exist.

Replacement Chain. Method of comparing the NPVs of mutually exclusive projects with unequal lives. The method is used by carrying the analysis out to a common denominator year.

Required Rate of Return. The rate of return that stockholders expect to receive on common stock investments.

Residual Theory of Dividends. The theory that dividends paid should equal the excess of earnings over retained earnings necessary to finance the optimal capital budget.

Residual Value. The value of leased property at the end of the lease term.

Restrictive Covenant. Provision in debt contracts, including bond indentures, that constrains the actions of a borrower.

Retained Earnings. That portion of earnings not paid out in dividends. The figure that appears on the balance sheet is the sum of the retained earnings for each year throughout the company's history.

Return on Common Equity. Income available to common stockholders divided by common equity.

Revolving Credit Agreement. Formal line of credit extended to a firm by a bank.

Right. A short-term option to buy a specified number of shares of a new issue of securities at a designated "subscription" price.

Rights Offering. A securities flotation offered to existing stockholders.

Risk. The probability that actual future returns will be below expected returns. Risk is measured by standard deviation or coefficient of variation of expected returns or by the beta coefficient.

Risk-Adjusted Discount Rate. The discount rate that applies to a particular risky (uncertain) stream of income; the riskless rate of interest plus a risk premium appropriate to the level of risk attached to the particular income stream.

Risk Aversion. A dislike for risk. Investors who are averse to risk have higher required rates of return for securities with higher risk.

Risk Premium. The difference between the required rate of return on a particular risky asset and the rate of return on a riskless asset with the same expected life.

Risk, Relevant. Risk of a security that cannot be diversified away, or market risk. Risk premiums are thought to apply only to relevant risk.

Risk-Return Tradeoff Function. *See* Capital Market Line.

Risk, Total. The total of market and nonmarket risk of a security.

Safety Stock. Additional inventories carried to guard against changes in sales rates or production/shipping delays.

Sale and Leaseback. An operation whereby a firm sells land, buildings, or equipment to a financial institution and simultaneously leases the property back for a specified period under specific terms.

Salvage Value. The value of a capital asset at the end of a specified period. It is the current market price of an asset being considered for replacement in a capital budgeting problem.

Scenario Analysis. Short version of simulation, where bad and good sets of financial circumstances are compared to a most likely, or base, case NPV.

Seasoned Issue. Outstanding bonds—bonds which have been on the market for a while.

Secondary Market. In investment terminology, the "market" in which stocks are traded after they have been issued by corporations. When a company sells a new issue of stock, the transaction is considered a "primary market transaction."

Securities and Exchange Commission (SEC). The U.S. government agency that regulates the issuance and trading of stocks and bonds.

Securities, Junior. Securities that have lower priority in claims on assets and income than other securities (senior securities). For example, preferred stock is junior to debentures, but debentures are junior to mortgage bonds. Common stock is the most junior of all corporate securities.

Securities, Senior. Securities having claims on income and assets that rank higher than certain other securities (junior securities). For example, mortgage bonds are senior to debentures, but debentures are senior to common stock.

Security Market Line. The line that shows the relationship between risk and rates of return for individual securities.

Selling Group. A group of stock brokerage firms formed for the purpose of distributing a new issue of securities; part of the investment banking process.

Sensitivity Analysis. Simulation analysis in which key variables are changed and the resulting change in the rate of return is observed. Typically, the rate of return is more sensitive to changes in some variables than to changes in others.

Service Lease. A lease under which the lessor maintains and services the asset.

Short Selling. Selling a security that is not owned by the seller at the time of the sale. The seller borrows the security from a brokerage firm and must at some point repay the brokerage firm by buying the security on the open market.

Simulation. A technique whereby probable future events are simulated on a computer. Estimated rates of return and risk indexes can be generated.

Sinking Fund. A required annual payment designed to amortize a bond or a preferred stock issue. The sinking fund may be held in the form of cash or marketable securities, but more generally the money put into the fund is used to retire some of the securities in question each year.

Small Business Administration (SBA). A government agency organized to aid small firms with their financing and other problems.

Social Responsibility. The idea that businesses should be partly responsible for the welfare of society at large.

Sovereign Risk. Risk of expropriation of a foreign subsidiary's assets by the host company and of unanticipated restrictions on cash flows to the parent.

Specialists. Members on the stock exchange who facilitate the trading process by keeping an inventory of shares of the stocks in which they specialize.

Speculative Balance. Cash balance that is held to enable the firm to take advantage of any bargain purchases that might arise.

Spot Rate. The effective exchange rate for a foreign currency for delivery on (approximately) the current day. Distinguished from the forward rate.

Spread. The difference between the price a security dealer offers to pay for securities (the "bid" price) and the price at which the dealer offers to sell them (the "asked" price).

Standard Deviation. A statistical measurement of the variability of a set of observations.

Standard of Fairness. SEC doctrine that states that claims must be recognized in the order of their legal and contractual priority.

Standard of Feasibility. Test made by the SEC during a reorganization to determine whether fixed charges would be covered by earnings.

Stock Dividend. A dividend paid in additional shares of stock rather than cash. It involves a transfer from retained earnings to the capital stock account; therefore, stock dividends are limited by the amount of retained earnings.

Stock Repurchase. A means by which a firm distributes income to stockholders by buying back shares of its own stock, thereby decreasing shares outstanding, increasing EPS, and increasing the price of the stock.

Stock Split. An accounting action to increase the number of shares outstanding; for example, in a 3-for-1 split, shares outstanding are tripled and each stockholder receives three new shares for each one formerly held. Stock splits involve no transfer from surplus to the capital account.

Subchapter S. Section of the Internal Revenue Code that allows certain small business corporations to be taxed as either proprietorships or partnerships rather than as corporations.

Subjective Probability Distributions. Probability distributions determined through subjective procedures without the use of statistics.

Subordinated Debenture. A bond having a claim on assets only after the senior debt has been paid off in the event of liquidation.

Subscription Price. The price at which a security may be purchased in a rights offering.

Supernormal Growth. Part of the life cycle of a firm when its growth is much faster than that of the economy as a whole.

SWAG, or SWAG Method. A method of obtaining data (generally quantitative) such as subjective probability distributions, when these data are not otherwise obtainable. SWAG stands for "Scientific Wild A–– Guess." The SWAG method is often used to obtain inputs for GIGO analysis.

Synergy. A situation where the whole is greater than the sum of its parts. In a synergistic merger, the postmerger earnings exceed the sum of the separate companies' premerger earnings.

Takeover. The acquisition of one firm by another over the opposition of the acquired firm's management.

Tangible Assets. Physical assets as opposed to intangible assets such as goodwill and the stated value of patents.

Tender Offer. A situation where one firm offers to buy the stock of another by going directly to the stockholders, frequently over the opposition of the management of the firm whose stock is being sought.

Term Loan. A loan, generally obtained from a bank or insurance company, with a maturity greater than one year. Term loans are generally amortized.

Term Structure of Interest Rates. Relationship between yields and maturities of securities.

Terminal Value. The value of an asset at a future ending time. The value of an asset today is the present value of its terminal value discounted at its cost of capital.

Times Interest Earned. Earnings before interest and taxes divided by interest charges. This ratio measures the ability of the firm to meet its annual interest charges.

Trade Credit. Interfirm debt arising through credit sales and recorded as an account receivable by the seller and as an account payable by the buyer.

Transactions Balance. Cash balance associated with payments and collections; the balance necessary to conduct day-to-day business.

Translation Loss. Loss resulting from translating financial statements from a foreign subsidiary's currency to the parent's currency.

Treasury Stock. Common stock that has been repurchased by the issuing firm.

Trend Analysis. Analysis of a firm's financial ratios over time in order to determine the improvement or deterioration of the financial situation.

Trust Receipt. An instrument acknowledging that the borrower holds certain goods in trust for the lender. Trust receipt financing is used in financing inventories for automobile dealers, construction equipment dealers, appliance

dealers, and other dealers in expensive durable goods.

Trustee. The representative of bondholders who acts in their interest and facilitates communication between them and the issuer. Typically these duties are handled by a department of a commercial bank.

Underwriting. (1) The entire process of issuing new corporate securities. (2) The insurance function of bearing the risk of adverse price fluctuations during the period in which a new issue of stocks or bonds is being distributed.

Underwriting Syndicate. A syndicate of investment firms formed to spread the risk associated with the purchase and distribution of a new issue of securities. The larger the issue, the more firms typically are involved in the syndicate.

Unlisted Securities. Securities that are traded in the over-the-counter market.

Utility Theory. A body of theory dealing with the relationships among money income, utility (or happiness), and the willingness to accept risks.

Venture Capital. Risk capital supplied to small, growth companies by wealthy individuals, partnerships, or corporations, usually in return for an equity position in the firm.

Vertical Merger. A company's acquisition of one of its suppliers or one of its customers.

Warrant. A long-term option to buy a stated number of shares of common stock at a specified price. The specified price is generally called the *exercise price*.

Weighted Cost of Capital. A weighted average of the component costs of debt, preferred stock, and common equity. Also called the *composite cost of capital*.

Working Capital. A firm's investment in short-term assets—cash, short-term securities, accounts receivable, and inventories. *Gross working capital* is a firm's total current assets. *Net working capital* is current assets minus current liabilities. If the term *working capital* is used without further qualification, it generally refers to gross working capital.

Working Capital Policy. Basic policy decisions regarding target levels for each category of current assets and the financing of these assets.

Yield. The rate of return on an investment; the internal rate of return.

Yield Curve. Graph of the relationship between the yields and maturities of a security.

Yield to Maturity. Rate of interest earned on a bond if it is held to maturity.

INDEX

Frequently Used Symbols in Financial Management

b	(1) beta coefficient, a measure of an asset's riskiness;
	(2) the fraction of a firm's earnings retained rather than paid out
CAPM	capital asset pricing model
D	dividend per share of stock *(DPS)*. D_t is the dividend in period *t*.
EPS	earnings per share
EBIT	earnings before interest and taxes = net operating income *(NOI)*
FVIF	future value interest factor for a lump sum
FVIFA	future value interest factor for an annuity
g	growth rate, especially growth rate in earnings, dividends, and stock prices
I	interest (in dollars) on a bond
IRR	internal rate of return
k	a percentage discount rate, or cost of capital:
k_d	interest rate on debt (R_F = interest rate on risk-free debt)
k_s	cost of capital of common equity obtained by retaining earnings
k_e	cost of capital from sale of new common stock
k_p	cost of capital of preferred stock
k_a	weighted average cost of capital
k_M	cost of capital for "the market," or an "average" stock
$\hat{k}$	"k hat" is an expected rate of return
MCC	marginal cost of capital
NPV	net present value
P	price of a share of stock; P_O = price of the stock today
P/E	price/earnings ratio
PV	present value
PVIF	present value interest factor for a lump sum
PVIFA	present value interest factor for an annuity
r	(1) rate of return on investment; (2) the *IRR* on a new project
R_F	rate of return on a risk-free security
R	receipt, or cash flow
ROA	return on assets
ROE	return on equity
ROI	return on investment
S	sales
Σ	summation sign (capital sigma)
σ	standard deviation (lower case sigma)
t	(1) tax rate, or (2) time, when used as a subscript.
	For example D_t = the dividend in year t
V	value